Moving Politics

Moving Politics

Emotion and ACT UP's
Fight against AIDS

DEBORAH B. GOULD

THE UNIVERSITY OF CHICAGO PRESS   CHICAGO AND LONDON

DEBORAH B. GOULD is assistant professor of sociology at the University of California, Santa Cruz.

The University of Chicago Press, Chicago 60637
The University of Chicago Press, Ltd., London
© 2009 by The University of Chicago
All rights reserved. Published 2009
Printed in the United States of America

18 17 16 15 14 13 12 11   2 3 4 5

ISBN-13: 978-0-226-30529-5 (cloth)
ISBN-13: 978-0-226-30530-1 (paper)
ISBN-10: 0-226-30529-5 (cloth)
ISBN-10: 0-226-30530-9 (paper)

Library of Congress Cataloging-in-Publication Data
Gould, Deborah B.
    Moving politics : emotion and act up's fight against AIDS / Deborah B. Gould.
        p. cm.
    Includes bibliographical references and index.
    ISBN-13: 978-0-226-30529-5 (cloth : alk. paper)
    ISBN-13: 978-0-226-30530-1 (pbk. : alk. paper)
    ISBN-10: 0-226-30529-5 (cloth : alk. paper)
    ISBN-10: 0-226-30530-9 (pbk. : alk. paper)
    1. ACT UP (Organization)—History. 2. AIDS activists—United States. 3. AIDS (Disease)—Political aspects—United States. 4. Social movements—Psychological aspects. 5. Emotions—Political aspects. I. Title.
    RA643.83.G68 2009
    362.196'9792—dc22
                                                                    2009002576

♾ The paper used in this publication meets the minimum requirements of the American National Standard for Information Sciences—Permanence of Paper for Printed Library Materials, ANSI Z39.48-1992.

TO ALL WHO HAVE EXPANDED MY POLITICAL HORIZONS

Contents

Acknowledgments

A project of this scope is in many ways a collaborative endeavor, and it is a pleasure to thank the individuals and groups who helped bring this book into being. One of my greatest debts is to the members of ACT UP whom I interviewed. Not only did they give hours of their time, but they also shared with me the intimate and moving details of their experiences in ACT UP. I often returned to the interviews in order to nuance and sharpen my analysis. Thank you to Marion Banzhaf, David Barr, Gregg Bordowitz, Jeff Edwards, the late Ferd Eggan, Darrell Gordon, Mark Harrington, Carol Hayse, Jeanne Kracher, Billy McMillan, Tim Miller, Sarah Schulman, Frank Sieple, Peter Staley, Kendall Thomas, and Michael Thompson. Thank you as well to Tracy Baim, a journalist I interviewed because of her knowledge of Chicago's LGBT community.

The process of interviewing members of ACT UP evoked the absence of so many of our comrades who died. Their passion in fighting for their lives and for an end to the AIDS pandemic motivated this book, and I hope it comes through in these pages.

My thoughts about this project started years before the actual writing, during ACT UP/Chicago's last years when my closest friends and comrades in the movement would get together to discuss why ACT UP was in decline. Those politically and intellectually far-reaching discussions—really, a co-production of knowledge—were the crucial beginnings for me of making sense of my own experiences in ACT UP and of the movement as a whole. I am especially grateful to Jeff Edwards, Ferd Eggan, Jeanne Kracher, and Mary Patten.

Various groups that I have been involved in have shaped this project as well. The influence was not limited to a point here and a point there, but was comprehensive, shaping my ways of thinking as well as my aspirations about the world. Such influence is difficult to cite in the body of a text, and I am so happy to acknowledge these groups here. Participants in ACT UP/Chicago, Queer to the Left, COURAJ, Feel Tank Chicago, and various unnamed affinity groups and reading groups have profoundly influenced my thinking about existing social arrangements, alternative possibilities, and how to go about bringing such imagined worlds into being. It has been exhilarating to be in the conversation with them.

I owe my most recent collaborators, Feel Tank Chicago (Lauren Berlant, Mary Patten, and Rebecca Zorach), a special thanks. Our discussions have deeply influenced how I understand emotions, feelings, and affect, and surely have filtered into this book in ways of which I am not even aware.

Six people provided feedback on the entire manuscript—Jeff Edwards, Dawne Moon, Laurie Palmer, Mary Patten, Erica Rand, and Marc Steinberg. I am immensely grateful for the care each of them brought to the task, for their critical insights and suggestions, and for their encouragement.

Doug McAdam, an anonymous reviewer for the University of Chicago Press who later revealed himself to me, also gave me feedback on the entire manuscript. His enthusiasm for the project came at a perfect time, when my own sense of its unfinishedness threatened to stall my progress. The book benefited from insightful and generous feedback provided by the other anonymous reviewers as well.

Many others provided me with criticism on parts of the book or papers that got folded into the book. I feel lucky to have such astute interlocutors: Elizabeth Armstrong, Mohammed Bamyeh, Marion Banzhaf, Kathy Blee, Gregg Bordowitz, Lisa Brush, Cheris Chan, Ann Cvetkovich, Helena Flam, Kathryn Flannery, Bill Gould, Sue Gould, Cecilia Green, Randall Halle, David Halperin, Katie Hogan, Paul Hoggett, Jim Jasper, Jennifer Lee, John Markoff, Joey Mogul, Francesca Polletta, Bill Reddy, Assata Richards, Eric Rofes, Bill Sewell, and Stacey Waite.

I owe immense thanks to Bill Sewell, who supervised the dissertation out of which this book grew. Bill was an exceptional chair and is an even more extraordinary person. His intellectual generosity and creativity are remarkable, and this project has benefited immeasurably from his keen critical insights. I was lucky to have Leora Auslander, George Chauncey, and Michael Dawson on my dissertation committee as well. Their critical feedback, plentiful suggestions, and ideas for the book moved this project forward in important ways. I cannot imagine a better dissertation committee.

In addition to my committee members, a number of other people at
the University of Chicago asked me hard questions, pushed my thinking
forward, and provided me with encouragement: Norma Field, Sue Gal,
Andreas Glaeser, Gary Herrigel, Moishe Postone, Leslie Salzinger, Lisa
Wedeen, and the participants in the Social Theory, Lesbian and Gay
Studies, and Gender and Society workshops.

The book benefited as well from comments made at various confer-
ences. The "Emotions and Social Movements" conference at New York
University was especially important in that it introduced me to a number of social movement scholars similarly attuned to emotion. Special
thanks to the organizers of that conference—Jeff Goodwin, Jim Jasper,
and Francesca Polletta.

My appreciation for librarians and archivists grows and grows! Librarians at the Manuscripts and Archives Division of the New York Public Library, particularly Melanie Yolles, were a great help, as was the staff at Ger-
ber/Hart Library in Chicago. Susan Stryker and Willie Walker at the Gay
and Lesbian Historical Society of Northern California (now the GLBT
Historical Society) provided me with extensive assistance and stimulating
conversation. Many thanks as well to Kate Black, who gave me access to
interviews she conducted with lesbians in ACT UP, and to ACT UP/Chi-
cago member Lou Snider, who generously gave me his immense ACT UP
archive. Appreciations as well to Linda Miller, Ellen Neipris, Genyphyr
Novak, and Rex Wockner for the use of their photographs.

Two University of Chicago undergrads, Ryan Hollon and Justin Re-
inheimer, provided excellent research assistance. Sybil Sosin deserves
a mountain of praise for helping me edit the manuscript down by 150
pages. Thank you to Linda Miller, Ellen Neipris, Genyphyr Novak, and
Rex Wockner for the use of their photographs.

Working with Doug Mitchell has been a delight and a never-ending
source of encouragement. Responding to one of Doug's early queries
about my progress, I wrote that the process of turning the dissertation
into a book was more paralyzing and confusing than I had expected. His
reply: "You're obviously making good progress on the book; 'paralyzing
and confusing' is the tip-off. . . . Trust me." What more could one want
from an editor? Thank you as well to Tim McGovern, who has helped
the book wind its way through the publication process, to Nick Murray
for his superb copyediting, and to Erik Carlson for being calm, cool, and
collected through it all.

In its initial stages, this project benefited from a University Fellowship from the University of Chicago and from a Mellon "First Year" Dis-

sertation Fellowship. A James C. Hormel Dissertation Fellowship from the Lesbian and Gay Studies Project of the Center for Gender Studies at the University of Chicago allowed me to finish the dissertation. Invaluable as well was a stint as a Graduate Fellow in the Mellon Seminar on Contentious Politics at the Center for Advanced Study in the Behavioral Sciences, run by Doug McAdam, Sidney Tarrow, and Chuck Tilly.

My years as a Harper-Schmidt Fellow in the Society of Fellows in the Liberal Arts at the University of Chicago allowed me to continue the research and begin the process of turning the dissertation into a book. While at the University of Pittsburgh, a Type I Third-Term Research Stipend and a Junior Faculty Research Leave helped me to finish the book. Generous support for its publication comes from the University of Pittsburgh's Richard D. and Mary Jane Edwards Endowed Publication Fund and from Pitt's Women's Studies Faculty Research Fund.

Along the way, I needed all kinds of stimulants. Various reading and study groups have provided me with vital intellectual nourishment and necessary diversions. Friends and family have been an enormous source of sustenance throughout, and I am deeply appreciative that they have put up with this project for so long. For the many conversations, thank you to Lauren Berlant, Gregg Bordowitz, Tara Cameron, Jeanne Dunning, Jeff Edwards, Linda Evans, Helena Flam, Nicole Goldstein, Beth Gould, Pat Guizzetti, Jin Lee, Rachel Mattson, Joey Mogul, Beth Nugent, Caroline O'Boyle, Mary Patten, Jeannie Pejko, Erica Rand, Anne Redlich, Assata Richards, Eve Rosahn, Jeffrey Skoller, Brett Stockdill, Michael Tajchman, Therese Quinn, and Amy Wolfe.

My parents' intellectual curiosity, love of debate, and engagement with the world rubbed off on me at an early age. Most of all, they've been great parents—and words, of course, fail to convey what that means to me.

Finally, I am deeply grateful to Laurie Palmer, who knows best how many of my own preoccupations and aspirations are embedded in this project. Her inquisitiveness, unique insights, and critical sense have consistently pushed me forward. Our different interests have generated fertile ground on which my own thinking has grown and changed, and I know that such cross-pollination has seeped into this book. Her enthusiasm helped me to finish; her eager distractions kept me sane and more. Laurie has not only engaged me in fascinating conversations about the rational, the nonrational, and the irrational, but she has also been a wonderful companion in traveling to and fro.

Why Emotion?

I begin with a long quotation, both to set the scene and to indicate why this book about activism and social movements is also centrally about feelings, emotion, and affect. The speaker is artist and AIDS activist David Wojnarowicz, and the quotation is taken from a reading he did at the Drawing Center in New York City in 1992, shortly before his death from complications due to AIDS.

"If I had a dollar to spend for healthcare I'd rather spend it on a baby or innocent person with some defect or illness not of their own responsibility; not some person with AIDS . . . " says the healthcare official on national television and this is in the middle of an hour long video of people dying on camera because they can't afford the limited drugs available that might extend their lives and I can't even remember what this official looked like because I reached in through the T.V. screen and ripped his face in half and I was diagnosed with AIDS recently and this was after the last few years of losing count of the friends and neighbors who have been dying slow and vicious and unnecessary deaths because fags and dykes and junkies are expendable in this country "If you want to stop AIDS shoot the queers . . . " says the governor of texas on the radio and his press secretary later claims that the governor was only joking and didn't know the microphone was turned on and besides they didn't think it would hurt his chances for re-election anyways and I

wake up every morning in this killing machine called america and I'm carrying this rage like a blood filled egg and there's a thin line between the inside
and the outside a thin line between thought and action and that line is simply made up of blood and muscle and bone and I'm waking up more and more
from daydreams of tipping amazonian blowdarts in "infected blood" and
spitting them at the exposed necklines of certain politicians or government
healthcare officials or those thinly disguised walking swastikas that wear religious garments over their murderous intentions or those rabid strangers pa-
rading against AIDS clinics in the nightly news suburbs   there's a thin line a
very thin line between the inside and the outside and I've been looking all my
life at the signs surrounding us in the media or on peoples lips; the religious
types outside st. patricks cathedral shouting to men and women in the gay parade: "You won't be here next year—you'll get AIDS and die ha ha"   and the
areas of the u.s.a. where it is possible to murder a man and when brought to
trial one only has to say that the victim was a queer and that he tried to touch
you and the courts will set you free   and the difficulties that a bunch of republican senators have in albany with supporting an anti-violence bill that includes "sexual orientation" as a category of crime victims   there's a thin line a
very thin line and as each T-cell disappears from my body it's replaced by ten
pounds of pressure ten pounds of rage and I focus that rage into non-violent
resistance but that focus is starting to slip my hands are beginning to move
independent of self-restraint and the egg is starting to crack   america seems
to understand and accept murder as a self defense against those who would
murder other people and its been murder on a daily basis for eight count them
eight long years and we're expected to quietly and politely make house in this
windstorm of murder   but I say there's certain politicians that had better increase their security forces and there's religious leaders and healthcare officials that had better get bigger dogs and higher fences and more complex security alarms for their homes and queer-bashers better start doing their work
from inside howitzer tanks because the thin line between the inside and the
outside is beginning to erode and at the moment I'm a thirty seven foot tall
one thousand one hundred and seventy-two pound man inside this six foot
frame and all I can feel is the pressure all I can feel is the pressure and the
need for release. (Wojnarowicz 1992)

Affect. Being affected, being moved. Emotion. Motion. Movement,
from the post-classical Latin *movementum,* meaning "motion," and earlier, *movimentum,* meaning "emotion," and then later, "rebellion," or

"uprising."[1] The *movement* in "social movements" gestures toward the realm of affect; bodily intensities; emotions, feelings, and passions; and toward uprising.

Now a shift in registers, the first of many in this book, an indication of the uneasy relationship between scenes of affect, feeling, and emotion, on the one hand, and academic work, on the other. One of my goals is to make that relationship less uneasy. *Moving Politics* is about activism and political feelings, including not only expected and common feelings in the realm of activism, like rage, anger, indignation, hope, pride, and solidarity, but also those that might be less perceptible, like fear, shame, embarrassment, guilt, overwhelmedness, desperation, and despair. I begin from the premise that feeling and emotion are fundamental to political life, not in the sense that they overtake reason and interfere with deliberative processes, as they are sometimes disparagingly construed to do, but in the sense that there is an affective dimension to the processes and practices that make up "the political," broadly defined. Motivated by an interest in the processes of social change, the book is an inquiry into the affective stimuli and blockages to political activism. At its heart is the question of political imaginaries and their conditions of possibility: How do people come to their understandings of the world and their sense of what else might be possible and how to get there? What are the factors that make political action conceivable at all, or that make some forms of activism thinkable while others are, or become, wholly unimaginable? How do attitudes within a social group or collectivity about what is politically possible, desirable, and necessary—what I call a *political horizon*—get established, consolidated, stabilized, and reproduced over time, and with what sorts of effects on political action? What are the processes through which a prevailing or hegemonic political horizon might be challenged and even transformed? And what role do affects, feelings, and emotions play in generating, and foreclosing, political horizons? To get at questions of feeling and political (in)action, I analyze how political feelings are generated, sustained, and altered, or not; the ways in which power is exercised through and reproduced in our feelings; the processes through which ostensibly individual feelings take on a more col-

1. *Oxford English Dictionary Online,* s.v. "movement," at http://dictionary.oed.com/cgi/entry/00317198?single=1&query_type=word&queryword=movement&first=1&max_to_show=10 (accessed April 14, 2007).

lective character; and how affect, feelings, and emotions—individual and collective—articulate with more frequently studied factors that shape activism and movements (e.g., political opportunities, resources, ideology, frames). I explore as well a perhaps prior question: what are the processes through which the boundaries of "the political" are continually made, unmade, and remade, and the roles of affect, feelings, and emotions in those processes? My case is AIDS activism, and I focus in particular on the direct-action AIDS movement, ACT UP (AIDS Coalition to Unleash Power).

Arguing that confrontational direct action was needed to fight the exploding AIDS crisis, oppositional AIDS activist groups began to emerge in 1986–87 out of lesbian and gay communities around the United States. With cumulative deaths from AIDS-related complications nearing and soon surpassing twenty thousand nationally—the vast majority of them gay and bisexual men—lesbians and gay men formed direct-action AIDS groups in San Francisco (Citizens for Medical Justice [CMJ]), New York (the Lavender Hill Mob), and Chicago (Dykes and Gay Men Against Repression/Racism/Reagan/the Right Wing [DAGMAR]).[2] ACT UP formed in New York City in March 1987, and other chapters soon sprouted up across the country, quickly forming a national direct-action AIDS movement. Over the course of its life there were more than eighty ACT UP chapters in the United States and more than thirty internationally.[3] Through raucous demonstrations, acts of civil disobedience, zaps and disruptions, die-ins and other forms of street theater, meetings with government and other officials, and eye-catching agit-prop, ACT UP and similar direct-action AIDS groups intervened in every aspect of the AIDS epidemic, with tremendous effect. The movement's profound impact on the course of the epidemic is evident in the long list of victories it secured (sometimes working alone, sometimes in coalition). ACT UP forced the Food and Drug Administration (FDA) to speed up the drug-approval process and to adopt policies that allowed people with life-threatening illnesses access to experimental drugs *prior* to approval. The movement's efforts reconfigured scientific procedures, and thus scientific research itself, by securing the inclusion of people with HIV/AIDS in government and corporate AIDS decision-making bodies, allowing affected populations to have input into drug trial de-

2. Each of these groups was a precursor to an ACT UP chapter. DAGMAR formed earlier in the 1980s but shifted its focus to AIDS in 1987.

3. See ACT UP/New York n.d. b; and Halcli 1999.

sign and other aspects of drug research. ACT UP pushed the Centers for Disease Control (CDC) to expand the definition of AIDS to include infections and diseases commonly occurring in HIV-infected women and poor people. Direct-action AIDS activists succeeded in attracting greater attention to the needs of multiple populations with AIDS, including women and people of color, and won more funding for AIDS research, social services, and safe-sex education. ACT UP forced pharmaceutical companies to lower the prices of AIDS drugs; prodded insurance companies to reimburse for non-FDA approved, experimental drugs; pushed government bodies to create needle-exchange programs; and prevented the passage of extremely repressive AIDS legislation. Direct-action AIDS activists also altered public perceptions of people with AIDS (PWAs)—a less quantifiable result that nonetheless had life-and-death consequences.

In addition to the many crucial victories that prolonged and saved lives, ACT UP's interventions posed a powerful challenge to conventional understandings of homosexuality and of sexuality more broadly. [Indeed, ACT UP gave birth to a new *queer* generation that shook up straight *and* gay establishments with defiant, sex-radical politics] By re-eroticizing and revalorizing all kinds of sex, ACT UP queers furnished a strong response to the sex-negative early years of the AIDS crisis. In many ways, ACT UP could be credited as well with the birth and explosion of queer theory in the academy; during the ACT UP years the separation between the streets and the academy was less pronounced than in other periods, and learning happened across these more typically segregated worlds. ACT UP also brought a renewed militancy to lesbian and gay activism—unsettling "business as usual" in both straight and gay worlds. Demonstrating, literally, the efficacy of confrontational direct-action politics, ACT UP blew open political horizons that previously had extended only to voting, lobbying, and the occasional national demonstration or protest march. ACT UP queers opened up ways of being gay and of being political that had been foreclosed by the more mainstream-oriented lesbian and gay establishment, paving the way for new identity and political formations among sexual and gender outlaws of all ages. [In addition to influencing lesbian and gay politics, ACT UP also affected subsequent activists, particularly those in the alternative globalization movement, many of whom were inspired by ACT UP's theatrical, direct-action tactics and sleek, agit-prop style (Shepard 2002).]

Despite its impact and import, however, the origins, meteoric rise, development, and eventual decline of ACT UP have never received systematic scrutiny in the field of social movements.[4] This book explores why lesbians, gay men, and other sexual and gender outsiders became politically active in the face of AIDS, why they embraced confrontational, direct-action activism in the late 1980s after over a decade of engagement in more routine interest group politics, how the movement developed and sustained itself into the early 1990s, and why the movement declined in the early-to-mid-1990s despite the fact that the AIDS crisis was continuing with little sign of abatement.

When Your Data Make You Cry

I began this project in the fall of 1996, about two years after ACT UP/ Chicago, the chapter in which I participated, held its final meeting and disbanded. My initial intent was to explain the origins, development, and decline of the movement. That continues to be the narrative arc of the book, but the project has taken a number of twists and turns that I had not anticipated when I began.

Most of all, I had not expected to be moved by my research. But as I sorted through ACT UP's archives and thousands of news articles about AIDS activism, I repeatedly found myself dissolving into tears. I named what I was feeling "grief," although in retrospect I can see that, while predominant, it was accompanied by feelings of sadness, loss, despondency, longing, disbelief, regret, and surely others that remain unnamed. While reading something, often about people I had never met, I suddenly would start weeping uncontrollably, thoroughly undone. Or I would find myself astonished, in jaw-dropping disbelief about the sheer number and unrelenting reiteration of deaths within the movement. I would sit in an affect-flooded stupor, transported to a temporally disjunctive state, experiencing, in a way for the first time, the horrors of a recent past that I had lived through but on some affective level had refused.

---

4. While *Moving Politics* is the first book-length analysis of ACT UP's emergence, development, and decline, there is a rich scholarship on multiple aspects of ACT UP. See, for example, Black 1996; Bordowitz 1987, 2004; Cohen 1993; P. F. Cohen 1998; Crimp 1987a, 1987b, 1989, 1992, 2002; Crimp and Rolston 1990; Cvetkovich 2003a, 2003b; Edwards 2000b; Elbaz 1992, 1995; Epstein 1991, 1996, 1997; J. Gamson 1989; Halcli 1999; Harrington 1997; Hodge 2000; Patten 1998; Patton 1990; Reed 2005; Roth 1998; Saalfield and Navarro 1991; Stockdill 2003; Stoller 1998; Watney 1992a, 1994, 1995; and Wolfe 1990a, 1994.

I began to catalog the material that brought me to tears.

A remembrance by lesbian AIDS activist Jane Rosett of her close friend David Summers, an early AIDS activist, who died in 1986. David's lover, Sal Licata, had invited Jane and a few other close friends to David and Sal's seventh anniversary celebration, to, as Sal put it, "hang out in bed and hold David while he pukes." Jane wrote,

> Who could resist? It was a party. David held court and stressed how honored he was to have lured a lesbian into his king-size bed. Sal joked that David always did entertain best in bed. Vito Russo, Don Knudson, and I relayed the latest PWA dish. "More people are in love than in the hospital!" David cheered. Within a few days, David was dead, and within a few years, everyone else in David's bed that day—except me—was also dead. (Rosett 1997a, 40)

Resilience and buoyancy, and death . . .

A tribute to Danny Sotomayor, a charismatic member of ACT UP/Chicago who was well known, widely loved, and controversial, both within ACT UP and within the broader lesbian and gay community. Chicago gay journalist Rex Wockner wrote about his visit to Danny four days before he died: "He weighed 75 pounds, was bald from radiation treatment, couldn't talk because of a brain lymphoma, and was covered with tubes. 'Can you hear me? Do you know who I am?' I asked. . . . I sat down and found a tubeless place to touch him." (Wockner 1992a, 28–29). Illness, physicality, human touch . . .

A column about a lesbian and gay anti-violence march in Chicago in April 1992 where Mayor Daley showed up and was booed by the marchers. *Windy City Times* columnist Jon-Henri Damski found himself pointing at the mayor and echoing chants of "Shame, shame, shame!":

> Voices came from everywhere, like a disorganized chorus without a director. It was a flood of emotion coming from the deep tunnels of our grief. [Alderman Helen] Shiller was stunned, speechless for a moment, then said: "This is something different, it's deeper than anger." I agree. . . . Out of every corner of my eye, when I am at this kind of randomly attended queer gathering, I see the faces of people I have lost, and hug the bony bodies of guys who soon may be gone. The loss, the tears, the grief, the fear, the human terror and disbelief is constant. (Damski 1992b, 15).

ACT UP/NY member and cultural theorist Douglas Crimp's recollection about what a younger gay man in ACT UP had said to him after seeing an early 1970s gay film:

> [He] was very excited about what seemed to me a pretty ordinary sex scene in the film; but then he said, "I'd give anything to know what cum tastes like, somebody else's that is." That broke my heart, for two different reasons: for him because he didn't know, for me because I do. (Crimp 1989, 10–11)

A disappearing gay world. People, institutions, practices, ways of being, an entire alternative world . . .

A first-person account of ACT UP/New York's first political funeral, held in October 1992, where activists hurled the ashes of people with AIDS over the White House fence. On the day of the march, a small group of people who would lead the funeral procession met together. Arthur Gursch, from Chicago, held up a worn sack that contained the ashes of his lover, who had been a member of ACT UP/NY and later ACT UP/Chicago. "This is Ortez." (Finkelstein 1992b, 10)

At the many memorial services held to honor our dead, those of us in ACT UP had felt intense loss. We were constantly aware of the deaths that were devastating our lesbian, gay, queer communities—grief was never really absent. Still, as a movement, we did not dwell on it, and we certainly were not overwhelmed by it, at least not consciously and at least not in the early years. In the tumult of that time, we had had little time to reflect on what we were going through; we thought we only had time to act. As I discuss in chapter 4, many of us viewed mourning as cutting into our precious time, already in short supply. Indeed, just as an earlier generation of activists had advised "Don't mourn, organize,"[5] our common sense was to "turn grief into anger." With great empathy, but also out of concern, Crimp observed that mourning *became* militancy within the movement (Crimp 1989, 9). Such a channeling of feelings certainly describes my own nonconscious manner of dealing with the illnesses and deaths occurring within ACT UP/Chicago and the broader gay community. But as I got deeper into my research, I found myself staggered by the enormity of all those deaths from AIDS-related complications, by

5. Joe Hill, labor activist and member of the Industrial Workers of the World, is credited with the phrase.

what participants in ACT UP had been through, and by what we had been trying to achieve. I was overcome by the intensity of participating in a movement where so many members had been sick and dying, where so many were experiencing such immense loss, a movement that tried to fend off death but was manifestly unable to do so and instead was surrounded by it.

What is notable to me about my emotional reactions is that they occurred not while I was in the heat of the movement, with the urgency and intensity and death swirling all around, but years after the decline of ACT UP, while reading media accounts and activists' recollections of demonstrations and other events; looking at photographs and watching video footage of ACT UP actions; amid interviews with members of ACT UP/Chicago and ACT UP/NY; going through my folder of obituaries. I experienced profound sadness during my years in ACT UP, but mostly I remember feeling intense anger about the AIDS crisis. The onslaught of grief while doing research, then, was jarring and, perhaps counterintuitively, a source of knowledge that prompted a line of questioning about feelings and activism that has fundamentally shaped this project.

I wondered in particular about the seeming absence of grief in the movement, at least in the early years. During ACT UP's heyday, we only had had space for anger, for a sense of urgency, for action. Often when discussions in ACT UP meetings became long and sometimes tedious, someone would yell out, angrily, "People are dying!"—a reminder of the pressing need to act. I am not critical of ACT UP's elevation of anger above all other feelings—there was every reason to be furious—but the intensity and persistence of our anger over many years prompts the question of what we did with our grief. It evidently was channeled toward anger and confrontational action, but by what mechanism, and to what extent did such transformations in feelings "work"? And had such rechanneling existed since the beginning of the epidemic? My research clarified that it had not existed since the beginning. To the contrary, public expressions of fear, grief, and other feelings had prevailed in the earliest years of the epidemic; anger was only one of them. In fact, anger was often submerged (see chapter 1). That changed quite dramatically in the middle of 1986 (chapter 2), to such a degree that during ACT UP's heyday, anger was the norm, even normative (chapters 3 and 4). Years after the decline of ACT UP, a friend from ACT UP/Chicago watched Rosa von Praunheim's 1990 video *Silence = Death*—which documents the reactions of writers and artists to AIDS—and was astonished at how angry people had been—*we* had been—in those years. Commenting on the dearth of anger in the lesbian and gay community in the late 1990s, he wondered what had happened to alter our feelings.

[Indeed, the *emotional habitus* of lesbian and gay communities—by which I mean the socially constituted, prevailing ways of feeling and emoting, as well as the embodied, axiomatic understandings and norms about feelings and their expression—has shifted dramatically over the years of the AIDS epidemic.[6] Why, how, and with what effects? This project takes up these questions, providing an emotional history—keeping the multiple meanings of that phrase intact—of a political movement. An overarching argument of *Moving Politics* is that various constellations of affects, feelings, and emotions, as they shifted over time, decisively shaped the trajectory of lesbian and gay, and eventually queer, political responses to AIDS.

Emotion and Social Movements *Process Theory*

When I first envisaged this project, emotion was not at its center. The reigning paradigm in the study of social movements at the time was political process theory. Its proponents argued that "most political movements and revolutions are set in motion by social changes that render the established political order more vulnerable or receptive to challenge." They contended that such social changes—called political opportunities— were "a necessary prerequisite to action" (McAdam, McCarthy, and Zald 1996b, 8). Contrary to that paradigm's explanatory framework and predictions, however, ACT UP had emerged and developed *despite*, and indeed partially *because of*, tightly constricted political opportunities: lesbians, gay men, and AIDS advocates lacked (1) meaningful access to power and (2) influential allies, and they benefited from no (3) significant splits in the ruling alignment or (4) cleavages among elites.[7]

6. I first encountered the term *emotional habitus* in Kane 2001 (particularly 253–54), who derives it from the work of Norbert Elias, Pierre Bourdieu, and Thomas Scheff. I elaborate on my meaning below.

7. That listing of political opportunities is from Sidney Tarrow (1994, 18); he reaffirmed it in the second edition of his book (1998, 76), at which point he also reintroduced the concept of threat (to interests, values, and survival) and suggested that, when present in a context of increasing opportunities for action, threats too can stimulate contention by increasing the costs of inaction (72). For early articulations of the role played by political op-

The direct-action AIDS movement emerged during President Ronald Reagan's second term in office, a period when conservatives, often volubly hostile to lesbians and gay men, were ascendant. Liberals retreated as Reagan successfully united social and fiscal conservatives in what seemed to many to be a war targeting women, people of color, and poor people, as well as the welfare state. Democrats—hoping to shed the "liberal" appellation—were not inclined to support lesbians and gay men who were among those attacked as part of this conservative crusade.[8] Indeed in the early years of the AIDS epidemic, both parties at all levels of government responded to the health crisis with a deafening silence that was superseded in the mid-1980s by repressive legislation (some proposed, some enacted) that included mandatory HIV-testing, reports to state officials of the names of those testing positive, and quarantine. My archival research and interviews indicate that lesbians and gay men by and large experienced the 1980s not as a period of political openings but as one of increasing state repression and glaring government inaction in the fight against AIDS. People feared that the government would continue to allow massive numbers of gay men and others to die by not providing adequate funds for research, treatment, and social services—and that people with AIDS and gay people more generally might actually be rounded up. Following the political opportunity model, one would have to conclude that ACT UP emerged at an inopportune moment.[9]

That puzzle pushed me to consider other factors to explain not only ACT UP's rise but the earlier emergence of the broader AIDS movement as well. Influenced by the cultural turn then well underway both in the study of social movements and in the social sciences more broadly, I wanted to understand how those who constituted the early AIDS movement and ACT UP—self-identified lesbians, gay men, and other sexual and gender outsiders—had made sense of the AIDS epidemic from its first days in 1981. Issues of interpretation and meaning-making are central to the story of all social movements, remarkably so in the case of the AIDS movement because participants and the communities from which

---

portunities in social movement emergence, see Tilly 1978; and McAdam 1999. See also Tarrow 1994, 1998; and McAdam, McCarthy, and Zald 1996a, 1996b.

8. See Loughery 1999, 421–22 on the reluctance of democrats like Mario Cuomo, Michael Dukakis, and Ed Koch to address the AIDS crisis.

9. Epstein similarly notes that the Reagan/Bush years "marked a drastically constrained political opportunity structure for gay and lesbian . . . social movements in the United States" (1999, 52).

they came faced a new and mysterious cluster of diseases and symptoms that seemed primarily to affect gay men. How did they variously understand what has since come to be known as AIDS? What factors shaped those understandings, and why and how did their understandings shift over time? And what impact did that interpretative work have on their political responses to the epidemic? To answer these questions, I turned to lesbian and gay newspapers and combed through thousands of articles on every aspect of the AIDS epidemic, covering the period 1981 through the mid-1990s (see the appendix). I looked at mainstream media coverage as well. Along with reflecting on my own experiences in ACT UP/Chicago, I interviewed sixteen people who had participated in ACT UP, and read through dozens of interviews with others as well.[10] I also sorted through the extensive archives of ACT UP/Chicago, ACT UP/New York, and ACT UP/San Francisco.[11] Gay literature and memoirs from the period also enhanced my understanding of gay life in those years.

What immediately struck me as I pored over all of these primary sources was the emotionally saturated nature of lesbian and gay discourses about AIDS. The feelings expressed or evoked varied, especially across different periods—sometimes what was most pronounced was fear, other times gay shame and pride; sometimes grief, alternating with desperation and anger; sometimes fury, and then hope; sometimes despair; often, all of the above. The feelings indicated familiarity with and often expressed lesbian and gay ambivalence—a contradictory constellation of simultaneously felt positive and negative affective states about both homosexuality and dominant, heteronormative society.[12] My

10. I read interviews conducted by Kate Black in 1993 of lesbians from ACT UP chapters in Chicago, New York, and San Francisco, as well as interviews of ACT UP/NY members conducted by the ACT UP Oral History Project (coordinated by Sarah Schulman and James Hubbard), available at http://www.actuporalhistory.org/.

11. ACT UP/Chicago member Lou Snider kindly gave me his personal archive of materials covering AIDS activism in Chicago and nationally; in combination with my own, there now exists a substantial ACT UP/Chicago archive. I initially accessed ACT UP/NY's archive at the New York Public Library (Manuscripts, Archives, and Rare Books Division), which is now on microfilm (Thomson Gale, Gay Rights Movement, Series 3. ACT UP: The AIDS Coalition to Unleash Power). I accessed ACT UP/San Francisco's archive at the Gay, Lesbian, Bisexual, Transgender Historical Society of Northern California in San Francisco. (In the late 1990s, after the period under study, ACT UP/SF became dominated by people who believe HIV does not cause AIDS.)

12. The idea that ambivalence—the simultaneous existence of contradictory feelings in relation to a single object—is a constitutional part of all human beings is central to psy-

growing archive, in short, repeatedly pointed me toward emotion. The emotionally saturated nature of the discourses was in part due to the specifics of the case, but efforts to make sense of events and phenomena are never without feeling. Indeed, emotion incites, shapes, and is gener-ated by practices of meaning-making. That general principle, then, invites scholarly attention to the affective dimensions of sense-making.

In the late 1990s when I was beginning this project, emotion was hardly on the radar screen of theorists of social movements and other forms of contentious politics. Indeed, as I discuss below, the prevailing models in the field either implicitly or explicitly assumed the rationality of protesters, and their construals of rationality excluded feeling and emotion. As others have noted, even movement scholars who foregrounded culture were neglecting emotion (Jasper 1998; Goodwin, Jasper, and Polletta 2000, 2001b; Aminzade and McAdam 2001). Once again, I was coming up against limitations of the social movement literature. The kinds of knowledge I had acquired through my own activist engagements and was acquiring as I sorted through my growing archive were at odds, strikingly so, with the social movement literature. Indeed, while that literature offered many valuable insights and interesting lines of inquiry, its omissions and shortcomings were even more useful and productive at these early stages of the project. My initial goal, then, was to advance social movement theory both by providing a critique of the political process theory and its political opportunity thesis as well as by developing an alternative approach that foregrounded the important role of emotion in movement processes (Gould 2000). By the time

---

choanalytic thinking; see Freud 1953, 1955, 1958 , 1963; and Laplanche and Pontalis 1973, 26–28. My concept of lesbian and gay ambivalence draws from that literature, especially its foregrounding of unconscious processes, psychic conflict, and the fractured nature of the self. I also derive the concept from more sociological understandings that see ambivalence as socially structured (see Merton and Barber 1963; and Smelser 1998, for example). A sociological approach forces a recognition of the social factors that generate and structure lesbian and gay ambivalence: heteronormativity and consequent social nonrecognition, even social annihilation. But sociological theories do not provide a sense of ambivalence as it operates at an unconscious level and the profound psychic conflicts associated with it. Hence my turn to psychoanalytic theory, which also improves on theories of socialization by reminding us that the internalization of norms is a project that never fully succeeds and indeed generates psychic conflict (see Rose 1987, 90; quoted in Butler 1999, 200, n. 51.) Psychoanalytic theory illuminates the *force* of the feelings that were in play in this history; sociological theory allows us to see these feeling states as *social* phenomena whose contours can be mapped in social space. See Warner 1999 for another discussion of lesbian and gay ambivalence.

I finished that stage of the project, critiques of political process theory were increasing, a trend that has continued in the years since;[13] taking on that paradigm thus no longer seems as necessary. But the project of integrating feeling and emotion into our conceptual frameworks for analyzing contentious politics continues to be pressing.

Irrational Crowds, Rational Movements: Emotion before the Emotional Turn

An abbreviated history of the study of protest begins to suggest what is at stake in placing feeling and emotion at the center of an account of movement emergence, development, and decline. Prior to the 1970s, the dominant theories in the study of what was called "collective behavior" tended to depict protest as the result of a structural strain—for example, industrialization, urbanization, economic depression—that was said to produce abnormal psychological conditions in individuals, leading them to engage in rash, frenzied, disruptive, violent group behavior.[14] From this perspective, individuals participated in protest not because they had valid political grievances but because they were psychologically unstable or otherwise susceptible to being swept up into a "crowd." In contrast to legitimate actors in the polity, protesters were alienated from society and unfulfilled in their personal lives; narcissistic and arrested in their development; perhaps even latently homosexual.[15] Emotion, typically understood as natural impulses that interfered with reason—emotion as irrationality, in other words—was at the heart of this literature.[16] Motivated by psychic conflicts and unruly passions rather than reason, protesters were deemed unstable deviants who posed a threat to social order and thus should be feared.

13. For a passionate debate about the strengths and weaknesses of political process theory and its political opportunity thesis, see the special mini-symposium on social movements in *Sociological Forum* (1999, 14, no. 1:27–136) edited by Goodwin and Jasper and later extended and published as a book (Goodwin and Jasper 2004). For a self-critique by leading political process theorists, see McAdam, Tarrow, and Tilly 2001.

14. For a succinct and lucid analysis of different classical models of protest, including mass society, status inconsistency, and collective behavior models, see McAdam 1999, chap. 1; see also Goodwin and Jasper 2006, 612–14; and Emirbayer and Goldberg 2005.

15. See, for example, Lasswell 1986; Hoffer 1951.

16. Not all classical theorists set emotion and reason in opposition; Turner and Killian, for example, note that "emotion and reason today are not regarded as irreconcilable" (1957, 17; quoted in Emirbayer and Goldberg 2005, 510, n. 4).

Distinguishing itself from this earlier collective behavior literature, the new field of social movement studies that emerged in the 1970s responded to the former's disparaging portrayals of protest and protesters by adopting paradigms that assumed, even if implicitly, the rationality of protesters. Resource mobilization and political process models, for example, posit that participants in collective action are ordinary actors in the polity who, blocked from engaging in routine interest-group politics, unite and prudently turn to extra-institutional politics to press their demands.[17] Protesters are construed as rational actors in the sense that they engage in reasonable, thoughtful, strategic behavior designed to achieve their sensible political goals. [These rational-actor models usefully countered the classical paradigms' depictions of protesters as impulsive, irrational deviants, but, as others have noted, they simultaneously entailed an evacuation of emotion from research into contentious politics.] Pointing out that the new generation of social movement scholars "shared with the older ones one big assumption, namely, that emotions are irrational," Goodwin, Jasper, and Polletta note that "while the earlier theorists had portrayed protesters as emotional to demonstrate their irrationality, the new theorists demonstrated their rationality by denying their emotions" (2000, 71).[In light of prevailing understandings that oppose emotion to reason, acknowledging that protesters have feelings and might even be motivated by them risked painting activists as irrational, and so the dispassionate and calculating rational actor replaced the unthinking and irrational psychological misfit.]

The assumption of rationality was an important corrective, but it has produced a flat, thin picture of protesters and provides little insight into why such ostensibly dispassionate people would ever be motivated to engage in collective action. To be sure, protesters and activists are, in the broadest sense, rational actors: in various ways and to one degree or another, they calculate costs and benefits of action and strategize about how to secure their interests, but why, how, and under what conditions they do so is not self-evident and cannot simply be asserted or assumed.[18] Nor is rationality the whole story.

17. Early articulations of the resource mobilization model include McCarthy and Zald 1973, 1977. On the political process theory, see the sources cited in note 7.
18. For an early, insightful critique of the assumption of rationality in the dominant social movement models, see Ferree 1992.

The Emotional Turn

This is the terrain on which an *emotional turn* in the study of social movements and other forms of contentious politics has occurred, beginning in the late 1990s and continuing today.[19] The turn toward emotion is a response to the excesses of the rationalist paradigms, but it is an effort to offer a corrective without resurrecting the problems presented by the classical collective behavior models. To further situate this emotional turn, I sketch out below how scholars within this literature understand emotion and briefly consider some of the important contributions of the emotional turn. Then I lay out my own approach to the question of emotion and political (in)action, drawing from this literature and attempting to extend it both through explicit attention to the nonconscious, noncognitive, nonrational aspects of feeling and through provision of a framework for thinking about the emotional and the social together that takes seriously the bodily components of emotion.

EMOTION IN THE EMOTIONAL TURN.   What distinguishes literature in the emotional turn from previous scholarship on protest are its understandings of emotion and reason.[20] Where scholars of crowd behavior coded institutional politics as the realm of reason and maligned protest as the

19. A conference in February 1999 on emotion and social movements, organized by Jeff Goodwin, James Jasper, and Francesca Polletta and held at New York University, was especially important in launching the emotional turn. Prior to that conference, a number of pioneering social movement researchers had published pieces that foregrounded feeling and emotion (Brysk 1995; Flam 1990; Goodwin 1997; Groves 1995; Jasper 1997, 1998; Morgen 1983, 1995; Taylor 1995, 1996; and Taylor and Whittier 1995), but the NYU conference, perhaps because it drew together a group of scholars to think collectively about the topic, created a critical mass as well as a sense of momentum. The publication of a volume of essays largely from that conference—*Passionate Politics* (Goodwin, Jasper, and Polletta 2001a)— further advanced the emotional turn. The following list of other publications that focus on emotion and contentious politics is incomplete but indicates the emergence of a lively arena of scholarly inquiry and debate: Aminzade and McAdam 2001; a special issue of the journal *Mobilization* on emotions and contentious politics, edited by Aminzade and McAdam (7, no. 2 [June 2002]); Emirbayer and Goldberg 2005; Flam and King 2005; Goodwin and Jasper 2006; Goodwin, Jasper, and Polletta 2000, 2004; Gould 2000, 2004; Klatch 2004; Reed 2004; Reger 2004; Yang 2000. For histories of the social movement field that contextualize the emotional turn, see Aminzade and McAdam 2001; Calhoun 2001; Goodwin and Jasper 2006; Goodwin, Jasper, and Polletta 2000, 2001b; and Jasper 1997, esp. chap. 2.

20. Scholars in the emotional turn draw from the wealth of research on emotion conducted in fields as diverse as anthropology (e.g., Lutz 1986, 1988; Lutz and Abu-Lughod 1990; Rosaldo 1984), feminist philosophy (e.g., Jaggar 1989), history (e.g., Reddy 1997, 2001; Stearns and Lewis 1998; Stearns and Stearns 1986); neuroscience (e.g., Damasio

realm of emotion and thus unreason, and where the next generation of movement scholars simply wrote emotion out of their accounts, scholars in the emotional turn begin with the premise that emotion suffuses all aspects of social life. As Jasper puts it, "General affects and specific emotions are a part of all social life as surely as cognitive meanings and moral values are" (Jasper 1998, 405). Scholars accordingly cannot ignore emotion or relegate it to one arena (e.g., protest) that can then be disparaged and dismissed. In a related vein, where earlier research depicted protesters as emotional and assumed that other individuals and political actors were rational, and where the next generation of scholars assumed everyone was a rational actor, period, research in the emotional turn understands all human beings to be both rational and emotional, having the ability to reason, to think strategically, to assess and pursue their interests, to feel, and to emote. Even more, drawing from neuroscientific research, which has found that rationality *requires* emotion (e.g., Damasio 1994, xiii), scholars in the emotional turn challenge dualist oppositions that pit feeling and emotion, on the one hand, against thought, cognition, and reason, on the other. They similarly challenge both the equation of emotionality with irrationality and the notion that emotion necessarily engenders irrational behavior, arguing that *both* thought and emotion can be irrational, and *both* can lead to irrational behavior, although neither necessarily is or does so.

   In short, rather than being a force that interferes with reason that should therefore be sequestered from the public, political realm, emotion here is viewed as a crucial means by which human beings come to know and understand themselves and their contexts, their interests and commitments, their needs and their options in securing those needs. Scholars in the emotional turn challenge the rationalist assumption of the dominant paradigms without returning to the worst aspects of the collective behavior literature, which reduced protesters to psychologically broken individuals and understood protest in a depoliticized fashion as simply a form of acting out. A focus on emotion and feeling, then, need not, and *should* not, negate the rationality of protesters or the political nature of social movements and other forms of activism.

CONTRIBUTIONS OF THE EMOTIONAL TURN.   The most important contribution of the emotional turn is that it introduces a different ontology, a

---

1994, 1999), and sociology (e.g., Barbalet 1998; Collins 1990, 1993; Hochschild 1979, 1983; Kemper 1990; Scheff 1988, 1990a, 1990b; Thoits 1990).

different conception of social reality, into the study of social movements and other forms of contentious politics. Scholars in the emotional turn offer a multifaceted picture of human beingness that, without denying the rationality and ability to reason of social movement actors, recognizes emotion as a ubiquitous feature of human life that is present in, influences, and brings meaning to every aspect of social life, including the realm of political action and inaction.

This challenge to a rationalist ontology leads to a second important contribution. As others have argued, the factors that movement scholars deem important for mobilization have force precisely because of the feelings that they elicit, stir up, amplify, or dampen (Goodwin and Pfaff, 2001, 283; see also Jasper 1998, 399, 408 ff.; Goodwin, Jasper, and Polletta 2000, 74, and 2001b, 6; Aminzade and McAdam 2001, 17). Opening political opportunities, for example, will be an important factor in the emergence of a social movement only to the extent that an emotional charge attaches to those openings. Similarly, grievances are grievances only because they generate specific feeling states (Jasper 1997, 126). In short, attention to emotion is needed in order to understand the workings of the key concepts in the field. Because feelings are sometimes the primary hindrance to political mobilization and at other times the key catalyst for it, a third, related contribution of the emotional turn is that it points us toward a new, relatively unexplored arena for analyzing crucial sources of activism and blockages as well.

New Curves in the Emotional Turn

My own approach draws from the literature in the emotional turn while also extending it, both through explicit attention to what I call *affect* and by providing a framework for thinking about the bodily and social nature of emotion together. I contend that these new curves in the emotional turn illuminate aspects of human motivation and behavior as well as important social processes that we must consider if we want to understand political action and inaction.

Affect, Feelings, and Emotions

Most scholarship in the emotional turn uses the words *feeling(s)* and *emotion(s)* interchangeably, and the word *affect(s)* usually is absent.

Even when distinctions are made, there is a tendency to ignore or min-
imize their important implications.[21] My view is that some definitional
distinctions among these terms and, especially, acknowledgement of the
specific qualities of *affect* will enrich our studies. Concerned that social
constructionist understandings of emotion, which dominate the literature, have tended to tame feelings by rendering them in overly cognitive terms, my interest is in carving out a conceptual space within the
emotional turn for the noncognitive, nonconscious, nonlinguistic, and
nonrational aspects of the general phenomenon of emotion.[22] The definitional distinctions I offer here are in no sense "real," of course; like all
definitions, they are artificial namings, conventions. Each term, in fact,
has been defined in a variety of ways. But I am less interested in which
term gets attached to which definition than I am in pulling out certain
distinctions in order to strengthen our understandings of the emotional
dimensions of political action and inaction. The stakes are high in the
sense that how we use concepts influences how we understand and attempt to intervene in social reality. Below, I elaborate on the importance
of these definitional distinctions and argue that attention to what I am
calling *affect* illuminates important aspects of social life and dimensions
of political behavior that are otherwise obscured.

DEFINITIONS.   Drawing on the work of philosopher Brian Massumi
(1987, 2002, 2003), I use the term *affect* to indicate nonconscious and unnamed, but nevertheless registered, experiences of bodily energy and intensity that arise in response to stimuli impinging on the body.[23] These

21. In an early, programmatic statement advocating that social movement scholars attend to emotions, Jasper made distinctions within the category of emotion, but he only partially addresses the implications of those distinctions and in the end seems to obviate them
when he states that "even the most fleeting emotions are firmly rooted in moral and cognitive beliefs that are relatively stable and predictable" (1998, 421). As will become apparent,
this statement downplays the affective components of emotion. Goodwin, Jasper, and Polletta (2004) and Goodwin and Jasper (2006) explicitly distinguish different types of emotion, discussing each in relation to different social movement processes. That sort of typol-
ogy is not part of my project, but I share with these later pieces a desire to disaggregate the
category of emotion.

22. Scholars in the emotional turn draw from the sociological literature on emotions,
which also has a cognitive bias; for critiques, see Scheff 1988; Barbalet 1998, 80; Turner and
Stets 2006, 47; and Turner 2007, esp. chap. 2.

23. Although my perspective has been shaped by the many other scholars who write
about the nonconscious, physiological, bodily energetic aspects of emotion (e.g., Barbalet 1998; Collins 1993, 2004; Scheff 1988; and Turner 2007 in the sociology of emotions;
James 1890; Scherer 1984; and Tomkins [in Sedgwick and Frank 1995] in psychology; and

experiences are *registered* in that the organism senses the impingement
and the bodily effects, but *nonconscious* in that this sensing is outside
of the individual's conscious awareness and is of intensities that are inchoate and as yet inarticulable.[24] Affect, then, is the body's ongoing and
relatively amorphous inventory-taking of coming into contact and inter-
acting with the world. Drawing from psychoanalytic theory, I see affect
as unbound: it has no fixed object, no prior aim; rather, it is unattached,
free-floating, mobile energy (Laplanche and Pontalis 1973, 13–14, 50–
52). To get a better idea of affect, consider how we often experience our
feelings as opaque to ourselves, as something that we do not quite have
language for, something that we cannot fully grasp, something that escapes us but is nevertheless in play, generated through interaction with
the world, and affecting our embodied beings and subsequent actions. I
call that bodily, sensory, inarticulate, nonconscious experience *affect*.

As unspecified and unstructured bodily sensation, affect is bursting
with *potential* (that is what most interests Massumi). Another way to put
it is that affect colors nonlinguistic sensory experience by giving it a quan-
tity of intensity, and thus force, that prepares the organism to respond to
that which is impinging on it, *but in no predetermined direction.*[25]

I use the idea of an *emotion* or *emotions* to describe what of affect—
what of the potential of bodily intensities—gets actualized or concret-
ized in the flow of living. Emotions, Massumi writes, are "the expression
of affect in gesture and language, its conventional or coded expression"
(Massumi 2003, 232). Where affect is unfixed, unstructured, noncoherent, and nonlinguistic, an emotion is one's personal expression of what
one is feeling in a given moment, an expression that is structured by
social convention, by culture. The distinction here between *affect* and
an *emotion* can be illustrated through a discussion of one way we get
from the one to the other. Affect is outside of conscious thought, but,

---

Damasio 1994, 1999 in the field of neuroscience), I have been particularly influenced by
Massumi's discussion of what is at stake *politically* in this rendering of emotion (more on
that below). Massumi, incidentally, draws from Spinoza and Deleuze. Shouse 2005 is helpful for clarifying Massumi's argument.

24. Like Massumi, I use the word *nonconscious* rather than *unconscious* to reference
that which is outside of conscious awareness; the difference is that nonconscious perceptions do not require repression (Massumi 2002, 16).

25. Psychologist Silvan Tomkins contends that "the affect system provides the primary
motives of human beings" (Sedgwick and Frank 1995, 36); he too sees affects as indeterminate in their objects and aim, arguing that this quality grants human beings enormous
freedom (esp. chap. 1).

as sensory intensity, it can stir an inchoate sense that we are experiencing something, a vague stirring that, if forceful enough, can induce efforts—more or less conscious—to figure out what we are feeling and how to express it. In that figuring, we necessarily draw from our storehouse of knowledge, habit, and experience, as well as from culturally available labels and meanings, through which a gesture or linguistic naming that "expresses" what we are feeling emerges. This expression is never complete, never an exact representation of our affective experience (hence the scare quotes); it is better thought of as an approximation.

In this process of naming or approximately expressing what we are feeling, a transformation occurs, a reduction of an unstructured and unrepresentable affective state with all of its potential into an emotion or emotions whose qualities are conventionally known and fixed. Language and conventionalized bodily gestures thus in a sense "capture" affect, or attempt to. And that attempt gives specific form to an inchoate but pressing bodily sensation, shaping it, delimiting it, fixing it into the emotion or emotions that have been named or expressed. An emotion, in other words, brings a vague bodily intensity or sensation into the realm of cultural meanings and normativity, systems of signification that structure our very feelings.[26]

The unboundedness and nonfixity of affect, in contrast, provide it with enormous play, allowing it to move—and to be used, directed, mobilized—in a variety of nonpredetermined ways. The "capture" of affect, catching it up in culture, diminishes potential through inhibition and subsequent channeling of that which is actualized. But every "capture" of affect coincides with an escape of affect as well. Due to that escape, indeterminacy, and thus potential, accompany the processes through which something takes determinate form within culture (Massumi 2002, 8). There is always something more than what is actualized in social life.

The distinction I am drawing here between affect and emotions is not a temporal one, where, for example, first you have affect and then a fixed emotion in its place. Affect is always in play, even if not actualized. Indeed,

---

26. Geertz also has noted the role that language plays in ordering (and thereby altering) our feelings: "The achievement of a workable, well-ordered, clearly articulated emotional life in man is not a simple matter of ingenious instrumental control, a kind of clever hydraulic engineering of affect. Rather, it is a matter of giving specific, explicit, determinate form to the general, diffuse, ongoing flow of bodily sensation; of imposing upon the continual shifts in sentience to which we are inherently subject a recognizable, meaningful order, so that we may not only feel but know what we feel and act accordingly" (Geertz 1973, 80).

affect is what makes you *feel* an emotion (Shouse 2005); if there were no intensity to an emotion, it would not register as such. What that means is that nonconscious, noncognitive, and ultimately uncontainable bodily sensations that do not necessarily line up with our rational selves are a constant motivational force in individual lives and thus a force in social life as well.

We need an overarching term that encapsulates the entire phenomenon of affect and emotions, including those instances when the distinction is not of immediate import. I sometimes use the term *sentiment* in that manner, but more often I use the nouns *feeling* and *feelings* because they connote bodily, felt experience and also have been used in ways that reference the conventionality of felt experience.[27] The broad term *political feeling(s)* in my usage encompasses both affect and emotions. At this point my use of terms becomes a bit more complicated. I want to distinguish between the term *emotion(s)* when preceded by an article (e.g., *an* or *the*), and the term *emotion* in the singular when not preceded by an article. Where I define "an emotion" as affect actualized, I use *emotion* in the latter sense as an additional word for encapsulating the entire phenomenon of affect and emotions. I also use the term *emotional* in a broad sense: an *emotional habitus*, for example, includes both affect and emotions.

[In practice, affect and emotions usually are simultaneously in play and can be difficult to distinguish.]Affective states, for example, often generate immediate emotional displays, creating a sense that affect and emotional expression are one and the same. In addition, because human beings are oriented toward making sense of their experiences and expressing them to others, affective states can instantaneously be fixed into named emotions (although always incompletely). It is easy, then, to understand a named emotion or an emotional display as an expression of, and thus evidence of, a specific affective state or as the sum total of what someone is feeling.[Doing so would ignore the unstructured, indeterminate, nonlinguistic, and noncognitive nature of affect, but I raise the point here to indicate that, in the flow of living, it is often difficult to disentangle affect and emotions and precisely demarcate one from the other]

Why Affect?

Nevertheless, even with these empirical difficulties, making some *conceptual* distinctions is important, particularly because the category of af-

27. Hochschild (1979, 1983) speaks of *feeling rules,* for example.

fect has specific qualities of import in social life that are minimized and even obscured if we collapse all distinctions into one broad, undifferentiated category. With the term *affect,* I am trying to preserve a space for human motivation that is nonconscious, noncognitive, nonlinguistic, noncoherent, nonrational, and unpredetermined—all qualities that I argue play a role in political action and inaction. An affective ontology opens up a conceptual space that has shrunk considerably with the rise of rational-actor theories in the social sciences and has been difficult to inhabit in light of the important claims of the cultural and linguistic turns about the centrality of linguistic meaning-making practices in social life. Influenced by these latter intellectual developments and by an apparent anxiety that emotion will be construed as irrationality, scholars in the emotional turn sometimes have overly cognitivized and rationalized political feelings and downplayed what I call affect.[28] Goodwin, Jasper, and Polletta, for example, argue that "the emotions most relevant to politics . . . fall toward the more constructed, cognitive end" of a "dimension" at the other end of which are more automatic emotional responses (2001b, 13). For them, cognitive processing precedes and induces political emotions, making the latter in a sense rational: given the situation that one has now assessed, it is logical and expected that one would feel indignant or proud or ashamed. While I do not deny that political feelings can flow somewhat directly and expectedly from one's cognitive processing, this perspective masks the ways in which our feelings—political and otherwise—frequently diverge from our reasoning selves. In my view, if we neglect affect and fold feelings into cognition, or emphasize the cognitive dimension of feelings and how individuals' feelings align with their reason, we not only lose sight of the bodily, visceral qualities of feelings, but we also obscure a number of insights that an affective ontology provides for understanding political action and inaction.[29]

What, more precisely, is at stake in introducing an affective curve into the emotional turn? Let me begin to answer that question through

28. I am sympathetic to this anxiety about reintroducing emotion into the study of political activism, especially because ideas about the irrationality of protest and protesters are still so prevalent in the United States, and there is such a strong tendency to equate emotion with unreason. Making a distinction between the *non*rational and the *ir*rational, which I do below, helps to address this anxiety.

29. Calhoun also cautions against an overly cognitive cultural approach: "We will lose something of the specific idea of emotions if we lose touch with their bodily dimension" (2001, 47). See also Appadurai, 1990, 92.

a consideration of a structuring factor in lesbian and gay communities—
lesbian and gay ambivalence, mentioned earlier—a constellation of contradictory feeling states, including shame about homosexuality along
with gay pride, as well as desire for social acceptance along with repulsion from a society that oppresses sexual minorities. My research indicates that in the early years of the AIDS crisis, affective states circulating in lesbian and gay communities—including what in retrospect I
would call gay shame, a corollary fear of intensified social rejection, and
a frustrated desire for some sort of reciprocal recognition—had tremendous political import. So did gay pride, which was often expressed. But,
although the more negative feelings were rarely explicitly articulated and
seemed to operate primarily on a nonconscious, noncognitive level, they
course through lesbian and gay public discourses about the crisis in this
period. In chapter 1, I argue that this structure of ambivalence helped to
establish a political horizon that included caretaking, lobbying, and candlelight vigils, and made anything more confrontational largely unimaginable in the 1981–86 period.[30] Here I simply want to note that this politically consequential constellation of contradictory and unsettling feelings
operated more at the level of affect than at the level of named or name-
able emotions, more at the level of inchoate but pressing bodily intensities than at the level of cognitions.

Now, this might seem a risky proposition. With the collective behavior literature in mind, to propose lesbian and gay ambivalence as an important factor shaping lesbian and gay political responses to AIDS, and
to emphasize its affective dimensions, might be to approach too closely
the realm of the irrational. I see no reason to deny the irrational components of human motivation and action—*all* human beings have the capacity to be irrational if by that term we mean something like engaging in
illogical, senseless, and unreasonable behavior that goes against one's interests. But my rendering of affect actually is agnostic with regard to irrationality. Affect *may* generate irrationality, but it does not necessarily do
so. Affect is always *non*rational, however, by which I mean *outside of*—
but not necessarily *contrary to*—conscious, cognitive sense-making.[31]

---

30. This concept of lesbian and gay ambivalence—attentive to the psychic conflict generated by living in a heteronormative society—provides more traction for understanding
fluctuations in the form that lesbian and gay politics takes, it seems to me, than approaches
that posit an assimilationist/liberationist divide in lesbian and gay communities.

31. Berezin (2001, 93) similarly distinguishes between the nonrational and the irrational.

Pointing toward affect and the nonrational, then, need not return us to the problematic aspects of the collective behavior literature.[32]

But again, what does affect get us? What traction does it provide for thinking about social movements and other forms of contentious politics? How does attention to inchoate bodily sensation, to the nonrational, nonconscious, noncognitive aspects of emotion, advance our understandings of political action and inaction? I delineate here three of the important insights that an affective ontology provides.

THE COMPLEXITY AND INDETERMINACY OF HUMAN MOTIVATION AND BEHAVIOR. First, attending to affect advances our scholarship by pointing us toward politically important aspects of human motivation and behavior that a rationalist ontology and more cognitive renderings of feelings tend to obscure or misunderstand. Continuing the discussion of the political contours of lesbian and gay ambivalence will help to clarify this point. At the beginning of the AIDS epidemic, when the cause of AIDS was unknown but prominent scientific and media discourses suggested that homosexuality itself was the culprit, lesbians and gay men scrambled to make sense of what was happening and to figure out how they should respond. They drew from gay-liberation inspired discourses as well as from dominant, homophobic discourses, neither entirely subduing the other. But more was in operation than competing discourses. Affective states generated by lesbians' and gays' experiences of social nonrecognition and rejection—largely unacknowledged shame and associated anxiety about further social rejection, for example—made some lesbians and gay men receptive to the ideological claim that gay men were responsible for AIDS.[33] Indeed, the affective resonance of that prevailing discourse gave it a good deal of force, even for people who rejected its message on a cognitive level. People, of course, are affectively complex, subject to multiple and even contradictory affective states simultaneously. Feelings of pride, for example, were in play as well. I discuss these emotion dynamics in the following chapter, but what is notable at this point is that the emotional intensities provoked by the AIDS crisis, the multi-

32. The collective behavior literature, in my view, was problematic not because of its emphases on psychic conflict and irrationality but because it divided human beings into groups, preserving rationality for some (usually those invested in the status quo) while disparaging others (e.g., protesters) as irrational. Another problem is that it tended to posit feelings as prompting actions in an unmediated way.

33. On unacknowledged shame, see Scheff 1988; and Lewis 1971.

ple and often ambivalent affective states it stirred, influenced in complicated ways lesbians' and gay men's political responses to the crisis by shaping how they understood themselves and their world in this moment and thus their sense of political possibility.

As this example indicates, attending to affect rather than assuming rational actors or rendering emotion in cognitive terms illuminates a great deal by forcing consideration of the multiplicity and indeterminacy of human needs and desires; the often ambivalent and contradictory nature of our feelings; our more bodily and nonconscious forms of knowing and sense-making; inconsistencies and noncoherences within our thoughts and between our cognitive and felt responses to the world; our nonrational attachments (e.g., to normativity, to the social order); and the noninstrumental components of human behavior—all phenomena that have political consequences.

SOCIAL REPRODUCTION AND SOCIAL CHANGE.   Second, attention to affect illuminates an important source of social reproduction and social change that scholars of contentious politics have not yet explored very deeply. Regarding social reproduction, for example, affective states generate attachments to leaders, to reigning ideologies, to the existing social structures and hierarchies, and to normative ways of being.[34] Affect actually may be one of the most important sources of political *inaction*, a topic that needs much more attention both for its own sake and as an important point of comparison to analyses of the emergence of movements and other forms of contentious politics.

Affect is also a key force in social change. Ideas about the need for change and movement toward bringing it about often begin with an inarticulate and inarticulable sensation that something in the established order is not quite right. By signaling that something is awry, that things could be and perhaps should be different, affective states can inspire challenges to the social order. Affect, here, works as what Raymond Williams (1977) calls *structures of feeling.* The tension between dominant accounts of what is and what might be, on the one hand, and lived experience that contradicts those accounts, on the other, is not always con-

---

34. Some discussions of affect fail to recognize how affect can, in this sense, be nonliberatory (e.g., Massumi 2003). Discussions with Lauren Berlant have helped me to think about how affective states—a desire to feel reciprocity and a sense of belonging, for example—can generate attachments to normativity and current social arrangements, even those that create the stressful conditions of one's life. See Berlant 2007.

sciously understood; rather, it is often experienced "at the very edge of semantic availability," felt as "an unease, a stress, a displacement, a latency" (134, 130). These emergent, inchoate, not yet articulable ways of feeling (what Williams calls "structures of feeling," and what I am suggesting can also be understood as affective states) fail to reflect or identify with the existing order.[35] Even in their embryonic state, prior to, in Williams' words "definition, classification, or rationalization" (132)— that is, prior to being fixed in language—structures of feeling or affective states can shake one out of deeply grooved patterns of thinking and feeling and allow for new imaginings. A specific focus on affect, then, opens up an avenue of research into mobilization and social change that is obscured by rationalist ontologies and by renderings of feelings that downplay elements that may not be articulable but that nevertheless exert force, shaping people's experiences and knowledges of the world as well as their actions.

A focus on affect can help us to understand the workings of ideology, an important factor in both social reproduction and social change. Communications scholar Lawrence Grossberg argues that "affect is the missing term in an adequate understanding of ideology, for it offers the possibility of a 'psychology of belief' which would explain how and why ideologies are sometimes, and only sometimes, effective, and always to varying degrees" (1992, 82–83). Again, our affective states are what temper and intensify our attentions, affiliations, investments, and attachments; they help to solidify some of our ideas and beliefs and attenuate others. Affect, then, greases the wheels of ideology, but it also gums them up. As a result, attending to affect can illuminate how hegemony is effected but also why it is never all-encompassing.

A focus on affect retools our thinking about power. Power certainly operates through ideology and discourse, but it also operates through affect, perhaps more fundamentally so since ideologies and discourses emerge and take hold in part through the circulation of affect. Even more, affective states, unfixed in their directionality, can be molded and manipulated and then harnessed to the desired objectives of a leader,

35. Aligning Williams' *structure* of feelings with affect might introduce some terminological confusion insofar as I have described affect as *unstructured*, so let me clarify. In describing affect as *unstructured*, I mean that it is not within or contained by a semantic system. But affective states that are widely experienced in a given spatiotemporal context might be understood as a *pattern* (i.e., *structure*) of feelings, which is how I understand Williams' term.

the state, capital, or a movement. And of course, given the unfixed, fluid nature of affect, such efforts do not always succeed. An affect-inflected notion of power sheds new light on processes of social reproduction and social change.

MOVEMENTS AND MEANING-MAKING. A third benefit of attending to affect directly concerns social movements as sites where meaning is generated and disseminated. As mentioned earlier, affective sensations can incite attempts to figure out what one is feeling. The force of affect, along with its bodily, nonconscious, nonlinguistic, inchoate, and nontransparent qualities, is particularly motivating in this regard: you sense that you have been moved, that you are feeling something, but you do not quite know what it is because you lack immediate access to it; those qualities spur and give force to the impetus to make sense of the affective state(s). Social movement contexts provide a language for people's affective states as well as a pedagogy of sorts regarding what and how to feel and what to do in light of those feelings.[36] Movements, in short, "make sense" of affective states and authorize selected feelings and actions while downplaying and even invalidating others.

As an example consider the "emotion work" that occurred in women's consciousness-raising groups in the late 1960s and early 1970s.[37] Feminists challenged individualized and psychologized understandings of what many women were experiencing as depression, pointing to the social origins of that feeling state and renaming it *anger*. That interpretive emotion work encouraged women to understand themselves and their situations in new ways and indeed to feel differently, to feel angry rather than depressed and self-questioning. The sentiments of depression that many women were feeling might best be understood as affective states that arose from the conditions of life in a male supremacist social order, were attuned to the contradictions within that order, if only inchoately, and were full of potential in terms of reinscribing or inspiring challenges

36. What I am calling an *emotional pedagogy,* Polletta calls an *emotional propaedeutic* (2002, 36), and Geertz calls a *sentimental education* (1973, 449; see also Berezin 2001, 92). All of these terms point toward the training of feelings and sensations.

37. Sociologist Arlie Hochschild defines *emotion work* as "the act of trying to change in degree or quality an emotion or feeling," "the act of evoking or shaping, as well as suppressing, feeling in oneself" (1979, 561). I use the term to refer to efforts, conscious and not, to alter *others'* emotions and feelings as well. See also Goodwin and Pfaff 2001.

to that order. The context of the women's liberation movement helped direct that potential by naming a complex affective state as anger. The unstructured and unbound characteristics of affect—affect as potential, as not-yet-qualified intensities—allow and invite that sort of interpretation and reinterpretation. Movement contexts are sites where inchoately felt affective states get translated into named emotions, guiding the indeterminate potential of bodily intensities in directions that tend to align with the movement's goals. Attention to affect, then, directs social movement scholars to this very important arena of movement activity.[38]

This discussion gives a sense of how a focus on affect can strengthen our understanding of political action and inaction. To be clear, in arguing for an affective ontology, I am not suggesting that we disregard human rationality or that we ignore the cognitive aspects of feelings; attention to affect needs to accompany and qualify such perspectives, not supplant them. My point here is that, as rational and cognitive as we human beings are, we also are moved affectively, and any inquiry into political action and inaction thus needs to attend not only to feelings, but as well to the affective aspects of feelings.

Studying Affect

If its shaping role in political action and inaction indicates the need to study affect, its nonconscious, noncognitive, and nonlinguistic qualities raise the question of how to do so. To get a sense of the affective states in play in a given scene, close readings of texts, speech, and bodily action that are sensitive to affect are necessary. Feeling states do not need to be stated for us to suspect they are present. To study shame that occurs outside of conscious awareness, for example, sociologist Thomas Scheff describes a method based on attending to bodily "emotion markers"— gestures that are suggestive of what one is feeling (1988; Scheff draws from Lewis 1971; see also Ahmed 2004, 19, n. 23). Texts have emotion or affective markers as well. I read through hundreds of lesbian and gay newspapers to ascertain how people were making sense of and understanding AIDS at different points in the crisis, and was struck by the fre-

38. Taylor and Whittier (1995) do not speak in terms of affect *per se,* but they emphasize the role played by social movements in transforming and channeling feelings (see also Jasper 1998, 417).

quent expressions of gay pride in the early and mid-1980s; pride clearly was in play, but *how* lesbians and gay men expressed it—that is, what they attached pride to, the contrasts they drew, their tone, the aspirations that their expressions of pride conveyed—suggested that largely noncognitive, nonconscious states like anxiety and shame about gay difference were operating as well (see chapter 1). *How* they expressed pride, in other words, signaled that various affective states were in play, prompting me to investigate further. As another example, in the early 1990s, the way different sides in ACT UP's internal conflicts expressed anger toward one another—for example, the tenor and content of their angry expressions, each side's responses to the other's anger—indicated that sentiments of nonrecognition and even betrayal were in play but apparently were *felt* as anger and thus remained beneath conscious awareness, largely unarticulated and unacknowledged (see chapter 6). Reading in a manner that was attuned to the silences, to the inarticulable, to the inchoate, to the less-than-fully conscious, as well as to the specific (and changing) context of lesbian and gay communities amid this crisis, allowed me to get a sense of the preoccupations, fears, aspirations, and needs—whether expressed or not—that operated at various points in this history.

As I sorted through mountains of material and got a feeling for how lesbians and gay men were making sense of and responding to the crisis, initial hunches about the sorts of affective states in play either fell by the wayside or gained plausibility as the material repeatedly yielded corroborating evidence. To build a persuasive account about something as slippery as affect may require assembling a critical mass of material.

Introspective, emotional self-knowledge allows one to observe and read in a manner that can pick up the unspoken, the repressed, the less-than-fully conscious, the inarticulable. We are all emotional beings and as such have implicit knowledge about feelings, about what gives rise to various feeling states, about what sorts of actions they tend to prompt, and about how they tend to be expressed in various contexts. We also have self-knowledge about inchoate affective states, at least the knowledge that they exist and affect us and some sense of how they make us feel. In addition, because affects always arise in context, knowledge about the context one is studying, coupled with emotional self-knowledge, can point one toward the possible or probable affective states, given the specific historical conditions. In short, then, the opacity and untidiness of affect need not preclude its study.

Affect and the Social

Arguing for an affective ontology raises the question What of the social? After all, affect gestures toward the visceral, the bodily, the physiological, all of which seem to align affect with the natural, the innate, the raw, the individual—what might be understood as the presocial. The place of the social is similarly brought into question by a notion of affect as unrealized potential, which gestures toward the unruly, the wild, the indeterminate. Scholars in the emotional turn have joined others in challenging conventional understandings of feeling states that fail to recognize their social dimensions and construe them as the untamed wild.[39] Does an emphasis on the more bodily, affective components of emotion return us to a notion of feelings as individual and presocial? It need not, but the very question clarifies that we need a way to think of the bodily and the social components of emotion together.[40] In what follows, I provide a framework for doing so. I first offer a brief challenge to the idea that affect is presocial. I then introduce the concept of emotional habitus as a fruitful way to approach the question of the relationship between affect and the social. I conclude the section with a discussion of emotion and power, placing the bodily components of emotion firmly within view of scholars of contentious politics.

THE STATUS OF AFFECT VIS-À-VIS THE SOCIAL.   Affect is autonomic, involuntary, and physiological, but it is also inseparably intertwined with the social. Indeed, affect presupposes sociality: a body's affect system is about being affected and able to affect in turn, and thus is all about being in relation to a world populated by other beings and things. It would not exist in their absence. In other words, affects arise from social conditions as those conditions are encountered by a being with physiological properties; affect is a body's processing of social conditions, of its context. Affect *is*, then, about bodily, physiological processes, but those processes, and affect itself, can be considered presocial only by ignoring their relation to social phenomena.

Moreover, affect is shaped by social phenomena. *Shaped* by, not *determined* by—a distinction of key importance. As mentioned earlier, af-

---

39. For two examples, see Jasper 1998; and Emirbayer and Goldberg 2005.
40. For the purposes of this discussion, I am using *bodily* and *affective* interchangeably.

fect is not subsumable by the social: social conventions and practices to
some degree capture affect, but there is always an accompanying escape.
That escape is in relation to—indeed, is a by-product of—the capture of
affect, but those escaping intensities continue as unrealized potential
rather than being actualized as determinate emotions. Thus there is an
openness, indeed an unruliness, to affect, an indeterminacy and unpre-
dictability about it, even as affect is shaped by the social. The issue, then,
and this is what I take up in the following sections, is how to think of the
affective and the social together, in ways that account for the relative autonomy of affect (Massumi 2002, 35) as well as its intertwining with the
social.

Scholars in the emotional turn argue for an understanding of feelings
that recognizes their social dimensions. My goal here is to extend those
insights by providing a framework for thinking of the emotional and the
social together while simultaneously foregrounding the bodily, affective
dimensions of emotion. I develop the concept of emotional habitus for
this purpose.

EMOTIONAL HABITUS: BRINGING THE BODILY AND THE SOCIAL TO-
GETHER.   A central argument of *Moving Politics* is that the emotional
habitus of lesbian and gay communities, and shifts therein, shaped both
lesbian and gay attitudes about, as well as engagements in, distinctive
forms of AIDS activism from the recorded beginning of the epidemic
in 1981 through the early-to-mid-1990s. With the term *emotional habitus,* I mean to reference a social grouping's collective and only partly
conscious emotional dispositions, that is, members' embodied, axiomatic inclinations toward certain feelings and ways of emoting. By directly
affecting what people feel, a collectivity's emotional habitus can decisively influence political action, in part because feelings play an important role in generating and foreclosing political horizons, senses of what
is to be done and how to do it.[41] There are also moments when the hold
of an emotional habitus is loosened, especially due to the unruly qualities of affect. Here, I further lay out what I mean by the term *emotional
habitus,* discuss its relation to affect, and suggest the value of the con-

41. With his concept of *cognitive liberation,* McAdam (1999) noted the importance of
coming to believe that change is possible; my introduction of feelings into the mix challenges the cognitive bias in that important concept.

cept for analyses of social movements and other forms of contentious politics.[42]

Pierre Bourdieu defines a *habitus* as the socially constituted, commonsensical, taken-for-granted understandings or schemas in any social grouping that, operating beneath conscious awareness, on the level of bodily understanding, provide members with a disposition or orientation to action, a "sense of the game" and how best to play it (Bourdieu 1977, 1990; Bourdieu and Wacquant 1992). From living and acting within various social contexts—what Bourdieu calls *fields,* each with its hierarchical structure, regularities, logic, and stakes—one acquires a practical sense of "things to do or not to do, things to say or not to say" (Bourdieu 1990, 53), a sense that is obvious and goes without saying, given your location in a particular field and what seems (im)possible from there. A habitus thereby structures individual and collective practices. It is itself also structured by such practices and thus as well by the social conditions that shape people's dispositions. The habitus concept encapsulates the dialectical relationship between structure and practice: they make, unmake, and remake one another. [Social structures do not come into being or survive except through human practices which, while creative and improvisatory, are themselves structured and not reducible to the conscious, willed, independent actions of rational actors in pursuit of their interests (Bourdieu 1990).]

The habitus, this practical sense, is acquired—and thus has a relation to the social—but it is also embodied, inculcated at the level of nonconscious, bodily knowledge. It is acquired almost as a direct feed into the body that bypasses more conscious thought processes. That noncognitive process of embodiment, a literal *incorporation* in Judith Butler's words (Butler 1997, 154), is what makes the social in us *feel* like "second nature," like our own individual thoughts, values, feelings. [Indeed, that acquired practical sense to a large degree *becomes* one's "nature," one's dispositions, one's axiomatic orientation toward action in the various fields that one traverses.]

What I especially like about the habitus concept is that it illuminates the noncognitive, nonconscious, bodily, and indeed affective processes

---

42. I only recently came across the work of Nick Crossley, who also uses Bourdieu's notion of habitus to think about social movements. See in particular Crossley 2002, 2003. Thanks to Marc Steinberg for introducing me to Crossley's work.

through which we become enculturated. The very obviousness of certain
practices—obviousness at the level of the viscera—means that their enactment tends to occur without much thought or reflection. Take norms
for example. The concept of habitus provides great insight into how normativity works and why it is so powerful. People rarely engage in conscious, rational calculations about whether to follow social norms. From
acting within various fields, we get a bodily sense of how we must be,
what we must do, to get by, to survive, to be intelligible, to fit in, to be
heard, to be loved, to gain respect, or to be recognized. That bodily, practical sense does not have the coherence or directiveness of a blueprint—
it can be fuzzy and ambiguous, even contradictory, and of course changeable as well—but it nevertheless provides force to our orientation to practical action. To be more precise, it is the emotional charge attached to
our practical sense that gives the latter such force. The affects and feelings that attach to abiding by norms—bodily intensities that we might
call recognition and belongingness—as well as the promise or threatened withdrawal of such feeling states, catch us up in normativity.[43]
The habitus concept illuminates the processes—bodily, nonconscious,
affective—through which actors are conscripted, unwittingly but will-
ingly, into the social.

The term *emotional habitus* extends the habitus concept into the
realm of feeling. Operating beneath conscious awareness, the emotional
habitus of a social group provides members with an emotional disposition, with a sense of what and how to feel, with labels for their feelings,
with schemas about what feelings are and what they mean, with ways
of figuring out and understanding what they are feeling. An emotional
habitus contains an emotional pedagogy, a template for what and how
to feel, in part by conferring on some feelings and modes of expression
an axiomatic, natural quality and making other feeling states unintelligible within its terms and thus in a sense unfeelable and inexpressible. [A
social group's emotional habitus structures what members feel and how
they emote. It is structured as well, shaped by the field(s) in which it operates, and instantiated, stabilized, reproduced, and potentially transformed through practices like enactments or intimations of feelings and

43. This does not preclude defiance of norms, which of course occurs; but even here the
concept of habitus is useful in that such defiance perhaps occurs most readily when there
is a subgroup with another habitus orienting members toward different sorts of practical
action.

statements about what is (non)normative regarding feelings and their expression.]

Also important to note is that a collectivity's structural positioning within a field influences its emotional habitus.[Lesbians' and gay men's positioning within a heteronormative society, for example, has helped to generate an ambivalent emotional habitus in lesbian and gay communities that includes contradictory feeling states about both homosexuality and dominant heterosexual society, as I mentioned above.[44] The emotional habitus of marginalized groups are influenced by the reigning emotional habitus in a society, but their contours derive as well from specific experiences of oppression.

[One reason that I like the term *habitus* for thinking about feelings is that it locates feelings within social relations and practices, thereby pointing toward their conventionality and countering a standard understanding of feelings as wholly interior to the individual.] I am especially drawn to the concept because it forces us to consider *together* phenomena that are often opposed to one another: the social and conventional aspects of emotion, on the one hand, along with the nonconscious and bodily components, on the other.[45] [Indeed, an emotional habitus has force precisely because its bodily and axiomatic qualities obscure the social, conventional nature of feelings and generate the sense that what one is feeling is entirely one's own.]★

While I argue that the axiomatic and nonconscious qualities of an emotional habitus give it a force that shapes how members of a social group feel, emote, label, and understand their feelings, I also want to note, especially in light of more totalizing usages of the habitus concept, that variability of feeling and contestations of emotional norms are always present within a collectivity. The tendency within a social grouping will be toward similar ways of feeling and emoting, but people's different histories influence how a reigning emotional habitus shapes their particular feelings and practices. Habitus, as systems of dispositions, are not

44. The work of Du Bois (1989), de Beauvoir (1989), and Fanon (1967) indicates ambivalent emotional habitus within other oppressed groups, each with its specific shape and content.

45. I prefer the term *emotional habitus* to a concept from the sociology of emotions literature that on its face might appear similar—*emotion culture* (Gordon 1989)—because the former, by emphasizing practices, especially those that are nonconscious and noncognitive, offers an account of why and how specific feelings become widespread within a collectivity and why and how they sometimes change.

exact blueprints but consist of "virtualities, potentialities, eventualities" whose actualization is contingent (Bourdieu and Wacquant 1992, 135).[46] Emotional habitus shape ways of feeling and emoting; they do not produce them in a mechanical, deterministic way.

I veer from standard usages of the term in two related ways. First, Bourdieu developed the concept to account for social reproduction, but I also consider how a habitus might be instrumental in generating social change. Social movements, for example, generate schemas of perception, ways of understanding the world, sentiments—habitus—that dispose participants to question the status quo and to engage in specific forms of activism and other movement practices that can lead to social transformation.[47] Second, while Bourdieu emphasizes the durability of habitus and of the dispositions toward practical action that they engender, part of my focus is on their malleability. I agree that habitus tend to be more or less stable, but because they are constituted through human practice, they are dynamic and always subject to alteration. For their reproduction, habitus must be reinstantiated, and that need to be repeated creates the possibility for, in Butler's words, "a variation on that repetition" (1999, 185). Bourdieu agrees in principle insofar as any habitus, as knowledge of the game and how to play it, requires and ensures an ability to improvise within the contours set by the game itself; that improvisation can alter the habitus (as well as broader social arrangements). Habitus, then, are historically contingent, requiring us to investigate the practices that generate, stabilize, reproduce, and sometimes transform them. Precisely that sort of analysis of lesbian and gay community emotional habitus is at the core of *Moving Politics*.

AFFECT, EMOTIONAL HABITUS, EMOTIVES.   In stating that our feelings, including our affective states, are influenced by the reigning emotional habitus and to that extent are cultivated, I might seem to be contradicting my earlier claims about the open-endedness and unruliness of af-

46. Because emotional habitus shape the feelings and emotions of *all* of us, the concept usefully challenges any notion that social movement "leaders" are strictly rational, while "followers" are emotional. As Emirbayer and Goldberg write, activist leaders "are not quasi-divine unmoved movers; they, too, are formed within the flow of emotional engagement and located inside the very configurations of passion that they seek to manipulate and control" (2005, 479).

47. Crossley (2003) makes a similar argument. Butler (1997, 141–57) also indicates the possibility of transformative habitus when she challenges Bourdieu's suggestion that performative utterances are only effective when spoken by those with social power.

fect.[It is difficult to think of the capture and escape of affect together, to think about affect as caught up in but not subsumed by the social.]Because the concept of emotional habitus requires us to think about that relationship between the bodily and the social, it can help us to bring affect into our analyses in sociologically productive ways.

Earlier I discussed how our experiences of affect can prompt attempts to make sense of what we are feeling. That experience is part of what provokes a given emotional habitus into action insofar as the latter is what provides us with schemas for interpreting and naming our affects, and for figuring out what to think and do about what we are feeling. In other words, the unintelligibility and forcefulness of an affective experience urges sense-making, and the emotional habitus obliges. In the subsequent process, the emotional habitus shapes one's affects, effectively altering one's feeling experience.

William Reddy's notion of *emotives*—emotional statements like "I'm angry," in which the referent changes with the emotional statement itself—helps to illuminate how an emotional habitus and the emotives it makes possible and probable can alter affects (Reddy 1997, 1999, 2000, 2001). (Terminology is somewhat problematic here in that Reddy and I use different terms: where I use *affect,* Reddy uses both *feeling* and *emotion.* I will stick to my terminology as much as possible and clarify when my use of a term might be unclear.)[An emotive is an attempt to name an affective state that is forceful but as yet illegible.]Reddy (1997) labels such emotional utterances *emotives* to evoke their performative quality: [an emotive actually *does* something;]rather than merely describing or representing one's preexisting affective state—an impossible task given the nature of affect—an emotive alters it. As Reddy argues, "the 'external referent' that an emotive appears to point at . . . emerges from the act of uttering in a changed state" (1997, 331). When someone utters an emotive like "I'm angry," she attempts to make legible and verbal what was previously nonverbal and unable to be directly observed by anyone, including herself, but this effort to name and categorize necessarily elides the gap between language and the felt affect.[48] Many components of affect fail to be brought into the verbal realm. From a psychoanalytic perspective, we might understand them as being repressed; from a compatible but more affect-oriented perspective, we might understand them as simply remaining outside of awareness, not made meaningful through

48. Barbalet (1998, 24) makes a similar point.

language. The emotive, then, purporting to *describe* an affective state, enacts a slippage and thereby actually *alters* the affect(s) to which it refers (Reddy 2000, 117).[49]

This always imperfect naming and categorization process brings into being a named, legible, definite *emotion* (in my terminology) in the place of a felt but amorphous and uncategorized affective state. It also produces a "residuum" (Reddy 1997, 333)—the unnamed excess of the interpretive process—which remains opaque, perhaps forceful enough to prompt further efforts at interpretation, perhaps simply remaining at the level of a felt but relatively faint bodily intensity. Probably because it is extradiscursive, Reddy does not say much about the character of this residue or what exactly happens to it. In Massumi's terms, what the emotive does is effect the simultaneous capture and escape of affect, so the residue is affect—uncontained potential. It continues to be experienced, however nonconsciously or inchoately, and may continue to exert force and motivate. This affective residue, then, is an extradiscursive by-product of discursive processes and in that sense is molded by social processes. At the same time, noting that it is extradiscursive allows us to see that affect is not encompassed by the linguistic processes that partially capture it but that it also escapes.

To summarize: Affect can generate a strong desire to make sense of itself. That desire mobilizes the emotional habitus. With its matrix of possible and probable emotives and other interpretive schema, an emotional habitus provides means for interpreting and naming one's affective states. But such efforts at capturing an affective state in language never simply *describe* an (indescribable) affective state, but in fact actually *alter* the affective state that initiated the search for its meaning. An emotional habitus, in short, encourages practices that themselves shape affect.[50] Affect, importantly shaped by emotional habitus, is inextricably intertwined with, although not subsumable by, the social.

Emotives, emotional displays, and other sorts of practices are made possible or probable through an emotional habitus, and their enactment

49. Reddy has more recently noted that second-person emotion claims, for example, "You are angry," have emotive-like effects on the hearer if she or he reflects on the claims (2000, 117); I would add that first-person plural emotion claims, for example, "We are angry," are also emotives, potentially affecting the feelings of the speaker and of those hearing the claim.

50. As will become apparent in my narrative of AIDS activism, emotives operate at a collective level too; public claims of lesbians' and gay men's pride, for example, can generate a widespread gay pride along with an affective residue that remains unnamed.

in turn tends to stabilize and reproduce that habitus by reinstantiating the prevailing affects and emotions, their axiomatic quality and naturalness, and the reigning schemas and attitudes about emotion and emotionality. But a social group's improvisational practices regarding feelings can also unmake and transform the emotional habitus, allowing for new affects and emotions, for new attitudes about feeling and emoting, for the development of new emotional taken-for-granteds. Affect is particularly important in this regard. A forceful bodily intensity might contradict the established emotional habitus and jar one out of axiomatic ways of feeling and emoting that come to feel overwrought, inadequate, or simply off base. That strong affective state might succeed in puncturing the dominant emotional habitus with its prevailing attitudes, norms, and ways of feeling and emoting, and inaugurate a new constellation of feelings, emotions, and emotional postures. It might challenge the more general reigning dispositions and orientations to action as well. Affect, in short, has the potential to escape social control, and that quality creates greater space for counter-hegemonic possibilities and for social transformation.[51]

EMOTION AND POWER. The idea that affect can and cannot be tamed raises the question of power, both as a repressive and productive force. As the discussion of habitus indicates, one of the ways in which power operates is affectively: power is exercised through and reproduced in our feelings, and it is forceful and effective precisely because of that. The power of a habitus to structure human behavior, for example, derives from the fact that it operates at the visceral affective level, often bypassing conscious thought altogether.[52] We acquire a *feel* for the game, meaning that on a bodily, affective level we gain a sense of what is possible and probable, and thus of what to do and what not to do, given the circumstances; we all tend to be compelled by that sort of bodily information and thus tend to follow it, thus reproducing the existing social order. If we accept that affect helps to secure a given habitus, then we can see that social forces are powerful to the extent that they are able to manipulate the affective charges that get attached to all aspects of living. Because an

51. The direction of change, of course, can be in a reactionary or more liberatory direction.

52. That is not to deny that domination is sometimes actualized through thought and beliefs, but simply to note that ideology or hegemony are not the whole story with regard to domination.

emotional habitus can structure people's feelings, including those affective charges, it is especially important for the operations of power. And
an emotional habitus is thus a critical arena of political struggle. As an
example, consider how an emotional habitus that generates fear of terrorism can enhance a regime's power to regulate and control its population. This ability to evoke affective states and emotions, as well as
to establish and enforce norms about feelings and their expression—the
power of an emotional habitus—is a dimension of power that we tend to
overlook. But that ability may be more than useful; it may actually be a
requirement for the operation of some forms of power. Reddy contends,
for example, that any enduring political regime "must establish as an essential element a normative order for emotions," what he calls an "emotional regime" (Reddy 2001, 124). Reddy is speaking of political regimes
specifically, but other sorts of social formations similarly need individuals to feel and emote in certain ways and not in others. Also pointing
to the exercise of power through emotion, sociologist Helena Flam discusses "cementing emotions," those that "uphold social structures and
relations of domination," feelings like loyalty, gratitude, faith in the system (Flam 2005, 19–20; see also Berezin 2001).

More particular forms of domination are also upheld through control
over or production of emotion. In this regard, sociologists Mustafa Emirbayer and Chad Goldberg flag as particularly insightful Bourdieu's analysis of symbolic violence: "Actors often enjoy a certain emotional power
over others, [Bourdieu] argues, and this is facilitated by the fact that the
latter's very dispositions and habitus are often constituted in such a way
as to 'predestine' them to modes of emotional engagement and response
that leave them complicit in that domination" (Emirbayer and Goldberg
2005, 492). Bourdieu discusses how, for example, masculine domination
is perpetuated in part through the socially constituted dispositions of
women that orient them toward "feminine submissiveness," a habituated
compliant and subservient mode of being that manifests and is reiterated in women's bodies in the form of "*bodily emotions*—shame, humiliation, timidity, anxiety, guilt—or *passions* and *sentiments*—love, admiration, respect. These emotions are all the more powerful when they are
betrayed in visible manifestations such as blushing, stuttering, clumsi-
ness, trembling, anger, or impotent rage, so many ways of submitting,
even despite oneself and 'against the grain,' to the dominant judgment"
(Bourdieu 2001, 38–39, emphases his; quoted in Emirbayer and Goldberg 2005, 492). Our affective states and emotions, shaped by the social

world but experienced as solely our own, can smooth the workings of power in part by obscuring its very operations.

Our feelings can disrupt the operations of power as well, of course. While it is true that emotional habitus may be nonconsciously absorbed by individuals, and thus quite forceful, it also is true that people sometimes actively resist them. Hochschild, for example, notes that people can intentionally defy what she calls *feeling rules* by refusing to manage their feelings appropriately (Hochschild 1979, 567). More involuntarily, people may experience feelings that are conventionally unacceptable, and they might not submerge them. Such *outlaw emotions,* as feminist philosopher Alison Jaggar calls them, have subversive potential in that they can "enable us to perceive the world differently from its portrayal in conventional descriptions. They may provide the first indications that something is wrong with the way alleged facts have been constructed, with accepted understandings of how things are. . . . [They] may lead us to make subversive observations that challenge dominant conceptions of the status quo" (Jaggar 1989, 161).[53] Similar to Williams's structures of feelings, outlaw emotions can help to unravel hegemonic ideologies. One of the most significant aspects of social movements is that they are sites for nurturing counter-hegemonic affects, emotions, and norms about emotional display, as mentioned above.

We can, and need to, think affect and the social together. Affect is open-ended and polygenerative but also capturable and able to be made determinate, if incompletely, within an actually existing context. The concepts of emotional habitus and emotives provide us with a way to understand that simultaneous capture and escape of affect.

One of my contentions in this book is that insofar as emotional habitus shape what people actually feel, they can have tremendous effects on political action and inaction, generating, for example, fear of the unknown, high expectations regarding change, satisfaction with the status quo, angry dissatisfaction with the status quo, or political depression— feelings that, each in its own way and in combination with others, help to establish a given political imaginary and block others. This was certainly the case with regard to the different emotional habitus that prevailed in lesbian and gay communities across the 1981–1995 period. Each emotional habitus, and the emotives each made possible and probable,

53. On the political implications of this sort of emotional "deviance," see also Thoits 1990.

offered, for example, different ways to navigate the feeling states that make up lesbians' and gay men's ambivalence, sometimes elevating their desire for social acceptance and anxiety about social rejection, at other times submerging those feeling states and instead elevating rage against those who had socially annihilated them and were now physically annihilating them as well. One important task, then, is to explore these emotional habitus, the practices through which they were generated, reproduced, and sometimes transformed, how the different emotional habitus shaped the affective states and emotions widely circulating in lesbian and gay communities, and the ways in which the different emotional habitus influenced attitudes about and engagements in distinct forms of AIDS activism.

The Movement of Movements into History

The movement of movements into history is not without its affective dimensions. That became clear to me in June 1994 when I saw an exhibit at the New York Public Library commemorating the twenty-fifth anniversary of the 1969 Stonewall Riots, the legendary beginning of the modern lesbian and gay liberation/rights movement.[54] The exhibit, *Becoming Visible: The Legacy of Stonewall,* creatively documented a century of lesbian and gay history in the United States. It was magnificent. You could listen to eight decades of music of historical importance to lesbians and gay men, thumb through lesbian pulp novels, and enjoy male physique magazines. There were photographs of bars, bath houses, and political meetings. Much of the exhibit focused on the lesbian and gay movement, starting with the homophile organizations of the 1950s. There were ephemera from the women's and gay liberation movements as well, including buttons, protest posters, and other agit-prop. I remember a letter from Huey Newton of the Black Panther Party expressing his support for gay liberation and gay lib material voicing solidarity with the Panthers and other movements.

Immensely enjoying myself, I was winding my way through the exhibit when I turned the corner and came face to face with images, doc-

---

54. The exhibit was curated by Fred Wasserman, Molly McGarry, and Mimi Bowling, with support from a number of scholars and lesbian and gay cultural institutions. See McGarry and Wasserman 1998, a book based on the exhibit.

uments, and ephemera from ACT UP, included as a part of this history. I stopped, stunned, overtaken by ambivalence. On the one hand, I felt the sweet surprise of recognition: what an honor that ACT UP was being placed within this history, a successor to previous social movements that had fought for various types of liberation and helped to change the world. But this recognition of the historical import of ACT UP was bittersweet in that it was occurring at the painful moment of the movement's decline. A few of us were still struggling to keep ACT UP/ Chicago together, and a number of other ACT UP chapters were similarly hobbling along, but many chapters had already dissolved, and as a national movement, ACT UP was no longer what it had been. We were moving from the streets into history, a shift made quite apparent in this museum-like exhibit, where ACT UP joined other movements safely encased behind glass. Given the continuing AIDS epidemic,[55] history was not exactly what or where we wanted to be, and my immobility was due in part to a belated realization that the movement was indeed coming to an end.

An event a few years later indicated that the issue of ACT UP and history evoked ambivalence among other former participants as well. Fearing the erasure of ACT UP from official Chicago lesbian/gay/bisexual/ transgender (LGBT) history, some former ACT UP/Chicago members nominated the group, posthumously, to the City of Chicago's Lesbian and Gay Hall of Fame, and the nomination was accepted. Significantly, previous nominations of ACT UP—during the period when it was an active, vibrant organization (frequently targeting Chicago's Mayor Daley)—had been rejected. Upon the acceptance of its nomination this time, former ACT UP/Chicago members got together and composed a statement that we read at the induction ceremony.[56] Part of it follows:

> Many people see this event tonight as a celebratory occasion, part of a long process of honoring LGBT individuals and organizations who have contributed to "our community." But for us, this event is full of tragic ironies. At the very point when there seems to be a "consensus" that "the AIDS crisis is over," a point of view with which we profoundly disagree, it finally seems

55. This was before the advent of protease inhibitors. There were few anti-HIV treatments, and those that did exist were not particularly promising; people were still dying all around us, from among us.

56. I was not one of those who nominated ACT UP, but I did participate in the subsequent meetings and the event itself.

"safe" enough, "distant" enough, to include ACT UP/Chicago in the "official" LGBT pantheon. To us, however, this occasion is more like a political
funeral.

This official commemoration of ACT UP, even though initiated by
former members, felt painful and politically suspect, coming as it did in
relation both to ACT UP's decline and to the ongoing AIDS crisis with
its continuing political dimensions.

I recount these stories in order to raise questions about the movement
of movements into history and about my own role as a historian of the
direct-action AIDS movement. Where the timing of the above incidents
provoked ambivalence about the potentially depoliticizing effects of the
assignment of ACT UP to history, the issues in the current moment—
twenty-plus years after the emergence of the direct-action AIDS movement and more than a dozen since its decline—revolve around questions
of authorship and voice. Whoever tells the history of a movement shapes
it as well. There is an immense responsibility, then, in recounting the history of a movement that was made up of thousands of participants, each
with his or her own rendering of ACT UP. The responsibility is magnified in light of the fact that many participants are dead; we will never
know the content, sound, and texture of their histories of the movement.
My hope is that by integrating voices and perspectives other than my
own—via archival research and in-depth interviews—a more complex,
multilayered picture of ACT UP will emerge. But this account is necessarily partial. My own perspectives, understandings, preoccupations,
feelings, and desires, and changes in all of them over time, have shaped
this project in specific and probably peculiar ways. Some who participated may not recognize their own experiences in what I relay here.
This book, then, stands as an invitation to further discussion and debate
about ACT UP (and an invitation to a more general discussion of the
emotional dimensions of political action and inaction).

Why Study Early AIDS Activism?

This book also argues against a type of forgetting that frequently characterizes the way we Americans deal with our country's often horrific
past (and our present as well). Where once I was stopped in my tracks
by what seemed like a premature induction of ACT UP into lesbian and

gay history, I now am concerned that the early years of the AIDS crisis, along with AIDS activism from the 1980s and 1990s—phenomena that defined lesbian/gay/queer politics and were important contours of the U.S. political landscape in that period—are being forgotten. As early as 1990, AIDS activist and cultural theorist Cindy Patton wrote that an amnesia regarding the early history of AIDS activism had set in. She saw its origins in the growing professionalization of the AIDS service industry but argued that the loss of this history was reinforced by progressives who "[had] begun to locate the beginning of AIDS activism in 1987 or 1988, with the emergence of ACT UP" (Patton 1990, 19–20). Early AIDS activist history has been eclipsed even further since 1990 as part of the erasure from national consciousness of AIDS as a crisis. The history of ACT UP also has started to disappear, in a manner similar to the erasure from official history of other defiant social movements and practices of resistance in the United States.[57]

What we lose if the history of AIDS activism in this country is forgotten is the memory of a government of a wealthy, ostensibly democratic country unmoved by the deaths of hundreds, thousands, and finally hundreds of thousands of its own inhabitants, largely because the overwhelming majority of them were gay and bisexual men, and the others were seen as similarly expendable: drug users as well as poor men and women, a disproportionate number of whom were black and Latino/a. We are at risk of losing as well the history of lesbian/gay/queer collective political resistance in the face of the government's aggressive indifference, extreme negligence, and punitive policies regarding AIDS. Along with my goal of thinking broadly about the emotional sources of political action and inaction, then, I aim to document a disappearing history and hope that *Moving Politics* will help us to think about activism in the current moment as well.

The book is divided into three parts. In part 1, I analyze the earliest days of the AIDS epidemic when mysterious diseases afflicting gay men were first reported, and proceed to the caretaking, service-provision, and lobbying efforts of the early and mid-1980s (chapter 1). I then explore the emergence of more confrontational, direct-action AIDS activism in the middle of 1986 and its rapid dissemination across the coun-

---

57. Those movements that have been enshrined in the official history have often been sanitized or used to advance a developmental narrative that relegates the need for confrontational activism to the distant past.

try after the founding of ACT UP/New York in 1987 (chapter 2). These two chapters attempt to explain the emergence of AIDS activism, the forms it took in the earliest years, and the expansion of the political horizon that occurred five years into the crisis and ushered in a period of more contentious activism. Both chapters track the various feeling states circulating in lesbian and gay communities in this period. Part 1's conceptual focus is the generation, reproduction, and transformation of an emotional habitus, and the effects those emotional processes had on political imaginaries and on political activism. In part 2, I examine the development and flourishing of the national direct-action AIDS movement into the early 1990s (chapters 3 and 4). Conceptually, part 2 is centrally concerned with activism as world-making and the feeling states that it generates. It also considers how activists' emotion work helps to secure an emergent and counter-hegemonic emotional habitus. In part 3, I investigate the decline of the national movement in the early-to-mid-1990s (chapters 5, 6, and 7). The conceptual focus is on the affective dimensions of movement decline. I explore how changes in a movement's context can generate affective states that are difficult to address and that profoundly challenge the movement's viability.

Emotion and Activism

There are strong biases in U.S. society against anger and protest, and, not surprisingly, against the two in combination. Angry protests violate norms of decorum and typically are seen as unnecessary in a democratic polity like the United States. In part as a result, shame, embarrassment, and fear of social rejection readily attach to political activities that occur outside routine channels. In that sense, feelings, which might seem trivial when exploring all things political, are profoundly consequential. Given their consequentiality, it seems vital to think about the ways in which feelings are produced; the ways in which power relationships are exercised through and reproduced in our feelings; the ways in which a society's or social group's emotional habitus disciplines us; and how our feelings, as well as a given emotional habitus, shape our views of what is politically possible, desirable, and necessary, thereby helping to establish a political horizon and to determine whether we turn to political activism—and in what forms, if we do. One of the political goals of this project is to expose feeling states as sites of power, demonstrating their role in regulating political behavior, particularly in terms of foreclosing senses of political possibility and blocking contentious politics. At the same time, an emotional habitus is never totalizing, and a social order's attempts at control through affect and emotions are never thoroughly successful. Another goal of this project, then, is to show how affect and emotions also nourish resistance by prying open ideas about what is to be done and spurring people into action.

PART I

The Affects and
Emotions of Mobilization

The emergence of ACT UP in New York in 1987 and its rapid spread across the United States initially presented no puzzle to me. The AIDS crisis was exploding by that point, and the devastation in lesbian and gay communities, especially in large cities, was immense. Gay men in particular were suffering extreme and multiple losses as close friends, lovers, ex-lovers, acquaintances, neighbors, and co-workers died painful and early deaths; by this point, some gay men had lost their entire social circle to AIDS. At the same time, AIDS-related discrimination, ostracism, and violence were on the rise. And yet, almost six years into the epidemic, President Reagan, intent on preserving close relations with leaders of the religious right, had yet to make even one policy speech on AIDS.[1] Worse yet, his administration did not request an appropriation to fund AIDS research until May 1983—nearly two years after the official start of the epidemic—and in subsequent years the administration consistently attempted to cut already inadequate Congressional appropriations to deal with the exploding crisis. The National Institutes of Health (NIH)—the federal agency responsible for conducting and sup-

---

1. Reagan had hardly even mentioned AIDS in public prior to an April 2, 1987, speech. Reagan's first public mention of AIDS was in September 1985, in response to a reporter's question (Beegan 1985; Boffey 1985); his only other public mention of AIDS prior to April 1987 was in February 1986, in a message to Congress (http://www.aegis.com/topics/timeline, accessed July 1, 2007).

porting medical research—did not begin a concerted research effort until 1983 (McGarry and Wasserman 1998, 225). Here is a telling comparison: in 1976, the CDC spent nine million dollars within months of the initial outbreak of what became Legionnaires' Disease, an outbreak that killed thirty-four people; in contrast, during the entire first year of the AIDS epidemic, when more than two hundred people died, the CDC spent just one million dollars on AIDS (Rimmerman 2002, 93). All levels of government were either aggressively ignoring the AIDS epidemic or using it as an opportunity to attack those suffering most. Indeed, rather than providing adequate funding for AIDS research, treatment, and other services, by the mid-1980s all levels of government were increasingly considering punitive laws that called for mandatory HIV-testing and even quarantine. Right-wing pundits were calling for extreme measures, including tattooing HIV-positive people. A prevailing sentiment among lesbians and gay men during the mid-1980s was that their community was under attack. There also was a strong and growing sense that the government was neglecting the health crisis and that routine political channels—lobbying and letter-writing and the occasional march, for example—would not change that.

In a sense, then, it is no surprise that lesbians, gay men, and other sexual and gender outlaws took to the streets in 1987. That would seem to be the rational course of action. In the face of mounting deaths, and frustrated by the limited effectiveness of routine political tactics like lobbying, why not act up?

But why *then,* in March 1987, rather than earlier? Lesbian and gay communities were experiencing devastation well before the emergence of ACT UP. The number of AIDS cases and deaths had been exploding for years. An explanation that simply looks to grievances or strain to account for the turn to more confrontational activism only begs the question: Why take to the streets when 20,000 had died rather than 1,000 or 10,000 or 100,000? After all, from the first years of the epidemic, lesbian and gay leaders had denounced as inadequate the amount of government funding allocated to address the health crisis. Serious concerns about quarantine also long predated the emergence of ACT UP. Reports of repressive AIDS legislation pervaded lesbian and gay newspapers by 1985. It seems plausible, then, that lesbians and gay men might have turned to confrontational activism years before the emergence of ACT UP—in 1984 for example, when Reagan and Bush were running for reelection, or in 1985, when Congress's Office of Technology Assessment (OTA) issued a report that strongly criticized the Reagan Administration's handling of the AIDS crisis. These were moments that pointed toward possible political allies, potential political openings, yet they did not inspire the emergence of the direct-action AIDS movement. An adequate explanation of its emergence must explain its timing.

Actually, the emergence of ACT UP at all is a puzzle insofar as governments frequently display indifference to the hardships and untimely deaths of members of the populace, embracing punitive rather than ameliorative policies, and yet people do not respond with confrontational activism. In fact, the emergence of political activism of any sort—whether in the form of service provision, lobbying, or direct action—is never inevitable; individuals and organizations, affected by the conditions around them, have to make activism happen, and they do not always do so.[2]

The rise of AIDS activism from the first days of the epidemic and the turn to more confrontational direct action in the mid-to-late 1980s, then, present us with a number of puzzling questions that I address in the following chapters. Why did lesbians, gay men, and other sexual and gender outlaws become politically active in the face of AIDS, and why did their early activism take the forms it did, marked by caretaking and service provision, candlelight vigils, and lobbying? Why did thousands then turn to direct-action politics beginning in the middle of 1986, embracing disruptive demonstrations, civil disobedience actions, die-ins, and other modes of intervention designed to shift understandings and policies with regard to the epidemic? Why did ACT UP, which exemplified these forms of activism, initially receive widespread support in lesbian and gay communities, even from mainstream, establishment-oriented leaders and organizations?

The last two questions are especially pressing in light of the gay movement's rejection of militancy and turn toward professionalism and routine interest-group politics in and since the mid-1970s. Part of the general post-1960s shift away from radical left politics, the change from gay liberation to gay rights politics involved adopting an agenda oriented toward gay inclusion rather than broader social transformation, a concom-

2. Social movement scholars' focus on movements *per se* can narrow our vision of political action to that which is undertaken by existing social movements, leading us to neglect questions about political activities that are engaged in *prior* to the emergence of a given movement or outside of a movement context altogether, as well as questions about political *in*action and the *non*-emergence of movements. I try to avoid these problems by focusing more broadly on the factors that shape political action and inaction.

itant focus on the legislative realm, and an embrace of what some have called a "politics of respectability" that required downplaying gay sexual difference.[3] ACT UP, in contrast, drew from and in many ways marked a revitalization of early gay liberation politics.

My account moves between national and local scales, recognizing that lesbian and gay responses to AIDS occurred simultaneously and in an interrelated manner at both levels. My local focal points are Chicago, New York, and San Francisco, but I draw on evidence from other cities as well. My focus on multiple cities is partly intended to counter existing accounts that tend to conflate ACT UP with ACT UP/New York. As the first, largest, most visible, and in some ways most influential chapter, ACT UP/NY had a tremendous effect on the movement, but it was part of a larger phenomenon, a national movement made up of dozens of local chapters.

Much of the evidence that I use to construct my narrative comes from lesbian and gay newspapers because they provide a useful lens into early lesbian and gay understandings of and responses to AIDS (see the appendix). The gay press was the primary site where lesbians and gay men learned about this new epidemic, got information about state and societal responses to the crisis, tried to figure out how to respond to the epidemic, challenged mainstream media and medical constructions of AIDS, expressed opinions and debated the issues, and solicited volunteers and activists in the fight against AIDS.[4] News articles, editorials, opinion columns, letters-to-the-editor, and public service announcements illuminate the texture of lesbian and gay sentiments about and understandings of the AIDS epidemic. Individually and cumulatively, they display the shifting contours of lesbian and gay ambivalence about self and society in the context of AIDS. In particular, they show how feelings were articulated and evoked, often nonconsciously and unintentionally, in a manner that affected the emotional habitus and helped to shape lesbian and gay political responses to AIDS. Lesbian and gay newspapers not only recorded such emotional dynamics; they simultaneously reenacted them and thereby multiplied their potential effect by relaying such emotional dynamics to their readers. Editorials and opinion columns that articulated or elicited feelings played a special role: in offering in-

3. See, for example, Bronski 1998, 70–74.
4. Political scientist Cathy Cohen (1993) argues similarly that gay newspapers were an important site where new discourses about AIDS developed (258–59); see also Altman 1994, 21; Gross 2001, 103; and Tester 2004, 67.

sight into the editor's or the writer's feelings, they more overtly articulated norms about feelings and their expression, suggesting to readers how they should and should not feel, how they should and should not express those feelings, and how they should and should not act.[5]

A given emotional habitus and a social group's political horizon are tightly coupled, each feeding into and bolstering the other. At the conceptual core of these two chapters, then, are the following questions: how was an emotional habitus established and stabilized within lesbian and gay communities during the early years of the epidemic, what caused that habitus to shift over time, how was the newly emergent emotional habitus installed and sustained, and how did those processes shape both lesbian and gay attitudes about, as well as engagements in, distinctive forms of activism? Those questions form the narrative arc of the following two chapters.

5. See Hall 1974 on the role of the media as primary and secondary agents of signification; part of what I want to emphasize is the role the media play in both reflecting and constructing emotional habitus.

Pride and Its Sisters
in Early AIDS Activism

The response to AIDS by lesbian and gay communities was immediate. Within months of the first recorded cases of what soon came
to be known as AIDS, gay men in particular began questioning medical professionals, raising money for research, and organizing needed
services. Within the first few years, thousands of lesbians, gay men, and
other sexual and gender outlaws took on vital activities like caretaking, service provision, and lobbying. Why and how did this early mass
mobilization occur? The more general aim of this chapter is to analyze how a social group's political horizon—its sense of political possibilities and the sorts of activism thus deemed doable, desirable, and
necessary—is established and reproduced over time. I contend that emotional habitus are decisive factors in the generation of any political horizon, in part because they provide an affective charge to pedagogies of political behavior. This chapter explores the establishment of an emotional
habitus in lesbian and gay communities, the emotional practices it generated, its own reproduction over time, and how that habitus established one
political horizon and foreclosed others, effectively (and affectively) shaping the forms of AIDS activism from this early period of the epidemic.[1]

Before turning to my analysis, I want to acknowledge the difficulty of
writing about AIDS activism during the 1981–86 period without distort-

---

1. Parts of this chapter come from Gould 2001 and Gould 2009.

ing that analysis by anachronistically examining it from the vantage point
of what immediately followed: more confrontational direct-action activism exemplified by ACT UP. In part because of many ACT UP members' self-understanding that they were doing activism where others were
providing social services, but also because of ACT UP's dramatic successes, earlier AIDS activism—including service provision—tends to be
overshadowed. At this point, no one can write about the earliest AIDS
activism without knowledge of ACT UP's subsequent emergence, but I
have tried to counter the teleological tendency by treating the 1981–86
period with its own integrity, valuable in its own right, rather than seeing it as "not ACT UP" or as simply laying the ground for ACT UP's en-
trance onto the historical stage (although it certainly did that).

One difficulty, however, is that a retrospective appraisal of the growing
devastation of the AIDS epidemic itself as well as events that occurred
within lesbian and gay communities that I discuss in this chapter do raise
the question of why lesbians and gay men did not take to the streets earlier. My approach to this question is historical rather than moral, an inquiry into what *did* happen and *why* rather than a claim about what
should have happened. Again, my main interest in this chapter is to understand how a social group's political horizon is established, recognizing that the establishment of one is the foreclosure of others. As early as
1983, a few lesbians and gay men began to advocate taking to the streets,
but in that moment such tactics were unappealing to most. The existence
of this competing framing about what should be done to address the crisis and its initial nonadoption, followed a few years later by a widespread
embrace of it, pose an interesting question: what made street activism
largely unthinkable in one moment but thinkable, and even desirable, in
another? Indeed, because of the contingent nature of any mode of activism, each period of AIDS activism presents its own puzzles. Rather than
establishing means for caring for people with AIDS, lesbians and gay
men instead might have distanced themselves from AIDS and its stigma
altogether in the early years. Why did thousands mobilize into AIDS
service organizations (ASOs)?

The Heroic Narrative of Early AIDS Activism

I begin with what I think is the dominant, heroic, narrative of lesbian
and gay AIDS activism between 1981 and 1986. At its simplest, the nar-

rative goes like this: from the earliest days of the AIDS epidemic, amid the incredibly hostile and budget-cutting climate of the Reagan years and in the face of almost no governmental or other outside help, lesbians and gay men—friends and lovers of people with AIDS (PWAs), community activists, sympathetic medical professionals, and PWAs themselves—worked together to provide services and care to people who were ill and dying. Facing government inaction, and out of gay pride, self-respect, and love for their sick brothers and for their beleaguered communities, they immersed themselves in emergency caretaking and formed the earliest ASOs. They assembled vital information and distributed it in their communities and to the larger public. Even before an infectious agent had been identified and isolated, they invented safe sex. They also lobbied for government funding and held the government accountable for its negligent and punitive responses to the crisis.

Much in this narrative is accurate, and, most important, it challenges the common perception that AIDS activism began in 1987 with the founding of ACT UP/New York. Still, it is worth revisiting and revising, first because it overlooks lesbians' and gay men's often contradictory sentiments about self and society, sentiments that AIDS reinforced; indeed, the heroic narrative obscures the ways in which unmentioned *bad* feelings like shame about gay sexual difference and a corollary fear of ongoing social nonrecognition and rejection, along with feelings like love, self-respect, and pride that are included in the narrative, shaped early lesbian and gay political responses to AIDS. Second, the heroic narrative disregards the tensions that existed within lesbian and gay communities about how to respond. And third, in light of the emotional valence that attached to it during the period of its unfolding, as well as the emotional charge that still attaches to it today, we might better understand this narrative as a quasi-accurate historical depiction that itself manifests both a promise of, as well as a bid for, gay respectability.

Feelings about Self and Society amid an Epidemic

I complicate the heroic narrative by considering how painful experiences of social annihilation and nonrecognition by heteronormative society and the consequent desire for relief from that condition through some degree of social acceptance and reciprocal recognition shaped lesbians' and gay men's political responses during the early years of the epidemic. With the term *nonrecognition,* I mean to reference the experience of wishing to be in a genuinely mutual and communicative relation with another but being deemed unworthy of such a reciprocal connection for whatever reason.[2] The evidence indicates that affective states that flowed from the experience of social ostracism and nonrecognition—feelings like gay shame and a related fear of social rejection that are absent from and masked by the standard heroic narrative—influenced the form and content of early AIDS activism.[3] My analysis, then, begins with an acknowledgment of the painful experience of nonrecognition that lesbians and gay men sometimes experience in a heteronormative society and a consequent structure of ambivalence about both self and society that is evident in lesbian and gay communities.[4] Many feelings might flow from the experience of nonrecognition: shame, as Sedgwick emphasizes, but also anger, contempt, sadness, frustration, resignation, and despair. I contend that the experience of social annihilation and nonrecognition importantly structures the emotional habitus in lesbian and gay communities. In this chapter I explore the formation of that emotional habitus and how it helped to establish, reinforce, enlarge, and circumscribe the collective political horizon at this moment in the fight against AIDS. We can imagine how the experience of nonrecognition and consequent contradictory feelings about self and society might affect lesbian and gay politics as well as the political activism of other socially marginalized groups. How do you confront a society when you feel unrecognized and desire relief from that painful condition, when you want to be part of society but simultaneously reject it, in part because it has rejected you? How do you make demands of state and society when you simultaneously feel, in this case, proud *and* ashamed of your homosexual identity and practices? More broadly, this chapter sheds light on the relationship between the affective dimensions of oppression and political action and inaction.

2. The literature on recognition begins with Hegel and is very long and rich. The sources I have found most useful that consider the psychic effects of nonrecognition include Fanon 1967; Tomkins (in Sedgwick and Frank 1995); and Sedgwick 2003.

3. Here I draw on the work of queer theorist Eve Sedgwick (2003), who draws on the work of psychologist Silvan Tomkins (in Sedgwick and Frank 1995) to argue that gay shame derives from nonrecognition. On the central role of shame in human behavior, see Scheff 1988, 1990a, 1990b.

4. I assume that most human beings, gay and straight, need and want some form of recognition. Within this universal claim, there is a lot of space for variability. While nonrecognition is a familiar and possibly acute experience for people who are socially marginalized, not all of them experience the same felt need for reciprocity and recognition from mainstream society.

Fear amid Chaos

Given our current vantage point, from which some have (prematurely) declared "the end of AIDS,"[5] it might be easy to forget the bafflement, terror, and panic that surrounded the first years of the epidemic.[6] The magnitude of the health crisis was unclear, but the forecasts were dire. Dozens and then hundreds of previously healthy gay men were suddenly being diagnosed with mysterious and rare diseases that indicated a breakdown in their immune systems; the mortality rate was unknown, but some thought it might be close to 100 percent. Within the first year, the CDC declared AIDS an epidemic, and the CDC's James Curran warned, "The epidemic may extend much further than currently described and may include . . . thousands or tens of thousands of persons with immune defects" (Mass 1982, 17).

There was tremendous fear in lesbian and gay communities. In one of the first lengthy articles on the epidemic in the national lesbian and gay news magazine the *Advocate,* the reporter stated that "a profound panic has crept over men in the major centers of the outbreak. Few know what to do or not to do" (Fain 1982, 20). When interviewed in 1994, Peter Groubert, a gay man living in San Francisco, remembered those early years: "People were afraid of themselves. They were afraid of everyone else. Fear truly gripped the city" (quoted in Shepard 1997, 66). Also interviewed in the mid-1990s, San Francisco gay activist Cleve Jones recalled the apocalyptic feelings he experienced after discussing the mysterious diseases affecting gay men with AIDS doctor Marcus Conant during the first year of the epidemic: "I thought that I would be killed by it, that everybody I knew would be killed by it. . . . I was very frightened" (quoted in Shepard 1997, 63). ACT UP/New York member Kendall Thomas recalled the everyday life of gay men in New York in the early 1980s: "People were terrified; I know I was. . . . There was a *palpable* sense of anxiety. . . . Death, or dying, was literally all around me. . . . There were moments of utter terror which would descend upon me without warning" (Thomas 2002; emphasis his). Gay communities were being decimated. Many gay men were attending memorial services every week. People who volunteered as "buddies" to assist people with AIDS with their daily tasks

5. There was a spate of such declarations by some prominent gay journalists beginning in 1996 (see Sullivan 1996; Savage 1997).

6. For an account of lesbian and gay responses to AIDS during the early-to-mid 1980s, written during that time, see Altman 1987, esp. chap. 5.

were experiencing multiple deaths, again, sometimes every week.[7] Cleve
Jones indicated how unrelenting were the deaths: "Everyone's address
books were a mass of scratch-outs" (C. Jones 2000, 101).[8]

The mystery, ambiguities, horrors, and devastation of the epidemic
alarmed and terrified gay men, and lesbians as well, particularly those
living in the urban centers most affected by AIDS. Equally troubling,
the diseases seemed to be striking gay men in particular, suddenly reinforcing implausible antigay rhetoric that linked disease to gay identity itself.[9] Indeed, along with the medical aspects of AIDS, lesbian and
gay communities simultaneously had to face the social and political dimensions of the epidemic. From the first reports about what was initially
dubbed the "gay plague," understandings of the epidemic have almost
never focused solely on its medical aspects; as others have noted, discourses about AIDS have consistently overflowed with metaphors and
moralizing stories.[10] Initial medical and mainstream media reports included a heavy dose of homophobic sensationalism about gay male sexual practices, foregrounding social taboos such as anal sex, anonymous
sex, and public sex. The media focused on the most stunning and dramatic cases of gay men with histories of more than one thousand sexual
partners while ignoring those whose sexual histories were more conventional.[11] Their hysteria reflected and reinforced discourses that equated
homosexuality and homosexuals with disease and perversion.[12]

7. See, for example, GMHC's 1990–91 Annual Report, "The First Ten Years," 16.

8. In 1994, artist and ACT UP/Chicago member Mary Patten showed a piece at the Fis-
chbach Gallery in New York City—*Untitled (names and addresses)*—an address book, Patten's own, with every name whited out, "a quiet testimony to . . . the erasure of an accu-
mulated and dense personal history" due to AIDS (e-mail correspondence with Patten,
5 August 2006).

9. By categorizing those affected in terms of sexual *identity* rather than sexual *practices*, the initial medical and media reports created the impression that the diseases were
affecting gay men specifically, and *because of* their identity rather than because of specific
practices. The policy ramifications were significant: government and other institutions' responses to this ostensibly "gay" epidemic were slowed immeasurably, and safe-sex information likely was less effective at reaching men who had sex with men but did not identify as gay.

10. See, for example, Treichler 1987; Ross 1988; Watney 1989; Loughery 1999.

11. Men with modest sexual histories were among the first reported cases of what later
became AIDS. Of four of the first patients seen by clinicians in Los Angeles, for example, "one had been monogamous for four years, two had several regular partners, and only
one 'was highly sexually active'" (Epstein 1996, 380, n. 15, quoting Gottlieb et al. 1981).

12. Hysteria about lesbians being "AIDS carriers" also indicates how the equation of
homosexuality with disease shaped understandings of AIDS in the early years.

Meanwhile, the Reagan administration was displaying monumental indifference to the epidemic.[13] Most local and state governments were similarly failing to respond to the crisis; indeed, by the mid-1980s, it was clear that legislators were focused less on addressing the needs of people who were sick than on proposing and enacting repressive laws, including calls for quarantine. The grief, fear, and overall trauma in lesbian and gay communities was enormous.

Making Sense of AIDS

Lesbians, gay men, and other sexual and gender minorities could not easily assimilate this new, mysterious phenomenon and its many implications. The feelings associated with sex are profoundly disruptive and contradictory in any case, even moreso here where gay sex was linked so intimately to death. Add to that the highly ambiguous nature of the situation, the frightful conjectures, and the implausibility of a syndrome of illnesses attacking gay men in particular, all of which was tremendously unsettling. The epidemic itself and responses to it by state and society called into question lesbians' and gay men's everyday routines and practices, and generated immense self-doubt as well as anxiety about their relationship to mainstream society. It was an open and undefined moment when, because previously fixed ideas were uprooted and confusion and uncertainty reigned, the need to make sense of oneself and of one's world was greatly intensified.

Amid the insecurity and dislocation of the AIDS epidemic, and in the context of vitriolic and homophobic reactions from the dominant institutions of mainstream society, sexual and gender minorities had to reconsider who they were and where they fit within society, and to think about their relationship to this epidemic, how they should respond to it, and how they should *feel* about it. Those practices of meaning-making happened in a collective and ongoing way at community meetings, in AIDS organizations, in the pages of lesbian and gay newspapers, through broadsides, leaflets, safe-sex education materials, calls for volunteers, and in everyday conversations. Lesbians and gay men confronted serious questions that centered on gay identity and politics: To what extent

13. Evidence indicates that when mentioned at all, AIDS was treated as a joke by members of the Reagan administration. In 1982, in answer to a reporter's question about the epidemic, the White House press secretary, Larry Speakes, joked that no one in the White House had AIDS. See the transcript in the *Washington Blade,* 11 June 2004, 28.

should they identify with and mobilize around this health crisis, given the immense stigma of AIDS? How would the epidemic and society's responses to it affect each of them individually and lesbian and gay communities more broadly? What, if anything, was "the meaning" of AIDS? What did AIDS reveal about them? How should they approach the question of the relationship between gay sexual practices and these deadly diseases? How should they respond to the epidemic if they decided to "own" the issue? How should the government address the crisis?

Although moments of dislocation and insecurity can engender "collective creativity" (Sewell 1996, 867), where new ideas and ways of being are invented and tried out, those trying to make sense of themselves and the world amid such conditions also draw from readily available assumptions and common sense. In the early years of the AIDS epidemic, lesbians, gay men, and other sexual and gender outlaws did create new knowledges while also pulling from contradictory but well-worn and deeply ingrained patterns of understandings and feelings about lesbian and gay selves and about mainstream society. Gay liberationist ideas that criticized dominant heterosexual society, foregrounded gay community self-determination, and celebrated gay sexuality and gay difference helped shape their understandings and feelings about AIDS.[14] But so did more conventional heteronormative ideas that disparaged gay sexuality, gay culture, and the gay community, ideas that were pervasive, albeit usually subterranean, in lesbian and gay communities. The decline of gay liberation in the early 1970s, of course, importantly shaped the discursive context. It perhaps is no surprise, then, that gay discussions about AIDS were saturated with ambivalent language that indicated gay pride as well as shame, and animosity toward society as well as a strong desire for social acceptance and a related anxiety about intensified social rejection.

Emotives, Feelings, and the Establishment of a Political Horizon

We can get a sense of how important ambivalent feelings have been in shaping lesbian and gay political responses to AIDS by looking at public, largely internal discussions in lesbian and gay communities about the crisis—as recorded in the gay media and in ASO literature, for example. These discussions are a window into the often unarticulated but force-

14. Brier 2007 explores gay liberation- and feminist-inspired discourses of early AIDS activists.

ful affective states coursing through lesbian and gay communities in this period. Although debates revealed divergent views and feelings, and showed that there was no self-evident, widely accepted response to the crisis, repeated articulations of what soon became the normative emotives did help to shape a political horizon.

The pre-AIDS emotional habitus among lesbians and gay men was structured by ambivalence, and AIDS created conditions for the heightening of some of those contradictory feelings. Reddy (1997) argues that when the standard emotives in a community repeatedly name and evoke feelings particular to one side of a deep ambivalence while submerging or repressing feelings specific to the other side—a navigation, of sorts, of the experience of ambivalence—individuals' affective states and emotions can be affected. When repeatedly named and evoked, certain emotional states are elevated and made meaningful while others are repressed or simply remain unintelligible because they are not brought into language. Emotives, again, do not simply describe feeling states but can affect how people are able to, and actually do, *feel*. In addition, the emotional practices of a social group encourage members to align their feelings and emotional expression with the emotional norms and orientation of the group. These emotion dynamics can thereby foster a particular resolution to a widespread ambivalence.[15]

Here, then, is the heart of the argument of this chapter. During the early years of the AIDS crisis, as activists and others repeatedly articulated and evoked certain feelings and suppressed others, they generated and reproduced a particular emotional habitus. They expressed love of their gay brothers and of the community, as well as gay pride, especially when noting and encouraging the community's responsible efforts to fight AIDS and its stoicism in the face of death; many also expressed and elicited shame about gay sexuality and anxiety about social nonrecognition and rejection; a few individuals publicly articulated anger toward state and society, but their expressions often were suppressed or defused. This emotional habitus—with its implicit pedagogy about what to feel and how to express one's feelings about self and society—influenced lesbians' and gay men's self-understandings as well as their attitudes about homosexuality, AIDS, and dominant society. In crystal-

15. To be sure, any such "resolution" would be temporary and unstable insofar as the repressed or submerged sentiments are not actually purged. On the irresolvability of ambivalence, see Freud 1955; Laplanche and Pontalis 1973, 28; and Smelser 1998, 6.

lizing lesbian and gay ambivalence, this emotional habitus offered a resolution of sorts to the political dilemmas posed by the experience of such
contradictory feelings. That is, this constellation of feelings, repeatedly
expressed and evoked in the lesbian and gay press and in pronounce-
ments by lesbian and gay leaders and AIDS activists, helped to establish
a political horizon that authorized some forms of activism while delegitimizing others—that, for example, encouraged lesbians and gay men to
focus on the vital work of caretaking and service provision, to embrace
routine interest-group tactics such as voting and lobbying, to equivocate
about gay male sexuality, and to suppress more confrontational rhetoric
and activism that might compromise their social acceptability.[16]

Recalling the bodily, nonconscious nature of a habitus, I am not arguing that lesbians and gay men *intentionally* mobilized certain affective
states and emotions and downplayed others in order to direct lesbian
and gay politics toward service provision and lobbying and away from
confrontation. Some may have been so strategic and deliberate, but most
simply drew from and echoed existing, familiar, emotionally charged
discourses. Gay shame and fear of social rejection, for example, were
nothing new; they had figured prominently in lesbian and gay experience
for decades and were then heavily reinforced by the dominant society's
responses to AIDS. Those feeling states, in short, were recognizable. We
might even say they "made sense." They could be readily expressed all
the more persuasively in the context of a health crisis in which lesbian
and gay communities had significant reason to be concerned about societal perceptions and acceptance. In other words, regardless of intent, such
expressions of feelings were available and resonant, and their articulation or elicitation required little if any reflection. Indeed, the force of an
emotional habitus derives from operating beneath conscious awareness,
from being absorbed into individuals' bodily sensations and thereby nat-
uralized. The effects of the repeated evocations of specific feeling states,
more important than the intentions lying behind them, bolstered such
feeling states among lesbians and gay men. I contend that we need to explore the workings of such emotional processes in order to understand
the sources and forms of political action.

The remainder of this chapter continues my analysis of early AIDS

16. The multiple and often contradictory feelings present in this emotional habitus
should dispel any idea that specific emotional states lead to specific types of activism (e.g.,
shame leads to inaction, pride leads to the streets). We can say that feelings *do* shape political (in)action, but *how* they do so is always contingent.

activism. Initially, I stick closely to the heroic narrative, simply providing an analysis attuned to the emotions—especially gay pride—involved in that heroism. I then explore some of the unacknowledged feeling states that I argue decisively shaped lesbian and gay political responses to the crisis.

GAY PRIDE AND ITS SISTERS IN EARLY AIDS ACTIVISM. As the heroic narrative suggests, in the terrifying and politically hostile context of the Reagan/Bush years, the mobilization in lesbian and gay communities to deal with the crisis on its many fronts was extraordinary and indispensable in the fight against AIDS. Following an ethos—forged in the gay and women's liberation movements—that made them wary of government involvement in what they saw as internal lesbian and gay community affairs, the earliest AIDS activists educated themselves, alerted gay men to the epidemic, and taught doctors how to diagnose symptoms. Drawing from existing community resources and finding new ones, they raised consciousness as well as money. In the face of government inaction and hoping to preserve their besieged communities, they created autonomous, grassroots, community-based service organizations to take care of gay men with AIDS, providing numerous ways for others in the community to volunteer their time and donate resources to fight the crisis.[17] That work was groundbreaking. In historian John D'Emilio's words, "Within a few short years, the community was able to build from the ground up an extraordinary network of service organizations that cared for many of the sick and educated the community" (1997, 83). Regarding questions of gay sexuality, gay men's previous experiences with state surveillance had created suspicion of government agencies, and, at least in the earliest years, there was "a general consensus that gay men could and should work out their evolving sexual norms within the private confines of their community" (Patton 1990, 15). Even before the identification of HIV, gay men invented safe-sex materials that suggested "how to have sex in an epidemic."[18] As Cindy Patton has written, "Informed by a

17. In the first year or two of the epidemic, some AIDS activists believed that they would be able to provide services and information without government assistance, upholding a valued principle among gay and lesbian liberationists of noninterference by the state. That belief faded as the number of cases exploded.

18. That was the name of a pamphlet compiling safe-sex information for gay men, produced by Richard Berkowitz, Michael Callen, and Richard Dworkin (1983); on early safe-sex campaigns in gay communities, see Patton 1987, 1990, and 1996.

self-help model taken from the women's health movement and by the gay liberation discussion of sexuality, safe sex was viewed by early AIDS activists, not merely as a practice to be imposed on the reluctant, but as a form of political resistance and community building that achieved both sexual liberation and sexual health" (1989, 118; quoted in McGarry and Wasserman 1998, 229).

Lesbians participated in AIDS activism from the beginning, many of them bringing expertise from years of involvement in other movements, especially the women's health movement. In the words of writer and activist Jewelle Gomez, "This moment of mutual political recognition between lesbians and gay men signaled a new era of activism" (1995, 57). Lesbian participation is particularly notable because, in the years prior to AIDS, lesbians and gay men typically were not engaged in political activism *together*.[19] Why did numerous lesbians now get involved in an issue that had been gendered as male by the scientific-medical establishment and the straight and gay media?

On the most mundane level, many of the existing lesbian and gay social service organizations that responded to the epidemic had lesbians on their staffs (Stoller 1997). But many lesbians who joined early AIDS activist efforts had more passionate reasons to become involved. One early activist, Amber Hollibaugh, notes that she and many lesbians were drawn to AIDS activism because of the "shared *gay* identity we felt with gay men" (1995, 220, emphasis hers). Some lesbians got involved because "they saw their community under assault" (Patton 1990, 21), and many recognized a personal interest in opposing the religious right's use of AIDS to forward its homophobic agenda. In the early years of the epidemic, lesbians were often constructed by the media and right wing pundits as "AIDS carriers," and thus, in a manner similar to gay men, as "degenerates," "perverts," and "deviants."[20] Although the epidemic had

19. The reasons for this are many; one is that throughout the 1970s, lesbian politics were centered in lesbian feminism, some versions of which were separatist, and gay male life was focused on building gay (male) community institutions, including bars, baths, and other sites where the growing gay male sexual subculture might further develop.

20. Even health and scientific institutions linked lesbians to AIDS. In 1982–83, the American Red Cross advised lesbians as well as gay men to refrain from donating blood. The debate about lesbians and blood donation was occurring as late as 1986 in the pages of the British medical journal, the *Lancet*. In 1987, the Sonoma County (California) Red Cross turned down a women's motorcycle club offer to do a blood drive, again fearing "lesbian blood" (Grover 1987, 25). See also Byron 1983; reprinted in Blasius and Phelan 1997, 589.

ostensibly been gendered as male, many lesbians recognized that in fact the epidemic had been "queered" and they too were being targeted.

In addition, a number of early lesbian AIDS activists identified as sex-radicals—feminists who were interested in the pleasures and diversity of female sexuality and who challenged other feminists' opposition to pornography, butch/femme roles, and sadomasochism.[21] Dominant discourses about AIDS that disparaged gay male sexuality reinforced the need to tie the fight against AIDS to the fight for sexual freedom. Sociologist Nancy Stoller suggests that lesbians' "interest in AIDS politics and the organizational milieu of AIDS work was fueled by a belief that AIDS organizations would be groups that were more open about sexual diversity" (1997, 179). Lesbians who had antiracist and feminist politics also got involved because they saw through the gendering of the epidemic and very early in the crisis recognized that women, particularly poor women of color, were going to be affected by AIDS in ways that were inflected by race and class. In short, lesbians joined the fight in these early years "out of compassion, solidarity, the link they saw between gay men and lesbians, and political concern" (O'Sullivan and Parmar 1992, 12).

In many ways, AIDS sparked greater contact between lesbians and gay men, and the category "lesbian and gay community" became more accurate (although it continued to exclude other sexual and gender minorities). Drawing from her experiences as a lesbian archivist during this period, ACT UP/New York member Polly Thistlethwaite notes that "in the 1980s—you can see it from the organizational files in the [Lesbian Herstory] Archives—things were 'gay *and* lesbian' instead of 'gay' *or* 'lesbian'. There was a lot more coming together like that" (Thistlethwaite 1993, emphasis hers; see also McGarry and Wasserman 1998, 239).[22]

Seeing the destruction that this new epidemic was wreaking and fearing that government involvement would lead to government control, these early AIDS activists mobilized past political experience, indigenous resources, and lesbian and gay volunteers to address the crisis.[23]

21. On feminist sex-radicalism, see essays in Vance 1989; and Snitow, Stansell, and Thompson 1983. On lesbian sex-radicals and AIDS activism, see Stoller 1997; and Hollibaugh 1995.

22. For more on lesbian AIDS activists, see Black 1996; Patton 1990; Rieder and Ruppelt 1988; Stoller 1998; Wolfe 1990a; and Yingling 1991, 293–94.

23. Patton has noted that their approach ironically "dovetailed with the Reagan plan to shift virtually all government services into communities under the guise of Christian charity and volunteerism" (1990, 16).

Although in the first few years most people were busy digesting what was happening around them, caring for friends and lovers, and building community-based ASOs, by 1982–83 some early AIDS activists were engaging in externally oriented activism as well, mobilizing lobbying efforts and candlelight vigils. In 1983 the PWA self-empowerment movement emerged, issuing a founding statement, the "Denver Principles," that, along with making policy recommendations, condemned attempts to label people with AIDS "victims" and urged people with AIDS to assert control over their own health care.[24] By the mid-1980s, some people with AIDS and their allies were engaging in illegal direct action by smuggling experimental AIDS drugs that were either unapproved in the United States or cheaper outside its borders. Buyers' clubs then distributed the drugs to people with AIDS across the United States.[25]

The efforts of these early AIDS activists were heroic indeed, and the movement of thousands of volunteers into ASOs in these early years should be understood as a successful mass political mobilization— political in the sense that to love and care for those whom state and society have betrayed, for those deemed better off dead, is a forceful refusal to accede to existing notions of worthiness. How can we account for this mass mobilization? The need to respond in the face of government inaction helped to animate it, and the community's resources certainly enabled it to occur, but this political response was never inevitable. Activists were already confronting other pressing issues, including violence against lesbians and gay men and the lack of civil rights protection. Traumatized by the sicknesses and deaths, and afraid of renewed political attacks against the lesbian and gay community, activists and nonactivists alike simply might have stayed away from AIDS.

Crucial to the mobilization effort, in my view, were feelings like gay pride and love for one's sick brothers and for the community at large. Activists and service providers frequently articulated and elicited feelings of pride and love, helping to counter the shame and fear surrounding AIDS. By linking ways of feeling to specific forms of action, such expressions enlisted massive numbers of lesbian and gay volunteers and community resources to address the health crisis. The following invocation of pride in the community's efforts against AIDS in a report to

24. The "Denver Principles" are reprinted in Crimp 1987a; see also Chambré 2006, chap. 2.

25. See Epstein 1996, 188–89; and Chambré 2006, 138–40 for brief discussions of buyers' clubs.

the lesbian and gay community from the San Francisco AIDS/KS Foundation in December 1983, used an emotional style that was widespread in this period: "We as an entire community can be proud . . . of the cooperation within all segments of the gay and lesbian community. . . . Alone, this community has educated, lobbied, demonstrated and fought for government action. The only services that have been delivered are those which have been demanded or those which have been provided by the community itself" (San Francisco AIDS/KS Foundation 1983, 1, 3).[26]

In gay politics, and likely in other movements of socially marginalized people, public discussion about the movement's political actions—even a mere description—is usually more than it purports to be. Such discussions in gay politics, for example, often additionally express, or gesture toward, lesbian and gay ambivalence: they contain implicit or explicit judgments about how gay people should or should not present themselves and act in the public realm. For example, when *Advocate* reporter Larry Bush asserted in a 1983 news article how unique the gay community spirit was in motivating individuals to unite in order to provide services for people with AIDS, and when in the same article the executive director of the National Gay Task Force, Virginia Apuzzo, was quoted as saying that "the community has responded, with its heart, with its pocketbook, with its political savvy" (Bush 1983a, 19), both were speaking in an emotional register that expressed and evoked gay pride. On one level, expressions of gay pride simply acknowledged that lesbians and gay men involved in caretaking and service provision had reason to feel proud: their efforts were prolonging and saving lives.

At the same time, the many expressions of pride in this moment were doing more than acknowledging these efforts. They offered lesbians and gay men a pedagogy of feeling: rather than feel ashamed, as mainstream discourses suggested, they should feel proud of the community's efforts in the face of immense adversity. In offering a way to feel and a template for what to do with gay pride, those expressions of pride effectively, and affectively, encouraged lesbians and gay men to volunteer and to donate money and services rather than to disidentify from the mobilization around AIDS. The fact that some lesbians and gay men did disidentify— which I discuss below—puts pressure on any account that naturalizes this

26. Originally the Kaposi's Sarcoma Research and Educational Foundation, it changed its name to the San Francisco AIDS/KS Foundation and ultimately became the San Francisco AIDS Foundation.

massive mobilization. The proud emotional register of much lesbian and gay rhetoric about AIDS in this period helped to define what it meant to be gay and thereby encouraged these forms of early AIDS activism. The model of gayness enacted here did not offer a radical reconstitution of U.S. American citizenship in the way that Berlant and Freeman (1993) describe Queer Nation as doing, but it did make possible a parallel citizenship whose practices explicitly recognized the value of gay lives and countered the sense of lesbians and gay men as irredeemably "other."[27] In a period of virulent homophobia, these enactments of gay dignity and self-recognition offered an antidote.

Thus far, my account fits squarely within the heroic narrative. As Patton has argued, early AIDS activism had "liberationist roots" (1990, 19), and at first glance, little or no gay shame is evident in these early lesbian and gay responses to the epidemic: activists were proudly defending their communities and gay male sexuality in the face of the homophobic hysteria that permeated medical and media reports. In primarily pursuing community self-determination rather than government action, they indicated suspicion of and animosity toward the state and scant concern with social acceptance. If we extend the heroic narrative in a manner that attends to the important role of emotional states in political activism, we might read the attitudes and actions of these activists as an indication that they had achieved a resolution to lesbian and gay ambivalence that was grounded in gay pride and a loving respect for one another and that encouraged a politics of community autonomy and disengagement from the state.

Such an account usefully challenges a linear retelling of history that would suggest that the story of lesbian and gay responses to AIDS began with shame and political inaction and moved to gay pride and antipathy toward society, exemplified by ACT UP's militant street activism. All of the components of ambivalence and political activism in these early years contradict any such linear narrative: gay pride and antipathy toward society were apparent in the earliest lesbian and gay responses, and they were linked to a community self-help form of political resistance inspired by gay liberation rather than to street activism which was not yet even on the horizon.

Still, while this heroic narrative provides some sense of the motivations that lay behind early AIDS activism, the picture it draws is incom-

27. I thank Mary Patten, who suggested I think about this idea of parallel citizenship.

plete. Although pride was one of the most pervasive and motivating sentiments at the time, it was not the only sentiment evoked in these early public discussions. Pride helped to establish responses like service provision, volunteer caretaking, and lobbying as forms of AIDS activism that were thinkable and desirable. But other affective states that are largely absent from the heroic narrative—what in retrospect we could call gay shame and a corollary fear of social rejection, for example—also contributed to establishing and limiting lesbians' and gay men's sense of the possible.

GAY SEX AND ANXIETY. Discussions in lesbian and gay communities about AIDS and gay sex indicate the forcefulness of emotional states besides pride in this moment. Early medical and media reports linked AIDS to gay sex and even to gayness itself, and that association fed an unspoken but widespread anxiety in lesbian and gay communities that maybe homosexuality really was abnormal, unhealthy, and in this case, even deadly. AIDS, of course, did not introduce shame and guilt about gay sexual difference. Rather, it played on fertile ground. A little over a year into the epidemic, Michael Lynch, a reporter for Toronto's left-leaning gay paper *The Body Politic,* suggested that the mainstream media's coverage of AIDS that equated gayness with pathology resonated with gay men: "Within the hearts of gay men" there was already "a persistent, anti-sexual sense of guilt, ready to be tapped. . . . Deep within ourselves lingered a readiness to find ourselves guilty. We were ripe to embrace a viral infection as a moral punishment" (Lynch 1982, 35, 37). A few years later, gay writer and activist Darrell Yates Rist similarly argued that mainstream society's homophobic constructions of AIDS "corroborated understandings we somehow profoundly held—had *always* held—about ourselves. . . . [AIDS] taps a dark, cold well, a bottomless intelligence that nurtures our conception of ourselves: Sadly, we are moral aberrations, flaws in nature's scheme" (Rist 1986, 45; emphasis his).

Writing in 1985, Cindy Patton argued that this anxious affective state was widespread, even affecting those with a strong gay pride: "Lurking deep in the heart of even the most positive and progressive lesbians and gay men was the fear: maybe they are right, homosexuality is death" (Patton 1985, 6). Although such affective states did not exist across the board, mainstream society's homophobic understandings of AIDS tapped into feelings of guilt and shame about homosexuality and anxiety about social rejection that already were present within the lesbian and gay affective landscape. AIDS, a crisis inescapably related to gay male sexual practices, unsurprisingly exacerbated feelings of shame and fear of rejection.

Prior to the 1984 isolation and identification of the human immuno-deficiency virus (HIV), the scientific-medical establishment's theories of causation included frequent exposure to sexually transmitted diseases, antibiotic overload, recreational drugs popular among gay men, "the fast gay lifestyle," gay male sexuality itself, and an unknown infectious agent.[28] Although uncertainty about the causes of AIDS pointed in a number of directions, lesbians and gay men, influenced by their own anxiety about gay difference and attendant social rejection, often echoed mainstream media and medical reports, fastening on gay male sexual practices and the supposed "gay lifestyle" with its easy sex, ostensibly higher rates of sexually transmitted diseases, and recreational drug use. For example, the cover of the March 18, 1982, issue of the *Advocate* ominously asked, "Is the Urban Gay Male Lifestyle Hazardous to Your Health?" Its answer was, plainly, "yes." As sociologist Steven Epstein has argued, "when a mysterious illness appears in a specific social group, it makes eminent sense to ask what distinguishes that group from others not affected, or less affected, by the illness" (Epstein 1996, 49), and lesbians and gay men understandably joined the scientific-medical establishment in that line of questioning. But as Epstein also points out, and as examples I discuss here illuminate, that process is inevitably *normalizing* insofar as it considers the ways in which the assumed-to-be homogeneous social group ostensibly deviates from the norm. Difference easily slides into deviance. In this case, for example, lifestyle theories tended to draw their assumptions from existing discourses that cast homosexuality and gay male sexual practices as abnormal and unhealthy.

Heated debates among gay men about their sexual practices had occurred before the epidemic, but AIDS intensified them. Articles about AIDS in lesbian and gay newspapers as well as statements from gay leaders and AIDS service providers often revealed anxieties about anonymous sex, promiscuity, and, *even after the development of safe-sex measures,* specific gay male sexual practices, particularly those that ostensibly

28. See Epstein 1996 for an excellent analysis of how AIDS activists, people with AIDS, scientists, the media, pharmaceutical companies, and public health officials, in cooperation and in competition with one another, have constructed our knowledge about AIDS. He shows how an initially unpopular hypothesis—that an unknown infectious agent was causing AIDS—became credible.

set gay men apart from heterosexuals like anal sex, rimming, and fist-ing.[29] The frequent inclusion of "anonymous sex" in gay-produced warn-ing lists of potential risk factors is particularly significant, for it reveals that many wove together their moral beliefs or anxieties with their health concerns; anonymity, *per se*, does not transmit disease—introducing oneself to a sex partner does not stop disease transmission—so its in-clusion derived less from health concerns than from gay anxiety, even shame, about public perceptions of gay male sexual practices.[30]

Some gay community leaders expressed fear that gays had somehow brought AIDS on themselves. Less than one year into the epidemic, and two years before the identification of HIV, David Goodstein, the editor of the *Advocate,* pronounced, "Whether we like it or not, the fact is that aspects of the urban gay lifestyle we have created in the last decade are hazardous to our health. The evidence is overwhelming" (1982). By "ur-ban gay lifestyle," Goodstein probably meant the existence of venues like gay bathhouses and bars where men could meet to have sex with one an-other. The "evidence" that the growing epidemic was the result of such venues or more generally of gay male sexual culture was, in actuality, not "overwhelming," and rather than speaking the "truth" about AIDS, Goodstein's statement and others like it, drawing from heteronormative understandings of gay male sexuality, both revealed and likely reinforced gay shame and anxiety about society's perceptions of gay sexuality.[31]

Shame, guilt, and self-blame were even more pronounced in an explo-sive manifesto—"We Know Who We Are: Two Gay Men Declare War on Promiscuity"—that was published in the *New York Native* in Novem-ber 1982 by two gay men with AIDS:

29. Rimming is oral-anal sex; fisting is when one person inserts his/her hand into an-other's anus or vagina. See Rubin 1991 on the irrationality of placing fisting in the "unsafe" category in safe sex literature.

30. Many of the earliest lesbian and gay newspaper accounts about the new epidemic among gay men included "anonymous sex" as a risk factor. See, for example, Kelley 1981; DiPhillips 1981; William 1982; Sonnabend 1982; and Mass 1983. For a contemporaneous critique, see Berkowitz, Callen, and Dworkin 1983.

31. Because the once-common view that gay male sexuality is innately "perverse" and that gay men brought AIDS on themselves may still have traction, I should note that AIDS is not caused by homosexual sex *per se* or by the so-called "gay lifestyle," but by a virus (HIV) that has a standard disease transmission route. Anyone who engages in any activ-ity with an HIV-positive person where body fluids like blood or semen are exchanged can become infected with HIV. See Crimp 1987c, 253; and Bérubé 1988, 18, for arguments about how promiscuity among gay and bi men actually may have helped to *curtail* HIV transmission.

Those of us who have lived a life of *excessive promiscuity* on the urban gay
circuit of bathhouses, backrooms, balconies, sex clubs, meat racks, and tea-
rooms know who we are. . . . [W]e have been unwilling or unable to accept responsibility for the role that our own *excessiveness* has played in our present
health crisis. But, deep down, we know who we are and we know why we're
sick. . . . *Our lifestyle has created* the present epidemic of AIDS among gay
men. (Callen, Berkowitz, and Dworkin 1982, 23; emphases mine)

Their statement was ambivalent rather than simply self-deprecating: the
manifesto trafficked in shame about gay male sexual practices and pulled
from readily available homophobic and erotophobic discourses to support the authors' "lifestyle" hypothesis about AIDS, but it also indicated
self-love and grave concern about the gay community. Their statement,
for example, acknowledged that gay promiscuity had been "a healthy reaction to a sex-negative culture"; the problem, from their perspective,
was that promiscuity now threatened "to destroy the very fabric of urban gay male life."[32]

Callen and his colleagues were clearly trying to save gay male lives,
and their love for the urban gay community and for themselves was
likely motivating their manifesto. Of course, we cannot know precisely
what they were feeling, but it is perhaps more important to consider the
effects that their manifesto and similar statements from others had on
those who read it. If, as my argument about lesbian and gay ambivalence and the above comments by Lynch and Rist suggest, lesbians and
gay men have a reservoir of guilt and shame about their sexual identities
and practices, then any suggestion by gay men that gay men's sexual "excesses" had brought AIDS on themselves would in a sense speak to gay
men and possibly have the effect of reinscribing and elevating gay shame,
guilt, and self-doubt. That "shame-effect" is perhaps inevitable in a homophobic, heteronormative society where gay identity, in queer theorist
Judith Butler's words, is produced and riven at once (Butler 1999, 192,
n. 11). To identify as gay, lesbian, or queer is to travel close to, and sometimes fall over, the precipice of abjection. As much as many of us embrace our own difference, the ongoing straddling of a line between being
accepted and being rejected takes its emotional toll. It generates, at least

32. Notably, the manifesto authors wrote a safe-sex booklet in 1983 that challenged the
way that antigay, antisex moralizing was masquerading as medical advice (Berkowitz, Callen, and Dworkin 1983).

occasionally, ambivalence about our sexual difference, about that which generates social nonrecognition and thwarts (some) desired human connection. In this context, even cautionary warnings designed to save gay lives could unintentionally heighten gay shame.

Shaming often seemed to be the intention. Gay newspapers from that period, as well as interviews and oral histories, reveal that shame-filled discourses were pervasive in lesbian and gay communities. Their own worlds turning upside down, many gay men cast blame on those who supposedly lived in the gay "fast lane." Anthropologist Gayle Rubin has noted that in the San Francisco lesbian and gay community, "the most popular group to blame for AIDS was 'sleazy South of Market [gay] leathermen'" (1997, 111). If it was not leathermen, it was the sexually voracious. A gay man from San Francisco recalled the blaming and shaming that went along with such distancing from AIDS: "Those first years of the disease, the conversations over dinner and at the bars were basically denial. You know, 'So and so I know has got the gay cancer but he was a slut.' It was that kind of a reaction, 'He deserves it.' It just reinforced what we had been told" (quoted in Shepard 1997, 68). Shame and moralizing condemnation were apparent as well in the following statement by a gay doctor: "Perhaps we've needed a situation like this to demonstrate what we've known all along: Depravity kills!" (quoted in Bronski 1982, 9). Larry Kramer, a playwright and later a cofounder of Gay Men's Health Crisis (GMHC) and then of ACT UP/New York, revealed his ambivalence about, perhaps even his aversion to, his own and other gay men's sexual practices when he wrote a "personal appeal" in the *New York Native* that stated, "It's easy to become frightened that one of the many things we've done or taken over the past years may be all that it takes for a cancer to grow from a tiny something-or-other that got in there who knows when from doing who knows what" (Kramer 1981).

There was nothing inevitable about the tone and content of that prevalent paradigm for understanding the epidemic, evident in the fact that not all gay and lesbian public discussions of AIDS sounded the same. Indeed, some challenged this tendency to blame and shame gay men. For many gay men, free sexual expression was central to the definition of being gay; they had fought for gay sexual liberation throughout the 1970s and, while sexual freedom might threaten mainstream acceptance, it remained at the heart of gay male politics, and many were not willing to relinquish it. That motivated them to challenge others who were warning gay men to stop having sex, or at least stop having sex in certain ways.

Playwright Robert Chesley wrote a letter to the *New York Native* challenging what he saw as Kramer's self-hatred and shame about homosexuality: "Read anything by Kramer closely. I think you'll find the subtext is always: the wages of gay sin are death. . . . I am not downplaying the seriousness of Kaposi's sarcoma. But something else is happening here, which is also serious: gay homophobia and anti-eroticism" (Chesley 1981).[33]

Other gay liberationists challenged the homophobia and erotophobia of the more prevalent discourses as well, pointing out that morality was being pushed "under the guise of medical expertise" (Lynch 1982, 36; see also Scannell 1983). Rather than countering shame by disavowing what society deemed shameful and unworthy of recognition, they celebrated gay sexuality and challenged society's understandings of what was shameful. In left-leaning, gay liberationist publications like Boston's *Gay Community News* and Toronto's *Body Politic*, and sometimes in more moderate gay publications like the *New York Native*, gay liberationists pointed to the panic-mongering of terms like *epidemic* and *plague* and challenged the idea that the community was facing a crisis.[34] From our current vantage point, these liberationist arguments sometimes read as a form of denial. But we should recall that people initially had no idea what AIDS was or how people were "catching" it, and in 1981 and 1982 they had no idea about the scale of the problem or about the devastation that was to come. Given the medical profession's history of pathologizing gay male sexuality, it was understandable, and indeed vitally important, that people in the community questioned the accuracy and panic-mongering of medical reports. They were certainly correct about the homophobic distortions in these reports, and they were right to point to the ways that a health issue was being used by the state, the media, and the right wing to attack homosexuality. Their concerns about civil liberties were well-founded, especially given the revelation in 1985 that the Reagan administration had seriously considered mass quarantine of people with AIDS (Altman 1987, 64; cited in Epstein 1996, 95). In any event, although their defense of promiscuity and other components of

33. In a heteronormative context that generates contradictory sentiments about self and society, it is not surprising that accusations and counteraccusations with regard to gay sexual practices—that which distinguishes gays from straights—traffic in a discourse of self-hatred. The emotional register of these internal community debates both revolves around and navigates lesbian and gay ambivalence.

34. See, for example Bérubé 1984; Bronski 1982; Jurrist 1982; Lewis 1982; and Lynch 1982.

gay male sexual culture were audible within gay communities during the
first two years of the epidemic, theirs was not the dominant discourse or
the prevailing sentiment at this time.

(NOT) DEFENDING GAY SEX.   The question of the closure of the gay
bathhouses became a potent controversy in lesbian and gay communities
in San Francisco in 1984 and in New York City in 1985. Those defending the baths included not only their owners (who of course had a financial interest) and gay liberationists, but also more rights-oriented activists. Many lesbian sex-radicals, familiar with attacks on queer sexuality
from experience in the feminist "sex-wars,"[35] joined in the defense of gay
male sex establishments as well. At a demonstration in the spring of 1984
against the threatened closure of the bathhouses in San Francisco, protesters wearing only towels held up signs that read "Today the Tubs, To-
morrow Your Bedroom" and most ominously, "Out of the Baths, Into the
Ovens?" (Thompson 1994, 262; Shilts 1987, 442). In October 1984, three
hundred protested the San Francisco Department of Public Health's order to close the bathhouses (Mendenhall 1984, 3).

     Given heightened concerns about social acceptance in the early years
of the AIDS epidemic, why were some lesbians and gay men willing to
articulate a defiant, non-compromising position regarding questions of
sexual expression? First, as I suggested above, sexual freedom was an
important component of many gay men's self-identity. Second, from the
beginning of the epidemic, many liberationists fought the equation of
homosexuality with AIDS and argued that AIDS must not be seen as
proof that gay sexual liberation was a mistake. They pointed out that
AIDS provided a political pretext, but no medical rationale, to condemn
practices like promiscuity and anonymous, public sex. Given the pervasive articulations of shame, guilt, and blame in this period, their rhetoric
of sexual liberation might have been a conscious or unconscious attempt
to counter those feelings with pride in gay sexual difference. Third, and
related, gay men had already invented safe sex, thus undermining the
public health rationale for closing the bathhouses and limiting sexual
partners. Fourth, from past experience with homophobia in the medical
establishment, many lesbians and gay men distrusted the medical ratio-
nales given by the public health officials who advocated bathhouse clo-

35. For accounts of the sex wars, see Snitow, Stansell, and Thompson 1983; Vance 1989;
and Duggan and Hunter 1995.

sure. Finally, many lesbians and gay men were more focused on threats to civil liberties than on AIDS at this point in the epidemic, and many opposed state intervention everywhere, including in gay sex venues.[36]

As striking as the defense of the gay bathhouses is in the larger context of concern about social acceptance, any perusal of gay newspapers in San Francisco or New York from the mid-1980s will reveal that the community's response to the crackdown on gay sex clubs was, in sex theorist Pat Califia's words, "fraught with ambivalence" (1994, 276). Califia writes, for example, "Many segments of the gay community had never approved of the sexual license the bathhouses represented. The fact that the Mineshaft [a gay bar in New York City] was an S&M club made many gay men and lesbians reluctant to defend it" (276).[37] The public scrutiny of gay sex venues prompted some lesbians and gay men to call for a return to monogamy, to question experimentation with S&M and leather, and in other ways to disavow gay sexual culture.[38] In writer John Loughery's words, on the bathhouse issue, "gay men themselves were divided, even self-divided" (Loughery 1999, 431).

Perhaps that self-division explains Patton's observation from the period: "Lesbian and gay activists are not yet free from erotophobia, not yet convinced by their own rhetoric of sexual liberation" (1985, 13). It is difficult to rid oneself of gay shame, perhaps even impossible. As Eve Sedgwick writes, "The forms taken by shame are not distinct 'toxic' parts of a group or individual identity that can be excised; they are instead integral to and residual in the processes by which identity itself

36. In his account of lesbian and gay community debates about the closure of gay bathhouses, Shilts (1987) disparaged those who argued against closure. He suggested that bathhouse activists irresponsibly cared more about civil rights than gay lives, but, unfairly, he failed to mention that safe-sex practices were already well-established when the issue arose. More generally, Shilts's *And the Band Played On* (1987) can be read as a challenge to the heroic narrative of early AIDS activism, but Shilts and I proceed from very different standpoints. Whereas he castigates activists for being "in denial" about AIDS and for caring more about gay liberation-inspired sexual politics than gay lives (thereby setting himself up as the lone voice of reason in the gay community), I am more interested in explaining how anxiety about the possible further withdrawal of social recognition as a result of gay sexual difference shaped the early mobilization of lesbians and gay men to fight AIDS. For trenchant critiques of Shilts, see Crimp 1987c, 2002; Gross 2001, 101; and Rubin 1997.

37. Califia's comments about reasons for the lack of community response to the closing of the Mineshaft are corroborated in Schulman 1985b. See also Freiberg 1985b, 14: "The Mineshaft was defended by virtually no activists, many of whom in fact have long hoped the baths and backroom bars would close for lack of business."

38. For critical accounts of such moralizing within lesbian and gay communities, see Bronski 1986, and 1994, 260; Bersani 1995; Rubin 1997.

is formed. They are available for the work of metamorphosis, reframing, refiguration, transfiguration, affective and symbolic loading and deformation, but perhaps all too potent for the work of purgation and deontological closure" (Sedgwick 2003, 63). Again, those who identify as lesbian or gay come into being as such in a world in which they are abjected and hence often denied recognition, even—indeed, especially—from those with whom they are most intimate. Sentiments of gay shame are therefore an ongoing, ever-present possibility, more than ever amid an epidemic linking gay pleasure to death.

SHAME EFFECTS. The evidence indicates that AIDS itself along with mainstream and gay shaming and blaming had monumental psychic effects on lesbian and gay individuals. In a 1983 interview in *Newsweek,* Richard Failla, a New York City gay judge, suggested that shame and self-doubt among gay men were widespread: "The psychological impact of AIDS on the gay community is tremendous. It has done more to undermine the feelings of self-esteem than anything [homophobic crusader] Anita Bryant could have ever done. Some people are saying, 'Maybe we are wrong—maybe this is a punishment'" (quoted in Andriote 1999, 70). A couple of years later, Patton similarly noted "intense ambivalence" about sexuality among gay men, and suggested the following analysis: "Regardless of the medical facts . . . there is an inescapable feeling that sex, the thing which to some important degree defines gay identity and community, is the cause of the killing. It is extremely difficult to escape this sex-negative ethos when people are dying of AIDS every day" (1985, 16–17).

The perplexing and ambiguous nature of AIDS elicited understandings that perhaps inevitably were filled with gay shame. ACT UP/New York member Gregg Bordowitz recalled how his early affective states and thoughts about AIDS in part derived from his own "internalized homophobia": "I thought there would probably be retribution for living out a gay sexual life. So I was kind of concerned that maybe there was a 'gay cancer.' . . . You know, maybe there was something wrong with getting fucked. Maybe there was a price to pay" (Bordowitz 2002a).

SEX AND RESPECTABILITY. This widely experienced psychic distress affected lesbian and gay sexual politics in this period, shaping debates about such matters as how lesbians and gay men should conduct themselves sexually and how they should present their sexual selves to straight society. Some lesbians and gay men argued not only for sexual restraint, but for specific measures to be taken to "clean up" the image of the lesbian and gay community as well. Ignoring the gay community's development of safe-sex practices, many lesbians and gay men, including activists, condemned the 1970s—the years of gay "promiscuity"—as a period of adolescence, and advocated that gay men embrace "mature," "responsible," monogamous sexual behavior.[39] A letter-writer to the *Bay Area Reporter* indicated fear of AIDS along with desire for the straight world's respect; he suggested that a rejection of promiscuity, and indeed of the entire gay subculture, was necessary to earn that respect:

> AIDS . . . attacks the very root of who we are as gay men and women. It points at our sexuality . . . with an uncompromising gesture. As much as we may know and justify to ourselves that AIDS is not god's wrath on gays, there is that itching question mark in our conscience. "What if . . . ?" it asks. . . . Our entire subculture seems to be based on prosexual scenes: bars, baths, parks. . . . At what point is the sexuality going to become secondary to knowing one another as people? We are lacking in a structure by which to promulgate the idea that being gay is all right and that one need not engage in sex with many different people in order to be gay. As I was coming out, I rejected the idea that this was one of the rights of passage. Sex to me was special—and in times since, its specialness has been compromised by too many (although less than two dozen) sexual partners. Yet I have some swollen lymph glands and I am frightened. . . . In what ways do we encourage through action . . . the by now understood necessity that promiscuity is to be avoided and that a life of moderation . . . is the one to be followed? *In what way have we proven to the straight world that we are worthy of respect?* (Freeman 1983, 8; emphasis mine)

A letter to the *New York Native* calling on that newspaper to cease printing personal ads similarly suggested the writer's AIDS-heightened shame as well as his anxious belief that social and political acceptance of gays by the straight world would come only if gays changed their ways, raised their morals, and presented themselves as "decent" human beings rather than the sexual "perverts" that they very well might be:

39. Seidman cites numerous examples during the first years of the crisis of gay men criticizing promiscuity and using AIDS "as a pretext to speak critically about homosexuality and to advocate reforms of the gay subculture" (1988, 197). See also Patton 1985, 107–8; Rofes 1990, 15; and Padgug and Oppenheimer 1992, 261.

You fill the front pages asking for gay people to be accepted by the general public . . . then make gay people seem like the sexual perverts they are considered to be by filling the last 14 or 15 pages with ads that put you and us on a lower level than *Screw.* If I were straight and read the ads I'd say, "The gays deserve AIDS". . . . It is your duty to try to put us in a good light and not make us look like a bunch of perverts—unless that's what we are. . . . The AIDS crisis is a most important time for gay people medically and socially. . . . Your paper is being read by straight people, and printing those ads can only bring down or confirm the general public's opinion of us. Doors will be closed to us socially and politically. (Bengston 1984)

From this writer's perspective, straight people's rejection of gays derived not from straight prejudice, heterosexism, or erotophobia, but from gay sexual behavior. Even more, gay sexuality evidently was so perverted that gays might actually *deserve* AIDS.

Gay public discourses indicate that, in this period when gay men were getting sick and dying from mysterious illnesses and when AIDS and gay identity were tightly bound together in people's minds, it was extremely difficult for gay men not to read AIDS as a morality tale with certain 1970s-inspired gay sexual practices as the villains and adoption of straight society's sexual mores as the path to gay redemption.

An editorial in Chicago's lesbian and gay newspaper, *Gay Life,* similarly revolving around questions of sex, respectability, and gay redemption through a renunciation of the "gay lifestyle," called on the community to "encourage gay businesses to de-emphasize some of their anonymous- and group-sex components." The editors revealed their concern with societal perceptions when giving the following rationale: "This may be good for health and will certainly be good for . . . public acceptance" ("Stay" 1983). Apparent in all of these examples, concerns about AIDS as a medical problem were frequently articulated side by side with anxieties about social acceptance; indeed, anxiety that AIDS proved gay deviance and might jeopardize lesbians' and gay men's social standing often discursively trumped fears about the syndrome itself.

My argument here is not about specific individuals' affects or emotions, although the preceding quotations are at least suggestive in that regard. Rather, this material provides evidence about the characteristics and texture of the prevailing emotional habitus within lesbian and gay communities in this period. It illustrates in particular how the felt experience of living as sexual "others" in a heteronormative society that viewed AIDS as "proof" of gay abnormality shaped how lesbians and gay men made sense of the epidemic, their relation to it, and how they might respond to it. Whether or not one completely bought society's homophobic ideas about AIDS, gay sexuality, and normalcy—and many, of course, did not—it was exceptionally difficult to escape the affective charge attached to such ideas. These examples also illustrate the emotional dimensions of social reproduction: feelings that lesbian and gay individuals expressed and evoked in public forums, like shame and a corollary fear that visible gay difference threatened social acceptance, helped to establish and reinforce an emotional habitus that encouraged many gays to embrace respectable sexual mores, at least in their public statements; indeed becoming sexually respectable was posited as a ticket to gay redemption.

DISTANCING.   Such expressions and feelings of shame and fear shaped lesbians' and gay men's attitudes about how to respond to the AIDS crisis. One response was closer to a nonresponse, a distancing from AIDS. The heroic narrative of early AIDS activism implies that lesbians and gay men had no qualms about "owning AIDS." Padgug and Oppenheimer argue, for example, that the gay community "was incapable of constructing AIDS as a disease of 'the other'" because it simply had to address the crisis (1992, 256). That became more true as the epidemic wore on, but in the early years, powerful psychic mechanisms against "owning" AIDS were in play. The feelings brought on by the crisis were too much to bear: the fear of AIDS and of premature death; the loss of loved ones; the anger and guilt over having engaged in actions, even unknowingly, that might have put you at risk for illness and death; the shame of associating yourself with what mainstream institutions and even other lesbians and gay men, and perhaps you as well, construed as shameful, perverse, hedonistic behavior, behavior that seemingly was what spurred nonrecognition and rejection of lesbians and gay men. One might understandably ward off such painful feeling states by disidentifying from AIDS.

Discussing his own distancing from AIDS, cultural theorist and ACT UP/NY member Douglas Crimp notes how powerful such unconscious processes are, even when one rationally knows that AIDS might affect one personally:

As it became more and more evident that an epidemic disproportionately affecting sexually active gay men was spreading, I reacted, as did many of my

gay friends, with my own version of the us/them mechanism. "It's only happening to those guys who go to sex clubs." "It's only happening to those guys
who take lots of drugs." "It's only happening to those guys who've had lots
of sexually transmitted diseases." I reassured myself that I was not one of
"those guys," the ones who get AIDS. And I did so even though I went to sex
clubs, I took drugs, and I'd had my share of sexually transmitted diseases.
But somehow, by some form of magical thinking—*this is the force of the
unconscious*—I exempted myself from the category of "those guys," the others, the ones who get AIDS. (Crimp 2002, 260; emphasis mine)

Anxiety that AIDS "proved" the equation of homosexuality with abnormality and perversion, and therefore justified lesbian and gay exclusion from society, also made identifying with AIDS less automatic and
more problematic than the heroic narrative suggests. Some of the comments cited earlier that disparaged aspects of gay male sexual culture
associated with AIDS and distinguished the speaker/writer from those
with AIDS suggest distancing incited by that sort of anxiety. That seems
to have been the case as well when *Advocate* editor David Goodstein
proclaimed in 1982 that the urban gay lifestyle and its ethos of sexual liberation was hazardous to gay men's health and concluded with the statement, "I shudder at the political implications of this notion" (Goodstein
1982). In his view, AIDS and what it ostensibly revealed about gay lives
posed a threat to lesbians' and gay men's political access, access that was
now needed more than ever. In 1985, Cindy Patton noted this concern,
writing, "At a time in lesbian and gay movement history when the trend
is toward hiding or disguising *sex* under the rubric of 'lifestyle,' a 'gay
disease' that is somehow linked with sex is [viewed as] an embarrassment
and a political liability" (1985, 6; emphasis hers; see also Heim 1982a and
1982b). Some of the distancing from AIDS and the sexual "lifestyle" that
ostensibly caused AIDS seems to have been both spurred by and part of
a politics of respectability.
   Concerns that gay sexual practices themselves might hinder social acceptance and political access had a longer history, drawing on an anxiety about rocking the boat that had taken root by the second half of the
1970s as lesbians and gay men succeeded in attaining the status of a recognized minority group and gained acceptance in some quarters of society. As gay activist and writer Alan Bérubé critically noted in 1984,
"The success of our minority politics strategy has left us ambivalent toward our sexual desires and practices. . . . We often see our sexual de-

sires as threats to our hard-won political victories and the recognition
we've gained as a minority group" (Bérubé 1984). Increased social acceptance encouraged a downplaying of gay sexuality and attempts to be
seen as "normal," as "just like everyone else." AIDS only intensified this
anxiety about social and political refusal.

Distancing behavior was physical at times. G'dali Braverman (later a
member of ACT UP/New York and ACT UP/Golden Gate) got involved
with GMHC in the middle of 1982. On weekends he and other GMHC
volunteers sat at tables in Greenwich Village handing out AIDS information and soliciting donations. In a 1994 interview he remembered,
"Most gay men would pass by the table or would cross the street to avoid
the table. . . . [W]omen with babies with strollers would stop; younger
heterosexuals seemed to be interested or accessible on some level that
most gay men weren't. Literally you could spend entire Saturdays and
Sundays with maybe only three or four gay men ever stopping to talk or
donate money" (quoted in Shepard 1997, 72).

Again, in the first years of the crisis, lesbians and gay men had no
way of understanding the devastation that was to come, and initially they
may have believed that AIDS had nothing to do with them. But as the
scope of the epidemic became clearer, many indicated hesitancy about
"owning" AIDS. Fear of the illnesses and death certainly was in play.
But the ways in which some distanced themselves suggested an anxiety that something about homosexuality—something that was revealed
by AIDS—was indeed shameful and must be obscured in order for gays
to be deemed deserving of rights and state assistance. Erving Goffman
argues that one way that people express and respond to stigma and resulting identity ambivalence is by distancing themselves from that which
most visibly stigmatizes them (1963, 106–8). AIDS increased the stigmatization of gay men by pointing to the difference of homosexuality and
the ostensible cost attached to that difference. In so doing, AIDS magnified gay men's shame about their sexuality and their sense that their
social ostracism was their own fault. Some navigated their ambivalence
by engaging in what Goffman calls "in-group stratification," distinguishing between their own behavior—increasingly suspect in the eyes of the
straight world—and the behavior of those whom they could construct as
even more "deviant." As Epstein notes, "The AIDS epidemic has engendered fear and prejudice and has sparked the necessity, on a massive
scale, for what Erving Goffman has called 'the management of spoiled
identity'" (Epstein 1996, 11). Distancing allowed those who blamed

their own marginalization on the characteristics and practices of *other* gays, especially gay men with AIDS, to imagine that their taint would not rub off. Usually spurred by nonconscious processes, distancing from AIDS offered a way to portray a cleaned-up version of homosexuality to the world, *and to oneself,* presenting the possibility of resurrecting gay respectability and self-respect; it offered a much desired route to gay redemption.

Attempts to salvage the damaged reputation of gay men by distancing from AIDS had significant emotional and political effects. The sort of distancing that created a good gays/bad gays dichotomy corroborated homophobic stereotypes and fostered heteronormativity, even among lesbians and gay men. This reproduction of heteronormativity, in turn, (re)generated gay shame and further encouraged politics that demonstrated lesbian and gay "normalcy" and "respectability."

THE TROPE OF RESPONSIBILITY.   The first and largest community-based institution addressing the AIDS crisis, New York's Gay Men's Health Crisis, did not distance itself from AIDS, of course, and neither did many lesbian and gay organizations and individuals. To the contrary, their actions give substance to the heroic narrative of early AIDS activism. Nevertheless, their responses to AIDS were partly shaped by the contradictory feeling states that make up lesbian and gay ambivalence. And in turn, their frequent articulations of gay pride and evocations of feelings like gay shame, fear of social rejection, and desire for gay redemption and social acceptance produced and reproduced an emotional habitus in lesbian and gay communities that helped to enlarge, but also to limit, the political horizon. We can begin to analyze these emotional and political dynamics by looking at the emotional resonances of the pride-infused trope of responsibility that figured prominently in gay newspapers' and AIDS organizations' rhetoric about the gay community's efforts to fight AIDS in the early and mid-1980s.

For example, in 1982, at one of GMHC's earliest fund-raisers, its president, Paul Popham, gave a speech in which he noted that the community, by coming together in a spirit of cooperation during this health crisis, had shown that "we *can* get things done, that we *can* act responsibly, and that we *do* care about each other" (Popham 1982; emphases his). Similarly, a GMHC advertisement proudly asserted that GMHC and its volunteers were "showing the world that the gay community is as cohesive, strong, determined, and responsible as any other" (Gay Men's Health

Crisis 1983). Gay newspapers and ASO literature were filled with such proud proclamations about gay efforts to fight AIDS. Ed Power of the Kaposi's Sarcoma Research and Education Foundation wrote a column for the San Francisco *Sentinel* in 1983 that similarly presented the AIDS crisis as an occasion both to convince gay people of their own worth and to prove something to the straight world: "This crisis presents us with the opportunity to show ourselves—and the world—the depth and strength of our caring" (Power 1983, 4). A letter to a gay paper in Los Angeles that was reprinted in San Francisco's *B.A.R.* echoed GMHC's and the KS Foundation's tone, indicating the wide circulation of such sentiments and suggesting their resonance. Urging lesbians and gay men to volunteer their skills, time, and money to the cause, it implored, "The world is watching us. . . . Let's show them how we *can* take care of our own" (Rogers and Selby 1984, 7; emphasis in original).[40]

Although not the only gay discourse about AIDS in this moment, such proud rhetoric about gay responsibility occurred so frequently in lesbian and gay communities that we need to ask what was motivating it and, more importantly, what kinds of effects it had. Its recurrence certainly can be understood as a rebuttal of dominant society's homophobic rhetoric about AIDS that constructed gay male sexual practices, gay culture, and the gay community as a whole as irresponsible: excessive, hedonistic, immature, and dangerous.[41] In that context, lesbians and gay men understandably attempted to bolster lesbian and gay self-esteem and to fight the even greater stigma that now attached to homosexuality.

Proud expressions of the community's responsible efforts against AIDS were part of an internal community conversation, one that offered a pedagogy of how to be gay and how to respond to AIDS. The trope of responsibility also was part of a conversation that individuals were having with themselves, an attempt at salvaging self-respect by those gays who themselves blamed AIDS on the "fast gay lifestyle" and the "irresponsible promiscuity" of the 1970s as well as those who simply feared such a link. In his 1982 speech, before extolling the gay community's responsible efforts against AIDS, Paul Popham indicated his anxiety about

---

40. See also Ford 1986.

41. Sociologist Gary Kinsman notes that the discourse of "responsibility" has been a strategy of governance of PWAs in Canada, as it has been in the United States: "Those who acquired HIV infection through gay sexual activity or injection drug use are already constructed as more 'irresponsible' than those who were infected through the blood supply" (Kinsman 1996, 396).

gay sexual practices, including his own, when he stated, "Something we have done to our bodies, and we still don't know what it is, has brought us all, in a sense, closer to death" (Popham 1982, 13).[42] Given the pervasiveness of such sentiments in lesbian and gay communities, not to mention the homophobic hysteria of mainstream rhetoric, it is likely that the promotion of an ethic of responsible behavior was a retort to prevalent straight *and* gay discourses about AIDS that, by placing gay men far outside of "respectable" and "normal" personhood, heightened gay shame and an already pervasive fear of social rejection. Proud assertions that gay communities were responsibly addressing the crisis shifted the lens from scrutiny of the shameful sexual gay past to approbation for the respectable (i.e., desexualized, caring) gay present.[43] They thereby offered an antidote to gay shame, likely eliciting pride while also spurring lesbian and gay involvement in AIDS organizations.

The rhetoric of gay responsibility had other effects as well, however, something that we might expect in a context where lesbians and gay men have contradictory sentiments about both gay sexuality and dominant society. In emphasizing that the community's efforts "showed the world" how responsible the gay community was, this rhetoric elicited concern about social acceptance, and held such acceptance out as a prospect, but only if the community continued to act respectably. Such expressions thereby raised hopes about social acceptance, and indeed about gay redemption, while simultaneously eliciting shame about gay difference and fear that continual social nonrecognition and rejection would follow if that difference were not buried or at least counterbalanced by gay respectability. Of course, mainstream discourses about AIDS already were shaming of gay men, and thus gay shame likely would have been one of

42. Even as the head of GMHC voiced anxiety about gay male sexual practices and their role in the epidemic, GMHC as an organization issued a letter that countered precisely that sort of self-blaming: "Unsettling though it is, *no evidence exists* to incriminate any activity, drug, place of residence or any other factor, conclusively, in the outbreak facing us" (quoted in Epstein 1996, 54; emphasis in original GMHC letter). Voices were cacophonous in this period, even within any one individual.

43. The rhetoric of gay responsibility in the early 1980s helps to explain why by the late 1980s, as Seidman has noted, AIDS was seen by many gays as marking "the beginnings of a new maturity and social responsibility among homosexuals" (Seidman 1988, 189). Crimp levels the following retort to such narratives: "AIDS didn't make gay men grow up and become responsible. AIDS showed anyone willing to pay attention how genuinely ethical the invention of gay life had been" (Crimp 2002, 13, 16). Crimp argues that moralizing gay narratives about AIDS can be understood as a psychosocial response to the ongoing AIDS crisis.

the key affective states among gay men in this period. But my claim is
that assertions of gay responsibility further entrenched gay shame.

A column from 1985 in the *New York Native* about volunteer AIDS
work being done by gay men and lesbians in San Francisco indicates how
articulations of gay pride about the community's efforts to fight AIDS
often simultaneously enlisted other feelings: shame about sexual difference, fear that the painful state of social nonrecognition might continue,
and faith that gay redemption was possible through good deeds and the
suppression of gay difference. The columnist wrote: "Not surprisingly,
the AIDS struggle has given [gay] San Franciscans new cause for civic
pride, pride of a deeper sort than the pride we felt when we were the gay
party capital of the world." The writer then approvingly quoted a friend:
"'We have a chance to prove something now, to show the world that we
aren't the giddy, irresponsible queens it often takes us to be. Sure, AIDS
has changed things here, but not necessarily for the worse'" (Hippler
1985, 31). The writer encouraged lesbians and gay men to see the silver
lining of AIDS, indeed, perhaps even to be grateful for it, because they
could now feel proud that their efforts to address the crisis had earned
them respect and recognition from a society that previously had misunderstood them, or perhaps had understood them only too well.[44]

Some of the proud rhetoric of responsibility in this period reads as a
disavowal of gay sexual cultures, even of gay sexuality itself, and seems
to have been motivated, unconsciously, by the felt need to "resolve" the
contradictory feeling states that make up lesbian and gay ambivalence.
But some of these efforts entailed a degree of conscious and strategic
maneuvering. According to AIDS and gay activist Eric Rofes, lesbians
and gay men constructed "public relations campaigns repeatedly reminding the world that gay men had responded 'responsibly' to a burgeoning
epidemic" (1996, 2). He continued, "In 1985, AIDS educators in the gay
community began to declare victory over the transmission of HIV and
touted a dramatic decline in new infections as a sign of successful education efforts taken up by a 'responsible' gay community" (145). Rofes's
knowledge derived from his own experience: in his job as executive director of the Los Angeles Gay and Lesbian Community Services Center,
he too made such claims, in part to justify expanded federal funding and

---

44. A 1988 article by Alan Bérubé suggests that this reading of AIDS was aired with
some frequency in that moment (17).

to rally heterosexual participation in donor events, but also to present "a 'good boy' image of the gay community in the mainstream media" (145).

None of this is to deny that these articulations of pride revolved around the community's tremendous response to AIDS, and, in rebutting antigay stereotypes, they likely restored a sense of pride and dignity to the gay community. But a politics of respectability is almost always deeply ambivalent; concerned above all with social acceptance, it entails efforts of some members of a marginalized group both to disprove dominant stereotypes about the group and to regulate and "improve" the behavior of its members in line with socially approved norms.[45] Articulations of pride in this moment exceeded their ostensible topic, evoking more than the feeling of pride: they conveyed an unspoken but palpable sense of relief that gays could now be construed by others as (almost) normal, and they indicated a widespread hope that such an appearance of normalcy would override gay difference and thereby invite recognition and even redemption. As such, they evoked and magnified shame about gay sexual practices and the ostensibly "irresponsible" gay past, as well as a corollary fear of ongoing social rejection if gays failed to act in a respectable manner. Traversing questions of gay selves in relation to dominant society, the proud assertions of gay responsibility provided an ideal of how to be gay and an accompanying emotional orientation.[46] Pride and respectability became tightly linked to one another: a proud gay identity now derived from gay respectability and required it as well. The trope of responsibility, then, played into the shame-imbued idea that gays, somehow undeserving, had to be "good" in order to get a proper response to the AIDS crisis from state and society. Respectability, on straight society's terms, was the price of admission.

Articulations of gay pride were of course cacophonous in this period, drawing from gay liberation discourses as well as from well-worn, deeply ingrained mainstream understandings of gay sexuality and from main-

45. See Higginbotham 1993 on the politics of respectability in black, middle-class communities. For a rich analysis of the role of concerns about respectability in black political responses to AIDS, see Cohen 1996, 1999. See Warner 1999 for an analysis of sexual shame and the contemporary mainstream gay movement's consequent embrace of a politics of respectability.

46. Philosopher Barbara Koziak's analysis of Homeric *thumos* (1999) crystallized for me the idea that a way of life has an accompanying emotional orientation.

stream values more generally. It is likely that people were experiencing both types of pride. But pride in gay difference was not backed by mainstream values, whereas pride in the gay community's responsible efforts against AIDS, precisely because of its easier alignment with mainstream norms, may have been a more compelling feeling for many. The latter pride certainly had more institutional backing and a more prominent place in the community's emotional habitus during this period than did pride in gay difference.

A contrast to earlier articulations of gay pride is instructive. When gay pride was coined as a slogan by lesbian and gay liberationists in 1969, it pointed to, and celebrated, gay sexual difference and politics that affirmed that difference. It often was linked to defiant and oppositional activism. Gay pride in the early and mid-1980s had a different flavor. Expressions of pride now frequently pointed toward gay similarities with dominant society—gays as responsible, mature caretakers. In that sense, it was a pride that was premised on a nonconscious agreement with dominant views about what is shameful, about what is beyond the pale and thus unrecognizable, and deservedly so, by "normal" society. In a moment when a public health epidemic intensified gay shame and fear of social rejection, gay pride now encouraged a politics of respectability.

That is to say, the emotional habitus that these articulations helped to establish simultaneously enabled and circumscribed political behavior, helping both to set and to delimit the political horizon. It authorized and validated reputable activism, such as provision of services, care-taking, candlelight vigils, and tactics oriented toward the electoral realm, while delegitimizing and thereby discouraging less conventional political actions that might jeopardize gay respectability. Reddy points to the regulatory role that shame can play and suggests its potential effect on political activism: "Shame can lead to . . . action aimed at managing appearances; such action can, in turn, take the form of emotive utterances and behavior that drum up and intensify socially approved feelings and play down or deny deviant ones. Local varieties of shame are therefore, in many cultural contexts, a principal instrument of social control and political power, even where shame is disavowed" (Reddy 1997, 347). *Even where shame is disavowed:* indeed, expressions of gay pride in this moment exerted a form of social control by presenting a normative vision of how to be gay, and how to address AIDS, foreclosing other ways that risked social rejection.

FRAME FAILURE: THE SUPPRESSION OF ANGER AND CONFRONTATIONAL ACTIVISM. Continuing this investigation of the role that emotion played in establishing a political horizon in this moment in lesbian and gay communities, I turn next to an analysis of how these communities navigated anger as it emerged among some lesbians and gay men. Notably, criticism of the government's response to the epidemic was fairly muted in the first couple of years. In fact, opinion leaders in lesbian and gay communities often bent over backwards to emphasize the commendable job being done by the government. Their expressed faith in the government stood in stark contrast to criticisms from other quarters. For example, in 1982 Representative Henry Waxman (D-CA) argued that state and societal responses to AIDS would have been different if the epidemic had "appeared among Americans of Norwegian descent, or among tennis players, rather than among gay males" (Heim 1982b, 9, 11). Waxman's indignation contrasts with the more laudatory, accommodating tone of a contemporaneous editorial in Chicago's *Gay Life:* "Many good people, the government of the United States included, are trying to do something about the disease. More than $1 million has been allotted by the government to study AIDS and attempt to find a cure" ("Support" 1982). In a moment when a U.S. congressman was pillorying the federal government's response to the crisis, a lesbian and gay newspaper articulated and solicited "cementing emotions" (Flam 2005) like faith in the government's goodwill.

This slowness to anger derived in part from mainstream discourses that equated homosexuality itself with illness—thereby naturalizing gay deaths from AIDS—coupled with nonconscious anxiety among many gay men that perhaps those mainstream appraisals of homosexuality were correct, as proven by AIDS. As philosopher Naomi Scheman notes, it is hard to be angry if one thinks that what is happening to oneself flows naturally from what one is (Scheman 1993, 26). Feeling anger is sometimes an achievement, and not always easily accomplished.[47]

Nevertheless, by the spring of 1983, a growing anger about the slow pace of scientific research and the low level of government funding threatened to destabilize the prevailing emotional habitus and to shift the political horizon in lesbian and gay communities. In this section I explore responses to that threatened destabilization and how they af-

47. For a slightly different perspective on "emotional achievement," see Yang 2000.

fected AIDS activism. Important to consider in this regard is that heteronormativity makes feelings such as anger among lesbians, gay men, and
other sexual and gender outlaws both likely and unacceptable. Naviga-
tions of anger, then, are endemic in lesbian and gay politics.

In the spring of 1983, two people proposed an expanded political horizon: Larry Kramer, cofounder of GMHC, and NGTF Executive Director Virginia Apuzzo. In his widely published and lengthy call to
action—"1,112 and Counting" (Kramer 1983a; reprinted in 1990a)—
Kramer offered a scathing indictment of the federal and New York City
governments, the scientific-medical establishment, the media, and the
gay community itself for allowing AIDS to become a crisis. He called on
lesbians and gays to take to the streets, to commit civil disobedience in
order to save gay men's lives. Similarly, Apuzzo concluded a New York
candlelight vigil in May 1983 with a rousing speech that offered lesbians and gay men a new political imaginary that included confrontational
activism: "If something isn't done soon, we will not be here in Federal
Plaza at night in this quiet, we will be on Wall Street at noon! . . . [N]o
politician will be immune to a community who will not take no for an
answer" (Berlandt 1983, 4).

At Congressional hearings on AIDS in May 1983, lesbian and gay
leaders criticized the federal government's response to AIDS. Apuzzo
expressed her pride in the gay community's response to AIDS and her
anger and frustration that "gay people have had to be self-reliant if for
no other reason than they are intentionally and systematically denied
their rights" (National Gay Task Force 1983, 2). She called on Congress
to appropriate at least $100 million for AIDS research (National Gay
Task Force 1983; "Apuzzo Testifies" 1983, 4; "Apuzzo, Enlow Testify"
1983, 3).

Also in May 1983, lesbian and gay communities in a number of cities held large candlelight vigils. Press accounts and photographs suggest
that the mood was typically solemn, and grief about the ever-increasing
deaths was prevalent; still, people with AIDS spoke about their dissatisfaction with the government's response to AIDS, and reports of a vigil in
New York indicate that the mood during the march of several thousand
shifted from solemnity to vocal chanting for more federal funding.[48]
Kramer spoke at the New York vigil, comparing the $600 million that

48. For press accounts of early candlelight vigils, see Chibbaro and Martz 1983; "Central Park Memorial" 1983; Walter 1983. On the New York vigil, see Arvanette 1983.

the Reagan administration was spending in military aid to the El Salva-
doran army and the $10 million to fight the Tylenol poisoning scare to
the "'princely pisspoor sum' trickling down for AIDS research;" he also
called AIDS "our Vietnam" (Berlandt 1983, 4). In a speech at the Fifth
National Lesbian/Gay Health Conference in June, Apuzzo repeated her
call to take to the streets (Martz 1983a).

Lesbian and gay leaders and AIDS activists and lobbyists returned
to Capitol Hill in August of 1983 and again slammed the federal government's response as "too little, too late" (Martz 1983b, 1). Apuzzo blasted
the federal government, claiming that its inadequate response to the crisis stemmed from its view that those affected by AIDS were "expendable." An unnamed source quoted in *Gay Life* said that Apuzzo's comments amounted to calling government officials "murderers" (Streips
1983a, 14).

By the spring of 1983, then, a new framing of the crisis was emerging
in some quarters of the lesbian and gay community: anger at the government was beginning to crystallize, and some started to express that anger and to link it to calls for more confrontational activism.[49] Apuzzo
threatened an escalation in tactics, some type of defiant direct action
on Wall Street rather than the more somber candlelight vigils then occurring across the country; Kramer called for civil disobedience. In
speeches and articles in the months and years following his call to action, Kramer compared AIDS to the Nazi holocaust and continued to
implore lesbians and gay men to take to the streets to demand a response
to the AIDS crisis.[50]

Their calls to action, especially Kramer's, had an impact. Kramer's
article "spread like wildfire across Gay America" and acted as a "dramatic wake-up call" (Streitmatter 1995, 255). George Mendenhall, reporting for the *B.A.R.* in that period, remembers, "Suddenly, gays talked
of nothing else. After that one article in the *Native*, gay phone lines to
the West Coast were burning up. No doubt about it—he got us talking
about AIDS" (Streitmatter 1995, 255).[51]

Nevertheless, Kramer's and Apuzzo's calls to action did not move lesbians and gay men to embrace confrontational activism in 1983, or 1984,
or 1985. Writing in the mid-1980s about gay AIDS activism in that pe-

49. For more evidence, see Ortleb 1982; Pierson 1983; D'Eramo 1983, 13; and Bush
1983b.
50. Many of Kramer's early speeches and articles are reprinted in Kramer 1990a.
51. See also Clendinen and Nagourney 2001, 480–81.

riod, political scientist Dennis Altman noted, "Perhaps the greatest gap in AIDS politicking is the lack of a genuine mass mobilization behind demands for a greater government response to AIDS" (Altman 1987, 107). How might we account for this "frame failure"? Because it was widely circulated and generated considerable response in lesbian and gay communities, my focus here is on Kramer's 1983 call to action—on its reception and its failure to mobilize confrontational street activism. The more general question here is about how a political horizon is generated.

There are a number of plausible reasons why Kramer's frame failed to mobilize in this moment. It is possible that others simply did not see AIDS as a crisis at that point. While true in some cases, the evidence I discuss below indicates that many actually agreed with Kramer's analysis if not his prescription for action.[52] Another possibility is that lesbians and gay men were too overwhelmed with caretaking to consider more externally oriented activism. That is true to some degree, but it overstates the case: not everyone was overwhelmed; thousands of lesbians and gay men were beginning to engage in AIDS activism such as candlelight vigils and, to a smaller degree, lobbying. When ACT UP did emerge years later, many participants simultaneously engaged in caretaking.

One factor that I think better explains this framing failure is that Kramer had no background in lesbian and gay politics and thus had little political credibility among lesbians and gay men.[53] Many activists who had built the gay rights movement and community institutions during the 1970s simply did not know Kramer. Those who did may have been alienated by his disparagements of the movement (Clendinen and Nagourney 2001, 461). Of those who knew Kramer, many viewed him as espousing antisex and antigay viewpoints. Many gay men were infuriated by his 1979 novel, *Faggots,* which condemned gay male sexual culture as unable to nurture the type of stable, loving relationship that the main character desperately seeks. Reviews slammed Kramer as puritanical and self-hating. As D'Emilio writes, *Faggots* shaped many people's reactions to Kramer's framing of the health crisis (1997, 75), and their suspicions were corroborated by the way that Kramer's ambivalence about gay male sexuality peppered his calls for militant action. Many may have

52. For evidence that people in lesbian and gay communities saw AIDS as a crisis in this period, see the *Advocate* from February 17, 1983, especially Bush 1983a; see also Power 1984; and Odets 1996.

53. Thanks to an anonymous reviewer who pointed this out to me.

dismissed his seemingly extreme claims about the scope of the epidemic and about government genocide as the rhetoric of someone using AIDS as a way to get gay men to "clean up their act."

Moreover, Kramer turned people off with his homophobic and sexist language. In "1,112 and Counting," Kramer impugned the manhood of those who warned against rocking the boat too vigorously, suggesting they were like sheep led to slaughter: "I am sick of 'men' who say, 'we've got to keep quiet or *they* will do such and such.' *They* usually means the straight majority. . . . Okay, you 'men'—be my guests: you can march off now to the gas chambers; just get right in line" (Kramer 1983a, 22; emphases his). Kramer's alignment of masculinity with his favored forms of activism and of femininity with passivity and inaction undoubtedly was offensive to many lesbians and gay men.[54]

Why would gay people listen to someone whose rhetoric echoed mainstream society's homophobic characterizations of gay men and of gay male sexual culture, whose rhetorical style was hectoring and hyperbolic, and who had little political credibility? All of these factors undoubtedly help to account for the failure of Kramer's militant collective action frame in 1983.

But these explanations do not address the fact that some lesbians and gay men actively discouraged confrontational activism in ways that suggest that the rejection of Kramer's call to action was animated in part by anxiety about the angry and militant forms of activism that he advocated. In posing challenges to mainstream (gay and straight) norms about political activism and about emotional expression, Kramer's call to action generated uneasiness and apprehension, perhaps about the indeterminate potential inherent in people angrily taking to the streets, perhaps as well about the threat to social acceptance that angry gay activism might pose.

Consider, for example, letters and an editorial published in the *New York Native* in response to "1,112 and Counting." Some letters applauded Kramer, while others accused him of ranting and raving. One credited him with igniting his own rage, but confessed hesitancy about his proposed political course of action. More critically, one writer accused Kramer of being blinded by "self-righteous rage," while another countered his "preposterous" criticism of New York City Mayor Edward Koch, praising the Mayor's funding of AIDS research ("Letters" 1983).

54. On Kramer's "fag-baiting" with language of sissies and wimps, see Bergman 1991, 130.

A *Native* editorial expressed ambivalence about Kramer's emotional tenor and activist incitements. It acknowledged that the piece had generated controversy and stated that the *Native* had published it to raise awareness of the threat of AIDS, "in spite of some reservations about [Kramer's] attacks on public officials." The editorial called on everyone to "cool the rhetoric" and concluded by commending Mayor Koch for appearing at an AIDS symposium and for having recently appointed a gay man to direct a new city office that would focus on AIDS ("Editorial" 1983). Discrediting Kramer's denunciation of Koch by strongly praising the mayor's (relatively minor) recent actions on the AIDS front, the *Native*'s editorial seemed intent on generating faith in the government and quelling anger and any street activism that might follow in the wake of Kramer's call to action. Its praise for Koch is particularly striking, considering that San Francisco's Mayor Dianne Feinstein had by then committed $1 million to AIDS research and patient care, while Koch had released a scant $25,000, despite the fact that New York City had the highest caseload in the country (Berlandt 1983, 4).

Bart Church of the Gay Rights National Lobby's AIDS Project wrote a letter ostensibly praising Kramer's article, but Church seemed most intent on defusing Kramer's anger and advocacy for militant activism (Church 1983). Ignoring Kramer's calls for various types of action—including donating money, volunteering, lobbying, and engaging in civil disobedience—Church wrote that Kramer had failed to provide a clear idea of how people could fight AIDS; the bulk of Church's letter was thus a checklist of things people could do: donate money, volunteer, lobby. Notably, Church avoided listing confrontational actions like civil disobedience that Kramer had emphasized. Church also praised the federal government's CDC for having "done all it can" (Church 1983). Where Kramer's essay was intended to arouse gay men's anger toward the government and fear about their own political inaction, Church's letter expressed gratitude and faith in the government's goodwill, feelings that contradicted and could defuse any anger that Kramer's essay might have aroused. Church thus indicated concern about Kramer's political project and offered an emotional pedagogy that discouraged confrontation and helped to reaffirm the existing political horizon.

The editors of Chicago's *Gay Life* similarly downplayed and marked as extreme Kramer's rhetoric. They did place his article on the front page, but their edits of his article along with the editorial in the same issue are easily read as an attempt to counter Kramer's interpretation of the crisis and his confrontational rhetoric and propositions for action (Kramer 1983c). The editors removed his specific appeals for sit-ins, traffic tie-ups, and volunteers willing to be arrested in acts of civil disobedience.[55] More tellingly, the same edition contained a by-then-standard AIDS editorial that encouraged people to call the White House to demand increased AIDS funds ("Call" 1983). The editors made no mention of Kramer's scathing article and indeed struck an entirely different tone. They lauded Chicago's Mayor Jane Byrne and the city's Department of Health for their response to the AIDS crisis, although the city of Chicago had yet to allocate even one dollar of city funding specifically to AIDS. Further dampening any local anger that might be directed at the city government, the editors asserted that the idea for the national phone drive to the White House "arose out of anger and dissatisfaction in *other* parts of the country . . . where AIDS and AIDS-related fatalities have been reported in high numbers, and where the city governments have been slow in acting with the community to attack the problem." They continued, "Chicago has been more fortunate than others. . . . Mayor Byrne's administration has responded effectively" ("Call" 1983, 4; emphasis mine). Anger, perhaps legitimate in other cities, was unnecessary in Chicago, despite the fact that there were by then dozens of diagnosed cases but no city AIDS office or city AIDS funding.[56] *Gay Life*'s editors seemed intent on curbing the affective and activist surge some readers might have felt upon reading Kramer's article. By evoking feelings like gratitude toward the City of Chicago and satisfaction with its efforts to address AIDS, the editorial discredited Kramer's outrage and propositions for action, potentially lessening any anger that Kramer's article might have generated and validating the existing, comparatively staid political course of action rather than the more confrontational efforts that Kramer advocated.

Most striking about these responses to Kramer's call to action is the way emotion figures in them. His entreaty to take to the streets in order to pressure the government animated some in the community to de-

55. The version of Kramer's article that ran in the *Bay Area Reporter* (Kramer 1983b) also made no mention of civil disobedience, but the edits differed from those in *Gay Life*, suggesting that the editors of *Gay Life* and the *Bay Area Reporter*, rather than Kramer himself, did the editing.

56. For reports on the lack of any Chicago City funding allocated to AIDS, see "City" 1983; "Pros" 1983; and Robles 1988, 7. For Chicago AIDS statistics from the period, see City of Chicago Department of Health 1991.

fend existing government responses to the AIDS crisis, and they did so in an emotional register seemingly designed to dampen the discontent and defuse the anger that Kramer, Apuzzo, and a few others started to air in this moment and that might catch on with others.[57] These efforts, in my view, were shaped by the existing emotional habitus in lesbian and gay communities, which was heavily colored by gay shame, fear of intensified social rejection, and desire for social acceptance. Responses to Kramer's call to action also helped to bolster and reproduce that emotional habitus by elevating socially acceptable feelings like stoic nobility and gratitude toward the government, making anger seem unnecessary and overwrought. Whether intentionally or not, their responses also helped to reaffirm and delimit the political horizon, promoting the existing repertoire of community-based service provision, caretaking, lobbying, and candlelight vigils, and arguing against the unconventional, disruptive activism that Apuzzo and Kramer urged.

Kramer's article sent a shock wave through lesbian and gay communities, and animated and energized many lesbians and gay men to get involved in AIDS activism, but it did not lead to the kind of confrontational activism that Kramer advocated, largely because his outrage and call to action so forcefully contradicted lesbian and gay emotional and political norms. Some may have felt as angry as Kramer, but the prevailing emotional habitus tended to suppress those feelings, or at least their expression. The sense of political possibilities in that moment extended only to actions that stayed within the confines of accepted political behavior, discouraging anything that might "rock the boat."

This more temperate political horizon held even for those who indicated that they shared Kramer's analysis and some of his anger. For example, Wayne Friday, a political columnist in the San Francisco *B.A.R.*, acknowledged how much Kramer's article had affected him and even revealed that he was enticed by Kramer's call to action: "I agree with Kramer and the others who are screaming the loudest that soon—very soon—we had better wake up those in power . . . who should be doing something" (1983, 17). But Friday immediately moved away from that precipice with an assertion of how much San Francisco's congressman, Phil Burton, was doing on the AIDS front. His praise for Burton was perhaps well-deserved,

---

57. D'Emilio similarly argues that this and others of Kramer's statements about AIDS "have repeatedly evoked . . . angry, defensive denunciations" from within the gay community (1997, 79).

but in dramatically shifting gears, Friday effectively, if inadvertently, deflated Kramer's critique of government responses as well as his call to action. Friday's voice had no trace of Kramer's anger. He quoted Burton's gay aide, Bill Kraus, about the efforts underway to get the foot-dragging NIH to fund AIDS research proposals, but Friday did not then circle back to Kramer's article (which had excoriated the NIH). Although Friday began by agreeing with Kramer's call to action, by the end he had steered his readers away from confrontational activism and toward satisfaction with and gratitude toward a local politician. Like others, his sense of political possibility remained in the electoral realm.[58] His column not only reveals the strength of the existing political horizon, but also indicates how that political imaginary was simultaneously reproduced.

The actions at this time of Gary Walsh, a person with AIDS in San Francisco, are perhaps the exception that proves the resilience of the existing political horizon. Walsh had participated in some AIDS lobbying and then, furious about the federal government's continuing failure to act, he "deluged the Washington office of Margaret Heckler, Secretary of Health and Human Services, with phone calls, insisting she hear one-to-one what it's like to have a friend die of AIDS" (Shilts 1983). His action was perhaps the first AIDS-related "phone zap," a tactic later frequently deployed by ACT UP, but it was conducted by one person, on his own, rather than collectively by a movement. In 1983, there was little space for collective expressions of militant, confrontational anger.

In noting that people generally want to be proximate "to the sacred center of the common values of the society" in which they live, Goffman suggests that conformity exerts a formidable pull on most individuals, under *any* circumstances (Goffman 1959, 36). How much stronger might be the pull toward that sacred center for those who have been cast out to the margins of society? In a country such as the United States, where voting, lobbying, and an occasional rally are the acceptable avenues for trying to effect change, engagement in more militant collective action violates political norms and suggests a too severe, and possibly even subversive, critique of what is at the sacred center of the United States—the image of a flourishing democracy and the land of freedom and equality. To question the sacred, the inviolable, is to bring suspicion on oneself.

Adopting Kramer's angry and militant collective action frame would have placed lesbians and gay men outside of American emotional and

58. See Power 1983; and Crane 1983 for more examples.

political norms and thus even further outside of dominant society. It is no surprise, then, that his exhortation to militant and angry activism had little play among lesbians and gay men in 1983. In a moment when social perceptions had life-and-death consequences, most lesbians and gay men, all too familiar with social nonrecognition and desiring relief from that painful affective state, were not inclined to veer too far from conventional forms of political action.

PRACTICES OF SOCIAL REPRODUCTION. The prevailing emotional habitus and political horizon made it probable that some public expressions about a political course of action would click while others, like Kramer's, would generate defensiveness and attempts to discredit his emotional pedagogy and political proposals. Consider the moving speech that Robert Cecchi, a gay man with AIDS and a volunteer at GMHC, gave at the May 1983 candlelight vigil in New York City. Cecchi addressed his remarks to President Reagan. He began by saying that he was "a feeling, thinking, God-loving man with AIDS" and continued, "I love my country. I've worked hard for it. I've paid my taxes, voted in every [election], and I never threw garbage in the streets." He then talked about his volunteer work to help other people with AIDS. Evoking the desire for love and recognition, along with the fear of rejection, that a gay son might experience in relation to his heterosexual father, and suggesting parallel feelings on the national, political level, Cecchi concluded by imploring Reagan to increase funding for AIDS research: "Like our first president, you are the father of this country. Do you hear me when I say your children are dying? This problem transcends politics. In asking you to release monies, I am asking for an act of love. If you are my father, Mr. President, I am your son. Please help me save my life."(Cecchi 1983; quoted in part in Román 1998, 29).

Cecchi's words indicate the complicated political relationship of lesbians and gay men to dominant society—standing precariously both inside and outside—and suggest how that ambiguous relationship, and its psychic force, affected lesbian and gay communities' early AIDS politics. In part, Cecchi's declaration that gays were part of society was a defiant assertion of national belonging. At the same time, in describing himself and, implicitly, other gay men as upstanding and patriotic citizens of the country, as loyal sons, Cecchi was in effect saying, "We are good, upright citizens and *thus* you should love and help us." State assistance in a time of crisis should be forthcoming *not* because gays are citizens, whether straight society likes it or not, but because gays are *good* citizens. He was asking for love and suggesting that gays are lovable *because* they are contributing members of society, because they are, in fact, the children of dominant society; the state should thus provide financial help to its children, who, like any other children, are innocent. In equating gay men to children, Cecchi challenged dominant constructions of the depraved, predatory homosexual, but that equation also reads as a bid for gay respectability premised on a denial of gay difference. Cecchi was saying in effect that the state should assist gays in this moment of crisis not because that was the state's job, but because gays were childlike and thus, Freud notwithstanding, nonsexual and pure. Criticism of government inaction was implicit in Cecchi's request, as was a sense of entitlement. But both were tempered by a suggestion of shame about sexual otherness and a desire for the love and acceptance of heterosexual society, even at the cost of suppressing gay difference. Cecchi's dissatisfaction with the government's inaction was accompanied by the belief, or perhaps simply the hope, that aligning gays with normative citizenship and submerging gay difference would prod the government into action.

In using this example, I am not arguing that Cecchi himself was ashamed of gay difference and feared social rejection. Indeed, it is possible that his speech was primarily a rhetorical strategy rather than a heartfelt expression of his own feelings. Regardless of Cecchi's feelings and intent, his speech is interesting for my purposes because it indicates the difficulties that hated and oppressed social groups face when confronting the state. They have to navigate their own contradictory status as both members and outsiders, and that entails a navigation of their own sentiments about self and society, which are often contradictory as a result of that status.

My contention here is twofold. First, the prevailing emotional habitus and political horizon in lesbian and gay communities made comments like Cecchi's intelligible and encouraged their expression. Second, such comments, in turn, buttressed both feelings like shame about gay difference and fear that such difference would translate into continued social rejection and reinforced assumptions about what lesbians and gay men should be feeling and about what forms of political activism were acceptable and desirable. This habitus and political horizon also help to explain why some gays emphatically praised the federal government's responses to the health crisis during this period.[59]

59. Contrast Beardemphl 1983, 5; Schweikhart 1983, 5; Lorch 1983, 6; "Congratulations" 1983; and Streips 1983b, 8, for example, with Kramer 1983a and "Apuzzo Testifies" 1983.

What most interests me is how the repeated expression and elicitation of certain feelings helped to establish and bolster a given political
horizon and foreclose another. The evidence suggests that this largely
nonconscious mobilization of feelings had a greater effect on lesbians'
and gay men's political imaginaries than did some concrete factual information that others were stating. In "1,112 and Counting," for example,
Kramer angrily noted that the government had spent $10 million dur-
ing the first two weeks of the Tylenol scare to find out why fewer than
ten people had died but only $1 million over an entire year to investigate
why hundreds had died of complications from AIDS (Kramer 1990a, 26,
39; see also Deitcher 1995, 142). And again, Kramer, Apuzzo, and a few
others criticized the government for its low level of funding for AIDS
research. One might thus conclude that gay praise of the federal government in this moment was overly generous, even farfetched. But it is
more interesting, I think, to consider the factors that trumped negative
appraisals of the government and the angry feelings attached to them.
The evidence shows that cognitive appraisals of a situation are not the
only factors that influence people's political (in)action. Any investigation of political behavior needs to acknowledge that people are simultaneously cognitively and affectively driven; that is true of Kramer and of
Cecchi, Apuzzo and lesbian and gay newspaper editors. Our thoughts
and our feelings together shape our political imaginaries and courses of
action. In this case, the structure of lesbian and gay ambivalence and attempts to navigate its contradictory affective states played a significant
role in shaping what was politically (un)thinkable.

My purpose in analyzing how lesbians and gay men dealt with Kramer's call for militant AIDS activism is to explore why activist responses
took the specific forms they did in these early years of the AIDS crisis.
I am not positioning Kramer as an example of an ambivalence-free gay
man who felt no compunction about engaging in militant politics that
threatened gay respectability. First, this is simply not true of Kramer.
Indeed, he is a prime example of an individual who is self-divided, an
affective state that is familiar to the socially marginalized.[60] His writings repeatedly suggest his own ambivalence about being gay.[61] Second,
in arguing that there is a link between ambivalence and politics, I am

---

60. Frantz Fanon's *Black Skin, White Masks* (1967) is a moving study of the relationship between social marginalization—in his case due to colonialism—and identity ambivalence. See also Du Bois 1989.

61. As just one example, see Kramer's 1985 play, *The Normal Heart*.

not saying that engagement in particular politics reveals a given individual's psychic state. Neither am I arguing that a particular "resolution" to an individual's ambivalence would automatically lead to a particular response to AIDS. My argument is not at the level of the individual. Rather, what I am arguing is that when a given constellation of feelings and related emotional practices becomes widespread within a social group, the emotional habitus that is established creates a space for some forms of activism and forecloses others. Even then, of course, a given resolution to ambivalence, should one arise, and a concomitant emotional habitus do not drive members of that group inexorably toward a particular and predictable course of political action. The task, then, is to trace how a given emotional habitus comes into being and is stabilized, how it helps to establish a political horizon, and how those processes affect people's modes of activism and whether or not they engage in activism at all.

My hope is that this example of frame failure will help us to sharpen our analyses of frame success. In his "insider's critique" of the framing perspective, social movement scholar Robert Benford notes the lack of attention to the question of frame failure: "Instead, movement framing studies often are plagued by circular claims in which unverifiable causal relationships are implied. That is, we tend to work backward from successful mobilization to the framings activists proffered and then posit a causal linkage between the two" (Benford 1997, 412).[62]

We may be able to avoid such tautological reasoning by exploring how a community's emotional habitus animates and sustains certain framing efforts while discouraging or discrediting others. By analyzing reasons for the initial failure of Kramer's and Apuzzo's frame, I hope to avoid circular reasoning when later talking about the resonance of a similar framing offered by direct-action AIDS activists in 1986 and 1987. The initial failure and subsequent success of this more confronta-

---

62. Social movement scholars Hank Johnston and John Noakes agree, writing, "A constituency that finds a frame compelling usually becomes apparent to researchers by its mobilization, but those social actors for whom the frame is not compelling are generally lost to history" (Johnston and Noakes 2005, 16). The only work I know of that has begun to theorize frame failure specifically is that of Glenn (1999), Diani (1996), and Koopmans and Duyvendak (1995). My work differs most from that of Koopmans and Duyvendak who, drawing on the insights of political process theory, link frame failure to tightening political opportunities. Kramer's frame did not fail for that reason, which will become apparent in the next chapter when I discuss the success of a Kramer-like call to activism in the context of constricting political opportunities.

tional collective-action frame allow me to consider factors that shifted in the interim—primarily the structure and content of the emotional habitus—and to explore why and how such factors help to account for frame resonance.

As the remainder of this chapter will show, during this period lesbian and gay communities continued to pursue activism that consisted primarily of caretaking and service provision, along with lobbying and occasional candlelight vigils. The emotion work (Hochschild 1979, 1983) of various AIDS professionals, newspaper editors and columnists, and other lesbians and gay men seems to have submerged any stimulus toward confrontational street activism that Kramer's article and Apuzzo's call for action might have inspired.

THE CONSOLIDATION OF THE EXISTING POLITICAL HORIZON: DEALING WITH GROWING ANGER, 1984–85.   Disturbing AIDS statistics were issued at the beginning of 1984. Total reported AIDS cases had tripled during 1983. The number of AIDS cases was exploding in Boston, Chicago, Los Angeles, New York, San Francisco, and Washington, D.C., affecting people from all walks of gay life, from the most strait-laced professionals to drag queens, activists, men who frequented gay baths, and men in monogamous relationships.[63] By 1985, the number of reported AIDS cases nationally had exceeded eleven thousand, and the number of AIDS-related deaths was nearing six thousand (Centers for Disease Control and Prevention 1997, 14). Death and illness among gay men were by now commonplace in the epicenters of the epidemic. The CDC estimated that five hundred thousand to one million people were already infected with HIV and that AIDS cases would double over the next year (Beldekas 1985). Gay and AIDS activist Eric Rofes painted a vivid picture of gay life during this period. "By 1985, many gay men over the age of thirty were facing decimation beyond their wildest imagination. Over 10,000 had been diagnosed with this frightening syndrome and tens of thousands more were infected with HIV and feared for their lives. Even more men had lost lovers, best friends, neighbors, coworkers, and entire social networks" (1996, 157). Rofes continues, "Gay men struggled to accept the overwhelming horrors accumulating all around: contemporaries dying painful deaths, acts of desire becoming acts of contagion, the homophobe's wildest dreams finding fulfillment" (232). Lesbian and

63. See Bommer and Williams 1984.

gay newspapers around the country started obituary sections in 1984 and 1985.

Ever greater numbers of lesbians and gay men were involved in care-taking and were losing friends and lovers to AIDS. Cindy Patton's account of her day at the 1985 Gay Pride march in Boston provides a vivid illustration of what it felt like to be involved in AIDS work during this period. "At this year's lesbian and gay pride march, I see the lover of a man I know who has just died . . . walking silently, in tears, carrying the placard bearing the date of his lover's death. One of the staffers from the AIDS Action Committee looks tired and I ask her what's wrong. 'We were up late last night,' she says. 'We had to add two new placards from yesterday'" (Patton 1985, 162). Patton then ran into a friend whose lover had died the previous year. And she learned that another friend had been diagnosed with AIDS. Even for those not living with AIDS, personal contact with people living with and dying from AIDS was increasingly familiar to many lesbians and gay men.

It is no exaggeration to say that by 1985, AIDS was devastating lesbian and gay communities across the United States. There was palpable desperation along with panic and intense fear about AIDS itself and about the social and political repercussions for lesbians and gay men. Also evident in this emotional mix is a mounting anger among lesbians and gay men about the government's negligent responses to AIDS. In Rofes's words, "Rage began to sweep over the tribe during these years" (1996, 45). Criticism of all levels of government by lesbians and gay men became more scathing.[64]

As I indicated earlier, along with Kramer's and Apuzzo's calls to action, debates within lesbian and gay communities in 1984 and 1985 about whether or not to close gay bathhouses revealed a growing willingness among some lesbians and gay men—particularly in San Francisco—to use more confrontational activism to fight the state's response to the AIDS epidemic. But activism on these fronts was not yet widespread or sustained, and the growing anger and defiance of some lesbians and gay men may have encouraged others to attempt to dampen and rechannel such sentiments. As occurred in response to Kramer's 1983 call to action, statements from lesbian and gay leaders and newspaper editorials during this period suggest such efforts—both conscious and not—to manage affects and emotions. Most specifically, a number of other feelings—an in-

64. See, for example, "$10 Million" 1985; and Freiberg 1985a.

ternally oriented pride in the community's responsible efforts in addressing the AIDS crisis, faith in the government's goodwill, love for one's
brothers, and a stoic nobility in the face of death—were frequently elicited and articulated. That emotion work, I believe, effectively channeled
the growing anger among lesbians and gay men toward service provision
and lobbying, and away from less conventional street activism. Even as
the exploding AIDS epidemic and people's growing anger about government inaction were putting enormous strain on the emotional and political norms then prevalent in lesbian and gay communities, lesbians and
gay men generally continued to abide by and reinstantiate those norms—
evidence, perhaps, of the force and weight of structure and of the tendency of social action to reproduce the status quo.

A more general comment on anger might be useful here. Histori-
ans Carol and Peter Stearns (1986) have argued that during the last two
hundred years, attitudes in the United States about anger have shifted;
whereas the colonialists viewed temper as a sign of manliness, anger
is currently regarded as a feeling that needs to be restrained and controlled.[65] Anthropologist Catherine Lutz (1986, 1988) has written about
the gendering of anger, noting that its expression by men is more acceptable than by women; still, she agrees that the dominant American attitude toward anger is that it should be controlled. Lesbians and gay men,
like others, are influenced by this hegemonic emotional habitus, and perhaps more intensely so in moments when they seek acceptance by mainstream society. That helps to explain why discomfort and hesitation
about gay anger and attempts to control it have been part of the gay community's emotional habitus since the early 1970s when the gay movement
shifted its quest for sexual liberation and broad social transformation to
the fight for lesbian and gay rights. It should be no surprise, then, that in
the mid-1980s many lesbians and gay men, particularly those who were
part of the gay establishment, were concerned about the negative social repercussions of gay anger, particularly if linked to confrontational
activism.[66]

65. Stearns and Stearns attribute the shift in part to concern about the destructive force
of human aggression evident during World War II and the Nazi holocaust and to concern
about black and student unrest during the 1960s.

66. I have not done the research, but my guess is that because the emotional habitus of
the more radical women's movement validated feelings of anger, lesbians who had some
contact with that movement may have been more attuned to anger and may have had a critique of social norms against its expression. The prevailing emotional habitus in lesbian
and gay communities, however, was more aligned with the dominant emotional habitus.

In this context, even as anger and criticisms were aired, lesbian and gay leaders issued few calls for any activist response beyond lobbying and voting. Confrontational activism was simply not part of many people's political imaginaries in this moment. When the *Advocate* interviewed twenty lesbian and gay "leaders and thinkers, movers and shakers" about their predictions and thoughts for the new year, 1985, most anticipated a worsening AIDS crisis (Freiberg, Kulicke, and Walter 1985). But little anger was articulated and, in the rare instances when political action was mentioned, these leaders tended to advocate lobbying and involvement in the electoral realm. (Only two out of the twenty expressed anger and suggested the need for more confrontational tactics).

Street activism of the sort contemplated by Kramer and Apuzzo was rarely mentioned in the gay papers during this period, and then it was often immediately qualified or even discounted. In an article in the San Francisco *Sentinel,* Stonewall Gay Democratic Club Political Vice President Ralph Payne mentioned his disgust that the Democrats were scapegoating gays for losing the 1984 presidential election and stated, "It's time to take to the streets." But he immediately clarified that he "wasn't necessarily advocating civil disobedience, but rather the tactics of mass organizing—demonstrations, picketing, petitions" (Hass 1985, 6). The article concluded with information about how to get involved in AIDS lobbying and fund-raising. Payne himself may have favored more confrontational activism—indeed, two years later he was part of a civil disobedience action at the White House that I discuss in chapter 2—but he clearly felt the need to qualify his claim that it was time to take to the streets. Even mentioning street activism required an immediate disavowal.

San Francisco gay activist Cleve Jones gave a speech in November 1985 that helps to illuminate why more confrontational action was beyond many lesbians' and gay men's political horizon at this time. His speech appears as an attempt to defuse anger and militant action, and such a rerouting could understandably have been its effect. The occasion was a somber candlelight vigil to commemorate the 1978 assassinations of San Francisco Supervisor Harvey Milk—who was gay—and Mayor George Moscone. Jones recalled the White Night Riots in 1979 that occurred in San Francisco when the killer, Dan White, was convicted of manslaughter rather than murder and sentenced to only five years in prison: "That night we did not march in silence and the light that filled this plaza came not from candles but from burning barricades and exploding police cars.

All that is history now. . . . The candlelight march is an annual opportunity for us to face our community's loss together in a spirit of strength, love, and hope. Above all else, this march is a symbol of hope" (C. Jones 1985, 10–11). Jones criticized the state and federal governments for letting people with AIDS, including his friends, die. Rather than using his indictment as an opportunity to make demands or to call for community action targeting the government, Jones then simply concluded: "We send this message to America: we are the lesbians and gay men of San Francisco, and though we are again surrounded by uncertainty and death, we are survivors, we shall survive again, and we shall be the strongest and most gentle people on this earth" (11). Jones invoked the White Night Riots, but only to push them into the recesses of history, where, presumably, they belonged. Proud and gentle people do not riot, he suggested, no matter how angry they are about government negligence in the face of thousands of deaths. Jones named only two courses of action, street riots and gentle, dignified, candlelight marches, and only the latter was actually thinkable. Notably, in a 1995 interview, Jones said that he led such marches in a manner that would defuse lesbians' and gay men's anger (Shepard 1997, 39). His political universe, and the gay political universe more generally, allowed for no other options.

Others in the community encouraged the channeling of a growing anger among lesbians and gay men away from confrontational activism and into more reputable political work such as care for people with AIDS. At an AIDS memorial candlelight procession in Chicago in 1985, anger was articulated and elicited but then quickly defused and directed toward compassion and love: One speaker asked the crowd, "Are you mad? Are you angry?" He said he was "pissed" because no one outside the lesbian and gay community was doing anything about AIDS. The crowd loudly agreed with him. He concluded by advising: "Take your anger and turn it into love for your brothers." The procession concluded with marchers singing the refrain "We are a gentle, angry people" from Holly Near's *Singing For Our Lives* (Cotton 1985a).[67]

---

67. Near's song, in various versions, was popular at lesbian and gay candlelight vigils during this period. De la Vega remembers singing "We are a gentle, *loving* people, singing for our lives" after the New York City Council passed a gay rights bill in March 1986 (de la Vega 1986; emphasis mine). Other versions of the refrain similarly excise anger from lesbians' and gay men's affective experiences: "We are gay and lesbian people"; "We are a loving, healing people"; "We are a justice-seeking people"; "We are a peaceful, loving people." During the late 1980s and early 1990s, AIDS activists spoofed the song, singing: "We are a gentle, angry people, and we are *whining, whining* for our lives."

A remarkably similar emotional dynamic occurred at an AIDS memorial candlelight vigil and march the same year in San Francisco. The five thousand marchers somberly proceeded with "an almost painful slowness" from the gay Castro neighborhood to the Civic Center. When Dean Sandmire, the co-chair of the PWA Caucus of Mobilization against AIDS (MAA), announced that Governor George Deukmejian would not be attending the march, "there were loud catcalls and hisses" from the crowd.[68] The press report noted that Sandmire "rose to the occasion quickly" and yelled to the crowd, "This is not why we're here. We're here to honor the dead and those who are still living" (Linebarger 1985a, 3). Both Sandmire and the reporter expressed concern about an angry gay crowd. Anger and whatever actions anger might prompt when expressed in a mass of people were pitted against the more appropriate feelings—love and respect for one's brothers—and thereby affectively defused.

San Francisco is an interesting case in that comparatively more anger was expressed in its gay newspapers, particularly the *B.A.R.*, during the 1984–85 period. Much of the anger was about the closing of the bathhouses. A number of editorials, opinion pieces, and letters-to-the-editor also expressed anger about low levels of government AIDS funding, attempts to implement repressive measures, including quarantine, and the growing power of the right wing. How did that slightly different emotional landscape affect the sense of political possibilities among San Francisco's lesbians and gay men? My sense is that the anger that some in San Francisco were articulating both expanded the political horizon to include more confrontational activism and also mobilized others in the community to counter, actively, that anger and its political potential. Attempts by Cleve Jones and Dean Sandmire to defuse gay anger, for example, might have been prompted by the perceived shakiness of the existing political horizon. There seems to have been an emotional and political jostling within the community, perhaps between gay "leaders" who were anxious over the growing anger and its possible political explosiveness and more "rank and file" members of the community who were increasingly angry and more willing to embrace confrontational tactics.

In addition, gay San Franciscans who voiced anger in this period fre-

68. MAA formed in San Francisco in late 1984; along with testifying at hearings and lobbying, MAA mobilized a number of AIDS vigils around the country, including those that occurred in May 1985.

quently connected it to action in the electoral realm, probably because of the community's access to the San Francisco political establishment, which helped to produce a political horizon that for many began and remained in the electoral arena.[69] A 1984 editorial in the *San Francisco Sentinel*, for example, warned of the growing power of the homophobic right wing and defiantly proclaimed that "we will not be denied our rightful place as members of . . . society" (Murray 1984). Given the editorial's title—"The Real Revolution"—one might expect a call to lesbians and gay men to take to the streets to fight the right and the Reagan administration, but the writer instead pointed toward voting: "Justice can only be achieved through the political process. Elections this year are crucial. We must educate ourselves and each other to issues and candidates, and vote wisely. . . . This is an exciting time for us as a community. The stakes are high, the possibilities for progress greater than ever before. The real revolution has just begun" (Murray 1984). In setting the electoral realm as the appropriate political horizon, the pedagogy of this and similar statements translated anger into a predictable form. Rather than an explosive anger that might encourage unconventional political activism, this anger was contained and channeled toward the electoral realm. This evidence also indicates that there is no necessary relationship between a given emotional state and specific forms of political activism. Anger can go in many different activist directions.

In this period, New York City was hit particularly hard by AIDS, and the local government's response was woefully inadequate.[70] Lesbians and gay men living in this epicenter of the epidemic increasingly expressed anger at the local, state, and federal governments, but there as well such expressions tended to confirm, rather than alter, the existing political horizon, as the following example indicates. Charles Ortleb, publisher and editor-in-chief of the *New York Native*, wrote an editorial about press reports that Robert Gallo of the National Cancer Institute had "stolen" a sample of HIV from its French discoverers and thereby had set treatment and research back "immeasurably." Ortleb concluded with the following exhortation to action: "Get angry, as angry as you'd

69. Sociologist Elizabeth Armstrong discusses the ascendance of gay political power and access to the Democratic Party in San Francisco during the 1970s (2002, esp. chap. 6).

70. See Shilts 1985 for a comparison between the official government responses to AIDS in San Francisco and New York City. See also Gay Men's Health Crisis 1991, 16; Loughery 1999, 428.

be if someone had just killed your lover. Then call up every Senator, every Congressman you can get on the phone and demand an immediate investigation of Robert Gallo . . . before this fraud and this scientific standstill in fact does kill you, your lover, and millions of other Americans" (Ortleb 1985). Anger, even in the face of the death—indeed, the *murder*—of one's lover and perhaps oneself, should be channeled toward phoning one's elected representatives.

The words of Nathan Fain, a gay man who worked at GMHC, offer some insight into gay anxiety about anger and confrontational politics and the resulting political horizon that excluded militancy. Speaking about gay anger and AIDS politics at an AIDS conference, Fain revealed unease with anger that seemed to derive in part from his own anxiety about gay difference and gays' relationship to dominant society. Darrell Yates Rist reported on Fain's speech and included excerpts from a conversation he had had with Fain a few days before:

> Fain told me that gay men's anger over AIDS had begun, he knew, to seethe. . . .
> He was perturbed: "factions" in the gay community had out of hand condemned the government and its scientists—"offended many of our friends"—when they didn't have an inkling of how much the government had been doing and was, he was convinced, about to do. Today his speech concedes that some of us have reason to be angry. But, he says . . . we must grow up, "assume the responsibilities of adulthood." . . . We must turn our backs on the politics of our "collective childhood," and not permit ourselves to be rebellious—like a bunch of "drag queens throwing bricks at cops." If we don't behave, the "*real* world" won't respect us. (Rist 1985a, 77; emphasis his)

To be accepted and respected, lesbians and gay men should assume the proper emotional demeanor and engage in activism sanctioned by mainstream American political norms. Even as the AIDS epidemic was exploding across the country, some seemed most anxious about alienating straight society with angry and confrontational activism.[71]

GAY PRIDE AND ITS SISTERS (REDUX): MANAGING ANGER AND MAINTAINING THE EXISTING POLITICAL HORIZON.   The growing frequency of articulations of anger in the mid-1980s threatened the prevailing emotional habitus and political horizon, and in that context, expressions of

71. See also Merla 1985.

pride again played an important role. Often immediately following some lesbians' and gay men's expressions of anger, others evoked and affirmed pride in the community's response to AIDS as the proper feeling to feel amid this crisis. As in the early 1980s, such expressions both acknowledged how much lesbians and gay men were doing to respond to the crisis and simultaneously engaged questions about gay selves in relation to dominant society. And, as before, the emotional tenor of this pride authorized and validated certain political tactics while delegitimizing others.

Editorials in Chicago's *Gay Life* throughout 1985 offer good examples of how the emotional habitus itself was bolstered during this period and how it incited feelings that helped to reproduce and simultaneously circumscribe the political horizon. The newspaper's editorials consistently criticized the government's negligent response to AIDS, for example, but answered a growing frustration among lesbians and gay men with exhortations to persevere, to continue along the path of "taking care of our own," and to feel pride in the community's efforts in the face of the growing disaster. None made the case for stepped-up activism. One, for example, angrily indicted the government for hesitating "to do for AIDS what it doesn't think twice about doing for other diseases," but rather than stoke readers' anger, the editors shifted the emotional register: "Where others might have caved in under the pressure of the killer AIDS, our community has grown in strength during this tremendous crisis.... June is Gay and Lesbian Pride Month, and in Chicago we can truly be proud" ("Off" 1985). In editorial after editorial, *Gay Life* repeatedly mobilized gay pride about "taking care of our own" in a manner that skirted the possibility of turning to angry, confrontational activism.[72]

But by the second year of the epidemic, it was clear that lesbian and gay communities simply could not "take care of their own" any longer. As early as August 1982, Tim Westmoreland, an aide to Rep. Henry Waxman (D-CA), had told AIDS activists that the gay community could not "go it alone," stating, "You need the federal government involved in this" (Clendinen and Nagourney 2001, 468–69).[73] Lesbians and gay organizations were aware of the vast financial needs. In public testimony before Congress in 1983, NGTF's Virginia Apuzzo challenged the Reagan

72. See "AIDS" 1985; "Health" 1985"; "We've Got to Help Ourselves" 1985; "1985" 1985; and Cotton 1985b.
73. See also Bush 1983a, 21.

administration's neoliberal efforts to privatize government social programs when she stated, "We are not dealing with a problem which can
be addressed only by volunteers from the private sector" (National Gay
Task Force 1983, 3). In this light, gay newspaper editorials in 1985 that
made no demands of the government but instead expressed an internally
oriented pride along with an almost stoic nobility in the face of death
and government inaction seem oddly placid, likely to submerge anger
and defuse any impulse toward confrontational activism. Claims made
in the emotional register of stoic pride were pervasive, not only revealing some of the character and texture of the existing emotional habitus,
but likely helping to secure that habitus as well, along with its attendant
political horizon. Confrontational tactics were almost never mentioned
publicly by leaders, activists, or others during this period.[74]

The contemporaneous comments of some lesbians and gay men—
including the quote of Nathan Fain above—suggest that lesbian and gay
ambivalence was a factor in establishing this political horizon. In a column in the *Native,* David Scondras, an openly gay member of Boston's
City Council, called on lesbians and gay men to engage in "protest and
vocal, direct confrontation" in response to the Massachusetts House of
Representatives' rejection of a gay rights bill. Scondras countered "those
among us . . . who caution 'restraint' and 'moderation' . . . [those who]
worry that we might alienate some lawmakers" with the following logic:
"Our ultimate goal in initiating gay rights legislation is, after all, not so
we can act more 'respectable' or learn how to 'fit in,' but to protect ourselves from homophobia" (Scondras 1985). Virginia Apuzzo's comments
at a meeting of elected and appointed lesbian and gay officials similarly
revealed her perception that widespread ambivalence about self and society had translated into anxiety about lesbian and gay expressions of
anger tethered to militant political activism:

74. In all of 1985, Chicago's lesbian and gay press printed only two articles that raised
the prospect of militant action in response to AIDS: see Baim 1985 and Quinby 1985. It
was similar in the *Advocate* and in the *New York Native,* which recorded growing articulations of anger but only a few calls for more militant activism in 1985. Only four articles in the *Advocate* indicated that some lesbians and gay men felt the need for militant
action to fight AIDS: Freiberg, Kulicke, and Walter 1985; Walter 1985; Freiberg 1985b;
and Linebarger 1985c. Thirteen articles in the *Native* indicated a growing militancy, but
nine of them were reporting on the formation and actions of the Gay and Lesbian Anti-
Defamation League (GLADL), which I discuss below. See Merla 1985; Scondras 1985;
Morris 1985; Adkins 1985; Fall 1985a, 1985b; Schulman 1985a, 1985b; Jefferson 1985a,
1985b; Brown 1985; Rist 1985b.

For those of us who have earned—for whatever silly, transient, cheap reason—the respect and regard of [the political] system, we must be willing to
spend it on this [AIDS] issue. . . . Yes, we must negotiate. Yes, we must lobby.
Yes, we must litigate. . . . But we must also remember where we come from,
and return to allowing that rage to be expressed and not think for a minute
that there is something not respectable about that. (Walter 1985, 11)

Apuzzo attempted to broaden the sense of political possibilities by directly challenging the logic that pitted gay expressions of rage against respectability. The comments at the same meeting by Massachusetts Congressman Barney Frank, however, sounded the more typical cautionary
note: "The political system has responded better to [the AIDS crisis] at
this point than I would have hoped. . . . [That means] in my judgment,
that the political course of action that has been chosen [by the lesbian
and gay community] is correct" (Walter 1985, 13). The comments of
both Apuzzo and Frank indicated their awareness of the beginnings of
rumblings among some lesbians and gay men for more militant action;
Apuzzo attempted to alleviate lesbian and gay anxiety about rocking the
boat, while Frank's ratification of the existing order encouraged staying
the non-confrontational course.

Cracks in the Emotional Habitus and Openings toward a New Political Horizon

The second half of 1985 and first half of 1986 mark a transitional emotional and political moment in lesbian and gay communities characterized by growing lesbian and gay anger, local outbreaks of more confrontational activism, and efforts to contain those developments.

In June 1985, one gay man with AIDS, John Lorenzini, chained himself to the old Federal Building in San Francisco to protest the Reagan
administration's failures to address the AIDS crisis (Snyder 1985; Wetzl
1985). Lorenzini was the first activist arrested while protesting the AIDS
crisis. Although he asked others to join him, no one was "seriously interested," and his act of civil disobedience was a solitary action (Lorenzini 1987, 24). Rather than marking a broader shift to militancy, then,
Lorenzini's action was an exception that indicated widespread reluctance about engaging in such defiance. But the tide was definitely turning, and fairly soon afterwards, more than two hundred people gathered
in San Francisco's Castro neighborhood in response to a call from MAA

to protest California Governor George Deukmejian's veto of much of the state's AIDS budget. A frequent chant among protesters was "We say fight back!" Speaking at the demonstration, John Wahl of MAA compared the Deukmejian administration to the Reagan administration, stating that both "stand for letting us die." Urging the crowd to up the ante, Wahl continued, "we can let them know we are not going to go peacefully" (Linebarger 1985b). Maggie Rubenstein, also from MAA, was met with "wild applause" when she addressed the crowd: "We have a fascist state in this country for people like us. We're tired of this bullshit. The government, the medical profession, and the scientists don't give a shit about our lives" (Linebarger 1985b).

Four months later, at the end of October, nine individuals "spontaneously decided to spend the night in front of the old Federal Office building" (Hippler 1986, 43) in San Francisco for an indefinite period of time to protest the federal government's negligent response to the AIDS crisis.[75] Their demands included $500 million in federal funding for AIDS research and services, release of experimental AIDS drugs by the FDA, and extension of benefits like disability payments to people who did not yet have CDC-defined AIDS but had what at that time was called AIDS Related Complex (ARC). Two gay men with AIDS chained themselves to the doors. Neither was arrested, but those at the vigil indicated their determination to stay until their demands were met. The peaceful vigil was joined by more protesters and soon grew into what became the San Francisco AIDS/ARC Vigil.[76] A few months into the vigil, participants described their motivation:

> The feeling was that the time for inaction was over. Something, no matter how desperate, had to be done and it had to be done immediately. . . . People were tired of watching their friends suffer and die, tired of the labeling of a new disease as being a result of the "gay lifestyle," tired of government inaction, and tired of the timid responses of the existing leadership of many (if not most) lesbian and gay organizations. (ARC & AIDS Vigil, n.d., "Background")

75. The nine had been participating in a one-night vigil called by MAA. Their decision to continue the vigil the next day, after its official end, apparently surprised members of MAA, who were initially hesitant in their support but quickly became supporters of the vigil (ARC & AIDS Vigil, n.d., 1–2).

76. On the San Francisco AIDS Vigil, see ARC & AIDS Vigil, n.d.; Linebarger 1985c; and Hippler 1986.

Over the next weeks and months, the vigil received enormous support from lesbian and gay newspapers, politicians, businesses, political organizations, and other individuals.

Meanwhile, in the fall of 1985 activists in New York City who were "fearful, angry and frustrated over mushrooming AIDS hysteria" in the media, particularly the *New York Post,* formed the Gay and Lesbian Anti-Defamation League (GLADL) (Freiberg 1985b, 14).[77] In announcing its formation, the new chairman, Gregory Kolovakos, stated that GLADL was embracing more militant political action and countering the recent complacency within the lesbian and gay community. One GLADL organizer saw the group as "a vehicle for gays and lesbians to channel their anger" (Adkins 1985). Lesbians were prominent in GLADL's early meetings and protests, in part because, as writer and activist Sarah Schulman noted, there was a growing sense among some lesbians that AIDS was their issue, not least because they too were feeling the effects of AIDS-related homophobia (Schulman 1985b, 27). More than six hundred lesbians and gays attended a meeting called by GLADL in November 1985 to discuss AIDS hysteria; many speakers invoked the Stonewall Riots and suggested that a new militancy was emerging. The next day one hundred activists protested outside City Hall during a committee hearing on closing the gay baths and other sex establishments.[78]

GLADL's propaganda suggested that a new emotional habitus and political horizon were in formation, and GLADL was helping them along. On a poster announcing a demonstration targeting the *New York Post,* GLADL criticized the *Post*'s AIDS hysteria, writing that it "defames us in a manner that no self-respecting community should have to bear." It then called on lesbians and gay men to join the protest to express "our outrage" at the *Post.* "In memory of our loved ones whose voices have been silenced, and for the love of ourselves, we must say enough is enough. DEMONSTRATE" ("Protest" 1985). GLADL's message was clear: any self-respecting gay man or lesbian should feel outraged by the *Post*'s sensationalistic, antigay AIDS coverage and should direct that outrage into protest. GLADL's linkage of pride and self-respect to protest stands in stark contrast to contemporaneous emotional

77. In 1986, GLADL changed its name to GLAAD, the Gay and Lesbian Alliance Against Defamation. On GLADL/GLAAD, see Adkins 1985; Freiberg 1985b, 1986a; Fall 1985a, 1985b; d'Adesky 1986a; Gross 2001, 105–6; and Wolfe 1997.

78. As far as I can tell, this protest was not organized by GLADL, but it was in the same spirit and it similarly suggested cracks in the political horizon.

evocations that joined pride and self-respect to service provision and volunteer caretaking. Two distinct ways of being a political gay person, each
with its particular emotional sensibility, were jostling with one another.

In December, between five and eight hundred lesbians and gay men
joined GLADL in an emotional demonstration against the *Post*. Again,
a GLADL speaker joined feelings about self and society to political activism: "Men and women who protest lies about themselves are men
and women who respect themselves and demand respect from others"
(Fall 1985b, 11). Clendinen and Nagourney note that the rhetoric and actions of GLADL suggested that political anger, and not only grief and
despair, was an appropriate sentiment to feel vis-à-vis the AIDS crisis (2001, 525–26). In this moment of increasing protests, lesbian writer
Joan Nestle remarked, "There's a real chance here for street responses
like we used to have, by an angry mob. I think we have the potential to
be an angry mob, and I use that in the best sense of the word" (Schulman 1985b, 28).

In May 1986, inspired by this activism and contending that it needed
to proliferate throughout the United States, AIDS and gay activist Eric
Rofes issued a call to resistance. Raising the possibility that this more
resistant activism might be "too extreme for the lesbian and gay politicos
of the 1980s," Rofes nonetheless made a case for "creative forms of militancy, including passive resistance, high-visibility zaps and outrageous
street dramas" about gay and AIDS issues:

> For the lesbian and gay community throughout America, resistance is a con-
> cept whose time has come. Working within the system doesn't bring the re-
> sult it used to. It's time to develop a strategy of resistance applicable to the
> challenges we face. If you are a gay man or lesbian in America today, your
> rights are threatened more than they've ever been during the past 15 years. . .
> *How much are you willing to take before fighting back?* (Rofes 1986; empha-
> sis his)[79]

As Rofes's appeal indicates, the more oppositional politics that some
in San Francisco and New York were advocating was not yet widespread,
and their actions themselves did not grow *directly* into the street AIDS
activist movement, but their occurrence indicated a shifting mood among

79. For a similar appeal in this period by gay San Francisco Supervisor Harry Britt, see
Mendenhall 1986.

some lesbians and gay men who were reconceptualizing themselves and dominant society in ways that prompted expansion of their sense of what was politically possible, desirable, and even necessary.

The exploding AIDS epidemic itself, of course, was a huge factor shaping how lesbians and gay men were understanding AIDS and the crisis. The number of AIDS cases and deaths recorded during 1985 alone surpassed the number of cases and deaths that had occurred during the entire epidemic through 1984 (Centers for Disease Control and Prevention 1997, 14). State and societal responses were also playing a role. Nationally, 1986 began with more calls for repressive legislation and with the Reagan administration attempting to cut AIDS funding by 20 percent ("Reagan" 1986). A *Los Angeles Times* poll found that 51 percent of Americans favored quarantining people with AIDS and other polls indicated that 15 percent of the population supported tattooing people with AIDS (McGarry and Wasserman 1998, 230). By late spring of 1986, a quarantine initiative sponsored by Lyndon LaRouche had received many more than the 394,000 signatures required to be placed on the California ballot (Freiberg 1986c, 10; Fall 1986, 9).

However, even as local and national lesbian and gay leaders intensified their criticisms of all levels of government, and despite the fact that some new gay and AIDS organizations had started to practice a more oppositional politics, the publicly articulated political horizon of most lesbian and gay leaders stopped at lobbying, organization building, and service provision. When interviewed by the *Advocate* in the spring of 1986 about the state of their movement, the leaders of the major national lesbian and gay organizations focused on professionalism, lobbying, electoral strategies, and increasing their membership base (Giteck 1986). Some lesbians and gay men, perhaps recognizing the growing instability of the still-prevailing emotional habitus and political horizon, acknowledged the growing anger but offered suggestions for a political response to the AIDS crisis that delinked anger from militant tactics or confrontational activism. In Chicago, for example, criticism of the government continued, but leaders in the community continued to offer love and pride in the community, rather than angry political action, as solutions to the growing crisis. A typical editorial in the *Windy City Times*, for example, advocated "loving ourselves, as a community" as "the only way through this crisis." Grief over the mounting deaths was similarly redirected toward community pride: "Yes, we mourn the loss of thousands of good men and women. But we do not let their deaths set us back. Instead, we gain from their loss, and as a community we get ever-stronger" ("Memorials" 1986).

An editorial in the *B.A.R.*'s 1986 gay pride issue by Bob Ross, the publisher, similarly expressed pride in "the love and caring our community has shown in the AIDS crisis" (Ross 1986). In San Francisco, of course, the AIDS/ARC Vigil was underway, and some lesbians and gay men were publicly contemplating angry activism to fight the LaRouche quarantine initiative. Ross acknowledged neither activist trend, instead commending lesbian and gay volunteers and the local government: "The main thanks should go to the thousands of men and women who volunteer incredible amounts of their time and energy. We have seen the community donate millions of dollars to help their own, and we have seen local government come up with millions more to help" (Ross 1986). He concluded with a call for lesbians and gay men to donate more money to help fight the LaRouche initiative.

Emotion and the Establishment of a Political Horizon

A collectivity's emotional habitus not only shapes how members feel and express their feelings, but also helps to establish their sense of political possibility and attitudes about what forms of political activism are viable and desirable in a given moment. An emotional habitus is neither given nor static, of course. Human practices—emotional, discursive, interpretive, bodily—produce, reproduce, and sometimes transform a specific emotional habitus. Those processes, in turn, help to explain both the on-goingness of, as well as shifts in, forms of political (in)action. What gets called rational calculation is a factor in these processes as well, but we often neglect to consider the ways that emotion thoroughly influences our rational calculations regarding "what is to be done." In that capacity, and in others as well, emotion helps to structure the politically thinkable, the horizon of political possibilities and of imaginable futures. Two important tasks, then, are to explore how people come to feel as they do and how those feelings affect their political imaginaries and political actions.

An emotional habitus can strongly influence individual and community-wide affects and emotions, but it does not determine them. The articulations of gay pride and evocation of sentiments like gay shame and fear of rejection shaped what lesbians and gay men were feeling, but they did not rid lesbian and gay communities of anger or animosity toward mainstream, heteronormative society. Emotive conventions hindered their expression and likely reduced such feelings themselves, but, as Reddy points out, individuals vary in their responses to emotive convention. That variation "provides an initial reservoir of possibilities for change . . . that can be drawn upon when ideological, economic, or political factors put pressure on the system" (1997, 334–35). In other words, emotive conventions are subject to contestation, particularly in times of crisis.

A Shifting Emotional Habitus and the Emergence of the Direct-Action AIDS Movement

In constitutional terms there is no such thing as a fundamental right to commit homosexual sodomy. . . . Decisions of individuals relating to homosexual conduct have been subject to state intervention throughout the history of Western Civilization. Condemnation of those practices is firmly rooted in Judeo-Christian moral and ethical standards. Homosexual sodomy was a capital crime under Roman law. During the English Reformation . . . Blackstone described "the infamous crime against nature" as an offense of "deeper malignity" than rape, an heinous act "the very mention of which is a disgrace to human nature," and "a crime not fit to be named." . . . To hold that the act of homosexual sodomy is somehow protected as a fundamental right would be to cast aside millenia [*sic*] of moral teaching. ("Supreme Court Opinion" 1986, 13)

Thus wrote Chief Justice Warren Earl Burger in an opinion concurring with the U.S. Supreme Court's majority decision upholding the constitutionality of the state of Georgia's statute prohibiting homosexual sodomy. The Court's June 30, 1986, ruling animated a decisive and dramatic shift in lesbian and gay collective political responses to AIDS. In the context of ever-increasing AIDS-related deaths, continuing government failure to address the crisis, and increasingly repressive legislation, the *Bowers v. Hardwick* decision was a turning point, an event that profoundly affected the emotional habitus in lesbian and gay communities and the prevailing political horizon. Drawing from a wealth of evidence that indicates that in the wake of *Hardwick* there was a marked and widespread transformation in lesbian and gay rhetoric and sentiments about the AIDS crisis, I argue that primarily as a result of its emotional effects, the *Hardwick* ruling contributed to the emergence of the confrontational and defiant direct-action AIDS movement.

Events and a New Constellation of Feelings

Bowers v. Hardwick: *The Event and Its Aftermath*

On August 3, 1982, Michael Hardwick was in his bedroom in Atlanta, Georgia, engaging in oral sex with another man.[1] Hearing a noise, Hardwick looked up and found a police officer standing in his bedroom and staring at him. The police officer arrested the two men for violating Georgia's antisodomy statute, took them to jail, and threw them into a holding cell, announcing to others in the cell and to the guards that the men were in for "cocksucking" (Deitcher 1995, 147). The charges against the two men were eventually dropped, but Hardwick (with the backing of the American Civil Liberties Union) sued to challenge Georgia's antisodomy statute, and the case made its way to the U. S. Supreme Court.

Comparing gay sex to "adultery, incest, and other sexual crimes" and noting that "proscriptions against [homosexual sodomy] have ancient roots" ("Supreme Court Opinion" 1986, 13, 12), the Court upheld with a five-to-four majority a statute that denied homosexuals the right to engage in consensual sex in the privacy of their homes. The justices thereby left intact antisodomy laws in twenty-four states and Washington, D.C. Provocatively, although Georgia's law prohibited heterosexual and homosexual sodomy, the Court applied its decision only to the part of the statute that prohibited the latter (18). The majority argued that the state of Georgia need not offer any "compelling interest" for the statute other than the state legislature's moral sense that homosexual sodomy is wrong (Keen 1986a, 6).

Lesbians, gay men, and other sexual and gender outlaws around the country experienced the decision as "a declaration of war" (Deitcher 1995, 140); their response was immediate and more anger-driven and dramatic than any lesbian/gay activism for nearly a decade. Outraged queers held spirited demonstrations in cities around the country.[2] Linking the

---

1. I draw here from Deitcher 1995. See also Halley 1993; Leonard 1986; and Walter 1986.

2. For accounts of these demonstrations, see Burkes 1986, 2; Byron 1986; d'Adesky 1986b; Deitcher 1995, 150; Freiberg 1986b; O'Loughlin 1986b; Wetzl 1986; and Wolfe 1990a, 234. Chicago lesbians and gay men did not immediately protest the *Hardwick* de-

protests to growing gay fury about the AIDS crisis, writer and critic David Deitcher argues that "news of the *Hardwick* decision was enough to awaken the radical in most apolitical queers. . . . Protests erupted in cities across the country as the news reached communities in which frustration and rage had been mounting over the loss of lovers and friends, the accelerating rate and intensity of bias-related violence, and the unprecedented challenge to queer social identity that the epidemic posed" (1995, 148–49).

As many as two thousand lesbians and gay men participated in a "militant" demonstration in San Francisco the evening of the *Hardwick* ruling (d'Adesky 1986b, 9; O'Loughlin 1986b). Arguing that the Supreme Court had revoked lesbians' and gay men's "rights to privacy and to life" and had "slapped us in the face," Pat Norman, a lesbian running for the San Francisco Board of Supervisors, expressed her outrage and warned, "when I'm slapped, I fight" (O'Loughlin 1986b; Wetzl 1986, 2). Gay and AIDS activist John Wahl asserted that gay activists would unleash "social disorder and chaos" across the United States, adding, "That's not a threat; that's a prophesy" (Wetzl 1986, 2, 4). The crowd hissed and booed when San Francisco Board of Supervisors President John Molinari told the protesters that "the system still works"—Molinari had never before been booed at a gay event—indicating shifting feelings among lesbians and gay men as well as an expanding sense of political possibilities (O'Loughlin 1986b; Jones 1987, 16). In Washington, D.C., protesters gathered in front of the Supreme Court, leaving reluctantly only late at night. One activist, describing the collective sentiments of the protesters, noted, "I think some people would have stayed until midnight. The feeling in the crowd was so strong—more than any one speaker" (Byron 1986, 7). Hundreds marched in Boston the evening of the *Hardwick* ruling, expressing anger and staging a defiant kiss-in to protest the ruling (7).

In New York City, lesbians and gay men "took to the streets for two angry, militant demonstrations" (Freiberg 1986b, 12), the largest since the 1970s (see figs. 1 and 2). Notably, people who had never before been involved in gay politics participated in these and subsequent protests. As many as three thousand gay men and lesbians demonstrated in Greenwich Village the night after the Court's decision (Keen 1986b). Protesters stopped traffic, sat down in the street, and, according to a *New York Native* reporter, "in a theme sounded time and again," called for "a 'new

cision. Chicago gay activist Darrell Gordon (2000) attributes this to the fact that activists were absorbed in local politics, attempting to pass an anti-discrimination ordinance.

FIGURE 1. Demonstration in New York City against the *Bowers v. Hardwick* decision, July 1, 1986. Photo by Ellen B. Neipris.

FIGURE 2. Protesters sitting in the street during *Bowers v. Hardwick* demonstration, New York City, July 1, 1986. Photo by Ellen B. Neipris.

militancy,' for fighting back" (d'Adesky 1986b, 8). During the sit-in, some participants urged lesbians and gay men to disrupt the July 4 celebration of the one hundredth anniversary of the Statue of Liberty, to be attended by President and Nancy Reagan and perhaps a few Supreme Court justices. On July 4, as many as ten thousand lesbian and gay protesters marched toward the site in lower Manhattan where hundreds of thousands of people were celebrating. Ignoring warnings by police and protest leaders, thousands of participants angrily chanting "Civil rights or civil war!" circumvented police barricades that had been installed to prevent protesters from reaching the celebration (Freiberg 1986b, 12; Byron 1986, 7).

The striking change in tone and sentiment in lesbian and gay communities is evident in the following story, which invites a contrast with earlier candlelight vigils. During the July 4 demonstration in New York City, Andy Humm of the Coalition for Lesbian and Gay Rights asked the crowd "Are you angry today?" and the crowd shouted back "Yes" (Finder 1986). After a speaker asked precisely the same question at a candlelight vigil in Chicago one year earlier and the crowd replied "Yes," the speaker attempted to channel the expressed anger into love for one's brothers and stoic nobility in the face of death. In the midst of this post-*Hardwick* demonstration, no one submerged or redirected the anger; along with other feeling states, that anger animated protesters' efforts to evade police barricades, march toward the Fourth of July celebration, and confront straight America with queer fury.

Demonstrations continued in cities around the country throughout the summer, sustained by and nourishing outrage among lesbians, gay men, and other sexual and gender outlaws. A few weeks after the *Hardwick* ruling, as many as four thousand demonstrators protested a visit to San Francisco by Supreme Court Justice Sandra Day O'Connor. Police tried to block the protesters with their motorcycles, but to no avail; protesters, simultaneously angry and playful, chanted "What do we want? Sodomy! When do we want it? Now!" (Linebarger 1986, 1, 2). According to a *Washington Blade* report, "the [San Francisco] protesters . . . displayed emotions that many observers compared to the community's anger in 1979 over the lenient sentence given to Dan White, assassin of gay officeholder Harvey Milk" (Helquist 1986, 13).[3] Speakers accused the

---

3. At demonstrations in 1979 to protest White's conviction for manslaughter rather than murder, thousands of lesbians and gay men marched to San Francisco's City Hall,

Supreme Court of violating lesbians' and gay men's fundamental right to privacy, noting that the Court had simply written them out of the Constitution. Others stressed that the time for massive civil disobedience was at hand. In August 1986, thousands joined the New York–based lesbian and gay direct-action group, the Lavender Hill Mob, in a protest at Lincoln Center where Chief Justice Warren Burger was being honored (Lavender Hill Mob 1987).[4] Protests occurred in other cities as well throughout the summer, each amplifying the others.

Anger and calls for militant political activism in response to *Hardwick* were widely and fervently expressed in lesbian and gay communities across the country throughout the summer and fall of 1986. The *Advocate* reported that "the Supreme Court decision infuriated many New York gays more than . . . anything else in recent years" (Freiberg 1986b, 12). Jim Owles, a founder of the 1970s gay rights group Gay Activists Alliance, remarked that the protesters' fury made him "feel more than ever that there's a time again for a new militancy in the gay and lesbian community" (Freiberg 1986b, 13). The *Washington Blade* quoted Andy Humm saying that the gay movement would now need to rely on "massive civil disobedience" and "street protests" (Keen 1986b). *New York Native* columnists called for massive protests, law-breaking, boycotts, and a march on Washington.[5] Letters to the editor printed in the *Native* from gays in cities around the country similarly expressed anger and explicitly linked it to the need for "active resistance," "riots," "protest," "another Stonewall," a "return to the streets."[6] An anonymous letter-writer to the *Washington Blade*—a gay person in the military—called for "greater militancy" in the form of protests and massive boycotts, encouraging all gays to "let your rage be turned to activism, not depression" (Anonymous 1986, 21). The publisher of San Francisco's *Sentinel* wrote a column about his own growing fury in the wake of *Hardwick*, emphasizing that the decision had come down in a period when "we are busy caring for our sick brothers." He continued, "anger is appropriate—even rage" (Murray 1986).

---

where at least eleven police cars were set on fire, and protesters smashed City Hall windows (Adam 1995, 114).

4. The Lavender Hill Mob formed out of GLAAD in the wake of *Hardwick*. Activists who formed the Mob were key participants in the demonstrations after *Hardwick*, and they soon turned their attention to confrontational AIDS activism.

5. See, for example, Apuzzo 1986; Gans 1986a; Morris 1986; Bockman 1986.

6. See, for example, letters in the issues for July 21, July 28, and September 1, 1986.

Compared to other lesbian and gay newspapers, Chicago's *Windy City Times* offered comparatively thin coverage of the *Hardwick* ruling, and anger was less explicitly articulated. Still, a scathing (if too facile) editorial argued that lesbians and gay men in the United States were living under an apartheid that was similar to, albeit less violent than, apartheid in South Africa. It also supported an escalation in political activism: "The Supreme Court has sent us a message—we as a community have been too complacent, have trusted that the courts and legislatures would see the light eventually" ("Celebrating" 1986).

Arguing that lesbians and gay men should embrace "militancy" as some in the black community had done twenty years earlier, an editorial in the usually staid *Advocate*—headlined "The Time for Gay Rage Is Now!"—urged gays to use "massive, widespread, creative acts of civil disobedience." The editor acknowledged that lesbians and gay men were hesitant about confrontational tactics, but the Court ruling prompted him to egg them on: "This doesn't mean we should abandon our traditional efforts at political organizing, coalition-building, and education. But push has *already* come to shove, and gay people had better be prepared to do a little pushing and shoving of their own" ("Time" 1986; emphasis in original).[7] National leader Virginia Apuzzo offered a plan for what to do with "gay rage," emphasizing "ritually repeated" acts of civil disobedience (Apuzzo 1986). Within a month of the Court's decision, national lesbian and gay leaders, responding to "the anger stirred nationwide by the . . . ruling," issued a call for a march on Washington (Halberstadt 1986, 6).

Many of those who urged a new gay militancy linked the *Hardwick* ruling to the ongoing AIDS crisis. One speaker at the first rally in New York, referring to the *Hardwick* ruling as well as other recent repressive legislation concerning AIDS, noted that "the atmosphere in the country is parallel to pre-war Germany. Don't anybody think it can't happen here 'cause it's already started" (d'Adesky 1986b, 8). Keith Griffith, a member of a newly formed AIDS activist group in San Francisco, Citizens for Medical Justice (CMJ), wrote a letter to the San Francisco *Sentinel* that encouraged lesbians and gay men to up the ante with activism targeting the Supreme Court's decision as well as the AIDS crisis. Knitting the two together, Griffith wrote,

---

7. Clendinen and Nagourney write that the *Advocate*'s editorial was "uncharacteristically strident" (2001, 538).

When one combines all the injustices committed against our community over recent weeks with news of a surge in AIDS cases in the city and the looming threat of the [LaRouche] AIDS [quarantine] initiative, it is hard to escape the feeling of being "shell-shocked." It should be readily apparent to all that now is the time to adopt bold new strategies in the struggle to be a free people. . . . We can no longer afford to work through proper channels, if we ever could. Our very right to exist is under fire in ways most of us have not seen since the modern gay rights movement began. (Griffith 1986, 2)

San Francisco activist John Wahl similarly advocated militant action to fight the Supreme Court's decision as well as the AIDS crisis, even as he acknowledged the ambivalence among many lesbians and gay men that historically had held some back.

We need to become aware of our own worth, and that means absolutely dumping the mental and psychological restraints we have adopted [from] conditioning by a culture that puts down same sex affection. . . . We also fear that if we become too uppity, we will lose the gains we've made. People who are constantly pushing very, very hard for their rights get them. You have to be vocal, you have to be confrontive, you have to be angry, you have to absolutely never accept second class humanity or second class citizenship for any reason whatsoever, not even for tactical reasons. . . . There are no tactics that are unacceptable or unusable if we find ourselves in a war situation. (Lowe 1986a, 5)

This angry rhetoric was not idle. Demonstrations against the Court's ruling were immediate, and within months of the *Hardwick* decision, direct-action AIDS groups emerged across the country. For example, a group of lesbians and gay men formed Citizens for Medical Justice in San Francisco, and in September 1986, CMJ staged a sit-in at California Governor George Deukmejian's office to protest his veto of an AIDS anti-discrimination bill and his lack of action on twelve other AIDS bills awaiting his signature; eight activists were arrested (ACT NOW 1990, 1).[8] In another indication of "the growing radicalization of the community," in the words of one *B.A.R.* writer, hundreds of lesbians and gay men in San Francisco signed pledges of "noncompliance" stating that

8. CMJ, perhaps the first direct-action AIDS group in the country, later changed its name to AIDS Action Pledge, which later changed its name to ACT UP/San Francisco.

they would commit acts of civil disobedience if the LaRouche initiative to quarantine people with AIDS passed in the November 1986 election (Jones 1987, 17).

Across the Bay in Oakland, activists chained themselves to the Alameda County Administration Building in December 1986, creating an AIDS/ARC Vigil—like the one in San Francisco—to protest a delay in a supplementary AIDS appropriation (Linebarger 1987a, 6). In the early months of 1987, a Chicago anti-imperialist group, DAGMAR, began discussing a militant response to the AIDS crisis; that summer they began to engage in confrontational AIDS activism, and they later joined with activists fighting for lesbian and gay rights to form the direct-action AIDS organization C-FAR (Chicago For AIDS Rights) which subsequently became ACT UP/Chicago.[9]

Confrontational direct-action AIDS groups also began to emerge in New York City. Longtime political activist Maxine Wolfe—later a participant in ACT UP/New York—linked their emergence to the *Hardwick* decision and the militant street demonstrations that followed, noting that after those demonstrations, the political horizon expanded: "There was a whole different sense in the community of what was possible" (Wolfe 1993). Wolfe connected those initial angry demonstrations and that new sense of possibility to the birth during the next six months of two precursors to ACT UP/New York: an AIDS activist artist collective, the Silence = Death Project, and the Lavender Hill Mob. At the end of 1986, the Silence = Death Project began to plaster New York City with posters that had the pink triangle symbol from the gay rights movement, with the point of the triangle facing up, above the slogan "SILENCE = DEATH" (see fig. 3). Text at the bottom reflected and reinforced the new mood in the community: it condemned the government's response to AIDS and encouraged lesbians and gay men to "turn anger, fear, grief into action."[10] Months later, members of the Silence = Death Project attended the founding meeting of ACT UP/NY and contributed their graphic to the burgeoning direct-action AIDS movement.

The Lavender Hill Mob, formed immediately after *Hardwick*, participated in the large demonstrations in New York after the ruling and

9. For a brief timeline of early AIDS activism in Chicago, see DAGMAR 1994; for more on DAGMAR, see Burkes 1988.

10. See Crimp 1987b and Crimp and Rolston 1990 for more on the Silence = Death Project. Some members of the Silence = Death Project later formed Gran Fury, another activist artist collaborative that produced much of ACT UP/New York's agit-prop.

FIGURE 3. SILENCE = DEATH poster, 1986. Silence = Death Project.

soon began to focus its direct-action activism on AIDS (Walter 1987a).
In February 1987, the Mob disrupted a CDC conference on mandatory
testing, demanding that the CDC turn its efforts to developing safe-sex
education programs and providing health care for those already suffering from AIDS. Mob members were present at ACT UP/New York's
founding one month later.

Amid this growing activist ferment, Larry Kramer gave a speech in
March 1987 at the Gay and Lesbian Community Center in New York

City that called for a militant activist response to the epidemic.[11] Already
angry and already "acting up,"[12] members of the Lavender Hill Mob attended Kramer's speech "as much to see who the other angry ones were
as to hear Larry speak" (Lavender Hill Mob, n.d.). Kramer quoted his
1983 article "1,112 and Counting," noting that reported AIDS cases had
exploded from 1,112 to 32,000, and made an almost identical exhortation
to action. In the spirited discussion that followed, a decision was made to
start a new organization to fight the AIDS crisis. Two nights later, more
than three hundred lesbians, gay men, and other sexual and gender outlaws attended the founding meeting of ACT UP, a self-described organization of people united in anger and committed to the use of civil disobedience and direct action to fight the AIDS crisis.[13] Two weeks later,
ACT UP held its first protest, targeting the FDA and the profiteering
of pharmaceutical companies. Virginia Apuzzo's threat from four years
earlier materialized with that first ACT UP demonstration, which shut
down Wall Street. The demonstration tied up traffic for several hours,
and seventeen people were arrested (Crimp and Rolston 1990, 28).

Throughout 1987, lesbians, gay men, bisexuals, transgendered people,
other queers, and straight allies formed ACT UP chapters and similarly
confrontational direct-action groups around the country. The October
1987 March on Washington for Lesbian and Gay Rights was important
in this regard, reflecting, reinforcing, and inspiring activist militancy.
The march drew hundreds of thousands and was led by people with
AIDS, many in wheelchairs. Most observers commented on its militant

11. His speech is reprinted, with commentary, in Kramer 1990a, 127–39; for coverage of
the speech, see Salinas 1987a.

12. As Kate Black notes, groups like the Mob "were acting up against AIDS before
ACT UP New York . . . was founded" (1996, 75).

13. Many who have discussed street AIDS activism and ACT UP, including Kramer
himself, place Kramer as the founder of the movement. This is both historically inaccu-
rate and preposterous. First, the historical record refutes the common belief that ACT UP/
NY was the first confrontational direct-action AIDS organization to form and that other
groups were simply knock-offs. Second, it is absurd to suggest that movements and activist organizations are founded by single individuals. Movements and activist organizations
are collective endeavors that develop out of a milieu and take hold only when the sensibilities they offer resonate with a social collectivity that either preexists the emergence of the
movement/organization or is brought into being through such an emergence. Kramer's incitement to action certainly was a factor in ACT UP/NY's emergence, and ACT UP/NY
played an important role in inspiring the emergence of similar organizations across the
country, but it is erroneous to cite Kramer as the sole founder of either ACT UP/NY or of
the direct-action AIDS movement as a whole. The question of Kramer's role in the founding of ACT UP/NY was contentious even early on; see Kramer 1990b and Epstein 1990.

tone. Drawing from conversations and interviews, Kate Black described the march as "feisty, militant, radical, and disruptive, fueled, in part, by lesbian and gay anger and despair over the AIDS epidemic" (1996, 27, n. 28). The organizers adopted nonviolent civil disobedience as an integral part of the march, a move that supports sociologist Steven Epstein's contention that the march "reflected a rare moment in which the mainstream lesbian and gay rights movement seemed to move in sync with more radical, grassroots activism" (Epstein 1999, 59). Explaining why they decided to adopt civil disobedience, a move that, by their own account, was "unprecedented in the his/herstory of the Gay and Lesbian movement," the organizers stated, "Traditionally, civil disobedience and non-violent resistance have been used as a last resort when all other remedies have failed. The feeling is that the *Hardwick* v *Bowers* decision, coupled with continued inadequate and inappropriate government response to the AIDS crisis, indicates that all of our previous efforts to secure our civil rights have failed" (National March on Washington for Lesbian and Gay Rights 1987, 42). The weekend of the march, more than four thousand people participated in a massive civil disobedience action at the Supreme Court and more than eight hundred were arrested—the largest act of civil disobedience in Washington, D.C. since the anti–Vietnam War demonstrations (Harding 1987, 26). "Human wave after human wave" of lesbians, gay men, and other sexual and gender minorities were arrested on the steps of the court as they were cheered on by thousands of supporters (d'Adesky 1987, 9). Many returned from the march and launched activist groups, especially direct-action AIDS groups.[14]

The direct-action AIDS movement officially became national in scope the weekend of the march when two hundred street AIDS activists from across the United States met to plan a coordinated series of AIDS demonstrations for the spring of 1988 (Zwickler 1987); a national umbrella organization for the movement emerged from that meeting, eventually taking the name ACT NOW, the AIDS Coalition to Network, Organize, and Win.

14. Many were inspired by ACT UP/NY's contingent at the march. For example, John Fall, a founding member of ACT UP/Los Angeles, attended the march six months after the death from AIDS of his gay cousin. There he "discovered the visceral politics of New York's ACT UP group and found fellow Angelenos seeking an organized channel for their own rage. The following month, Los Angeles's ACT UP chapter was born" (Ison 1990, 36). See also Deitcher 1995, 138–39. On the effects of the march in inspiring lesbian and gay activism, see D'Emilio 1992, 267.

The Puzzles Posed by Hardwick

If I am correct that the *Hardwick* ruling spurred the emergence of the
direct-action AIDS movement, it is notable that the spark was a Supreme
Court decision that was not explicitly about AIDS. How did lesbians, gay
men, and other sexual and gender outlaws understand the relationship
between this antisodomy ruling and the ongoing AIDS crisis? Also perplexing is that for years, queer folks had suffered through inadequate government responses to the AIDS crisis along with other assaults, including
calls for quarantine. In response, they had cared for their sick and dying,
created and staffed ASOs, strongly criticized the government, lobbied,
testified, held candlelight vigils, and sometimes held protests; there is no
question that the horrors of the AIDS crisis had been mobilizing them.
But there was a dramatic shift after *Hardwick:* lesbian and gay anger and
militancy were much more pronounced, widespread, and ongoing. Why
did the Court's antisodomy ruling prompt lesbian and gay communities
to shift course and embrace oppositional and defiant AIDS activism?

The prevailing model in the study of social movements, the political
process model and its political opportunity thesis, has a tough time answering this question. Social movement theorists would likely consider
the *Hardwick* ruling a tightening of the political opportunities facing lesbians and gay men. Doug McAdam, for example, has written that the Supreme Court decisions that negatively affected black people during the
period from 1876 to 1930 limited the opportunities for black political action (1999, 71); that constriction in opportunities helped him to explain
why a civil rights movement did not arise in that period. My research
suggests that queer folks experienced *Hardwick* as a further tightening
of the political opportunities that they faced, particularly in the context
of increasing calls for quarantine and government failures to address the
AIDS crisis. *Hardwick* unequivocally marked a further erosion of lesbians' and gay men's access to the political process. But rather than inhibit-
ing contentious political action, as the model would predict, this tightening of political opportunities acted as a crucial spark to the direct-action
AIDS movement. Given the model's definition of opportunities, it appears that ACT UP inexplicably emerged at an inopportune moment.

I draw from historian William Sewell's theory of the event (1996)
to explain why the *Hardwick* ruling provoked the turn to direct-action
AIDS politics and spurred the emergence of ACT UP. Sewell argues
that the defining feature of an event is that it transforms the underly-

ing social and cultural structures that shape human behavior. The *Hardwick* decision brought a turning point in AIDS activism because it transformed very specific structures—the emotional habitus and its attendant
political horizon in lesbian and gay communities—creating a space for
the emergence of new forms of AIDS activism. The Court's ruling shattered important components of the existing emotional habitus and crystallized and amplified feelings like anger and indignation that had begun to circulate but were still more or less inchoate and unfocused, and
in any case had been dampened by the prevailing norms in lesbian and
gay communities against public expressions of anger. *Hardwick* magnified and bolstered an emergent, new constellation of affects and emotions, effectively authorizing sentiments and expressions of gay rage and
indignation and directing them toward the government, the pharmaceutical industry, the scientific-medical establishment, the corporate media, and other institutions seen as contributing to the AIDS crisis. These
new emotional practices and new sentiments about gay selves and about
dominant society created a new, counterhegemonic emotional habitus
and challenged the limits of the previous political horizon, offering new
attitudes about what was politically possible, desirable, and necessary in
the fight against AIDS, and thereby creating fertile ground for the emergence and development of confrontational direct-action AIDS activism.

Bowers v. Hardwick *as a "Moral Shock"*

How did this work? The beginnings of an explanation are found in
James Jasper's concept of *moral shock,* a cognitive-affective state that
Jasper defines as occurring "when an unexpected event or piece of information raises such a sense of outrage in a person that she becomes inclined toward political action" (Jasper 1997, 106).[15] A moral shock jars
you into a state of disbelief that forces you to reconsider your habitual
going-along. After a moral shock, you might continue to go along, but
you might not. Queer folks, particularly those who believed in American
democracy's proclamation that equality was the law of the land, experienced *Hardwick* as an unforeseen, astounding, and outrageous legal decision, hardly to be believed. In denying homosexuals basic civil and human rights, and in the context of the government's increasingly apparent

---

15. As Jasper notes, moral shocks are similar to Edward Walsh's "suddenly imposed
grievances" (1981, 106).

willingness to sit by as thousands of gay and bisexual men died, the ruling brought into stark relief the contours and depth of homosexual exclusion and oppression. It decimated any sense of belonging to dominant
society that members of the mainstream gay community, particularly
those who were white, male, and middle-class, might have felt, if only
tenuously. Even lesbians and gay men who were highly critical of U.S.
democracy were stunned by the Court's decision; Jeff Edwards, a gay
man who had been involved in anti-imperialist activism and later participated in ACT UP/Chicago, recalled, "They took . . . commonplace stereotypes and hatreds and put them into a Supreme Court decision. . . .
It's not like [I thought] those thoughts weren't present in the society. . . .
What was shocking was that they were stated so plainly in a Supreme
Court decision" (Edwards 2000a).

As Jasper argues, a moral shock "helps a person think about her basic values and how the world diverges from them" (1997, 106). Extending Jasper's thought, I would add that, while feelings always prompt and
contribute to the work of interpretation, a moral shock creates such a
disjunctive experience that sense-making takes on greater urgency, and
new ways of understanding oneself and the world, and the relation between the two, are brought to the fore. In this case, by making plain the
degree of nonrecognition—indeed, social annihilation—that queers were
subject to, the shock of *Hardwick* heightened the salience for many lesbians and gay men of their gay identities to their own self-understandings.
Jasper notes that the word *shock* suggests "a visceral, bodily feeling"
that animates "strong emotions" (Jasper 1998, 409). A moral shock generates bodily intensities, affective states, that are themselves motivational and provide a strong impetus to make sense of what one is feeling.
I contend that the affective states roused by the visceral shock of *Hardwick* spurred a reconfiguration in lesbians' and gay men's feelings and
emotions about state and society as well as about themselves, heightening in particular gay anger, indignation, even rage. That reconfiguring
occurred on both an individual and social level. Individuals' emotional
states were matched, stirred, reinforced, and legitimized by repeated articulations of similar emotions by lesbian and gay leaders, by the lesbian and gay media, by protesters and other activists, by friends, lovers, co-workers, and neighbors who were discussing the ruling, trying to
make sense of the shock itself and the affective states it prompted. *Hardwick* incited an explosion of emotional expression—Reddy's emotives
(1997)—that shaped queers' feelings by naming, as anger and indigna-

tion, for example, the complicated constellation of affective states that they experienced after the ruling.

In effect, then, the moral shock of *Hardwick* propelled a rearrangement in the prevailing emotional habitus in lesbian and gay communities, in particular a reconfiguration of the contradictory sentiments that constitute lesbian and gay ambivalence. Because ambivalence is characterized by the simultaneous feeling of two contradictory sentiments, a "resolution" to it that effectively elevates one of the contradictory feelings and suppresses the other is necessarily unstable; any ostracized sentiment is always there, able to emerge if prompted. *Hardwick* had that effect. By exposing the disjuncture between American rhetoric and reality, by indicating that U.S. society was the "Land of Equality and Justice for All"—except queers—the *Hardwick* ruling spurred indignation among lesbians and gay men that their rights alone could be so thoroughly abrogated. In confronting lesbians and gay men with the extent of their outsider status, with their social nonexistence, *Hardwick* incited indignation, anger, and rage, feeling states that previously had been downplayed and submerged. Even more, the *Hardwick* ruling authorized their expression. After all, what more did queers have to lose? Insofar as the Court already had enacted complete social rejection, it wasn't as if they needed to worry any longer about possible social and political repercussions of feeling and voicing rage. Similarly, whereas prevailing gay attitudes about gay selves and AIDS previously had been colored in part by shame about gay sexuality, *Hardwick,* by providing an unambiguous look at state homophobia, encouraged lesbians and gay men to channel blame and shame about AIDS away from themselves and toward the homophobic state and other institutions of society. In short, by provoking, intensifying, and simultaneously authorizing feelings and emotions like outrage and indignation toward the state, the moral shock of *Hardwick* incited lesbians and gay men to understand themselves and their relation to dominant society in new ways. In this moment of government betrayal, as gay fury displaced shame, a sense of entitlement—of gays as fully deserving of state assistance—could be mobilized more easily.

Hardwick, the Ongoing AIDS Crisis,
and a Shifting Emotional Habitus

Two pressing questions remain unanswered. The first recognizes how tempting it might be to naturalize *Hardwick*'s moral shock factor, but cautions against doing so: Why did lesbians, gay men, and other sexual and gender outlaws experience *Hardwick* as a moral shock? That they would do so was never inevitable. Ten years earlier, the Supreme Court upheld Virginia's antisodomy law (D'Emilio 1992, 191), and that ruling does not seem to have been experienced in the same way by lesbians and gay men; it certainly did not spur them to hold massive demonstrations or to embrace confrontational activism to defend their rights. Moreover, in the few years just prior to the *Hardwick* decision, queer folks had experienced numerous indignities; although some voiced anger in those instances, public expressions and demonstrations of anger after *Hardwick* suggest an anger that was more widespread and more intensely felt. Why was this so?

Second, why did they react with confrontational activism, particularly given their most recent engagement in caretaking, service provision, and the gay movement's embrace for more than a decade of more routine interest-group politics? As Jasper recognizes, although the cognitive and emotional processes that attach to a moral shock *might* propel someone into political activism, "responses to moral shocks vary greatly" (1997, 106). Moreover, Jasper continues, "most people, in most cases" do not embrace confrontational activism in the face of such a shock, but "resign themselves to unpleasant changes" (106).

To answer these questions, we must consider the context in which the ruling occurred, specifically the political terrain of the AIDS epidemic in that moment and, in a related vein, the already shifting emotional habitus in lesbian and gay communities.[16] Both affected how queer folks experienced—cognitively and affectively—the ruling.[17]

When the *Hardwick* ruling came down in the middle of 1986, queer folks were facing a devastating crisis with numerous medical, social, and political dimensions. The number of AIDS cases had surpassed thirty thousand, the majority of whom were gay and bisexual men, and more than half of them had died (Centers for Disease Control and Prevention 1997, 14, 9). The thousands of deaths were all related: each death was another member lost to an imagined gay community (Anderson 1983), and

16. In addition to intense homophobia, other aspects of the context that created a sense of emergency for many lesbians and gay men included the Reagan administration's embrace of trickle-down economic policies and racialized attacks on the welfare state, the War on Drugs, an escalation in the Cold War, U.S. intervention in Central America, and the challenge to sexual freedom that the Meese Report on Pornography posed.

17. Experience, in my view, is in relation to interpretation, but not reducible to it.

the accumulating bodies were decimating real lesbian and gay communities. Many gay men were losing their entire networks of lovers, friends, and acquaintances to AIDS. Prospects for treating those living with AIDS were bleak: indeed, there were no FDA-approved treatments. And not only did it seem that HIV inevitably led to AIDS and AIDS to death, but studies suggested that fully one half of all gay men in large urban areas might be HIV-infected. As Epstein notes, "Such news can only be described as devastating" (Epstein 1996, 117).

Moreover, the state had relinquished its responsibility to its citizens, abandoning the gay community to address the crisis on its own. People with AIDS (or suspected of having AIDS or of being at risk) were being evicted from their apartments, fired from their jobs, dropped from insurance policies, denied health care by fearful doctors and nurses, disowned by their families, and physically attacked. One week before *Hardwick*, the Justice Department actually legalized discrimination against HIV-positive people, arguing that HIV-positive persons "could be fired by employers under federal government contracts if the employer simply believed—scientific evidence notwithstanding—that the so-called 'AIDS virus' could be casually transmitted" (Rist 1987, 13). Moreover, state legislatures were increasingly considering, and sometimes passing, laws to implement mandatory testing and quarantine of persons testing HIV-positive. Lyndon LaRouche's quarantine proposition, evoking the possibility of concentration camps for people with HIV/AIDS, had received many more than the necessary signatures and would be on the ballot in California in November 1986. In terms of the affective terrain, then, *Hardwick* occurred in a context of already existing fear, terror, grief, desperation, even despair, a time, in Epstein's words (1996, 117), of "deepening gloom" in lesbian and gay communities. Noting that context, national leader Virginia Apuzzo remarked, "There is more anger among our people than I've seen in over a decade." She explained why the rage was so deep and so pervasive: "It's not as if [*Hardwick*] happened in isolation. A week before, the Justice Department virtually provided a rationale for AIDS discrimination. Widely publicized AIDS caseload projections for 1991 soared to 180,000. And, through it all, the unrelenting funeral procession" (Apuzzo 1986).

Hardwick was the last straw, in part because its ramifications were especially shocking. In the absence of equality, the lesbian and gay movement in many ways had been banking on the liberal promise of privacy. In allowing government intrusion into gay bedrooms, the *Hardwick* ruling, emanating from the highest echelons of the state and offering the final word on gay rights, demolished the logic of a safe private sphere and forced a recognition of gays' *de facto* noncitizenship. In the words of Jean O'Leary, then the executive director of National Gay Rights Advocates (NGRA), "Even the closet [is] now unsafe" (O'Loughlin 1986a, 2). It was deeply shocking that the state would declare this lack of rights precisely when lesbian and gay communities were suffering such immense devastation and death and were desperately requesting state assistance that, it was assumed, would have been forthcoming for other citizen groups. The *Hardwick* ruling could not have enacted state betrayal any more forcefully. In short, the context of the ongoing AIDS crisis and the meaning that many attributed to the Supreme Court's ruling within that context, along with the array of affective states it generated and intensified, help to explain why queer folks experienced *Hardwick* as a moral shock.

Why and how did that experience prompt thousands to turn toward confrontational activism and thousands more to provide moral and material support? To answer those questions, we need to investigate more thoroughly the ruling's emotional effects, specifically the ways in which it reconfigured lesbians' and gay men's feelings about state and society, and themselves as well, in the context of the AIDS crisis.

The prevailing emotional habitus had already begun to be destabilized by the unending growth in cases and deaths, increasingly repressive legislation, and consistently inadequate government funding. In addition, isolated instances of more defiant AIDS activism were beginning to emerge at this point. *Hardwick,* then, occurred in a moment when new sentiments and political horizons were emergent but not yet widespread. By amplifying, accelerating, and generalizing these local, relatively small and isolated challenges to the existing emotional habitus and political horizon, *Hardwick* hastened their challenge to the status quo and extended their reach. Although itself not directly about AIDS, *Hardwick* punctuated and gave new meaning to the ongoing epidemic; it crystallized and heightened feelings about and interpretations of the epidemic that were taking shape but were still fairly embryonic and tentative.

Deitcher has noted that prior to *Hardwick,* "among gay men there had been no mass epiphany about AIDS" (1995, 140). The Court ruling changed that, bringing the political aspects of the health crisis into sharp focus, even for gay men who were only minimally politically attentive. The Court's evident willingness, even eagerness, to exclude a whole class of people from privacy protections encouraged lesbians and gay men to interpret the *Hardwick* ruling not as the logical result of some gay people's *individual* failings—their ostensibly extreme sexual practices, for example—but as unfair discrimination against and oppression of an entire social group.

The ruling also encouraged a politicized analysis of the government's response to AIDS, challenging understandings that reduced the epidemic to a shameful consequence of some gay men's sexual "extremity" or that depoliticized the crisis by construing it as a string of individual deaths accompanied by isolated feelings of fear and grief. The deaths of thousands of gay men may have been caused most directly by a virus and the consequent breakdown of people's immune systems, but in denying queers privacy protections and then defending that decision with bald-faced homophobia, the *Hardwick* ruling clarified the complicity of the government in the AIDS crisis. In that period, ACT UP/NY member Gregg Bordowitz saw a shift from individual, private sentiments of fear to collective and public rage, and suggested that this was part of what drew him into AIDS activism: "I was caught up with . . . the emotions at that time, which were reaching a critical boiling point. They were coalescing out of the fear and anxiety of atomized individuals into a kind of public rage" (Bordowitz 2002a). Interviewed by the *Advocate* in September 1987, Susan Cavin, an editor for *Big Apple Dyke News,* connected the emergence of militancy with *Hardwick*'s denial of privacy rights, the dire consequences of social exclusion amid the AIDS crisis, and the consequent felt urgency to challenge that exclusion:

> People feel up against the wall. [The Supreme Court] took away gay people's right to even be in the closet in the privacy of their own bedrooms. When they took away our closet, they really took away our right to exist at all. That has created a more militant stance among people who never had any intention of becoming militant. . . . [Gays] have nothing to lose at this point [by engaging in mass civil disobedience]. With so many gay men dying, people feel that the AIDS crisis has pushed them over the line. The urgency of winning some sort of decent treatment in this society has become apparent. (Vandervelden 1987b, 48)

The blatant homophobia of the *Hardwick* ruling shocked lesbians and gay men into a greater acknowledgment of the serious, indeed life-threatening, consequences of state-sponsored and socially sanctioned homophobia and nonrecognition.

The connection to AIDS was not hard to make. As the highest court in the land was now willing to espouse virulent homophobic justifications in denying privacy rights to a group of citizens, who was to say that quarantine of HIV-positive people—widely supported by the public and increasingly being called for in state legislatures—would not now be implemented? When interviewed, lesbians and gay men who later participated in ACT UP said they had believed that a quarantine might actually be implemented, and, for some, that fear was heightened after the *Hardwick* ruling.[18]

Within this increasingly ominous context, fear of the future intensified. In addition, it became increasingly hard for lesbians and gay men even to hope that state assistance would be forthcoming, especially if they simply continued along their current political path. If the government and society saw homosexual sex and love (and thus homosexual lives) as criminal, they certainly would not suddenly become concerned about homosexual deaths. To the contrary, *Hardwick* allowed an interpretation of the government's nonresponse to the AIDS crisis as evidence that state and society viewed gay men as expendable—indeed, as better off dead. The ruling also demolished any idea that gay respectability would lead to state assistance in gay men's hour of need. The Court even compared homosexuality to rape, suggesting that gay respectability was an oxymoron. The Court's message was clear: insofar as gay sexual practices were construed as unnatural and repugnant, gays could do nothing to redeem themselves.

Hardwick laid bare dominant society's hatred for lesbians and gay men, and made clear the hopelessness of a strategy for gay rights based on being "good" lesbians and gays. In doing so, *Hardwick* reconfigured lesbians' and gay men's feelings about state and society, and simultaneously rearranged their self-feelings, paradoxically, perhaps, easing gay shame and fear of further social rejection. At the point of complete social annihilation, there was no *further* to be feared. An immense transformation in sentiments about self and society challenged views long entrenched in lesbian and gay communities about what kinds of political

18. See Barr 2002; Bordowitz 2002a; Edwards 2000a; Eggan 1999; Kracher 2000; Mc-Millan 2000; Miller 1999; Patten 1993; Sieple 1999; Thompson 2000.

activism were acceptable, possible, desirable, and necessary, effectively breaking the hold of the gay establishment's politics of respectability on lesbian and gay activism and creating a space for the emergence of confrontational, direct-action AIDS activism.

As I suggested earlier, there was nothing inevitable about the political response of lesbians and gay men to the *Hardwick* decision, and there was no necessary connection between *Hardwick* and the emergence of confrontational AIDS activism. *Hardwick* might not have spurred thousands to take to the streets, especially if it had been decided a few years earlier, when it might have magnified gay shame about homosexuality and a sense that AIDS and social rejection were the high costs of the "gay lifestyle." The fact that the emotional habitus and political horizon in lesbian and gay communities were already shifting when the *Hardwick* ruling occurred is important for understanding why the Court's decision intensified lesbian and gay anger rather than shame and encouraged confrontational activism rather than staying the course. Activists' and other's pride in the lesbian and gay community's response to AIDS had already begun to alter ambivalence about self: people were feeling proud as lesbians and gay men who alone were responding to the crisis, gay shame could be destabilized as a result, and a sense of entitlement to citizen rights and privileges could now be mobilized more effectively. In this context, the homophobia of the Supreme Court's decision amplified and quickened a shift in what had been the prevalent lesbian and gay emotional habitus. *Hardwick* crystallized into anger the multiple affective states then circulating about the AIDS crisis, and that anger and indignation were no longer easily submerged. To the contrary, they quickly became normative, challenging and frequently displacing faith in the government's goodwill, gay shame, fear of social rejection, and stoicism in the face of death.

In addition, activists who observed in themselves and others these shifting sentiments intentionally named and mobilized gay anger and linked that emotion to the need for more oppositional activism. New York City's CLGR called for a demonstration against chief Justice Warren Burger with a flyer that stated, "The Supreme Court Comes to Town . . . and we're going to be there! Let's Show That Rage Once More" ("Supreme Court Comes" 1986). When national lesbian and gay leaders met after *Hardwick* and called for a march on Washington, they were well aware of the pervasive anger among lesbians and gay men and they too were hoping to harness it. Troy Perry, the national leader of the gay

Metropolitan Community Churches (MCC) commented, "I've never seen our people so pissed as they are because of the Supreme Court decision. I think we're missing the boat if we don't come out of this with a march on Washington" (Halberstadt 1986, 6). Vivian Shapiro, co-chair of the Human Rights Campaign Fund (HRCF, a national lesbian and gay PAC) expressed a similar desire to mobilize gay rage: "Everybody's frustrated; we have to mobilize the energy while it's here" (Halberstadt 1986, 6).[19] Feeling their own anger and seeing it among others, these activists worked to channel it into street activism. Rather than being out of step with the majority of lesbians and gay men, as Apuzzo's and Kramer's incitements to confrontational activism had been in 1983, such calls now were widely resonant, even among more mainstream gay activists.

Denaturalizing White, Middle-Class, Gay Male Indignation

One pronounced sentiment in this period was indignation. Indignation is a variation of anger that revolves around a sense that one has suffered an injustice, that one's rights have been unjustly revoked, for example, or that one's status has somehow been unfairly degraded or nullified, and that someone is responsible for that indignity; it is a form of outrage that stems from being spurned or rejected after having thought that you were a member of the club and thus entitled to membership rights and privileges. *Hardwick* denied lesbians and gay men constitutional protection, but even more than that, the ruling called into question their very status as human beings. In its aftermath, lesbians and gay men had to confront the reality that their claims to social belonging were fraught with ambiguity. Indignation, then, arose when lesbians and gay men were faced

19. It is particularly notable that in this period the leaders of the MCC and HRCF were intent on mobilizing lesbian and gay anger into potentially militant activism. In the year 2000, MCC and HRC (which by then had taken the *F* out of its name) spearheaded the Millennium March on Washington, a lesbian and gay march viewed by many queers as an attempt to convince mainstream (and corporate) America that lesbians and gay men are "just like them" and thus should have "a place at the table"; the goal was viewed by many as assimilation, on heteronormative terms, rather than societal transformation. The weekend of that march, Perry officiated at a massive lesbian and gay commitment ceremony, "The Wedding," a money-making venture for the MCC (Rand 2005, 162–63). From our current vantage point, then, Perry's and Shapiro's declarations after *Hardwick* are surprising, indicating that in the wake of that ruling, even relatively mainstream activists were intent on mobilizing anger and linking it to an activist response. Perry, notably, was arrested while demonstrating with ACT UP in Los Angeles in October 1989 (Dawsey 1989).

with legal and social rejection, indeed with thorough betrayal by state and society.

In the wake of *Hardwick,* Apuzzo responded to lesbian and gay indignation and evoked a sense of entitlement when, after acknowledging "gay rage," she suggested that during this year of celebrations marking the two hundredth birthday of the Constitution, lesbians and gay men "must claim some part of that" by "laying claim to the phrase 'We the people' early, often, and everywhere" (Apuzzo 1986). Kramer frequently articulated his indignation in relation to AIDS, particularly regarding the government's failure to provide services for its gay citizens, and he suggested that others should feel indignant as well. In one interview, for example, Kramer criticized the lesbian and gay community's approach of taking care of its own rather than fighting "to make the system accountable to us and to give us what's rightly ours" (Williams 1987, 23).

Jeff Levi, executive director of NGLTF, related the thwarting of this sense of entitlement to a growth in activism: "We are now seeing the politicization of a lot of white, middle-class gay men who never thought that issues such as access to health care, national health insurance and social security benefits were relevant to them" (Giteck 1986, 46). Many middle-class, white, gay men were accustomed to being addressed and listened to, especially in arenas where their sexuality might not be visible or especially relevant. *Hardwick* and the AIDS crisis revealed how precarious was their inclusion. Their growing anger, then, was inflamed by indignation that the government was neither listening to nor acting on their grievances and was actually denying them their rights.[20]

Noticing this indignation and construing ACT UP as a white, male, and middle-class organization, some have argued that a sense of entitlement that derived from being relatively privileged men motivated many participants' confrontational street activism.[21] There is some truth to that assessment, as many white, middle-class, male members of ACT UP would attest, but I want to address three troubling aspects of that assertion, one political, one empirical, and one conceptual. Politically, the claim that ACT UP members felt entitled to state assistance in a time of crisis sometimes contains a judgmental, moralizing strain that implies, in my view problematically, that being privileged is itself an irredeemably bad thing

20. Schoofs (1997) quotes AIDS activists as acknowledging that this sense of entitlement played a role in the emergence of ACT UP.

21. See, for example, Cohen 1998.

and a valid reason to disregard a person's political claims. The suggestion is that white, gay men should not have been fighting for their own lives, that to do so was somehow selfish.[22] My empirical point is that while ACT UP chapters often were *predominantly* white, male, and middle-class, many women, people of color, and working-class people participated in ACT UP.[23] Characterizations of the movement that ignore their presence and their leadership create a distorted picture of the movement.[24]

My conceptual intervention is to note that to foreground the role of a sense of entitlement among white, middle-class, gay men in their turn to the streets ignores the pervasive ambivalence in gay communities about sexual difference and thus cannot explain the timing of ACT UP's emergence. If middle-class, white, gay men felt entitled to a state response, why did they not pursue their interests and embrace confrontational street activism earlier, say in 1983, when many were noting the small amount of government funding for AIDS, or in 1985, when there were more frequent and more scathing indictments of government inaction?

It would be an error to naturalize gay, white men's sense of entitlement and consequent indignation about the government's inaction on AIDS. To be sure, in our hierarchical society, various social forces encourage white, middle-class men to feel a sense of entitlement and to feel indignation when something or someone thwarts their expectations. And many white, middle-class, gay men in the movement did indeed link their post-*Hardwick* indignation to a sense of entitlement betrayed. But neither the conviction that the government should assist gay men nor indignation at the government's failure to do so sprang forth naturally; both had to be mobilized, and any success in doing so was contingent on a reconfiguration of gay men's sentiments about themselves. In the early years of the AIDS crisis, society certainly was not encouraging gay men to feel indignation or a sense of entitlement, and the structure of ambivalence in gay communities made any mobilization of such affects and emotions all the more difficult. The race, class, and gender status of white, middle-class, gay men made their mobilization possible, perhaps even probable, but not unproblematic or inevitable.

22. In chapter 6, I discuss how this dynamic of shaming about privilege operated *within* ACT UP.

23. Cvetkovich makes a similar point (2003a); see also Hodge 2000, 361; Wolfe 2004.

24. Notably, a survey of the membership at an ACT UP/NY meeting found that one-third of those in attendance lacked health insurance. See Timour 2003, 14.

New Feelings and an Expanding Political Horizon after Hardwick

The Lesbian/Gay Media's Amplifying Role

The post-*Hardwick* shift in sentiments and attitudes about self, society, and what could and should be done politically extended far and wide. Lesbian and gay newspapers played a large role in this process. They ran ever more articles, editorials, opinion columns, interviews, and letters-to-the-editor that indicted the government, expressed dissatisfaction with the lesbian and gay establishment's relatively staid response to AIDS, and suggested the need for more confrontational AIDS activism. Indignation grew, as did anger and rage; editors and others heightened and encouraged animosity toward the government and society; they increasingly articulated fear about the consequences of lesbian and gay inaction in the face of the growing crisis. While expressions of pride about the community's caretaking and service provision continued, expressions and elicitations of shame and fear of social rejection took up comparatively less discursive space in the lesbian and gay media after *Hardwick*. Just as the content of lesbian and gay newspapers during the early and mid-1980s both reflected and bolstered the prevailing emotional habitus and its accompanying political horizon, their content in this later period both recorded and amplified the explosion of new feelings about self and society and the widespread sense that new, more confrontational tactics for addressing the crisis would be needed and should be welcomed.

I cite here a few examples that reveal this strikingly different tone and content in later AIDS coverage. Notably, these articles often compared the new sentiments and attitudes about activism to those that had prevailed earlier, and their tone indicated the writer's sense that the new constellation of feelings and its accompanying activist trajectory had the potential to force the government and other institutions to respond to the AIDS crisis. These published texts helped both to generate and to bolster the new feelings and new activist imaginaries.

Consider, for example, a front-page article in the *San Francisco Sentinel* about CMJ's first protest action in September 1986, which targeted California's governor for failing to sign a bill that would protect people with AIDS from discrimination. Citing no evidence, but suggesting his own sympathies, the reporter concluded that CMJ's action—a disruptive takeover of his office—had succeeded in making the governor aware that "the gay community is capable and willing to begin moving beyond traditional strategies" (Lowe 1986b, 4). Again suggesting that his sympathies lay with CMJ, the reporter quoted member Keith Griffith distinguishing CMJ's street activism from the tactics of the gay establishment. Griffith impugned the motives of the existing gay leadership, advocated gay militancy, and suggested that the stakes involved in adopting one mode of activism rather than another were high:

> It's time gay people in S.F. take note that their gay leadership is not taking an aggressive enough role in the fight against AIDS discrimination. Working through the system is not enough. . . . The community needs to become more militant on these issues. Our so-called leadership is so afraid we'll embarrass them and jeopardize the Stop LaRouche campaign. We think 13,000 AIDS-related deaths is enough and more aggressive actions like this one today are long overdue. We hope this is just the first of many more protests in the future. (Lowe 1986b, 4)

In this moment of transition in gay and AIDS activism, Griffith felt the need to justify CMJ's militancy, but the *Sentinel*'s placement of the article on the front page and the reporter's evident sympathies with CMJ indicate that more confrontational, street-based AIDS activism was ascendant.

In January 1987 the *New York Native* published Larry Kramer's "Open Letter to Richard Dunne and Gay Men's Health Crisis," in which Kramer criticized GMHC for becoming overly bureaucratic, conservative, and cowardly, and for focusing on providing patient services to the exclusion of political advocacy. In many ways the piece echoed the rhetorical style and emotional tenor of Kramer's 1983 call to arms, but in this later moment, Kramer's words fell on much more fertile ground. It expressed his sense of urgency in a manner that criticized and goaded: "I beg the board of GMHC to hear me. . . . The worst years of the AIDS pandemic lie ahead of us. . . . Please etch this thought on your consciousness: *There are millions of us yet to die*" (Kramer 1987a, 15; emphasis his). Where before Kramer had been largely alone in his scathing rhetoric and incitement to the streets, responses to his letter indicate the now more widespread challenge facing the older emotional habitus and political horizon. Some letters to the *Native* disagreed with Kramer's indictment of GMHC, but a majority endorsed his position and indicated that his views about the need for confrontational AIDS activism now were widely shared.[25] In a letter that echoed Kramer's challenge to GMHC, Vito Russo (a gay film critic and person with AIDS who later co-founded ACT UP/New York) bolstered the new emotional-political sensibilities with an analysis that accused the GMHC board and staff of refraining from expressing anger and engaging in political activism because they were wary of controversy and afraid of social rejection. He implored GMHC to expose the Reagan administration's negligent response to AIDS and to "fight like hell for my life and other people's lives." By deconstructing the impetus behind what Russo saw as the gay establishment's politics of respectability and by suggesting the ineffectiveness of that form of activism—even linking it to death in this time of crisis—Russo authorized angry, militant direct action: "Is there no place for anger in this battle? Must our lives be sacrificed in the name of good taste? Have gay people become so obsessed with a respectable image over the last few decades that the desire finally to be seen as good little boys and girls will cost us our very existence? Are we now *dying* just to be accepted?" ("Kramer and Russo vs. GMHC" 1987, 9; emphasis his). In invoking animosity toward society, Russo, like Kramer, offered a response to lesbians' and gay men's contradictory feelings about self and society, a new constellation of sentiments suddenly being aired with some frequency: our homosexual lives are worth saving; whether we are "good" or "bad" gays, we are entitled to a more urgent, compassionate, and effective response to the AIDS crisis; we must make "a lot of noise," "get [our] asses in the streets," and fight for our lives rather than strive for social acceptance; death is the too-high price of our inaction.

Interviewed in Chicago's *Windy City Times* in October 1986, gay writer Darrell Yates Rist similarly berated the gay leadership for being too apologetic in the context of the AIDS crisis. Making a point about a relationship between feelings and politics, and alluding to the ambivalence of gay leaders, he criticized those leaders "who have tried to muffle the anger of the gay community" and asserted that the community should move beyond "the passive and polite." He stated, "When we muffle our voices and pretend that we can be bankers over a bargaining table striking a deal on real estate, our success will remain limited. We have to be willing to slam our fists down on the table and say no to the lies that led to the hysteria, and no to the hatred that allowed the government to move so slowly" (Johnson 1986b). Being respectable not only seemed to

25. See letters to the editor in the *Native*, February 9 and February 16, 1987.

be failing as a strategy, it was increasingly tagged as too high a cost of admission into mainstream society.

The following is an interesting instance of a lesbian and gay newspaper shifting gears in a manner that reflected and buttressed the new emotional habitus and its new sense of political possibilities. In September 1986, the *Windy City Times* ran a feature article on John Lorenzini, a person with AIDS who had chained himself to the Federal Building in San Francisco in June 1985 and again in October to protest the government's negligent response to AIDS. In the interview, Lorenzini commended the lesbian and gay community's service-oriented response to the AIDS crisis, but called on the community to do more on a "political" level. He spoke of channeling his anger outward, toward the government, and appealed to others to do so (Johnson 1986a). What is most notable is that the *Windy City Times* published this interview with Lorenzini more than a year after his action (and just months after the *Hardwick* decision), *not* in the days or weeks following his action—which would have made sense for a time-sensitive news publication.

The headline of a story that ran in September 1987 in the *Advocate* posed the recent shifts in lesbian and gay activism as a question: "Civil Disobedience: Are We Entering a New Militant Stage in the Struggle for Gay Rights?" The reporter left no doubt that the answer was yes, asserting the existence of "a deepening recognition within the gay community that a more dramatic form of moral and legal resistance is needed" and noting that "even the most moderate gay leaders" were calling for "mass civil disobedience" in response both to the *Hardwick* decision and to the government's slow and inadequate response to the AIDS crisis (Vandervelden 1987b, 46). Taking the emotional and political pulse of the gay world, the reporter claimed that "more and more gay people are feeling a heightened moral outrage at a government—indeed an entire society—that denies them basic human dignity and civil rights. Many of these individuals, otherwise law-abiding citizens, now feel compelled to take public, unlawful action in response" (46). As evidence of the growing militancy, the reporter noted that ACT UP/NY and CMJ were both drawing large numbers of people to their meetings, and that gays in Washington, D.C., Boston, Los Angeles, Houston, and Denver already either had engaged in civil disobedience or were planning to in the near future. Perhaps because he could see that the tide was shifting, the reporter included a sympathetic meditation on both the history and the philosophical underpinnings of nonviolent civil disobedience.

The reporter asserted that the planned massive civil disobedience action to take place the following month at the Supreme Court signified "a watershed in the maturation and refinement of gay political sensibilities in America." Rather than representing a threat to gay respectability, the action would mark "a certain coming of age for the gay rights movement" (46). Whereas before *Hardwick,* maturity had pointed toward caretaking, it now went hand in hand with militancy.

In addition to running stories and features that indicated shifts in the community's emotional habitus and political horizon, the gay media also expressed strong support for the emerging direct-action AIDS movement, and that too helped to extend the new constellation of feelings and the new orientation toward AIDS activism. At the end of 1986, for example, the *San Francisco Sentinel* gave Keith Griffith—one of the founders of CMJ—their Man of the Year Award "for courageously steering the gay rights movement beyond the bounds of traditional political and legal response to threats to the community's civil rights" ("Man & Woman" 1986, 1). The newspaper specifically praised CMJ for its sit-in protest at California Governor Deukmejian's office. Similarly, a columnist for the *Sentinel* endorsed a June 1, 1987, national AIDS demonstration protesting the Reagan White House's failures regarding the crisis and proudly credited CMJ with showing "the rest of the nation's lesbian/gay communities that nonviolent civil disobedience is a viable option to advance our movement" (Lowe 1987, 7). *New York Native* publisher and editor Charles Ortleb voiced support and encouragement of militant activism in early 1987 when he thanked the Lavender Hill Mob "for making it clear that we will not go gentle into that good night" (Ortleb 1987). Anger no longer had to be tempered with gentleness.

The gay media in this moment did more than record the dramatic shift in the community's emotional habitus and political horizon. Coverage of the shifting sentiments, along with explicit support of confrontational activism, reinforced and broadened those shifts by encouraging lesbians, gay men, and other sexual and gender outlaws to embrace angry, direct-action AIDS politics.

The Gay "Mainstream" Embraces Militancy

More militant AIDS activist groups emerged in the wake of the *Hardwick* decision, but even more indicative of how widespread were the shifting sentiments and opening sense of political possibilities in lesbian and gay communities is that even gay politicians, mainstream gay activists, and leaders of establishment-oriented national lesbian/gay and AIDS organizations began openly embracing confrontational tactics. Angry street militancy suddenly was supported—publicly and sometimes even fervently—by prominent figures and institutions in lesbian and gay communities, further authorizing the turn toward confrontational activism. In San Francisco, for example, the Stonewall Democratic Club—a group traditionally oriented toward the electoral realm and aligned with the Democratic Party—invited the more militant activist group MAA to conduct civil disobedience training at the Stonewall Club's meeting following the *Hardwick* decision (Lowe 1986a, 11). Also in San Francisco, Harry Britt, a gay member of the San Francisco Board of Supervisors, publicly voiced strong support for the civil disobedience action by protesters conducting the ongoing AIDS/ARC Vigil in San Francisco, even in the face of the federal government's attempts to shut it down (Wetzl 1987, 8).

Consider as well that in March 1987, just after the emergence of ACT UP/NY and five days after its first action, Duke Comegys, the co-chair of the establishment-oriented HRCF and himself a registered Republican,[26] gave a keynote address at the National Lesbian and Gay Health Conference in which he accused the government of "killing us" and called for a nationwide campaign of civil disobedience. Comegys asserted, "We have tried rational discourse for six long years and it simply hasn't worked. . . . If reason alone can't do the job, then radical action— such as mass sit-ins and demonstrations with hundreds of us going to jail—is our only recourse." He continued, "I am personally ready to go to jail to save my life and the lives of my family and friends. I cannot take any more death" (Vandervelden 1987a; "More" 1987). Having hit bottom in terms of grief over the deaths and despair about the effectiveness of "rational discourse," Comegys advocated an expansion of the community's political horizon. After his address, he received an extended standing ovation from an audience of more than one thousand. A couple of months later, a California-based gay political action committee, the Municipal Elections Committee of Los Angeles (MECLA), held their annual awards ceremony—tickets were $225 per person—and gave Comegys an award, again suggesting widespread mainstream gay support for the turn toward militant AIDS activism ("MECLA" 1987).

26. Clendinen and Nagourney 2001, 556–57.

The Executive Director of HRCF, Vic Basile, expressed more ambivalence than did Comegys, but he too endorsed the recent turn to civil disobedience. "I believe that, for the most part, the traditional mainstreaming of our issues is the thing that is going to bring results for us. [Still,] civil disobedience is an appropriate tool in the arsenal of weapons that gay people could use to bring about political change" (Vandervelden 1987b, 46). Another mainstream gay activist, David Mixner, indicated ambivalence about militancy similar to Basile's; nevertheless, he also strongly endorsed confrontational activism. "If we had a lot of time, the existing process would be working fine. . . . But time is not on our side in this crisis. We can just accept that, or we can do something dramatic and powerful. We can say, 'Wait a minute, we can no longer continue with business as usual'" (46).

Similarly, GMHC, the largest ASO, supported ACT UP/NY from the beginning. Indeed, many GMHC volunteers and staff members participated in ACT UP/NY. Tim Sweeney, second in command at GMHC, facilitated the very first ACT UP/NY meeting (Petrelis 2003, 25; Nesline 2003, 7). In addition, ACT UP/NY member Michael Petrelis recalls that early on someone who worked at GMHC helped ACT UP/NY plan a small action during GMHC's annual AIDS Walk to target New York Mayor Ed Koch, whom GMHC had named the Honorary Chair of the event (Petrelis 2003, 29). GMHC also provided institutional support to the emerging direct-action AIDS movement. ACT UP/NY's meeting minutes from April 20, 1987—after just one month on the scene—indicate that GMHC donated one thousand dollars to the organization (ACT UP/New York 1987b). In the same period, GMHC's establishment-oriented executive director, Richard Dunne, wrote a letter to the editor of the *New York Native* stating, "The clear, angry, direct action of ACT UP is useful and necessary" (Dunne 1987). Dunne's articulation of support provides an interesting vantage point for understanding ACT UP's ascendance in this moment. During this time period, some members of ACT UP/NY repeatedly attacked Dunne and GMHC for being too accommodating and too reluctant to engage in political activism. Dunne articulated his support for ACT UP in the context of promoting GMHC's record in the fight against AIDS and took a defensive tone. After quoting mainstream press articles that praised GMHC's advocacy role, Dunne wrote, "Obviously, GMHC is expanding its advocacy role. We support the activism of groups like AIDS Coalition to Unleash Power. . . . We also believe that the follow-through on working out the specifics of policy implementation is as important as street demonstrations" (6). The content and tone of Dunne's reply to criticism from ACT UP raises the question of the extent to which Dunne genuinely supported ACT UP. He evidently had some reservations; he certainly was suggesting, for example, that street AIDS activists were not capable of follow-through. But in the face of ACT UP's criticism of GMHC, Dunne clearly felt the need to voice support for ACT UP. Whether or not he was being honest, Dunne's comments indicate that, while militancy was not the only game in town, it was the game that you now had to respond to, and there evidently was a sense that you at least had to appear to support ACT UP.

Even more striking than the outpouring of verbal support for ACT UP from the gay establishment is the fact that numerous gay leaders put their bodies where their mouths were. Again, many GMHC volunteers and staff members attended ACT UP/NY meetings and actions. ACT UP/NY member Jean Carlomusto recalls GMHC board members and its executive director Rodger McFarlane getting arrested at ACT UP/NY's first demonstration (Carlomusto 2002). The evidence belies the perception that GMHC and ACT UP were invariably at odds or that individuals had to choose one or the other. Also indicating how widespread were the transformations in political imaginaries after *Hardwick,* a diverse array of groups, including ACT UP/NY, MAA, and the establishment-oriented HRCF, together sponsored a national AIDS demonstration outside the White House in June 1987. Sixty-four activists were arrested for sitting in the street and blocking traffic, including a dozen prominent directors and board members of AIDS service and lesbian and gay organizations, along with lesbian and gay elected officials (fig. 4). Paul Boneberg of MAA noted how remarkable was this shift in tactics: "Today's action was a massive quantum step toward militancy. Never before has the collective gay leadership put itself on the line like this" (Linebarger 1987c, 5; see also Walter 1987b and Salinas 1987b). In Jane Rosett's words, "It was a time in AIDS activism when the suits hit the streets" (Rosett 1997b).

The following comments from Ralph Payne, one of those arrested at the June 1 demonstration, indicate just how new and different were the emergent emotional habitus and political horizon, and how much anxiety (as well as excitement) they provoked among some of the more establishment-oriented activists. In this period, Payne's activism spanned the spectrum from more moderate to more confrontational: he was vice

FIGURE 4. Virginia Apuzzo being arrested at a national AIDS demonstration in front of the White House, June 1, 1987. Photo by Ellen B. Neipris.

president of the gay Stonewall Democratic Club, a member of the board of the San Francisco AIDS Foundation, and treasurer of MAA. Recording his thoughts and feelings amid the action, Payne indicated that the emotional and political winds in the lesbian and gay community were shifting. "After participating in so many quiet and somber candlelight memorials, I am startled by the anger and militancy of the crowd as we begin our march to the White House" (Payne 1987, 8). The crowd chanted "We've got the power to fight back!" and, in a contrasting emotional tenor, sang "We Shall Overcome" and "We Are a Gentle, Angry People." Payne described the reasoning behind the decision to engage in civil disobedience as follows:

> For the first time since the Stonewall riots nearly 20 years ago, lesbian and gay representatives from around the nation came together to take a unified action. We consciously broke the law of this land to protest the injustice directed towards our people. We did so nonviolently. . . . For six years our community has stood virtually alone waging the war against this epidemic . . . . We have developed the services. . . . We have lobbied our elected officials demanding action. We have fought back lunatics wanting to put us into con-

centration camps. We have conducted the funerals. We have conducted the funerals! And we have exhausted all of the avenues available to us within the system. . . . So today, June 1, 1987, 64 frightened people took a risk and crossed a line, stepping into a space that has been waiting for us for some time. (Payne 1987, 8–9)

Perhaps nervous that straight observers, or maybe other lesbians and gay men, might construe their action and the militant tone of the demonstration as heralding some sort of dangerous and irrational mayhem, or perhaps himself worried that militant action might usher in social disorder, Payne seemed bent on softening the action and the anger that was driving it: "Our message is that the time has come to take the next gentle step in our liberation. We must let the system know that it is failing us, and that we can no longer stand by and watch our people die. If we have to, we will break the law—non-violently. Filling up the jails is preferable to filling up the hospitals. We are not going to just die" (Payne 1987, 9).

Simultaneously defiant and tempered, Payne asserted that gay anger, though present and growing, would be of the gentle sort. As a new emotional habitus and political horizon were emerging, anxiety about rocking the boat was diminished but clearly still in play. In that context, articulations of support for confrontational AIDS activism—including those like Payne's, which simultaneously reassured people who might be worried about angry queers engaging in street activism—helped to authorize the political turn toward confrontational direct action.

Growing Support for Direct-Action AIDS Politics

In its earliest weeks and months, ACT UP and similar direct-action AIDS groups garnered support not only from the gay media, other gay institutions, and gay leaders, but also from thousands of other queer folks from across the political spectrum. When DAGMAR held a twenty-four-hour vigil in front of Illinois Governor James Thompson's home in August 1987 to protest Thompson's impending signature on repressive AIDS legislation, "hundreds of protesters from a broad spectrum of the lesbian and gay community—including some who had previously considered DAGMAR too radical for them to join—picketed and camped out near the governor's house" (Burkes 1988).

There is also evidence that many who did not get involved in the movement were thrilled that others were now embracing confrontational

activism. Consider, for example, the following comments from Liddell
Jackson—an antiracist organizer and the founder of Jacks of Color, a sex
venue for men of color.

> When ACT UP first came around, people were like, "ACT UP, you go! I may
> not be able to go out there and scream but I'm behind you all the way." Be-
> cause nobody else was listening to us any other way. If you can get people to
> listen and get drug trials done and get drugs out there that are going to be af-
> fordable, thank you. So there was a lot of support for them, especially among
> the sex community. (Jackson 2002, 175)

ACT UP/NY sold one thousand SILENCE = DEATH buttons and collected
more than twenty-five hundred signatures on petitions during GMHC's
1987 annual AIDS Walk (ACT UP/New York 1987c). Members of ACT
UP/NY recall the huge impact that ACT UP had when it marched in
New York's Lesbian and Gay Pride Parade in June 1987, barely three
months into its existence. Michael Nesline remembers starting out with
between sixty and one hundred participants and ending with "hundreds
and hundreds of people who joined [ACT UP's contingent in] the parade" (Nesline 2003). Karl Soehnlein recalls "intense excitement from
other people . . . along the [parade] route." Soehnlein worked at the ACT
UP/NY T-shirt and information stand that day and felt that "everyone
wanted to know about ACT UP" (Soehnlein 2003). Even more, ACT
UP/NY's membership grew dramatically following the 1987 parade; at
the first ACT UP meeting after that parade, "hundreds of people were in
the room" (Nesline 2003).

Also suggestive of the widespread nature of the shifts in sentiment
and in political imaginaries then occurring is the fact that many lesbians got involved in the direct-action AIDS movement. Lesbians and gay
men mostly had stopped working together politically in the early years
of the gay liberation movement. This was partly because of sexism in the
movement and lesbian feminist critiques of the developing gay male sexual subculture. In my view, it was also because the gay rights movement
during the 1970s, led and populated primarily by gay men, had adopted
comparatively moderate tactics and goals and as a result became unin-
teresting and uninviting to many more politically radical lesbians. The
emotional shifts and political opening that occurred after *Hardwick* created a space in gay activism for those who had a more radical critique
of state and society. In part because anger had been explored and le-

gitimized in women's consciousness-raising groups during the 1960s and 1970s, a number of lesbians with experience in the women's liberation movement were particularly receptive to the anger then growing in lesbian and gay communities.[27]

The fact that many gay men who turned to AIDS activism had no previous activist history also indicates how different the post-*Hardwick* moment was. Gay men with political histories played an important role in the movement, but many were acting up for the first time.[28]

In short, the evidence indicates that shifts in sentiment and in political imaginaries in lesbian and gay communities were widespread. Over the five years preceding the emergence of ACT UP, isolated expressions of anger as well as a few instances of more militant AIDS activism occurred, but they were counterhegemonic challenges to the norm of gay and AIDS politics in the 1981–86 period. After *Hardwick,* anger, indignation, and rage took center stage, soon becoming the new norm. This emergent emotional habitus offered an alternative way to feel and to express one's feelings, joining self-respect, self-love, and pride to indignation, anger, and animosity toward society. This new constellation of sentiments, explicitly and unabashedly linked to militancy, ushered in a new political horizon that created a space for confrontational AIDS activism.

Contesting the New Emotional Habitus and Political Horizon

The earlier sentiments and attitudes did not disappear, of course, nor did the new militancy go uncontested. The emotional habitus and political horizon within a social group are never totalizing. Considering as well the structure and political contours of lesbian and gay ambivalence, it is no surprise that a struggle ensued about the necessity and validity of angry street activism. That struggle historically has been present in lesbian and gay politics, but what is notable about this moment is that, contestations notwithstanding, the new constellation of feelings and ideas about political activism not only took hold but also came to prevail. A discussion of the contestations reveals the shifting ground.

Directly following the *Hardwick* decision, when outrage and street demonstrations were the immediate response by thousands of sexual

---

27. For more on lesbian participation in ACT UP, see Black 1996.
28. See France 1988, 36.

and gender minorities, some in the community indicated their anxiety about defiant, oppositional politics. In fact, the night after the *Hardwick* decision was announced, protest organizers in New York tried to end the sit-in after half an hour. Maxine Wolfe recalled that members of GLAAD organized the rally but "panicked at the militance and the anger in the street" (Wolfe 1993) and tried to get people to leave, warning "You're gonna get into trouble" and urging "Go home, go home, go home" (Wolfe 1997, 417).[29] The mood, however, was decidedly more confrontational than it had been during the previous decade; protesters did not heed the call to disperse and continued blocking traffic for almost four hours (Wolfe 1993; Wolfe 1997, 417; see also Freiberg 1986b, 12). As one protester sitting in the street later wrote, "The crowd of about 3,000 was in no mood to listen to leaders. . . . It was a night for anarchy and open debate, not for leaders" (Rosco 1986, 11). In the eyes of *New York Native* reporter Anne-Christine d'Adesky, GLAAD's hesitancy about the sit-in and other protesters' refusal to follow GLAAD's attempts to disperse the protest indicated an important split within the gay community, even within its leadership. But, according to d'Adesky, "expression of anger and defiance was just the thing [that most participants] needed," evident in the following statement from one participant who was chanting "Civil rights or civil war!": "This morning I was feeling really depressed, now I feel great. We really needed this. We need to show we're not gonna take it. We're gonna fight back, and hard" (d'Adesky 1986b, 8). Older norms about political feelings and their expression were coming up against the newer habitus, and the latter was winning out.

Even so, when it soon became apparent that some lesbians and gay men were planning a disruption of the Statue of Liberty Centennial celebration on July 4, GLAAD leaders were "horrified," according to Wolfe (1997, 417). "They really did not want this to happen. . . . They said things like 'People are coming here and it's a big holiday, and you don't want to fuck it up for people; you're gonna ruin their party; you're not gonna get your point across'" (417; see also Wolfe 1994, 219). But their anxious attempts to contain people's anger and redirect the protest into more socially acceptable channels failed. In Wolfe's words, "Nobody listened to them" (Wolfe 1997, 417). Word about the protest spread quickly.

29. Wolfe's recollection is corroborated by accounts written during the period itself: see d'Adesky 1986b, 8; Gans 1986d; and a letter in the July 28, 1986, issue of the *Native*. See also Deitcher 1995, 150.

GLAAD got a police permit for a rally in Sheridan Square and for a march to Federal Plaza (many blocks north of Battery Park, the site of the Statue of Liberty celebration). Wolfe recalled her realization that the masses of lesbians and gay men were far ahead of their "leadership," writing, "As I arrived at Sheridan Square, the whispering said it all: 'Battery Park, Battery Park'" (1994, 219). Wolfe recalls,

> GLAAD had negotiated with the cops for a permit to march to Federal Plaza, about ten blocks north of where the Centennial Celebration was happening and to rally there. But people were determined to go down to Battery Park—to be a presence in the midst of the tourists at the Centennial. After the rally at Federal Plaza, GLAAD stationed marshals to block the demonstration from going downtown. This was just a totally spontaneous act of about five thousand people, who were communicating by passing the word back; these people broke through the marshal line. The cops formed a barricade around Trinity Place with cars and horses and were basically telling people that they weren't gonna let them go through. There were some people from GLAAD who were standing up and saying, "Break it up now, you don't want to do this stuff." (Wolfe 1997, 417)

Corroborating Wolfe's recollection, one participant commented that the formal organizers of the July 4 demonstration seemed "committed to containing and channeling, and maybe defusing, our anger" (Gans 1986d). Their efforts, however, again failed. After the rally at Federal Plaza, thousands of protesters did proceed to Battery Park, evading the police barricades and ignoring protest organizers' "pleas to obey" and attempts to "calm the crowd" and to contain protesters' anger and militancy (Byron 1986, 7).

The leadership of GLAAD may have been apprehensive about people getting hurt on GLAAD's watch if a confrontation broke out between protesters and Fourth of July Centennial celebrants. But their concerns during the July 4 demonstration seem of a piece with their attempts to stop the sit-ins the night of the *Hardwick* ruling, suggesting a more general concern about gay militancy in the streets. To me, the anxiety of GLAAD's leadership is striking; whereas less then seven months before, they had been furious about politicians' and the media's AIDS hysteria and had organized a number of demonstrations, they now wanted to control the anger and militancy of thousands of lesbians and gay men. In retrospect, there are indications that from the beginning, GLAAD leaders were more oriented toward institution-building than confrontational activism. Interviewed by the *Advocate* just months after its emergence, one leader of the group saw "the immediate task" for the new organization as being "to incorporate and raise funds to get the organization on a permanent footing" (Freiberg 1986a, 17). More critically, a Lavender Hill Mob document states that "GLAAD was promoted under the pretense of being a grass roots organization fighting homophobic oppression, yet suffered from disrespect for its own membership. GLAAD was controlled by a 'Star Board,' who fought intensely to control the movement" (Lavender Hill Mob, n.d.). Due to frustration about GLAAD's hierarchical structure and "unwillingness to do more direct action and civil disobedience," some members of GLAAD's direct-action committee left the organization immediately after the July 4 protest and formed the Lavender Hill Mob (Wolfe 1994, 219). Maxine Wolfe's description of the first GLAAD meeting[30] and of GLAAD demonstrations corroborates the Mob's appraisal. Wolfe indicates her sense that from the start, the GLAAD leadership organized meetings in an undemocratic manner, perhaps precisely because they were concerned that a non-hierarchical activist organization following no predetermined script—an organization populated by angry queers who might take their anger and their critique of state and society in any number of different directions— might get out of control.

> It was pretty tame. . . . There was already a board. They already had an idea about what they were doing. And basically, they wanted an army of soldiers. It was a very hierarchical organization. . . . [In the planning of GLAAD demonstrations,] there was absolutely no input from anybody [other than the leadership] into what was going to be done. The board of directors made the decisions. . . . [At the meetings] no one would even get a chance to get up and speak. (Wolfe 1997, 410)

About the GLAAD-organized protest at the *New York Post*, Wolfe recalled that GLAAD "organiz[ed] and orchestrat[ed] the whole thing. It was so frustrating. . . . And they weren't going to do anything that was going to get them into trouble. It was not about civil disobedience" (Wolfe 2004, 38). In this light, GLAAD's anxiety about the post-*Hardwick* demonstrations is less surprising.

30. GLAAD was calling itself GLADL at that point.

Several additional examples indicate the persistence of anxiety about confronting dominant society after *Hardwick*. When the Lavender Hill Mob disrupted the CDC's conference in February 1987, their first target was mainstream lesbian/gay and AIDS organizations that had attended the conference to argue against mandatory HIV testing. Lavender Hill Mob member Bill Bahlman indicted the mainstream groups for participating in this "travesty" that was the CDC conference; he excoriated their staid tactics, saying: "We should be yelling, we should be screaming about this issue. We shouldn't be sitting, talking rationally about this!" (Walter 1987a, 11). Reaction to the Mob's disruptions from the more mainstream lesbians and gay men was mixed, but many expressed anger. The extremity of the comments of Jeff Levi, executive director of NGLTF, indicated anxiety about gay militancy; he angrily equated the activists who disrupted the CDC press conference to right-wing extremists, saying, "Just as the CDC has to deal with [anti-gay, AIDS-hysterical California Representative William] Dannemeyer, we have to deal with the Lavender Hill Mob" (Walter 1987a, 11). While acknowledging that their tactics were "valid," deputy executive director of GMHC, Tim Sweeney, stated that the Mob "must realize that sort of stridency and anger and rage can do a lot to paralyze our supporters" in the heterosexual world (Walter 1987a, 11). Sweeney's concerns may have been practical and tactical, but they can also be read as having an ideological dimension that privileged non-confrontational activism over militancy. Nevertheless, just one month later, Sweeney, along with members of the Lavender Hill Mob, helped to found ACT UP/NY, an organization that unabashedly embraced anger, rage, and confrontational activism that many viewed as strident. I raise this not to point to Sweeney's internal contradictions—we all are self-contradictory—but to indicate that within the gay community and in the United States more broadly, hegemonic ideas against militant activism have such force that they often prevail even among individuals who are ambivalent about such activism but with some marked sympathies in that direction. Given a typically unfavorable environment, then, the very emergence of the new emotional habitus and the direct-action AIDS movement are especially stunning.

Hesitancy about confrontational rhetoric and tactics again was apparent in the 1987 Gay Pride edition of the *Windy City Times*, which ran two opinion pieces about AIDS politics side by side. In "Our Voice Is Our Power—Only If We Use It," Larry Kramer berated the lesbian and gay community for failing to fight back while the government was killing gay men. He accused gay men of colluding in their own genocide and asked how many needed to die before we "decide to stop just sitting quietly like the good little boys and girls we were all brought up to be—and start taking rude, noisy, offensive political action?" (Kramer 1987b, 22). He denounced the community's penchant for "kissing ass," for allowing political leaders to permit the deaths of tens of thousands of gay men. Kramer asserted, "AIDS is our Holocaust," and the necessary response is confrontational, defiant, political activism (33). Kramer received a standing ovation for this speech, which he gave at a Gay Pride celebration in Boston.

The column that ran next to Kramer's was by Chicagoan Paul Varnell. As the headline suggests, "We're Making Progress" was comparatively upbeat and reiterated what until recently had been the standard rhetoric, congratulating the gay community for its successes during hard times. Varnell's piece conveyed a nervousness about the recent turn toward confrontational AIDS activism. He criticized the Reagan administration's "reprehensible" failures to fight AIDS, but before his critique could generate gay anger, Varnell suggested that lesbians and gay men should be thankful that Reagan "has made no marked specific anti-gay efforts" (Varnell 1987, 34).[31] Notably, despite previously lambasting the State of Illinois' response to AIDS and claiming that "never has so little been done, so slowly, by so many people" (Regnier 1985, 8), Varnell now tempered his criticism and refrained from mentioning repressive measures—including mandatory testing and quarantine—that recently had been passed by, or were pending in, the Illinois legislature. In striking contrast to Kramer's plea for confrontational activism, Varnell called for what he labeled "decent" and "socially legitimate" activism (1987, 34), suggesting his anxiety that the recent upsurge in confrontational activism might threaten lesbian and gay respectability and risk further social rejection.

Similar anxiety may have been in play in the following instance of distancing from confrontational activism. In August 1987, DAGMAR held a twenty-four-hour vigil in front of the house of the governor of Illinois, James Thompson, to demand that he veto repressive AIDS legislation passed by the Illinois General Assembly. DAGMAR member Darrell Gordon recalled this action as "the first time in years that there was any kind of direct-action street activism in the Chicago queer scene" (Gor-

31. Varnell did not read Reagan's AIDS policies, or lack thereof, as "anti-gay."

don 2000). The Illinois Gay and Lesbian Task Force (the state branch of NGLTF) initially supported the vigil (Gordon 2000), but when they discovered that some DAGMAR members were planning to engage in civil disobedience, "IGLTF disassociated itself from [the] vigil," with the rationale that "people do have a right to privacy," although they did not specify how the vigil would violate Thompson's privacy ("IGLTF Delivers" 1987). Recalling IGLTF's back-peddling, Gordon (2000) suggested that members of the organization were worried that being associated with DAGMAR and its particular form of confrontational AIDS activism might hurt IGLTF's relationship to both the Democratic and Republican Parties.[32]

Individuals and the Social Space for Militancy

These examples remind us that the emergence of confrontational AIDS activism occurred within the structure of lesbian and gay ambivalence. In part as a result, while the new emotional habitus offered different ways to feel and helped to pry open the prevailing political horizon, not everyone embraced the turn toward militancy. Having said that, let me dispel any idea that I am claiming something about the affective states of those who did and those who did not participate in the direct-action AIDS movement. My argument is not about individuals but about the structuring potential of emotional processes, and more specifically of any given emotional habitus. To reiterate, I argue that *Bowers v. Hardwick* created a new emotional-political imaginative space in lesbian and gay communities that allowed for the emergence of angry, confrontational, street-based AIDS activism. With this idea of the creation of a fresh imaginative space, I am trying to bring to mind the new feelings and the sense of new political possibilities that were opened up and made culturally available by *Hardwick;* the new feelings and sense of possibilities quickly began to circulate among queer folks. Articulated repeatedly by community leaders, the lesbian and gay media, AIDS activists, and by gay friends, lovers, and acquaintances, they soon crystallized into a powerful counterdiscourse and alternative set of feelings to what had previously prevailed. As these different sentiments and ideas took hold,

32. AIDS activists were aware that their anger and militancy unsettled some, and they sometimes played into that. One ACT UP T-shirt, for example, stated, "DESPERATE DYING HOPELESS PEOPLE WITH NOTHING TO LOSE ARE DANGEROUS AND UNPREDICTABLE" (Kauffman 2002, 38).

growing into the reigning emotional habitus with its new sense of political possibilities, the conditions for new political responses to AIDS were created.

My claim is not that those who turned to the streets were experiencing emotional states different from those who did not. Neither am I arguing that feelings drive people inexorably toward a specific set of politics. Angry, defiant activism was newly authorized and legitimized, even valorized, by *Hardwick,* and some individuals moved into the emotional-imaginative space created by that event while others did not, but those motions cannot be mapped to specific feeling states.

Indeed, by speaking of this political opening in the 1986–87 period as the creation of a new imaginative space with a different emotional quality to it than what had existed previously, I am countering the idea that an analytical focus on affect and emotions necessarily leads to an individual-level explanation of social behavior. An emotional-political space creates imaginative possibilities for activism (and downplays or even forecloses others) that help to shape what sorts of activism people take up. Many of those who embraced direct-action politics felt immense anger (along with a host of other affects and emotions), but so did many who did not join the movement. An individual's political (in) actions are not transparent indicators of his or her feelings. And again, feelings alone do not determine a person's political actions. In discussing the emergence of a new emotional-political imaginative space, I simply wish to illuminate how an assemblage of affects and emotions circulating in a social group crystallizes into an emotional habitus and how new attitudes about activism, related to the new emotional habitus and similarly circulating, can become so widespread as to open a new political horizon. These processes, occurring at the level of the social/cultural *and* at the level of the individual are important in that they help to structure (but not determine) political possibilities and political actions in a given moment.

Those who participated in ACT UP felt a range of sentiments— anger, grief, despair, gay shame and pride, fear about the future, desperation, excitement, a sense of belonging, a desire for social acceptance and recognition. (A similar range of feeling states certainly was experienced by those who did not get involved in the movement.) I do not claim, then, that participants in the movement were free of shame about gay sexuality or that they had no desires for social acceptance. As I argue in the next two chapters, the emotional habitus of ACT UP did counter gay shame and fear of social rejection, but even those of us in ACT UP who embraced a queer "anti-identity" did not entirely cleanse ourselves of such bad feelings. As one example, consider the following comment by Gregg Bordowitz, written five years after he got involved in ACT UP/ NY and embraced its militancy and queer sensibilities. "It has been . . . difficult not to understand my HIV infection as a punishment, regardless of my sex radicalism" (Bordowitz 1993, 211). Activists and nonactivists alike are complicated emotional beings, influenced by our nonconscious affects, by our emotions, and by the emotional habitus of the different worlds in which we live. People can try to ascertain what they are feeling and can try to reconfigure their affects and emotions, but they do not always succeed. ACT UP offered a space for the reconfiguration of one's sentiments about self and society, but I do not contend that ACT UP activists were shame-free anti-assimilationists, while those outside the movement were not.

The Affects and Emotions of Framing

To further illuminate why thousands of queer folks now embraced confrontational AIDS activism, in this section I analyze lesbians' and gay men's increasing use of rhetoric that invoked the Nazi holocaust and constructed AIDS as genocide.[33] Epstein notes that "AIDS as genocide" became "one of the key frames employed by ACT UP in its formative years of mobilization" (Epstein 1996, 221–22). That framing of the crisis was shaped by and simultaneously strengthened the new emotional habitus and also helped to expand sentiments and ideas about what was politically possible and necessary.

The fact that this genocide frame resounded in lesbian and gay communities after *Hardwick* presents an interesting empirical puzzle. When Larry Kramer wrote "1,112 and Counting" in 1983, he equated AIDS deaths to murders and used the evocative metaphor of gay men marching off to the gas chambers to suggest that the AIDS crisis was a holocaust—assertions that he repeated in the subsequent months and years. At that time, although some lesbians and gay men agreed that the government exacerbated the crisis, most found it a stretch to claim that

33. See d'Adesky 1986b; DAGMARR 1986; Gans 1986b, 1986c; Michael 1986; Ruschmeyer 1986; and the many letters in the *Native* for July 21 and July 28, 1986.

government officials were directly responsible for deaths by disease, that the government was to blame for a syndrome that at that point was hypothesized as deriving from a virus in some circles and from immune suppression due to "the fast gay lifestyle" in others. Kramer was seen as a hyperbolic crackpot, and his framing of AIDS deaths as murders akin to the Nazi holocaust fell flat. It is quite possible to imagine lesbians and gay men continuing to reject the genocide frame even in light of the *Hardwick* ruling, calls for quarantine, government negligence, and the growing number of AIDS cases and deaths. Gay men were not being rounded up and put in concentration camps, and the deaths were not directly at the hands of the government. Why and how did an understanding of AIDS as genocide—an understanding that on its face might seem preposterous—now take hold in lesbian and gay communities?

The striking contrast in lesbians' and gay men's reception of the genocide frame in these two time periods also allows us to study the more general question of why and how frames do or do not take hold and mobilize. In my view, the best way to approach the question of frame resonance without imputing it from successful mobilization is to analyze strategic framing processes in the context of the broader practices of meaning-making in which activists and others engage. Only by attending to how people make sense of themselves and their worlds can we ascertain why a given frame succeeds or fails.[34]

AIDS as Genocide: Linking Fear, Grief, and Anger to Action

The ideas of genocide and holocaust are historical references familiar to many Americans and to lesbians and gay men in particular. Sociologist Arlene Stein has noted that the Nazi holocaust "has emerged as a familiar historical template evoking profound emotional associations. . . . The Holocaust stands out as an indisputable instance of immorality, evoking images of apocalypse" (Stein 1998, 523). Epstein has suggested the special resonance of the holocaust template for lesbians and gay men: "In

---

34. I agree with McAdam (1999, xxi–xxii) and Johnston and Noakes (2005, 5) who argue that social movement scholars have tended to emphasize the strategic components of framing, ignoring the broader interpretive processes in which both movement actors and potential participants engage. That tendency, in my view, has impoverished our understandings of the meaning-making dimensions of social movements. For a critique of the framing literature that explores the dialogic nature of meaning-making, see Steinberg 1999a, 1999b.

part because gays and lesbians were among the targeted victims of the Nazi holocaust, they have been particularly inclined to invoke the rhetoric of genocide in characterisations of present-day political challenges" (Epstein 1997, 417). In the 1970s, the lesbian and gay movement took as its symbol the pink triangle that male homosexual prisoners had been forced to wear in the Nazi concentration camps. During the late 1970s, the lesbian and gay press frequently compared the antigay crusades of the New Right to actions of Nazi Germany (D'Emilio 1992, 259). In the context of the AIDS tragedy, the Nazi holocaust was thus a familiar and available discourse for thinking about mass death of a scapegoated group of people. Still, lesbians and gay men did not widely adopt this framing of AIDS until 1986, and when they did so, they made, and seemingly believed, an extraordinary claim: that the deaths of thousands of gay men, apparently from a virus, was comparable to the intentional and systematic slaughter of millions of Jews, Roma, gays, and others whom the Nazis deemed undesirable.

To understand why what might be seen as an extreme framing now seemed a reasonable conceptualization of the epidemic, we must again consider the pivotal role played by specific historical events, focusing on how such events affected how lesbians and gay men interpreted and felt about their situation. In particular, the *Hardwick* ruling and calls for quarantine distinguish this period from the earlier 1980s. As mentioned previously, by the summer of 1986, LaRouche's quarantine initiative had gained enough popular support to be placed on the California ballot. Other state legislatures began to consider similar initiatives.[35] The *Hardwick* ruling and these increasing calls for quarantine suggested widespread social acceptance of a high level of state intrusion into lesbians' and gay men's so-called private lives; it evoked images of government lists and knocks on the door late at night to round up those who were breaking the antisodomy laws and those who were infected with HIV. Lesbians and gay men expressed concerns that after the bath-

35. These legislative moves are more evidence that lesbians' and gay men's access to the political system was tightly constricted. McAdam has noted that antiblack legislative action between 1876 and 1930, even bills that failed to pass, "severely restricted the opportunities for successful political action by, or on behalf of, blacks" (1999, 71–73). Again, my findings are exactly opposite those of political-opportunity theorists in that, in this instance, the further constriction in political opportunities actually encouraged political action and the formation of a movement.

houses and backrooms were closed, their bars, bookstores, and other gathering places might be next, indicating fear that even greater repression might follow.

In an *Advocate* article, gay writer Arnie Kantrowitz suggested why a comparison between gays and Jews was appropriate in this context, and in doing so, he provided insight into the source of these more apocalyptic thoughts and feelings. He quoted Nazi holocaust scholar Raul Hilberg's timeline of Jewish persecution, from the fourth century, when missionaries of Christianity said that Jews could not live among them as Jews, to the later Middle Ages, when the secular rulers said that the Jews simply could not live among them, and finally to the Nazi era, when Jews were told that they could not live, period. Kantrowitz drew the parallel between Jews and gays, writing:

> For centuries we have heard from the heterosexual majority, "You may not live among us as homosexuals," and the closet was our means of survival until we could tolerate it no longer. Now are we hearing, "You may not live among us," in the form of the threatened compulsory HIV testing and quarantine that several states are actively considering as law? Does it take much imagination to hear in the wind, "You may not live"?

Kantrowitz then pointed to additional similarities, finally asking, "Will there be a 'final solution' for American gays as there was for German gays and Jews?" (Kantrowitz 1986, 45). By this point, of course, thousands of gay and bisexual men had already died; to many, it *felt* like a holocaust, especially in the face of state inaction and repression. The words of Kantrowitz and others revealed fear and anger, echoing and amplifying such feeling states in other lesbians and gay men who were trying to make sense of these ominous judicial and legislative events.[36]

Lesbian and gay interpretations of and feelings about these events were corroborated by government negligence in the fight against AIDS, but also by the immensity of media hysteria. In a March 1986 op-ed in the *New York Times,* the "paper of record," William Buckley (1986)

---

36. A large number of ACT UP members were Jewish and, according to Bordowitz, "the holocaust metaphor [thus] was available [to many in the movement] as the most horrifying negative ideal. . . . [It played a] pivotal role in our understanding of the possibilities for civilized barbarity" (Bordowitz and Deitcher 1998, 30). Calls to tattoo and quarantine HIV-positive people may have raised fears among Jewish lesbians and gay men familiar with the history of the Nazi holocaust.

called for tattooing the buttocks of people with AIDS.[37] In June 1987, noting that a lead editorial in the *New York Times* had opined that while mandatory testing for HIV might be "a hasty step toward detention camps," it was not a "foolish" idea and "might one day be seen as brave," a column in the *Windy City Times* worried that this elite paper had opened the door to concentration camps for people with AIDS (Layman 1987, 7).[38] Concentration camps and tattooing as a means of identifying and separating populations were being considered, sometimes even advocated, in the pages of one of the most prominent newspapers in the United States.

A phenomenon with a different temporality also directed people's thoughts to the Nazi holocaust: the rising number of deaths. Michael Callen, founder of the PWA Coalition, suggested a visual reason why such analogies were increasingly resonant. He described the PWA "look," an image seared in his head after seeing many friends and lovers die: "The eyes are sunken with resignation and wasting, yet wide open with terror. . . . It is a look I've only seen elsewhere in gruesome photos from the holocaust" (PWA Coalition 1987, 162). The image of wasting bodies corroborated and intensified fears generated by state and society (non) responses to the crisis.

The use of genocide rhetoric was not limited to street AIDS activists, which suggests the widespread resonance of ACT UP's frame. A letter to President Reagan that was signed in the name of 431 people with AIDS, their friends, and relatives in Chicago, for example, accused the government of genocide for its foot-dragging in testing drugs (O'Connors and Johnson 1987). In 1988 when New York City Mayor Ed Koch unveiled his Five-Year Plan on AIDS, many in the AIDS service community characterized it as "genocidal in its inadequacy" (Hopkins and Zwickler 1988, 36). Similarly, the editor of the Chicago lesbian and gay newspaper *Outlines,* Tracy Baim, labeled AIDS "this generation's holocaust" (Baim 1988).

To summarize, given a context of immense and apparently intentional government neglect, popular and legislative support for quarantine, denial of basic civil rights by the Supreme Court, media hysteria, and horrific illnesses and ever-increasing deaths, lesbians and gay men

37. See gay responses to Buckley's op-ed in letters to the editor in the *Native,* April 7, 1986.

38. The *New York Times'* editorial "Forced AIDS Tests: Then What?" was printed on June 7, 1987.

no longer saw it as farfetched to compare thousands of deaths from a
virus with the millions of deaths due to intentional state murder. The
new constellation of feelings after *Hardwick* and understandings of
AIDS as genocide drew from and corroborated one another: in the context of this moment in the AIDS crisis, lesbians' and gay men's fear,
grief, and anger supported an interpretation of AIDS as genocide, and
that interpretation—which became a prominent framing of the crisis—
intensified those very feelings.

In addition, the genocide frame was particularly resonant because it
assuaged anxiety that gay male sexual practices might be responsible for
the epidemic and offered a retort that focused anger and blame on the
government and thus worked to assuage gay men's feelings of shame and
guilt. Epstein has noted that the charge of genocide inverted the standard accusations surrounding AIDS: "It wasn't immorality that 'caused'
AIDS, as popular discourse would have it; rather, gays, injection drug
users, people with haemophilia, and Haitians were all victims of a ma-
levolent conspiracy to eliminate undesirables" (1997, 418; see also Stein
1998, 525–26).

A remaining question concerns the relationship between the genocide frame and the turn toward confrontational, street AIDS activism.
If you believed that AIDS was a holocaust, then "business as usual" in
the political realm, which by then was clearly ineffective, was not much
of a response. In the context of a shifting emotional habitus, the genocide frame was a motivational call to action. More generally, I would argue that any given frame has an emotional tenor that is constitutive of
the frame itself, and that affective charge helps to account for the force
or effectiveness of the frame.

Social movement scholar Robert Benford has offered a more strategic reading of the framing processes that lead to participation in a social movement. He points out that there is a difference between "simply identifying a problem" and "convincing persons that it is so serious
that they must take ameliorative action." He continues, "Activists thus
attempt to amplify the problem in such a way that their audiences are
persuaded that any response other than collective action is unreasonable" (Benford 1993, 201). Strategic framing by activists certainly occurs
and surely is partly responsible for some mobilization. For example, in
ACT UP/NY's early years, member Herb Spiers suggested that AIDS
activists intentionally deployed holocaust rhetoric with mobilization in
mind: "'Genocide,' if used to describe governmental AIDS policy, is a

call to arms." He continued, "It is invoked heuristically, to guide our sense of outrage at the official neglect of a despised population" (Spiers 1988, 36). ACT UP's SILENCE = DEATH emblem might similarly be seen as a reference to the holocaust designed to make confrontational direct action seem imperative. Drawing on a perceived historical lesson—that the world and European Jews were too passive and quiescent in the face of genocide—the emblem indicts those who have been and might remain silent amid the ongoing AIDS genocide. The emblem in effect labels the government's, but also lesbians' and gay men's, silence and inaction as murderous, and suggests that confrontational activism is the only rational course. SILENCE = DEATH says to lesbians and gay men: Don't let your despair overwhelm you into doing nothing; you will be to blame if you do nothing while you or your friends and lovers die from AIDS; you'd better take to the streets and act up.

The "AIDS as genocide" frame, in short, was used by activists to motivate others. But why did their efforts work? We cannot answer that question without attending to broader practices of meaning-making, which occurs at multiple sites and in many different ways. How lesbians and gay men understood and then decided to respond to the AIDS epidemic at this moment was perhaps the product of some conscious and strategic framing, but it was also the product of interpretive practices that were less directed and intentional and included less-than-fully conscious processes. A frame is only articulable, resonant, and effective in light of those interpretive processes. In this case, in the context of *Hardwick,* government negligence and repression, and the exploding epidemic itself, an understanding of the AIDS crisis as genocide, deriving from and reinforcing a newly emergent emotional habitus, motivated confrontational street AIDS activism.

Activists do not pick their frames out of thin air. Like all of us, activists are constantly interpreting the world, trying to make sense of themselves, their situations, and their political options. Before subsuming all interpretive activity into conscious and strategic framing activities, students of social movements need to recognize that many of these processes are nonconscious. Moreover, if we believe, as I think we should, that thought requires feeling, then our conceptualization of framing needs to reflect this. If we want more insight into the crucial questions of frame resonance and shifts in frames over time, we must look more closely at how people understand and feel about themselves and their situations, why and how those feelings and understandings change, and how such dynamics affect political subjectivities and practices. In the case of direct-action AIDS activism, feelings played a significant role in interpretive and framing processes as lesbians and gay men attempted to understand, respond to, and mobilize others to fight the AIDS epidemic.

Conclusion: The Emergence of Direct-Action AIDS Activism

I have argued that a transformation in lesbians' and gay men's feeling states following *Hardwick* was a decisive factor in the emergence of the direct-action AIDS movement. Before concluding, I want to consider an alternative hypothesis. One could argue that the changed circumstances after *Hardwick* made the costs of pursuing only routine tactics prohibitively high, making it *rational* to take to the streets. My account does not deny the existence of rational calculation, but it raises and answers questions that a rational-actor explanation would have a hard time answering in its own terms. For example, if lesbians and gay men were simply rational actors, why did they not take to the streets earlier, in 1983 or 1984, when the crisis was exploding, and a number of gay leaders were voicing frustration with government inaction? The answer might be that their cost/benefit calculations militated against action in the streets, but that tautological reasoning—their actions must have been rational because humans are rational—raises more questions than it answers. For example, what factors entered into their definitions of self-interest? How did something like lesbians' and gay men's marginalized status and consequent ambivalent sentiments affect their cost/benefit calculations? And given the stark shift in tactics, we would have to ask what happened that allowed or pushed lesbians and gay men to alter their cost/benefit assessments about taking to the streets. If the answer is *Hardwick,* we would have to ask why *Hardwick* per se altered their calculations. My point in drawing attention to the proliferating questions is that rational-actor accounts beg these questions but cannot answer them within their own logic; yet such questions have to be addressed if we want to understand social life. Rational calculation is surely part of the story, but it seems reductive to claim individual self-interest as the most important and always present motivation that provides an answer to such questions. My explanation points toward factors other than self-interest that can be decisive in motivating specific forms of political behavior—factors like affective states and psychic conflicts that are part of being human. Even models with a soft assumption of rational actors simply ignore such nonrational phenomena and their effects on political action. As a result, their explanations seem one-dimensional and incomplete.

To repeat then, my central claim in this chapter is that the U.S. Supreme Court's *Bowers v. Hardwick* decision and the emotional dynamics within lesbian and gay communities that it set in motion sparked the direct-action AIDS movement. In the context of the ongoing AIDS crisis, *Hardwick* helped to transform lesbians' and gay men's sentiments about self and society, crystallizing more oppositional feelings and effectively reconfiguring the contours of the prevailing emotional habitus in lesbian and gay communities. The new emotional habitus offered a different assemblage of sentiments that profoundly shook up the orthodoxy of political restraint that had dominated lesbian and gay politics during the early 1980s.

As I detailed in chapter 1, the year immediately preceding the emergence of direct-action AIDS activism was colored by numerous attacks against the lesbian and gay community. Fighting the crisis through routine political channels that emphasized lobbying, letter-writing, and voting was proving to be utterly ineffective. By this point in the epidemic, grief and desperation were being experienced on a community-wide level: thousands of gay men had already died, and thousands more were gravely ill and would soon die; tens of thousands more were HIV-infected and might become ill at any moment. The unresponsiveness of politicians from both political parties was by now glaring in the light of the skyrocketing case load and the astonishing number of deaths. Calm and reasoned appeals for government action seemed more and more out of sync with the government's punitive and negligent response and with lesbians' and gay men's fear and swelling grief and anger. Feelings of anger could no longer be channeled so easily into an internally oriented pride about the gay community's extraordinary response or into noble stoicism in the face of death.

With illness and death swirling all around them, and facing vicious attacks from politicians, pundits, and the media, more and more queer folks were now personally confronting the AIDS crisis. The illnesses, deaths, repressive legislation, and climate of hostility toward queers could no longer be assessed as abstract phenomena. Many experienced a growing sense that their everyday routines—and, for ever-increasing numbers, their very lives—were imperiled. In 1985, AIDS activist Cindy Patton remarked on her own shifting understanding of AIDS, on her own growing awareness that the AIDS crisis was closing in on her. Remembering her reaction to the first reports of the mysterious diseases affecting gay men in Los Angeles, she wrote, "I don't recall having felt any personal connection to those six dead gay men on the other coast." She continued, "I did not know for over a year that while I pondered this abstraction, a close friend was becoming increasingly sick, and would ultimately be diagnosed with and die of AIDS. This experience of discovering information and then confronting its real life manifestation would be repeated for me at ever shortening intervals, and come increasingly closer to home" (1985, 5).

The crisis facing queer folks by the middle of 1986 was now acutely *felt*, by which I mean that people were living the crisis on an affective level, viscerally, in their bodies, whether infected with HIV or not. Intense dread, piercing grief, utter frustration, anxiety about the future, intensifying anger. These viscerally felt affective states, an emergent structure of feelings (Williams 1977), posed a challenge to the community's prevailing emotional habitus. Those bodily intensities and the new interpretations of the AIDS crisis derived from and buttressed one another.

Hardwick accelerated and amplified all of these emotional and interpretive transformations and helped to blow open the political horizon, creating a space for the emergence of defiant and oppositional AIDS activism. Feeling increasingly besieged, lesbians' and gay men's faith in the government and internally oriented pride transformed into disillusionment with the workings of democracy, a sense of entitlement betrayed, and anger. Following Gamson (1992), Jasper argues that "inchoate anxieties and fears must be transformed into moral indignation and outrage toward concrete policies and decisionmakers. Activists must weave together a moral, cognitive, and emotional package of attitudes" (1998, 409–10). That framing work—transforming unstructured affective states into legible emotions and interpretations—operated on fertile emotional and political ground after *Hardwick*.

Direct-action AIDS activists simply needed to echo and build on what other lesbians and gay men already were feeling and saying. Tapping into and simultaneously reinforcing the feelings of many queer folks, AIDS activists asserted that AIDS was genocide—a worsening medical and political holocaust caused by institutionalized homophobia, racism, and sexism; that the government and scientific-medical establishment would continue to treat "faggots" (and "junkies") as expendable and to be unresponsive to lobbying and other routine political efforts; that the costs

of "staying the course"—more deaths and increasing state repression—
were unacceptably high; that there was thus an urgent need for confrontational, collective action. Addressing people's growing despair about
the epidemic itself and about the government's unresponsiveness, activists suggested that there was nothing to lose by turning to the streets,
and indeed everything to gain. They thereby channeled a potentially demobilizing despair into action. "SILENCE = DEATH" was the much publicized call to arms. Insofar as activists were reflecting and bolstering
emergent interpretations of the AIDS crisis and new sentiments about
gay selves and about dominant society, it is no surprise that thousands
responded, no longer restrained by gay shame and corollary fears of social rejection, and evidently no longer willing or able to submerge their
indignation and anger. In the new, post-*Hardwick* emotional and political context, many came to see engagement in confrontational collective
action as imperative, and ACT UP became the organizational space for
that sort of angry militancy.

PART II
Activism as World-Making

Something that struck me during my research when I looked over my calendars from 1989 to 1995 was how many ACT UP meetings I attended on a weekly basis. There were times when I went to five meetings a week: a general membership meeting, a women's caucus meeting, a steering committee meeting, a meeting of those of us who were working on an upcoming action, and a subcommittee meeting for those working on a particular aspect of the upcoming action. I was not alone; attending as many as seven ACT UP meetings per week was typical for many members.[1] Then there were the actions themselves, the fund-raisers and benefits at various queer venues, the leafleting on street corners and in the bars, the posting of our latest agit-prop. A sense of urgency about the AIDS epidemic and about the need to save lives motivated this insistent pace, but other forces help to explain why we all put in so many hours and kept coming back week after week, for years.

The following two chapters address the question of movement sustainability.[2] That question, infrequently raised in studies of social movements, should intrigue scholars, particularly those who employ even a

1. Sarah Schulman, a cofounder of the ACT UP Oral History Project, arrived at the same conclusion after interviewing dozens of ACT UP/NY members (Schulman, April 14, 2005, program at New York University, "Read My Lips: Research and the ACT UP Oral History Project").
2. Both chapters draw from Gould 2002.

soft assumption of rational actors, since they might want to investigate why people continue to participate when they could easily take that proverbial "free ride" and reap the benefits of others' work. A few scholars who have explored the question of sustainability dispute the assumptions that underlie the free-rider problem—that people are autonomous and individualized utility-maximizers—and emphasize the importance of such factors as collective identity formation and activist culture and communities (see Rupp and Taylor 1987; Taylor 1989; Taylor and Whittier 1992; Whittier 1995). Their findings provide a sturdy base for the following two chapters, which argue for the vital role that emotion and emotional processes play in sustaining social movements. Factors like a collective identity or an activist community help to sustain movements principally because of the strong feelings that imbue and are evoked by such factors. To enhance our understanding of movement sustainability, then, we need to explore the generation of affects, emotions, and emotional habitus within movements and analyze how those processes shape attitudes about what is to be done politically.

Chapters 3 and 4 analyze social movements as sites of collective world-making, that is, as spaces in which the ongoing interactions of participants continually produce sentiments, ideas, values, and practices that manifest and encourage new modes of being. Movements are able to sustain themselves in part because, as projects in world-making, they are compelling to participants and prospective participants hungry to construct alternative worlds. Organized with the goal of bringing about other realities, movements often counter the common sense, the habits of feeling and emoting, and the ways of living that prevail in a given time and place.

ACT UP certainly did. From its start and throughout its life, ACT UP was a place to fight the AIDS crisis, and it was always more than that as well. It was a place to elaborate critiques of the status quo, to imagine alternative worlds, to express anger, to defy authority, to form sexual and other intimacies, to practice non-hierarchical governance and self-determination, to argue with one another, to refashion identities, to experience new feelings, to be changed.

The following two chapters explore what it felt like to be in the midst of that sort of world-making project within the collectivity of the direct-action AIDS movement. In chapter 3, I focus on the erotics of ACT UP, on its humor and playfulness and the sheer fun that participation in the movement often provided, and on the intensities of direct-action AIDS activism. In chapter 4, I continue the discussion of world-making with a focus on how ACT UP challenged the emotional habitus and the attendant political horizon that had until recently prevailed in lesbian and gay communities. My claim is that the feeling states, experiences, and qualities of ACT UP that I discuss helped to sustain participants' involvement and thus the movement.

It might be tempting to read the next two chapters as nostalgia, as an overly emotional (that is, sentimental) imagining of a better, more meaningful past. I have at times longed for this past—and why not?!—but my interest here, in addition to providing a history of ACT UP, is to plumb that history with an eye toward opening imaginative possibilities for the present. Regardless of whether the past was better or not, there certainly is room for improvement in the present. Social movements, as projects in world-making, offer insights that are easily forgotten in periods when social transformation seems impossible, at best distant. My intention here, then, is not only to provide an analysis that helps us to understand the affective dimensions of activism that help movements to grow and sustain themselves, but also to remind us about the pleasures and intensities of activism, even amid horrific conditions, and thereby to impress upon us that there is nothing inevitable or immutable about a given state of affairs.

CHAPTER THREE

The Pleasures and Intensities of Activism; or, Making a Place for Yourself in the Universe

What was it like to be in ACT UP, to protest in the streets demanding a response to the AIDS crisis, to participate in the construction of new identities and new ways of being? In this chapter I explore the strong sentiments that ACT UP participants felt amid the action, toward one another as well as about the significance of their activism, concentrating specifically on the pleasures and intensities generated through participation in a protest movement.

Before beginning, though, I want to note one difficulty in describing how it felt to be in ACT UP. For analytical purposes I break apart and analyze different aspects of what many of us experienced as a whole phenomenon. We did not necessarily experience a separation between, for example, the political intensities of ACT UP and its erotically charged atmosphere, or between our protest actions and the caretaking networks that we set up when members got sick. Lives are often lived in that sort of uncompartmentalized way, and perhaps even more so when lived at such a high level of intensity. With that in mind, and in order to address the damage that results from the sort of analytical separation presented in this chapter, in the first section I provide a general overview of how participants experienced ACT UP. I interpret participants' quotations only minimally and allow the complexity and multiplicity of their experiences to remain intact. Then, in the sections that follow, I analyze the role that ACT UP's erotic atmosphere, its campy humor, and the intensities of street-based AIDS activism played in the development and growth of the movement.

ACT UP, Circa 1987–1990

Because they provide excellent insight into the character and feel of the movement, I begin with quotations from a number of ACT UP participants describing meetings, protests, and other activities. Most of them come from retrospective interviews, but comments and reflections that were recorded or written amid the action sound similar, suggesting that the passage of time has not greatly distorted people's memories. Each is specific to one person's experience and in that sense is singular, but the affective energy that suffuses all of them indicates the shared dimensions of experiences in the movement. Indeed, across dozens of interviewees there is a remarkable consistency in people's positive memories of what ACT UP meetings and events felt like.

That is not to say that participants' experiences were all the same or that there were no bad feelings in the movement. Indeed, while some experienced ACT UP as a home, others felt like outsiders. In fact, after conducting dozens of interviews of ACT UP/New York members, Sarah Schulman, ACT UP/NY member and cofounder of the ACT UP Oral History Project, joked that 99 percent of ACT UP/NY felt left out.[1] The actual interviews do not bear that out, but several people do note their feelings of exclusion, and Schulman's statement serves as a reminder that ACT UP had in-crowds and cliques, and participants often had different experiences even while they shared others. Feelings of being an outsider were evident in some of my interviews as well, and cultural theorist Ann Cvetkovich found something similar when she interviewed lesbians from ACT UP/NY: "The powerful sense of belonging that some people found is . . . matched by the ambivalence of others" (Cvetkovich 2003a, 174; see also 179–80). It may be that in any situation of intense affilia-

1. The ACT UP Oral History Project "is a collection of interviews with surviving members of the AIDS Coalition to Unleash Power, New York. The project is coordinated by Jim Hubbard and Sarah Schulman, with camera work by James Wentzy (in New York) and S. Leo Chiang (on the West Coast). The purpose of this project is to present comprehensive, complex, human, collective, and individual pictures of the people who have made up ACT UP/New York" (http://www.actuporalhistory.org/about/index.html; accessed December 29, 2006). Schulman made this comment at a program at New York University, "Read My Lips: Research and the ACT UP Oral History Project" on April 14, 2005.

tion, individuals oscillate between a sense of belonging and feelings of alienation.[2] As well, many ACT UP chapters experienced painful internal conflicts in their later years (I explore those conflicts in chapter 6).

Nevertheless, almost all of the interviews I have conducted and read show remarkable similarity in people's descriptions of what it felt like to participate in ACT UP; interviewees repeatedly speak of the exhilaration of protest actions and meetings, the erotic atmosphere of meetings, feelings of camaraderie and connection with others in the movement, and a sense of fulfillment that derived from engaging in meaningful activities and taking part in something larger than oneself. In their repetition, the quotations provide a strong sense of how numerous participants—spanning racial and gender identifications, HIV status, age—experienced ACT UP.

To Jeff Edwards, ACT UP/Chicago meetings were "electric": "There were so many energetic and smart people doing so many things. . . . So much was happening in that room. There was so much passion, and imagination, and urgency" (Edwards 2000a). Kendall Thomas also used the metaphor of electricity to describe his first ACT UP/NY meeting, a metaphor that speaks to the affective charge of ACT UP: "It was just electrifying. The apparent democratic character of the gatherings, the apparent commitment to an egalitarian ethic in which who you were or what you were was secondary to the passion and strength of your commitment while you were there in that room or in a committee meeting. The sexiness of it, the libidinal energy was palpable, alongside the real anger" (Thomas 2002).[3] ACT UP/NY member Maxine Wolfe pointed to the "combination of serious politics and joyful living" as one of ACT UP's greatest qualities, something that she thought not only distinguished ACT UP from many left movements but that helped to sustain ACT UP as well.

> People would party really hard. We would go and do actions where we really put our bodies on the line, and then we'd go out and party all night. . . . If you don't have a community, if you don't have a way of being, of people that you can be with, who make you feel good about who you are, about what you're doing, as you're doing that stuff, you're not going to stay in it. You can't. It just becomes a drudge. And, I think that was one of the things that was amaz-

2. Thank you to Mary Patten who helped me to articulate it this way.

3. Thomas' use of the word *apparent* here is significant, indicating some of the critique that Thomas eventually developed of ACT UP/NY. I return to that in chapter 6.

ing about ACT UP. . . . We could have big parties at big venues, and people would come and dance their heads off, and then the next day, go out and get arrested. That combination is what you need, in order to continue. You need some life. (Wolfe 2004, 111–12)

Many participants look back on their years in the movement as a period when the multiple aspects of their lives were integrated, with ACT UP as the unifying force. Lei Chou's comments about the multiple ACT UP/NY meetings he attended every week were echoed by many others: "That was my whole life. Every night there was something going on." When asked what it was like "to live in ACT UP," Chou replied, "Well, you know, everybody in your phone book is somebody in ACT UP. When you go out to eat with friends, everybody at a table is from ACT UP. When you go out to bars, you see the other people from ACT UP" (Chou 2003, 24–25).

The following quotation from ACT UP/NY member Gregg Bordowitz conveys how enthralling and absorbing ACT UP was for him and for many of us:

ACT UP was everything. ACT UP was home. ACT UP was part of a supportive climate. It was a place to find sex. It was a place to have discussions. [To] form friendships which are still dear to me. I mean, it was just everything. It was all that it could possibly be. [ACT UP/NY] was huge. The meetings were just packed. You had to touch a hundred bodies to get across the room, it was a very erotically charged place to be. And that was part of it. I was into it. I was into that kind of politics. I had *heard* about revolutionary joy, but here was my time to experience it. I just loved it. . . . It was life-saving. It was a place to go to get support. It was a place to put all of my energies into. . . . ACT UP provided the possibility of not being alone. It was life-affirming. And yeah, it was everything. It was my world. . . . I went to an ACT UP meeting every night at some point, which was kind of a little bit crazy, but I needed to put my energy somewhere. . . . There were a lot of people who were throwing all of their energy [into ACT UP], like nothing else mattered. I don't remember anything else from that period. I was working full time. And I was in school. I dropped out of school—a college degree, anything for the future didn't seem necessary. I don't remember anything except going to meetings and actions during that time. (Bordowitz 2002a; emphasis his)

People *lived* ACT UP, and one reason was that the movement gave many people a sense of belonging, perhaps for the first time. David Barr walked into his first ACT UP/NY meeting in May 1987 and said to himself, "Oh my God, I'm home. . . . I had been waiting for this. I liked the energy in the room and I liked the approach. . . . It was really sexy. There were all these really cute guys and they were interesting and they were political and I had just never seen [anything like] it before. I thought, 'Finally, I've been looking for this all my life.' I really felt like I was home" (Barr 2002).

Charles King recalls being moved, bodily, at his first ACT UP/NY meeting: "Standing in the back of a packed room at the Gay and Lesbian Community Center, I found myself heaving dry sobs, hoping no one could see my visceral reaction. At last there was something I could do. I could fight back. And even if we didn't win, I wouldn't be going down alone" (King 2007). Moisés Agosto characterized his first ACT UP/NY meeting as "like a religious experience" in the sense that he had tested HIV-positive a few years earlier, had had almost no one with whom to discuss AIDS, and then he walked into a room with "a bunch of fired-up people" who "really wanted to make a difference, really fighting for their lives, literally," people to whom Agosto felt he could relate (Agosto 2002, 7).

ACT UP was an emotionally enticing place. Although ACT UP/NY member Allan Robinson was critical of the racism he encountered in ACT UP, he found that "an energy in the room" made him go back, "again and again" (Hunter 1993, 59). He recalled, "Outside of all my criticism, I found an energy in the organization that was frankly exciting. That energy helped me deal with the loss, anger, and the frustration with societal indifference I was encountering. I think that, in retrospect, ACT UP has satisfied that need for many people. So many people need that kind of conduit to deal with those feelings" (Hunter 1993, 60). As I discuss in the next chapter, ACT UP was a place that normalized and thereby authorized anger, that allowed people to shelve their grief for a period and instead "turn grief into anger," a place that generated pride in queerness and in defiant street activism.

Jim Eigo attended his first ACT UP/NY meeting by mistake but was so taken by it that he stayed.

> I went to the Gay and Lesbian Community Services Center in November of 1987. . . . I went there thinking I was going to a forum that Lambda Legal Defense was presenting on what we should do in the wake of the *Bowers v. Hardwick* decision. . . . This would have been about fifteen months after the deci-

sion, and yet Lambda was having a forum on it, and it was going to be on the second floor of the Community Services Center. But I thought it was on the first floor. So, I sat down in an ACT UP meeting, and I very quickly knew that this was not Lambda. It was the most vital political meeting—even before the meeting started—the most vital group of people I'd ever sat among in my life. The table by the entry was full of literature that everybody was producing themselves and had out. And there was a buzz everywhere. And then when the meeting started—and it was quite clear that unlike any political meeting I had ever been to in my life that this was really, actually being run by the people, from the floor, for themselves, for those concerns that were central to their lives at this time—it just blew me away. I knew right away that it was a group that I had to become involved with immediately. (Eigo 2004, 18–19)

After that first accidental meeting, Eigo did not miss a general meeting for "a few years," and then only because he was out of town on ACT UP business (Eigo 2002, 179).

Marion Banzhaf also experienced ACT UP/NY meetings as deeply compelling. Prior to participating in ACT UP, Banzhaf had engaged in various feminist and left movements, including international solidarity organizations. ACT UP meetings felt different to her primarily because people literally were fighting for their lives.

You can't get much more vibrant and immediate than people who are facing life-and-death situations. . . . In the international solidarity work I had done, I didn't actually ever go to any of the countries I did international solidarity work for. I didn't go to Zimbabwe, I didn't go to Namibia, I didn't go to Palestine. I still believed that those were life-and-death situations, but I wasn't experiencing it myself, so I think that was really what kept me [coming to ACT UP]. It was just so raw and immediate. People would report that so and so who had been to the meeting last week had died the following week. People would cry. People would scream. People would really respond and get angry and all, the whole gamut of emotions, and people were determined to work together to try to change this. (Banzhaf 2002)

Interviewed in 1990, ACT UP/San Francisco member Michael Shriver similarly indicated how important it was to be up close with AIDS and death. "We intimately understand the epidemic because it is sitting next to us at a meeting" (quoted in Whiting 1990).

ACT UP/Chicago member Jeanne Kracher noted that the immedi-

acy of the AIDS crisis for herself and her intimates gave AIDS activism a different feel than the anti-imperialist activism with which she
was familiar from years of doing international solidarity work. Kracher
had participated in actions that, for example, shut down the South African consulate on International Women's Day in protest of the treatment
of South African women living under apartheid. She continued to support that work, but she noted a difference, at the level of affect, between
work on behalf of people whom she did not really know and AIDS activism that was driven by the needs of her friends and her community.
The AIDS crisis, she noted, "was about me. And it was about people
who I [knew and] cared about." And, she added, it was about the lesbian and gay community. "It was about [homophobes] saying that lesbians and gays are bad because they're spreading this disease. . . . I think it
was about homophobia. . . . It was all about essentially how we were a pa-
riah in the world. . . . And so it was about me. I think I felt I owned it, the
issue, on some level" (Kracher 2000).

Like others, Billy McMillan was moved by the sense that people in
ACT UP/Chicago were in solidarity with one another, united in common cause: "I thrived on the camaraderie and needed it very much during that period of my life. People in ACT UP validated my feelings that
something was very wrong with the way things were. Our government
and society had failed us. I felt empowered that there were other gays and
lesbians who, like myself, . . . believed that we had to take matters into
our own hands to help our community." Being with others who shared
his views about the crisis and the need to address it with direct action
filled McMillan with hope: "I felt a sense of connection to the people I
was working with, and I felt that we were going to create change, that we
were really going to change the world. And, being involved in ACT UP
made me feel like I wasn't going to die yet." (McMillan 2000).

That sense of optimism, shared by many in the movement, was corroborated by the respect and praise that ACT UP quickly garnered from
people in the scientific-medical establishment, from pundits, and from the
media, which I discuss in chapter 5. Here I simply want to note the powerful effects that such mainstream recognition had on many in the movement who, as queers, were more than accustomed to being unaccepted,
unseen, unrecognized. Consider the following comment by ACT UP/NY
member Larry Kramer, quoted in a *New York Times* article that covered
an ACT UP member's disruption of Governor Mario Cuomo's State
of the State address in January 1990. Requesting that the sergeant-at-

arms stop dragging the protestor, G'dali Braverman, away, Cuomo paused to allow Braverman to speak. After responding with a defense of New York's AIDS policies, Cuomo became solemn and declared: "You can argue with [the protester's] timing and his taste. You cannot argue with his sincerity." The *New York Times* then quoted Larry Kramer, who had been watching the speech on TV. "I burst into tears when I saw it. It's just so moving to be taken seriously, to see Cuomo actually let the guy speak" (Sack 1990). ACT UP was a movement that empowered its participants, many of whom for the first time experienced what it was like "to be taken seriously" as openly gay people asking something of state and society, to be heard and even respected.

ACT UP's radicalism—in the realms of sex, tactics, critique, and vision—was vitally important to the movement's meteoric rise and flourishing. As I argued in chapter 2, in the wake of *Hardwick,* queer folks embraced a militancy that the mainstream lesbian and gay movement had rejected in the early 1970s. *Hardwick* opened a new emotional-political imaginative space, and ACT UP emerged within that space; as stated at the start of every ACT UP general meeting, we were united in anger and committed to direct action to end the AIDS crisis. ACT UP leveled a powerful critique against the state and its dominant institutions and ushered in alternative modes of feeling, thinking, and being for many lesbians and gay men, many of whom began to identify as queer. ACT UP's radical potential is part of what attracted Kendall Thomas to the movement. "I was invested in the idea of helping to create a queer public sphere that wasn't about civil rights, but rather was about freedom, which is larger and more audacious and bolder than a simple demand for civil rights. And ACT UP seemed to be an organizational framework for that kind of politics" (Thomas 2002). Many participants were drawn to ACT UP because it allowed, indeed encouraged, people to be angry at state and society, to embrace confrontational tactics, to be in-your-face queer. Even more, to be in a room overflowing with politically like-minded individuals, with people who shared your sense of political possibility, generated feelings of camaraderie and a strong sense of belonging.

Another aspect of ACT UP that participants frequently mentioned in their interviews and that drew many to the movement was its democratic character. As indicated in quotations above, both Kendall Thomas and Jim Eigo initially were struck by the democratic ethos within the movement. Other participants were as well. Contrasting ACT UP/NY to other political groups she had been in, Marion Banzhaf recalled ACT UP as "very exciting, because this was a different kind of group. It was not a top-down group, it was a bottom-up group, even though there were hierarchies within ACT UP about who was cool and who got to cruise whom and who got to do what. It was still a very democratic group" (Banzhaf 2000). Jeanne Kracher made a similar comparison regarding ACT UP/Chicago. "Compared to anything else I had been involved with, [ACT UP/Chicago meetings] were extremely democratic. In retrospect, I don't know how democratic they were, probably not as much as I would like to fantasize or romanticize that they were. But [in contrast to] the way certain groups are run, [in ACT UP] people got the chance to speak" (Kracher 2000). Jeff Edwards concurred, describing ACT UP/Chicago meetings as having an "egalitarian feel" to them: "Certainly some people had more power than others, but anybody could walk in and conceivably get a project going" (Edwards 2000a).

ACT UP/Chicago member Ferd Eggan described an instance when these democratic principles manifested themselves at a precarious moment during a national demonstration in Chicago. Because of its large size and ACT UP's militancy, the demonstration had flowed into the street by that point, but police officers on horses were blocking our way.

> We were surrounded by all the horses and everything. And so I got on the mike and just asked people whether they wanted to fight through the horses and take the streets, or not. . . . And we actually voted in the middle of the street that we would just take the street. . . . People decided that they would just fight through the horses and go take the street. And then we did. And I think that was my favorite moment, really, because it was like people deciding what to do, *en masse,* right in the middle of this demonstration. (Eggan 1999)

I remember the exhilaration of that moment as well—more than a thousand activists collectively deliberating in the street and ultimately deciding to push our way through the phalanx of cops and horses. The sense of freedom generated through defiant and collective self-determination was thrilling. We had a tactical leadership team for every protest action, the members of which rotated from action to action, but they were never authorized to control the demonstration or its participants; their job was to be attuned to all facets of the demonstration, to facilitate decision-making on the spot if necessary, to assist affinity groups if asked, and more generally to ensure that the action went off smoothly. As a movement, ACT UP was committed to democratic practices in meetings and during actions, and that enactment of a participatory form of decision-making was exciting in part because collective self-rule is generally absent from most of our lives. Remarking on her interviewees' enthusiasm about ACT UP/NY's democratic, fast-paced, and action-oriented meetings, Cvetkovich suggests that participants were taken by "the utopian sense of the possibility of a collective" (Cvetkovich 2003a, 184).

As a collectivity, ACT UP participants shared many values, but the movement fended off groupthink more or less successfully with its caucus and affinity group structure—a facet of the movement that contributed greatly to ACT UP's non-hierarchical, decentralized, and democratic character and that participants found particularly compelling. Caucuses of women, people of color, and people with immune-system disorders (PISD) provided a degree of autonomy to those underrepresented groups and allowed differences of identity to flourish, at least initially, within the collectivity of ACT UP. Self-organized affinity groups of people who wanted to engage in civil disobedience or direct action together similarly operated relatively autonomously from the larger group. They had great latitude in designing actions and projecting messages. In a given action, one group might block the door to a building, another might scale the building to hang a banner, another might block traffic with street theater, while another might take over an office inside the building. This cellular, self-organizing structure engendered creative, exciting, and mediagenic demonstrations, but more than that, it allowed for multiplicity within the movement—in terms of priorities, tactics, demeanor, and identity. Gregg Bordowitz favored this decentralized model of activism in part because it allowed "affinity groups [to] do anything they wanted," although of course "within parameters" such as adhering to principles of nonviolence. "ACT UP [New York] was not one monolithic institution. It was a group of people who met every Monday night. Many of them were parts of smaller groups, or cells, or affinity groups within the larger group. And those affinity groups to some extent had, if not a separate life, a life outside the group. So it was much more molecular in structure" (Bordowitz 2002b, 26, 29).

Affinity groups often stayed together for years, and strong bonds of affection developed among members. Jim Eigo recalled a member from his affinity group, Wave 3, becoming ill and the other Wave 3 members becoming that person's support system. "We were there at the hospital the whole time. And the months that he was at the hospital, we pretty much transfigured the AIDS ward over at Beth Israel, and all the doctors, after being pretty wary of us at the beginning, came to like us. . . . We were virtually the support system for Brian, who was estranged from his family" (Eigo 2004, 52). Eigo noted that those sorts of affinity group activities, along with small social gatherings of affinity group members, created "close-knit communities within communities" and tremendous feelings of trust and solidarity.

> They really mortar a group together. And when you're getting arrested, there might be a few people who are out there, who are gung-ho about getting arrested and really have no fear, but I was never arrested when I didn't have fear. . . . If an affinity group did something that put your bodies on the line, . . . I'll speak, at least for myself, my fear level was always very high, and I don't know if I could have done it without a group of people [with whom] I felt close. . . . Some of them were people I was as close to as any people I've been to, in my life. So, those, in some ways, were the little cells within ACT UP. And, I think, many people within ACT UP could tell you similar stories about the affinity groups, the special caucuses, the committees, the subcommittees that they worked in, within ACT UP. (53)

FIGURE 5. A PISD Caucus affinity group action at a national ACT UP demonstration in Chicago, April 23, 1990. Photo by Rex Wockner.

Indeed, from Eigo's perspective, affinity groups and caucuses were the crucial glue holding ACT UP together: "The only way you could get four hundred people coming together weekly—and at our height, we could draw on about fifteen hundred people coming to our biggest demonstration—the only way you could do that, I think, is if there were these small, hyper-active groups of people who felt really close to each other" (53–54).

These quotations, largely unadorned, provide a sense of how participants experienced ACT UP. The content of these quotations and of others below, especially their repetition of similar sentiments, forcefully attests to the important role that feelings played in spurring and sustaining participation in the movement. They show that ACT UP, filled with people fighting for their lives and their community, was emotionally intense: participants felt a strong sense of urgency and solidarity, meetings were heady and affectively rousing, the movement enticed through its sexual and creative atmosphere. Itself a project in world-making, participation in ACT UP was life-affirming and engendered optimism that activists might be able to stop the AIDS crisis and save lives. The quotations themselves, saturated with these sentiments, provide some explanation for why queer folks flocked to ACT UP and remained into the 1990s. In what follows, I extend this analysis of the affective dimensions of ACT UP, first considering how ACT UP's sexual culture helped the movement develop and flourish.

ACT UP's Erotics

Participants consistently remark on ACT UP's vibrant sexual atmosphere, suggesting that its erotic climate played a powerful role in attracting people and sustaining their participation.[4] Ferd Eggan described ACT UP meetings as filled with "a lot of sexual feeling and validation," observing that the movement provided "an opening for a lot of people, of possibilities, and a lot of people took advantage of them" (Eggan 1999). Marion Banzhaf recalled, "It was a time that I was exploring non-

4. In terms of movement sustainability, it is important that ACT UP itself was a sexualized space. See Goodwin 1997 for an account that illustrates how sexual and affectual ties between movement members and those outside the movement led to "libidinal withdrawal" from the group and contributed to the *disintegration* of the Huk movement in the Philippines. I found no evidence that that played a role in ACT UP's decline.

monogamy for myself in a different way than I had ever done. . . . I had more queer sex in ACT UP than I had had in my whole life" (Banzhaf 2002). Karl Soehnlein of ACT UP/NY recalled having sex "with dozens and dozens of guys in ACT UP." In a challenge to negative ideas about promiscuity, and reflecting ACT UP's sex-radical ethos, Soehnlein described himself during this period as "really promiscuous, in a really exciting, great way" (Soehnlein 2003, 28). ACT UP/Chicago member Michael Thompson described Chicago's meetings as "really sexy," adding, "there were just a lot of hormones [in the air] at all times." He was particularly taken with the sexual expressiveness of lesbians in ACT UP: "To be around lesbians who were also being sexy was really cool. Because that [intermixing of men and women] is not something that generally happens in the queer world. It was generally segregated" (Thompson 2000).

Polly Thistlethwaite fondly remembered ACT UP/NY's meetings at the Gay and Lesbian Community Center in Greenwich Village: people sat in each other's laps, brushed up against one another, and cruised each other (Thistlethwaite 1993). In 1988, ACT UP/NY member Maria Maggenti described the sexual feel of the meetings and the effect it was having on her: "I [leave] the meetings feeling incredibly sexy. . . . [F]eeling sexy, feeling beautiful, makes you feel very much alive. . . . It's the most subversive way anyone could respond to this crisis" (France 1988, 36). Jeff Edwards remembered ACT UP/Chicago meetings as occurring in a "very sexually charged environment." He noted in particular the effect that the positive sexual atmosphere had in countering earlier discourses that had made gay men ashamed of their sexual desires and practices, and afraid to have sex: "That was great, I think especially because . . . I was listening to people having discussions in the mid-'80s saying, 'You can't kiss anybody.' [In ACT UP] there was an opening up of a greater sexual freedom again" (Edwards 2000a). Edwards credited ACT UP with helping him and other gay men to "push ourselves beyond" a "cloudy period" that had prevailed during the first years of the epidemic. "The whole issue about shame and isolation and the anti-sex stuff. I really think that we brought something back, about being open about being sexual beings and having fun. I think ACT UP made that happen" (Edwards 2000a). Jim Eigo similarly noted that ACT UP/NY "was in some ways almost the first place that you could celebrate sexuality, after AIDS hit" (Eigo 2004, 56). He credits ACT UP/NY's erotic atmosphere with the meteoric rise of the movement: "One reason ACT UP took off so quickly was be-

cause its weekly meeting was the sexiest space in the city for a gay guy
to be on a Monday night. Urban gay men had seen their community sex
spaces erode in the age of AIDS. ACT UP would be a first stand in reclaiming that space, in asserting our right to it" (Eigo 2002,184). A statement from ACT UP/NY member David Robinson in 1988 supports Eigo's claim: "On Monday nights, the place to be is at one of our meetings"
(France 1988, 36). Noting that an ACT UP activist played a role model
for a confused young man in the 1990 porn film *More of a Man*, political
scientist Dennis Altman argued that this indicated that "the gay/AIDS
politics of the current period has now been integrated into sexual fanta-
sies in a quite remarkable way: 'the activist' now becomes defined as an
object of desire, thus legitimating political activity at the level of the li-
bido" (Altman 1994, 91). ACT UP's erotic atmosphere made its politics
sexy too.

Given the prevailing climate of sexual fear in the late 1980s—in both
gay and straight worlds—ACT UP's celebration of queer sexuality was
a political act. Indeed, many ACT UP members experienced their bodies as the battleground on which the AIDS war was being fought, both
in terms of HIV and its related illnesses, and in terms of sexual freedom.
Jeanne Kracher saw ACT UP's sexual culture as a form of resistance to
dominant society's efforts to "shut us down sexually" (Kracher 2000).
Maria Maggenti viewed ACT UP's sexual politics similarly:

> Here are all these people who are coping with an illness that is transmitted
> sexually. So, to be sexual in defiance of that, happily sexual, using condoms
> or other forms of safe sex, was extremely bold. And, it was especially bold to
> say that you were still going to have sex and fuck and be a cocksucker and all
> these things, when there was so much shame attached to the fact that this dis-
> ease was sexually transmitted. (Maggenti 2003, 52)

ACT UP recuperated queer sexuality in part by creating a new venue
where sex and activism were thoroughly joined. B. C. Craig, a lesbian
who was a member of both ACT UP/NY and ACT UP/Boston, pointed
to this connection: "Especially in a time when gay bars and baths had
such a bad reputation because of the scare of AIDS, ACT UP was a place
that you could go and be sexy and sociable and still feel like you were
dealing with the crisis instead of denying it. And so, ACT UP has always
had a real history of a lot of sexual dynamics going on" (Quoted in Cohen 1998, 138). Karl Soehnlein noted that his erotic desires helped to ani-

mate and sustain his involvement in ACT UP/NY. At the very first meeting he attended, in June 1987, a man stood up and asked for volunteers for a task related to the upcoming Gay Pride Parade. Soehnlein recalled:

> And he's blonde and hunky and muscle-y, and I was like, "I'll sign up! You're sexy." And that was part of [the excitement], too. It was sexy. I was 21 and surrounded by all these men who were so attractive to me, and that was part of it, absolutely, that was part of it . . . for many of us who were involved in ACT UP, who were in our early 20s. It was this sexy place to go. You didn't have to always go to clubs and bars. We would go to an ACT UP meeting, do something important, be part of that, but also get this kind of jones off the whole thing. (Soehnlein 2003, 7)

Sex and politics went hand in hand in ACT UP, and this characteristic of the movement challenges standard dualisms that suggest that the presence of supposedly private phenomena like intimacies threatens the ostensible rationality of the political public sphere. Rather than impeding ACT UP's political activities, the sexual and social climate in many ways was, in Cvetkovich's words, a "foundation of the group's power" (2003a, 185), a force that invigorated many activists. Rather than posing a threat to group solidarity—here I recall Freud's arguments about group cohesion being threatened by non–aim-inhibited libidinal ties among some members (1959, esp. 92–97)—even dyadic sexual relations among ACT UP members seem to have bolstered participation in the movement, in part because ACT UP's self-identity entailed a celebration of queer sexual expression of all sorts. In line with the movement's ethos, having queer sex enacted, simultaneously, sexual desire for another individual as well as love for the group and its sex radicalism. When asked if the socializing within ACT UP ever distracted from the activism, ACT UP/NY member Trina Johnson replied,

> I would say that actually the passion fuels us, that passion and desire keep us going. We want to keep having sex, we want to keep being queer. . . . And seeing people we can fuck right in front of us almost makes you want to say, "This is really important, I want to live this way, I've got to be able to continue living, and so I've got to work on these issues." (Quoted in Cohen 1998, 143–44)

Having sex surely satisfied individuals' libidinal desires, but it also contributed to group cohesiveness. Jean Carlomusto noted the following about ACT UP/NY's sexiness: "It was a great part about being involved with ACT UP. The men were having sex with men, the women were having sex with women, men and women were having sex with each other.[5] It boiled down to the Emma Goldman saying, 'If I can't dance, I don't want your revolution.' If we can't fuck, what are we doing here?" (Carlomusto 2002, 23). For many of us, there was no distance between sex and politics: meetings were filled with flirtation, cruising, touching, and kissing, along with heady discussions with life-and-death stakes, discussions that themselves were sexy in their intensity. ACT UP's ethos made having queer sex, and lots of it, feel like a political act, and the close physical contact of our civil disobedience actions, along with our chants and propaganda and the ACT UP uniform itself—T-shirt, jeans, leather jacket, combat boots—sexualized ACT UP protests. There was an erotic charge to everything we did. Probably as a result, even meetings that went on for hours often felt electrifying rather than tedious. Participants recall how exciting it felt simply walking into the room just prior to the start of the meeting—people kissed and hugged hello—and that energy often continued after the meetings, as people hung around socializing and then went out for a late-night dinner. That continuous sexual energy drew people to the movement and helped to sustain our participation.

ACT UP's Humor

Along with its erotics, the movement was awash in campy humor, as well as sheer fun. Jeanne Kracher contrasted her experience in ACT UP to other social movements and suggested that ACT UP's humorous and joyful atmosphere, especially given a context where death was ever-present, played an important role in sustaining people's participation. "Given all the death and everything, we had an incredible amount of fun. And there was a lot of humor. The movement just had so much humor. . . . I think people could laugh at themselves. . . . And all the gay cultural stuff, from the dancing to the drag stuff to the sex stuff made it all a much more fun movement to be a part of" (Kracher 2000).

In the face of homophobia and other indignities, AIDS activists camped it up. At a national demonstration at the White House in June

5. Carlomusto's remark here refers to queer men and women having sex with *one another*. I discuss the sexual fluidity within ACT UP in the next chapter.

1987, activists sitting in the middle of the street chanted, "Your gloves don't match your shoes, you'll see it on the news!" as police wearing bright yellow rubber gloves moved in to arrest them, apparently warned that they otherwise might "catch" AIDS in the process. Gilbert Martínez, a founding member of the Latino Caucus of ACT UP/NY, recalls flirting with the police officer who arrested him at a demonstration targeting the NIH in 1990: "When I was arrested at NIH, this real hunky cop asked me if I wanted to walk or be carried. And I said, 'Are you kidding me? I would never walk and pass up the opportunity of being held in your arms'" (POZ 1997, 63). Activists sometimes even responded to death and grief with humor. Marion Banzhaf remembered a New York affinity group satirizing the frequent ACT UP chant "How many more must die?!" when it made a T-shirt that said, "Harmony Moore Must Die." It was an instance of "turning this expression about genocide and loss into an internal satire" that only ACT UP members would understand. In a climate of bigotry, antigay violence, illness, death, and unending if submerged grief, campy humor was a creative response that offered much-needed psychic relief and release. Humor was a way of making the pain that queers were suffering in this moment less painful. Banzhaf put it this way: "Even in the face of all the loss, we still had fun, and we needed to create fun in order to continue to deal with the loss, actually" (Banzhaf 2002). Writer and ACT UP/San Francisco member Benjamin Shepard concurs: "That was the beauty of ACT UP. The group offered an outlet for an otherwise horrendous situation. Sometimes it was through humor, style, and camp; sometimes it was through direct action" (Shepard 2002, 13).

ACT UP's direct action and protests frequently combined the serious with the humorous. In October 1989, ACT UP/Chicago unveiled its "Freedom Bed" (fig. 6) in downtown Chicago at a demonstration organized with an abortion rights organization, Emergency Clinic Defense Coalition (ECDC). The protest was for abortion rights and for comprehensive and free medical treatment for people with AIDS, both issues with high stakes. Activists performed safe-sex skits on the bed, with lots of rollicking about, sexiness, and occasional fighting off of intrusions from Supreme Court Justices, Jesse Helms, and local politicians who were anti-abortion, antigay, and standing in the way of the fight against AIDS. Photographs show the crowd of demonstrators laughing hysterically as those in the performance wrestled Chief Justice Rehnquist out of the bed. ACT UP's street theater often included scathing and comical sat-

FIGURE 6. ACT UP/Chicago members performing on the "freedom bed" at a demonstration for AIDS and abortion rights held by ACT UP/Chicago and the Emergency Clinic Defense Coalition, downtown Chicago, October 6, 1989. (Photographer unknown.)

ires of people we were targeting, along with lots of drag, sexual innuendo, and jokes.

Even ACT UP's "unsexy" and unglamorous actions often combined the sobering and the humorous. At a September 1991 demonstration in Madison, Wisconsin, to protest Governor Tommy Thompson's inaction in the face of the AIDS crisis in Wisconsin prisons, members of ACT UP staged a grim mock suffocation-by-towel in protest of the death of Donald Woods, smothered to death by prison guards allegedly attempting to prevent contracting HIV from Woods' saliva (Schmitz 1991).[6] More humorously, demonstrators also smeared peanut butter and jelly sandwiches on the walls of the state building and threw additional PBJ sandwiches at the governor's office in protest of the Department of Corrections' assertion that PBJ was a sufficient nutritional supplement for prisoners with AIDS.[7]

ACT UP participants sometimes injected queer sensibilities and hu-

6. It was known at that time that HIV could not be transmitted through contact with an HIV-positive person's saliva.

7. ACT UP's demands included investigations into the deaths of two people with AIDS in Wisconsin prisons, compassionate early release of terminally ill prisoners, adequate nu-

mor into the most unreceptive of places. At a national ACT UP action in April 1990 for universal health care, close to one hundred and
fifty AIDS activists from across the country were arrested in Chicago,
effectively overwhelming the city's jail system. Because there were not
enough jail cells for all of us, the police put everyone into a large room,
unsegregated by gender. We were euphoric from the protest action and
happy to be together, so there was a lot of animated discussion along
with hugging and kissing and general excitement. Our jubilant conversations quickly reached a high pitch, and the officer in charge tried to gain
control over the room by demanding that we cease kissing and that we sit
"girl-boy-girl-boy." His order was met with giggles as we all rearranged
ourselves like obedient school children (the gender queers among us ensured that we weren't *that* obedient). Then, at frequent intervals, ACT
UP/Chicago member Ortez Alderson stood up and reminded us all that
"there is to be noooooo same-sex kissing in the jail," and on cue we all
resumed kissing, boys with boys, girls with girls, girls with boys, gender
queers with all.

Those lighter parts of ACT UP were attractive even to people who
were more on the margins of the movement. Bill Snow, for example, always felt "somewhat out of place" in ACT UP/NY. He went to meetings
and stood in the back, mainly listening and watching the process, as well
as checking out the guys. "It wasn't my social life, it wasn't my social circle," Snow recalled, but he continued to attend meetings, in part because
he was HIV-positive and was seeking information, but also because "it
was fun. It was always exciting" (Snow 2003, 4, 13). ACT UP/NY member Larry Kramer credited the fun that people had in the movement with
helping to sustain ACT UP: "A great part of what keeps us together, besides our common goals, is that it's a lot of fun" (quoted in Solomon 1989,
121). Years later, Maria Maggenti concurred. After describing an ACT
UP road trip that included being refused service by motel managers who
did not want gay men with AIDS staying in their rooms, Maggenti described the wonderful time they had when they took a day off from activism and went to the beach:

> That to me was the glue that kept that group together. From the outside, it
> looked like everyone was always yelling, "Fuck you, government, and fuck

---

tritional supplements for people with AIDS, and provision of safe-sex information and
condoms to prisoners.

you _____," but in fact, the kind of behind-the-scenes of it was a lot of parties, a lot of drinking, a lot of eating, a lot of love affairs, and extraordinary friendships. That's what kept me in it for so long. It couldn't just have been "doing the right thing," although that was obviously a motivating factor, and a significant factor. That was also the glue. But it was also a lot of fun. (Quoted in Cvetkovich 2003a, 172)

ACT UP's Intensities

ACT UP was affectively intense, and that quality, inextricably intertwined with ACT UP's sexiness, humor, and fun, drew people to the movement and inspired them to return again and again.[8] Being surrounded by illness and death and collectively fighting the state and dominant social institutions on issues with life-and-death stakes filled our lives with meaning and purpose and generated immense feelings of connection and love toward one another. Gregg Bordowitz was exaggerating only slightly when he remarked, "everybody was in love with everybody."

> There was this intense sense of comradeship and closeness. We were all brought together and felt close because of the meaningfulness of the work, and the fact that people were dying, and people in the group were getting sick. It created this feeling, a heightened intensity. Emotions were very powerful within the group, and they were on the surface of the group. Often people would cry in meetings, or people would get enraged in meetings. It was intense that way. And also, that fuels Eros. That fueled attraction, people clung to each other, not necessarily in a desperate way, but people found comfort in each other. They enjoyed each other. It was very physical. (Bordowitz 2002b, 52)

Love drove and sustained our activism.

Artist and ACT UP/Chicago member Mary Patten has written about the intensity of life in ACT UP, highlighting the ways in which our activism and every other aspect of our lives were inseparably, and deliciously, entangled: "A friend remembers: 'Those were the days when we would

8. Collins 2004 discusses the attraction of situations that fill individuals with emotional energy.

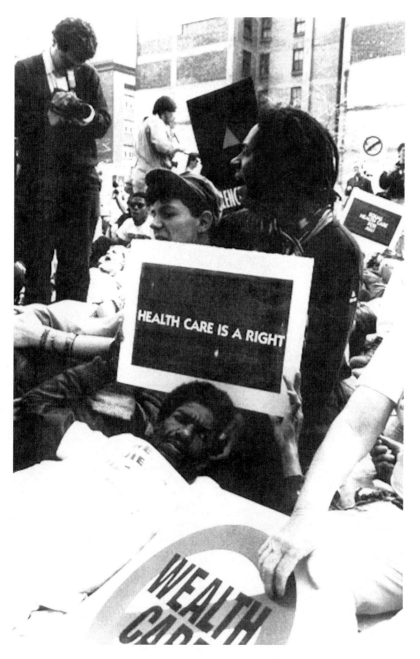

FIGURE 7. Die-in at national ACT UP demonstration in Chicago, April 23, 1990. Photo by Linda Miller.

go into Suzie B's (a since-closed dyke bar), and we knew everybody (and everyone knew us).' The connective tissue between our 'private' and our 'public' lives—between the ways we did political work and organizing, had sex, played, theorized, and mourned—was strong, elastic, sometimes barely noticeable" (Patten 1998, 389). Patten's friend is *me,* and I recall the loss I was feeling when I said that to her after ACT UP's decline. As Patten notes, our social, sexual, emotional, intellectual, and political lives were tightly interwoven. It bears repeating that ACT UP meetings were more than meetings; they were a place to fight AIDS, and they also were cruising grounds, a chance to channel one's grief and frustration and to revitalize feelings of anger and pride, a place to struggle, learn, and grow, an opportunity to enact newly emerging queer identities,[9] and a place to reimagine the world. Sexual liaisons were a chance to have sex, and also a way to learn more about safe sex as well as an opportunity to elaborate queer theory. Parties allowed us to dream up our next action and to mourn the most recent deaths. Creative demonstrations provided fodder for theorizing, while study groups reinvigorated our street activism. Every aspect of our lives connected to every other, and it all seemed vital. Engaged in world-making with like-minded people, we felt exuberant, joyous, engaged, connected to one another, sexy, and consequential. Ferd Eggan put it this way: "People reveled in that sense of accomplishment, sense of being together, sense of transgressing, being able to express sexuality in a bigger way than they had ever been able to before" (Eggan 1999). To be sure, there were conflicts within the movement, but for a number of years we addressed them in a manner that, for many members, maintained strong positive feelings and identification with the movement and with one another.

Maxine Wolfe described the feel of the early years in this way:

> [In] the beginning [there] was an incredible sense not just of empowerment but of connection, of collectivity. . . . On [ACT UP's] first year anniversary, we had a party at this little teeny club. . . . And you know at the end this guy Brad Ball . . . sang ["Getting To Know You."] People cried. Cried. I mean you know it was like finally having a group to do something about this epidemic, to be lesbian and gay in, to connect with on more than the isolated level that people had been dealing with in the lesbian and gay community

---

9. I discuss the rebirth of *queer* in the following chapter.

here for years. Okay. For years. . . . [T]hat was 1988 and you know people hadn't felt that connected since the early '70s. (Wolfe 1993)

ACT UP/NY member Vito Russo recalled people camping it up and singing Broadway tunes, Motown hits, and pop classics at that same first year anniversary party: "People were really celebrating their friendship. And I'll never forget, this quiet guy in glasses who never said much sat down at the piano and sang, 'I Got You Babe.' And said, 'I just want to tell you all how happy I am to be with you.' It was a group that had been strangers a year before" (quoted in Span 1989, D4).

ACT UP/Chicago member Carol Hayse recalled the strong sense of solidarity that developed between gay men and lesbians, the "joy in rediscovering each other" (Hayse 2000). ACT UP/Chicago's Frank Sieple also recalled the intense connection he felt with other members of ACT UP: "The camaraderie just can't be replaced. It's like going, I'd imagine, you know, people that go into some sort of battle together. . . . World War II, or something. And you're with these people and planning things, and going through these things. And some people die, you know, it's just like a war" (Sieple 1999). Karl Soehnlein came to think of ACT UP/NY as his "chosen family."

> I quickly understood that I was closer to these people than I was to my own family at that point. My family was kind of coming along, slowly, with dealing with having a gay son—and not only a gay son, but a gay son who was an activist. . . . Meanwhile, I was finding all of this closeness, like I had never known with any friends before, with my comrades in ACT UP. "Comrades" seems like a good word for it. . . . It became a family. They were the people I wanted to be with at holidays. . . . Yeah, you know, we did things families do. We broke bread and we supported each other and we fought. It was a family. (Soehnlein 2003, 16)

Moved by one another's courage and defiance, we also brought one another to tears. Gay novelist and ACT UP/NY member David Leavitt marked the aftermath of a demonstration in South Carolina to protest that state's AIDS policies—including a quarantine measure—as the moment that will stay with him the longest. After being bailed out of jail, ACT UP/NY members were in a motel room listening to radio coverage of their action. A native Carolinian who had participated in the protest was being interviewed. At the end of the interview, the reporter asked him if he wanted to say who he was. Leavitt wrote,

> He hesitated, explaining that coming out was something one had to do one step at a time; he paused; then he said his name and the town where he lived. The report ended with those words. . . . He'd spoken out, branded himself, gone public. Too many people in his life had died brutal deaths for him ever to be silent again. The radio switched off, we all sat there, humbled, pensive. Then a rustling broke the quiet, "Walter's lost a contact," someone said. Of course—like most of us, he was crying. That's what I'll always remember best—the way, within a second, we were all on the floor, feeling for that missing lens. (Leavitt 1989, 83)

The feelings spanned the spectrum. Bill Jesdale from ACT UP/Rhode Island recalled that after ACT UP benefits his cheeks would hurt because he had spent the whole night laughing and smiling. "I just really felt like I had found where I belonged" (quoted in Cohen 1998, 129). Frank Sieple emphasized how participating in ACT UP's street protests filled him with feelings of self-respect: "It was very liberating because you were obviously standing up for something. And willing to get arrested for something. So you've got all this psychological stuff going on about standing up for yourself" (Sieple 1999). In a world that so emphatically enacted disregard for gay men, lesbians, people with AIDS, a world that despised queer folks, to stand up for yourself and proudly and defiantly demand that state and society respond to the AIDS crisis was exhilarating.[10]

Most ACT UP participants were brought up in the United States, where radical politics and street activism are often derided as unnecessary and overwrought, so to be in a group that shared your values and your commitment to direct action was immensely important. That sense of connectivity and unified purpose generated strong sentiments of solidarity and intensified identification with the movement. John Weir recalled ACT UP/NY as "the one place I could be where people had the same understanding of the world that I had" (quoted in Cohen 1998, 139). That sense of meaningful connection stayed with ACT UP/NY member Zoe Leonard even after she left ACT UP: "I have so much fondness and respect for the people I worked with in ACT UP. I feel like there's something really special when I run into them. . . . You took a stand with this

10. For another example, see Members of C-FAR 1988, 10.

FIGURE 8. National ACT UP demonstration, Chicago, April 23, 1990. Photo by Linda Miller.

person. It's knowing that in some very, very important way you shared at least some basic values with this person" (quoted in Cvetkovich 2003a, 168). In the early years a sense of similar values and shared purpose, arrived at through working together, generated and nourished strong sentiments of connection and camaraderie.

Such feelings helped encourage participants who might have been hesitant or fearful about engaging in confrontational activism. ACT UP/ Chicago member Tim Miller recalled the "excited and jubilant and congratulatory and welcoming" atmosphere at the rally prior to the 1988 FDA demonstration, noting how important it was that there was a "sense of community," given people's anxieties about engaging in activism that defied authority and transgressed norms of public decorum: "I think parts of [the activism] were terrifying. You know. To certain people. I mean none of us were raised to be activists. We were always [taught] to be nice and considerate, and follow the rules. And we weren't doing any of that all of a sudden" (Miller 1999). Practices of solidarity validated and encouraged defiant challenges to mainstream society's norms regarding emotional comportment and political activism.

The sense of camaraderie also created a context that made it safer and easier for people with health-related needs to engage in civil disobedience. An HIV-positive man from ACT UP/Rochester, N.Y. described the solidarity he felt with members of the PISD Caucus who were arrested during the 1988 action at the FDA.

> I feel a strong allegiance with the other people in PISD. . . . [A] number of us in PISD got arrested at the civil disobedience. . . . [T]he police tried to isolate and separate us. . . . [We made a number of health-related requests of the police.] It empowered me to be with people who supported me about what I needed, and it was empowering to be able to support the rest of the group with what they needed. I feel really alone sometimes; this gave me a wonderful sense of connecting. (Hiraga 1988, 8, 10)

The importance of practices of solidarity, especially across lines of difference, is evident in the following comments from Jeanne Kracher about a rally on the eve of a large national demonstration in Chicago at which different affinity groups announced their actions:

> The people of color caucus, which was calling itself the Harriet Tubman/ James Baldwin Brigade . . . got up and said, "Whatever the women are doing at this demonstration, we're going to support their action." And then the PISD Caucus did the same thing. . . . They took this big stand which was: whatever action women are doing at this thing, we're going to stand behind them and support them in any way we can. (Kracher 1993; see also Kracher 2000)

Kracher was moved by that show of solidarity: "It was the HIV-positive and immune-compromised people, and the people of color caucus, saying 'This is the moment that we put our bodies between the cops and the women so the women can accomplish what they're going to do.' And it was very meaningful" (Kracher 2000). An affinity group of women from around the country were planning to build an AIDS ward for women in the street in order to draw attention to the issues facing women with HIV/AIDS and to challenge, directly, the fact that women were being denied entry into Cook County Hospital's AIDS ward. The spoken solidarity from affinity groups that had several HIV-positive gay male members helped to validate the women's emphasis on women with HIV/AIDS, an issue that by then had become a bone of contention in some ACT UP chapters.

People's descriptions of what it felt like to participate in ACT UP recall Durkheim's notion of *collective effervescence*. The term conveys the "transports of enthusiasm" and "a sort of electricity" that comes from people amassing and being physically close to one another in a manner that "launches them to an extraordinary height of exaltation" (Durkheim 1995, 217).[11] Ferd Eggan, for example, recalls being awash with feelings of "solidarity, comfort, and belonging" when he joined other people with AIDS in the civil disobedience action at the Supreme Court as part of the 1987 March on Washington. "In the midst of those kinds of mobilizations, it's possible for me to feel angry. Angry at the government, but also sort of buoyed up by this feeling of connection, of solidarity. . . . [I was] swept up into the power of this immense group of people. It was a great feeling. It's a terrific feeling to be surrounded by this sea of humanity who are doing what you're doing" (Eggan 1999). The amassing of large numbers of people who see themselves as in some way connected and acting together for a collectively desired end generates, in Randall Collins' words, a "bodily awareness of copresence" that can unleash immense "emotional energy" (2001, 28). Movements, in that sense, are locations for the "transmission of affect" (Brennan 2004), sites where bodily intensities are relayed among participants.[12] Demonstrations felt euphoric to ACT UP/NY member Marina Alvarez, an affective state generated by sentiments of camaraderie and identification, especially across difference:

11. Durkheim discusses collective effervescence in the context of native Australian religious ceremonies that draw members of a clan together. A man of his time, he problematically asserted a thought/emotion dichotomy, privileging the former by suggesting that reason should be able to subordinate emotion, and ascribing to "primitives" in particular an inability to control feelings. We can dispense with that baggage, however, and retain the term itself since it usefully describes important emotional synergies that can occur when masses of people come together in common cause.

12. Here it is useful to note again the distinction I made in the introduction between affects and emotions. Feminist philosopher Teresa Brennan argues that affect, unlike emotions, can be transmitted. Emotions are not transmissible between people because an emotion is an individual's naming of a personal physical sensation. That naming is personal even if the names one uses are culturally shared. A particular emotion, then, is simply a linguistic phenomenon, a naming that another might adopt to describe her own feelings but not transmissible in the way that, say, energy, is. As an example, let's say you happen upon a protest and see baton-wielding police poised to begin making arrests. Your body registers the intensities circulating within that scene and under some circumstances produces analogical affects that prepare your body to respond. Your body takes in, literally, the scene and its circulating intensities, making them your own and preparing you to respond. What is infolded are intensities, affects, rather than someone else's named emotions.

I've never felt energy like the energy that we had in those marches. There was
an energy that was exhilarating. . . . People were dying, and we were fighting
for people who were dying. We were from all kinds of backgrounds, all kinds
of cultures. Who had red hair? I dyed my hair whatever—Spanish orange.
Who had purple hair? Who was black? Who was poor? We were all together.
Do you know the power I would feel when I would come back [from a dem-
onstration]? I tell you, I was on a natural high for about a week. (Quoted in
Cvetkovich 2003a, 187)

Carol Hayse experienced an adrenaline rush during demonstrations,
an exhilaration that stemmed in part from a sense of purposefulness
and political efficacy: "It's a very existential feeling of freedom and
joy and liberation . . . when you know that what you're doing is righteous
and correct and historic, that what you're doing matters, and that people
can impact policy" (Hayse 2000).

Sentiments of exhilaration and elation stemmed in large part from
being engaged in defiant, confrontational activism with other social
outcasts who were committed to fighting the AIDS crisis and building
a more just and joyous world. Mark Harrington's memory of an after-

FIGURE 9. National ACT UP demonstration, downtown Chicago, April 23, 1990. Photo by
Genyphyr Novak.

demo dérive through the streets of New York points toward the sheer euphoria in collectivity:

> My favorite part [of ACT UP/NY's 1989 "Stop the Church" action] was after-
> wards, when we got away from the church, started marching around the city
> and sat down in Times Square. Because it seemed like we were free, we were
> happy, we were all together, and nobody could stop us. It was just one of those
> nice moments that happens when you do things in activism, where there isn't
> any reason for what you're doing, it's just an expression of collective joy or
> power. (Handelman 1990, 117)

ACT UP/Chicago member Sharyl Holtzman's comments about the aftermath of a national ACT UP demonstration in San Francisco against
Secretary of Health and Human Services Louis Sullivan similarly convey the intensity of feelings of joyousness and collectivity within the
movement.

> When Sullivan was finished, [the members of ACT UP who had partici-
> pated in the demonstration] marched out of Moscone Center, feeling abso-
> lutely ebullient, and walked down Fourth Street to join the [Lesbian and Gay
> Pride] Parade. As we neared Market [Street], we saw the ACT UP colors, the
> SILENCE = DEATH signs, and for a split second we froze in amazement. Out
> of over 200 entries in the Parade, ACT UP was crossing the intersection just
> as we were arriving. . . . Like lovers who had been kept apart in a battlefield,
> we ran toward them—our friends, our fellow warriors, our family. It was exu-
> berant and unbelievable. People were jumping in the air, they were hugging,
> they were crying, they were laughing through their tears. (ACT UP/Chicago
> 1990, 4)

A movement's demonstrations, actions, and other events—its rituals—
allow participants to move outside of the everyday mundane, or, more
apt in this case, out of everyday devastation, and to be transported into
a more meaningful existence that holds out potential for self and social
change. Such happenings have an almost sacred quality to them, part
of what gives them tremendous intensity. In describing the feelings he
experienced during an affinity group action, ACT UP/NY member Jon
Greenberg provided a glimpse into such ecstatic affective states. Prior to
the risky action, everyone was afraid, but, Greenberg states,

[We] knew that it was only fear, and rather than let that stop us, we used it to propel us into further action, to confront and push through the barrier of our fear and be liberated even as our bodies were being arrested and jailed. There was an otherness about those moments. We all felt it. We all knew that we had, if only for a moment, an hour, a day, become larger than we had been the day before. We each became part of the other, and as a unit our collective spirit crossed an illusory boundary which we only knew was an illusion after we had crossed it. . . . Through collective empowerment we declared who we were and how we felt and made a place for ourselves in the universe. (Greenberg 1992)

Greenberg's description of ACT UP actions recalls Clifford Geertz's description of religious rituals as dramas in which humans "attain their faith as they portray it" (1973, 114). Those who engaged in an action were already sympathetic to ACT UP's worldview, but the experience of doing the action—of "becoming caught up in it not just imaginatively but bodily" (116)—often amplified people's identification with the movement and with their comrades and intensified their commitment to fighting AIDS. Durkheim noted a self-perpetuating dynamic to collective effervescence: "The very act of congregating is an exceptionally powerful stimulant. . . . The initial impulse is . . . amplified each time it is echoed, like an avalanche that grows as it goes along" (1995, 217–18). In the early years, ACT UP's demonstrations and other actions, the weekly meetings, the unplanned moments of connectivity, together were that avalanche, continually generating strong feelings of collective euphoria.[13]

In a world where impersonal, abstract forces shape daily lives and can generate sentiments of being out of control, of inefficacy, of helplessness and hopelessness, social movements are often a space that engenders rich and textured counterfeelings. In addition to filling our lives with intensity and a sense of meaning and purpose, the exciting swirl of ACT UP's protest actions and meetings allowed us to reinvent ourselves, to carve out a place where we could be angry, oppositional, defiant, hopeful, sexual, and happy, a place where we could engage in collective projects of world-making. The intense emotional energy that is generated when people join in pursuit of a common end helps to explain why people engage in collective action even when they could easily take the proverbial "free ride."

13. On the strong feelings evoked by movement rituals, see Jasper 1998, 418.

When interviewed, former ACT UP participants invariably comment on the important role the movement played in their lives and specifically recall the intensity of their feelings while in the movement. Jeff Edwards remembers that participation in the movement "felt really powerful. I really felt like we were making history." Moreover, "being an AIDS activist was just central to my identity" (Edwards 2000a). Ferd Eggan described ACT UP as changing his life (Eggan 1999). Michael Thompson noted how intense it was to be involved in a movement where participants were dying: "It was a very special time to be with people who you knew might not live through their lives. . . . To be in a political movement where the movement was dying. There's nothing quite like that" (Thompson 2000). Jeanne Kracher echoed Thompson's sentiments about the illnesses and deaths of comrades in the movement.

> We were experiencing things that for people our age were very heavy. I mean, when I think about how you and I went and took care of Ortez and changed his diaper five times in one night and carried him to, . . . all of that stuff, how old were we then? I was in my early 30s and you were in your mid-20s. I mean, there's a way that you don't experience that in this society . . . coming from the background we come from. (Kracher 2000)

Carol Hayse recalled that the deaths, while sobering and saddening, also reinvigorated her activism: "It helped keep me going to know that you have to fight this thing that's killing people" (Hayse 2000). For Billy McMillan, his years in ACT UP were the best of his life. "They were very empowering years, years of self-growth. I felt as an HIV-positive person that my life really had meaning and purpose and that I was part of something larger than myself" (McMillan 2000).

Perhaps I should emphasize that the feelings generated in ACT UP's meetings and actions were not a natural result of people joining together in common cause. Those sentiments of exhilaration, love, and camaraderie derived in part from the narratives we had constructed about ourselves as angry, proud, and defiant, and from each individual's growing identification with those emotions and with others who felt them. The extraordinary feeling of being part of something larger than yourself derived in part from our constructions of our political work as important and world-changing. My point here is that those intense bodily feelings that occur amid the action, read and shaped (although never entirely) through culture, help to sustain movements over time. In this case, the affects and emotions generated in and by ACT UP also helped to secure the movement's emotional habitus, its potentially unstable resolution to lesbians' and gay men's contradictory feelings about self and society, and its political horizon. It is hard to dispute the righteousness of angry, queer, defiant AIDS activism when, through such engagement, participants also experience sentiments of camaraderie, of political efficacy, of making history, of being changed, and of living meaningful lives. ACT UP participants faced both a society where street activism was frequently disparaged and a community that had a history of hesitancy about angry, confrontational activism. Direct-action AIDS activists were bucking both systems, and they took some heat for that. The intense feelings generated in the movement—of self-affirmation, purposefulness, connection to others, shared resolve, love—fortified a commitment to ACT UP, helping the movement to flourish into the early 1990s.

There is no fixed recipe for sustaining a movement, but the case of ACT UP indicates the importance of feelings in nourishing activism—feelings that derive from being recognized and affirmed in one's self, from connecting to others and becoming part of a "we," from engaging in something larger that oneself, from experiencing self-organization and autonomy within collectivity, from being enticed to change and try out new ways of being. I would venture that social movements sustain themselves at the level of desire. A movement milieu—shaped in large part by its emotional habitus—expresses desire for different forms of social relations, different ways of being, a different world. In doing so, a movement allows participants to feel their own perhaps squelched desires or to develop new ones that through articulation can become contagious, flooding others' imaginations and drawing them into the movement. In articulating and enacting what previously might have been unimaginable, a movement offers a scene and future possibilities that surprise, entice, exhilarate, and electrify. One general lesson, then, is that movements enhance their sustainability when they speak to people at the level of desire, allowing, or better, enticing, participants to collectively develop and pursue their aspirations for a different world.

The Emotion Work of Movements

To grasp the sources of political action and the various forms it takes requires attending to the emotion work in which activists and others engage, as the previous chapters suggest.[1] In this chapter I focus on the central role that emotion work plays in sustaining social movements. The fact that part of the work of social movements is *emotional* is infrequently considered by scholars of contentious politics.[2] But consider that in order to attract and retain participants and to pursue a movement's agenda, activists continually need to mobilize affective states and emotions that mesh with the movement's political objectives and tactics, and suppress those that do the opposite. Social movements provide affective pedagogies to participants and supporters, authorizing ways to feel and to emote that often go against the grain of dominant society's emotional norms. They offer, in anthropologist Clifford Geertz's phrase, "a vocabulary of sentiment," a "sentimental education" (Geertz 1973, 449). More than *manage* emotions—a term that implies a preexisting emotional state that then is amplified or dampened—the emotion work of movements frequently *generates* feelings.

ACT UP had its emotion work cut out for it in relation to the broader U.S. context and to that of the more mainstream lesbian and gay com-

---

1. I define the term *emotion work,* drawing from Hochschild 1979, in the introduction.
2. But see Aminzade and McAdam 2001; Goodwin and Pfaff 2001.

munity. Like other social movements in the United States, ACT UP confronted a dominant emotional habitus that typically disparages angry people, seeing anger as chaotic, impulsive, and irrational, and thus "something which a mature person ideally can or should transcend" (Lutz 1986, 180). Anger takes on an especially negative cast when expressed by people whom mainstream society marks as "other," particularly when large numbers of them are taking to the streets and breaking the law in order to disrupt "business as usual." ACT UP also confronted an American ideology of democracy that locates legitimate political activity in the halls of legislatures and in the voting booth, and maligns street activism as unnecessary and extreme, a threat to social order. ACT UP's task was complicated even further by the recently prevailing emotional habitus in lesbian and gay communities that had suppressed anger and in other ways made a confrontational political response to AIDS largely unimaginable.

Within this context, the work of AIDS activists that illuminated, embodied, augmented, and extended the newly emerging emotional habitus and explicitly linked that set of feelings to confrontational street activism was crucial in strengthening the direct-action AIDS movement. The *Bowers v. Hardwick* decision opened an imaginative space that allowed for confrontational AIDS activism, but the new feelings and political attitudes that *Hardwick* animated were not universally accepted within lesbian and gay communities, something we might expect in most communities and certainly in one where social marginalization produces ambivalent feelings about self and society. Within this contestatory moment, ACT UP's emotion work, its affective pedagogy, played a crucial role in securing the new emotional habitus and attracting participants into the direct-action AIDS movement.

I investigate the ways direct-action AIDS activists—sometimes consciously but often less purposively—nourished and extended an emotional habitus that was both amenable to their brand of confrontational activism and responsive to the contradictory feelings that make up lesbian and gay ambivalence. I analyze, for example, how ACT UP marshaled grief, tethered it to anger, and linked both sentiments to confrontational AIDS activism; relocated the feeling of pride from a politics of respectability to a celebration of sexual difference and confrontational activism; and altered the subject and object of shame from gay shame about homosexuality to government shame about its response to the AIDS crisis.

ACT UP's emotional pedagogy offered new ways for queer folks to feel about themselves, about dominant society, and about political possibilities amid the AIDS crisis, offering a "resolution" of sorts to lesbian and gay ambivalence: it emphasized self-love and self-respect over shame and self-doubt, authorized antagonism toward society, eased fear of social rejection, and challenged the desire for acceptance on straight society's terms. The new matrix of feelings, expressed repeatedly in the movement's rhetorical and ritual practices, affected how people felt not only by legitimizing these feelings, but by naming and enacting them and thereby bringing into being and elevating those emotions while suppressing other feeling states. ACT UP also gave birth to a newly politicized *queer* sensibility that crystallized this new set of feelings and furnished a powerful response to lesbian and gay ambivalence. Foregrounding angry, confrontational activism as well as sex-radicalism, *queer* offered a compelling vision of "how to be gay" in this moment of crisis. ACT UP's emotion work—intertwined with and inseparable from its interpretive work—helped the direct-action AIDS movement to flourish into the 1990s.

Emotion work is typically less visible than the other tasks of a movement, which is one reason why scholars have tended to overlook it. But attention to the rhetoric and actions of movements illuminates the emotional dimensions of their work. The ephemera that materialize and instantiate a movement's collective action frames—its leaflets, fact sheets, T-shirts, stickers, buttons, posters, banners, speeches, chants—are particularly rich sources for exploring a movement's emotion work since framing entails mobilizing some feelings and suppressing others. Something else to consider is that although terms like *emotion work, mobilize,* and *suppress* might suggest conscious, purposive behavior, much of a movement's emotion work is nonstrategic and unpremeditated. Indeed, the generation of some feelings and the suppression of others often are crucial *effects* of a movement's many activities rather than the *intention* lying behind them. I return to this point below. A final point before turning to the case concerns the importance of studying a movement's emotion work in relation to other factors. Emotional dynamics and processes do not operate in isolation. Thus the task is to explore how a movement's emotion work articulates with other factors—for example, political opportunities and activists' interpretive practices, including framing—to affect movement sustainability.

ACT UP and a New Emotional Habitus

How did the movement respond to the emotional habitus that had until recently prevailed in lesbian and gay communities and to the one that still prevailed in larger society? How did ACT UP augment and amplify the emergent emotional habitus with its pedagogy of emotional and political practices, and how did ACT UP's preferred ways of feeling, being, and doing activism become axiomatic to large segments of lesbians and gay men? In the following sections, I pursue such questions, first through an exploration of vying emotional and political norms in lesbian and gay communities, followed by an analysis of ACT UP's surprising success in securing—however provisionally and incompletely—the ascendance and preeminence of its own. The story of ACT UP's emergence challenges the social movement literature's political opportunity model, as does an analysis of its meteoric rise and development. The perception of constricting political opportunities helped to nourish, rather than squelch, the direct-action AIDS movement largely because that hostile environment bolstered queer anger and validated activists' claims that confrontational protests were now imperative.

Feelings in Flux

Although its emotional habitus and confrontational activism were ascendant and marked a new, more defiant moment in lesbian and gay politics, ACT UP had to vie with others in mainstream lesbian and gay communities who continued to be influenced by and reaffirm the previous emotional habitus and the more staid politics it encouraged. Even during ACT UP's heyday in the late 1980s, this struggle persisted. Most revealing are those instances when speakers or writers acknowledged the pull of the older constellation of feelings and its attendant political horizon but nevertheless encouraged lesbians and gay men to embrace the turn to angry militancy. Consider the following excerpt from an op-ed by Achy Obejas in Chicago's *Windy City Times*, which disparaged the continuing popularity of the song "We Are a Gentle, Angry People."[3]

3. This song, also called "Singing for Our Lives," had become meaningful in the discourse of lesbian and gay politics. For some it signified activism and respectability; for others, it signified political passivity, complacency, and assimilationism. What it means to those singing it, however, is often ambiguous. Some who participated in the massive civil disobedience at the Supreme Court during the 1987 March on Washington sang it along

Obejas wrote the piece in the summer of 1987, a few months after the emergence of ACT UP in New York and contemporaneous with organizing by DAGMAR for its first public demonstration about AIDS.

> When I realized Holly Near's "We Are a Gentle, Angry People" had become the unofficial anthem of the lesbian and gay movement, I was not proud. . . . Gentle anger, methinks, is repressed anger. . . . Too often in the lesbian and gay movement, we shy away from making a little noise, always fearful that we will lose more than we gain. . . . Pretending we are not angry—and we can do this so well we actually believe it—is the greatest tragedy that can befall us: it will keep us from being free. . . . The anger, that feeling of madness at the realization of how we're denied, how we're left to die, how we're bleached out even when it's impossible to totally erase us—that should never, ever be the gentle sort. Sure, it's going to make some people a little scared, a little nervous. That's OK. (Obejas 1987)

Its tone and content indicate that Obejas wrote the piece during a period of emotional transition; she acknowledged, but challenged, one set of affects and emotions and its accompanying politics, and advocated another.

Where Obejas extolled a righteous and raucous anger to disparage what she saw as gay quiescence, the following example reveals another side in the struggle, the exaltation of gay love and gentleness, seemingly mobilized as a challenge, perhaps even a reproach, to the confrontational anger that was becoming more prominent. In describing the sorrowful, somber, and love-filled mood of a Memorial Day AIDS service and candlelight vigil in Chicago in 1988, *Windy City Times* columnist Lawrence Bommer implicitly called into question the growing anger and embrace of militancy among some lesbians and gay men. Bommer described the speeches of two men with AIDS who marveled at the love they experienced from God and from friends once they fell ill: "Given that reservoir of love, any self-pity, even anger, turned irrelevant. The fact that these young men could rise above so much pain to thank their friends—when it would be just as understandable if they raged against the dying of the

---

with "We Shall Overcome" and "America the Beautiful," changing the refrain to "we are a gentle, *loving* people," (Johnson 1987, 1). People perhaps sing that song in such circumstances in order to ameliorate the anxiety that comes from being seen as a troublemaker, in the hope of conveying to passers-by and to oneself that one's actions are not really threatening since they are performed by gentle, loving people. Or, maybe, it's just a song to sing.

light—that, too, proves we are a gentle, loving people" (Bommer 1988, 10). While anger was perhaps understandable, it verged on the disreputable, and lesbians and gay men should strive instead to prove their gentleness and lovingness. Prove to whom? we might ask. Bommer does not say, but the imagined audience might range from oneself to other lesbians and gay men and to the straight world.

A *Windy City Times* editorial in its 1988 Lesbian and Gay Pride Day issue suggested an ongoing struggle between competing emotional ways of being. The editors acknowledged lesbian and gay discomfort with activism fueled by gay rage while indicating their own support for and pride in the new, angry activism. The editors reflected on the 1969 Stonewall Rebellion (the date commemorated by lesbian and gay pride parades) and drew connections to Chicago's upcoming Pride Parade.

[Reliable sources] record that the [Stonewall Riots] began with the last patron the police rounded up, a lesbian who was too proud to submit to the humiliation of being forced like a criminal into the waiting squad car. At the moment, no doubt, she did not feel particularly proud. . . . What welled up inside [felt] like anger and frustration and a rage blind to the consequences of fighting back. She had simply had enough. But the wellspring of that rage and frustration . . . was pride—was a sense that she was a person of equal stature to the cops . . . a sense that her way of expressing intimacy was fundamentally and profoundly good. . . . It was this same pride which erupted in her fellow patrons and inspired them to rush to her aid. . . . Even more than in 1969, we have had enough. But the battle no longer occurs in a moment, culminating in a street riot. The struggle now is less dramatic and more drawn-out. . . . When we fight back now, it is not in a moment of passion; it is calculated and planned, leaving time for a thousand rationalizations to sap our wills. . . . The City of Chicago still lacks legal protection for lesbians and gay men. Seven years into the most severe epidemic of this century, the United States has authorized only one AIDS treatment drug. . . . We all know the statistics and we all know that we have had enough—but when the anger from the latest insult subsides and we are left in the hollow of reflection, we decide all too often that we can take some more. We *cannot* take any more. Pride week must mean more than a parade. . . . We have an ordinance to pass, and our aldermen need letters. We have AIDS funding to secure, and our activists need demonstrators. . . . So march in the parade—but when it's over, take another step. ("Our" 1988; emphasis in original)

The editorial's tone and content indicate two vying emotional habitus, with the newer one calling into question emotional norms and a concomitant political horizon that had prevailed in lesbian and gay communities since the earliest days of the epidemic.

A forum at Harvard's Kennedy School of Government in early 1988 also revealed emotional and political sparring, this time among elected officials and other lesbian and gay leaders. From the podium, openly gay U.S. Congressman Barney Frank (D-MA) criticized recent gay and lesbian civil disobedience actions in his state. According to the *Windy City Times,* Frank "drew hisses from the crowd when he said that such actions often amount to nothing more than 'therapy' for the movement and may actually set back the struggle for lesbian and gay rights" ("Frank" 1988). Other lesbian and gay panelists disagreed with Frank. Virginia Apuzzo, for example, stated, "We are not angry about one precipitous act, we are angry about a lifetime, a century, two centuries' worth of deliberate oppression in its most fundamental form, saying, 'You cannot be'" ("Frank" 1988). Apuzzo joined AIDS activists in justifying and promoting lesbians' and gay men's anger, explicitly linking it to confrontational activism. As I noted in chapter 1, a similar debate between Frank and Apuzzo had been publicly aired in 1985, at a point when Frank's belief in moderate politics was widely shared in lesbian and gay communities and the rare articulations of anger were typically submerged. By 1988, the relative positions of these contending emotional habitus and political horizons had been reversed.

Clearly, then, a struggle in lesbian and gay communities over the proper emotional demeanor and the acceptability of various forms of activism persisted, but opposition to angry and confrontational activism was no longer axiomatic. ACT UP's style of activism was ascendant, erupting around the country as more people joined direct-action AIDS organizations and formed new ones where they did not already exist. An *Advocate* article written less than two years after the *Hardwick* ruling, "The New Gay Activism: Adding Bite to the Movement," registered the growing militancy:

> They're picketing, protesting, chanting, and rallying. They're holding sit-ins, "kiss-ins" and "die-ins." New groups have formed across the country in unexpected places like Kansas, Maine, Minnesota, Missouri, and Vermont. In the South, often regarded as politically inactive, groups have sprung up in

Georgia, Tennessee, and seven cities in North Carolina alone. Even places such as Boston, New York, and Washington, D.C., which have had strong gay organizations for years, have recently seen the creation of new, more militant groups. . . . All across the United States, gays and lesbians—fed up with the ineffectiveness of traditional lobbying tactics—are taking their case to the streets. . . . Groups are staging radical demonstrations that more often than not end up on the front page of newspapers or on the local news. And in almost every case, the new organizations are dedicated either wholly or largely to direct political action. . . . The new era in gay activism may have reached a high point the week of April 29, [1988] when more than 30 new and established groups across the country staged a series of direct actions [about AIDS],[4] including rallies, protests, and acts of civil disobedience. (Freiberg, Harding, and Vandervelden 1988, 10–11)

In its last issue of 1988, the *Windy City Times* ran an article with the headline "ACT UP Proliferates Nationwide" that began with the statement, "They were everywhere." It continued, "All year long, they kept showing up in the news. . . . AIDS Coalition to Unleash Power, better known by its acronym ACT UP, is the fastest-growing grass-roots political organization in the world. Chapters are everywhere, from one newly formed in Palm Springs, California, to those in all of America's major metropolises" (Schoofs 1988, 16). In an article entitled "A Decade of Rage" that commemorated ACT UP's tenth anniversary, a *Windy City Times* reporter noted that the new militancy, while controversial, was undeniably popular within lesbian and gay communities. "From [ACT UP's] beginning, the concept of direct-action activism divided the gay community"; nevertheless, "in its heyday during the late 1980s and early '90s, ACT UP was ubiquitous in the consciousness of gay America." Indeed, "the group's firebrand style of activism rallied a generation" (Weisberg 1997).

ACT UP was able to draw enormous support throughout the late 1980s and into the 1990s.[5] Increasingly calling themselves *queer*, lesbians and gay men, along with other sexual and gender outlaws who were politicizing bisexual and transgendered identities, embraced the new mil-

4. This article conflated gay activism with AIDS activism: the new activism was focused on AIDS.

5. I provided examples from the period of the movement's emergence in chapter 2. I return to this question of community support for ACT UP, and its later withdrawal, in chapter 5.

itancy. ACT UP drew enthusiastic praise even from more mainstream leaders, individuals, and institutions.

The emotional and political terrain for direct-action AIDS activism certainly was fertile, but that alone cannot explain ACT UP's ability to sustain itself and flourish into the 1990s. After all, the moral shock of *Hardwick* might have worn off quickly, and the confrontational activist response consequently might have lost support. Moreover, the militancy that emerged on the heels of *Hardwick* might have been extremely brief, given the emotion and political norms that prevail in mainstream American society and given the structure of lesbian and gay ambivalence and the instability of any temporary resolution to it. Additionally, from a historical perspective, anything more than a burst of militancy seemed unlikely: accounts of the lesbian and gay movement demonstrate that the allure of more routine and staid political activism has typically exerted a greater pull on the lesbian and gay movement than has confrontational politics.[6] But in this case, angry militancy won out for an extended period of time, and its predominance asks to be explained.

The Strategic Uses of Emotion

A possible explanation that takes emotion and emotion work seriously raises a question about intention and emotion work that I want to address at the outset. One might suppose that ACT UP was able to sustain itself because direct-action AIDS activists appreciated an emotional imperative: to generate support for their street activism, they had to challenge how lesbians and gay men understood and felt about the epidemic; they thus consciously set out to do so, and their strategic efforts to mobilize anger and suppress feelings not amenable to ACT UP's form of activism were successful.

I have strong reservations, which I discuss shortly, about limiting my analyses of emotion work to strategic efforts, but this explanation is worth exploring, especially because AIDS activists' emotion work sometimes was manifestly calculated and instrumental. That sort of intentionality, for example, was evident at ACT UP/NY's first meeting, where participants discussed how to shift the focus of the upcoming Gay and Lesbian Pride Parade from "Gay Pride" to "Gay Rage" (ACT UP/ NY 1987a). In a similar vein, the meeting minutes from a C-FAR meet-

6. See, for example, D'Emilio 1998.

ing in October 1988 record the following rationale for an outreach proposal to change C-FAR's name to ACT UP: "the name [ACT UP] gives
us a sense of anger which the name 'C-FAR' . . . is lacking" (C-FAR
1988b). Even the emotional demeanor projected in demonstrations was
sometimes quite conscious. In discussing a nationally coordinated day of
AIDS actions across the United States, ACT NOW leader and member
of ACT UP/Los Angeles, Mark Kostopolous, stated, "We want to present a picture to the nation that we're not just sorrowful, but that we're
angry and expecting change" (Wockner 1989a, 40).

    More generally, each exhortation to feel a given sentiment and every
expression of a feeling could be read as an attempt by activists to mobilize specific feelings with the goal of garnering support for the movement. Viewed from this strategic angle, feelings might fit quite neatly into
political process and political opportunity models via the framing concept. Along these lines, leading political-process theorist Sidney Tarrow
has pointed to the intentional emotionality of collective action frames,
writing, "The culture of collective action is built on frames and emotions
oriented toward mobilizing people. . . . Symbols are taken selectively by
movement leaders from a cultural reservoir and combined with action-
oriented beliefs in order to navigate strategically. . . . Most important,
they are given an emotional valence aimed at converting passivity into
action" (Tarrow 1998, 112). Robert Benford argues for a similar recognition of the role of feelings, writing that they are "a vital social movement
resource" that movement actors "produce, orchestrate, and strategically
deploy" (Benford 1997, 419).

    That sort of instrumentalizing of feelings certainly occurs in move-
ment contexts, but beginning and ending our analyses there forecloses
important avenues of inquiry and leaves crucial questions about emotion
work unasked and unanswered. Any exploration of the strategic deploy-
ment of feelings, for example, begs the question of what we might call
emotional resonance: why do people sometimes respond to such deployments of emotion—feeling the anger that organizers ask them to feel, for
example—and why does this purposive mobilization sometimes fail? Investigation of these questions demands an analysis of the workings of
feelings—of the ways they are generated, intensified, or dampened—that
necessarily takes us out of the realm of instrumentality. Even if emotions sometimes are deployed strategically, we risk neglecting much of
what is rich and significant about emotion if we reduce it to another tool
in the social movement entrepreneur's framing toolkit. For example,

an angry chant at a demonstration might mobilize participants' and by-
standers' anger toward the target of the protest, but rather than a strategic intent, the stimulus behind the chant simply might have been a felt
need by demonstrators to express their own anger. A view of feelings
as strategic deployments strips them of all of their bodily, noncognitive,
non-instrumental attributes, thereby depleting them of some of their
most interesting characteristics and diminishing much of their conceptual force. If we stick to an instrumentalist rendering, we will lose sight
of the sensuous experience of feelings and thus of their power or force in
stimulating and blocking activism.[7]

Grief into Anger

I return, then, to the question of how ACT UP, with its angry militancy, captured the imagination and secured the enduring participation
of thousands of queer folks. Direct-action AIDS activists' responses to
the grief pervading lesbian and gay communities provides a useful entry
point for exploring how ACT UP buttressed and extended the emerging
emotional habitus and its concomitant politics. In its rhetoric and protest
actions, ACT UP harnessed grief to anger and both feelings to confrontational action. Attention to how it did so and why this emotion work
was effective can help us to explain why and how ACT UP was able to
develop and grow into the early 1990s.

COMPETING APPROACHES TO GRIEF.   Within lesbian and gay communities, there have been two fairly distinct modes for dealing with the constant grief surrounding the epidemic. Both provide an opportunity for
public, collective grieving; the difference lies in their emotional tone and
political sensibility. The first approach emerged in the early 1980s: candlelight memorial vigils that lesbians and gay men held to honor those
who had died from AIDS-related complications (fig. 10). This approach
was reinvigorated in the late 1980s with the Names Project Memorial
Quilt, which has afforded lesbian and gay communities a similar opportunity for public and collective grieving. Initiated and first shown in 1987,
the quilt contains thousands of patches—each a unique, creative expres-

---

7. In his insider's critique of the framing perspective, Benford initially seems to make
a similar point, but his instrumentalist view of emotion quoted above undermines his own
argument and simply magnifies, rather than rectifies, our existing "overly cognitive conception" of social movement participants (Benford 1997, 419).

FIGURE 10. "An AIDS Candlelight March," poster, author unknown, 1983.

sion, made by friends, lovers, admirers, family members—that commemorate people who have died from AIDS-related complications. At each showing, the names of the dead memorialized in the quilt are read; in 1987, there were 1,920 panels, and the names were read almost continuously for more than three hours (d'Adesky and Zwickler 1987, 8). As at candlelight memorial vigils, the mood at quilt showings has tended to be solemn.[8]

Implicitly (and sometimes explicitly) criticizing what it suggested was the depoliticizing nature of those rituals, ACT UP offered an alternative route for grief: confrontational AIDS activism. Consider the following example. Direct-action AIDS activists from across the country converged in Washington, D.C., on the weekend of October 10–11, 1988, to "seize control of the FDA."[9] That same weekend, the Names Project

8. For more on the quilt, see Jones 2000 and Sturken 1997.
9. Activists demanded, among other things, that the FDA shorten the time taken to approve drugs and refuse data from drug trials that used placebos and prohibited enrollees from taking concurrent prophylactic drugs to protect against opportunistic infections. See Crimp and Rolston 1990, 79, 81.

Quilt was displayed on the National Mall. As part of its mobilization for the FDA action, ACT UP passed out a leaflet at the quilt showing (fig. 11). One side blared, "SHOW YOUR ANGER TO THE PEOPLE WHO HELPED MAKE THE QUILT POSSIBLE: OUR GOVERNMENT." Text on the reverse read, "The Quilt helps us remember our lovers, relatives, and friends who have died during the past eight years. These people have died from a virus.

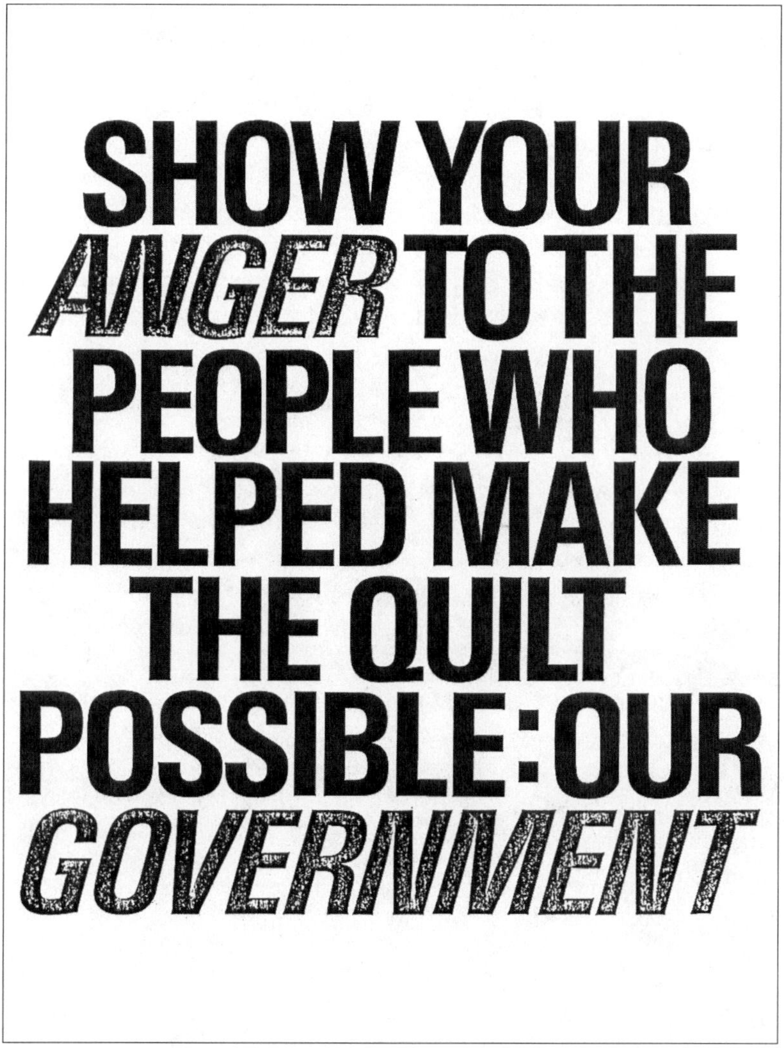

FIGURE 11. "SHOW YOUR ANGER," leaflet, ACT UP/NY, 1988.

But they have been killed by our government's neglect and inaction. . . .
More than 40,000 people have died from AIDS. . . . Before this Quilt
grows any larger, turn your grief into anger. Turn anger into action. TURN
THE POWER OF THE QUILT INTO ACTION" (ACT UP/NY 1988b, emphases
theirs).

Here, ACT UP acknowledged lesbian and gay grief about the deaths
of people with AIDS, and then attempted to transport them to another
place, figuratively from grief to anger, literally from the quilt and the
deeply felt grief manifest there to a demonstration at the FDA where
that grief could be expressed in angry, confrontational political activism.
The ACT UP leaflet located the source of lesbian and gay grief at the
government's doorstep, and then offered a clear, logical response: if you
feel grief, as we all do, then you should also feel anger toward those who
have caused you to feel grief; and if you feel anger, you should join us in
confrontational activism to fight those who are responsible for turning a
public health issue into the AIDS crisis. Rather than regarding the quilt
as a memorial to gay men and others who had died, ACT UP suggested
it be viewed as a chronicle of murder that necessitated a forceful activist response. In beginning with a prevalent and more or less acceptable
feeling—grief—and then linking that grief to anger—a more disreputable
feeling—ACT UP authorized anger. ACT UP's emotional and political
pedagogy both acknowledged and addressed lesbians' and gay men's ambivalence about political confrontation: given our grief and under these
dire circumstances, where we and our loved ones are being murdered by
our government, anger and defiant activism targeting state and society are
not only necessary, they are legitimate, justifiable, rational, and righteous.

THE POLITICS OF GRIEVING.   Direct-action AIDS activists' criticisms of
grieving rituals like vigils and quilt showings were often scathing and
laid the ground for ACT UP's different approach to grief. For example,
founding member and longtime administrator of ACT UP/New York,
Bradley Ball, disparaged a Memorial Day AIDS candlelight vigil that
occurred in 1987:

A handful of people clustered at Sheridan Square and sang a pretty song
and lit candles. . . . I [handed] out leaflets for the Washington demonstration
[about AIDS, to occur on June 1, 1987]. I had intended to participate [in the
vigil], but I simply could not. The opening lines of the pretty song [are]: *We
are a strong and gentle people. Singing, singing for our lives.* . . . How can we

be singing for our lives? I'm so upset. . . . I've spent this weekend [handing out leaflets] on streetcorners and in barrooms confronting apathy and hostility, and now I find out we're singing for our lives. . . . Oh God, I'm tired and angry. I've been living AIDS for so long. . . . I want to go back to that mysterious time when I didn't have this virus inside of me that is slowly and surely and quietly destroying my system. I want out. Goddammit, I'm so fucking angry! Stonewall was supposed to bring us out of the closet and into the streets. In 1977 it was Anita Bryant. . . . And now there's this awful disease that is knocking us over like dominoes. . . . And we're lighting candles and singing songs. (Ball 1987; quoted in Goldberg 1997, 63–64; emphases his)

A year later, Ball continued his criticism: "We have spent many years mourning and bereaving, and have developed that into a high art. A lot of AIDS benefits like candlelight vigils have pretty names, but they don't express the fact that massive sectors of society are dying and that no one seems to care" (Anger 1988, 10).

Jeanne Kracher recalls having "very mixed emotions" about the candlelight vigils in Chicago:

They were very sad, they were very solemn. It was heavy. . . . It was a moving experience. But on another level, I remember all of us [members of DAGMAR and C-FAR] being very critical about it. We were very tough, and felt like if you're gonna get two hundred people marching through the street with candles, have them say something. . . . But, I also think that I thought this is a good thing that people are paying attention to [AIDS]. [We] were trying to figure out politically what all of this meant, and sort of having contempt for people that were singing that "we are gentle, angry people," and I'm sure we were making all the jokes that we always made about [that song]. [Our perspective was that] people should be angry. (Kracher 2000)

Kracher, in retrospect, emphasized the need for people to express grief, but in the moment itself, "I think there was this tendency [on our part] to want everything to be angry, and [we thought] that there was something that was extremely passive about these candlelight vigils" (Kracher 2000). Ferd Eggan had a similar recollection of a candlelight vigil he attended: "I remember feeling, 'Well, this is very nice, and it's sad, and it's nice to be with these people.' . . . But [I remember feeling] that it was pretty tame" (Eggan 1999). ACT UP/Chicago member Darrell Gordon thought that people at the vigils "had this kind of defeatist attitude, instead of this empowerment idea of taking back, and trying to fight, the system. . . . It wasn't about trying to fight the Reagan-Bush administration, or fighting the pharmaceutical companies, or anything of that nature at all" (Gordon 2000).

Many were similarly skeptical about the Names Project Memorial Quilt. Carol Hayse, a member of DAGMAR and later of C-FAR and ACT UP/Chicago, saw the quilt at the 1987 March on Washington. When interviewed, she recalled the deep sadness she felt: "I just cried and cried . . . I mean, you just can't stop crying. I'm tearing up now. It's very sobering" (Hayse 2000). Her sadness, however, was tempered with a political critique that she described as follows:

> I generally remember being a little contemptuous of the Quilt. A little. I also cried at the Quilt. I mean, I was aware that these were people's lives being represented. . . . But I was a little contemptuous of the Quilt, 'cause in some ways, it seemed to divert energy from anger. It seemed to say 'mourning is the valid response,' and *not* say the other thing that needs to be said with that: . . . 'turn your mourning into anger.' . . . And so it seemed a bit reformist and diverting of energy to a lot of us. (Hayse 2000; emphasis hers)

Hayse's recollection of ACT UP's way of dealing with death provides some insight into her own, and other ACT UP members', mixed feelings about the Quilt: "There was a great great deal of collective mourning in the queer community at that time. . . . So, if my memory serves, we were bending the stick in the other direction. We were saying, 'Mourning's fine. No problem. Make your space for mourning. But then, you know, get out, grab a rock and throw it through the window of the FDA'" (Hayse 2000).

In later years, some activists became even more disparaging of these more somber expressions of grief. In an article that began with the news that his entire immune system was shot, ACT UP/NY's Bob Rafsky offered a fantasy: "I'd like to find a few people who have sewn Names Project Quilt panels but now see such gestures as inadequate. Then, the next time the Quilt is unrolled—with their permission, for all our dead and our dead yet to come—I'd piss on it." Rafsky provided the following emotional and political reasoning in support of that fantasy:

> It's not grief itself we should shed; we need our grief. But if we can't leave behind all the false comforts, the easy, symbolic embodiments of our grief, most

of us will never feel our anger at full force for very long. Our anger, even the knowledge some of us have of our own forthcoming deaths, gets mixed up too easily with other agendas. . . . I [want] to take AIDS militancy further than it's ever gone. (Rafsky 1992, 51)

Another person with AIDS angrily expressed his desire that someone "just burn that stupid blanket" (quoted in Patten 1998, 403). Even people who made quilt panels sometimes indicated ambivalence. A panel for ACT UP/San Francisco member Terry Sutton read, "Terry Sutton. He hated this quilt. And so do we! ACT UP."[10]

Returning to the leaflet that ACT UP distributed at the quilt showing in 1988, its emotion work should now be clearer. Confrontational AIDS activists initially operated in a context in which public grief among lesbians and gay men was articulated in a somber emotional register and from a political position that stopped short of oppositional activism. Many activists deemed these public grieving rituals a hindrance to the forms of activism that they thought might actually save lives. Despite sometimes being contemptuous of these rituals, they too felt the grief and knew how deeply felt and widespread it was. The ACT UP leaflet acknowledged lesbian and gay grief, but in affixing grief to anger and confrontational activism, it offered an alternative.

MARCHING WITH DEATH IN THE STREETS. ACT UP's political funerals— introduced into ACT UP's tactical repertoire in the early 1990s—offered an emotional and political sensibility that acknowledged, evoked, endorsed, and bolstered lesbians' and gay men's anger. Carrying the remains of their loved ones through the streets in a powerful joining of grief with anger, ACT UP drew on a tradition used by liberation movements from South Africa to Ireland and El Salvador that underscored the political nature of the deaths of their comrades.[11] ACT UP/New

10. See the photograph in Sturken 1997, 187. Some who were not in ACT UP also criticized the quilt. Urvashi Vaid, for example, contends that the quilt "didn't do enough to politicize people" (Andriote 1999, 367).

11. There are, of course, important distinctions between these traditions as carried out by ACT UP and by liberation movements in other countries. In the latter, political funerals have been used in the context of an armed struggle and they mark the murder of comrades at the hands of the state or opposition forces. ACT UP's political funerals marked the deaths of comrades, but, despite movement rhetoric that they were killed by government neglect, they were, of course, not directly killed at the hands of the state. As with all tactics, the political funeral has a different meaning in different contexts.

York issued an invitation/leaflet announcing the first of its political funerals, the October 1992 "Ashes" action:[12] "BRING YOUR GRIEF AND RAGE
ABOUT AIDS TO A POLITICAL FUNERAL IN WASHINGTON D.C." (fig. 12). The
image that accompanied the headline was modest, the outline of an urn,
with the following text as its contents:

> You have lost someone to AIDS. For more than a decade, your government
> has mocked your loss. You have spoken out in anger, joined political protests,
> carried fake coffins and mock tombstones, and splattered red paint to repre-
> sent someone's HIV-positive blood, perhaps your own. George Bush believes
> that the White House gates shield him, from you, your loss, and his respon-
> sibility for the AIDS crisis. Now it is time to bring AIDS home to George
> Bush. On October 11th, we will carry the actual ashes of people we love in fu-
> neral procession to the White House. In an act of grief and rage and love, we
> will deposit their ashes on the White House lawn. Join us to protest twelve
> years of genocidal AIDS policy. (ACT UP/New York 1992)

In using the ashes of dead people, the action was an escalation in tactics, a shift from actions that deployed representations of death (e.g.,
mock tombstones and fake coffins) to a funeral procession that carried
the actual bodily remains of loved ones dead from AIDS-related complications. The leaflet offered the appropriate feelings and the appropriate activist response to "twelve years of genocidal AIDS policy": a love-
inspired and grief-filled rage channeled into a funeral march that would
force AIDS into the national consciousness.

Held in Washington, D.C., the same weekend as the annual display
of the Names Project Quilt, ACT UP's "Ashes" action implicitly drew
a distinction between the quilt's encouragement of grief and its own enactment of a grief-inspired rage. ACT UP/NY member David Robinson's announcement that he planned to scatter his lover's ashes on the
White House lawn inspired the "Ashes" action. Interviewed the day of
the march, Robinson explicitly drew a contrast between the political implications of the quilt and of ACT UP's funeral march: "George Bush
would be happy if we all made Quilt panels. We're showing people what
the White House has done: they've turned our loved ones into ashes
and bones" (Wentzy 1995). During the procession, participants angrily
chanted that message: "Bring the dead to your door, we won't take it

12. I am drawing here from Gould 2004.

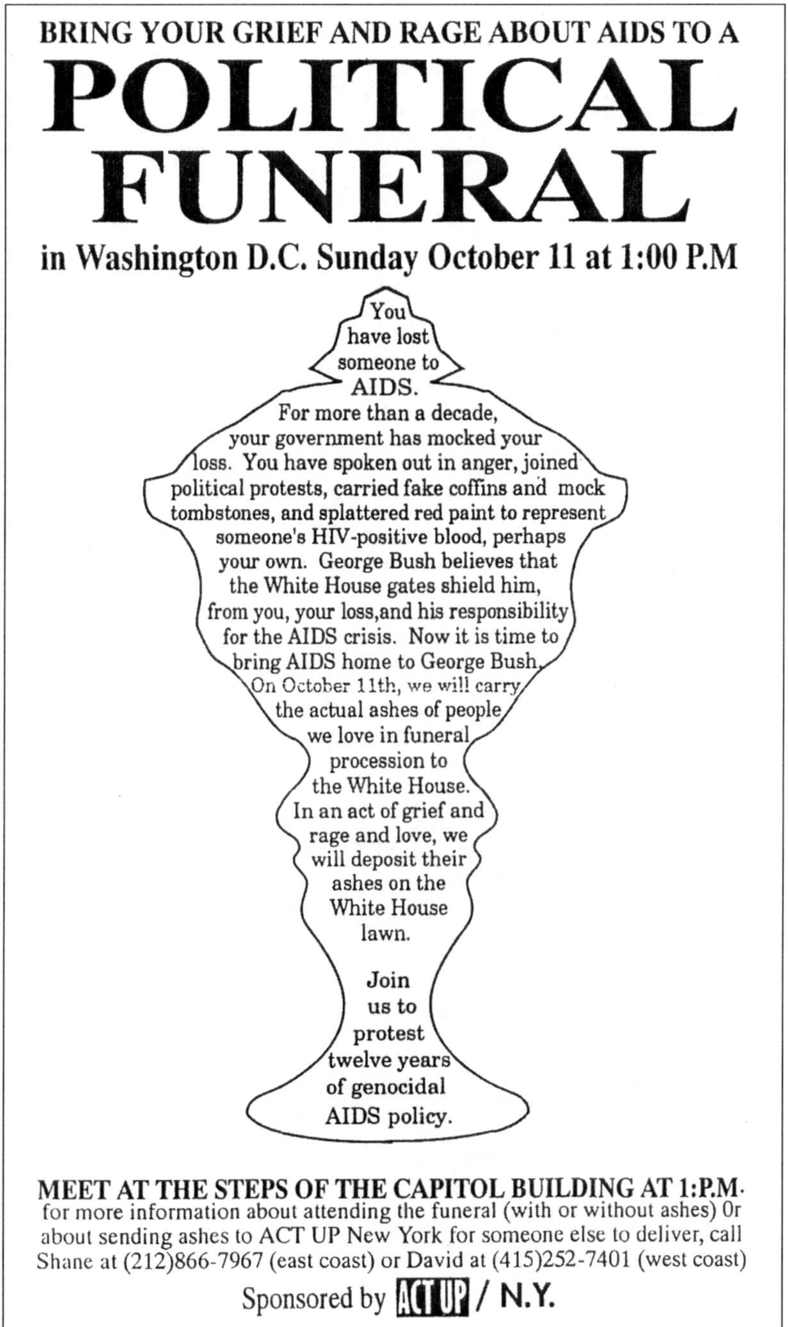

BRING YOUR GRIEF AND RAGE ABOUT AIDS TO A

POLITICAL
FUNERAL

in Washington D.C. Sunday October 11 at 1:00 P.M

You have lost someone to AIDS. For more than a decade, your government has mocked your loss. You have spoken out in anger, joined political protests, carried fake coffins and mock tombstones, and splattered red paint to represent someone's HIV-positive blood, perhaps your own. George Bush believes that the White House gates shield him, from you, your loss, and his responsibility for the AIDS crisis. Now it is time to bring AIDS home to George Bush. On October 11th, we will carry the actual ashes of people we love in funeral procession to the White House. In an act of grief and rage and love, we will deposit their ashes on the White House lawn.

Join us to protest twelve years of genocidal AIDS policy.

MEET AT THE STEPS OF THE CAPITOL BUILDING AT 1:P.M·
for more information about attending the funeral (with or without ashes) Or about sending ashes to ACT UP New York for someone else to deliver, call Shane at (212)866-7967 (east coast) or David at (415)252-7401 (west coast)

Sponsored by ACT UP / N.Y.

FIGURE 12. "Bring Your Grief and Rage about AIDS to a Political Funeral," leaflet, ACT UP/NY, 1992.

anymore" (Wentzy 1995). ACT UP/NY member Avram Finkelstein also contrasted the funeral march to the quilt:

> One by one, we called out the names of the dead: without a podium, a loud-speaker or celebrity spokespeople. The procession was the Quilt come to life—walking, shouting and storming the White House. . . . The ash bearers charged the gate, surrounded by crews [of activists] with linked arms. A fog of ashes blew through the fence and the urns were hurled. . . . I saw some-one actually scaling the fence. . . . We chanted and cheered and our dead floated over the immaculate green sod. . . . [After the action] I walked back to the Quilt, hoping to see [my deceased lover] Don's panel before the rains came. . . . I wanted to snatch it up and heave it over the fence, where it really belonged. . . . [The "Ashes" march] has defined AIDS memorials for me. It connected me for the first time to the anger and grief of thousands of others, and reconfirmed what I have always known . . . action is the real Quilt. (Fin-kelstein 1992b, 22)

ACT UP's message was clear: the way to grieve the endless deaths is with confrontational activism that angrily forces the reality of AIDS deaths into public view.

ACT UP/NY soon escalated further, shifting from ashes to dead bod-ies. Two weeks after the "Ashes" action, an anonymous person with AIDS issued a statement, "Bury Me Furiously," calling on AIDS activ-ists to hold a political funeral when he died, carrying his body in an open casket through the streets. The person, later revealed to be ACT UP/NY member Mark Fisher, wrote,

> I want to show the reality of my death, to display my body in public; I want the public to bear witness. We are not just spiraling statistics. We are people who have lives, who have purpose, who have lovers, friends and families. And we are dying of a disease maintained by a degree of criminal neglect so enor-mous that it amounts to genocide. . . . Oppressed people have a tradition of political funerals. . . . Everyone who sees the procession pass knows that the living, those who love the deceased, are bereaved, furious and undefeated. . . . I want my own funeral to be fierce and defiant. (Anonymous 1992)

Weeks later, the funeral for Fisher slowly wound through the streets of Manhattan, "urged on by a single drum" (Finkelstein 1992c), ending at George H. W. Bush's reelection campaign headquarters. Over the next few years, ACT UP chapters held a number of political funerals, carrying the bodies of their dead through the streets and attempting to deposit them at strategic sites, including the White House.

ACT UP's political funerals, perhaps the most spectacular enactment of the movement's conjoining of grief and anger in direct action, offered stark foils to the modes of grieving manifest at the quilt and candlelight vigils. In enacting the turning of grief into anger, these funerals transformed the staggering personal losses into a political as well as personal tragedy, into an injustice that should motivate lesbian and gay indignation, fury, and direct-action activism.

How Emotion Work Works

Through leaflets, speeches, chants, demonstrations, and other types of actions, AIDS activists encouraged queer folks to transform painful feelings of grief into anger and action. Why and how did the movement's emotion work *work*? How did ACT UP's emotion work further the shift in tone from somber grief to confrontational anger, and how did it animate and sustain a new, more confrontational activism? More generally, why is emotion work sometimes able to alter people's feelings, and how does it do so?

We can begin to answer those questions by attending to the relationship between language and feelings, as Reddy's notion of *emotives* does (1997). AIDS activists' repeated naming of their grief as anger effectively and *affectively* altered how some queer folks were actually feeling. Like other feeling states, grief is a complicated matrix of sentiments that includes sadness, loss, depression, fear, anger, dread, and a host of others. Activists altered the meaning and experience of grief by renaming as "anger" that complicated constellation of feelings. Their repeated expressions of anger elevated the emotion of anger and suppressed sentiments of sadness, despair, despondency, and loss, temporarily eclipsing those aspects of grief. Lesbians, gay men, queers could then reexperience a potentially paralyzing affective state of grief as outward-directed, action-oriented anger. Ferd Eggan described ACT UP's angry activism as both a buffer against and a channel for grief (1999). Jeanne Kracher recalled that "in the early days [of ACT UP], it was all about anger," but she noted that the anger should be recognized as, at least in part, "a form of grief" or a stage in the grieving process (Kracher 2000). Through activists' continual expressions, grief in a sense *became* anger. The way that

ACT UP/Chicago turned grief about the deaths of its members into angry activism greatly appealed to Frank Sieple, providing him with a politicized route for his grief: "It's almost like we didn't have time to grieve, you know, turning that grieving into the energy to move on. . . . One way, at least with me, of grieving, was taking that energy that I would use on grieving and putting it into action to prevent, or to make their deaths not seem in vain. . . . I think a lot of people did that" (Sieple 1999). As Douglas Crimp (1989) has noted, many in ACT UP turned away from the pain of mourning; indeed, mourning became militancy. Reiterated over time, anger became defining of ACT UP's emotional habitus, and linking grief to anger and both to action became axiomatic to many.

Of course, AIDS activists' naming of anger and urgings to turn grief into anger did not result in the complete disappearance of feelings of sadness, loss, and devastation that help to make up grief. Consider the following recollections of the "Ashes" action by Bob Rafsky.

> At the front of the march was a single line of people carrying urns. . . . Behind them were about a hundred of us who were willing to be arrested helping them to the White House fence. Behind us were three drummers playing rhythmic patterns that worked into our bodies: 1-2-3, 1-2-3, 1-2-3-4-5. Finally came the supporting marchers, more than 1,500 of them. . . . A few feet from me a young man in a white T-shirt was shouting at an imaginary George Bush, "It's your fault! It's your fault!" before he broke down and sobbed. . . . The action had been coordinated by a 22-year-old classics graduate student at Columbia University who had joined ACT UP. . . . I saw him pressed by our bodies against the White House fence, kneeling and weeping as ashes soared over him. (Rafsky 1992, 22–23)

Similarly, a demonstrator at a 1987 protest by CMJ to protest the federal government's inactivity on AIDS threw himself against the door of the Federal Building in San Francisco, sobbing and holding up a sign that demanded medical care (Linebarger 1987b).[13]

The fierce anger expressed by confrontational AIDS activists never entirely suppressed and was never completely divorced from the intense grief that many felt. Still, activists' repeated expressions of an-

---

13. These examples of manifest grief during demonstrations challenge any attempts to domesticate the feelings of protest by rendering them as merely one more strategic tool deployed by movement entrepreneurs trying to mobilize support.

ger elevated that feeling and submerged grief. The two emotional states were tightly coupled in ACT UP's emotional habitus; indeed, activists so forcefully harnessed and subordinated grief to anger that grief could hardly be felt as something other than anger. That configuration transformed people's feelings and also offered a powerful impetus to confrontational activism.

Emotion Work and the Feelings of Disjuncture

We also need to consider how the context in which activists' emotion work occurs might affect their success in inciting, amplifying, and regenerating specific feeling states and dampening or suppressing others. Significant characteristics of that context include the makeup of the prevailing emotional habitus, the sorts of emotives that are available and authorized or can be made so, the sorts of discourses that are widely circulating, and aspects of the environment and of people's everyday lives that are especially emotionally charged. Activists' creative emotion work is constrained and enabled by such contextual factors, and its success is shaped by them.

An important contextual factor for AIDS activists in the late 1980s and early 1990s was the disjuncture between queers' ongoing experiences with the epidemic and the dominant discourses about AIDS popularized by the mainstream media, politicians, and the scientific-medical establishment. The emotion work done by direct-action AIDS activists was compelling to wide segments of people within lesbian and gay communities largely because it spoke from and to the experiences of that disjuncture. Through their emotion work, AIDS activists gave shape to the affective experience of the disjuncture, naming as outrage what might have been experienced more amorphously as a mixture of incredulity, disappointment, and frustration that the government and mainstream society could be so unaware and uncaring about life for queers amid the AIDS crisis.

By the late 1980s, many lesbians and gay men had experienced the deaths of friends and lovers, caretaking of those who were ill, overflowing obituary pages in local lesbian and gay newspapers, and an endless succession of funerals. For those who were infected with HIV and symptomatic, taking care of their own health was a daily effort and often an emotional roller coaster ride. Medical and scientific breakthroughs were few, and when they did occur, the hopes they raised were soon dashed.

Moreover, lesbians and gay men were inundated with mind-numbing and grim statistics on deaths and new cases. Week by week, people were witnessing both the devastation of their community and the deaths of friends and loved ones. And there was no end in sight to any of it, only ongoing devastation. Such emotionally charged experiences, especially when widespread and frequent within a social group, can themselves motivate activism as well as create a reservoir of feeling states that are ripe for mobilization.

But even more was at play here. Dominant understandings of AIDS tended to blame gay men and gay male sexual practices for the spread of the virus. The media and politicians, not only those from the religious right, consistently made distinctions between "innocent AIDS victims"—children, hemophiliacs, and other ostensibly straight, middle-class people—and queers, junkies, and prostitutes, the lowlifes of society who were "guilty" not only of bringing AIDS on themselves, but of spreading the plague to the innocent. Dominant discourses sanctioned repressive and punitive measures—including quarantine—to deal with the epidemic. As well, there were frequent assertions by the media, politicians, and bureaucrats that the scientific-medical establishment was doing all it could to fight the epidemic. There was no public acknowledgement of the role that homophobia, racism, and sexism were playing in the government's and other institutions' handling of the crisis.

Dominant discourses about AIDS simply ignored lesbians' and gay men's daily experiences with the epidemic, implicitly deeming the experiences as well as those having them inconsequential. Queer folks already were familiar with social nonrecognition, but the felt disjuncture between their own emotionally wrenching experiences and dominant understandings of AIDS was, for many, staggering. How could state and society negate the horror they were living through? Dominant AIDS discourses seemed increasingly nonsensical: people were sick and dying as the result of a virus and government inattention to the crisis, *not* as the result of sexual deviance; gay men with AIDS were as innocent as anyone; lesbians and gay men were virtually alone in responding to the crisis; the government's homophobia was having deadly consequences; the scientific-medical establishment was *not* doing all that it could. In explaining his decision to join C-FAR, Frank Sieple noted this disconnect between his lived experiences with AIDS and dominant discourses that commended the government's response to the crisis: "[I was] really tired of seeing friends diagnosed and dying while the newspaper wrote about the good things the government was doing" (Wockner 1990a, 35).

By the late 1980s, this disjuncture was large enough to create an affective and conceptual space from which queers could launch a strong challenge to hegemonic constructions of AIDS and a scathing critique of the state's and other institutions' paltry efforts to address the epidemic. Also important in wrenching that fissure wide open were the years of lesbian and gay discourses applauding the community for its responsible efforts against AIDS, which had bolstered lesbian and gay pride and helped to create a massive chasm between lesbians' and gay men's self-understandings and the construction of homosexuality in the dominant discourses. Gay shame was not purged, of course, but it was being challenged, and ACT UP built on and continued that fight.

ACT UP/NY member Dudley Saunders credits the movement for naming and authorizing the fury that many gay men were unconsciously experiencing but had suppressed largely because of gay shame. "Most people did not believe they had the right to be angry. . . . I think for a lot of gay men, there was such shame around being gay. And then, to have gotten yourself infected, even if you'd [gotten infected] before you knew anything. You'd done this dirty thing, and gotten this dirty disease, just as, you know, you deserved to get. You had nothing to be angry about. [ACT UP] did these things that tapped into this rage that people didn't know they had, didn't know they could have" (Saunders 2003, 37–38).

During a speech at a 1988 ACT UP/NY demonstration, Vito Russo pointed to the enormous disconnect between queers' everyday lives amid the crisis and dominant society's unwillingness to grasp or care about those horrors. The emotional effects—primarily anger and contempt toward dominant society, coupled with pride about being an AIDS activist—animated his activism.

> Living with AIDS is living through a war which is happening only for those people who are in the trenches. Every time a shell explodes you look around to discover that you've lost more of your friends. But nobody else notices— it isn't happening to them—[and] they're walking the streets as though we weren't living through a nightmare. Only *you* can hear the screams of the people dying and their cries for help. . . . It's worse than wartime because during a war the people are united in a shared experience. This war has not united us—it's divided us. It's separated those of us with AIDS and those of us fighting for people with AIDS from the rest of the population. . . . It's not

happening to *us* in the United States—it's happening to *them*—to the dispos-
able populations of fags and junkies who deserve what they get. . . . And the
days and the months and the years pass by—and *they* don't spend those days
and nights and months and years trying to figure out how to get ahold of the
latest experimental drug and which dose to take it at and in what combination with what other drugs and from what source and for how much money
because it isn't happening to them so they don't give a shit. . . . They don't
spend their waking hours going from one hospital to another, watching the
people they love die slowly of neglect and bigotry because it isn't happening
to them so they don't give a shit. They haven't been to two funerals a week for
the last three, four, or five years so they don't give a shit. It's not happening to
them. . . . AIDS is a test of who we are as a people. When future generations
ask what we did in the war, we have to be able to tell them that we were out
here fighting. . . . I'm proud to be out here today with the people I love and to
see the faces of those heroes who are fighting this war and to be a part of that
fight. (Russo 1988b, 10; emphases his)

In lesbian and gay communities, ACT UP's emotionally charged
frame—which built on earlier AIDS activists' challenges to dominant
AIDS discourses—became the alternative to dominant understandings
of the epidemic. It took hold in large part because its outrage offered recognition of, and gave voice to, queers' daily experiences of devastation.
Street-based activists' outraged framing of the AIDS crisis addressed
queers' fears, anxieties, and desires about their lives, their survival, their
identities, their communities, their sexual practices, their relationship to
dominant society, and their political options. Their framing was faith-
ful to queers' daily experiences of AIDS, and that made it emotionally
resonant. That is, activists' emotion work *worked:* their vocal acknowledgement of the chasm separating queers' experiences from the straight
world's constructions of AIDS, and their expressed fury about that disjuncture, echoed what some in the community were feeling, in some cases
amplified people's feelings, and generated feelings of outrage among others. This successful emotion work animated many lesbians' and gay men's
support for ACT UP and their enduring participation in the movement.

The Emotion Work of Reconfiguring Death

The creative interpretive work of direct-action AIDS activists not only
reconfigured many lesbians' and gay men's understandings of the crisis,

but also reconfigured people's feelings. The following example illustrates the emotionally charged nature of AIDS activists' interpretive work and provides another opportunity to analyze why and how ACT UP's emotion work worked.

Direct-action AIDS activists resignified AIDS deaths, as sociologist Josh Gamson (1989) has noted, from death caused by deviance or virus, to murder by government neglect. Where contemporaneous constructions of AIDS blamed a virus and gay male sexuality, AIDS activists blamed the homophobic government and other institutions. In 1988, for example, an autonomous, activist artist collaborative within ACT UP/ NY, Gran Fury, designed a sticker that sandwiched a bloody handprint between blocks of text that read "The government has blood on its hands. One AIDS death every half hour" (Crimp and Rolston 1990, 80; see fig. 13).[14] The graphic suggested that AIDS deaths should be viewed as less about infected blood than about government negligence and genocidal complicity in the murder of thousands.[15]

Likewise, posters at ACT UP demonstrations often were in the shape of gravestones with the names of people who had died and the epitaph, "Killed by Government Neglect." ACT UP's die-ins, where demonstrators would lie in the street while others outlined their bodies with chalk, similarly conjured up a murder scene rather than death by disease or by "deviance." Chants at ACT UP demonstrations drew attention to the government's role in the crisis and in the accumulating deaths: "Land of the free, home of the brave, is putting queers in the grave;" "Justice, equality, it's all a fucking lie, our homophobic government is letting people die." A chant at a funeral march for ACT UP/San Francisco member Terry Sutton indicted a pharmaceutical company as well as the FDA: "We're Terry's friends, and we're here to say: we blame Astra and the FDA" (Marquardt 1989). At a 1988 rally in Albany, N.Y., Vito Russo attributed his own illness and possible death to the social response to AIDS rather than to a virus:

If I'm dying from anything it's from homophobia. If I'm dying from anything it's from racism. If I'm dying from anything it's from indifference and red

14. The text of Gran Fury's bloody hand graphic was changed over the years to reflect the accelerated pace of AIDS deaths.

15. Gamson (1989) also discusses ACT UP's resignification of blood. In this section I extend Gamson by investigating the *emotional* components of ACT UP's resignification work.

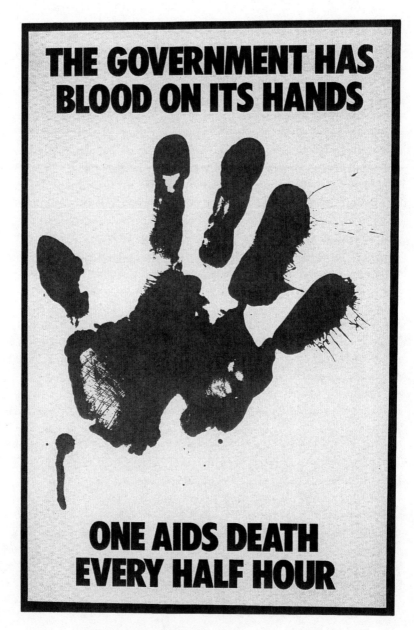

FIGURE 13. "The Government Has Blood on Its Hands," Gran Fury, 1988.

tape. If I'm dying from anything it's from Jesse Helms. If I'm dying from anything I'm dying from Ronald Reagan. . . . If I'm dying from anything I'm dying from the fact that not enough rich, white, heterosexual men have gotten
AIDS for anybody to give a shit. (Russo 1988b, 10)[16]

All of these transformations in the meaning of AIDS deaths had an
emotional charge. Where an understanding of death as the result of deviant sexual practices typically evoked shame, and where an understanding of death as the result of a virus might evoke terror and despair, an
understanding of death as produced by government neglect—that is, of
AIDS deaths as *murder*—stirred indignant outrage.

The mutual reinforcement of ACT UP's interpretive and emotion
work created a robust, tightly knit system: If you shared ACT UP's interpretation of the AIDS epidemic, you were encouraged to feel angry about the crisis and to embrace direct action as the appropriate response. As an ACT UP/Los Angeles banner put it: "Angry? ACT UP!"
(Sprecher 1990). Individuals could of course place themselves outside of
this system: as tightly woven as the component parts might have been,
the system was never totalizing, and an individual could embrace one
part while ignoring or even rejecting the others. Still, once someone inclined toward one of the components, the tightly knit nature of the system bolstered adherence to the others as well.

The Emotion Work of Rituals

Rituals, as Durkheim argued, are important to emotional transformation, reminding us that the places and times in which activists' emotion
work occurs affect its success.[17] Reddy's concept of emotives highlights
how language shapes feelings, but sometimes people experience affective states that become legible and motivating through a more bodily experience than naming, such as attending a meeting or a protest action.
Avram Finkelstein credited his engagement in AIDS activism with producing that type of emotional transformation in himself: "Eleven years
ago, I met my soulmate and fell madly in love. . . . Four years later, he
was dead. . . . My landscape was flattened by loss. When the dust finally
cleared, two things were apparent to me: I was not alone, and something—

16. For another example, see "Heckler" 1992, 9.
17. On emotions and rituals, see Collins 2004.

besides support work—had to be done about AIDS. Fear and grief faded away when I discovered action" (Finkelstein 1992a, 48). A person's enactment of anger at a demonstration—through chants and facial and bodily gestures, for example—may suppress other feelings, making the anger physically legible to oneself while displacing the sensation of other feelings that simply are not enacted, at least not in a culturally recognizable form. ACT UP's meetings and actions were ritualized happenings where that sort of emotional transformation could occur.

It is clear that ACT UP's emotion work succeeded in part because it was tapping into and echoing what many queer folks already were feeling. In some cases the key was ACT UP's authorization of queer rage and its expression. Sometimes what mattered most was ACT UP's naming as anger a complex matrix of unstructured feelings that became intelligible through that naming; named political emotions gave form to more amorphous affective states. The movement also intensified, and even produced, feelings. ACT UP's meetings and actions were especially emotionally generative.

The following account of one HIV-positive gay man's decision to join ACT UP indicates the sort of emotion work that occurs during activist actions and how effective that work can be in transforming people's feelings. In a 1994 interview, G'dali Braverman described his initial contact with ACT UP/NY: "I had received a couple of flyers in the mail about ACT UP. I breezed through them and, basically, tossed them" (quoted in Shepard 1997, 113). Braverman experienced an emotional transformation while watching New York's Gay and Lesbian Pride Parade in 1988. "When ACT UP passed . . . I took one look and said, 'I am going to go to the next meeting of that organization.' There was a sense of power, a sense of action. It didn't appear to be about pity or shame or sadness or guilt. It seemed to be about anger and action" (113). Braverman's witnessing of ACT UP/New York's anger in the streets seems to have altered his previous disinterest. Having tested HIV-positive the previous year, Braverman may have been feeling a variety of sentiments about AIDS and the epidemic, perhaps including the shame and guilt that he mentioned. ACT UP's expressive demonstration of anger may have allowed Braverman to *feel* anger, by legitimating that feeling but also by *enacting* it.

In the ritualized happening of a meeting or action, ACT UP's emotion work linking anger to engagement in street activism might generate precisely those effects. In his memoir, *Queer in America,* Michelangelo Signorile indicates as much. He talks about becoming increasingly scared about AIDS in 1987. He and a friend were invited to an ACT UP/ NY meeting, and they decided to go even though they had been told that ACT UP was a protest group "and we weren't sure how we felt about that" (Signorile 1993, 53). Signorile had no experience with activism and believed that ACT UP was a bunch of crazy radicals (Signorile 2003, 5–6). In his memoir, Signorile notes that the politics articulated at that ACT UP meeting were unfamiliar to him, but the anger being expressed with "passion and fervor" was exhilarating. "The meeting went on for hours. I'd never experienced anything like this, and hadn't felt as stimulated by anything I'd done before. . . . When the meeting was over, . . . [I was] filled with energy" (1993, 54–55). That affective state prompted him to go to a demonstration discussed at the meeting that was to be held later that night. "I didn't know the first thing about protesting and I still wasn't sure about it. I certainly didn't like the idea of getting arrested" (56). But as he watched other protesters disrupt the targeted official's speech and get arrested, his own anger began to swell; he jumped up on a platform and began to shout, and was soon arrested. By his own account, Signorile quit his previous life entirely after that action and joined ACT UP.

Braverman's comments help to explain why Signorile suddenly felt enough anger to engage in an action that would likely result in his arrest: "We helped perpetuate . . . anger in the discussions that we had around the actions so that you [became] a bottle of emotions with a great sense of purpose" (quoted in Shepard 1997, 114). ACT UP chapters across the country began their meetings with a statement of purpose that always included the phrase, "We are united in anger and committed to direct action to end the AIDS crisis." Members repeatedly exhorted one another to feel their anger. Emotionally prescriptive statements like this one from a letter to ACT UP/NY written by member David Robinson were common: "To survive, to save our queer lives, love is not enough; we must be 'united in anger,' we must feel and use our rage" (Robinson 1990, 4).

Although ACT UP's emotion work was sometimes conscious and calculated, it was often the unintended by-product of ACT UP's other activities, as the following stories illustrate. When Terry Riley happened upon an ACT UP/NY demonstration in April 1987, he stopped to watch, struck by participants' unquenchable anger, "the kind of anger not seen on white American faces since Vietnam" (Green 1989, 21). After fifteen minutes, he found himself walking toward the protesters and joining them. He began to chant, loudly and angrily, and did so for forty-five minutes, not knowing who he was with but feeling their anger, and now his own anger, about the AIDS crisis. Although not in a calculated, strategic manner, ACT UP members were engaging in emotion work through their action. Public demonstrations with angry, chanting amassed bodies encouraged public and collective expressions of anger about AIDS and were also a vehicle for the "transmission of affect" (Brennan 2004), allowing energy to cross bodily borders and incite others to join in. Riley happened upon the demonstration and became enthralled, evidently overtaken by the anger on protesters' chanting faces. Their bodily expression seems to have generated in him an affective state that he had not been feeling just moments before, animating him to move toward them and become a chanting participant. He joined ACT UP soon thereafter.[18] Again we should recall Durkheim's notion of collective effervescence, particularly his idea that the experience of coming together alters people's psychic activity and subsequently their actions: "The vital energies become hyperexcited, the passions more intense, the sensations more powerful; there are indeed some that are produced only at this moment. Man does not recognize himself; he feels somehow transformed and in consequence transforms his surroundings" (1995, 424).

Billy McMillan had a similar experience that prompted him to join C-FAR. He was in Los Angeles and decided to go to an ACT UP/Los Angeles demonstration against presidential candidate George H. W. Bush, who was holding a fund-raiser at the Bellaire Hotel. Some of the protesters' signs were simple crosses, with somebody's name written on one axis and the date of death on the other. Someone gave McMillan a cross to hold, but another protester asked him if he would mind switching crosses. McMillan said "OK," but then asked why, and the man replied that the guy on McMillan's cross was a friend of his. That exchange, in the midst of this ACT UP/L.A. demonstration, stirred McMillan:

> Here I was in the middle of this demonstration where I didn't know anyone.
> That guy's words really struck me, and I just started crying. This was so real,
> and so personal; so many people were affected by AIDS and so many more
> were going to be affected. I felt a great sense of loss. And then I began to get

18. This story comes from Green 1989.

real pissed off at all those greedy, wealthy people going into this presidential fund-raiser. I felt that they didn't care if we all died right then and there. . . . I came back [to Chicago] and I hooked up with my friend Adam Burck, who was involved with this group called C-FAR, Chicago For AIDS Rights. . . . They were the only group in town doing anything proactive. . . . So I went to their meeting . . . and I was all fired up because of this demonstration in L.A. (McMillan 2000)

The repeated expressions of anger at ACT UP meetings and actions made anger normative and intensified the feeling itself, suppressing other feelings that might have arisen or become intensified during the AIDS crisis—grief, shame, fear—or that might accompany participation in confrontational activism—fear and anxiety about defying authority, uncertainty about the utility or necessity of the action, or embarrassment about appearing crazy, foolish, or politically impassioned. Through the emotional preparations, each participant's feelings were given meaning through language—labeled as anger—and thus could be felt as anger, perhaps producing the sense of being "a bottle of emotions with a great sense of purpose."

Participation in ACT UP meetings and actions also provided an outlet, "a vent for rage and frustration" (Span 1989). Meetings and actions helped to address the painful feeling states that were part of daily life for many queers. Ray Navarro, a person with AIDS and member of ACT UP/NY, found activism to be "a way of healing, . . . a way of dealing with the fear" (quoted in Span 1989). ACT UP activists engaged in emotion work with regard to other feelings as well, especially gay pride, shame, and fear of social rejection.

ACT UP's Transmutations of Pride, Responsibility, and Shame

ACT UP's emotional pedagogy authorized anger and confrontational activism in part by making angry direct-action activism an object of lesbian and gay pride. In doing so, ACT UP dramatically dislodged pride from its place within what in some ways was a politics of respectability during the early 1980s. At an HRCF dinner held seven months after the formation of ACT UP/NY, Larry Kramer concluded a speech by encouraging attendees to join ACT UP/NY, partly by expressing his pride about confrontational AIDS activism:

With pride, I close by acknowledging ACT UP, the AIDS Coalition to Unleash Power—now almost 1,000 very energetic men and women who glory in nothing more than protesting in the streets. I cannot tell you how infinitely moving this organization is. . . . Their commitment is astounding. They have picketed and yelled and screamed and even been arrested on some dozens of occasions. . . . I beg all of you to come and join us at [our upcoming demonstrations] and at our Monday night meetings. (Kramer 1987d, 16)

An ACT UP button that said "I was arrested fighting AIDS"— pinned by activists onto one another as they were released from jail— also linked pride with confrontational activism and encouraged (re)commitment to the fight. A C-FAR leaflet announcing a meeting elevated its direct-action activism by making an implicit comparison between possible objects of gay pride. It blared, "FIGHT BACK, FIGHT AIDS!" followed by smaller text that read, "We MUST keep the pressure on in order to bring about the government and institutional responses necessary to combat the AIDS crisis. PLEASE JOIN WITH US and experience the satisfaction and pride of helping your brothers and sisters. . . . LET'S FEEL RIGHTFULLY PROUD BY FIGHTING FOR OUR RIGHTS TOGETHER!" (C-FAR, N.D.; capitalization in original). C-FAR's use of the qualifier *rightfully* before the word *pride* raised questions about previous objects of lesbian and gay pride and offered a new orientation: pride about collective and confrontational activism.

Repeated articulations and evocations of this new pride valorized direct-action AIDS activism, fortified commitment to the group, and encouraged others to support, and even join, ACT UP. Tim Miller recalled the pride he felt after joining C-FAR: "I think there was an incredible sense . . . of being proud that I'm doing something" (Miller 1999). Expressions of pride about AIDS activism were echoed by those not directly involved in the movement, suggesting that ACT UP's pride was migratory. For example, in June 1988 *Outlines* columnist Rex Wockner distinguished C-FAR as "the most exciting new development in the Chicago gay movement" and continued with an assertion of pride about confrontational AIDS activism: "C-FAR's Carol Jonas, Ferd Eggan, Lou Snider, . . . Paul Adams, . . . and countless others make us very, very proud this June" (Wockner 1988, 29).[19]

Emotional expressions have emotional effects. Repeated articula-

19. See also Markson 1987.

tions of pride about angry activism counteracted lesbian and gay shame, whether about sexual difference or about noisy activism that threatened to shake up the status quo. They thereby helped to authorize ACT UP's direct-action politics, in part by supplanting, or at least suggesting the limits of, the previous emotional habitus and displacing the prior object of pride from its preeminent position. The frequent articulations of pride seem to have enlivened that feeling among street AIDS activists and among other lesbians and gay men as well.

Direct-action AIDS activists also resignified the terms *responsible* and *responsibility*, and here again—strengthening the link between pride and confrontational activism by labeling the latter as *responsible*—this emotion work helped to generate support for ACT UP. In the mid-1980s, responsible gay men and lesbians took care of their dying friends and lovers, volunteered to be buddies for people with AIDS, and supported the work of ASOs. AIDS activists declared that responsible queers now took to the streets and were the new source of pride. Responsible queers might still take care of ill friends and lovers, volunteer at an ASO, and so on, but direct-action AIDS activists shifted the emphasis, privileging confrontational activism. Indeed, directly challenging the trope of responsibility that prevailed in the early 1980s, AIDS activists sometimes derided ASOs for not doing more to save actual lives. ACT UP/NY member Steven Webb wrote a letter to the *New York Native* expressing his beliefs about what responsible lesbians and gay men should be doing. He described a recent ACT UP action and then asked, "Where were you?" He continued,

I get the impression that the New York community looks to the Gay Men's Health Crisis (GMHC) to lead the way in all issues concerning AIDS. The GMHC provides patient services and education. Their agenda has been to offer any person with AIDS high-quality care and a dignified way to die, and preventive education to those not yet infected. Laudable. Necessary. But this community must understand that what the GMHC does has next to nothing to do with saving the lives of those who are dying. It is within their substantial power to do more to save lives; it is simply not their priority. . . . We are at war and we are losing: 21,000 dead, at least one million walking wounded. We are at war. Will you enlist? (Webb 1987, 6)

Larry Kramer drew a connection between responsibility and activism in a speech that he gave to the annual Gay and Lesbian Town Meeting in Boston in June 1987 (reprinted in the *New York Native*): "Why are there so few people out there screaming and yelling? . . . We are going to die because we refuse to take responsibility for our own lives" (Kramer 1987c, 37). Although Kramer suggested that responsibility included actions like writing letters and giving money, his view that confrontational activism was the truly responsible act is clear. After listing all of the governmental agencies that were supposed to be conducting research on drugs, and all of their shortcomings, Kramer asked,

> What the fuck is going on here and what the fuck are you doing about it? . . . Twenty-four million gay men and lesbians in this country, and who is fighting back? We have a demonstration in Washington and we have 300 people. . . . How many dead brothers have to be piled up in a heap in front of your faces before you learn to fight back and scream and yell and demand and take some responsibility for your own lives. . . . [T]hey are killing us and we are letting them. (Kramer 1987c, 40)

Taking up Kramer's equation of responsibility with confrontational activism, a man wrote the following in a letter to the editor: "I was so impressed by Larry Kramer's article 'Taking Responsibility for Our Lives' that I could no longer sit by as others did something. I went to my first meeting of . . . ACT UP last Monday" (Franetic 1987, 6). In many contexts, the hectoring, shaming register that Kramer used might fail to mobilize, but in this moment the aligning of pride and responsibility with ACT UP inspired some to get involved.

The following example suggests how articulations of the righteousness and necessity of activism (and thus of the responsibility to participate) invigorated those already involved. In a keynote address to a national meeting of direct-action AIDS activists in 1988, C-FAR member Ferd Eggan declared,

> The fact, dear friends, is that AIDS has taught us how to live and how to be well—by fighting for what's right. It is our society that is truly sick—sick with oppression and exploitation. The government is not interested in helping us— they would prefer that we curl up and die. In the face of cruelty and injustice, it's right to rebel. We all have to act and act now. There is hope for this sick society—the healing power of our anger and love. Love does not mean being nice, it means seeing what's wrong and trying to change it. (Eggan 1988, 2)

The crowd then cheered loudly, "giving Eggan a standing ovation and chanting, 'ACT UP, fight back, fight AIDS'" (Olson 1988, 6).

Eggan's statement knit together many components of ACT UP's emotional habitus and its concomitant politics. Acceptance by an oppressive and exploitative society should not be the goal; the course of action instead should be to reject and fight to change that "sick" society. Lesbian and gay anger and love must inspire a rebellious activism. Never mind dominant society's emotional and political norms: angry, confrontational activism is the responsible thing to do given the injustices and cruelty of the AIDS crisis. Gay love must be a love committed to social change and righteous rebellion.

Along with resignifying responsibility in a way that valorized defiant street activism, activists also altered a previously used meaning of responsibility by laying the blame for the AIDS crisis at the doorstep of the government. Rather than claiming community responsibility in caretaking as an indirect way to counter dominant discourses that blamed gays as *responsible* for AIDS, AIDS activists directly countered the accusations against gay men: gays were not responsible for the AIDS crisis; rather, the government's negligence and *irresponsibility* were to blame, and the government should be held responsible for resolving that crisis.[20]

In its reconfiguration of the trope of responsibility and its reorientation of pride, ACT UP challenged the normative affective ties that lesbians and gay men might have felt with regard to dominant institutions like science, the media, and the state. Rather than trusting them, ACT UP suggested that skepticism, doubt, and distrust would be more appropriate feelings with which to approach and assess such institutions. Indignation and outrage also were appropriate, of course, as were hostility and disgust. Targeting them for their genocidal policies was proper and responsible.

ACT UP also transformed the subject and object of shame. ACT UP

20. The trope of responsibility was also used against ACT UP. Politicians and the mainstream media frequently constructed AIDS activists as irrational and irresponsible. For example, after heated exchanges with lesbian and gay activists, Chicago Mayor Richard Daley walked out of a town hall meeting and stated that he would meet with "responsible gay activists but not with those who wanted confrontation [i.e., ACT UP]" (Hanania 1989, 3). Expressions about the responsibility of confrontational street activism should thus also be seen as a response to mainstream views that construct activism as irresponsible. ACT UP engaged this discursive struggle over the meaning of responsibility (see chapter 5).

inverted gay shame by asserting that the (in)actions of the government
and other institutions responsible for the AIDS crisis were shameful. A
frequent chant at ACT UP demonstrations was "shame, shame, shame,"
said while pointing to a specific target. The alteration of shame was connected to ACT UP's other emotion work: lesbians and gay men angrily
fighting back were righteous and responsible, and rather than feeling
ashamed, they should feel proud of both their sexual practices and their
confrontational activism.

The audiences for ACT UP's rhetoric of shame were both the targets
of its protests and its own members. An ACT UP/Los Angeles document
written as an internal educational piece about the FDA evoked shame in
a manner that seemed aimed at influencing how ACT UP members understood the government's role in the epidemic, but as an internal document, it may as well have been designed to counter gay shame. "The
shameful fact remains that no new drugs are being released to PWARCs
[people with AIDS-related complex] or PWAs. . . . Homophobia, sexism,
and racism have all contributed to mismanagement, delays in funding,
and shameful neglect of those who are suffering" (ACT UP/Los Angeles, n.d., 2, 6). The shame was on the government and other institutions,
not on those who were suffering through this epidemic.

AIDS activists also invoked shame to criticize lesbians and gay men
who were critical of ACT UP. Many lesbians and gay men, for example, were critical of ACT UP/NY's 1988 disruption of a speech by New
York City's Mayor Ed Koch, during which the mayor declared June
"Gay Pride and History Month" and unveiled a new photo exhibit.
ACT UP zapped the mayor because of his "failed leadership on AIDS"
(Kirschenbaum 1988, 6), but others in the community felt that the may-
or's actions bestowed "official recognition of our status as an honorable,
distinguishable community with a heritage of activism and pride" and
should therefore be celebrated (Conkey et al. 1988, 6). In response to the
heated criticism, Vito Russo wrote a letter to the *New York Native* that
took ACT UP's detractors to task and ended by shaming them:

> I would like to register my wholehearted support of ACT UP for their appro-
> priate and well-timed zap of Mayor Koch. . . . All those good and polite lit-
> tle boys and girls who have been whining about how ACT UP trashed its own
> party and how this wasn't the time or the place to zap the mayor are not ac-
> tivists, they're a bunch of politically naïve asswipes. . . . These people are like
> the Jews who said, 'Don't throw rocks at the Nazis. You'll make them mad

at us.' How much worse can this administration possibly be? . . . I would like
to remind all of these so-called "activists" what activism means. Activists do
things that you're not supposed to do. Activists are not respectable. . . . Activists are not dazzled by the crumbs off a table from a mayor who is allowing their friends to die. Activists are not grateful for some rinky-dink exhibit
which "allows" us to celebrate our history while our history is being systematically wiped out. . . . These prim and proper fans of gay history should take
note. History will record that, like the Jews who did nothing during the Holocaust, they are the traitors and fools in our midst. Shame on them. (Russo
1988a, 6)

Such articulations of shame redirected the feeling away from self-
doubt and self-hatred. Not queers, but the government and other institutions should feel ashamed for failing to address the AIDS crisis, and
those who were continuing to kowtow to dominant society should feel
shame as well. Gay journalist Jon-Henri Damski recorded the shifting
subject of shame in a column he wrote about an eruption of sentiment
against Chicago's Mayor Daley who made a surprise appearance at a
lesbian/gay antiviolence march. There were approximately a thousand
participants, and when the mayor unexpectedly showed up, there was an
outburst, fueled by the mayor's negligence with regard to AIDS. "I found
myself with the crowd around me, automatically pointing my finger at
the mayor, and echoing 'Shame, Shame, Shame!'" (Damski 1992b, 15).
Damski noted the queer transformation of shame:

In the old days, we felt shame for our queer sexuality. And if a politician even
came to talk to us, . . . we would be silent with respect. But today queers
are standing up and demanding more of their public servants. We know the
shame is not on us, we who have led the fight against this pandemic plague.
But the shame is on them . . . who run a health department that still offers us
nothing but timid avoidance. The shame is on their neglect, not our sexuality.
That's why we have the courage to stand up and put the shame where it be-
longs. (Damski 1992b, 15)

As with activists' articulations of anger and pride, their articulations
of shame seemed to affect their own and others' sentiments about themselves and society. From the vantage point of Betty Berzon—a psycho-
therapist who had worked in the lesbian and gay community for years—
ACT UP's actions and rhetoric profoundly affected their feelings of

shame. Reflecting on ACT UP's actions and slogans, its popularity, and its fervor, Berzon noted, "I began to see the effects of these developments in the new ways my clients talked about being gay. I was hearing more pride of ownership in a community feeling its strength, speaking out, acting up, demanding attention to its needs. Clearly this transition . . . from a victim's mentality to an activist mindset was having a positive impact on the self-esteem of many gays" (Berzon 1994, 307–8).

I am not claiming that ACT UP successfully eradicated gay shame; that would be impossible in a heterosexist world where queers, like any other social outcasts, sometimes experience shame due to living in a state of nonrecognition and social erasure. Nevertheless, ACT UP's reconfiguring of shame had the effect of ameliorating the feeling for many queers, and its work in that arena generated immense appreciation.

ACT UP's Response to Mainstream Emotional and Political Norms

ACT UP also had to navigate the emotional habitus and concomitant political norms of mainstream society. In Western societies, and in the United States most specifically, anger is commonly disparaged when expressed by members of groups that are themselves socially devalued. Anthropologist Catherine Lutz lists several factors that contribute to the "generally negative evaluation of anger" in the United States (1988, 180). First, there is the dominant culture that "portrays much emotion as chaotic and irrational" (180). People expressing anger in public seem particularly out of control. Second, "anger is often seen as an antisocial emotion because it can involve protest against restraints that are social" (180) and seen as necessary to the smooth functioning of society. Lutz notes that there is some ambivalence here because the prevailing individualistic ethos in the United States sometimes legitimizes protest against "the system." Nevertheless, *who* can challenge state and social regulations is severely prescribed by social hierarchies of race, gender, class, sexual orientation, and the like. Only some groups of people are authorized to express "righteous anger" and even then only in certain ways and for a specific period before they too are derided as overwrought and crazy. A view of anger as *righteous* seems to be the exception rather than the rule. Lutz also lists a third factor that produces a negative evaluation of anger: "the strong association posited between anger and aggression" (180). In general, then, anger is suspect.

Thomas Scheff argues that "rationalism has come to be the dominant attitude in our present status quo, the social arrangements that go without saying in our society. One such arrangement is the suppression of emotions" (1992, 102). We uphold rationality as the ideal way to be, and "being rational"—assessing, evaluating, adjudging, considering, appraising—is equated with being unemotional. In the United States we are particularly inclined toward the suppression of strong feelings (103). We are made uneasy by expressions of intense grief, loudly articulated anger, enacted rage and fury. Emotionality in the streets—most obviously in the case of riots, but also in the case of confrontational protests—is even more unsettling because it seems to signify a breakdown in social order. In addition, street protest is often cast as unnecessary and dangerous, partly because of its emotional valence. As social movement theorists Frances Fox Piven and Richard Cloward have argued, "The ideology of democratic political rights, by emphasizing the availability of legitimate avenues for the redress of grievances, delegitimizes protest" (1992, 313). ACT UP, then, confronted a prevailing emotional habitus and dominant political norms that tend to discourage emotional protest politics.

AIDS' activists might have responded by tempering ACT UP's emotionality. Other movements have certainly followed that route. Julian McAllister Groves found that the animal rights activists he studied tried to manage the expressive tone of their movement so as not to appear overly emotional. "Activists learned to manage their own emotional responses to animal cruelty, and find emotional dispositions that appeared more legitimate. . . . [They also] learned how to identify in others the emotional traits appropriate to animal rights activism, and avoided interactions with those who did not conform to the correct emotional disposition" (Groves 1995, 443). Activists made conscious attempts to appear rational and dispassionate, grounding their arguments in rights-based philosophy and drawing boundaries between an acceptable concern for animals and an overly emotional concern (447–49, 456).

Direct-action AIDS activists, in contrast, authorized ACT UP's emotionality and political defiance by flipping conventional understandings on their head and asserting the *rationality* of their angry and confrontational activism. Recall Ferd Eggan's assertion that "in the face of cruelty and injustice, it's right to rebel," and the standing ovation he received. Aware of the discrediting potential of dominant emotional and political norms, ACT UP participants repeatedly justified the movement's militancy by pointing to the extremity of the AIDS crisis, to the genocidal actions of people and institutions targeted by the movement, to the wholesale slaughter of their community, and to the effectiveness and necessity of ACT UP's angry activism.

In many cases, the target audience was other lesbians and gay men who were skeptical about ACT UP's emotionality and confrontational politics. In response to a gay man's assertion that "action born of anger was ineffective," lesbian AIDS activist Denise Kulp explained the link between her anger and her decision to commit civil disobedience. "People I love are dying, and that makes me angry. I am making my anger powerful by turning it into action, to change the way things are" (Kulp 1988, 22). Angry activism, Kulp contended, was an obvious and rational response to death. ACT UP/Chicago used its allotted speaking slot during the 1992 Pride Rally to counter criticism about its confrontational activism.

> Some people in this community say we should stop rocking the boat. But the ship is already sinking, folks. They say we should shut up, tone it down, be more civilized, and grow up. We cannot be calm and polite when four people die of AIDS every day in Chicago, deaths that could have been prevented; when almost 200,000 people have already died of AIDS in this country alone. Why should we be nice and sweet when Mayor Daley and his Health Commissioner Sister Sheila Lyne fought us every step of the way as we demanded an increase in their measly one million dollar AIDS budget? They told us that they would not and could not increase the AIDS budget just as they hadn't in the last four years. But we forced them to increase it by 2.5 million dollars. We disrupted Mayor Daley's appearances and shouted him down while he tried to ignore us. We invaded City Council meetings. We barged into the Health Department while they locked their doors on us. . . . We won the additional AIDS funding because we were loud, disrupted their business as usual, and took to the streets!!! (ACT UP/Chicago 1992, 5)[21]

ACT UP's leaflets and other agit-prop that used rhetorics of murder and government-sponsored genocide similarly challenged conventional emotional and political norms and justified defiant activism. Its repeated expressions of anger and indignation toward state and society, and of pride about both confrontational activism and sexual difference, coupled

21. This months-long campaign resulted in the city of Chicago more than tripling its 1992 AIDS budget. Full disclosure: I co-wrote this ACT UP/Chicago speech.

with ACT UP's assertions about the rationality, necessity, and responsibility of activism, together valorized what is often derided as emotionally overwrought and politically unnecessary. ACT UP's challenge to mainstream norms provided a language of resistance and an emotional pedagogy to lesbians and gay men, ways of feeling and acting that addressed those who were hesitant about engaging in ACT UP's activism.

Summary: ACT UP and a New Emotional Habitus

Social movements face emotional imperatives, and their response to such constraints and opportunities affects their development. In their emotion work, direct-action AIDS activists addressed lesbian and gay grief by naming it as anger and tying it to confrontational activism; gave voice to queers' infuriating experience of having their daily encounters with the horrors of AIDS ignored by mainstream society and simultaneously being blamed for the crisis; offered a response to lesbian and gay ambivalence by elevating anger at state and society and pride about sexual difference and confrontational activism, while suppressing shame about homosexuality and fear of social rejection; and countered mainstream American emotional and political norms, most effectively with rhetoric that asserted the necessity and rationality of emotion-driven, confrontational activism.

ACT UP's emotion work was a crucial and necessary element in its meteoric rise in the late 1980s and growth into the early 1990s. If ACT UP had not engaged in this constant and extensive emotion work, it would not have been able to garner and sustain the support and participation of large segments of lesbian and gay communities across the United States. Arising in a moment of emotional transition but within both a structure of lesbian and gay ambivalence and a context of mainstream American emotional norms, the direct-action AIDS movement had to engage in the struggle between competing emotional habitus, each with its attendant politics. ACT UP's emotion work, sometimes strategic and premeditated but often simply the unintended by-product of its various activities, provided thousands of lesbians and gay men with a new set of affects and emotions that authorized angry, confrontational street activism. Activists' repeated articulations and bodily enactments of this new emotional habitus helped to animate and sustain their own engagement in and others' support for confrontational AIDS activism.

The (Re-)Birth of Queer

ACT UP not only inaugurated a new era in lesbian and gay politics and in AIDS activism, it also was the site from which a new, *queer* sensibility emerged and took hold, a sensibility that was embraced by lesbians, gay men, and other sexual and gender outlaws across the country. *Queer* wove together the new emotional habitus and the movement's oppositional politics and sex-radicalism, creating a collectivity that set queer-identified folks apart from the more establishment-oriented gay leadership and institutions. Rather than an identity, or even an *anti*-identity in the way that queer theory posits, *queer,* in its moment of rebirth circa 1990,[22] might best be understood as an emotive, an expression of self and collectivity that created and regenerated feelings that were a powerful and alluring response to lesbian and gay ambivalence about self and society: fury and pride about gay difference and about confrontational activism, antipathy toward heteronormative society, and aspirations to live in a transformed world. This new sensibility grew out of the political exigencies of the moment. The deadly consequences of existing as a despised population were by then unambiguous and staggering; there was a dire need to up the ante in the fight against AIDS. Also apparent were the repercussions for gay activism of the painful psychic effects of living as a despised group—most especially a widespread anxiety about acting up. *Queer* not only challenged the vehement homo-hatred that structured state and societal responses to the crisis; it also offered emotional, political, and sexual ways of being that addressed that anxiety. Even more, as a shared sensibility, *queer* generated a sense of connection with others in the room who were as angry, as willing to be defiant, as willing not only to celebrate gay difference but to believe that the world needed that difference. In a context of social nonrecognition, *queer* invited and intensified our recognition of one another.

As an affective antidote to the bad feelings that flow from social annihilation, the new queer sensibility helped to generate broad appeal for ACT UP and, largely as a result of its emotional effects, was a vital force sustaining the movement into the early 1990s.

22. I say *rebirth* to indicate that the term *queer* was embraced by some sexual and gender outlaws in earlier historical moments (Chauncy 1995); I focus here only on its usage circa 1990.

Queer: Anger, Political Opposition, Sex-Radicalism

By 1990, to identify as queer was to embrace righteous anger about homophobia and the AIDS crisis as well as political defiance; it was to feel
proud about sexual difference and relatively unconcerned about social
acceptance. With that sensibility, the new queer generation proudly and
joyously shook up norms in straight and gay society.[23]

ACT UP queers reeroticized sex and catapulted their proud sexual
difference into the public realm, challenging the tendency of the gay establishment to downplay gay difference in a bid for mainstream social
acceptance. In Steven Epstein's words, "Queerness connoted a provocative politics of difference—an assertion that those who embraced the
identity did not 'fit in' to the dominant culture *or* the mainstream gay
and lesbian culture and had no interest in doing so" (Epstein 1999, 61;
emphasis his). ACT UP's queer stance also fought the AIDS-era equation of sex with death and made a clear link between confrontational
AIDS politics and liberatory sexual politics. ACT UP/Chicago's speech
at the 1992 Lesbian and Gay Pride Parade knit the two together:

> Fighting the AIDS epidemic must go hand-in-hand with fighting for queer
> liberation. And we mean liberation for all queers! Queers of all colors and
> sexes, leather dykes and drag queens and radical faeries and bulldaggers
> and dykes on bikes and poofters and fish and studs and butches and femmes
> and clones from the 1970s and the 1990s. We need to celebrate our sexuality,
> our erotic innovations created out of this epidemic, our fantasies and fetishes,
> our particular ways of fucking, sucking, and licking. It is our queer love that
> has made us capable of fighting the insurance industry, the drug companies,
> the government, the bureaucracies, the gay-bashers, the right-wing zealots,
> the AIDS crisis. (ACT UP/Chicago 1992, 5)

The new queer sensibility unabashedly drew sex and militant politics together. ACT UP/Chicago member Mary Patten extolled ACT UP's conjoining of the two: "ACT UP combined the red fists of radical 1970s feminism and the New Left with the flaming lips of neo-punk, postmodern,

23. I use the term *generation* not as a marker of age, but as a way to indicate the ascendance at this time of a queer emotional and political sensibility and its widespread influence on sexual and gender outlaws of many ages.

222222222222222222

pro-sex queer politics. . . . Red now stood for lips, bodies, and lust as well as anger and rebellion; fists connoted not only street militancy, but sex acts" (Patten 1998, 389).[24]

ACT UP also unleashed a queer coming together of lesbians and gay men, dykes and fags, and that made the movement enormously compelling for many. ACT UP/NY member Polly Thistlethwaite spoke about gay men's and lesbians' "passionate respect for each other," recalling in particular how "revered" many lesbians in the movement were: "Faggots were crazy about these girls" (Thistlethwaite 1993; see also Moore 2003, 4). Jeanne Kracher recalled that gay men's openness about their sexuality had a strong influence on her own sexuality.

> I think for me, one of the earliest memories I have of really feeling like, "Huh, this is interesting, this is something I haven't experienced before, and this is something I better be open to and learn from," was all the sex-positive stuff [in ACT UP]. . . . Sex certainly was never the basis of anything that I had organized around. Certainly not as a feminist. And there was a way that these guys were so expressive about their sexuality, which helped to free me. . . . There was something about being in that crowd that was very freeing, about being a lesbian, about being gay, that this was about sex on a very deep level. These guys . . . would take their shirts off at the first possible moment at a demonstration and would have a million nipple rings and were making out whenever they could possibly incorporate that into anything. And there was a way that that was very freeing. (Kracher 2000)

Ferd Eggan credits lesbians for the movement's embrace of queer sexuality: "I think that one of the reasons why ACT UP and the AIDS movement in general became a movement about gender and sexuality was because of lesbians. And all the advance work that people had been doing during the '80s, like *On Our Backs* [a lesbian sex magazine]" (Eggan 1999).

Challenging the recent attacks on queer sexuality, gay men brought their highly developed (and much maligned) sexual cultures to the movement; lesbians brought their experience from the feminist sex wars and the recent renaissance in lesbian sexual experimentation; and both brought

24. Patten (1998, 405) credits lesbian pornography editor Susie Bright with popularizing the red fists/red lips metaphor as a way to signal the transformation in lesbian identities in the late 1980s and early 1990s.

FIGURE 14. ACT UP/Chicago's Power Breakfast T-shirt. Produced by ACT UP/Chicago Women's Caucus, design by Mary Patten and Jeanne Kracher, photography by Shelley Schneider-Bello, 1990.

an openness about learning from one another in the sexual realm. United (at least temporarily) by their activism, feelings, and sex-radicalism, lesbians and gay men in ACT UP turned to each other as political allies and friends, embracing and even trying on each other's identities. Men in ACT UP/Chicago wore the Women's Caucus "Power Breakfast" T-shirt, which pictured two women engaged in oral sex (fig. 14).

Around the country, dykes wore "Big Fag" T-shirts, and fags wore "Big Dyke" T-shirts. Queers embraced gender and sexual fluidity. Some queer dykes and fags started having sex with one another (see Black 1996).[25] That is not to say that ACT UP created an utterly accepting and experimental sexual environment. Men and women having sex together often felt the need to hide their relationships; some of these liaisons I learned about only in interviews. Ann Cvetkovich notes that there was "a significant discrepancy between ACT UP's professed reputation as

25. This phenomenon may have been more frequent on the coasts than in the Midwest. Although some gay men and lesbians had sex with one another in ACT UP/Chicago, we often joked that we were more "conservative" in the Midwest, where girls do it with girls and boys with boys.

a model for queer intimacies, including relationships between lesbians and gay men, and the actual practice, which involved a lot of secrecy" (2003a, 194). Still, my recollection is that many of us, although somewhat uncomfortable with the "hetero" queer sex going on in our midst, were trying to interrogate our gut reactions. Zoe Leonard's reflections about the difficulties she faced in being "out" about having sex with a man in ACT UP/NY indicate some of the complexities of sexual ecumenicalism. At the time, she experienced people's attitudes as "small-minded and painful," but she came to an understanding of why these sexual relationships were difficult for some in the movement to accept: "We had created a safe queer space and now there were people having heterosexual sex within that space, occupying that space. I can understand now why that was threatening" (quoted in Cvetkovich 2003a, 193). *Queer* had its sexual limits, then, but there was nevertheless an immense opening out toward sexual and gender outlaws of *most* stripes, especially those who were outcasts in the mainstream lesbian and gay community—drag queens and kings, trannies, S&M practitioners, butches and femmes, bisexuals, leather dykes, nelly boys, public sex lovers, sluts, dykes donning dildos and other sex toy aficionados, man/boy lovers.[26]

While the new queer attitudes about sexuality, society, and politics took shape in the emotionally charged atmosphere of ACT UP meetings and actions, they quickly spread to people not directly involved in the movement. And to be sure, as a provocation to both gay and straight establishments, ACT UP was often challenged by lesbians and gay men who disputed its representation (in both senses of the word) of the lesbian and gay movement and community. Still, ACT UP's queer sensibility momentarily overturned the gay status quo, effecting sweeping changes in many lesbians' and gay men's sexual and political subjectivities and practices.

The Emotion of Queer

The emotional effects of reclaiming a queer sensibility were perhaps what most attracted lesbians, gay men, and other sexual and gender outlaws

---

26. *Queer* also had its racial and gender limits, a point I take up in chapter 6. Although for some it signified a political stance for radical social transformation, including challenges to white and male supremacy, for others *queer* elevated oppression due to sexuality above all other oppressions. See Barbara Smith (1993) for an analysis of how *queer* became raced as white and gendered as male.

to embrace the term as well as the movement from which it grew. The AIDS epidemic had ravaged lesbians' and gay men's already conflicted feelings about homosexuality. *Queer,* as an emotive, offered a new sensibility that allowed, encouraged, and in a way *enacted,* a changed orientation both to self and to dominant society for those within as well as outside the movement. Artist and ACT UP/NY member Gregg Bordowitz has written eloquently about his need, after testing HIV-positive in 1988, to fight "an internal conclusion that my pleasure had led to my death" (Bordowitz 2004, 126). He describes "the discourse of blame that would judgmentally bring sentence down upon me for getting fucked up the ass, liking it, and getting a fatal disease from it," asking, "Where did this discourse exist?" He answered, "Among the homophobes. Among the right wing. And in my own mind. Sometimes, I believe that my homosexuality is a disease and that I deserve to get sick from it. This thought can overtake me at any time. I think it in my dreams. I hear it in the voices of kind friends and see it in the faces of my relatives. It's always present." But, he writes, "I am not resigned to it. I fight it" (126–27). *Queer* offered a potent emotive for the fight. Bordowitz suspects that his embrace of ACT UP's queer fashion was primarily about repudiating the shame he felt about his sexuality (Bordowitz 2002a). ACT UP/NY member Peter Staley credits the movement with queering him, both politically, by enticing him to become a confrontational activist, and in terms of his self-understanding and self-presentation: "ACT UP has had a dramatic effect on my life. I left Wall Street altogether and am doing ACT UP activities full-time, getting arrested, and wearing an earring" (Anger 1988).[27] ACT UP's queerness, along with the feelings of solidarity generated in the movement, encouraged ACT UP/NY member Michelangelo Signorile to embrace his sexuality. "I'd never felt so close to people I worked with. . . . We were putting our bodies on the line for each other, going to jail for each other. I loved these people—and was loved back—in a way I had never known. I was feeling powerful about being gay. Feelings from when I was a child came back. I had longed for people to tell me that being gay was great. My closet was opening. These people were the most out-of-the-closet, in-your-face people in the world" (Signorile 1993, 63). ACT UP's queer sensibility created the means for recognition

---

27. Before joining ACT UP/NY, Staley worked as a bond trader. By his own account, he was deeply closeted while working on Wall Street before joining ACT UP (http://blogs .poz.com/peter/archives/2008/06/peter_staley_ai.html; accessed June 29, 2008).

of both self and one another, generating forceful feelings of solidarity within the movement.

Lesbians' and gay men's appropriation of the label *queer,* as with the appropriation of any collective identity or sensibility, entailed both "an affective as well as [a] cognitive mapping of the social world" (Jasper 1998, 415). *Queer* valorized anger, defiant politics, and sexual nonconformity, and displaced gay shame, self-doubt, fear of rejection, and the desire for social acceptance. As queer theorist Judith Butler has noted,

> The increasing theatricalization of political rage [e.g., in disruptions of politicians' speeches, die-ins, etc.] in response to the killing inattention of public policy-makers on the issue of AIDS is allegorized in the recontextualization of "queer" from its place within a homophobic strategy of abjection and annihilation to an insistent and public severing of that interpellation from the effect of shame. To the extent that shame is produced as the stigma not only of AIDS, but also of queerness, where the latter is understood through homophobic causalities as the "cause" and "manifestation" of the illness, theatrical rage is part of the public resistance to that interpellation of shame. (Butler 1993, 23)

With outrageous, in-your-face, sexy, and angry activism, queers reappropriated *queer,* expurgating it of its shame-inducing power and, in the process, suppressing feelings of shame they might have had. Where mainstream discourses and some prominent lesbian and gay discourses had earlier blamed gay sexuality for AIDS, *queer* valorized non-normative sexuality and suggested the positive role of gay male sexual culture in the AIDS epidemic. Similar to Crimp, who asserted that "it is our promiscuity that will save us" (1987c, 253),[28] Ferd Eggan challenged criticisms that depicted the 1970s as "a death trip of ruttish sexuality and alienation," urging queers to remember that "gay men's sexual networks in particular were the foundation to build the communities that care for each other now" (Eggan 1988).

As became evident during the feminist "sex wars" that raged during the 1980s, numerous lesbians had already been engaging in a sexual

28. Crimp's reasoning was that promiscuity taught gay men about sexual pleasures and also about the varied ways to seek and attain those pleasures. "It is that psychic preparation, that experimentation, that conscious work on our own sexualities that has allowed many of us to change our sexual behaviors [amid AIDS]" (1987c, 253).

renaissance that foregrounded a multiplicity of sexual pleasures, some of which had been disparaged in some lesbian feminist circles—use of dildos and other sexual accessories, penetrative sex and fisting, S&M, butch/femme, bondage, use of pornography. The rebirth of *queer* extended these and other lesbian sexual practices, and discussions about them, to many more lesbians, and marked a new explosion in lesbian sexual experimentation. Celebrations of queer sexuality united lesbians and gay men in a common cause: the fight against the stigmatization of their sexual practices and identities and the fight for sexual liberation. For both lesbians and gay men, characteristics that queers were supposed to be ashamed of now became sources of pride.

Pride in queer sexuality was pronounced, for example, in a demonstration that ACT UP/Atlanta hosted against Georgia's sodomy law. Five hundred activists from ACT UP chapters across the country demonstrated at the Georgia state capitol on the opening day of the legislature in 1990. Holding signs that read "Sodomy: the law is the perversion" and chanting "Suck my dick, lick my clit, sodomy laws are full of shit," demonstrators simulated sex acts as they blocked traffic (Gerber 1990, 1). In response to the governor's description of the action as "repulsive," one demonstrator stated, "it was an audacious affirmation of lesbian and gay *sex*" (quoted in Gerber 1990, 1; emphasis in original). Chip Rowan, an ACT UP/Atlanta organizer of the protest, called the demonstration "a source of strength and pride for gay people in the South who want to take the risk of coming out publicly" (3). After the sodomy action and a demonstration the next day that targeted the CDC, Rowan remarked, "Everywhere we went today and last night, people were applauding us, saying we had to continue this, saying how good ACT UP made them feel" (3). The pride demonstrated in ACT UP actions—whether it attached to queer sexuality or to confrontational activism—was infectious.

The embrace of a queer, anti-assimilationist, and oppositional sensibility also addressed lesbians' and gay men's fears of social rejection: as they themselves were rejecting society, they were less concerned with society's rejection of queers. To feel and express anger was now normative. The queer embrace of defiant activism valorized as rational and indispensable that which mainstream society typically disparaged as irrational, dangerous, and unnecessary. *OutWeek* columnist Nina Reyes registered the psychological and political shift that had occurred through ACT UP and that was propelling this new queer sensibility forward:

It took us years to realize that in our attempts to check the ravages of AIDS, we had contributed to the repression of our own queer sexuality. We have had to come to terms with the pall of fear that had descended upon our collective psyches, demonizing promiscuity and equating all of our sexual experimentation with death. Then, in 1986, the U.S. Supreme Court affirmed that we have no basic right to our sexual self-expression. . . . When it became clear that AIDS would decimate not only individual queer lives but our sexually queer culture, ACT UP was spawned. The flickering spirit of liberation ignited queer rage, and our community developed a self-consciously sex-positive movement. . . . The AIDS-activist group has rebaptized the liberation impulse. . . . ACT UP erupted into activism with the incendiary passions of individuals united in anger, unwilling to take it anymore. . . . It gave lesbians and gay men who had had enough of the [gay rights] movement's reservation and politesse the chance to fight hard and dirty and without apology. (Reyes 1990a, 41, 44)

Intense affective states of eroticism and sexiness, exuberance and euphoria, pride and self-respect, now attached to the term *queer* and animated identification with and the embrace of both this new sensibility and ACT UP, the site where new queer selves were being publicly and passionately enacted. The queer and confrontational components of ACT UP were part of what drew many young queers to ACT UP. Polly Thistlethwaite indicated this when she explained her attraction to ACT UP/NY: "The thing that appealed to me about ACT UP when I first started . . . was that it was in the streets and it was queer, it was gay and lesbian, and I had never had the courage or the opportunity to demonstrate around that. And that was great" (Thistlethwaite 1993).

In sum, the new queer sensibility—born within ACT UP and championed by the movement—offered an emotionally compelling response to lesbians' and gay men's often contradictory feelings about self and society. Additionally, as a collective identification that embraced opposition and an outsider status, queerness appealed to those who historically had been marginalized by the mainstream lesbian and gay movement and community. It validated those who held radical politics, who refused assimilation, and who celebrated sexual difference. Eliciting and fortifying a fierce pride in bucking political, emotional, and sexual norms, *queer* exerted a strong affective pull that enticed thousands to adopt the label and to support the movement out of which it emerged. For all these reasons, the rebirth of *queer* helped to generate and maintain support for ACT UP.

Conclusion

ACT UP's rise in the late 1980s and sustained growth into the early 1990s was contingent on the generation and regeneration of intense sentiments among thousands of queer folks. This was true in part because ACT UP was operating in a society that typically disparages angry street activism, but it also was necessary in light of the gay world's history of anxiety about rocking the boat. In their rhetoric, agit-prop, and actions, AIDS activists normalized and valorized anger and confrontation, making them sources of pleasure and pride. My contention is that ACT UP's emotion work helped it to secure and extend the new emotional habitus and its attendant political horizon and was thus a crucial factor in the movement's growth and sustainability. Its affective and political pedagogy had force: ACT UP became one of the important places to be if you were a self-respecting queer concerned about the AIDS crisis.

Emotional imperatives exist for all movements: like other organizations, including political regimes, social movements must establish a normative emotional order if they are to survive (Reddy 2001). We thus need to investigate how movements respond to such emotional exigencies, exploring the affective pedagogies they offer and how that largely nonconscious work influences movement sustainability.

PART III
The Feelings of Decline

The last meeting of ACT UP/Chicago is seared in my brain. It was in January 1995, and there were fewer than ten people there. Most of us had been involved for many years, but there were also two men attending their first ACT UP meeting. ACT UP/Chicago had been declining for quite awhile by this point. We probably peaked in 1990 but had been able to pull off a number of large and successful actions through 1992; during the next couple of years, even as a core group continued to meet, our numbers shrank and we held very few demonstrations.[1] ACT UP chapters around the country had a similar trajectory; nationwide, the direct-action AIDS movement dwindled markedly after 1992. Not expecting that this January meeting would be our last, we started with a report from Ann Bata, our treasurer. We had a small amount of money in our bank account and a number of bills coming due. We owed Ann Sather's Restaurant rent for our meeting space. The group approved paying the bill, and after a brief discussion, decided to stop meeting at a public venue because we no longer could afford it, and with such small meetings, we could meet at someone's house. Ann then reported on the monthly charges for our post office box; she noted that we were receiving almost no relevant mail. We voted to close the P.O. box. Ann next

---

1. The last ACT UP/Chicago demonstration was in December 1994, against the Illinois Department of Corrections.

reported on the monthly charges for our voice mail. We were receiving almost no phone messages, so we decided to cancel our voice mail account. Ann then reported on the monthly charges our bank was deducting from our account because our balance was below the minimum. Saving money was costing us money and no new money was coming in, so we decided to close out our bank account as well.

That's when I started to laugh, simultaneously amused and distraught by the irony of the situation. ACT UP/Chicago was disintegrating right before our eyes as we closed account after account . . . and here were two new members, eager to fight the AIDS crisis! Soon, all of the old-timers were laughing hysterically, tears streaming down our faces, down mine because here were two new enthusiastic members attending what seemed to be ACT UP/Chicago's final fizzle, but also because I sensed that this was it for ACT UP/Chicago.[2]

At the moment of this writing (2008), a few chapters of ACT UP still exist. During the last few years, ACT UP/New York and ACT UP/Philadelphia, for example, have targeted profiteering by the transnational pharmaceutical industry and have fought for domestic and global access to AIDS drugs. But as a national movement, ACT UP had largely declined by the mid-1990s. The three chapters that make up this part of the book explore factors that contributed to its decline.

The decline of ACT UP might be dated in 1992 or 1993, but it began before that and went on for a number of years after. In fact, some factors contributing to its decline began as early 1989–91, years during which local ACT UP chapters and the national movement kept up a flurry of activity, registered a number of victories, and continued to grow. ACT UP was still in existence during 1993–94, but it was unquestionably in decline by then, if not yet entirely finished. Many participants had already left the movement and it had become harder to attract new members, and by that point, although a number of ACT UP chapters were continuing to act up, the movement had a changed feel about it and seemed altogether different. ACT UP's decline, then, extended over a number of years. The following discussion attends to the different temporalities of factors like social, cultural, and political openings toward lesbians and gay men (chapter 5); conflicts and fracturing solidarity within the movement (chapter 6); and the growth of despair within ACT UP (chapter 7).

2. Edwards 2000a has a similar recollection of this last meeting.

Two points need to be mentioned from the outset. First, many assume that ACT UP declined because it succeeded. There is some truth to this; ACT UP's many victories provided more treatment options, allowed some activists greater input into the workings of AIDS research and drug development, and in other ways beneficially altered the AIDS landscape. Some surely left the movement as a result. But as I discuss in chapter 7, in the years of ACT UP's decline many in the movement reached a point of despair about the AIDS crisis; they did not think the movement had succeeded in saving lives, and they were losing hope in its ability to do so. It is important to note that ACT UP declined before the advent of protease inhibitors in 1995–96, drugs that have helped people to live longer. ACT UP's activism was a crucial factor in the development of this new class of drugs, but that extraordinary success was not yet known during the years of ACT UP's decline.

A second point is that other factors contributed to ACT UP's decline that I do not discuss here. In particular, I do not explore the role played by state repression. The police presence at ACT UP demonstrations often was enormous, and there were frequent incidents of police brutality. As just one example, the City of Chicago paid tens of thousands of dollars to settle a lawsuit brought by members of ACT UP/Chicago, ACT UP/Kansas City, and ACT UP/New York against the Chicago Police Department for brutality during a demonstration in June 1991 targeting the American Medical Association. ACT UP/Chicago member Jeanne Kracher recalls people being "freaked out" by that and other incidents of police brutality and notes that "fewer and fewer people . . . [came] to demonstrations" as a result (Kracher 2000).[3] My hunch is that FBI surveillance of ACT UP and the sense among participants that we were being watched also affected the sustainability of the movement.[4] I hope that future analyses will explore the role of these factors in ACT UP's decline.

An overarching theme of these three chapters is that changes in a movement's context *and the affective states generated as a result* can

3. On police brutality at ACT UP actions, and police surveillance of ACT UP, see Olson 1990a; Chibbaro 1990; Alexander 1991; Barron 1991; Bull 1991; Halley 1991; Millenson and Alexander 1991; Olson 1991a; "Police Committee" 1991; Yang 1991; Bowden 1992; and Olson 1992.

4. On FBI surveillance of ACT UP, see Kaplan 1991; Osborne 1993; "FBI" 1995; Hamilton 1995.

challenge the practices, feelings, habitus, and imaginaries that organize and indeed constitute the movement, making it difficult for the movement to persist. These affective states—emergent, amorphous, operating largely beneath conscious awareness—may be difficult to assimilate and address even as they exert pressure on the movement's existing customs, routines, systems, rituals, procedures that hitherto have worked. In the case of ACT UP, real and perceived political, social, and cultural openings toward lesbians and gay men, along with our increasing knowledge of the growing enormity of the AIDS crisis, even in the face of our victories, created an affective landscape that was difficult to navigate. The movement's emotional practices were oriented primarily toward generating and heightening anger, but that emotion work was less successful in a changed context of apparent openings, of growing desperation and consequent competition over the movement's focus, of despair about the never-ending deaths and our inability to stop them. My discussion of movement decline sticks closely to the case of ACT UP, but the argument is portable: to understand why movements wane, we need to investigate how they navigate the feeling states that arise from their changing contexts.

Writing about ACT UP's decline has been excruciating at times. The movement filled my life during six intense years, and its decline was devastating for many more years afterward. The continuing deaths made the absence of ACT UP incomprehensible. As well, where once my life had been filled with intensity, a sense of purpose, and collectivity, the emptiness after ACT UP was disorienting and hard to bear. Many people I interviewed had similar difficulties adjusting to "life after ACT UP." Sometimes the pain was in the form of regrets over what the movement might have achieved if we had been able to navigate the in-fighting, if ACT UP had been able to build stronger alliances. Often it was utter sadness about the deaths. After our interview, Marion Banzhaf wondered about all the people ACT UP lost to AIDS and about the possibilities foreclosed by those deaths: "If only Aldyn was still alive. If only Ray were here, all those people" (Banzhaf 2002). Some spoke about the void in their lives after ACT UP. Recalling his experience in ACT UP, David Barr noted that he "lived with this sense of passion that has not been replaced and probably won't be replaced, and coming to terms with that loss has been really hard and has taken a really, really long time and it's still not over" (Barr 2002). Jeff Edwards recalled his feelings of depression and a sense of aimlessness after ACT UP. But knowing that those of us who were shaped politically by ACT UP bring those experiences into our subsequent work is one thing that has allowed Edwards, finally, "to be able to rest easy with the fact that it's over" (Edwards 2000a). One of my hopes in the following chapters is that thinking about movement decline and the feelings of loss that often accompany it might open out toward new political horizons and creative, new forms of activism.

Openings and Movement Decline

The ideological environment in which ACT UP operated contributed to its decline. Like other confrontational activist movements in the United States, ACT UP faced a political landscape that is frequently hostile toward oppositional street activism or, when perhaps more supportive, nonetheless often characterizes such activism as worrisome, unseemly, and acceptable only under the narrowest of circumstances. In a country where democratic procedures ostensibly provide effective institutionalized means for addressing conflict, where routine interest-group politics establishes and demarcates the political horizon, defiant extra-institutional politics breaks the rules. Politicians, the corporate media, and other dominant institutions frequently condemn protest politics as extremist, particularly when they understand democracy in terms of harmony and unity of the population rather than as a form of governance that follows an indeterminate path.[1] From the perspective of the reigning ideology, a functioning democracy has little need for confrontational protest politics.

This ideological context undoubtedly discourages militant, confrontational activism, but history shows that it does not prevent it. Indeed,

---

1. Because there is no agreed upon content to the "good life" or the best means of achieving it, democracy necessarily (and positively) entails friction, dissension, and conflict.

ACT UP initially operated quite effectively in this milieu. Nevertheless, disparagement of ACT UP and its methods of activism—from both gay and straight worlds—eventually contributed to the decline of the direct-action AIDS movement. The question, then, is why that larger political milieu posed little hindrance to militant AIDS activism in one moment but became an impediment in another.

The difference was not primarily within the ideological climate itself, which remained fairly constant over time, at least in important respects. What gave traction to the disparagements of ACT UP in its later years were real and perceived political, cultural, and social openings for lesbians and gay men. A widespread sense in lesbian and gay communities that greater acceptance by society was forthcoming gave discourses against confrontational activism a renewed emotional and psychic force. This chapter explores these dynamics, focusing on why and how the ideological context came to matter and contributed to the movement's decline. An ideological climate like that in the United States nearly *always* affects activism, discouraging some potential participants from involving themselves in or even associating with a confrontational movement's activities. Apart from those effects, the consequences of the ideological milieu vary depending on the material conditions facing the movement and participants' and potential participants' understanding and framing of the overall environment. This chapter, then, explores how the ideological context of politics articulates with other factors in a movement's environment to affect its viability.

Against Confrontation

Confrontational movements like ACT UP operate in ideological environments made up of mainstream attitudes and discourses as well as those generated from the margins of society that sometimes echo conventional wisdom but also offer alternative perspectives. Even mainstream discussions about militant movements are often polyvalent. In the case of ACT UP, for example, mainstream newspaper editors, scientists, and government officials frequently criticized its agenda and tactics, but they often praised ACT UP as well. The ideological climate that confrontational movements like ACT UP face—even as constituted through mainstream discourses—is not always thoroughly negative. Nevertheless, the privileged discourses tend to be those that naturalize and sanction political practices like lobbying, fund-raising, and voting and paint street activists as dangerous, immature, unreasonable, irrational, foolish, and uninformed.[2]

In light of biases against confrontational activism, we should read derisive portrayals of such activism not as accurate descriptions but as operations of power whose effects require study. I begin, then, with an analysis of the disparagements that ACT UP faced. What was their content and why, how, and to what extent did they affect the movement's viability?

Disparagements in the Period of ACT UP's Decline

DERISION FROM THE MAINSTREAM. When ACT UP began to decline, direct-action AIDS activism was being vilified by people and institutions from various echelons of society, which plausibly contributed to its decline. The most famous incident was an aggressive denunciation by President George H. W. Bush during a meeting with journalists from the religious press in March 1991. In response to a question about condom distribution in New York City's public schools, the Catholic Church's opposition, and alleged "Catholic-bashing" by groups like ACT UP, Bush stated,

> I think ACT UP resorts to tactics that are totally counterproductive. To the degree that the AIDS question should be treated as a health question, they work even against that because of their outrageous actions. . . . [I have had my] own meetings broken up by them. . . . It's an excess of free speech . . . to resort to some of the tactics these people use. And I've tried to be very sensitive to the question of babies suffering from AIDS—innocent people that are hurt by this disease. (Quoted in Wockner 1991b; see also Dowd 1991; Wockner 1991d, 13)

Bush later indicated that he was particularly upset by *who* was in the streets engaging in this "excess of free speech." ACT UP demonstrated at Bush's vacation home in Kennebunkport, Maine during Labor Day weekend, 1991, and in response Bush defended his AIDS policies and

---

2. Protest politics, such as the sit-ins for civil rights, are sometimes constructed as noble, but in dominant discourses, protest usually becomes noble only in retrospect, if at all, after the movement has disappeared and can be safely idealized.

then said, "I'm in favor of behavioral change. Here's a disease where you can control its spread by your own personal behavior." He then indicated that he had been "more moved" by another demonstration staged in Kennebunkport earlier that summer by people who were unemployed. "That was the one I was concerned about. That one hit home because when a family is out of work, that's one I care very much about" (Wockner 1991e). Irrespective of his actual policies regarding employment, Bush's rhetorical point was clear: queers had brought AIDS on themselves, and queer AIDS activists, a group seemingly excessive in and of itself, had no legitimate reason to take to the streets.

As is often the case when elites disparage confrontational protest, Bush's statements deriding ACT UP conflated oppositional politics with civil disorder, raising the specter of violence and danger. ACT UP demonstrations across the country typically were policed heavily (figs. 15 and 16). Depictions of ACT UP as an extremist organization rationalized such an extreme police presence, and the extremity of the police presence in turn secured the image of ACT UP as a violent organization whose actions threatened to unleash civil disorder.[3]

In addition to being construed as dangerous and threatening, ACT UP often was portrayed, contradictorily, as simply ridiculous or silly, and most frequently as uninformed, overwrought, unreasonable, irrational, and childish. That sort of infantilizing differs dramatically from characterizations that see militancy as closer to terrorism, but both are strategies of governance that attempt to dampen support for contentious politics. In June 1991, one Bush administration official dismissively suggested that ACT UP's actions were no more than childish acting out, and no one, including the media, should pay ACT UP any mind: "They're a nuisance and that's all. They're irrelevant" ("Quotelines" 1991a). More vitriolically, House of Representatives member Robert Dornan (R-CA) claimed in July 1991 that "ACT UP [is] the most arrogant, discriminating, disgraceful homosexual group in this country" ("Quotelines" 1991b).

Ignoring ACT UP's analyses and grievances—disseminated in carefully crafted fact sheets, press releases, letters, and policy statements that sometimes ran as long as sixty pages[4]—commentators repeatedly

3. See Hartley 1982 for an analysis of the mainstream British media's tendency during the Thatcher era to depict political opposition in a manner that raised the specter of violent disorder.

4. See, for example, ACT UP/NY's *A Critique of the AIDS Clinical Trials Group* (ACT UP/New York 1990).

FIGURE 15. Police at ACT UP demonstration at the Democratic National Convention, Atlanta, 1988. Photo by Rex Wockner.

FIGURE 16. ACT UP demonstrator being arrested during national action, downtown Chicago, April 23, 1990. Photo by Genyphyr Novak.

challenged ACT UP participants' capacity to reason. After an ACT UP demonstration in June 1991 that targeted the American Medical Association for its punitive positions regarding HIV testing and for its historical opposition to national health insurance, a spokesman for the AMA denounced ACT UP's protest and suggested that the AMA would have responded to the protesters' demands if they had acted in a more reasonable manner: "We suggested to them they'd make more of an impact if they discussed it with us rationally than if they did what they've chosen to do [i.e., hold a protest]" (Wockner 1991c, 28; see also Yang 1991).[5] A *Washington Post* columnist suggested that ACT UP activists at the Seventh International AIDS Conference in Florence (June 1991) had "failed to use [their] brains," were "self-defeating" and acting "nonsensically," and had created an atmosphere in which there was "no place for reason" (Cohen 1991). A *Chicago Sun-Times* columnist labeled AIDS activists "zealots" and said that the uproar they were creating was "deafening and drown[ed] out the facts" (Kilpatrick 1991). In the same period, a *Philadelphia Inquirer* columnist painted ACT UP as an irrational, self-absorbed organization that was overcome by misguided rage, little interested in facts, and engaging in self-defeating tactics (Sutherland 1991).[6]

PLAUSIBLE EFFECTS OF DERISION FROM THE MAINSTREAM.   My point in providing details of such disparagements is not to address the accuracy or fairness of the media's representations of ACT UP. Rather, I aim to demonstrate that the ideological environment facing the direct-action AIDS movement frequently constructed the movement and its confrontational tactics as dangerous, illogical, juvenile, and so forth. My interest is in the effects on the movement of those negative portrayals.

ACT UP encountered both vitriolic and subtle derision, and we can imagine that the latter had a greater impact on ACT UP's viability. While the tirades of politicians, newspaper editors, and government bureaucrats might have hurt ACT UP's recruiting efforts, such invective surely *inspired* movement participants and potential recruits who

5. This AMA spokesman was being particularly disingenuous. Prior to the demonstration, members of ACT UP/Chicago demanded, and won, a meeting with AMA officials. At that meeting, we presented our grievances and demands, and they responded with their public positions on the issues. We held the demonstration because *rational* discussion did not help us achieve our ends.

6. See also Bowden 1992. Others who have noted the negative media depictions of ACT UP include Gross 2001, 108; Erni 1994; and Cohen 1998.

were happy to defy mainstream society. It can be exhilarating to interrupt the workings of power to such a degree that it froths at the mouth in response. More subtle disparagements—of the sort that define politics narrowly and play on commonsense ideas of proper political behavior—deauthorize contentious activism. They work to make activism threatening in some instances and simply unintelligible in others, turning activism itself into something embarrassing, something that mature adults do not do. In doing so, they privilege, and potentially bolster, the electorally bounded political horizon, foreclosing other, more oppositional activist imaginings.

Members and potential members of confrontational activist groups encounter such subtle derision all the time: at the dinner table and the water cooler, in the news, in Hollywood films, at school, in the pomp and ceremony of elections, in history books that perhaps make civil rights sit-ins honorable but do so by exceptionalizing them and relegating them to the past. Cultural theorist Stuart Hall remarks that the dominant ideology of a society often appears redundant: "We know it already, we have seen it before, a thousand different signs and messages seem to signify the same ideological meaning. It is the very mental environment in which we live and experience the world" (Hall 1973b, 186). Their axiomatic quality is what gives hegemonic ideologies against defiant activism their power.

ACT UP frequently was labeled as excessive, inappropriate, and unreasonable in relation to a conception of politics that circumscribes the political within the electoral realm. As Hall writes, "These acts of labeling in the political domain, far from being self-evident, or a law of the natural world, constitute a form of continuing political 'work' on the part of the elites of power: they are, indeed, often the opening salvo in the whole process of political control" (Hall 1974, 262). I would extend Hall's analysis by noting that the techniques of control here operate not only through ideological means but at the level of affect. The agents conjured up by construals of a protest event as serious and peaceful are different from those evoked by a description that construes activists as violent, militant, excessive, hysterical, irrational, or immature.[7] Feelings of affinity and identification are, of course, less easily generated

7. Étienne Balibar's discussion of the uprisings/riots in France in the fall of 2005 (at a lecture at the University of Chicago on May 10, 2006) helped me to articulate this in this way.

in the latter case. Although we do not know people's intentions, the symbolic delegitimation of ACT UP's confrontational tactics appeared to be attempts—conscious and not—by those invested in the status quo to, in Hall's words, "'distance' the mass of the public from any commitment to the event" (286). Movements need that kind of commitment to the event; disparaging criticism that succeeds in unraveling feeling states of affinity, identification, and commitment can thus pose a challenge to a movement's viability.

It is plausible, then, that the ideological environment in which ACT UP operated contributed to the decline of the direct-action AIDS movement. The plausibility of this hypothesis is further strengthened by considering as well lesbian and gay criticism of ACT UP during this same period of the movement's decline.

LESBIAN AND GAY DERISION.   In her book *Virtual Equality: The Mainstreaming of Gay and Lesbian Liberation*, Urvashi Vaid, former Executive Director of NGLTF, maintains that while ACT UP was controversial from its start, "the pages of the gay and lesbian press in the early 1990s are filled with . . . criticism of ACT UP as a strategy that had outlived its purpose" (1995, 104). Vaid concludes that "by 1992 . . . the consensus among gay people was that direct action was no longer an effective strategy" (104), and ACT UP was consequently on the decline. Vaid presents no evidence to support her claims, nor does she discuss what she means by "consensus" or who is included in the category of "gay people"—*all* lesbians and gay men?—and how one might determine what gay people in 1992 were thinking about ACT UP and direct-action activism. The truth of her assertions is thus questionable. But insofar as Vaid, an important and well-connected leader in national lesbian and gay politics during this period, was traversing the country and conversing with large numbers of lesbians and gay men, including activists, officers of organizations, newspaper reporters and editors, politicians, and other leaders, her assertion, even if an exaggeration, does suggest a negative shift in attitudes about ACT UP's confrontational, direct-action tactics in the early 1990s.

There certainly was a great deal of criticism. Gay and lesbian critics sometimes, as Vaid notes, "picked up and repeated" the Bush administration's rhetorical attacks on ACT UP (104). Most frequently critics marked ACT UP's actions as excessive and consequently a threat to lesbian and gay respectability. Consider, for example, an editorial in the

Windy City Times that defended the initially "widespread" booing and name-calling that greeted Chicago's Mayor Daley when he showed up at a lesbian and gay antiviolence march in April 1992 ("Daley" 1992). Acknowledging a queasiness within the community about confrontational activism, the editors began by writing that it may not have been "polite," but "booing and hissing at public events . . . [is] often the only way that people can let their political leaders know that they're angry and frustrated." In the editors' view, the initial heckling and jeering that met Daley "sent a strong signal to the mayor that many in the gay and lesbian community—and not just a few street activists—have serious concerns with his administration's handling of gay and AIDS issues." Their parenthetical point suggests that the editors were most intent on drawing a distinction between "street [AIDS] activists"—who evidently continued heckling the mayor throughout the march—and "most people in the crowd"—who apparently were part of the jeering initially but then stopped. Yes, the anger directed toward the mayor was understandable, the editors acknowledged, but AIDS was not the only issue facing lesbians and gay men, and "by hijacking an anti-violence march, AIDS activists muted the strong message that 1,000 people could have sent to millions of Chicago area residents watching the television news or reading the newspapers: that the gay and lesbian community is fighting back [against antigay violence] and that the city's political leaders are standing behind the community" ("Daley" 1992). The persistent heckling certainly may have muted that message, but what seemed most disconcerting to the editors was that the activists' feat conveyed another message, one that broadcast queer defiance and anger toward the mayor rather than gay harmony with City Hall. AIDS activists had veered from acceptable into unacceptable activism; they had exceeded the bounds of good taste, and had done so in front of TV cameras.

During the early and mid-1990s, ACT UP chapters that participated in campaigns to pass anti-discrimination ordinances or to defeat antigay ballot initiatives often faced criticism from more establishment-oriented gay activists in their locales. ACT UP/Portland member Erica Rand, for example, recalls that mainstream gay groups in Maine tried to discredit groups like ACT UP, viewing the direct action of AIDS activists as simply "acting out" and as a risk to their more mainstream strategy: "They were afraid that we would use tactics that would validate the negative images a homophobic public had of us" (personal correspondence, December 28, 2008).

Gay conservative commentator Andrew Sullivan was a vocal critic who marked ACT UP participants as extreme and out of step with most lesbians and gay men rather than as thoughtful, legitimate, and efficacious political actors. In a 1993 article in the *New Republic,* Sullivan wrote that the liberationist politics of ACT UP and similar radical queer activist groups distanced such "'queer' fundamentalists" from "the vast majority of gay people" who, Sullivan claimed, "wish to be integrated into society as it is" (Sullivan 1993).

While some lesbian and gay critics reproached ACT UP's confrontational tactics specifically, other appraisals during the years of ACT UP's decline were filled with condescension and scorn as well as antileftism and red-baiting, all of which, as with mainstream criticism, might distance lesbians and gay men from the movement. Gay journalist Randy Shilts—who, in addition to writing for the gay press, was the first reporter to cover AIDS regularly for a daily newspaper, the *San Francisco Chronicle*—stands out in this regard. In a January 1991 cover story for the national lesbian and gay magazine, the *Advocate,* Shilts claimed that the militant AIDS activist movement was demonstrating its "growing irrelevance" in the gay community by, ostensibly, being more concerned about poor blacks and Hispanics with AIDS than about gay white men with AIDS (Shilts 1991, 37). He continued with an assertion of ACT UP's demise: "By the end of 1990, it was clear that the SILENCE = DEATH crowd was losing its grip on the gay imagination" (38).

During this period, individual ACT UP chapters often faced criticism from within their local lesbian and gay communities that echoed critiques aimed at the direct-action AIDS movement as a whole. For example, in an editorial that challenged ACT UP/Chicago's priorities and insinuated that the organization was veering from its mission to fight AIDS, the *Windy City Times* adopted the criticisms that Shilts had aired in the *Advocate.* It began with a quote from Shilts charging that ACT UP was no longer relevant because it had put the issue of AIDS drugs on the back burner. It continued:

> We thought that fighting AIDS was the purpose . . . [of ACT UP]. But now that the New York City chapter has made national health care its priority, we're wondering what ACT UP/Chicago has as its top priority for 1991.[8] . . .

8. I have come across no evidence indicating that ACT UP/NY made national health care its top priority as Shilts argued in his *Advocate* essay (1991, 37) and the *Windy City*

We're wondering where [the need to get more and less costly drugs approved by the Federal Drug Administration to treat AIDS] falls on ACT UP/Chicago's list of priorities. At last check, ACT UP was leading a protest march . . . against the Persian Gulf war. . . . We're proud that ACT UP has seen the potential threat that the war has on funding AIDS programs. . . . But what is confusing to us is not knowing if ACT UP has made a long-range commitment to protest the war. What would such a commitment mean to its ability to agitate the government to provide more AIDS drug therapies? Closer to home, would such a new international emphasis prevent ACT UP/Chicago from demonstrating on the city's lack of a health commissioner or the ongoing privatization of its health care services? ("ACT UP, AIDS, and the Persian Gulf" 1991, 11)

Although this editorial was not as biting as Shilts' *Advocate* article, it painted the Chicago ACT UP chapter as politically errant and unsophisticated. It also pointedly ignored ACT UP/Chicago's numerous, ongoing AIDS-related campaigns.[9] Although it did not focus its critique on ACT UP's confrontational tactics, its derision nonetheless created a distance between the direct-action AIDS movement and those lesbians and gay men who wanted to see themselves as politically savvy and fighting the AIDS crisis "correctly." Moreover, by aligning itself with Shilts' critique of ACT UP, the *Windy City Times* editorial joined its concerns about ACT UP/Chicago to a larger antileft critique in Shilts's article. During this time period conservative commentators were waging war on liberals and leftists concerned with issues like racism, sexism, and homophobia; the right trivialized people with such concerns by labeling them "politically correct." The *Windy City Times* editorial aligned itself with such forces by suggesting that participating in ACT UP might paint one with the socially disreputable brush of leftism, political correctness, and feel-good (rather than pragmatic and smart) activism. Widely read Chicago gay journalist Rex Wockner waged a similar campaign against ACT UP/Chicago throughout 1992, accusing the organization, particularly the lesbian participants, of "political correctness."[10]

Times echoed here. The evidence suggests that it was *one* priority for many in the movement from about 1990 on.

9. ACT UP/Chicago addressed *Windy City Times'* criticisms in a letter to the editor two weeks later (ACT UP/Chicago 1991a).

10. See, for example, Wockner (1992a, 1992c). I return to Wockner's critiques of ACT UP in chapter 6.

In the period of ACT UP's decline, then, the movement faced criticism from both gay and straight worlds. It seems plausible that this inhospitable environment contributed to the decline of ACT UP by turning away participants, potential participants, and supporters. But two aspects of the data trouble any simple association between the ideological environment and ACT UP's decline. First, derision of ACT UP by politicians, the corporate media, high-ranking members of the scientific-medical establishment, and lesbian and gay critics also occurred in the years before ACT UP's decline, during its heyday from 1987 through 1990. Second, ACT UP received a considerable amount of mainstream and lesbian and gay praise throughout its life. I argue that the more or less hostile ideological milieu in which ACT UP operated *did* contribute to the movement's decline, but, given these confounding data, why and how it did so are questions we will need to address.

Earlier Disparagements of ACT UP

Criticism leveled at ACT UP was often scathing, even in the movement's early years. I discuss the widespread condemnations at some length, again, not to assess their truth but because they raise questions of whether a hostile ideological context matters at all with regard to movement viability, and if so, how and under what conditions.

EARLIER MAINSTREAM CRITICISM.   Contending that "ACT UP is probably the most widely reviled" activist group, a writer for *New York* magazine noted that New York City Mayor Ed Koch called ACT UP a group of "fascists" after some members disrupted him at the opening reception to a gay history exhibit in 1988 (Taylor 1990, 67).[11] A number of opinion pieces by *U.S. News and World Report* columnist John Leo were strikingly vitriolic. In one titled "Today's Uncivil Disobedience" (Leo 1989), Leo characterized as "simple tantrums" actions like blocking traffic on the Brooklyn Bridge, using rhetoric like "murder" and "genocide," and harassing politicians. In 1990 in a column headlined "When Activism Becomes Gangsterism," Leo conceded that "every so often, ACT UP undertakes some campaign that lends itself to rational analysis." But the thrust of his column was a construction of ACT UP as a group of gangsters, "the No. 1 loose cannon of local [New York City] politics," a group

11. On ACT UP/NY's zap of the mayor, see letters in the *New York Native*, 4 July, 1988.

that engages in "troublemaking that makes no sense in traditional political terms" but should not be underestimated because, as a crowd of "brownshirts," ACT UP is indeed a dangerous menace to society (Leo 1990a; see also Leo 1990b).

Like critiques of ACT UP in its declining years, these earlier ones also ignored AIDS activists' political analyses of the government's and other institutions' handling of the AIDS crisis. As Hall (1973a, 91–92) suggests, the media's failure to provide contextualizing background information about a movement's confrontational protests effectively casts them as meaningless, as senseless acting out. In failing to discuss ACT UP's political analyses, critics of the movement reduced it to its tactics and portrayed AIDS activists as dangerous deviants engaging in disruptive, inappropriate, meaningless behavior.

In the United States, confrontational activists frequently face such denials of political intelligibility, denials that should be understood as an operation of power insofar as they discourage participation in such activism and build opposition to it. A San Francisco-based direct-action AIDS activist group named Stop AIDS Now or Else (SANOE) was reviled by the *San Francisco Chronicle* for two actions in 1989, one that shut down the Golden Gate Bridge and another that disrupted the opening night at the San Francisco Opera. The actions were purposefully dramatic, projecting a level of desperation that AIDS activists and people with AIDS were feeling. Providing no context for SANOE's disruption of the Opera, the *Chronicle* editors described the action as "mindless" and SANOE as "an irresponsible fringe group" ("Opera" 1989).[12] Ignoring their political goals and analyses, the media depicted the protesters as social deviants rather than rightful political actors who felt compelled to go outside routine political channels.

The response by politicians and the media was similar in December 1989 when ACT UP/NY protested at St. Patrick's Cathedral in collaboration with the group WHAM!—Women's Health Action Mobilization (fig. 17). The action was designed to raise issues about the Catholic Church's opposition to safe-sex education, homosexuality, and abortion. Thousands demonstrated outside St. Pat's, and several protesters went inside and disrupted the service; one dropped a communion wafer to the

12. The *Chronicle* erroneously claimed that the protesters had punched patrons and sprayed tear gas at an opera singer but issued a correction and apology the next day, clarifying that according to an eyewitness "a member of the audience, not a demonstrator, used a chemical spray during the protest" ("Reporting" 1989).

floor in protest. Almost every local politician and daily newspaper railed against the action (Handelman 1990). New York City Mayor Koch, Mayor-elect David Dinkins, and New York Governor Mario Cuomo condemned it, as did Vice President Dan Quayle (Taylor 1990, 73; DeParle 1990, B1). The mainstream media coverage constructed ACT UP (and WHAM!) as irrational, unreasonable, and immature. If the protesters were seeking to persuade, a *New York Daily News* editorial asserted, they should know that "persuasion is done through reasoned arguments, not adolescent acts" ("Civil" 1989; see also "Storming" 1989).

Dr. Anthony Fauci, the Director of the National Institute of Allergy and Infectious Disease (NIAID), the AIDS research arm of the NIH, sometimes constructed ACT UP similarly. After ACT UP demonstrated at the NIH in May 1990 to protest the slow pace of AIDS drug research and the exclusion of women of child-bearing age from drug trials, *USA Today* quoted Fauci as saying, "A demonstration on the campus of the place that is doing the most to help them . . . is quite inappropriate" ("AIDS Activists" 1990). Failing to acknowledge ACT UP's stated reasons for holding the protest, and once more impugning ACT UP protest-

ers' discretion and maturity, Fauci, according to the *New York Times,*
said that "he knew the leaders of the protest [at the NIH] well and was
surprised to hear 'irrational' language on the street from people he had
worked with in meetings" (Hilts 1990). Fauci and others also suggested
that ACT UP's tactics were a threat to the conduct of science. The *Washington Post* quoted Fauci trivializing and discrediting ACT UP's NIH
action by calling it an "inconvenience that could undermine the morale
of federal AIDS researchers" (Jennings and Gladwell 1990).[13]

ACT UP's disruption of a speech by Health and Human Services Secretary Dr. Louis Sullivan at the Sixth International Conference on AIDS
in San Francisco (June 1990) drew heated criticism. Sullivan's speech
was entirely drowned out by the chants of ACT UP activists, after which
the secretary labeled the protesters "un-American" (Zonana 1990) and
ACT UP a "fringe group" (O'Neill 1990b), vowed never to meet with
ACT UP, and asked government officials to avoid all but "necessary and
productive" dealings with the group ("Health" 1990; "Sullivan" 1990).[14]
Later, Sullivan derided AIDS activists as "adolescent" ("ACT UP Disrupts Yale" 1990).

A *New York Times* editorial sounded the familiar theme of activist
excessiveness (fig. 18). Asserting "It's not as if society had turned its back
on AIDS and those whom it strikes," the editors wondered "what could
have caused such a pointless breakdown in sense and civility" ("AIDS
and Misdirected" 1990). The editors were eliding even recent history,
failing to mention, for example, that on the eve of the San Francisco
conference President Bush had indeed turned his back on people with
AIDS by announcing his opposition to a large federal AIDS disaster-
relief bill that had passed through Congress (Zonana 1990) and by shun-
ning the AIDS Conference in favor of a fund-raiser for arch-homophobe
Senator Jesse Helms.

Perhaps wanting to assure its readers that the *New York Times'* criticism was not based on homophobia, the editorial drew a contrast between good gay groups—who used "conventional political methods" and
successfully garnered more AIDS research funds—and the militant and
unreasonable gays in ACT UP who ostensibly had nothing to show for
their efforts. Indeed, according to the editors, "there is little value in

13. See also O'Neill 1990a, 1990b; Specter 1990b; and Kolata 1990. For a critique of Kolata's journalism, see Dowie 1998.
14. Sullivan apparently refused contact with ACT UP *prior* to the June 1990 disruption. See ACT UP/NY member Peter Staley's comments in O'Neill 1990b.

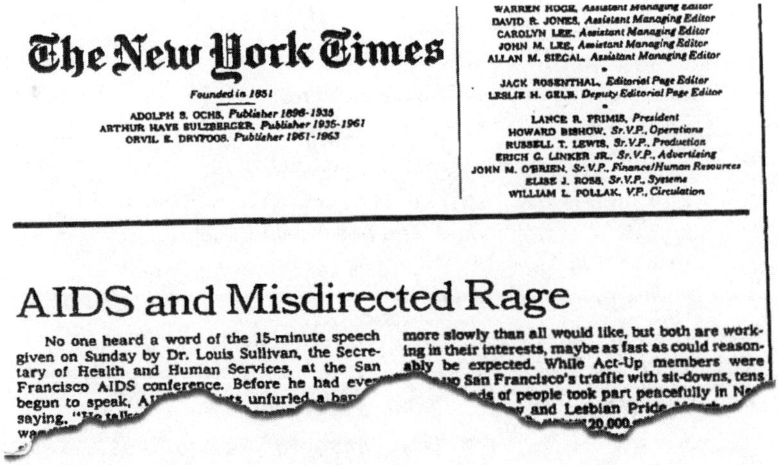

The New York Times

AIDS and Misdirected Rage

No one heard a word of the 15-minute speech given on Sunday by Dr. Louis Sullivan, the Secretary of Health and Human Services, at the San Francisco AIDS conference. Before he had even begun to speak, A[...]'s unfurled a ban[...] saying, "He ta[...] w[...] more slowly than all would like, but both are working in their interests, maybe as fast as could reasonably be expected. While Act-Up members were [...]o San Francisco's traffic with sit-downs, tens [...]ds of people took part peacefully in N[...] y and Lesbian Pride [...] 20,000 [...]

FIGURE 18. Lead editorial in the *New York Times*, June 26, 1990.

ACT UP's disruptions." Even as the editors acknowledged that ACT UP members had reasons to feel rage and despair, they cautioned against ACT UP's emotionality, offering reason as the more effective route for ACT UP to take: "But for all their righteous rage, it's important for them to see that shouting down Dr. Sullivan is counterproductive. If ACT UP's members would only keep their faith in education and hard lobbying and put down their bullhorns, they might find their rage surprisingly well understood, and effective when focused in the right way on the right targets" ("AIDS and Misdirected" 1990). The exclusion of any discussion of government foot-dragging or of ACT UP's actual effectiveness over the years was necessary to uphold the editors' faith in the democratic process and their related assertion that the movement's use of the "right" tactics on the "right" targets—as defined by the editors, apparently, and seemingly limited to "hard" lobbying, whatever that might mean—would certainly lead to success. As portrayed by the *New York Times*, ACT UP's militancy was incomprehensible and ineffective.

The *San Francisco Chronicle* wrote an editorial against ACT UP's disruption of Sullivan's speech that similarly constructed ACT UP as outside the bounds of civility and propriety. ACT UP's action, they wrote, "exceeded the limits of acceptable behavior." Indeed, ACT UP was dangerously beyond the pale, its disruption "little more than incipient *fascism*" ("Offensive" 1990; emphasis mine). ACT UP, using tactics

that ostensibly resembled the violence of a fascist state, was clearly reprehensible and dangerous.

The criticism came not only from people in positions of power. It was
also articulated by individuals writing letters to the editor and in face-
to-face interactions.[15] These people also often equated ACT UP's militancy with violence. For example, a member of the studio audience at
the February 9, 1990, *Phil Donahue Show* shouted at members of ACT
UP on the panel: "Stock exchanges and cathedrals—where do you stop?
Bombs, buildings? Militancy can turn into terrorism" (quoted in Erni
1994, 96). Ignoring the fact that ACT UP was committed to nonviolent direct action,[16] commentators suggested that confrontational tactics
would inevitably lead to terrorist bombings. Equally inaccurately, critics suggested that ACT UP's confrontational activism itself was indistin-
guishable from violent, destructive tactics.[17]

EARLIER LESBIAN AND GAY DISPARAGEMENT.   Turning to earlier lesbian and gay criticism of ACT UP, one of the first instances occurred
when ACT UP/NY zapped New York City Mayor Ed Koch at a City
Hall event inaugurating Lesbian and Gay History Month with an unveil-
ing of a lesbian and gay history photo exhibit. AIDS activists targeted
Koch because they saw him as doing almost nothing to deal with New
York City's then-exploding AIDS crisis. As in later criticism, lesbian
and gay critics castigated ACT UP for being excessive, extremist, im-
proper, disrespectful, politically unsavvy, and immature. At the June 1,
1988, zap, more than fifty ACT UP members began chanting as soon as
Mayor Koch walked to the podium, effectively disrupting the event. The
local WNBC news reported a strong negative reaction from many lesbian and gay leaders in attendance. The July 4 issue of the *New York*

15. For examples of letters to the editor, see Dessau 1990; Braverman 1990; and Roeder
1992. Face-to-face interactions are harder to document because they usually are not recorded by the media, but my interviews revealed that some ACT UP participants experienced conflict about their activism with their families and friends, in their workplaces, and
in other interactions; my own experiences corroborate this finding.

16. As I discuss in chapter 7, some individuals with AIDS did consider armed suicide
missions, and Larry Kramer did call for riots at the Sixth International AIDS Conference
in San Francisco in 1990, but ACT UP *as an organization* never seriously considered political violence.

17. I am not commenting on arguments for or against political violence here, but rather
simply noting critics' erroneous conflations.

FIGURE 19. *San Francisco Chronicle*, June 26, 1989.

Native contained letters that vehemently criticized ACT UP. One, written by four veteran lesbian and gay activists, compared ACT UP/NY to hateful antigay bigots and accused it of deploying "fascistic tactics" (Conkey et al. 1988).[18]

The psychologizing of ACT UP participants was a standard genre of critique, a mode that echoes mainstream denunciations of militant activists and trivializes activists' commitments by emptying their analyses of political content. Randy Shilts early on began charging that ACT UP's actions served more of a therapeutic than political purpose. The scientific-medical establishment and the mainstream media provided Shilts a ready platform, likely because of his stature as a mainstream journalist, but perhaps more importantly because he was gay and willing to denounce and scorn other gays. Shilts, invited to give a speech at the closing ceremony of the Fifth International Conference on AIDS in Montreal in June 1989, "obliged his hosts with an attack on the militancy of international AIDS activists attending the conference" (Crimp 2002, 142), arguing that ACT UP's dissent had gone too far and was "beginning to backfire" (Shilts 1989; see fig. 19). From the Conference stage Shilts warned, "expressing anger can give you a warm, fuzzy feeling inside, but this conference isn't supposed to be a therapy session" (Chase 1989a). In Shilts' rendering, "in the political arena, expressing anger for the sake of expressing anger is infantile, and sometimes counterproductive" (Shilts

18. See also Friedlander et al. 1988; Davidson 1988; and letters in the same issue of the *New York Native* from ACT UP/NY members that laid out ACT UP's reasoning behind the zap.

1989; quoted in Cohen 1998, 21). ACT UP, Shilts asserted, was becoming too "confrontational," prompting a "backlash," and in the end "may ultimately be counted as among the forces of death" (Shilts 1989). Over the years, Shilts continued his attacks on ACT UP, asserting that its actions were nothing more than a form of self-indulgent and infantile personal therapy, with little to show in terms of political accomplishments.[19]

In pitting the therapeutic against the political and aligning AIDS activism with the former, Shilts was drawing from and bolstering existing mainstream discourses that cast politics in terms of dispassionate, reasoned deliberation engaged in by elevated and high-minded *men* as against the mob in the streets, where individuals—feminized by their emotionality and apparent lack of reason—are moved by their passions, as in the therapeutic situation. Drawing on a perceived split between emotion and reason, this discourse places the therapeutic and the political at odds with one another; there is no possibility that emotional, collective street activism is sensible, that it can be both cathartic for participants (liberating, invigorating, restorative) as well as politically motivated and politically effective. Of course, Shilts's rendering also failed to recognize the emotional components of what he construed as politics.

In the movement's early years, others also disparaged direct-action AIDS activism by characterizing participants as immature. Local gay newspapers repeatedly labeled activists "juvenile," "childish," and "insane." Again and again, they were told to "grow up" and frequently were admonished with statements like "You can't just act up, you've got to act smart."[20]

Mainstream and lesbian and gay criticisms of the direct-action AIDS movement did not change dramatically between the period of the movement's emergence and development, from 1987 through approximately 1990, and the period of its decline, from approximately 1991 through 1994. A second point confounding the hypothesis that ideological work against defiant activism contributed to ACT UP's decline is that, although criticism was plentiful and often quite vitriolic, ACT UP also received a surprising amount of praise.

19. See, for example, Salholz, et al. 1990; Price 1990. Retrospective accounts by some gay critics are similarly infantilizing of ACT UP; see, for example Andriote 1999, 244.

20. See, for example, Karlin 1990; Wockner 1990b, 1990d; Dunne 1989; Alexander 1989; Warner 1989; and numerous letters about the actions of SANOE in the *B.A.R.* and the *San Francisco Sentinel* from February, September, and October 1989.

For ACT UP

The praise that both gay and straight individuals and institutions directed toward ACT UP acted as a counternarrative to the dominant ideology that derides contentious, confrontational activism. The amount of
praise is striking in that regard. In terms of effects, the praise may have
helped to bolster the movement's emotional habitus and political horizon. I focus closely on how those praising ACT UP did so, especially
how they aligned themselves with or distanced themselves from ACT
UP's tactics. Those aspects of the praise provide important insights into
the forcefulness of disparaging criticisms. Attending to them will help us
to understand why such criticisms eventually did gain traction and play a
role in ACT UP's decline.

Mainstream Praise for ACT UP

What is perhaps most surprising about the ideological milieu in which
ACT UP operated is that the movement received a good amount of
mainstream praise and even support. Some even applauded it for its
noisy disruption of Secretary of Health Louis Sullivan in June 1990.
The *San Francisco Examiner* endorsed ACT UP's action, even echoing
the movement's cries of shame directed toward Sullivan and his boss,
President Bush. The editors wrote that the protesters had "nothing to
be ashamed of and nothing to apologize for." Suggesting an astonishing
degree of sympathy with confrontational, disruptive activism in general,
the editors asserted,

> Protest is rarely pleasant; it is frequently annoying to people who regard
> themselves as innocent, put-upon bystanders who may even be sympa-
> thetic to the goals of the protest. But it has been effective in the fight against
> AIDS, a fight that has been waged by hard-working and dedicated physi-
> cians, nurses, medical researchers and activists. They all have played impor-
> tant roles. . . . The frustration of those most affected is palpable and under-
> standable. They demand and deserve more from Bush than a slap in the face.
> ("Bush" 1990)

An op-ed piece in the *Examiner* called ACT UP the "heroes of the epidemic" (Kirp 1990).
Others who have commented on media representations of ACT UP

tend to overlook such praise.[21] But given the pointed hostility that con-frontational movements typically face, the extent of praise conferred on ACT UP is extraordinary. ACT UP/NY member Peter Staley re-calls watching television news reports of the group's first demonstration in March 1987, which essentially shut down Wall Street in lower Man-hattan. According to Staley, all three TV networks covered the action sympathetically, "saying the FDA was slow and Burroughs Wellcome shouldn't be charging this much for the first drug for AIDS" (quoted in Kastor 1993). By 1989, mainstream newspapers and magazines regularly acknowledged ACT UP's influence and effectiveness. As one *Washing-ton Post* article noted with some surprise and awe, "leading government AIDS researchers read [ACT UP's] frequent manifestoes with interest and admiration" (Specter 1990a). News articles, editorials, and op-ed pieces admiringly noted that ACT UP's pressure had forced the phar-maceutical company Burroughs Wellcome to reduce the price of AZT, and that ACT UP's confrontational actions, combined with compelling research, had succeeded in pushing the FDA to revamp its drug test-ing system and implement the ACT UP–devised "parallel track" pro-gram, which allowed more people with HIV/AIDS access to experimen-tal drugs.[22] Scholars who studied the three major television networks' nightly news programs found that "ACT UP, particularly in its earliest stages, often received respectful coverage," a finding that they found "striking," given its members' "penchant for disrupting speeches, con-ducting sit-ins (or 'die-ins'), and getting arrested" (Cook and Colby 1992, 114). The media sometimes even echoed ACT UP's demands (e.g., "Getting" 1990).

The media amplified the praise by reporting that ACT UP was draw-ing acclaim from leading members of the science establishment. In an article about the Sixth International Conference on AIDS in San Fran-cisco, a *Los Angeles Times* reporter noted that "speaker after speaker paid homage to the activists' contributions in confronting the epidemic" (Zonana 1990, A23). The media frequently quoted scientists' and health bureaucrats' acclaim for ACT UP. For example, the *New York*

21. See, for example, Erni 1994; Cohen 1998; and Gross 2001; for an exception, see Cook and Colby 1992.
22. On Burroughs Wellcome see "Acting" 1990; Chase 1989b; Kirp 1990; and Taylor 1990. On ACT UP's effectiveness with the FDA, see "Acting" 1990; DeParle 1990; Garri-son 1989; "Getting" 1990; Kirp 1990; Salholz et al. 1990; Span 1989; Specter 1989, 1990a; Taylor 1990; and Zonana 1990.

Pressure From AIDS Activists
Has Transformed Drug Testing

Experimental Medicines More Accessible

By Michael Specter
Washington Post Staff Writer

With success that has surprised
even the most radical among them,
AIDS patients and their relentless
advocates have in less than three
years transform...the way exper-
im... ...ested

cleared we realized that much of
their criticism was absolutely valid."
  Over the past two years, AIDS
activists have forced a fundamental
shift in the way drugs f... ...tal illnesses are tested.
  Before AIDS, experi
could only be giv...
fo...nal   ...w...

FIGURE 20. *Washington Post*, July 2, 1989.

Times quoted the New York City Health Commissioner Dr. Stephen
Joseph (a sometime target of ACT UP) acknowledging that ACT UP
had successfully forced important changes in the testing and distribution of AIDS drugs (DeParle 1990, B1). Newspapers repeatedly quoted
Dr. Fauci—also a sometime target of ACT UP—praising the direct-
action AIDS movement. An article in the *Washington Post* headlined
"Pressure from AIDS Activists Has Transformed Drug Testing" (fig. 20)
quoted Fauci as follows: "In the beginning, those people had a blanket
disgust with us. And it was mutual. Scientists said all trials should be restricted, rigid and slow. The gay [*sic*] groups said we were killing people
with red tape.[23] When the smoke cleared we realized that much of their
criticism was absolutely valid" (Specter 1989, A1).[24] Fauci actually credited ACT UP with positively transforming the FDA's drug-testing procedures. Quoted in the *New York Times*, Fauci rhetorically asked, "Did
ACT UP play a significant role in the whole idea of expanded access to
experimental drugs?" Fauci's unhesitant reply: "The answer is yes" (De-
Parle 1990, B4). The *Los Angeles Times* quoted Fauci lauding ACT UP

23. During the 1980s and 1990s, the media and others consistently conflated AIDS and
gay identity by failing to recognize the difference between AIDS and gay organizations.
24. See also Garrison 1989, A1.

in the speech he gave at the Sixth International Conference on AIDS in San Francisco: "When it comes to clinical trials, some [activists] are better informed than many scientists can imagine. [Scientists] do not have a lock on correctness. Activists bring a special insight into the disease that can actually be helpful in the way we design our scientific approaches" (Zonana 1990, A23). More than broadcasting the praise of others, such news articles suggested that the news organization concurred with the acclamation.

EXPLAINING MAINSTREAM PRAISE OF ACT UP.   Given the hostile context in which confrontational protest groups in the United States frequently operate, mainstream praise of ACT UP requires explanation. It is less surprising once we acknowledge that the dominant ideology against confrontational activism, while pervasive, is not totalizing. There are always cracks in a dominant ideology. Alternative perspectives and counterdiscourses about society, the polity, and events always compete for consideration. Even people with an orientation toward the establishment may support confrontational activism in some circumstances. In this case, some politicians, some news editors and reporters, some scientists and bureaucrats sometimes held a perspective that differed from the dominant one, and they sometimes got airtime.

Still, most confrontational activist movements in the United States simply do not garner much acclaim. ACT UP did. The following reasons begin to explain why. First, from its earliest months, ACT UP was undeniably effective. Effectiveness in itself is not enough to elicit praise, but as soon as a well-known establishment figure like CBS News anchor Dan Rather credited ACT UP with forcing Burroughs Wellcome to drop the price of AZT, and as soon as Fauci, the government's chief AIDS scientist, stated that AIDS activists had some valuable ideas, other people in power had a harder time dismissing the movement.

A second reason is the shared interest between activists who wanted to accelerate the testing of experimental AIDS drugs in order to save lives and supporters of government deregulation. A striking example of this appeared in a March 1991 *Wall Street Journal* editorial criticizing the FDA's "foot-dragging" in approving an experimental drug for Alzheimer's disease: "The more you watch the federal government handle matters relevant to sick patients and new drugs, the more you come to see why AIDS advocates act up so much" ("Alzheimer's" 1991).

Third, the perception that ACT UP's membership was white, male, and middle-class helped the movement to draw mainstream support. Editors, reporters, scientists, and bureaucrats who shared some of those characteristics and who were not virulently homophobic may have identified with AIDS activists, especially when the latter articulated their grievances and demands in terms of a sense of entitlement as U.S. citizens. It is hard to imagine similar acclaim being conferred on a defiant, direct-action AIDS movement perceived to be populated by African Americans, or on any confrontational activist group made up of people of color, women, poor people, young anarchists, or any combination of such marginalized groups.

THE AMBIVALENCE OF MAINSTREAM PRAISE FOR ACT UP. We should note, however, that mainstream praise for ACT UP almost always was surrounded by a more general criticism corroborating the view that confrontational activism is both unnecessary and dangerous. Indeed, the praise usually was articulated in a strikingly ambivalent manner that revealed anxiety about and subtly disparaged precisely that sort of defiant activism. Much of the praise implicitly assumed that confrontational activism is typically the work of uninformed, unreasonable, immature individuals. The acclaim, then, derived in part from the perception that ACT UP was different in this respect, at least to some degree, and praise was thus due it precisely for overcoming its activist origins and character. I provide a number of examples because I think understanding the ambivalent nature of this praise will help us to explore why and how the ideological environment, inclusive of this vocal mainstream acclaim, eventually did contribute to the decline of the movement.

Fauci's praise of ACT UP often voiced precisely this sort of ambivalence, simultaneously expressing support for ACT UP and anxiety about its tactics. When in 1988 the FDA restricted the availability of ganciclovir, an experimental AIDS drug that seemed promising in fighting infections leading to blindness in people with AIDS, ACT UP members went to the NIH campus and decided to try to meet with Fauci, anticipating that they would be thrown out of the building. Instead, Fauci agreed to meet with them and then to contact the FDA; a few weeks later the FDA announced a plan to maintain the availability of ganciclovir. Quoted in a *Washington Post* article, Fauci stated how positive that outcome was, crediting ACT UP. But Fauci was not endorsing confrontational activism; indeed, he suggested that he had listened to ACT UP and responded to its demands only because ACT UP had behaved itself: "When ACT

UP acts in a *reasonable* way, when it has a *reasonable* concern, it can be an effective catalyst" (Span 1989, D4; emphases mine).

Fauci similarly suggested his ambivalence about ACT UP and discomfort with confrontational activism in a 1990 article in *Rolling Stone.* The reporter noted that ACT UP's action at St. Patrick's Cathedral had "caused many to write off the group as radical lunatics," and then quoted Fauci as saying, "That's made my job more difficult because I have to go back to the conservative establishment and say, 'We need to work with these people,' and they look at me like I'm crazy. They don't see the side of ACT UP that I do—intelligent, gifted, articulate people coming up with good, creative ideas" (Handelman 1990, 85). By couching his praise in an implicit and sometimes explicit critique of confrontational activism, Fauci suggested that ACT UP's effectiveness singularly derived from the rational research and argumentation of some of its members. In such statements, Fauci was both deriding confrontational activism and suggesting that he himself was not influenced by that form of AIDS activism—that he was not susceptible to pressure (i.e., weak)—but by sensible and reasoned debate alone. (Fauci, of course, failed to acknowledge that AIDS activists gained access to him initially only through their confrontational demonstrations and disruptions.)

Fauci was not alone in his ambivalent admiration. Indeed, most of the praise directed toward ACT UP was hesitant and qualified, illustrating the parameters of mainstream support for the movement.[25] For example, in a May 1990 column about the upcoming International AIDS Conference in San Francisco headlined "Protests Threaten to Drown Science at AIDS Conference," *Chicago Tribune* contributor Joan Beck credited AIDS activists with spurring scientists to action. "Would this extraordinary progress have happened without the impatient demands and provocations of protesters—primarily gays with their political skills and sense of aggrievement? Without them, would the nation's research have been channeled so quickly into the battle against AIDS? It's not likely" (Beck 1990). But as the title of her column signaled, Beck simultaneously echoed a standard disparagement of ACT UP by casting AIDS activists as engaging in antics that might pose a threat to scientific progress. "It's increasingly obvious that many AIDS activists are willing to sacrifice some of the conference's scientific potential to make their political points."

25. The stunningly positive and unambivalent *San Francisco Examiner* editorial cited above ("Bush" 1990) stands out as an exception.

Were protesters to interfere with "the serious science at the San Francisco meeting," Beck argued, the results "would be devastating." Although in one breath Beck credited AIDS activists with many important successes, she simultaneously trivialized their activism, labeling it "theatrics" and "high-spirited high jinks"—in contrast to "serious science"—and casting protesters as players in an "AIDS carnival sideshow." Activist "nagging" that had led scientists and society to focus on AIDS was at once good and excessive, skillful but simultaneously a threat to science (Beck 1990).

ACT UP's tactics posed some difficulties for mainstream commentators who applauded the movement. It was hard to deny the efficacy of its tactics and the inadequacy of more routine efforts like lobbying, but confrontational activism raises the specter of social disorder, and thus many are uncomfortable with it. One way mainstream commentators navigated that difficulty was by conceding the admissibility of certain defiant tactics, but only for a period already past, rarely for the here and now. Along these lines, a December 1990 column in the *Economist* described ACT UP as "among the most effective" pressure groups in the United States but suggested that "ACT UP's extremism" in the present was threatening to undermine support for condom distribution in New York City's schools. Intertwining praise of ACT UP with unsubstantiated claims that the movement's tactics had alienated supporters, the column contended,

> ACT UP's all-or-nothing tactics sometimes work. Its unrelenting pressure has persuaded the federal government to change its procedures for testing and distributing experimental drugs so that AIDS patients get them faster. But sometimes its extremism backfires. Demonstrations that prevented Dr. Louis Sullivan . . . from being heard at an AIDS conference in San Francisco in June cost ACT UP much sympathy. Its disruption of services in . . . St. Patrick Cathedral has outraged Jews and Protestants as well as Catholics. ACT UP looks set to go too far in its campaign for condoms as well. ("A Condom" 1990)[26]

The thinly veiled message in mainstream commentators' ambivalent support for ACT UP was a quasi-warning that AIDS activists walked precipitously close to the edge of acceptability and could easily be re-

26. For another example of ambivalent praise for ACT UP, see "Harassing" 1990.

coded as objectionable extremists. This ambivalent praise muddied the ideological waters, simultaneously endorsing and undermining ACT UP.

Lesbian and Gay Praise for ACT UP

Along with mainstream praise, another stunning aspect of ACT UP's environment that confounds any simple notion that the ideological environment contributed to ACT UP's decline is that the movement—characterized by unremitting anger and defiant, in-your-face tactics—received tremendous support from mainstream ASOs and from more establishment-oriented lesbian and gay organizations, leaders, and individuals. On the heels of the 1988 FDA demonstration, a *San Francisco Chronicle* article claimed that "most gay leaders—even those well within the political establishment—say support for more protests is broadbased" (Tuller 1988, A4). Indicating support from across a wide political spectrum, *New York Native* reporter Kiki Mason wrote, "ACT UP and similar militant organizations across the country have turned the tide of AIDS activism and forever changed the traditional gay movement. . . . Even those of us who are conservative have been pulled, inch by inch, toward defiance" (Mason 1988, 16). At the start of 1990, gay San Francisco Supervisor Harry Britt perhaps overstated the case but he indicated vast support among lesbians and gay men for ACT UP's emotional habitus and political repertoire: "They're [ACT UP] putting out for the rest of us some very fundamental anger. . . . Within the lesbian/gay community there is a universal sense that civil disobedience will be a fundamental strategy among our people in the next decade" (Whiting 1990). Notably, Britt made his comments *after* the uproar in San Francisco's lesbian and gay community over SANOE's Golden Gate Bridge and Opera actions; insofar as people often conflated SANOE and ACT UP, Britt's comments here can be construed as at least in part a counter to those who earlier had vilified SANOE. In a 1991 essay, historian John D'Emilio noted this widespread embrace of more militant tactics:

> Most closely associated with ACT UP, direct action has been reincorporated among the spectrum of tactics considered permissible even by the reform wing of the movement. Indeed, the most notable feature of the growing militance of the last few years has been the approval of it even by those organizations and activists who do not engage in such tactics themselves. The movement seems willing to tolerate both insider and outsider strategies, rec-

ognizing the necessity of both in order to reach common goals. (D'Emilio 1992, 267)

Urvashi Vaid argues similarly that direct-action activism—best exemplified by ACT UP—"took center stage in national gay politics" from 1986 to 1992 (Vaid 1995, 94). So, while criticism of ACT UP was widespread among some in the lesbian and gay community, others—including many with comparatively traditional activist histories—expressed strong solidarity with confrontational AIDS activists from the earliest days, sometimes even participating in ACT UP's actions and getting arrested.

The content and texture of this support is interesting because it reveals that lesbian and gay organizations, leaders, activists, and other individuals were engaged in a struggle—at the level of ideology and at the level of emotion—about what constituted proper political activity. Indeed, critics and defenders alike almost always raised the topic of the propriety of ACT UP's tactics. Critics usually indicated their anxiety about how mainstream society would perceive confrontational, disruptive, AIDS activism. Backers frequently indicated their awareness of that anxiety, and sometimes revealed that they too shared it to some degree but nevertheless supported confrontational activism. They often defended ACT UP and similar groups by attempting to answer that anxiety with claims about the effectiveness, necessity, and sometimes even nobility of confrontation. Their vocal support likely helped to legitimize and authorize ACT UP's mode of activism. I analyze it in some detail because the contours of that support provide insight into the instabilities and precariousness of ACT UP's emotional habitus and political horizon, allowing us to consider how derisive criticisms of the movement gained traction in the early 1990s.

An interesting example of support occurred around the militant actions that SANOE did in 1989. SANOE's lesbian and gay supporters took on gay and straight critics by arguing for the legitimacy and necessity of confrontational activism, even though it might alienate and anger mainstream society. An editorial in the *San Francisco Sentinel* that endorsed SANOE's action on the Golden Gate Bridge acknowledged "commuter ire" but noted that the media rushed to cover the action, providing front-page coverage of the AIDS crisis that was "desperately needed." Accordingly, the *Sentinel* wholeheartedly endorsed SANOE's action and confrontational activism more generally. "Would civil rights have been hurried along if Martin Luther King thought his Montgomery March bridge blockades too much an inconvenience [for commuters]? No. Would the Vietnam War have been stopped without unpopular protests? No. Will public demand for quicker AIDS drug testing move medical bureaucrats to action without civil disobedience? No" ("From" 1989). The editors authorized disruptive and militant street AIDS activism by placing it within what they saw as a noble lineage of effective protest politics.

In a second editorial one week later, the *Sentinel* again countered the critics and amplified its endorsement of SANOE by crediting its Golden Gate Bridge action with helping to push the FDA to approve an experimental treatment for AIDS-related pneumonia (PCP), aerosolized pentamidine.

> For all the lambasting of the bridge protest as not the way to do this, we must ask: Didn't it work beyond all expectations? Finally, finally, finally, the dismal state of getting FDA-approved treatments for those living with AIDS made every front page, every major news program. . . . Outpourings of protest—including the closure of the Golden Gate—spurred the Food and Drug Administration to approve [aerosolized pentamidine]. . . . We are on the right track, and if the bridge has to be closed again, then we say close it. The true revolutionaries—those who helped change the course of history—never gave up, no matter how much they were criticized or punished or told that they were going about their quest in the wrong way. There is no violence in this protest, only a sense of urgency. ("Sense" 1989)

The following *Windy City Times* editorial also indicated that lesbian and gay communities were engaged in a struggle about the propriety and value of direct-action AIDS activism. The editorial, written after a national ACT UP demonstration held in Chicago in April 1990 about the inadequacies of the for-profit and public health systems and the need for universal health insurance, praised the protest while simultaneously broaching a discussion of ACT UP's confrontational tactics.

> Some individuals feel uncomfortable with ACT UP's tactics. They say that ACT UP angers too many people. . . . And there are those who sincerely disagree with the appropriateness of some of the more extreme civil disobedience activities taken on by ACT UP. . . . But surely no one should have

to take to the streets to protest such obvious injustices as the ones demonstrated against last month. Alas, it's often the only way to get important issues brought to public attention. ("Turning" 1990)

The editors then credited previous civil disobedience by ACT UP
with successfully pressuring Burroughs Wellcome to drop the price of
AZT and with influencing the FDA to expedite its drug-approval process. "Likewise, the recent ACT UP demonstrations [in Chicago] have
highlighted several injustices that otherwise might not have been put
before a mass audience. . . . The Chicago demonstration was an excellent example of bringing an on-going issue into sharper focus for everyone" ("Turning" 1990). Even as they praised and thereby validated ACT
UP's confrontational tactics, the editors clearly felt a need to justify such
activism, acknowledging—and attempting to address—the anxiety that
ACT UP raised for many lesbians and gay men.

During her time as executive director of NGLTF, Urvashi Vaid sometimes seemed intent on assuaging lesbian and gay anxiety about confrontational politics as well. Interviewed about ACT UP in *Newsweek,*
she said, "My view is that you need to use all the tactics available, even
when you know that some of the things you do will antagonize and even
repel potential supporters" (Salholz et al. 1990).

As these examples indicate, expressions of support for ACT UP from
various quarters in lesbian and gay communities often had a protective
tone that indicated a need to defend its tactics.[27] ACT UP's defenders
were attuned to the context in which it was operating and intent on countering the anxiety generated by its violations of emotional and political
norms.

When the Ideological Context Matters

Where the general bias is against militancy, a lot of work—emotional
and ideological—is required to authorize confrontational politics. When
successful, that work can make defiant activism axiomatic within a social group for a time. The emotional and ideological work that ACT UP
did succeeded in that way, successfully draining criticisms leveled at the

27. For additional examples see Obejas 1991; Damski 1992a; Smith 1992; Garcia 1992;
and Baim 1993.

movement of their affective charge. But the biases against militancy are robust, especially because they are affectively compelling, and they can easily be reinvigorated and regain their preeminent position.

Disparaging criticisms of ACT UP from gay and straight worlds had little effect during the movement's early years, but they did later on because of significantly changed conditions and the feeling states provoked by those changes. Specifically, in ACT UP's later years a perception took hold in lesbian and gay communities that state and society were finally responding to AIDS and, even more important, were becoming more accepting of homosexuality. This changed context impaired ACT UP's emotion work.[28] Derisive criticisms of direct-action AIDS activism started to resonate and to have negative effects largely because perceived openings in the social, cultural, and political realms raised hopes of imminent social acceptance and a correlative anxiety about social rejection.

Having Nothing, or Something, to Lose

The situation was very different in the years of the movement's emergence when doors to the state and to mainstream institutions were mostly closed to lesbians and gay men. Direct-action AIDS activists made a case that the conditions facing queers and people with AIDS were dire and were not being addressed effectively by a homophobic government and scientific-medical establishment. Tens of thousands of queer folks agreed. Their frustration, anger, and desperation—and indeed the sense of outsiderness from a society that seemed unmoved, even gladdened, by their deaths—made them willing to defy mainstream emotional and political norms or at least to support wholeheartedly the angry direct action of others.

In a context where the political system denied them access, there was very little to lose, and much to gain, by acting up, and that is a key reason why criticism of the movement had very little traction early on. Mainstream gay activists' adamant support for an ACT UP/Chicago civil disobedience action at City Hall in November 1989 probably stemmed from their lack of access to Mayor Daley. The action occurred the day after

28. The broader political context was important as well; by the early 1990s, progressive politics had been largely shut down, and ACT UP thus was unable to draw sustenance from any broader movement culture. See Edwards 2000b.

Daley stormed out of a forum designed to address thorny relations between the mayor and the lesbian and gay community (Damski 1989). Under Mayor Harold Washington, gay activists had, in their view, "direct
and virtually unlimited access to the mayor's office" (Wockner 1989c,
26). Under Daley, in contrast, the mayor's own Committee on Gay and
Lesbian Issues (COGLI) had not been granted "a single meeting in the
first seven months of the administration" (26). At the same time, AIDS
activists were furious about the city's recently unveiled AIDS education
campaign which many saw as useless because it offered no information
about how to have safe sex and dangerous because it implied that monogamy could protect one from AIDS (Wockner 1989d). Speaking at
the action, Laurie Dittman, vice chair of COGLI, countered those who
advocated being "good little queers" and justified militancy in the face
of blocked political access: "We are not going to be quiet. We are not going to be patient. We are not just going to wait outside the door" to City
Hall (Wockner 1989c, 27; Craig 1989, 1). Rick Garcia, from the group
Catholic Advocates for Lesbian and Gay Rights, was arrested along with
members of ACT UP. He commented on the breadth of support for the
action: "The unity is unprecedented in this community. Most expect
ACT UP to take direct action. We don't expect it from the [lesbian and
gay] mainstream, and it's time" (Craig 1989, 8).

When even establishment-oriented lesbian and gay activists were being iced out by government bodies at federal, state, and local levels, and
when routine interest-group tactics were failing to achieve demands or
even gain access, criticism of ACT UP had little traction, and support
for the movement was forthright and extensive. Art Johnston, a Chicago
gay activist whose access to City Hall had been cut off and who became
a supporter of ACT UP/Chicago, interpreted the growing gay militancy
in the 1980s through the lens of AIDS: "All of a sudden people were
fighting for their lives or for the lives of their friends. Suddenly there
was an army of people with nothing to lose. With a death penalty hang-
ing over your head, suddenly you aren't so concerned about being polite
to politicians" (Pick 1993, 14). Beyond the terror of that death sentence,
an important aspect of the context that allowed many establishment-
oriented lesbians and gay men to move away from "polite" politics in this
period was that the political system was largely closed to lesbians and
gay men, and in that sense too, people had, in Johnston's words, "nothing to lose." In that context, ACT UP's defiant, oppositional tactics were

compelling, and ideological arguments against confrontational activism that were then circulating in both straight and gay worlds had little affective charge and thus held little sway.

A Changed Context: Partial Openings

The criticisms of the movement gained traction and had a corrosive effect only at the point when many lesbians and gay men sensed that the political, cultural, and social realms were opening toward them. The ideological biases against confrontational politics came to matter in the context of shifting material conditions and people's perceptions of those conditions. Stuart Hall's notion of *articulation* (1986) is useful here for pointing to the conjunctural nature of my analysis. Neither ideological nor material conditions alone determined the types of AIDS activism that queer folks pursued; rather, in these two different historical moments (the period of ACT UP's emergence in the late 1980s and the period of its decline in the early-to-mid-1990s), the ideological and material contexts articulated differently to one another, differentially shaping people's attitudes about their place in society and about what political activism they might engage in or support. The sense of openings in the later period heightened desires for social acceptance and anxieties about social rejection, reinvigorating a politics of respectability that dissuaded gays from confrontational action.

OPENINGS.   Bill Clinton's campaign for the presidency, and indeed the entire 1992 primary race for the Democratic Party nominee, marked a moment of significant political opening for lesbians and gay men. In an article in the *New York Times Magazine* just before election day—headlined "Gay Politics Goes Mainstream"—reporter Jeffrey Schmalz noted this opening and the fact that lesbians and gays were becoming a potent political force.

> For the first time in a race for the White House, gay and lesbian issues are being raised—and fought over. During the primaries, the five leading Democratic contenders . . . actively courted the gay vote. All five endorsed a repeal of the ban on homosexuals in the military, as eventually did [Independent candidate] Ross Perot. Questions about gay and lesbian issues, virtually unbroachable just four years ago, are now asked routinely of candidates, includ-

ing the President. For years, politicians of all stripes hid or returned financial
contributions from homosexuals for fear of being tainted. Today, they seek
them out. (Schmalz 1992, 20)

Schmalz described gay activists' optimism in the context of these openings, a growing confidence that no matter who won the presidential election, "the homosexual rights cause [would] continue to advance" (53).

In this period, the entire Democratic Party seemed to be courting
gays and lesbians, enacting a form of political recognition that queers
had never before received. During the primary season Bill Clinton gave
a speech to a gay group in Hollywood where he told attendees, "I have
a vision, and you are a part of it," opening, in the words of sociologist
Suzanna Walters, "a door that had never even been cracked before"
(Walters 2001, 31). At the Democratic National Convention that summer, lesbians and gay men held seats in all of the powerful organizing
committees, demonstrating "an unprecedented show of influence in the
Democratic Party" according to the *Advocate* (Purnell 1992, 42). Thirteen speakers at the convention mentioned lesbians and gays in their
speeches; an openly gay man with AIDS spoke, as did an open lesbian
who accused the Bush administration of scapegoating people like her.
Ted Kennedy talked about gay teenagers in his speech, as did Paul Tson-
gas. Candidate Clinton pledged to overturn the military ban on lesbians
and gay men.[29]

To be sure, the Republican National Convention that summer was a
homo hatefest; conservatives Patrick Buchanan and Pat Robertson gave
vitriolic prime-time speeches that brazenly attacked lesbians and gay
men. President George H. W. Bush and Vice President Dan Quayle also
maligned lesbians and gay men, although through a more veiled "pro-
family" rhetoric. The religious right placed referenda on the 1992 ballot
in several states and cities designed to deny lesbians and gay men protection against discrimination; some were defeated, but others passed. Even
with this backlash—which some wrote off as a retrograde, unsustainable
motion—lesbians and gay men felt that the political system was opening
toward them, especially within the Democratic Party.

Clinton's electoral victory bolstered that optimism, and when, just
months after assuming the presidency, Clinton invited prominent mem-

29. See Minkowitz 1992 for more on lesbian and gay political optimism generated by
the DNC.

bers of the gay and lesbian community to a meeting in the Oval Office, social acceptance seemed to be at hand. In Urvashi Vaid's words, "the meeting was historic, the first of its kind in the Oval Office, an important nod of recognition from the President of the United States at a crucial time in our movement" (Seabaugh 1993). Although it became clear early in his first term that Clinton would fail to come through on many of his promises to lesbians and gay men—lifting the ban against gays and les- bians in the military is the most famous, but Clinton also disappointed on AIDS policies—many continued to hold out hope for Clinton, in part because his gay-friendly image presented such a contrast to the unabash- edly homophobic Reagan/Bush years. Even with the setbacks, many in the gay community still felt that the political system was opening toward them.

The cultural realm was also becoming more gay-positive, most evi- dently on network TV. The fall 1991 TV season, for example, witnessed an explosion in gay content: a star football player came out as gay on *Coach,* a father embraced his gay son on *Dynasty,* a bisexual lawyer re- united with her female ex-lover on *L.A. Law,* episodes of *Designing Women* and *Seinfeld* explored gay stereotypes, and Roseanne's boss on *Roseanne* announced that he was gay (McConnell 1992, 70). Accord- ing to the *Advocate,* "TV viewers tuned in more gay themes and char- acters than ever before" during the fall 1991 season (70). Roseanne's friend Nancy, played by Sandra Bernhard, came out as a lesbian, becom- ing the first regular lesbian character on a sit-com. During sweeps month in 1992, an episode of the show *Northern Exposure* focused on the nineteenth-century founding of the town Cicely, Alaska—where the show takes place—by two lesbian pioneers (Sparta 2002).

The state of affairs on network TV had been dramatically different just a few years before. In 1987, for example, before the first episode of *Roseanne* aired, Roseanne Arnold proposed that her sister on the sit- com be a lesbian. She was met with "embarrassed silence." "Objections were raised. Would it be unacceptably rude? Why risk turning off a large segment of viewers?" (Kastor 1993). The idea was nixed. When the show *thirtysomething* depicted two shirtless men sitting in bed together in a 1988 episode, the network lost $1 million in advertising revenue. "The gay characters were written out of the show, and the offending snippet became non-history, scissored out of the reruns" (Kastor 1993). Gay lives simply could not be depicted on network TV. In contrast, by 1992, *TV Guide*'s Hollywood bureau chief suggested that gays and lesbians on

TV no longer caused a sensation: "there have been enough gay-themed episodes over the last year so that they are no longer headline-grabbing events. It's a more normal situation now" (McConnell 1992, 70).

According to the *Advocate*, there were also openings toward lesbians and gay men in the worlds of fine art, film, literature, music, dance, and theater in 1991 (Perry 1992). With gay-themed movies like *Paris Is Burning* and *My Own Private Idaho* playing to large crowds, major museums and galleries showing the work of lesbian and gay artists, and big publishing houses pronouncing the 1990s as the decade of gay and lesbian writers, the *Advocate* proclaimed, "It's been a banner year for up-front queer culture in the mainstream" (68). Suzanna Walters discusses the contradictoriness and limits of these cultural openings (2001), but many experienced them as a hopeful and promising form of public recognition.

Connected to these political and cultural openings was a sense that broader social acceptance of lesbians and gay men was imminent. More people seemed to be "coming out of the closet" and finding acceptance from their families, friends, employers, co-workers, and neighbors. As the February 7, 1993, cover of the *Chicago Tribune Magazine* blared, lesbians and gay men were moving "into the mainstream" and, the reporter noted, "gaining acceptance—and power" (Pick 1993, 12–13; see fig. 21). Institutions that lesbian and gay activists previously had criticized for their homophobia seemingly were changing. In May 1992, for example, ACT UP/NY member Michelangelo Signorile argued that "a 'lavender enlightenment' is under way at America's newspaper of record" (Signorile 1992, 34). He noted that the *New York Times* opened its pages to gay themes in 1991, publishing editorials and front-page stories on subjects like gay-bashing, children growing up with gay parents, the military ban on lesbians and gays, domestic partner benefits, hate-crimes bills, President Bush's fumbling on the AIDS crisis, and civil rights for lesbians and gay men. Media stories bolstered the perception that society was becoming more accepting of homosexuality.

OPENINGS? And yet, even as acceptance was growing in some quarters of society, homosexuality was not close to becoming normalized. Lesbian and gay visibility might have been increasing, but so were gay bashings, and the religious right was amping up its use of homophobia to fuel its push into the Republican Party. When Clinton assumed the presidency, he met with fierce resistance when he tried to implement some of

FIGURE 21. *Chicago Tribune Magazine*, February 7, 1993.

his anti-discriminatory policies, and he quickly reneged on many of his promises to lesbians and gay men. While the changes at the *New York Times* may have suggested a growing acceptance of lesbians and gay men by the "paper of record," Signorile quoted gay leaders who indicated that they thought there was a long way to go. Robert Bray of NGLTF called the *Times'* improvement "episodic." Stephen Miller of GLAAD noted

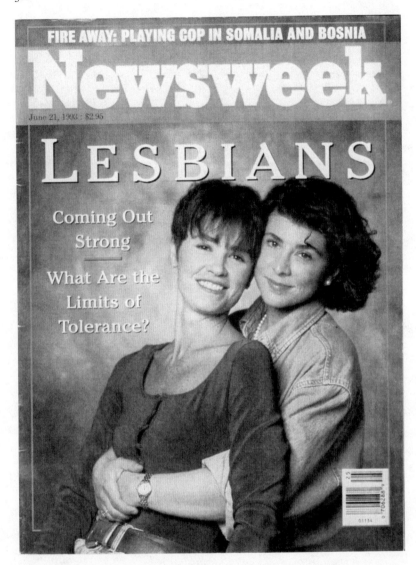

FIGURE 22. *Newsweek,* June 21, 1993.

that the *Times'* "political and Washington reporters don't ask the presidential candidates—or even the President—about gay civil rights, about gays in the military, or even about AIDS" (Signorile 1992, 39–40). *Newsweek* placed two embracing lesbians on its June 21, 1993 cover with a headline that said "Lesbians: Coming Out Strong," but the headline also asked: "What Are the Limits of Tolerance?" revealing continuing main-stream ambivalence about homosexuality (fig. 22). Social acceptance seemed simultaneously imminent and a long way off.[30]

The Allure of Social Acceptance

For lesbians and gay men, a massive shift was underway, from almost complete exclusion to a state of partial acceptance and partial exclusion. Lesbians' and gay men's continuing outsider status amid growing social acceptance set emotional dynamics in motion within their communities that allowed derisive criticisms of direct-action AIDS activism to gain traction. The biases against militancy that ACT UP's emotion work had successfully challenged began to exert a pull again. Partial social accep-tance buttressed what I would call an anxious calculus of moderation. In a context where social acceptance was not yet a reality but seemed within reach, some indicated their belief that queers might secure that acceptance if we all simply behaved ourselves, played by straight rules, and submerged gay difference. Political scientist David Rayside argues, for example, that as openly gay Massachusetts Representative Barney Frank "saw gay and lesbian issues coming closer to mainstream legiti-macy," he became "more vocal in his critique of certain aspects of the confrontational politics of the [gay] left" (Rayside 1998, 277). The var-ious openings and the feelings they prompted encouraged moderation and distancing from ACT UP's confrontational activism. An editorial in the New York Times after the April 1993 March on Washington for Lesbian and Gay Rights noticed and challenged (!) this turn toward nor-malcy and moderation:

This march was Ozzie and Harriet compared with the Stonewall days. . . .
As the Los Angeles Times's Bettina Boxall wrote: "They wanted to show to America that they were 'regular' people, the kind that live next door, go to work every day and pay their taxes." "Ordinary" and "The People Next Door" were mantras of the weekend, as though the right of full citizenship depends on how one chooses to dress. It doesn't. And it's a dangerous idea. The fixation on "normalcy" is understandable given how gay Americans have been demonized in recent years. But the measure of a just society is not how

30. See Walters 2001 on the paradoxical nature of growing gay visibility in this period. See also Vaid 1995.

it treats people who look like Ozzie and Harriet. . . . A just society must offer the same full citizenship to the flamboyant dressers in last weekend's parade as it does to those who looked "just like the people next door." ("Washington" 1993)

Although the *Times* highlighted lesbians' and gay men's embrace of "normal" dress and appearance and ignored their adoption of mainstream political norms, the emotional and psychic dynamics I am describing encouraged both forms of "mainstreaming." Partial social acceptance gave lesbians and gay men a taste of recognition and offered the promise of more of the same, contingent on "good" behavior, but it also threatened continuing social rejection should gays not fulfill their end of the bargain. In that economy, rocking the boat in any manner—through flamboyant dress, queer sex-radicalism, aligning too closely with other socially marginalized groups, or challenging society's emotional and political norms through angry and defiant street activism—generated anxiety that could easily become opposition. In short, with social acceptance in sight but not yet in hand, conditions favored a strategy of moderation, and non-normative behavior—including confrontational activism—could now easily be construed as jeopardizing what had already been gained.

Just as the pull of inclusion foreclosed the possibility of confrontational AIDS activism in the early 1980s, a similar pull contributed to the withdrawal of support for ACT UP and the decline of the movement in the early 1990s. An additional factor in the later period was that queer folks were exhausted, having fought the AIDS crisis by then for over a decade. In that context, the prospect of social acceptance promised more than inclusion; it offered a retreat from politics as well, and that was especially enticing after years of doing battle on multiple fronts.

I have said this before, but it bears repeating: the seduction of social acceptance needs to be understood within a context of social rejection. Writing in 1993, lesbian activist and writer Amber Hollibaugh acknowledged the allure of recognition in this period even as she counseled lesbians and gay men to be wary of it.

The good news is, we finally exist to people other than ourselves. The bad news is, on what terms? It is giddy-making to be written up as "the new power brokers" in *Newsweek*, to have the cover of *New York* magazine read, "The Bold, Brave New World of Gay Women," to be invited inside the White

House rather than carrying signs or lying down outside it—to be consulted as the experts on our own lives and needs. This is heady stuff. . . . It is a piece of what we have fought to accomplish, what we have struggled for and died to achieve, and it is momentous and valuable. But in this new period of returning Democratic Party dominance, the temptations for us to "go straight" also seem tremendous. Already we are being asked to clean up, dress up, compromise, bargain gratefully with the boys already at the table, the boys who own the table. . . . This faint call finally to be included and respected is like a siren song to those of us who have been written out of history. . . . It is thus ever more vital for us to sustain a long view of the struggle and to define what is *key* to us, what our commitment is as a movement to breaking the boundaries that block our liberation as gay people. (Hollibaugh 1993, 27–28; emphasis hers)

Although the acceptance being offered was not entirely, or even nearly, on any gay person's terms, its seduction was powerful, given the experience of stigmatization and social annihilation. Even those lesbians and gay men who rejected many aspects of mainstream society were subject to this seduction.

The structure of lesbian and gay ambivalence always made support for ACT UP precarious. Goffman sees that phenomenon as general among stigmatized groups: "Given the ambivalence built into the individual's attachment to his stigmatized category, it is understandable that oscillations may occur in his support of, identification with, and participation among his own" (1963, 38). In this period, the sense that social acceptance was imminent intensified many lesbians' and gay men's anxiety about and need to distance themselves from anything or anybody who seemed to threaten full admission. ACT UP fit that bill. In a context of greater openings toward lesbians and gay men amid continuing social disapproval and hostility, the occurrence of an ACT UP action had parallels to a situation that Goffman calls "nearing," where a stigmatized individual is "coming close to an undesirable instance of his own kind while 'with' a normal" (108). Goffman argues that identity ambivalence may become acute in such a situation: "The sight may repel him, since after all he supports the norms of the wider society, but his social and psychological identification with these offenders holds him to what repels him, transforming repulsion into shame, and then transforming ashamedness itself into something of which he is ashamed. In brief, he can neither embrace his group nor let it go" (108). For a collectivity that is experiencing increasing social acceptance—which is similar to Goffman's stigmatized individual being "with" a so-called normal—a public event like a defiant demonstration that violates propriety is comparable to the experience of "nearing" and might similarly intensify identity ambivalence among those oriented toward and perhaps partially identifying with "normal" society.

Precisely such dynamics are apparent in the following incident. In February 1992, six members of ACT UP/Chicago disrupted Mayor Daley as he gave a speech to a lesbian and gay business group, the Chicago Professional Networking Association (CPNA). ACT UP was in the midst of a campaign demanding that the city increase the AIDS budget, which at that point had been stagnant for three years even as the AIDS caseload had jumped 155 percent (Olson 1991b, 1). The ACT UP members and Daley engaged in a vociferous back-and-forth until the CPNA president intervened, simultaneously distancing himself from the AIDS activists and indicating his anxiety that his organization's good standing might be undermined by being associated with the manifestly disreputable ACT UP in the presence of a "normal," Mayor Daley: "The mayor is here, and our reputation, . . . and I can see from the people who are standing [i.e., those disrupting the event], you're wearing blue tags, which means you're not members of our organization, you are visitors this evening" (from transcript printed in Wockner 1992b, 25, ellipses in original).[31] The CPNA President felt compelled to ensure that the mayor not misconstrue the "visitors" as members of CPNA and mistakenly put his upstanding and professional organization in the same basket with ACT UP.

In the changed context of the early 1990s, anything seen as jeopardizing the realization of the newly offered promise of social acceptance might elicit anxiety and prompt vocal disparagement. Indeed, as Goffman writes, "it is only to be expected that this identity ambivalence will receive organized expression in the written, talked, acted, and otherwise presented materials of representatives of the group" (1963, 108). What is striking about criticism of ACT UP from lesbian and gay individuals and institutions is how often they expressed shame and embarrassment. Even when not explicitly expressed, people articulating critiques almost always suggested that they were feeling such sentiments, usually by distancing themselves from ACT UP through some form of dispar-

31. Full disclosure: I participated in this action.

agement that placed direct-action AIDS activists outside the community
of proper and legitimate political actors. Its emotionally inflected content and tone indicated that much of this criticism revolved around lesbians' and gay men's felt exclusion from mainstream society and consequent shame, as well as anxiety about further stigmatization and social
rejection.

Tactical Disputes or Something More?

A plausible alternative hypothesis, however, is that these critiques,
rather than deriving from gay anxiety, derived from simple tactical disagreements between ACT UP and its gay critics about how best to force
the government and other institutions to respond to AIDS. The following criticism of direct-action AIDS activism does indeed seem to revolve
around tactical differences alone. In response to SANOE's action blocking the Golden Gate Bridge, the director of public policy for the San
Francisco AIDS Foundation (SFAF), Pat Christen, stated, "We're very
supportive of civil disobedience, but disagree with the location [of this
action] for public safety reasons. However, in terms of the AIDS agenda,
in terms of the need for civil disobedience and future activities of this
kind, we're very supportive" (quoted in Conkin 1989). Christen and the
SFAF disagreed with SANOE's tactics in that instance, but they did not
distance themselves from SANOE. They expressed neither shame nor
embarrassment about its action and unequivocally endorsed civil disobedience and other forms of confrontational activism.[32]

Contrast Christen's criticism with the following letter to the *B.A.R.*
that also expressed tactical disagreement with SANOE's action but indicated anxiety about sharing an identity with angry lesbian and gay activists. The writer suggested that San Francisco AIDS activists should
not be so confrontational toward the people of "the city that has done
more and showed more compassion and interest in caring for AIDS victims than any other in the country." This writer distanced himself from
SANOE, whose action, he suggested, would only "confirm the negative
image that much of the country has of San Francisco." Further revealing
his concern with public perceptions and his own fear of being associated
with SANOE, he asserted that SANOE's behavior "can only be perceived

---

32. See also the comments of Steve Morin, an openly gay legislative aide to Representative Nancy Pelosi, about ACT UP's disruption of Secretary Sullivan in Zonana 1990.

as juvenile" (De La Roche 1989). Sentiments like these that disassociated
the critic from militant AIDS activism were articulated in almost every
letter to the lesbian and gay press that was critical of SANOE.[33]

The emotional valence and specific content of most of the gay criticism of direct-action AIDS activism indicate that much more was usually at stake than simple tactical disputes. Many of the critiques indicate
that ACT UP's confrontational tactics provoked anxiety and guilt by association. Critics often indicated their shame about ACT UP, sometimes
saying as much. An editorial in the *Windy City Times* asserted that more
moderate lesbian and gay activists tended to be "embarrassed by the in-
your-face tactics" of groups like ACT UP ("Yin" 1991). Several writers
who criticized ACT UP in letters to the gay papers apologized about
AIDS activists' actions.[34] Although they did not indicate to whom or
why they were apologizing, their apologies, a form of distancing behavior, indicate anxiety about activist behavior that might risk further social
rejection. Powerful unconscious processes may have been in play: such
apologies can furnish people with a developmental narrative that sepa-
rates them from their own childish (that is, outrageously gay) past, per-
formatively confirming their entry into an adult present where they become socially acceptable, even if gay.

Even critics of ACT UP who seemingly were expressing simple tactical differences sometimes seemed motivated in part by their own negative affective responses to ACT UP's activism. In a January 1989 article in *Spin* magazine about ACT UP's confrontational activism, Barney
Frank admonished that "the wrong kinds of demonstrations can make
people angry, rather than being helpful. Simply getting people's attention
isn't always a good thing" (Ford 1989). One could argue that Frank simply was expressing a view that diverged from ACT UP's about which tactics would best bring about changes in the government's AIDS policies.
He was asserting that lesbian/gay and AIDS activists should not engage
in activism that might make people—that is, straight people—angry because doing so would be harmful to the cause. Frank did not make clear
exactly what confrontational activism might put at risk, but this is precisely what shows that more was at stake for Frank than political inefficacy. Frank's talk of anger conjures up the anger that has been directed at

33. See letters about SANOE's actions in the *B.A.R.* and the *San Francisco Sentinel*
from February, September, and October 1989.
34. See, for example, letters by Douthwaite and Everett 1989; Roberts 1989; and Youngblood 1989.

one—perhaps from one's parents, but also from other authority figures—potentially flooding one with feelings like shame and anxiety. Frank's comments prompt the question, What might incensed straight people do? More than risking political failure, militant activism that maddens risks punishment, ridicule, nonrecognition, and continued social rejection.

In another instance when Frank was questioning ACT UP's (and Queer Nation's) confrontational tactics, he reportedly complained to *Miami Herald* reporter Eleanor Burkett, "When was the last time the American Association for Retired Persons had a die-in? Does the National Rifle Association have shoot-ins? 'We're here,' everyone knows we're here. That's not the point. The point is to forge an effective political force" (Burkett 1995, 312). Again, Frank articulated his critique of direct action in terms of tactical differences. But Frank was not only impugning the political savvy of direct-action AIDS activists; he also insinuated that they were more interested in childishly acting out than in being "politically effective," however the latter might be defined. More than engaging a tactical disagreement, Frank's comments about direct-action activists—questioning their effectiveness, relevance, political savvy, rationality, and psychological maturity—suggest a need to disassociate from such activism.

Tracy Baim, a long-time Chicago lesbian and gay newspaper publisher and editor, corroborated my sense that much lesbian and gay criticism of ACT UP stemmed from people's anxiety that ACT UP's ill-repute might rub off on other lesbians and gay men. An active presence in Chicago lesbian and gay community affairs since the mid-1980s, Baim is well positioned to discuss lesbian and gay attitudes toward groups like ACT UP. Recalling the first AIDS action engaged in by ACT UP/ Chicago predecessor DAGMAR, at which members chained themselves to the house of Governor James Thompson in the summer of 1987, Baim remembered, "That pissed off a lot of people"—specifically "the people that think that [actions like that give] a bad name to gay people." Suggesting that such attitudes were widespread, particularly among lesbian and gay community leaders, Baim noted, "Everybody's so worried about what the mainstream thinks about us" (Baim 2001). In Baim's eyes, people were worried that ACT UP's actions would tar them with the brush of disrepute, an anxiety that she attributed to "self-shame." Disparaging ACT UP as immature, irrational, and ineffective offered a psychic boost to the movement's lesbian and gay critics, positioning them as mature, reasonable, and respectable.

ACT UP, of course, is not the only oppositional social movement criticized for being too confrontational by members of the community from
which it emerged. Here, using a more general discussion of such criticism, I further interrogate the hypothesis that lesbian and gay critics of
ACT UP's militant activism were motivated primarily by tactical issues.
This discussion of people's reasons for criticizing confrontational activism also provides insight into why such criticism gained traction in lesbian and gay communities in the early 1990s when social acceptance began to seem imminent.

Critics of direct-action and militant activism almost never provide
empirical evidence to substantiate their claims that confrontational activism angers and offends potential supporters, that it provokes a backlash, that it simply does not work. Their assertions are not objectively
true; to the contrary, historical examples like the civil rights sit-ins and
protest marches demonstrate that oppositional and defiant, street-based
activism is often politically efficacious.

There also are no a priori grounds on which to make such a claim.
Sweeping claims about street-based activism like the ones made in a
Windy City Times editorial that hedged its praise of ACT UP simply
cannot be substantiated: "While protests work on the visceral level, they
miss the mark in other ways. They don't provide the opportunity for dialogue, for addressing and overcoming objections. They don't present arguments or solutions" ("Yin" 1991). That might be an accurate description of a specific protest action, but it fails as a general claim. The aims
and success of any form of activism depend on a number of contextual
factors that must be explored before any claims about the political effectiveness of a given course of action can be made. As a result, tactical disputes are inherent in activism. But there is an enormous difference between a critic who claims that a given moment is or was not the best time
for a specific action and one who dismisses militant activism out of hand
by claiming, for example, that it simply does not work. ACT UP's lesbian
and gay critics almost always were in the latter camp, and that is probably true about criticism directed toward other movements as well. Critics rarely said things like "taking to the streets is an option, but ACT
UP simply doesn't have the numbers to make it effective and therefore
shouldn't do it." Instead they made unsubstantiated claims like "taking
to the streets makes the community look bad; people won't listen to lesbians and gay men if we make them angry; ACT UP's tactics alienate
mainstream society; street activism risks a backlash."

The historical record shows that, while not always successful, confrontational activism often achieves its goals and is sometimes the decisive factor in a given struggle. As well, lobbying and similar tactics are
not always effective, something that critics of confrontation rarely if ever
mention. Insofar as the theoretical and evidentiary bases for their claims
are dubious, why do people—in this case, some members of the mainstream lesbian and gay community—dispute the political efficacy of militant activism? Some of them surely *think* they are correct. Given the
historical evidence to the contrary, however, one has to question what
forces other than tactical disagreements might be in play.

Hegemonic political ideologies contending that all grievances can be
resolved through the electoral process certainly foster unfounded claims
that confrontational activism "simply does not work." Equally important, in my view, is the affective charge that attaches to notions of order
and disorder. Anxiety about confrontational activism and the disorder
it allegedly unleashes can be readily mobilized, and that helps to explain why people disparage confrontational activism and why those criticisms sometimes hold sway. Additionally, in the case of ACT UP and
probably other movements of socially marginalized groups, ambivalence
about self and society and its circulation in community discourses play
an important role in negative constructions of confrontational activism.
The emotional valence and content of much lesbian and gay criticism of
ACT UP indicated as much. For lesbians and gay men living in a heteronormative society, anxiety and other feelings about one's relationship
to mainstream society may recede at different moments, but they rarely
disappear entirely. We may disdain society's norms and take pleasure in
defying them, but for those deemed abnormal, the emotional and psychic pull of being seen as normal, of fitting in, is a strong counterforce;
after all, as Goffman noted, great awards accrue to those considered
normal (1963, 74). Queer folks who feel the stigma of difference might
both value their own outsiderness and simultaneously feel invested in
the mainstream norms that categorize them as "other." As an example
of the latter, consider that much lesbian and gay criticism of ACT UP
echoed mainstream society's derision of lesbians and gay men as immature and childlike.

Some lesbian and gay criticism of ACT UP in this period was motivated by strategic attempts to promote the adoption of mainstream
norms as the ticket to fuller social acceptance. But we should not under-
estimate the force of the nonrational, nonconscious processes that par-

tial social acceptance set in motion. The promise of social acceptance, contingent on good behavior, amplified the desire for such acceptance and heightened anxiety about anything that might jeopardize its fulfillment. The evidence suggests that those affective states were very much in play in the disparaging critiques of ACT UP that circulated in lesbian and gay communities. The real and perceived openings toward lesbians and gay men beginning around 1991, then, altered the affective landscape in a manner that allowed disparaging criticisms of ACT UP to gain more of a foothold than they had in ACT UP's first few years.

ACT UP's Isolation

Disparaging criticisms of ACT UP contributed to the decline of the movement indirectly as well by producing feelings of isolation and betrayal among many AIDS activists who dealt with those feelings in part by becoming contemptuous of other lesbians, gay men, and AIDS advocates. Many of us in ACT UP felt that lesbian and gay disparagements were growing and were helping to shrink our membership. We sensed that the greater openings toward lesbians and gay men were not only siphoning off support for our activism but also prompting a conservative turn within the community that threatened to displace ACT UP. From our perspective, we had been on the front lines for years, our actions had forced government and the scientific-medical establishment to respond to the AIDS crisis, and all we were getting from other lesbians and gay men was criticism and disrespect. Many of us were perplexed. In the words of ACT UP/Chicago member Billy McMillan, who encountered many gay men who condemned ACT UP as an "embarrassment" to the lesbian and gay community, "We were the only ones out there doing anything. . . . Most of the time I felt like, why aren't other people doing this [i.e., taking to the streets]? Why don't they help us? Don't they see what's happening all around us? By that point, everyone knew someone who had died from AIDS or was dying. I felt like ACT UP/Chicago was really maligned" (McMillan 2000). In this context, where we felt unsupported, indeed, betrayed, we became increasingly self-righteous and disdainful of ASOs and mainstream lesbian and gay activists and institutions, probably alienating potential supporters in the process.

An ACT UP/Chicago flier distributed at Chicago's Lesbian and Gay Pride Parade in June 1991 indicated such feelings of isolation and betrayal vis-à-vis the broader lesbian and gay community. Bracketed with bold-lettered text that said "The AIDS Epidemic, Eleven Years Later" on the top and "This War's Not Over"[35] on the bottom, the leaflet asked lesbians and gay men to "take a reality check" about the AIDS epidemic, listing the numbers dead from AIDS and the failed policies of the federal and Chicago governments. A heading in the middle read "So what do we do about it?" and the text underneath berated other lesbians and gay men for going to fancy AIDS benefits, appeasing their guilt by writing checks to AIDS service organizations, voting for Richard Daley for mayor despite his failure to increase Chicago's AIDS budget, and gossiping and rumor-mongering about divisions in the AIDS movement "rather than getting off *your* butts and doing something" (ACT UP/Chicago 1991b; emphasis mine). Although the heading asked, "What do *we* do about it?" the voice quickly shifted to a more accusatory tone and replaced "we" with "you" in three places, indicating ACT UP members' sense of separation—and self-righteousness—vis-à-vis the broader lesbian and gay community. A contrast to earlier movement-produced documents is instructive; where this 1991 leaflet conveyed disdain and feelings of betrayal, for example, a C-FAR letter and flyer from 1988 repeatedly used the pronoun "we" to link activists with the community, communicating respect, camaraderie, and love toward other lesbians and gay men.[36]

Years after the decline of the direct-action AIDS movement, while recalling the later tensions between more establishment-oriented lesbians and gay men and ACT UP, Jeanne Kracher addressed the topic of ACT UP/Chicago's contemptuousness and provided a way to understand its source. By the early 1990s, many ACT UP/Chicago members felt "used and discarded" by ASOs; these more establishment-oriented AIDS advocates "would call us [ACT UP] in" when they needed help bringing attention to an issue, when they needed public support for their position, when they thought civil disobedience and arrests might be the way to get what they needed. But then at other times "they wouldn't call us in to have a discussion about anything" because "they were afraid that we would be too, . . . our demands would be too radical or too. . . . You know, [they thought] we couldn't really be diplomatic with the right people" (Kracher 2000). Feeling used and disrespected, and believing

35. This was in contrast to the 1991 Persian Gulf War, which was declared to be over at that time.
36. See C-FAR 1988a; and C-FAR n.d. (ca. April 1988).

that many ASOs were more concerned with maintaining their funding than with holding government bodies responsible for addressing the epidemic, many participants in ACT UP/Chicago began to construe the more establishment-oriented gays working in "the AIDS industry" as, in Kracher's words, the movement's "worst enemies." Feeling betrayed by them, we accused them of having betrayed us and people with AIDS, of having sold out. In retrospect, Kracher believes that "we were right a lot, but we also were obnoxious sometimes" (Kracher 2000).

ACT UP/Chicago member Jeff Edwards saw the relationship between establishment-oriented gays' derision of ACT UP and ACT UP's growing contemptuousness similarly, specifically pointing toward the role that ACT UP's growing sense of isolation played in the dynamic. "I think we were being self-righteous and narrow-minded. But I also think what maybe drove that was our sense of increasing isolation. . . . There was this process where we were vilified and then we called them traitors and sell-outs. . . . I think our sense of self-righteousness rose as we were more and more isolated" (Edwards 2000a). Edwards suggests that we responded to the disrespect we were experiencing by throwing it back at those establishment-oriented lesbians and gay men who questioned our political savvy and the value of our activism. As we felt increasingly politically isolated, we consoled ourselves by portraying ACT UP as authentically committed to people with AIDS while accusing everyone else of betrayal and caving to the status quo.

The feelings of isolation and self-righteousness were operative in other ACT UP chapters as well. ACT UP/NY's Mark Harrington articulated the following critique of ACT UP/NY. "We were always right and other [lesbian/gay and AIDS] groups were almost always too moderate and too sold out and too much part of the system. There was this sort of righteous rightness about us all the time and it became a real weakness of ours" (Harrington 2002b).[37] Other ACT UP/NY members' comments suggest that ACT UP's contemptuousness similarly derived from the

---

37. I agree with Harrington's critique, but his retrospective appraisal of ACT UP may be motivated in part by a desire to distance himself from aspects of ACT UP that now seem embarrassing to him. For example, he offers a developmental narrative of AIDS activism that characterizes the treatment activism he engaged in after ACT UP as more mature and sophisticated than ACT UP's confrontational actions; see Harrington 1996, 1997, 1998. In an interview, Harrington stated, "It was great to get arrested and . . . do tons of zaps and demos and then move on to grown-up strategies" (Harrington 2002b).

disdain that other groups directed toward ACT UP/NY. Peter Staley, for example, argued in a 1991 *Advocate* column that ACT UP's "arrogance" and consequent inability to listen to constructive criticism from outside the movement had arisen in large part because ACT UP "was left in virtual quarantine by the rest of the AIDS establishment and much of the gay community" because of their refusal to respect what ACT UP had accomplished (Staley 1991).

The context was different in ACT UP's early years. In that period, in the face of the manifest limitations of lobbying intransigent federal, state, and local governments, there was excitement among lesbians and gay men about the emergence of more theatrical and forceful forms of AIDS activism. The direct-action AIDS movement was growing quickly, attracting new participants throughout the country. Criticism of ACT UP from more mainstream lesbians and gay men seemed inconsequential. That changed in the early 1990s when societal openings toward lesbians and gay men seemed to siphon support away from ACT UP. Feelings among ACT UP members of being isolated and betrayed by other lesbians and gay men were important effects of the disparagements in this period, and ACT UP's disdainful rejoinders—understandable as they were—likely alienated potential supporters and isolated ACT UP even further.

Activism and Presentation of Gay Selves in a Moment of Openings

As support for ACT UP began to wither and the movement began to decline in the early 1990s, there was a surge in gay activism against the ban on gays in the military. The psychic dynamics set in motion by openings toward lesbians and gay men in this period help to explain this turn toward other forms of activism, which took off in the very moment of ACT UP's decline. As I discuss in greater detail in chapter 7, Crimp argues that this shift in attention can be attributed to many gays' desire to defend against painful feelings of grief and despair regarding AIDS. They were understandably redirecting their energies to lifting the ban, substituting "the image of the healthy body for that of the sick body" (Crimp 2002, 228). Crimp emphasizes that the images deployed by opponents of the military ban desexualized lesbian and gay soldiers in an attempt to displace the stereotype of gays as sexually obsessed and predatory. He also notes that lesbian and gay soldiers were depicted as true patriots who simply wanted to serve their country. I agree with Crimp that AIDS had become unbearable by then, and many lesbians and gay men simply had to turn away from AIDS and the grief and despair connected to the epidemic; other activist battles were comparatively less emotionally wrenching.

A point that Crimp suggests but that I want to emphasize is that the images used by the campaign to lift the ban directly countered the image of the AIDS activist that had dominated media images of lesbians and gay men beginning in 1987. Where ACT UP and the media tended to portray AIDS activists as militant, oppositional, angry, and sexually radical, the campaign to lift the military ban depicted lesbians and gay men as normal, desexualized, conservative, all-American patriots with great love for their country. The military ban example indicates how, in this moment of openings, the allure of social acceptance and a corollary anxiety about social rejection shaped the presentation of gay selves to the outside world. In the period from 1987 to 1990, when society seemed closed to lesbians and gay men and people with AIDS, ACT UP offered ways of being and feeling that rejected many mainstream norms and appealed to many lesbians and gay men. By the early 1990s, when different sectors of society began to seem more accepting of homosexuality, confrontation no longer seemed quite as necessary or compelling, making ACT UP's ethos only one among many possibilities. One could be loyal to one's people without acting up. One no longer had to reject mainstream society, which heretofore had rejected lesbians and gay men. Now one might begin to make some sort of peace with the mainstream. One could more easily be openly gay in the Democratic Party, on the job, at mixed social gatherings. As corporations began to see lesbians and gay men as a niche market and started advertising to them, new, corporate-mediated ways to be gay hit the mass media and filled the lesbian and gay press. Writer and activist Liz Highleyman argues that this commodification of gay identity and increasing consumerism "encouraged the movement to play down its radical edges to position itself as a more attractive market" (Highleyman 2002, 109).

It seems important to recognize that these pulls toward moderation and normativity, while they sometimes operated on a conscious, strategic level, primarily work on an affective level where the need to be recognized and accepted and a related anxiety about social rejection play out. During the early 1990s many lesbians and gay men felt increasing recognition from families, friends, employers, and society in general, and many of us did not want to lose that, did not want to risk renewed nonrecognition and rejection. Despite ACT UP's role in pushing mainstream society to recognize lesbians and gay men in the first place, in many people's minds ACT UP threatened social acceptance. In that context, criticism of the movement gained traction and broad support for the movement declined.

The following *Philadelphia Inquirer* column, written in October 1992 by Donna Gallagher, a lesbian member of the Philadelphia Mayor's Commission on Sexual Minorities, illustrates how openings toward lesbians and gay men in this moment amplified anxiety about ACT UP's confrontational activism. Gallagher both articulated that anxiety and simultaneously elicited it by linking ACT UP's continuing activism to social rejection of lesbians and gay men. She began the column with a standard insinuation of ACT UP's immaturity: "Yo ACT UP: Grow up or shut up." She then indicated that while she had once respected ACT UP, conditions were now different—most people in society no longer wanted gay men to die—and ACT UP's tactics thus were not only no longer necessary, they actually posed a threat to lesbians and gay men:

> The shock protests you pioneered in the '80s have grown not just tired and divisive in the '90s, but are increasingly damaging to the very people you purport to support. . . . As a lesbian, I have a tremendous amount of pride in your history. You changed the world. And you did it under the most extreme opposition imaginable and within a society that at the time seemed to tolerate only one thing in our community—the deaths of our gay brothers. Tragically, many in society still do. Fortunately now, most don't. . . . Wake up, ACT UP: You no longer need to shock people to get them to listen. . . . The image you choose to project to the world as self-anointed representatives of the gay and lesbian community is not just misleading, but selfish and ultimately destructive. . . . As long as many heterosexuals' sole vision of gays and lesbians is that of anger and rudeness and a complete disregard for the expression of any opinion other than those endorsed by ACT UP members, you only add fuel to the fire of hatemongers. (Gallagher 1992)

Gallagher argued that the use of reason would bring about any further social change that was necessary and that the time for confrontation was thus over; now lesbians and gay men could, and should, enter into the

326

CHAPTER FIVE

mainstream of society: "The time has come for leaders of the sexual minority community to replace raised fists with extended hands. We must stop trying to dictate by intimidation, and instead begin to persuade through reason. This ain't a sellout, it's reality. Wake up, ACT UP. If not, R.I.P." (Gallagher 1992).

Conclusion

Disparaging criticisms of ACT UP, present throughout the movement's life, had more or less traction not on the basis of their "truth" or "falsity" but on the basis of queers' perceptions about their standing vis-à-vis mainstream society. One might expect that the effect of the criticism would depend on what actions ACT UP was actually doing; if ACT UP escalated its tactics, for example, some might have become more uncomfortable with the movement and more inclined to agree with the critics, therefore withdrawing support from the movement. But the evidence shows otherwise. Some of the movement's most militant and controversial actions—for example, the shut-down of the Golden Gate Bridge and the protest inside St. Patrick's Cathedral—occurred in 1989, and while they were heavily criticized in lesbian and gay communities, the movement experienced no net loss in support. Disparagement of ACT UP simply did not matter very much in the 1987–1990 period. The decisive factor in the influence of such criticism on the movement's viability was the growing social acceptance of lesbians and gay men in the early 1990s.

In studying the disparagements that confrontational movements encounter, we learn not about the "rightness" or "inappropriateness" of militancy but about biases against contentious dissent, about what issues militancy raises for people and why, about the conditions under which disparaging criticisms affect a movement's viability and why they sometimes simply do not matter. We discover how one must act in the public realm in order to be considered rational, adult, reasonable, and normal in a given context, allowing us to observe how power operates through the very ideas of rationality, reasonableness, maturity, and normalcy. It becomes apparent that rather than being true reflections of the phenomena being described, those categories are strategies of governance, affective technologies of domination that, when deployed, tell us more about the anxieties of those doing the disparaging than about the movement itself.

What we also learn is that the space carved out for militancy is extremely fragile in the U.S. context. Confrontational activism raises anxiety and frequently faces a hostile environment. Sometimes that environment is relatively inconsequential, but it can contribute to the unraveling
of a movement. Part of the political project for such movements, then, is
to contest society's notions of proper political behavior, to dispute reigning ideas about what is rational and reasonable, to oppose the prevailing
ideology that disparages confrontational activism and maligns militant,
direct-action movements. What the case of ACT UP indicates is that the
context in which movements operate affects how and whether their efforts to expand the sense of political possibilities will succeed.

CHAPTER SIX

Solidarity and Its Fracturing

I just was amazed. It was home right away. It was vibrant. They all felt that anger that I had felt alone about. . . . It just felt so powerful and so alive. I was glued. . . . We knew we were building something huge and powerful. . . . This wild sense of community and this fellowship was intoxicating. . . . It was just a thrill.

—ACT UP/NY member Peter Staley, talking about his first ACT UP meeting in March 1987 and about the early years of ACT UP/NY

The fun was gone completely. The sense of family was gone; there was lots of in-fighting, lots of rumors, lots of bitterness. . . . It was very rough.

—Staley again, discussing how he felt in 1991–92, just prior to leaving ACT UP/NY to form another group, Treatment Action Group

T his chapter is about solidarity and its fracturing in activist contexts. Sentiments of solidarity are indispensable for many activist endeavors, and because such sentiments are never inevitable but always a question, we need to consider what generates and blocks such feelings. Solidarity is both an affective state—an inclination toward, and perhaps identification with—along with a set of practices—of mutual assistance and support, of having one another's back. In my view, the question of solidarity presupposes difference in the sense that the question concerns how two or more entities can come together in mutual support. I define solidarity, then, as affinities and reciprocities across difference.[1] What

---

1. That difference is *perceived*, of course, rather than essential.

I like about the word *affinity* is that thinking of its two primary meanings in relation to one another—affection for and being drawn toward,
and family resemblance or likeness—gives us a sense of one of the important issues when considering solidarity: an inclination toward another that is based on a perceived family resemblance might be lessened, even destroyed, if the indefinite edges that allow perception of a
resemblance are somehow made more distinct. Although the important
factors in solidarity formation and fracturing differ depending on the circumstances, we might fruitfully begin to conceptualize these processes
by investigating how people create a sense of family resemblance or
commonality, the factors that might threaten it, and the affective states
involved.

The two quotations that open this chapter speak to solidarity and its
fracturing in ACT UP. I explore both processes, focusing on how feelings and practices of solidarity were generated, why and how they unraveled, and the role that unraveling played in the movement's decline. Because ACT UP's later conflicts both revealed that solidarity within the
movement was fracturing and contributed to that process, I undertake
an analysis of those conflicts. I note the following puzzle at the outset.
On one level, the conflicts involved participants' different priorities and
differing ideas about the best strategies for fighting the AIDS crisis. That
is, they were in part about tactical and political differences. But similar
tactical and political conflicts had existed since ACT UP's earliest days
without destroying the movement. Their substance alone thus cannot account for the acrimony and destructiveness of the later conflicts. Why
were those later conflicts so damaging to local ACT UP chapters and
to the movement as a whole? And what caused the shift in internal relations, indicated in the quotations above, from euphoric camaraderie and
solidarity—even amid conflicts—to distrust, venomous personal attacks,
and divisive internal clashes?

Internal conflicts are a frequent feature of social movements and
other activist endeavors; sometimes they contribute to demobilization,
and sometimes they do not. To understand why and how internal conflicts contribute to the fracturing of solidarity and movement decline,
we have to analyze their affective dimensions. Scholars and activists
alike tend to focus on the substance of a movement's conflicts, neglecting the emotional undercurrents that play a part in structuring their substance and effects. With the term *emotional undercurrent* I mean to emphasize how the feeling states operating in a movement's internal conflicts

are often unarticulated, unacknowledged, and submerged, but nevertheless have force and direction, an insistence, affecting participants as well as things like the texture, tonality, intensity, velocity—the very content and character—of the conflicts. In the case of ACT UP, largely unstated and unrecognized feelings of betrayal, nonrecognition, resentment, mistrust, anger, and guilt were at the heart of the movement's later internal conflicts. This chapter explores why and how such sentiments took hold among participants, how they shaped ACT UP's internal conflicts, and how the conflicts and the feelings that spurred, shaped, and were evoked by them contributed to the demise of the movement. Analyzing the emotional hues of ACT UP's internal debates and conflicts also provides insight into more general processes of solidarity formation and fracturing. In addition, investigating the emotional workings of ACT UP's internal conflicts should furnish activists with ideas about how to deal with the bad feelings that can arise in the course of political work.

Looking at the affective dimensions of ACT UP's internal conflicts complements other scholars' analyses of ACT UP's decline. For example, political scientist and ACT UP/Chicago member Jeff Edwards (2000b) argues that as some in ACT UP turned their attention to AIDS among people of color, a general white racial backlash in U.S. society and in the lesbian and gay community penetrated ACT UP, generating intense conflicts within the movement that shattered solidarity among participants. A study of the emotional components of the conflicts about race in ACT UP—feelings of vulnerability, resentment, mistrust, betrayal, and guilt, for example—provides us with a mechanism that illuminates how such conflicts arose within ACT UP and became acrimonious. As another example, sociologist Steven Epstein argues that issues that could tear apart any social movement—"gender and racial divisions, as well as debates over internal participatory mechanisms, insider/ outsider strategies, and overall priorities and goals"—were overlaid in ACT UP by what he calls "the politics of expertise." Activists who gained access to the scientific-medical establishment mastered "specialized forms of knowledge" that separated them from and privileged them over their fellow activists (Epstein 1996, 292–93). Exploring some of the complex feelings among activists in this moment helps us to understand why and how a growing knowledge divide among activists (at least within ACT UP/NY) might have intensified conflicts and contributed to ACT UP's decline.

The following point bears repeating: Conflicts do not destroy movements. ACT UP's early conflicts prove as much. The emotional dimensions of these conflicts are decisive in distinguishing between those that do and those that do not fracture solidarity and contribute to movement decline.

Resisting Writing

I resisted writing this chapter, largely because ACT UP's internal conflicts were painful, wreaking havoc on the movement as a whole as well as on participants. In the midst of them, the conflicts often felt beyond our control, unstoppable, and yet they were playing out in our words and voices, with our tones and inflections, spurred by our bodily sensations, analyses, and emotions. The inability to deny activists' agency and responsibility in them—including my own—might be what makes these conflicts particularly painful to remember. During ACT UP/Chicago's disintegration and in the period immediately following, many of us tried to figure out what had happened. But in the years after, I unconsciously blocked the conflicts out.

My sense, though, is that we need to explore ACT UP's later internal conflicts if only because they played an important role in the decline of the movement. My intent here is not to resolve the conflicts—a task both impossible and irrelevant—but to consider why they arose and how they affected the movement. To do so, we have to explore the vulnerabilities, fears, and anxieties that participants on the different sides were experiencing. We need to understand the force of such affective states and how they might play out in a group dynamic.

I say how they *might* play out because the role of such feeling states in a movement's internal dynamics is indeterminate, largely because human beings have the capacity to attend to their own and to others' feelings. Put another way, even though our feelings are not transparent to ourselves or to others, we have multiple ways of paying attention to and listening to them. I do wonder how the course of ACT UP would have differed if we had better understood the different anxieties and desires that various participants were experiencing. ACT UP undoubtedly still would have been a contentious place, full of debate and disagreement and conflict. Trying to understand another's feelings and vulnerabilities does not mean that we will agree with the other's perspective. Caring for one another can include disagreement and expressions of anger toward one another,[2] which may be why ideological conflicts and political debates—even angry ones—are not in themselves a threat to an organization's viability. Indeed, conflict-free political activism is an oxymoron. Social movements typically are filled with contentiousness; conflict and debate are a primary means by which movements analyze the political terrain and figure out what to do. But in a context where sentiments of solidarity had once been so powerful as to be nearly unquestioned, ACT UP's internal debates and conflicts would have had a very different character and different effects if both sides had been able to acknowledge and address the complex feeling states that prompted and were evoked by competing strategies for how to fight AIDS.

These thoughts are more than a catalogue of my own regrets. I raise them because I think more attention to the emotional undercurrents that operate in social movements can help scholars and activists consider how internal movement dynamics themselves sometimes stymie activist efforts. There certainly are times when splits in a movement are productive and when the demise of a movement is a good thing, but that is not always the case. Analyzing the affective dimensions of internal conflicts will help activists to think differently about how to address them, perhaps thereby heading off some of the acrimony that they often engender.

Assuming Solidarity (and Feeling It Too)

Before turning to those conflicts and to the fracturing of solidarity within ACT UP, it is important to account for the tremendous solidarity felt within the movement in its early years. Those positive sentiments derived in part from a sense of commonality among participants, a sense that participants actively, but mostly nonconsciously, constructed. The movement's rhetoric, for example, emphasized that we all, as sexual and gender outlaws, were under attack, as was evident in the failures of state and society to respond to the AIDS crisis and in the right wing's use of AIDS to wage war against all things queer. The development in the movement of a queer ethos and a queer critique of straight society consolidated a shared sense of difference—and not only with regard to the straight world. ACT UP's turn to angry militancy, combined with the embrace of an in-your-face queer sensibility, set direct-action AIDS ac-

2. Thank you to Lauren Berlant for pointing this out to me.

tivists apart from many lesbians and gay men as well. A sense of difference from straight *and* gay worlds created a strong shared identity among participants. Conflicts within the movement were, in the words of cultural theorist and ACT UP/NY member Douglas Crimp, "mitigated by a queer hegemony" (1992, 15).

Two assumptions also helped construct a sense of commonality: first, that everyone in ACT UP agreed that the state and dominant social institutions were responsible for the AIDS crisis, and, second, that everyone present at meetings was there for the same reason: to use confrontational direct action to fight for all people with AIDS. Different participants surely had different understandings of what fighting the AIDS crisis meant, but a sense of shared principles and mission, along with a shared queer sensibility, made such differences largely inconsequential in the early years.

This constructed commonality did not negate identity differences. Indeed, it allowed sentiments of solidarity to develop across perceived differences. The caucus structure in particular provided a way for differences of identity to be recognized and for underrepresented subgroups to have a degree of autonomy within the overarching collectivity of ACT UP. Consider as well the following example. It was clear that some ACT UP members were struggling immediately and directly with AIDS-related illnesses, while others were not. Participants acknowledged that difference but simultaneously bridged it rhetorically by asserting that we were *all* living with AIDS: we were collectively experiencing the ravages of the epidemic, confronting a world that seemed to accept the deaths of gay people, living through and battling the attacks on our community. That claim indicated a recognition of the ways in which AIDS was shaping all of our lives, if differently. Even more, it asserted HIV-negative participants' strong identification with people with HIV/AIDS in the room. They and their bodies were the front line as well as living evidence, and sometimes dying evidence, of what was at stake in our activism. As the most vivid manifestation of why we were fighting this war against AIDS, people with HIV/AIDS evoked strong feelings of identification among those who were not HIV-positive, along with feelings of respect, sometimes even reverence, and a sense of responsibility to help them fight for their lives. Practices of solidarity across HIV status included HIV-negative participants taking to the streets, getting arrested, and forming support networks to care for ACT UP members who got sick. The widespread kissing in the movement—everyone was always

kissing everyone—was also a show of solidarity with people with HIV/
AIDS, a demonstration that, when elsewhere they were being demonized and viewed suspiciously as vectors of contagion, in ACT UP they
were loved, respected, and desired.

In a context of perceived commonalities, sentiments and practices of
solidarity extended across racial and gender lines as well. From ACT
UP's earliest days, for example, the movement characterized itself as
fighting for *all* people with AIDS—gay men of all colors, women, anyone
who was HIV-infected or at risk. A national meeting of direct-action
AIDS activists in October 1987 adopted guidelines for actions planned
for the spring of 1988 that placed ACT UP in solidarity with all people
with HIV/AIDS: "We recognize that AIDS has had a devastating impact
on the lesbian and gay community. We further recognize that the AIDS
crisis disproportionately affects men and women of color. Any strategies to fight the crisis must incorporate these understandings" (AIDS
Action Pledge n.d.).[3] ACT UP's rhetoric also connected the struggles by
women and by people with AIDS to control their bodies and sexualities.
Many ACT UP men joined ACT UP women to defend abortion clinics blockaded by Operation Rescue. Many also attended early teach-ins
that ACT UP women held about women and AIDS and about the role
of racism and sexism in the AIDS crisis. In the early years many men
looked to women for leadership in the movement, especially to the many
women who had extensive activist experience. Caucuses of women and
people of color formed early, sometimes in response to experiences with
racism and sexism within ACT UP,[4] but there was a sense among many
of the women and people of color during the early years that ACT UP
was a welcoming and receptive environment—not in the sense that ACT
UP was a place free of racism and sexism but in the sense that it was a
place for open and serious engagement with such issues.

The affective states stirred by perceived commonalities with movement comrades and difference from those outside the movement generated and regenerated solidarity. Members felt a sense of relief upon find-

3. See also Hansen 1987 and Richter 1987.
4. The Majority Action Committee—ACT UP/NY's first people of color caucus—
formed in late 1987. According to ACT UP/NY members Catherine Saalfield and Ray Navarro, it was formed in part because people of color found themselves combating racist
views within ACT UP that people of color were more likely to use drugs (Saalfield and Navarro 1991, 353). It was named to reflect the fact that in New York City, blacks and Latinos
made up a majority of AIDS cases.

ing others who, six years into immense devastation, wanted to take to the streets to fight the AIDS crisis. Being in the streets together, violating political, social, and emotional norms, was tremendously exhilarating, even euphoric. Important early victories also made many of us feel politically efficacious and optimistic about our collective ability to end the AIDS crisis, an alluring antidote to the despair pervading lesbian and gay communities. Important as well was the erotic electricity that coursed through ACT UP meetings and actions when in the gay community and in the world more broadly queer sex was so readily linked with disease and death. With commonalities established but differences allowed to exist, participants could feel recognized and cared for and experience a sense of belonging. Many people I interviewed described ACT UP as a home, a place to learn and grow and feel supported while fighting the AIDS crisis.

Such affective experiences were self-reproducing in that they created a strong desire to feel those feelings again. And they invigorated and reinvigorated sentiments of solidarity by creating a desire to be proximate to others who were feeling those feelings and creating conditions for you to feel them too. Being in the streets and getting arrested together, making demands and forcing change together, creating queer culture together, imagining and attempting to build a new world together— all of those practices generated affective intensities and a strong emotional identification among participants, regardless of HIV status or other identity markers.

Solidarity was assumed or, better, simply was not in question—at least not on a conscious level. ACT UP's emotional habitus contained an expectation of solidarity and hence impelled us toward it. So, for example, the respect granted to people with HIV/AIDS when they spoke in meetings along with practices like kissing not only demonstrated solidarity toward people with HIV/AIDS but also suggest that people in the movement on some level felt that they *should* demonstrate such solidarity. Gregg Bordowitz notes this: "I don't remember anyone ever saying this consciously. But in ACT UP, you had to kiss everybody because you couldn't be afraid of people with AIDS. So you had to kiss everyone you met. . . . I loved doing it. Even people you didn't even know very well. So there was a physical demonstrability that was part of the culture of ACT UP, that had to do with not fearing infection" (Bordowitz 2002b).

ACT UP/NY member Michael Nesline points to the "subliminal" aspects of the relationship between those with and without AIDS in ACT

UP's early years. "It seems to me that we strove to not differentiate and I don't remember if it was articulated so succinctly, but 'we all had AIDS' was sort of the operating fiction. There was no difference" (Nesline 2003, 21). And yet, people often simultaneously acknowledged the difference: "When somebody stood up and said, 'I have AIDS,' everyone would bow down to them and, by virtue of the fact that they had AIDS, everything that they said had extra weight" (21; see also Signorile 2003, 47). Perhaps most important was conveying solidarity by getting arrested. When asked if she thought that HIV-negative participants had a particular need or desire to prove themselves by "putting their bodies on the line," ACT UP/NY member Marion Banzhaf replied, "I don't think it was ever so conscious, but I think yes, unconsciously. I think that was true for me" (Banzhaf 2002). In the early years, solidarity across HIV status was simply a given, and it was *felt*. As ACT UP/NY member Gedalia Braverman recalls, although in later years "it became a point of division," HIV status was not a salient identity and did not make a difference in the early years because "it was clear that everybody was there for the same reason" (Braverman 2003, 10). The strong sentiments and practices of camaraderie that existed in ACT UP's first years—across HIV status as well as across race and gender lines—averted any need to query our ostensible unity.

Conflicts within Solidarity

Most important, in the early years, feelings and practices of solidarity were robust enough to survive conflicts. Indeed, in pointing to the importance of commonality or sharedness, I do not mean to suggest that solidarity requires sameness or complete agreement. Although ostensible synonyms of solidarity like unity, harmony, or accord suggest that solidarity entails the absence of discord, affinities and reciprocities across difference can, and often do, include disagreements and frictions.

ACT UP members recall contentious discussions and debates from the start, and many of these early conflicts involved the issues that were at the core of ACT UP's later bitter internal conflicts. Ferd Eggan remembers having a "heated" debate with Peter Staley and Chicago AIDS activist Danny Sotomayor at a national meeting of AIDS activists in 1988 about an issue that became divisive years later: whether the sole focus of the AIDS movement should be to fight for AIDS drugs, or whether the movement should also tackle health care access issues for people with AIDS. The latter approach required highlighting not only the role of homophobia but also the roles of racism, sexism, and poverty in the AIDS crisis since poor people, people of color, and women with AIDS were less likely than white, middle-class, gay men to have access to health care and thus to promising drugs (Eggan 1999). A similar debate occurred in May 1988 when ACT UP/NY devoted a meeting to a discussion of its goals and strategies (ACT UP/New York 1988a). The minutes from that meeting reveal wildly divergent opinions about ACT UP/NY's direction, with many arguing that its sole focus should be "getting drugs into bodies" and many others arguing for supplementing that goal with a focus on health care access issues—including access to treatments. Debates that occurred in 1990 and later about these issues were filled with personal attacks and accusations, but the minutes from this May 1988 meeting indicate strong differences of opinion but no vitriol.[5]

Mark Harrington remembers "very painful" conflicts in ACT UP/NY in 1989 about an experimental treatment, Compound Q. There were "battles on the floor [of ACT UP/NY], resolutions and counterresolutions" about the issue (Harrington 2002b). He also remembers ACT UP/NY having internal arguments about whether its "Stop the Church" action at St. Patrick's Cathedral in December 1989 had been effective or not; the conflict was about tactics and strategy (2002b).

But participants indicate that there was "a qualitative difference" between the early and later conflicts (Harrington 2002b; see also Crimp 1992, 15; and Velez 1991). Staley recalls that the earlier debates "were long and hard," but they "never became personal" (Staley 2002). Harrington remembers that initially ACT UP/NY "had been able to have a policy fight," but that "once [a fight] was over it was over, and we just moved on and started working together again." There was, he recalled, "a willingness to actually listen to criticism." That changed, however: "Later, it was factions, and people sort of got locked into their views and stopped really listening and really stopped being interested in real dialogue" (Harrington 2002b). Writing in 1991 amid ACT UP/New York's internal conflicts, Tony Malliaris similarly noted a closing down of the space for political disagreement and debate: "We *used to* brainstorm and debate our differences on issues together," but that no longer was oc-

5. Interviews I conducted corroborate this impression.

curring (Malliaris 1991; my emphasis). Initially, the contentiousness of ideological and political debates arguably strengthened the movement, allowing a diversity of perspectives to be aired and hashed out. Bordowitz recalls the earlier tensions in the movement being "good tensions, productive tensions" (Bordowitz 2002a). In contrast, the later conflicts, much more rancorous, strongly contributed to ACT UP's decline.

Fracturing Solidarities

A Changed Affective Landscape

What had changed was the affective landscape of the AIDS crisis. By the early 1990s, many activists started to feel desperate. It was becoming ever more clear that the battle was going to be long and hard and that many people in the movement and many other loved ones would not make it. I discuss the growing despair in the following chapter, but cite it here as an affective state circulating within the movement that intensified ACT UP's internal conflicts. Many activists felt more and more staggered by the scope of the crisis, by, in Crimp's words, "our constantly increasing knowledge of both the breadth and depth of the crisis—breadth, in the sense of the many different kinds of people affected by HIV disease; and depth, in the sense of the extent of social change that will be required to improve all these different people's chances of survival" (Crimp 1992, 14; see also Edwards 2000b). ACT UP/Chicago member Tim Miller notes how "overwhelming" it was to realize the scale of the epidemic, the different populations affected by it, and the fact that this crisis was not "some short-term thing" (Miller 1999). Mark Harrington believes that members began to lose their "native, . . . raw, untamed optimism" when they realized science wasn't going to "find a cure" anytime soon (2002b). The sense of political *in*efficacy that began to take hold was a shock.

Those overwhelming feelings of desperation and a growing sense of the movement's limited political efficacy created a scarcity mentality in which focusing on a particular issue came to be seen as *not* focusing on others. Earlier, ACT UP members had believed that they could and should take on any and all targets and issues related to the AIDS crisis. That was what the affinity group structure was about, after all. Any one group's victory was felt as sustaining the entire organization. It all seemed important. But in the changed landscape, others' actions, even when victorious, prompted anxious questions: what about *me* and the people *I* care about? This scarcity mentality brought complex emotional undercurrents into the political disagreements that previously had been absent—feelings of nonrecognition, betrayal, mistrust—intensifying the movement's internal conflicts.

Another important change that intensified ACT UP's conflicts occurred in 1989–90 when some ACT UP activists—primarily men in ACT UP/NY's Treatment & Data Committee (T&D), many of whom were HIV-positive—gained access to the top AIDS science researchers and government institutions against which ACT UP had protested. Such access introduced the possibility of getting AIDS treatments more quickly, but it also aggravated the scarcity mentality in the following way. In the initial years of the movement, activists made little separation between the scientific-medical and the political aspects of the crisis, convinced that both had to be fought together. Activists knew, for example, that getting AIDS drugs rapidly tested and released required tackling the heterosexism and homophobia that contributed to the sluggish government response and the slow pace of AIDS drug research. The newly acquired access changed some ACT UP members' political calculus. With several political barriers now removed, they believed they could focus their activities on the science of AIDS, specifically on improving and expediting AIDS drug research. Their goal became getting "drugs into bodies."[6] Indeed, as Edwards points out, for those who held this perspective, pushing for the testing and approval of new medical treatments became synonymous with "fighting AIDS" (Edwards 2000b, 495). Everything else was a distraction.

Others in the movement raised questions about this narrowing of focus, worried that it would mean neglect of important issues like unequal access to health care (and thus to effective AIDS drugs) and, more specifically, would result in less privileged AIDS-affected populations falling through the cracks. Noting that the epidemic was increasingly af-

6. The lore is that getting "drugs into bodies" was ACT UP/NY's original mission, but the evidence reveals that from its earliest days, ACT UP/NY and other direct-action AIDS organizations conducted numerous actions about other AIDS-related issues; see Banzhaf 2002; Harrington 1997, 275; Hodge 2000; and Wolfe 1993, 21. It may be that the meaning of "drugs into bodies" changed. Initially, it was a demand that ACT UP made of the federal bureaucracy and was based in the belief that people with a life-threatening illness should be allowed to take experimental drugs even if their efficacy had not yet been fully demonstrated. Only later did "drugs into bodies" become a position within ACT UP's internal conflicts, a stance that it should be the movement's only goal.

fecting black and Latino populations[7]—gay and straight, men as well as women—many ACT UP members across the country were focusing more of their activism on the AIDS issues most pressing for women, people of color, and poor people. Both sides saw themselves as "fighting AIDS," but each defined "fighting AIDS" differently.

In this changed affective landscape, different ideas about how to fight AIDS turned into acrimonious conflicts about who and what ACT UP should be fighting for and about how to deal with a system that was beginning to respond to (only) some of ACT UP's demands. Attempting to make sense of the ongoing epidemic and their inability to stop it, ACT UP members sometimes turned their attentions inward in search of obstacles within the movement. Perhaps our progress was being hampered because our energies were too dispersed, or because racism and sexism in the group were discouraging participation, or because some people were abandoning confrontational tactics (this last sentiment was more evident in ACT UP/NY).

Crimp (1992) notes that in this period identity categories took on new importance. It seemed to many in the movement that those focusing on AIDS drug research—who called themselves "treatment activists"—were primarily HIV-positive, white, gay men, and that those who came to be called the "social activists" were primarily HIV-negative, white lesbians along with people of color, some of whom were HIV-positive.[8] In reality, although some of the most visible participants tended to fit the dominant perception, there were lesbians, people of color, white gay men, and HIV-positive and negative people on both sides of the conflicts. Nevertheless, perceptions mattered, and each side appealed to fixed identity categories in order to bolster its side in the debate and deride its opponents. The actual and perceived *identifications* of each side also became important. While both sides claimed to be concerned about all people with AIDS— that was ACT UP's self-understanding, after all—each side came to be seen as emphasizing the needs of some populations at the expense of others: white, gay men vs. women and people of color. People began to feel that others in the movement had abandoned them; accusations of

7. Edwards notes that "by the end of the 1980s in the U.S., people of color were making up a rapidly growing proportion of new AIDS cases and constituted the overwhelming majority of the growing number of cases amongst women" (2000b, 502).

8. In general I avoid using these labels because they mislead by suggesting that the "social activists" were unconcerned with treatment issues and that treatment issues were not social justice issues.

betrayal flew from one side to the other. Because the feeling states structuring these conflicts were largely submerged and unacknowledged and because of the way ACT UP's emotional habitus was structured, it was extremely difficult to deal with the conflicts in a manner that would allow us to address the problems. Instead, moralizing emerged as a viable rhetorical register. In the end, these conflicts polarized numerous ACT UP chapters and played a significant role in the disintegration of several chapters and in the national movement's decline.

Of course, there were never only two sides in these debates. Some individuals had perspectives that simply did not fit neatly into either camp, but their perspectives were less audible. They might have felt cramped by the dominant voices in the conflicts and wary of being pigeon-holed into one camp or the other. Many others stayed out of the fracas: some were surely afraid of being exposed as having "bad politics"; others were probably upset by the rancor and wished that everyone could "just get along." With many people staying on the sidelines, the divergent perspectives of the two main camps shaped the tenor and content of the debates. Although the personalities of those most involved in the conflicts in different ACT UP chapters influenced the character of the clashes to some degree, the sound and texture of the conflicts were remarkably similar across the country.

Intensifying Conflicts and the Unraveling of Solidarity

FEELINGS OF BETRAYAL AND NONRECOGNITION. In September 1989, ACT UP/Chicago experienced an acrimonious conflict that foreshadowed conflicts that soon would explode in other chapters and at the national level.[9] The way this conflict played out illustrates how widely circulating affective states of desperation at the scope of the crisis intensified how participants experienced political differences within the movement. The key players were the Women's Caucus (I was a member) and a number of men in the organization, some of whom were HIV-positive. The flashpoint was a planned discussion on the role of sexism in the AIDS epidemic and in ACT UP/Chicago itself, and a boycott of this event by many of the men in the group. I discuss the incident and its aftermath at length because it illuminates how feeling states that had not been present earlier—especially feelings of nonrecognition and

9. Parts of this section draw from Gould 2006.

betrayal—shaped political disagreements about what "fighting AIDS" meant and how ACT UP should proceed with its work.

The original aim of the sexism discussion was threefold: (1) to increase knowledge within ACT UP/Chicago about the specific concerns of women with AIDS; (2) to explain why lesbians had gotten involved in AIDS activism; and (3) to discuss how sexism within the group was making it difficult for women to participate (ACT UP/Chicago Women's Caucus 1989). During the discussion, the Women's Caucus gave the men a questionnaire, in part an actual test of their knowledge about women and AIDS but also a bit of a setup, a way to catch them in their sexism. The questionnaire included some relatively straightforward questions about women with AIDS, but it also included the following more inflammatory questions: "If the AIDS crisis had hit primarily women, do you think that gay men would be responding to us in the numbers that we are responding now?" and "what adjectives are you familiar with that describe the smell of female genitals?"[10]

The sexism that had prompted us to call for the discussion in the first place, followed by the unreceptive and antagonistic behavior of some men during the discussion and the boycott by many others, felt like a betrayal to many of us in the Women's Caucus. We had felt unified with them in this battle, but suddenly it seemed that many men in the group did not care about us at all.

Feeling betrayed and outraged, we responded by reading a statement at the next meeting that took the men to task for their sexism. Acknowledging how much we had learned from them about fighting the epidemic and its antigay horrors, our statement revealed our sense that, in contrast to our respect for and commitment to them, many ACT UP men showed no respect or commitment toward us. Indeed, many seemed "clueless" about why lesbians, ostensibly at low risk for HIV, were involved. Not only did the men we were fighting side by side with appear not to know

10. This last question stemmed from knowledge among members of the caucus that women were referred to as "fish" in some gay male circles, a reference to the alleged smell of female genitalia; indeed, many of the men wrote "fish" as their answer. Although feeling unknown and misunderstood (and having one's body scents misconstrued) can make one feel humorless—a point suggested by Eve Sedgwick in a discussion of shame (2003, 64)—the ACT UP/Chicago Women's Caucus at times clearly had a more playful relation to the fish stereotype. For example, a banner made for the first Dyke March (in April 1993, in Washington, D.C.) declared, "Chicago Dykes Rule: Pussy by the Lake," and pictured a few catfish smiling and sunning themselves by Lake Michigan.

us, they seemed uninterested in knowing us or in understanding why we felt an urgency about fighting the AIDS crisis. Like straight men, they seemed to take for granted that women would support them, which made us feel resentful and angry, but they also seemed to be suspicious about why we were there, and that impugning of our motives made us feel misunderstood.[11]

A question that we raised during the sexism discussion and again in our statement—"What have the men in ACT UP learned from the women?"—revealed our strong sense of nonrecognition: "Need we remind you that women, and particularly many lesbians, have been there with you from the beginning, sharing skills, political experience and expertise, as well as compassion?" We wanted to feel "mutual solidarity and respect," but the men's failure to recognize us exacerbated our sense of unbelonging and insignificance. We indicated that, as lesbians, we were all too familiar with such disregard, and were not going to accept that from within what we considered to be our own shared organization: "Lesbians are made invisible in society at large; we are not willing to be made invisible in ACT UP as well." We indicated our anger toward them and our sense that they had betrayed us and that we could no longer count on them: "The Women's Caucus considers ACT UP's response to the sexism discussion an injustice and a violation of trust" (ACT UP/ Chicago Women's Caucus 1989, 2).

FROM SENTIMENTS OF BETRAYAL TO MORALISM. The constellation of sentiments that we were experiencing helps to explain the decision of the Women's Caucus to withdraw energy from "gay white men's problems," as we put it in our statement, and focus our efforts more on women and AIDS. I think the entire constellation of feelings also helps to explain the parts of our statement that seem to me now as moralizing of the sort that Crimp (1992) mentions in his discussion of ACT UP/ NY's conflicts. Consider, for example, the following excerpt from the statement:

11. Our feelings of nonrecognition from men in ACT UP may have been particularly distressing in a context where other lesbians, arguing that gay men were not concerned about lesbians, were questioning why lesbians were working on ostensibly "gay male issues" in the AIDS movement when lesbians were reportedly suffering a breast cancer epidemic around which a movement needed to form. See, for example, Brady 1991 and Winnow 1992; see also Stoller 1998, 15–21.

Gee, guys, you sure are good at spitting out rhetoric on the changing face of AIDS, but god forbid that the new face open its mouth![12] . . . Or is it truly asking too much of you that you take an interest in problems that do not directly affect you? Again we ask, if AIDS affected primarily women or ethnic minorities, just how many of y'all would be here? . . . Would YOU give money or time to combat it? (ACT UP/Chicago Women's Caucus 1989, 2; capitalizations in original)

This part of the statement called the men on their sexism and disregard for women and people of color with AIDS, and indicated our own identification with those populations, particularly women with AIDS. It also again revealed that we felt abandoned and betrayed by men in the movement, unappreciated, and disrespected as women. The statement indicated our sense that they were resistant to women's leadership. It conveyed as well our keen awareness of our position as lesbians in a heterosexist and sexist society, our desire that the structural position we occupied in society not be reproduced in ACT UP, and our fear that that was precisely what was happening. Such sentiments help to explain our turn to moralism. Our implicit answer to the question about whether the men would have gotten involved if AIDS was primarily affecting women was no, and in posing the question, the Women's Caucus suggested that we considered the men to be selfish while we, in contrast, had selflessly gone to the front-lines, in solidarity with gay men. Deploying a gendered notion of selflessness to our advantage, we were suggesting that the men should think about—and, in truth, feel bad about—the difference between their selfishness and our selflessness.[13] To be sure, parts of the statement read as a sincere attempt to engage in principled politi-

12. This is an interesting construction in that none of the women making the statement, as far as I know, were living with HIV/AIDS. We clearly felt a strong identification with women with HIV/AIDS. We also assumed their position for the following reasons: first, few in the scientific-medical establishment were addressing the epidemic among women, and the deadly consequences of that neglect made us acutely aware of the need to make women's concerns visible; second, many women with HIV/AIDS were rarely able to attend ACT UP meetings because they had children to care for; third, very few women with HIV/AIDS were "out" as such at this point. Women with HIV/AIDS with whom we worked closely thus wanted us to represent their concerns in ACT UP meetings.

13. Interestingly, many of the men answered "no" to the question. That is not proof that we were "right" in our construction of gay men as selfish. What their answers indicate, I think, is that highly gendered constructions of gay men as selfish and lesbians as selfless were widely circulating in this moment and easily latched onto by lesbians as well as gay men.

cal debate with the men about our political differences, but moralizing entered in when we interpreted the men's behavior in moral terms and found them wanting, while setting ourselves up as righteous: our understanding of the AIDS crisis was expansive, while theirs was narrow and selfish. We were politically advanced; they were politically flawed.

People arrive at moralism via different histories. Political theorist Wendy Brown, drawing from Nietzsche, reminds us that those occupying less privileged social positions, in their "impotent rage," may turn to moralism (Brown 2001, chap. 2). Power within ACT UP was less concentrated than this perspective suggests, however. Indeed, an interesting aspect of the conflicts within ACT UP was that some of those accused of being selfish and privileged were themselves occupying a precarious structural location; despite any race, class, and gender privileges they might have had, as gay men and/or people with HIV/AIDS they encountered a state and society whose indifference to them had deadly consequences. Although each side's situation was substantially different, both could claim that they were being disempowered.

WHAT ABOUT AIDS?   In November 1989, following the sexism discussion, Rex Wockner, a Chicago-based gay journalist whose columns were syndicated in gay newspapers around the country, wrote a story about what he called "a simmering ideological conflict among the leaders of ACT UP/Chicago" (Wockner 1989b). Wockner wrote that the conflict had come to a head and quoted a prominent member with AIDS, Danny Sotomayor, saying that he was "sick and tired" of racism and sexism issues getting in the way of the group's work on AIDS.[14] Sotomayor charged that ACT UP had been hijacked by "politically correct old dinosaurs with a leftist agenda." He continued, "The group is bogged down in rhetoric. People with hidden agendas dogmatically insist that we all have to go through a re-birthing around sexism and racism issues before we can even step out the door to work on AIDS." Wockner quoted Sotomayor as saying that he was considering "escaping" ACT UP/Chicago's "progressive focus" and starting another direct-action AIDS activist organization (Wockner 1989b).

In August 1990, Sotomayor angrily quit ACT UP/Chicago. His departure did not signal the end of ACT UP/Chicago; no other active ACT UP

14. Over the years, Rex Wockner's columns indicated his agreement with Sotomayor's critiques of ACT UP/Chicago. See, for example, Wockner 1992a and 1992c.

members left with him, even those who agreed with his criticisms. Still, debates similar to those that surrounded Sotomayor's exit continued to plague the group over the next couple of years, tearing at the organization and contributing to its decline. Featured in a cover article in an independent Chicago newspaper, Sotomayor explained why he left:

> I quit because I can no longer do the kind of AIDS work I want to do with the hostility that I feel within the group. People with AIDS are not setting the agenda of ACT UP. In fact, AIDS has become the fourth item on the ACT UP agenda, after racism, sexism, and gay and lesbian visibility. The group is being manipulated to suit the politics of a small group of people who don't even have AIDS. Part of my power within ACT UP was that I was speaking as a person with AIDS, with the power of genuine urgency. I still have that power, and I'll continue speaking out. But I have limited time, and I'm not going to spend it battling people's personal agendas and fighting people who claim to be my friends. Nothing lasts forever. Not me, and not ACT UP. In fact, I hope AIDS is cured forever so I never have to go out on another goddamned balcony [to defiantly hang a banner]. Fighting AIDS is not about climbing out on balconies. And that's the real tragedy of all this, because I think some people do think it's about street theater. But it's not—it's about helping people with AIDS. They're the only thing that's important in all this, and I know I haven't betrayed them. (Crump 1990, 21)

One thing that stands out in Sotomayor's statement is the sense that he had been betrayed by ACT UP, by people claiming to be his friends no less. He felt abandoned by members who did *not* have HIV/AIDS, people whom he alleged had manipulated ACT UP so that AIDS was no longer at the top of the organization's agenda, forsaking Sotomayor and others with AIDS just as the larger society had done. Quoted in an *Advocate* article a few months after leaving ACT UP, Sotomayor indicated that society's betrayal of gay men—evident in the fact that gay men with AIDS had become "yesterday's news"—amplified his anxiety that AIDS activists would do the same (Harding 1991, 21).

Also evident in Sotomayor's criticism of ACT UP/Chicago are ideas that were then circulating in the movement about how one must be— what principles one must uphold—in order to be an exemplary AIDS activist. The model ACT UP member believed that people with AIDS should be setting the agenda and leading the movement, and that ACT

UP's focus must be "fighting AIDS;" anything else was a betrayal of the principle of self-determination and, indeed, of people with AIDS. Almost everyone in the movement agreed with these principles; the point of contention was that different groups within ACT UP saw themselves as embodying or standing for different groups of people with AIDS— gay men, gay men of color, women—who sometimes had quite different concerns and needs. Because "fighting AIDS" was one of the group's highest principles but meant different things to different members, it became a rhetorical trope to bolster one's own side in the debates and accuse one's opponents of betrayal. In the last sentence of his statement, Sotomayor implied that he was following ACT UP's core principles; others, in contrast, were no longer fighting AIDS but actually were abandoning people with AIDS.

Sotomayor's critique had force. He was calling into question other ACT UP participants' loyalty and motives, charging them with being power-hungry and opportunist and, even worse, accusing them of betraying their dying comrades. Sotomayor may not have intended to impugn other participants' morals and thereby induce shame and guilt, but many saw that as his intent. His critique did have that effect on some and provoked anger among many.

Feelings of betrayal among people with HIV/AIDS were in the air, in Chicago and elsewhere. Sotomayor left ACT UP at a time when other chapters, including those in New York and San Francisco, were experiencing contentious conflicts about similar issues. Upon leaving ACT UP/SF in September 1990 and helping to form the more treatment-focused ACT UP/Golden Gate, Jesse Dobson wrote, "Despite its considerable past successes, for those who need to focus on fighting AIDS as a *personal* crisis, ACT UP/San Francisco was a trap" (Dobson 1990; my emphasis). Like Sotomayor, Dobson argued that his group had lost its way by focusing too much on racism and sexism to the neglect of AIDS: "AIDS is a horrific, immediate crisis! We cannot wait for anything to respond to it! I refuse to participate in the building of a coalition on the bodies of my community!" (Dobson 1990; see also ACT UP/Chicago PWA Caucus 1990; and Hardy 1991). Indicating the existence of feelings of abandonment within ACT UP/NY as well, Charlie Franchino stated the following in ACT UP/NY's internal newsletter/ suggestion box/venue for tirades, *Tell It To ACT UP* (*TITA*): "I personally feel more of a kinship with scientists I met in San Francisco [during

an international AIDS conference] than I do with certain members of
ACT UP" (*TITA* July 9, 1990, 1).[15]

THE EMOTIONAL UNDERCURRENTS OF POLITICAL CONFLICTS.   The different sides' sentiments of betrayal were not unconnected, of course.
Each side read the other's concerns and commitments as evidence of betrayal, an effect of the emergence of a scarcity mentality. Concerns about
women and people of color were heard as a lack of concern about gay
men with HIV/AIDS; concerns that the organization had become too focused on women and people of color were heard as an abandonment of
those people with AIDS in favor of white, gay men. And each side's sentiments of having been betrayed deflected charges of betrayal directed
against it, creating an impasse of bad feelings and no clear way to address one another across the growing animosity. Gay men with AIDS
in the United States, of course, have experienced profound betrayal by
state and society, and by family and friends. Betrayal is a painfully resonant affective state for lesbians and gay men more generally. Those resonances for everyone involved, as well as the contrast to previously experienced feelings of solidarity within and throughout the movement,
made the sense of betrayal by one's comrades especially crushing.

This dynamic of betrayal structured and intensified conflicts in ACT
UP. Earlier in the movement's life, when solidarity was felt and assumed,
different opinions about how to fight AIDS were not laden with much
significance. Different ideas about tactics or strategies did not prompt
people to question other members' identifications or their solidarity with
people with AIDS. But that changed as the affective landscape changed
and a scarcity mentality took hold. Without the assumption of solidarity, the question of solidarity itself became a contentious issue. Political
differences came to be seen as meaningful indicators of one's identifications, of the depth of one's feelings of solidarity with specific groups of
people with HIV/AIDS. Questions that previously were not at issue became pressing; indeed, they became the questions around which the different factions bolstered their positions and challenged their opponents.
Who was more committed to (which) people with HIV/AIDS; who in
the room had more at stake; who were the more legitimate or authentic

15. *TITA*, a weekly ACT UP/NY broadsheet, compiled complaints and suggestions
from ACT UP members. Many of ACT UP/NY's debates played out in its pages, often
through unsigned notes. Many thanks to Bill Dobbs, ACT UP/NY member and *TITA* publisher, for sending me copies of every issue.

AIDS activists? In that context, conflicts about ACT UP's direction and the tenor of the debates indicated that sentiments of solidarity were unraveling and also aided that painful process.

In retrospect it is apparent that what both sides were treating as political differences and a consequent power struggle was more than that. The disputes were being driven by unacknowledged but powerful feelings circulating throughout the organization. Each side felt betrayed by the other. The women felt that many of the men were unmoved by our concerns about women and people of color with HIV/AIDS. Given our strong identification with HIV-positive women, we probably experienced some of the men's apparent lack of concern as an abandonment not only of those women but of *us*. Various men in the organization felt threatened by the power of the Women's Caucus, which had shown leadership in the planning and execution of a national demonstration in Chicago in April 1990 that highlighted the effects of the AIDS crisis on women, people of color, and poor people. Some men likely were feeling that their own power was thereby diminished. But some also worried that actions like that national demonstration were distracting from the movement's focus on gay men with AIDS, that is, from a focus on *their* needs and those of their loved ones. They indicated a fear that ACT UP might betray them, with dire consequences.

Explosive, internal movement conflicts are almost always about more than political differences. Conflicts in ACT UP/NY and at the level of the national movement similarly illuminate how the emotional undercurrents of political conflicts help to constitute the substance, shape, intensity, velocity, and effects of those conflicts.

Political Access and the Further Unraveling of Solidarity

CONFLICTS IN ACT UP/NY, AND NATIONALLY. The unacknowledged emotional undercurrents of New York's conflicts were the same as those in Chicago: feelings of betrayal by activist comrades were especially widespread. And as in Chicago, the emotional intensity of these conflicts stemmed from the broader affective landscape of the AIDS crisis in that moment: a crushing sense of the immense scope of the epidemic, growing desperation and despair, and increasing feelings of inefficacy with regard to the ultimate goal of stopping the dying.

As Edwards (2000b) has noted, one important difference between conflicts in Chicago and New York stemmed from the fact that in 1989–90 a number of activists in ACT UP/NY's Treatment & Data Committee gained access to the top AIDS scientists and government institutions that ACT UP had previously targeted. T&D activists began meeting regularly with officials responsible for setting AIDS research priorities, designing clinical trials, and so forth. That newfound access to the federal AIDS bureaucracy held out hope that activists might now be more able to force changes that might save lives, *perhaps even their own*. But even as some activists gained access, women with HIV/AIDS and activists fighting on their behalf were increasingly frustrated by the scientific-medical establishment's refusal to address their concerns. Differential access to policymakers caused tensions in the movement about tactics and, in the context of a scarcity mentality, raised questions about the movement's focus as well.

Another part of the context that is important for understanding the conflicts is that during this period ACT UP, led by Women's Caucuses from around the country, was demanding that the CDC expand its definition of AIDS to include the opportunistic infections that were killing women and poor people with HIV. It ended up being a years-long campaign because of the CDC's unwillingness to budge.[16] The CDC's own *Morbidity and Mortality Report* indicated that 48 percent of women then dying of HIV-related conditions did not meet the CDC's definition of AIDS, which had been derived from the infections common to those first diagnosed: middle-class gay men. The ramifications of the CDC's exclusionary definition were serious: women were underrepresented in the official AIDS statistics, and they were consistently being misdiagnosed, undertreated, underresearched, excluded from clinical trials and other services available only to people with an AIDS diagnosis, and denied presumptive Social Security disability benefits. In part as a result, once diagnosed, women were dying more quickly than men (figs. 23 and 24).

The publication in this period of *Women, AIDS, and Activism* (ACT UP/NY Women & AIDS Book Group 1990) also drew attention to the complexities facing women with HIV/AIDS. A landmark book that grew out of a teach-in about women and AIDS that the Women's Caucus of ACT UP/NY conducted in March 1989, *Women, AIDS, and Activism* brought together discussions about the ways that racism and sexism operated in the epidemic, the treatment issues facing HIV-positive women,

16. Activists eventually were victorious: the CDC expanded the definition of AIDS in January 1993.

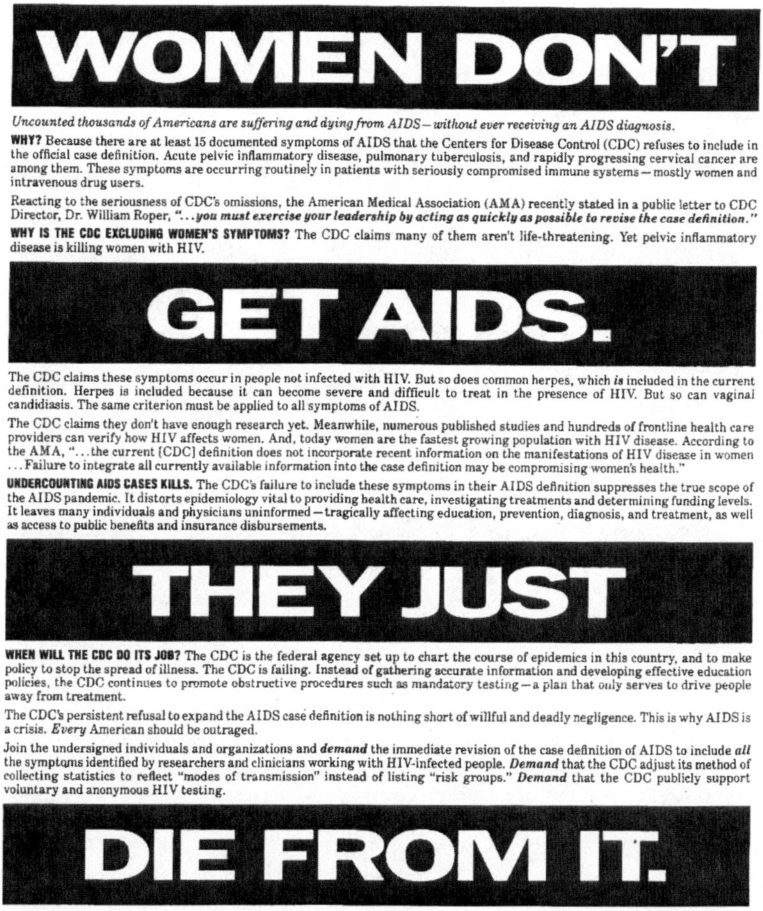

WOMEN DON'T

Uncounted thousands of Americans are suffering and dying from AIDS—without ever receiving an AIDS diagnosis.

WHY? Because there are at least 15 documented symptoms of AIDS that the Centers for Disease Control (CDC) refuses to include in the official case definition. Acute pelvic inflammatory disease, pulmonary tuberculosis, and rapidly progressing cervical cancer are among them. These symptoms are occurring routinely in patients with seriously compromised immune systems—mostly women and intravenous drug users.

Reacting to the seriousness of CDC's omissions, the American Medical Association (AMA) recently stated in a public letter to CDC Director, Dr. William Roper, "...*you must exercise your leadership by acting as quickly as possible to revise the case definition.*"

WHY IS THE CDC EXCLUDING WOMEN'S SYMPTOMS? The CDC claims many of them aren't life-threatening. Yet pelvic inflammatory disease is killing women with HIV.

GET AIDS.

The CDC claims these symptoms occur in people not infected with HIV. But so does common herpes, which *is* included in the current definition. Herpes is included because it can become severe and difficult to treat in the presence of HIV. But so can vaginal candidiasis. The same criterion must be applied to all symptoms of AIDS.

The CDC claims they don't have enough research yet. Meanwhile, numerous published studies and hundreds of frontline health care providers can verify how HIV affects women. And, today women are the fastest growing population with HIV disease. According to the AMA, "...the current [CDC] definition does not incorporate recent information on the manifestations of HIV disease in women ...Failure to integrate all currently available information into the case definition may be compromising women's health."

UNDERCOUNTING AIDS CASES KILLS. The CDC's failure to include these symptoms in their AIDS definition suppresses the true scope of the AIDS pandemic. It distorts epidemiology vital to providing health care, investigating treatments and determining funding levels. It leaves many individuals and physicians uninformed—tragically affecting education, prevention, diagnosis, and treatment, as well as access to public benefits and insurance disbursements.

THEY JUST

WHEN WILL THE CDC DO ITS JOB? The CDC is the federal agency set up to chart the course of epidemics in this country, and to make policy to stop the spread of illness. The CDC is failing. Instead of gathering accurate information and developing effective education policies, the CDC continues to promote obstructive procedures such as mandatory testing—a plan that only serves to drive people away from treatment.

The CDC's persistent refusal to expand the AIDS case definition is nothing short of willful and deadly negligence. This is why AIDS is a crisis. *Every* American should be outraged.

Join the undersigned individuals and organizations and *demand* the immediate revision of the case definition of AIDS to include *all* the symptoms identified by researchers and clinicians working with HIV-infected people. *Demand* that the CDC adjust its method of collecting statistics to reflect "modes of transmission" instead of listing "risk groups." *Demand* that the CDC publicly support voluntary and anonymous HIV testing.

DIE FROM IT.

FIGURE 23. "Women Don't Get AIDS, They Just Die From It," ACT UP flyer, ca. 1992.

the kinds of social services HIV-positive women needed, women and safe sex, the connection between reproductive rights and AIDS issues, and activism around women and HIV/AIDS.

The intensification of the conflicts, then, occurred in a period when different committees and caucuses within ACT UP/NY and across the country were highlighting different issues that to some degree divided along identity lines. But that intensification was not the result of activists focusing on different issues. Indeed, although a common misperception is that ACT UP/NY (and by extension, the entire direct-action AIDS

FIGURE 24. National ACT UP demonstration targeting the Centers for Disease Control, Atlanta, GA, December 3, 1990. Photo by Ellen B. Neipris.

movement) started with one focus—getting AIDS drugs tested and approved—and only later adopted a broader agenda, the reality is that ACT UP participants had focused on a range of issues from the start of ACT UP/NY. (This is true of other chapters as well.) Ample evidence dispels this misperception, and it is worth citing insofar as ACT UP/NY's conflicts were in part about precisely this issue of the organization's focus.

Minutes from the very first meeting of what would become ACT UP/New York indicate that issues on the agenda included women and AIDS, homeless PWAs, immigration, and race issues: "How can [the] lesbian and gay community coalesce with minority groups on AIDS issues?" (ACT UP/New York 1987a). Marion Banzhaf, who began attending ACT UP/NY meetings during its first year, recalls that

> from the beginning there were always people who were saying that AIDS was a mirror of everything that was wrong with society, and the beginning to me was never just about "drugs into bodies." It was about getting more beds in hospitals. It was about changing the attitudes of the healthcare providers to have them stop slipping trays of food under doors [to avoid physical contact with people with AIDS]. It was fighting against shame. . . . It was about who

gets access to the hospitals, versus who dies without ever being diagnosed. (Banzhaf 2002)

To be sure, some members originally were focused on treatment issues, but many saw AIDS as intersecting with large social problems and believed ACT UP should fight the crisis from that perspective.

Maxine Wolfe, who joined ACT UP/NY only a few months after its start, also has disputed the widespread perception that ACT UP/NY began with a single focus on AIDS drugs (Wolfe 1993, 21). She notes, for example, that ACT UP/NY initially did not have a separate committee working on AIDS drug-treatment issues. According to Wolfe, ACT UP/NY was originally and unproblematically focused on issues like housing for people with AIDS, needle exchange, and women with AIDS, as well as AIDS drug treatments. Interestingly, in a 1997 essay, T&D member Mark Harrington corroborated Banzhaf's and Wolfe's memories: "Among the elements and targets of ACT UP's *initial* activism were zaps and demonstrations about gay visibility, AIDS discrimination, drug companies, political leaders, the media, other AIDS organizations. Larry [Kramer]'s motto 'drugs into bodies' was often chanted, but there was little organized activism directed towards achieving that goal" (Harrington 1997, 275; my emphasis; see also ACT UP/New York n.d. a).

In my view, the misperception about ACT UP's original focus hinders any understanding of ACT UP/NY's conflicts. Indeed, the misperception helped foster the battles within ACT UP about the movement's priorities: some who wanted ACT UP to focus on getting AIDS drugs tested and approved argued that the movement had "gotten off track" by taking on issues that addressed the role of racism and sexism in the epidemic. Their accusations of other members' betrayal necessitated a view that ACT UP had abandoned what they claimed was its initial single focus on AIDS treatments.

ACT UP/NY's later internal conflicts did not derive, then, from the diverse focal points of various committees and caucuses within the group; while it is likely true that in the later years caucuses of women and people of color spent more of their time and resources on issues related to racism, sexism, and poverty in the AIDS crisis, those focal points had been there from the start. They became contentious only as a scarcity mentality took hold in the movement. A focus on one issue or on one population seemed to come at the expense of other people with AIDS, or at least could be read that way. Access to the federal AIDS bureaucracy by a few ACT UP members raised related concerns about whose needs would be brought to the table and whose ignored. Some members thus were wary of such "insider" tactics, while those who had gained access feared being hamstrung in their choice of tactics, especially now that meetings with officials actually might lead to beneficial changes in the AIDS drug-testing and approval process. Resulting feelings of betrayal, distrust, resentment, and anger intensified the political disagreements and made them extremely difficult to navigate.

In a June 1990 article, *Village Voice* reporter Donna Minkowitz— who attended ACT UP meetings regularly—characterized one side of the conflict as follows: "A powerful minority of the group's white men believes that ACT UP should concentrate on getting AIDS drugs approved by the federal bureaucracy—an issue that affects even the wealthiest AIDS patient—while subordinating other struggles, such as obtaining services for indigent PWAs or providing counseling and treatment to IV-drug users" (Minkowitz 1990, 20). To get a feel for the emotional undercurrents of ACT UP/NY's conflicts, imagine the feelings that might prompt advocacy of a single focus on getting "drugs into bodies," as well as the feelings evoked by that position among activists with other urgent focal points. Or consider the feelings that might motivate and be generated by the following anonymous missive published in ACT UP/NY's *TITA*. "Stop trying to save the world! ACT UP will not stop racism, sexism, the Contras, or save the whales. Concentrate our *few* resources on AIDS. That's what the A in ACT UP stands for. . . . The most important task of ACT UP is to pressure agencies to expedite drug-testing. Every other issue is a *distant* second to this" (*TITA*, March 19, 1990, 2; emphases in original). According to ACT UP/NY member Kendall Thomas, the Women's Caucus and Majority Action Committee responded to appeals to focus only on getting drugs into bodies by asking questions: "Surely, it can't [only] be about producing these drugs that can go into bodies, some bodies don't have insurance or some bodies are expressing a completely different range of illnesses, surely it can't be just about that" (quoted in Thomas 2002). Feelings of having been betrayed are met by feelings of having been betrayed. To understand why ACT UP's conflicts became explosive, we have to consider their emotional sources and undercurrents—what it feels like to anticipate your own death; to see no end in sight to the crisis; to sense a growing political inefficacy; to be told that your issues, your life and the lives of people you love, aren't as important as other's issues and lives; to feel betrayed; to be accused of having betrayed others.

INSIDE/OUTSIDE. The key players in the New York conflicts were members of T&D, which worked on AIDS treatment issues and was made up primarily (but not exclusively) of white, gay men, many of whom were HIV-positive, and members of the Women's Caucus, which primarily worked on issues about women and AIDS and was made up mostly (but not exclusively) of white lesbians, almost all of whom where HIV-negative. To be sure, neither T&D nor the Women's Caucus had monolithic memberships; there were divergent perspectives within each, and some members of both groups were not involved in the conflicts at all. As well, there were never only two sides to the debates, although the two main camps dominated the discourse. There were HIV-positive people, white, gay men, people of color, and women in both of the main camps. Maxine Wolfe recalls, for example, that the ACT UP/NY affinity group working on the CDC definition campaign had twenty-four members, only seven of whom were women, and several of whom were white, gay men with HIV (Wolfe 2004).

An exploration of the emotional undercurrents of an incident that occurred in the summer of 1990 helps to explain why conflicts within ACT UP/NY intensified in this period and contributed to the fracturing and eventual decline of the organization and, indeed, of the national direct-action AIDS movement. Responses by two women from ACT UP/NY and one from ACT UP/D.C. to a column in *OutWeek* by Mark Harrington revealed rising distrust and declining sentiments of solidarity among members of ACT UP/NY and within the national movement. In his weekly column, "Political Science," Harrington listed the tremendous advances that AIDS activists had made into the scientific labyrinth of the AIDS clinical trial system since ACT UP's May 1990 demonstration at the NIH. He noted in particular that activists now had access to those conducting AIDS research and setting research priorities. Pointing out that AIDS activists had made "more headway within the realm of science than in . . . local and state politics," Harrington posited that unlike politicians, scientists were capable of rational discourse and open to changing their minds (Harrington 1990, 34). In his list of activist victories, Harrington noted that more resources were going to be given to the Obstetrical and Gynecological Subcommittee of the Pediatric Committee of the ACTG (AIDS Clinical Trials Group) so that it could "expand its focus from pregnant women to all women with HIV" (37). He warned that the accomplishments did not mean "that activists have won an unqualified victory, or that the tasks before us are not as daunting as they ever were" (34). But, Harrington continued, "at least we will not have to skirmish over access to those who set research priorities, select drugs, and design and carry out clinical trials" (34). He acknowledged, "We must not abandon our criticism of the systemic flaws which continue to afflict the ACTG," but, he argued, "at least we will be able to bring our concerns and our demands directly to those responsible" (37).

Two weeks later, *OutWeek* printed three letters that took issue with Harrington's column. The first, by Linda Meredith from ACT UP/D.C., challenged Harrington's optimism that the changes he had detailed would amount to improvements for HIV-positive women. Meredith expressed anger that "although the advances outlined in Harrington's article are important, they will do little or nothing to improve the lives of women with AIDS, and nothing at all to implore [scientists] to wake up to the reality that lesbians are also at risk" (Meredith 1990, 5). She then described her own experiences at the recent ACTG meeting, to which she had been admitted as an observer, giving examples of the "ignorance and sexism" she encountered among government scientists and researchers, one of whom—Anthony Fauci, director of NIAID, the body overseeing the ACTG—Harrington had praised in his column. Meredith described an upcoming drug trial (ACTG #076) that would assess newborns of HIV-positive women but had no plans to provide necessary care for the women themselves. She also noted that researchers on the Obstetrical and Gynecological Subcommittee that Harrington had mentioned were pediatricians focused on children with AIDS and uninterested in the concerns of HIV-positive women. Expressing a strong identification with women with AIDS, Meredith wrote, "Women are the fastest-growing group in this country to be infected with HIV. *We* die six times faster than men, and *we* are denied access to Medicaid, Medicare, SSI [Social Security Disability Insurance], and ACTG clinical trials" (5; my emphases). Pointing out that she was one of the people whom the system had "let in," Meredith concluded, "I'm angry because the answer for us, sisters, is still on the outside. ACT UP!" (5).

Meredith's letter reveals a number of feeling states circulating among ACT UP women in this moment. Where concerns of T&D activists were seemingly being addressed, the concerns of Women's Caucus activists from around the country were slighted both within and outside the movement, creating sentiments among many women of nonrecognition and consequently of resentment, anger, and mistrust toward men in T&D. Also apparent is Meredith's identification with HIV-positive women, an identification so ardent that she used the pronoun "we" when referring to women with HIV/AIDS, as the ACT UP/Chicago Women's Caucus statement on sexism had done. Meredith's identification helps to explain why she experienced Harrington's failure to mention the problems still facing HIV-positive women—his seeming disinterest—as an affront, indeed, as a personal betrayal. Meredith's anger about lesbian invisibility in the AIDS epidemic—and her implicit critique of Harrington for not mentioning this issue—reflects feelings among lesbians of nonrecognition and lack of acknowledgement, both by others in the movement and by the scientific-medical establishment.[17]

Meredith's letter strikes me as a genuine attempt to engage in political debate with the members of T&D. She agreed that the advances outlined in Harrington's column were important, but questioned his optimism, particularly regarding HIV-positive women. The thrust of her letter was to counter Harrington's suggestion that the battle no longer needed to be conducted from the outside, arguing instead for the continuing necessity of engaging in confrontational demonstrations. Meredith's letter staked out a position in an ongoing debate in ACT UP about the merits of insider vs. outsider tactics now that some activists and people with AIDS had been allowed into the system.

In contrast to Meredith's letter, the other two were addressed directly to Harrington and struck more of an adversarial and reproachful tone.

17. This focus on lesbians and AIDS might seem odd, given that lesbians as a group have had a low rate of HIV-infection. One reason why some lesbians in ACT UP took up the issue was to complicate the category of "lesbian" by acknowledging that there are lesbians who have sex with men and lesbian injection-drug users who might be at risk, along with their partners. As well, the government was not collecting statistics about woman-to-woman HIV transmission, assuming its impossibility. Noting the government's ignorance about lesbian sexual practices and pointing out that there were HIV-positive lesbians who had no known risk factor, some women in ACT UP thought it was important to challenge this instance of lesbian invisibility and thus pushed the government to include a question about sexual orientation for women in its statistical accounting. Lesbians in ACT UP produced some of the first lesbian safe-sex materials, not only for educational purposes but also as part of ACT UP's more general pro-sex, pro-queer interventions. At the height of ACT UP's internal conflicts, British gay and AIDS activist Simon Watney criticized lesbians in ACT UP as having "AIDS envy." His reductive assertion failed to consider these points as well as the larger context in which lesbians were invisible in broader society (and often desexualized in contrast to gay men, who were hypersexualized) and experiencing nonrecognition within ACT UP.

One by ACT UP/NY member Heidi Dorow began as follows: "To Mark Harrington: Your 'Political Science' piece really pissed me off" (Dorow 1990, 5). Dorow insinuated that Harrington was being disingenuous, even dishonest, and that his comments might have dangerous effects: "You were trying to convince us that the big boys at NIH and NIAID have done a big turnaround and they are now interested in the needs of IVDUs [intravenous drug users], people of color and women in this crisis. Considering all the work that needs to be done, I think that's a very dangerous approach within the activist community" (5). In other words, Harrington's claim that activists' grievances would now be more readily heard and acted upon might undermine other activists' calls for confrontational activism targeting the federal AIDS bureaucracy, with dangerous effects for people with AIDS.

Countering Harrington's assertion that scientists were rational and open-minded and thus open to considering activists' demands, Dorow wrote about a recent meeting that she and other lesbian AIDS activists had had with Anthony Fauci, Dan Hoth and "other floundering NIH/NIAID blockheads" to discuss women and AIDS. Drawing attention to the fact that the scientists were treating male and female AIDS activists differently, she continued, "The 'rational discourse' of these scientists consisted of chastising us for having an 'attitude that will never get us anywhere.' The subtext to this whole exchange was, of course, 'You aren't going to get anything until you act like good girls'" (Dorow 1990, 5–6). Dorow's implicit suggestion here was that the ACT UP men who had gained access had done so by being "good boys," insinuating that perhaps they had made concessions that were politically unwise. Dorow then pointedly asked, "Do you really think that any of us should be satisfied with an Obstetrical and Gynecological Subcommittee of the Pediatrics Committee, which is made up of obstetricians—*not* gynecologists?!" (6; emphasis in original). Here, Dorow was challenging Harrington's optimism about recent changes in the ACTG regarding HIV-positive women while also intimating that he was not only ignorant about the difference between obstetricians and gynecologists, but that his ignorance revealed his lack of concern about HIV-positive women.[18] Dorow was suggesting that this male AIDS activist, like the misogynistic scientific-

18. Obstetricians specialize in pregnancy, delivering babies, and the care of women after childbirth; gynecologists specialize in women's reproductive health, whether they bear children or not.

medical establishment itself, viewed women with HIV only as vectors of HIV transmission to babies (hence the obstetricians on the committee), rather than as people with HIV who themselves needed services and treatment. Dorow then angrily challenged Harrington's claim that there was adequate access to the system: "Women don't have shit and won't until we stop settling for crumbs" (6). She concluded with an indirect call for (a renewed) solidarity among activists, suggesting that gay men had reason to identify with women with HIV/AIDS: "You can bet that if women don't have the care and access they need, there are a bunch of gay men out there who don't have it, either" (6).

Dorow's letter indicates strong sentiments of having been betrayed. She insinuated that Harrington was being dishonest and that the male activists who had gained access to the ACTG system had sold women out; her intimations suggested a belief that T&D was acting in bad faith and that its members were selfishly concerned only about their own health, at the expense of HIV-positive women. She accused him of having betrayed women with HIV/AIDS as well as T&D's female activist comrades. Where Meredith's anger seemed to be partly about Harrington's too easy optimism but mainly about the dire situation that HIV-positive women were facing, the more moralizing tone and content of Dorow's letter suggested that her anger was directed primarily at Harrington himself.

The third letter, written by ACT UP/NY member Tracy Morgan, was even more candid and acerbic in its accusations against Harrington and other gay, white, male activists, particularly with regard to abandoning HIV-positive women and, by extension, female AIDS activists. Addressed directly to Harrington, it began with an explicit assertion that he was "sell[ing] women's lives down the river" (Morgan 1990, 6). Morgan detailed numerous instances of sexism in scientific research that both challenged Harrington's assertion of scientists' rationality and rhetorically united all women—including those in ACT UP—as potential or actual casualties of Harrington's and T&D's too cozy relationship with the scientific-medical establishment. Morgan took Harrington to task for his claim that the increase in resources for the Obstetrical and Gynecological Subcommittee of the Pediatrics Committee was a victory. "This is not a victory in the least. . . . Placing the gynecological concerns of HIV-positive women under the wing of pediatrics is a sign of the utmost irrationality and indifference." Doing so, of course, was simply a continuation of seeing women as vectors of transmission. "Floored" by his

ignorance about the health issues of HIV-positive women, she continued, "Stop clapping for this crumb, and start holding out for some real
lifesaving maneuvers for women with HIV-related disease" (6). Morgan
concluded with an angry indictment of Harrington, as well as a threat:

> Like it or not, you are quickly becoming a colleague of rational scientists in a
> position that many other activists do not occupy. I do not see much difference
> between you meeting with Fauci and the other heavy hitters, and the boys
> from the neighborhood watching the game at the corner bar. What have you
> and other activists sacrificed to be accepted by this elite group? And accepted
> you have been. From your article, my fear is that you have sacrificed women.
> The sisterhood is watching, brother. Don't fuck us over. (Morgan 1990, 6)

Pronounced in this letter is Morgan's feminist critique of power—the
power of science in particular—and even more, of AIDS activists cozy-
ing up to power. It indicates Morgan's anxiety that proximity to power
might corrupt one and lead to an abandonment of important principles.[19]
Suggesting that acceptance into the system was itself evidence of some
type of compromise, Morgan insinuated that T&D activists had sold out,
sacrificing HIV-positive women as well as female AIDS activists, in order to be accepted by elite scientists. The accusation of "selling out"
had particular weight because it was one that ACT UP sometimes made
against certain ASOs as a way to distance ACT UP from more moderate AIDS organizations. To accuse other ACT UP members of selling out, then, was not only to accuse them of violating ACT UP's principles; it was simultaneously an accusation that they were in some sense
siding with people whom ACT UP criticized. Morgan was casting doubt
on T&D activists' motives, asking whose interests they had at heart. She
also noted that gender inequalities had crept into the putatively egalitarian ACT UP, sowing distrust and threatening movement solidarity.
    In concluding with the statement that "the sisterhood is watching,
brother," she not only issued a threat, she also insinuated that Harrington
was not to be trusted because he was male and was moving inside the
system. Morgan's suggestion was that the "sisterhood," ostensibly outside of and opposed to the system, untainted by power, was morally pure
and hence could be trusted. Morgan was claiming that women, experi-

19. Wendy Brown (2001, chap. 2) criticizes this construction that pits power and principle against one another and creates conditions for moralizing.

enced as they were with outsiderhood, were more likely to avoid the seduction of the inside, while men, even gay men with the experience of
exclusion, would be enticed by the proximity to power and the offer of
male bonding, and thus were more likely to succumb, sacrificing important principles as well as their activist comrades and less privileged people with AIDS in the process.[20]

An article written by Women's Caucus member Maxine Wolfe about
the July 1990 meeting between lesbian AIDS activists and Anthony
Fauci that Dorow mentioned suggests that the women from ACT UP/
NY and Washington, D.C., had good reason to be suspicious, both of the
federal AIDS bureaucracy and of men from T&D. Fauci evidently had
told women at the meeting that they "didn't get [the meeting with him]
because of our actions or pressuring but because of ACT UP" (Wolfe
1990b, 3). Fauci not only claimed that he had granted the women the
meeting as a result of his good relationship with some ACT UP men; he
also implied that the women themselves were inconsequential to ACT
UP. Wolfe reported that Fauci reiterated the divide between male and
female AIDS activists by stating that "he had an agreement with 'the
men in ACT UP, that is gay ACT UP,' about how they would deal with
each other in these interactions" (3).[21] The federal AIDS bureaucracy
was treating AIDS activists concerned about women and AIDS differently from the men in T&D, which would be reason enough for identity
categories to become a salient factor in ACT UP's internal conflicts. In
addition, Fauci's comments gave the women in ACT UP reason to suspect that the men in ACT UP were aligning themselves with the federal AIDS bureaucracy, despite that same bureaucracy's failure to respond to, or even to consider, the concerns of HIV-positive women. The
women understandably might have interpreted Fauci's comment that he
had "an agreement" with the men in ACT UP as saying that the men
from T&D had made concessions and cut some sort of a deal—the content of which was unclear—in order to be admitted into the system.

Comments about and by Fauci in a book suggest as much: the authors,
health specialists Peter Arno and Karyn Feiden, contend that Fauci indicated that he would integrate T&D activists into the ACTG process but
"in exchange, Fauci wanted the rhetoric toned down" (Arno and Feiden

20. Morgan again cast doubt on the motives of white male AIDS activists in an interview in the *Advocate* (Michaud 1990, 50).
21. See Corea 1993, 224–25 for a similar account of this meeting.

1993, 234). The authors quote Fauci: "If they [T&D activists] are trying to get into the system, they may have to modify some of their activist modes" (234). While suggesting that Fauci was unable to see direct-action activism or hear activists' emotional register as every bit as rational as scientific discourse, his comments also clarify more of what was at stake in Dorow's and Morgan's critiques of scientific rationality and of T&D's buying into that rationality. ACT UP men had a chance within that rubric, but ACT UP women and women with HIV/AIDS would always be short-changed.

The letters in *OutWeek* voiced a fear among many women and people of color within ACT UP that T&D members would not use their access to the federal AIDS bureaucracy to help push ACT UP demands regarding women, people of color, and poor people with AIDS. It appeared that they simply did not care about those populations and issues or those in ACT UP who were working on those issues. Gregg Bordowitz suggests reasons why that fear was legitimate:

> I do recall that the leadership in ACT UP and the general membership didn't always throw the entire weight of their support behind protests organized specifically to address women's issues or the concerns of people of color. . . . The general membership wouldn't vote against proposals brought forward by a people of color caucus—the Majority Action Committee—or a women's group. [But,] sometimes these actions drew small numbers or weren't the central focus of the group. And that sent a signal to the caucus that the majority of the group was not necessarily going to expend their energy or time on issues that [the caucus] cared about. And I think the same thing happened or occurred with women's issues as well. (Bordowitz 2002a)

ACT UP/NY member Ming-Yuen S. Ma echoes Bordowitz, noting that when action proposals from the Asian/Pacific Islander Caucus were discussed in the general group, "there was no opposition, but there was no enthusiasm, either" (Ma 2003). More generally, "I don't think that issues about women and AIDS, issues about AIDS and HIV in people of color groups [were] really on people's minds, other than the sort of litany of PC: oh, of course we have to care about women, or of course we care about people of color. But [were] they actually committed to it?" (Ma 2003; see also Agosto 2002, 28–29). That sort of discrepancy between ACT UP's rhetoric and actual practices regarding women and people of color might generate feelings of disregard and disrespect, of nonrecogni-

SOLIDARITY AND ITS FRACTURING

tion. These conditions created fertile terrain for the growth of mistrust and resentment.

The retrospective comments of T&D member Dudley Saunders also indicate that the antennae of the Women's Caucus and the different people-of-color caucuses were not far off the mark and that they had reason to be concerned about T&D's focus. Saunders acknowledged that in the context of desperation about finding AIDS drug treatments, the gender, race, and class privileges of many T&D members led them to dismiss issues not explicitly about getting "drugs into bodies":

> If you're a privileged white guy, . . . it's easy for you to focus on just making the science happen; just making a drug a cure, because you know you're going to get it. And of course, you believe that everyone should have access to it, but you're not going to think about that right now. You'll make sure you write in "access to people of color, and women and children." You'll throw that in every time. . . . But there was an enormous amount of distrust [between the different factions in ACT UP]. (Saunders 2003)

In Saunders' memory, T&D paid lip-service to the needs of other people with HIV/AIDS, but their feelings and practices of solidarity stopped there.

As with almost all of the flare-ups in ACT UP, this conflict revolved around political disagreements about whom ACT UP represented and how the organization should fight AIDS. But again such political disputes are rarely if ever the only thing at issue in conflicts as intense as these. As the letters by Meredith, Dorow, and Morgan reveal, movement conflicts frequently are driven and shaped by unarticulated and unacknowledged affective states. In this case, ACT UP women in New York and Washington, D.C. (and elsewhere), were being disregarded by the federal AIDS bureaucracy, and they felt similarly belittled and betrayed by some men in T&D. Despite the life-and-death urgency of the campaign to force a change in the CDC's exclusionary AIDS definition, despite the publication of *Women, AIDS, and Activism,* with its wealth of information about the severity of the epidemic among women, issues about women and AIDS continued to be ghettoized. Feeling disregarded and unrecognized, fearing that ACT UP was betraying HIV-positive women as well as female AIDS activists, many women in the movement became angry and distrustful. My sense is that those feeling states, in turn, prompted some to employ a moralizing rhetoric.

The letters published in *OutWeek* along with the turn to moralism indicate declining sentiments of solidarity within the movement across lines of gender. In terms of effects, the emotional dimensions of the conflicts likely contributed to the fracturing of the movement. It is difficult to imagine how activists can work together when some feel that others have disregarded and betrayed them. The subsequent distrust and anger can be navigated, of course, but probably only with some acknowledgement that the accusation is partially correct and that those accused are willing and able to change. In an interview years later, T&D member David Barr provided such an acknowledgement as he noted some of the emotional dynamics within ACT UP. In describing T&D's admission into the federal AIDS bureaucracy, Barr stated, "All of a sudden we were in this whirlwind and there was an arrogance that came with that that was not constructive, that made other people feel out of the loop, not considered, not respected, that their issues weren't important, that the work that they were doing wasn't important work" (Barr 2002). But at the time, the "arrogance" of some members of T&D—described as such by a number of T&D members themselves in retrospective interviews[22]—made it unlikely that they would acknowledge the women's accusations.

The following comments by another ACT UP/NY member also indicate how difficult it is to work across identity categories when those categories are the basis for moralizing.[23] I should note that this person saw himself as a leftist with antiracist and feminist politics. Also, he was HIV-positive and close to many of the men in T&D, but he was not involved in T&D. Although he understood and was sympathetic to its "drugs into bodies" focus, he was "not completely swayed" by it and did not orient his activism in that direction. To the contrary, he thought ACT UP could and should be "a catalyst for a renewed, reinvigorated relationship to other causes, like homelessness and the lack of drug treatment, and poverty, and racism," that ACT UP "would serve its highest purpose by being a catalyst for universal health care in the country" (Anonymous

22. When interviewed, David Barr (2002), Gregg Gonsalves (2004), Mark Harrington (2003), and Peter Staley (2002) all indicated that they now thought that T&D members, often including themselves, had at times been arrogant and had allowed their access to the scientific establishment and consequent power within ACT UP to go to their heads.

23. This person gave me permission to quote him and to include identifying information, but he asked that I not use his name.

2002). Still, he found himself "very challenged" by Morgan and Dorow's rhetoric, and not in a manner that prompted him to grow politically.

> They made certain kinds of arguments that . . . seemed to me to be very self-righteous and somewhat divisive at the time, that had to do with class and were, I felt, very blameful. . . . When they spoke, I felt implicated, let's put it that way. I felt like there was no way that I could get outside of my gender or my class. There was nothing I could do to redeem myself for being male and for being middle-class. And regardless of what I did, no matter how much I tried to raise my consciousness, . . . I would always be subject to a certain kind of castigation. And I think that to some extent, that kind of fueled a lot of these tensions. On both sides. There were also men who were very dismissive. . . . But for me, personally, sitting in the room, I always remember when they [Dorow and Morgan] would raise their hand and they'd get called on. I would prepare myself to be accused of being a racist, [of being sexist and classist]. . . . I think that a lot of the acrimony had to do with this dissonance, this inability to address each other. (Anonymous 2002)

The issue for this ACT UP/NY member was not that he was closed to being politically challenged. To the contrary, he recalls learning a great deal from many women in ACT UP "who made very similar arguments," but they did so without a castigatory tone, allowing him to hear them differently. His comments suggest that moralizing rhetoric not only signaled declining sentiments of solidarity but also furthered that unraveling.

Acrimonious debates in the spring of 1991 reveal that, as in ACT UP/Chicago, the moralizing came from both sides. And again, we need to contextualize that turn to moralizing by considering the content and emotional undercurrents of the conflicts. One particularly rancorous debate revolved around an action initiated by the ACT UP/NY Women's Caucus against an ACTG trial to test whether the drug AZT reduced transmission of HIV from mother to infant (protocol #076).[24] Another

24. Many AIDS activists—including members of New York's T&D Committee and Women's Caucus—thought that the #076 drug trial was unethical: it privileged the health of the fetus over the health of its HIV-positive mother. Women would not be warned about the risks to themselves and to their babies of taking AZT, treatment for the enrolled women would be discontinued soon after the birth of the child, and the trial had a placebo arm that would deny treatment to some trial participants. For critiques of #076, see Kirschenbaum 1990; Harrington 1991; and "ACTG 076 Is Bad Science and Unethical" 1991. The dispute was about the fact that the Stop #076 action had interrupted a conversa-

debate concerned a proposal initiated by a number of ACT UP women for a six-month moratorium on all meetings between ACT UP members and government officials at the CDC and NIAID about issues related to women and AIDS.[25] The debates, most generally, were about ACT UP/NY's focus and tactics, but they also involved questions of loyalties and commitments that placed different activists' ostensible ethics at the heart of the conflicts: Who truly had the interests of *all* people with HIV/ AIDS at heart; who really was committed to self-determination for people with HIV/AIDS?

Debates revealed enormous distrust and anger within ACT UP/NY, along with fears of betrayal and feelings of being disrespected and unrecognized, which created fertile ground for moralism. This mix of feelings and the turn to moralism are evident in minutes from an ACT UP/NY meeting and from a T&D meeting after the Stop #076 action. One participant in the action stated her opposition to #076 "as a woman [and] as a lesbian." Arguing that the trial was "racist science," she suggested that people who disagreed were themselves racist and sexist (ACT UP/NY 1991, 15). Marion Banzhaf—a member of ACT UP/NY and the director of the New Jersey Women and AIDS Network, which had conducted community meetings about #076 with HIV-positive African American women who were going to be recruited to be in the trial—was critical of #076 but, expecting that it might proceed, tried to push those designing it to revise its worst aspects. Banzhaf recalls another woman turning to her during a meeting and saying, "If you support this trial you don't support women!" (Banzhaf 2002).

T&D's meeting minutes after the Stop #076 action similarly indicate

---

tion about the trial between its principal investigators and a committee of representatives from affected communities. For more on the Stop #076 action and the ensuing conflict within ACT UP, see ACT UP/NY T&D Committee 1991; "As AIDS Treatment Activists" 1991; Auerbach 1991; Banzhaf 2000, 2002; Barr 2002; Cohen 1993; Harrington 2002b; Wofford 1991; and Wolfe 1992. The #076 study did proceed, and it found that AZT did help decrease the already low rate of HIV transmission from mother to child.

25. There was some confusion at the time, and it continues today, about whether the proposal was for a moratorium on all meetings or only those about women and AIDS. After sorting through the evidence, my sense is that the actual proposal may have been for a moratorium only on meetings regarding women and AIDS, but it seems clear that many people in ACT UP/NY thought that the proposal was about all meetings. That perception likely influenced their attitudes about the proposal. To get a sense of the contours and acrimonious tone of this debate, see: Banzhaf 2000, 2002; Barr 2002; Chou 2003; Cohen 1993; Cvetkovich 2003a, 199–200; Gonsalves 2004; Harrington 2002b; Link 1991a; Staley 2002; and Wolfe 1991, 1992, 2004.

the growing significance of identity categories and questions of solidarity within and across them. T&D member Derek Link stated,

> I feel like the motives of a lot of people in ACT UP . . . are questionable. And I've felt for a long time that ACT UP is not a safe place for HIV positives to be, and . . . I feel that very strongly. As an HIV-positive person, I [have] felt that myself. And I think a lot of people in ACT UP hold people with HIV in utter contempt. I think a lot of people [who were at the Stop #076 action] hold people with HIV in utter contempt. (ACT UP/NY T&D Committee 1991, 6)[26]

Although Larry Kramer countered that he felt "very safe in ACT UP" as an HIV-positive man (ACT UP/NY T&D Committee 1991, 7), Link's statement indicated that HIV status had become a salient identity category within ACT UP/NY and now was being mobilized as a marker of difference. Even though perceived divisions along lines of identity were often erroneous—not all white, HIV-positive men sided with T&D, and not all women supported the Women's Caucus positions—the perception made political differences extremely explosive, as well as ripe for moralizing.

With regard to the debate about the moratorium proposal, T&D member Gregg Gonsalves recalls feeling that the proposal positioned T&D members who sat on government committees as "collaborationists" (Gonsalves 2004, 43–44). He and others in T&D experienced the proposal as accusatory and castigatory, as calling their motives and ethics into question, and some responded by questioning their opponents' motives. Derek Link engaged in such emotional trumping when he wrote that the moratorium would "abandon people like me and my best

---

26. When interviewed, two people told me that Link was not HIV-positive. (See also Gonsalves 2004). Why Link may have lied about his HIV status is an interesting question that I can only speculate about. (See Odets 1995 for an excellent exploration of the psychology of HIV-negative gay men during the height of the epidemic.) If he did lie, it may be that, like other gay men of his generation, he thought that contracting HIV was inevitable. Or, perhaps the widespread equation of AIDS with gay male identity influenced his own self-identification. What is most important for my argument is that this statement and another that I discuss below indicate his own and other ACT UP members' view that having HIV/AIDS authenticated one's claims in debates about ACT UP's tactics and focus. The desire to be heard and respected may have moved Link to pretend he was HIV-positive. Whatever the reasons, when Link made this statement, he presented himself as HIV-positive and others perceived him to be HIV-positive, and that perception played a role in the effect of his statements.

friend who need ACT UP now—who can't wait 6 months for ACT UP's help in fighting for our lives" (Link 1991a). Disregarding the moratorium proponents' commitment to women with AIDS, Link implied that they were disconnected from and unconcerned about people with AIDS, period. More damning still, he suggested that the moratorium on meetings would put his life at risk (even though he noted earlier in the statement that the proposal only covered meetings with government officials about women and AIDS). He essentially accused those proposing the moratorium of abandoning and thereby threatening the lives of people with AIDS in ACT UP.[27]

Both sides in these debates seemed to feel betrayed, and each cast accusations of betrayal, either of HIV-positive women and female AIDS activists or of people with AIDS in ACT UP and gay men with AIDS more generally. Accusations of being racist came from both sides as well. The tone and content of the debates suggested a widespread belief that the position a person took revealed the truth of his or her political and ethical being. The effect was an unbridgeable gap between the two camps, with each side convinced of its own political righteousness even while standing accused of engaging in what both sides construed as shameful behavior. In interviews conducted years later, members of ACT UP/NY frequently mark the moratorium proposal and subsequent debates as a decisive moment in the organization's fracturing. Women closely associated with the moratorium proposal describe the debates as divisive, traumatic, and personally devastating (Cvetkovich 2003a, 199–200); T&D members echo those characterizations and describe the period as a turning point that induced some of them to leave ACT UP in January 1992 and form another organization (Treatment Action Group [TAG]). An editorial comment in *TITA* amid these debates noted the effects on membership: "The morale of the Floor is way down, more people are arriving later, leaving earlier and overall attendance is down" (*TITA*, April 22, 1991). The conflicts, and the manner in which they were playing out, were engulfing the movement.

27. There were more than two sides on the moratorium issue. For example, some people were concerned about how close T&D was getting to the scientific-medical establishment, but they opposed the moratorium because they thought that a ban on meetings was too sweeping and that the risks of insider tactics could be addressed through discussions about how to hold meetings with government and industry officials without being co-opted and in a manner that ensured representation of ACT UP's different constituencies. See, for example, Banzhaf 2002. The subtlety of that sort of argument was lost in the debates, which quickly polarized people into two opposing camps.

"HIV NEGATIVES: GET OUT OF OUR WAY". The growing salience of HIV status in ACT UP/NY's internal conflicts allows further analysis of the feeling states coursing through the organization in this moment and their role in the conflicts and in the decline of the movement. A written statement from Derek Link during this period—"HIV Negatives: Get Out of Our Way"—reveals a growing sense among some ACT UP/NY members that the organization was being hijacked by people who were HIV-negative and suggests sentiments of betrayal and desperation. It also indicates that at this point in ACT UP/NY's conflicts, as in ACT UP/Chicago, some were mobilizing HIV status in a manner that suggested a belief that being HIV-positive granted one greater legitimacy and authority in disputes about ACT UP's tactics and direction. Link wrote,

> HIV NEGATIVES LISTEN UP. ACT UP is not a game or a contest to see who can be the most PC [politically correct]. Many of you can waste time on these meaningless discussions because as one of you said last week "six months is not a life time." But, guess what? For those of us with low T-cells, it certainly is. Either help us to fight for our lives or get the fuck out of our way. (Link 1991b; capitalization in original)[28]

The sentiments expressed in his statement were shared by many members of T&D and ACT UP/NY; indeed, they existed throughout the movement, explicitly articulated in ACT UP/Chicago, ACT UP/San Francisco and other chapters as well. T&D's Mark Harrington recalls his own ambivalence about the statement because it had the potential to alienate many ACT UP members who were HIV-negative; nevertheless, he found it compelling (Harrington 2002b). He probably realized that because a number of HIV-negative people supported T&D, the statement would be interpreted as being directed only toward specific HIV-negative people—those most identified with the Women's Caucus for example. Gregg Gonsalves, an HIV-negative member of T&D, did interpret the statement that way, knowing that it could not be directed at him (Gonsalves 2004). In any event, Harrington's sense is that the claim that HIV-negative people were trying to hijack the movement "definitely resonated" with a lot of people in ACT UP/NY (Harrington 2002b).

28. The "six months is not a life time" reference is to an incident during the moratorium debates when a woman from the Women's Caucus said that six months was a justifiable trial period and unthinkingly added, "Six months isn't the end of your life." In response, others in the room angrily shouted "Yes it might be" (Cohen 1993, 315).

In some ways, "HIV Negatives: Get Out of Our Way" was in the
same emotional register as other ACT UP statements. It shares similarities in tone and style, for example, with a furious broadside, "I Hate
Straights," written by some ACT UP members and distributed by the
ACT UP/NY Pride Parade contingent in June 1990. Rhetorically dividing the world into straight and queer, the broadside was a fuming, outrageous (in the best sense) rallying call to all queers to feel their rage about
abusive treatment from the straight world. Link's statement also divided
the world into two camps of people, those with HIV and those without,
and it too had a furious tone and went to an extreme in order to make its
point: "Either help us to fight for our lives or get the fuck out of our way."
One key difference, though, was that "I Hate Straights" was written "by
queers to queers" and against straight society (Robinson 1990, 1), while
Link's statement enacted (or reinforced) an us/them divide within ACT
UP itself. ACT UP's main rhetorical style vis-à-vis its opponents—with
high doses of outrage, angry invective, and shaming—was now being deployed within the movement itself, by both sides in the conflicts, to disparage and discredit critics.

In enacting that split amid acrimonious political debate about ACT
UP's tactics and focus, Link's statement called the motives and loyalty
of HIV-negative people into question, suggesting that ACT UP members who were living with HIV/AIDS were the most legitimate voices in
the debate—perhaps the only legitimate voices. What made this statement so powerful was that everyone in the movement believed that people with HIV/AIDS indeed should be leading it. As Marion Banzhaf
states, "Being HIV-positive did give you an elevated status and I think
it should have." But while being HIV-positive needed to be privileged
within ACT UP, "it didn't need to be overvalued," as occurred when it
became "incorrect" for HIV-negative members "to challenge 'the HIV
positive position,' whatever it was, even if it was totally wrong" (Banzhaf 2002). The implication of much of the rhetoric about HIV status
was that if people with HIV/AIDS thought that some proposal was a
bad idea, or that ACT UP's sole focus should be "drugs into bodies," no
one else could or should dispute that. An unquestioning support of HIV-
positives' leadership was being asked of HIV-negative people.

ACT UP/Chicago member Michael Thompson recalled wanting to
leave the group when a similar conflict that revolved around HIV status occurred.

That was when the mostly white men within ACT UP/Chicago started saying that they were the ones who should be making the major decisions because they were HIV-positive. When that happened, I realized that something had gone wrong. I didn't know exactly what it was, but. . . . It's really
complicated. But when the HIV Caucus within ACT UP happened [and emphasized the difference between people who were HIV-positive and people
who were HIV-negative], I saw a split happening that I really didn't like at
all. I thought that they should be making decisions, but it was just the way it
was handled. It was very exclusive. It excluded the issue of women who might
have different issues, . . . the fact that women weren't even defined as having
AIDS, even though they were really sick and they were dying from it, they
didn't have the same symptoms as the men. I mean, that was so obvious. But
here the men are taking over, because they're HIV-positive. I thought, That's
not right. And that was one of the things that really turned me off about ACT
UP. (Thompson 2000)

The privileging of people with HIV/AIDS eventually became almost
synonymous with suspicion of those who were HIV-negative, at least
those who were not in or allied with T&D or similar groups in other
chapters. As Dudley Saunders, an HIV-positive member of T&D, recalled, "Being positive was almost a badge of honor, and you knew if
you were positive and doing this work, that you were serious. . . . People
believed that you were going to stay with it. And there was always a bit
of a feeling that if you were negative, maybe you were going to be out of
here" (Saunders 2003, 34). In this atmosphere, political disagreements
between people who were HIV-negative and people who were HIV-
positive became signs of betrayal of the latter. Of course, by presenting
HIV-positive people as a monolithic group, the "HIV Negatives: Get Out
of Our Way" statement skirted the question of *which* HIV-positive people should be listened to—those in the room, who were primarily white
and male and often affiliated with T&D, or those who often were not at
ACT UP meetings, particularly women and people of color. In any case,
there was almost no space for such discussions. Dividing the group into
those who were HIV-positive and those who were negative was a means
of shaming and silencing the latter.

Stock phrases like "What does this have to do with AIDS?" that consistently cropped up in ACT UP debates across the country in this period similarly functioned as divisive emotional trump cards. It was a

question that, as Kendall Thomas notes, was not really a question at all. "The aggressiveness of what dressed itself up as a question—'What does this have to do with AIDS?'—suggested that people had already reached a conclusion, which was not going to be subject to any kind of revision in a conversation of equals" (Thomas 2002). Rather than being an actual question inviting discussion, it was a rhetorical maneuver that shut down discussion by suggesting that some were there to fight AIDS, while others, shamefully, were not.

What it meant to "fight AIDS," of course, was in dispute. Those who asked "What does this have to do with AIDS?" tended to define "fighting AIDS" as getting AIDS drugs tested and approved, and they heard discussions about issues concerning women or people of color with AIDS as non-AIDS-related. Thomas recalls that topics about women and people of color "were always raised about a very specific HIV/AIDS-related issue." He remembers, for example, discussions about women getting sick and dying from infections that were not included in the CDC's definition of AIDS, about clinical drug trials that displayed more concern about babies than their mothers, about women and people of color being excluded from drug trials. Although these topics are AIDS-related, Thomas believes that "what people were *hearing* was something that, because they arrogated to themselves the right to define what AIDS was and to draw the boundaries of the proper domain of AIDS, had nothing to do with AIDS" (Thomas 2002; my emphasis).

The class dimensions of ACT UP's internal conflicts become clear here. For many in T&D, their focus on treatment issues derived in part from their economic status: middle-class or higher, they often did not have to worry about things that were life-and-death issues for other people with HIV/AIDS, such as access to health care and housing. What they needed more than anything were medications to which, once approved, they would have access. As a result their focus within ACT UP was on getting drugs tested and approved. As Gonsalves notes, "People felt like getting better treatments was more important than anything else, because it was a life-or-death matter for them." Having come to ACT UP "out of the fear of God that they were going to die" and going to T&D meetings "looking for treatment information" (Gonsalves 2004), some T&D members and their allies experienced the felt urgencies of other ACT UP members—for example, about PWA's access to health care, about the exclusion of women from AIDS drug trials—as either not about AIDS or as merely a diversion from T&D's important work.

Thomas notes the emotional trumping that entered in when some HIV-positive people suggested that "their experience of AIDS was *the* experience of AIDS and *the* way AIDS had to be talked about if we weren't to be diverted from it by something less urgent than the fact that they were dying." Thomas continued, "The fact that they were dying was tragic," but others were dying as well; moreover, the phrase "I'm dying" operated as a form of emotionalism, "a kind of trump card" that was mobilized whenever people demanded that ACT UP embrace an agenda that included fighting the AIDS crisis as it was affecting women and people of color (Thomas 2002; emphases his). A close reading of the documents and debates from this period indicates that HIV status became a contentious issue precisely at the point when other identities— race and gender, for example—were also becoming salient lines of difference within ACT UP. As Thomas notes, a number of the white men in the movement, wanting to hold onto the power that derives from being unmarked, simply did not want to deal with the issues of racism, sexism, and poverty in the AIDS epidemic. They

> clung to ACT UP as the one place in a time of crisis where they could find a certain comfort, and [they did not want] to come to ACT UP and be made uncomfortable by these women and people of color saying your analysis is wrong and you need to deepen your analysis so as to expand your field of political action. People didn't want to feel uncomfortable because they were people who had felt comfortable about most things most of their lives. (Thomas 2002).[29]

They resented being made to feel guilty about racism and sexism. ACT UP/NY member Robert Vazquez-Pacheco remembers that when issues of race would come up, "everyone would just sort of go into that stunned, 'Don't call me racist, don't call me racist' [mode]" (Vazquez-Pacheco 2002). In this context where white liberal guilt seems to have generated white resentment about being reminded of racism, it seems plausible that some responded by invoking HIV-status in a trumping manner that placed guilt on people who were HIV-negative—those who, from their perspective, had placed guilt on them.

29. In contrast, "the people of color in the room, whatever their class position, whatever their profession, their educational level, their gender, or their sexual affiliation and self-understanding, were simply more familiar with—you felt like Ishmael—you were just at home with discomfort" (Thomas 2002).

Although a statement like "HIV-Negatives: Get Out Of Our Way" indicated growing frustration and desperation among some members with HIV/AIDS, its moralizing quality may have obscured the affective states underlying it, and, in any event, many women and people of color in ACT UP/NY by that point felt furious about what they experienced as T&D's racism and sexism. Within this context, for example, Thomas came to feel that, as an African American member of ACT UP, he had been used by T&D activists: given the demographics of AIDS, "it was impossible in New York City in 1987, '88, '89, '90 for a group of white gay men to walk into a room demanding anything without the legitimacy of women and people of color around them." He had provided some of that legitimacy, and yet T&D was antagonistic toward or uncaring about what Thomas and others saw as pressing AIDS issues. At this point, Thomas grew so angry that he quit ACT UP: "I was angry a lot more often than even my best friends and closest comrades, white comrades in ACT UP, knew" (Thomas 2002).

IDENTITY, BETRAYAL, DESPERATION, AND MORALISM. In pointing toward the emotional trumping aspect of asking "What does this have to do with AIDS" and of raising distinctions along lines of HIV-status, I do not mean to suggest that those who invoked HIV status or raised that question were engaging in strategic, power-play maneuvering alone, consciously attempting to arouse shame and guilt in the hopes of undermining their opponents. That may have been the case in some instances, but also in play was real fear that ACT UP was being hijacked and sidetracked, with dire consequences for people with AIDS in the room. In discussing ACT UP/Chicago's internal conflicts, Tim Miller noted that we became "overwhelmed" as we grew increasingly aware of the different populations affected by the epidemic and that the AIDS crisis would not end anytime soon. Our knowledge led to debates about ACT UP's mission, Miller recalls, but he notes that more than political disagreements were in play:

> I don't think the HIV-positive people were trying to be difficult when they were saying, "Oh, we don't have time to do prisoners with AIDS. We don't have time to do women with AIDS." . . . I don't think it was a man against woman thing. I think it was the *desperation*, you know? I really feel like people felt, and they were in fact correct, the clocks were ticking. And a lot of them died. I don't think that they were trying to be anti-woman, or anti-black, or anti-Indian or anything. That may be the way it came across. That

may be what people heard. But I don't think that was the intention. (Miller
1999; my emphasis)

Miller is correct, I think, to note that people *heard* the challenges to actions about women and people of color with AIDS as sexism and racism.
And although Miller might be read as minimizing their role, sexism and
racism were certainly in play insofar as challenging such actions by asking "What does this have to do with AIDS" revealed a perspective that
generalized from the particular interests and worries of white, gay men,
thereby privileging their concerns over those of women and people of
color with HIV/AIDS. As Thomas' comments indicate, because of their
own race, class, and gender privilege, some people in the movement simply did not want to consider any aspects of the AIDS epidemic that were
beyond their own experience of it.

But we gain further insight when we consider the sense of desperation
that Miller suggested was in play among people with HIV/AIDS in ACT
UP, along with fear of abandonment and betrayal. In a December 1992
interview, Larry Kramer indicated that those feeling states were present
for him, and constituted "one of the subliminal reasons why ACT UP is
in such trouble." He continued, "The HIV-positives felt and feel betrayed
by their HIV-negative brothers and sisters. And I'm in total agreement.
I feel betrayed by my HIV-negative friends" (Zonana 1992, 45). Not only
were such feelings hard to experience, they also contributed to a scarcity
mentality that saw activism regarding issues of concern to one group of
people with HIV/AIDS in zero-sum terms, as diverting activist energy
and resources from other people with HIV/AIDS.

T&D member Gregg Gonsalves recalls an incident that indicated
how a strongly felt fear of death influenced ACT UP/NY's internal conflicts. "I remember being at a meeting with Bob Rafsky [who was in the
late stages of AIDS]. . . . Bob would go on these tirades. And somebody
said something, and he just turned and said, 'No, these people are going to save my life.' In retrospect, there was just such desperation. Bob
was sick, and there was a lot of faith put into what was happening at
T&D" (Gonsalves 2004). In a context where news on the treatment front
was often discouraging but sometimes offered a glimmer of hope, people with HIV/AIDS in the group might have experienced anything that
could be construed as slowing the work of T&D as a grave betrayal of
people with AIDS and a threat to their own lives. In a context where
many people with HIV/AIDS were desperate and placing their faith in

T&D, even *disagreement* with T&D by others in ACT UP could be experienced as betrayal and a dire threat.

The following comments by David Barr, an HIV-positive man who was in T&D, suggest that such feeling states underlay the turn to moralism by some T&D members and their allies throughout the movement. I asked Barr to consider the question "What does this have to do with AIDS?" and whether he thought ACT UP had gotten off the track of AIDS. He replied, "When you really deconstruct it and take it apart, at the time posing the question in that way seemed to make sense, and now in retrospect it doesn't really make any sense at all." Barr offered the following analysis of why that question nevertheless had resonated with many in ACT UP, particularly those who came to ACT UP because AIDS was directly affecting their lives:

> Most of them were white, middle-class. Most of them were men who had this sense of privilege, and all of a sudden they came up against a system that was saying, "We don't care if you die; we prefer it, and we're not going to help you." In addition to the rage about the disease itself, their rage about that [societal abandonment] was really overwhelming, and you can see them go through, "How dare they not take care of me." So when other people [in ACT UP] started broadening the agenda,[30] I think they felt like "Well, what does this have to do with *AIDS,* you know, what does this have to do with *me?*" (Barr 2002; my emphases)

Barr's analysis corroborates Thomas's: some people felt that if an issue had to do with AIDS, it had to do with *me,* and *only* if it had to do with *me* did it have to do with AIDS; therefore, because issues of racism, sexism, and poverty in the AIDS epidemic did not establish that link for the HIV-positive, white, middle-class men in the group, those concerns seemed to some to be "not about AIDS." As Barr said, those were AIDS issues, but getting people who feared betrayal as well as death to see that focusing on those issues would not detract from *their* issues required addressing people's fears, and "that process didn't happen" (Barr 2002; my emphasis).

---

30. Again, I believe the notion that some in ACT UP/NY wanted to "broaden the agenda" is a misperception; I do agree, though, that many in the movement *felt* that ACT UP was veering from what they saw as its original "drugs into bodies" mission.

Barr's comments indicate that white, male, middle-class privilege often motivated the "What does this have to do with AIDS" question, but more was involved. Also triggering that question about ACT UP's focus and priorities were gay men's rage about society's betrayal of them and their fear and desperation that ACT UP would abandon them too. Such feelings were constituent components of conflicts within ACT UP/ NY over racism and sexism and the organization's approach to fighting AIDS.

Because ACT UP fashioned itself as an AIDS movement that was fighting for all people with AIDS, people on the T&D side of the debates rarely argued that ACT UP should focus only on AIDS issues of most concern to white, gay men (who made up the majority of the organization). That argument was "politically incorrect" because it advocated that the movement put relatively privileged people with AIDS before other people with AIDS. The following letter to *TITA* from an anonymous "GWM" (gay white man) indicated irritation with what he construed as the "correct" line, as well as a willingness to buck it (although only anonymously). But his willingness and the content of his note perhaps also reveal the depth of some members' sentiments of having been betrayed by the movement's attention to AIDS issues among other populations: "Why is it that our discussions every Monday night are about children, women, prisoners, people of color, etc. with AIDS, yet the announcements of deaths of ACT UP members are, like the majority of ACT UP members, usually Gay White Males?" (*TITA*, July 15, 1991). His letter reminds us that ACT UP members were continuing to die, and that surely influenced the debates within ACT UP about its focus and direction. But the desperation felt by "GWM" and others was hard for other ACT UP members to attend to because it was articulated without acknowledging that, as a response from member Candido Negron to "GWM" put it, "African-Americans, Latinas/os, Asian and Pacific Islanders, we are all fighting AIDS, and we are also dying of AIDS" (*TITA*, July 29, 1991, 2).

Like other instances of moralism, the rhetoric about HIV-negative people hijacking the movement produced shame and indignation, unraveled sentiments of solidarity, and sowed divisiveness. Marion Banzhaf recalls feeling silenced when others would ask "What does this have to do with AIDS?" or assert that people with AIDS were dying while ACT UP was being diverted by battles against racism and sexism.

I mean it did shut you up. It shut me up for awhile. Sometimes I would say, "Well, but other people [with AIDS] are dying and they aren't in this room and so that's why I'm talking about racism and sexism." If I was feeling particularly feisty I would make a comeback like that. Otherwise you would just sort of hope that the facilitator would move the discussion along. And it couldn't be criticized exactly. You couldn't say, "Wait a second, let's do a hand count and see the difference between how many people are positive and negative here, and let's talk about the HIV-negative people's contributions to fighting AIDS. We shouldn't be made to feel bad that we are HIV negative." (Banzhaf 2002; see also *TITA*, April 15, 1991)

Accused of betraying HIV-positives, HIV-negative members of ACT UP felt misunderstood and unrecognized as committed AIDS activists. How could one reply sensitively to assertions that HIV-negative people were trying to build a social justice movement on the graves of gay men with AIDS? Rational responses that refuted the claim risked ignoring the feelings of betrayal that HIV-positive people articulated. Any refutation by someone who was HIV-negative could easily be heard as callous. And HIV-negative people who did feel guilt about their negative status may have felt that the accusation contained a grain of truth, insofar as they did indeed want to live out their lives in a more just world. Any sentiments of guilt, then, may have made it difficult to engage the accusation that they were trying to change the world and people with AIDS didn't have that kind of time. Indignation at the accusation was surely easier to feel than the more painfully self-critical guilt; guilt, then, might have been displaced into anger toward their accusers.

Moralism

Moralism was the emotional idiom of both sides in ACT UP's later internal conflicts, and it unquestionably intensified those conflicts, further unraveled feelings of solidarity, and contributed to the demise of the movement. Critical discussions of political moralism sometimes fail to illuminate the political struggles surrounding its emergence. I have tried to counter that tendency, drawing from evidence indicating how the emotional undercurrents of ACT UP's conflicts—feelings of being unrecognized, disrespected, and betrayed, and of resentment, mistrust and anger—created a fertile terrain for shaming and guilt-tripping.

In this section I explore the workings of moralism, the dynamics it sets in motion, and its potential effects in an activist context. I also analyze why it seemed to be a legitimate rhetorical register.

The Workings and Effects of Moralism

The structure of moralizing rhetoric within a social movement can unravel sentiments of solidarity or further such unraveling. How does this work? A moralizing claim always implicitly (and sometimes explicitly) poses the question: How could you? That is, it asks rhetorically, What kind of person are you that you could do such a thing or be such a way? Such a question often implies that your very being, your *essence,* is shameful. Political moralizing, a subgenre of more general moralizing, suggests a belief that a person's political attitudes and actions reveal one's true self: through your politics, you expose yourself as either a righteous human being or something less than that. The accuser need not actually believe the accusation for it to have shaming effects; it is enough for the accused to feel humiliated or embarrassed. Being shamed exposes one's failings not only to the other person, but to oneself as well, potentially forcing a process of self-questioning. When "successful," shaming can obliterate one's previous sense of self, replacing it with a sense of being disgraceful, reprehensible, dishonorable, in a word: bad. In this case, the response to the rhetorical question "How could you?" is "You're right, how could I?"

Common bodily manifestations of shame—described by Silvan Tomkins as dropping one's head and eyes and turning away from the one who has shamed you (Sedgwick and Frank 1995, 74 and chap. 6)—indicate that it can be hard to face whoever shamed you, making difficult any subsequent positive relationship. It is also difficult to face *yourself,* and rather than submitting to shame, one psychic response is to disavow the feeling and even turn it back on the shamer, attempting to shame him or her in return. As queer theorist Michael Warner argues, the usual response to shame is to "pin it on someone else" (1999, 3). Here, rather than acceding to the shame, the response to the question "How *could* you?" is an indignant and reproachful "How could *you*?" This dynamic of reciprocal recriminations describes what happened among the different factions within ACT UP.

A dynamic of responding to moralism with further moralism makes dialogue across political differences extremely unlikely. When each side

in a conflict presents its own position as morally superior, acknowledgement of other perspectives is blocked, effectively shutting down discussion. Even if you disagree with your critic's appraisal, how can you work
with someone who seems to see you as essentially and irredeemably
bad? And if you actually are shamed by your critic's reproaches, how do
you then engage with that person, with someone who has exposed your
shamefulness? Or, to shift the question slightly, how can you work with
someone whom *you* think is essentially and irredeemably bad or whom
you've leveled such charges against, whether you actually believe them
or not? The evidence indicates that in ACT UP, moralizing foreclosed
principled engagement with one another that might have addressed the
injuries that each side felt.

The Feelings of Fixed Identities

Wendy Brown argues that "contemporary political moralism tends to
conflate persons with beliefs in completely nonvoluntaristic fashion: persons are equated with subject positions, which are equated with identities, which are equated with certain perspectives and values" (Brown
2001, 38). That sort of conflation occurred in ACT UP. Both sides in
the conflicts assumed that women and people of color in the movement identified as such and thus were concerned about AIDS among
women and people of color, and that white, gay men identified as such
and thus were concerned about AIDS among white, gay men. Assuming that physical attributes translated into an identity, which translated
into a predictable set of identifications and politics proved to be divisive
in at least two ways. First, individuals whose identifications and politics
seemed to defy their identity category were seen as exceptions, and
sometimes suspected of "false consciousness" and betrayal of "their
people." Second, the assumption simultaneously presumed a connection
between specific identities and specific *disaffinities* or *disaffections*—the
absence of good feelings toward or concern about particular groups. So,
for example, shaming discourses from one side assumed that women and
people of color in ACT UP not only cared about AIDS as it affected
those populations, but that they did so *to the neglect* of white, gay men;
and if you were a white, gay man, especially if you were HIV-positive,
you were assumed to be racist and sexist, only concerned about getting
AIDS drugs into your body and the bodies of your similarly-situated
friends, and liable to sell out other people with AIDS. Even though

many people diverged from the simplistic and divisive schema that su-
tured together identities, identifications, disaffections, and politics, the
perceived linkage created immense distrust across lines of race, gender,
and HIV status.

As I discussed earlier, those identity categories initially were *not* salient markers of division within ACT UP. They became contentious only
as desperation about the enormity of the crisis and a resulting scarcity
mentality took hold. That changed affective landscape provoked the
emergence, in Crimp's words, of "competing identities," contributing to a
growing factionalization, particularly when activists presented identities
as fixed rather than fluid (1992, 14, 16). When Ferd Eggan tried to form
a PISD Caucus in ACT UP/Chicago at the start of 1989, no other people
with HIV/AIDS in the group were interested (Edwards 2000a). A caucus of people with HIV/AIDS formed only in the late summer of 1990, at
the height of ACT UP/Chicago's conflicts, when fixed identities became
an important means for challenging critics and bolstering one's own position in ACT UP's debates. Feelings of desperation produced different
urgencies among different groups of activists who used their identities
to drive home their particular urgency and to question other activists'
commitment to particular populations of people with AIDS. As Jeanne
Kracher recalls, the conflicts polarized quite frequently around "who
had more at stake in the room" (Kracher 2000).

Crimp does not elaborate on the feeling states underlying the identity
politics that took hold in ACT UP, but he does indicate a growing rancor, noting that the fixing of identities created an "impasse of ranking
oppressions, moralism, and self-righteousness" (1992, 16). I agree, and in
discussing conflicts in Chicago and New York, I have argued that to understand *why* different groups within ACT UP began to invoke identity
categories in sometimes rigid, divisive, and moralizing ways requires understanding the emotional undercurrents of the conflicts, in particular
the feelings of betrayal that both sides felt.

How to Be an AIDS Activist

Moralizing occurred through each side's insinuations that its opponents
were violating one or both of ACT UP's most sacred principles: that ACT
UP was a movement to "fight AIDS," and that the movement should be
led by people with HIV/AIDS. In this period, everybody in the movement seemed to feel some pressure to profess an identification with peo-

ple with HIV/AIDS. Contrast that with ACT UP's early years, when no one had had to declare their solidarity because it was assumed that if you were in ACT UP, whatever your HIV status, you cared deeply about people with HIV/AIDS. That assumption eventually was replaced by a series of litmus tests: if you did not agree with a specific committee, or caucus, or individual, if you did not support a specific action or proposal, then you obviously did not support people with AIDS. Both sides in ACT UP's conflicts upheld the same image of the ideal AIDS activist—utterly committed to *all* people with HIV/AIDS and to fighting the AIDS crisis—but each construed its side alone as embodying that ideal and thereby as being the true guardian of ACT UP's principles.

As Goffman notes in his discussion of identity performance, "to *be* a given kind of person . . . is not merely to possess the required attributes, but also to sustain the standards of conduct and appearance that one's social group attaches thereto" (1959, 75; his emphasis). Whereas in ACT UP's earlier years, membership in ACT UP provided one with an AIDS activist identity, and members assumed that everyone held ACT UP's core values, in ACT UP's later years that assumption crumbled. Self-fashioning became an important part of the conflicts as people worked to express their values and commitments. Each side's self-fashioning, however, simultaneously acted as an accusation. Put another way, moralizing was an available register in which to "enact the self" (Brown 2001, 23) and thereby "prove" one's own commitment to ACT UP's principles and challenge one's opponents.[31] Each side accused the other of forsaking some people with AIDS, and, given the sacred status of ACT UP's principles, to be accused of breaching any one of them was shaming. People did not necessarily end up feeling ashamed—they might have felt indignation at being shamed instead—but they were susceptible because no one wanted to be seen as violating ACT UP's core values.

ACT UP members held other principles that had important political content but also sometimes took on a moralizing tenor. Many participants, for example, determinedly and patiently drew attention to the ways that racism was affecting the AIDS epidemic and demanded that the movement deal with its own racism. Their more leftist perspective had a good deal of legitimacy within ACT UP and succeeded in creat-

31. For another example of enactment of the self through moralizing, see Mansbridge 1983, 152–55.

ing a context in which many white members educated themselves about racism and looked critically at their own racial privilege.[32] But commitments to antiracism sometimes became a tool for shaming others in the movement for not being antiracist enough or, worse, for being racist.

Of course, in some contexts simply raising issues of racism may seem to be moralizing. Whatever one's tone and intention, challenging whites to consider how they are actively working to erode their own privileged position in society might provoke or amplify already existing "white liberal guilt"—that is, whites' guilt about racism (and fears of appearing racist), along with resentment at being made to feel guilty about historical and contemporary events in which they may have had no part. That might have been especially true in the early 1990s when cultural conservatives were waging a campaign against what they called "PC" (political correctness), and fiscal conservatives were attacking social programs like welfare in their efforts to turn back the liberal-interventionist state (Edwards 2000b). The right's anti-PC campaign did have that sort of effect within the broader lesbian and gay community and within ACT UP. Many people felt resentful when issues of racism were raised, regardless of the tone of the discussion.[33] Allan Robinson, a member of the Majority Action Committee, heard something that suggested such dynamics were in play in ACT UP/NY:

> I heard a story about the first time I came to sit on the Steering Committee (the ultimate decision-making authority of ACT UP.) One of the most prominent members of that organization, a white man, who sits on that committee, said, "I'm not about to allow him to come here and have us feel guilty for 400 years of what he has experienced." I suppose that's what he saw me as, and the only thing I was bringing there. (Hunter 1993, 60–61)

ACT UP/Chicago member Darrell Gordon recalls that when discussions were raised about women and AIDS and about sexism within the movement, many men "became defensive and saw this as attacking them as men" (Gordon 2000). That was true regardless of the tone.

32. ACT UP was a crucial site for my own political awakening, and the antiracist, anti-imperialist politics of my closest friends and comrades in the movement greatly influenced me.

33. Edwards (2000b) provides a compelling account of how this broader political context penetrated the lesbian and gay community, spurring attacks on ACT UP from gay journalists as well as intensifying ACT UP's internal conflicts.

On Shame and Shaming

Queer theorist Judith Halberstam suggests that what I am calling moralism can, at times, have positive political effects. In a discussion that criticizes what she terms "white gay male identity politics," Halberstam argues that "we cannot completely do without shame" insofar as "shame can be a powerful tactic in the struggle to make privilege (whiteness, masculinity, wealth) visible" (Halberstam 2005, 220). There is some slippage in Halberstam's usage of *shame* here. At times she could be read as saying that we cannot do without shame *as an affect or feeling* insofar as it can force one who feels it to acknowledge one's privilege and to take on the responsibilities that such an acknowledgment generates. But in noting shame as a powerful *tactic,* she seems to shift its meaning from the feeling of shame to the process of *shaming* as a means for eliciting shame in those who then might become aware of their privilege. I am not sure which of the two Halberstam thinks we cannot do without. If shame, then I agree, and for exactly the reason that Halberstam offers. Shame may be a primary affective motivator for relatively privileged activists who target the social hierarchy that privileges them; shame, in that sense, does seem indispensable. But I am less convinced that we cannot do without shaming, understood as a means of eliciting shame through moral righteousness and judgementalism.

Do shame and shaming require one another, or might it be possible to retain one and dispense with the other? Shame, it seems to me, does not require shaming: a critical and impassioned but nonmoralizing discussion about racism might, through its educative effects, flood a white person with shame about her ignorance, about her complicity in structures of racism, about her previously unacknowledged white privilege. Here, in the absence of shaming, the feeling of shame itself might elicit a positive political effect—she might be de-centered, for example, suddenly mindful that her own reality perhaps is worlds apart from that of others. But, while shaming *can* evoke shame, and potentially political learning, it does not always succeed in doing so. The shaming in ACT UP might simply have made people feel resentful and angry about being shamed. Consider, for example, the comments of Bill Struzenberg, someone who left ACT UP/San Francisco to help found ACT UP/Golden Gate as an organization that would be "geared less to the 'isms' [i.e., issues of racism and sexism] and more to treatment issues." Noting that he personally prioritized finding a cure for AIDS over issues of "morality," Struzenberg stated, "I'd rather be tainted and alive than politically correct and dead" (Pepper 1990, 13). He indicated his sense that others had tried to shame him, perhaps about his white and male privilege, but rather than feeling ashamed, he simply dismissed other activists' concerns. Shaming might make someone so ashamed of his racism that he commits to fighting racism in a more active way; but it can also shut down discussion and lead to resentment rather than solidarity.

The shaming that occurred within ACT UP had that sort of negative effect. ACT UP's sacred principles regarding AIDS activism and people with AIDS, along with the feminism and antiracism of some members, created strong, if sometimes competing, ideas about how one must be to be an AIDS activist. People struggled with one another over these values, and a great deal of political growth—of unlearning and learning—occurred. But people shut down and stopped listening to one another when the rhetorical register became infused with the shaming and guilt-tripping that characterize moralism. Insofar as ACT UP members understood themselves to be progressive and compassionate, charges of being racist, sexist, and selfish, or, alternatively, of being opportunist, disloyal, and uncaring toward people with AIDS, trafficked in shame and guilt and impugned one's ethical being. Whatever feeling states were actually evoked, the moralizing rhetoric further unraveled sentiments of solidarity.

Moralism versus Political Dialogue

Even as I highlight the important role of moralizing in ACT UP's conflicts, we need to keep in mind the significant political differences at the center of these conflicts. That is, the whole of the conflicts cannot be reduced to the moralizing tone in which they sometimes were conducted. Sexism and racism, for example, were real problems in the movement, manifested in how people treated one another as well as in accusations that ACT UP was "getting off track" whenever the focus turned to issues like AIDS in women or in communities of color. There were power differences as well with regard to access to the federal AIDS bureaucracy (at least within ACT UP/NY). Add fear to this already combustible mix—fear of death and fear among gay men that ACT UP might abandon them—and we get a sense not only of the depth of the political differences regarding ACT UP's focus and direction, but of the stakes as well.

The political conflicts, then, were certainly substantive; members of the different sides had divergent analyses of the AIDS crisis and of how best to fight it. But as the discussion makes clear, political conflicts in movements are seldom only about divergent political analyses. More than tactical or strategic disagreements, political conflicts within a movement often revolve around the complex feelings evoked by the different positions of members within the movement and within society. Whether real or perceived, such differences can generate resentment, anger, guilt, hatred, fear of betrayal, and fear of loss of power and recognition. Left unaddressed, those feelings can prompt a turn to moralizing.

Political issues such as different access to resources or other power differentials within an organization cannot be addressed head-on when they are cast in moral terms. In the words of social theorist Peter Lyman, "As long as anger resolves its accusation through moralizing the world, it prevents the recovery of the history of the relation of domination, the nature of the violation, and thus the possibility of political analysis and action" (Lyman 1981, 70). Anger itself is not the problem, and, to be sure, people in ACT UP had many reasons to be angry at one another. The problem arose when anger was channeled into moralism rather than political debate. Any political solution to the conflicts became unlikely as both sides began to suspect that their potential interlocutors were irredeemably bad. Rather than engaging in dialogue to address people's feelings and real political disputes, each side in ACT UP's conflicts, convinced of its own righteousness, or at least presenting itself as such, dug in its heels. Each side retrenched indignantly, unwilling to acknowledge that the criticisms leveled against it might hold some truth or, in any case, needed to be addressed in a manner that would allow for continuing engagement with one another.

More important, the affects and feelings that had sparked the moralizing in the first place and that were at the core of ACT UP's political conflicts remained unacknowledged and unaddressed but nevertheless a powerful force in the conflicts. The sense of having been betrayed by one's alleged comrades, of one's activist work going unrecognized, of mistrust and anger toward fellow activists, together blocked compassion and unraveled sentiments of solidarity that most had once felt. The force of those bad feelings may have been particularly strong in light of the euphoria of the previously felt solidarity. The bad feelings certainly made us unwilling or, more accurately, simply unable to empathize. Moralizing displaced other sorts of conversations, about how best to fight AIDS, for example, and about what people in the movement were feeling about each other and about the AIDS crisis. ACT UP chapters became factionalized, with each side demonizing the other, personalizing and polarizing what otherwise might have been difficult, but navigable, political conflicts.

Political conflicts derive not only from divergent interests and identifications, but also from the affective dimensions of those interests and identifications and of the sense that they might be thwarted. The emotional undercurrents of ACT UP's internal conflicts were a constitutive component of those conflicts; if no one in ACT UP had feared betrayal or felt unrecognized, for example, the conflicts would have had an entirely different character and different effects on the movement, if they had existed at all. Unacknowledged and unaddressed sentiments of betrayal, nonrecognition, and mistrust spurred the embrace of a moralistic rhetorical register, and that entire matrix of affects and emotions decisively shaped ACT UP's conflicts, intensifying them in a manner that helped to fracture the movement.

The Non-Inevitability of Moralizing

Passionate, even angry, political conflicts within social movements are not inevitably carried out in a moralizing register. I mention this because the acrimony of ACT UP's conflicts indicates the difficulty of raising problems like sexism, racism, and feelings of marginalization in an organization without trafficking in shame. Because so many conflicts in progressive movements revolve around precisely such issues, I want to provide a counterexample to show that it is possible to confront such issues without shaming and guilt-tripping. At the beginning of 1990, ACT UP/NY's Majority Action Committee (MAC) wrote a memo to ACT UP. It began by claiming that recently there had been "an increasingly alarming pattern of culturally insensitive comments and actions by various members of our organization, ACT UP." It continued, "This pattern has called into question whether the AIDS Coalition To Unleash Power really does (or intends to) represent all persons affected by the HIV epidemic. (Note: 65% of persons with HIV illness are people of color.)" MAC then noted that ACT UP had missed an opportunity to build alliances with communities of color during the nomination process for New York's prospective health commissioner, Dr. Woody Myers, an African American. MAC continued,

Unfortunately, a few members of ACT UP chose to express their very legitimate opposition [to the nomination of Dr. Myers] in a manner that antagonized the communities of color involved in the decision process. Furthermore, they neglected to seek the input of MAC members regarding the possible ramifications of their actions. These actions proved divisive and led to internal turmoil along racial lines. This could have been avoided easily by communicating with persons from MAC and other AIDS activists in communities of color. In the future it is vitally important that we keep lines of communication open and MAKE USE OF THEM. (ACT UP/NY Majority Actions Committee 1990; capitalization in original)

The memo concluded, "Fight Back, Fight AIDS, Not Each Other," a twist on ACT UP's slogan, "ACT UP, Fight Back, Fight AIDS."

While insistent and forceful, the tone of MAC's memo steered clear of hostile personal attacks and moralizing. MAC certainly took ACT UP/NY to task, but did so in a straightforward manner. It seemingly did not pull any punches; indeed, MAC raised its own marginalization within ACT UP/NY, and called for that problem to be rectified. Still, it avoided personalizing the issue as well as any suggestion that MAC members were morally superior. It insisted that lines of communication should be opened and utilized, something that a moralistic accusation rarely suggests. It included no insinuations that ACT UP as a whole, or even specific members, were essentially and irredeemably racist. To the contrary, the memo explicitly argued for unity and against attacking one another ("Fight AIDS, Not Each Other"). The memo conveyed both MAC's agreement with the critique by other ACT UP/NY members of Woody Myers,[34] as well as MAC's desire to continue as part of ACT UP. Finally, the memo suggested practical ways to improve internal relations and move forward. In a context where moralizing rhetoric was beginning to take hold, MAC's memo may have been read differently than I have read it here, but it serves as an instance of engagement in political con-

---

34. Political scientist Cathy Cohen provides useful background information to ACT UP's opposition to Myers and to MAC's statement: "Many AIDS activists condemned the appointment of Myers who, while Indiana Health Commissioner, supported not only the recording of names of those infected with HIV so their sex partners could be traced, but also the quarantining of those with AIDS who 'knowingly' spread the disease. Black officials, however, defended Myers's appointment because they considered him to be one of the outstanding *black* doctors in the country. It was thought that his policies would enhance the condition of the black community; thus his seemingly conservative or reactionary positions about AIDS were to be tolerated" (Cohen 1999, 336; her emphasis).

flict about sensitive, complicated issues that did not traffic in shaming or guilt-tripping.

Why Moralism, Why Then?

Aspects of ACT UP's character as well as its context produced moralizing rhetoric as a legible and legitimate political idiom. In terms of its character, shaming, of course, was a political strategy that ACT UP used against its opponents and as such was a familiar and readily available style of political oratory.[35]

Aspects of the context in which ACT UP was operating also made moralizing an available and legitimate rhetorical register. Brown argues that righteous moralism is "the characteristic political discourse of our time," indeed "a hegemonic form of political expression" in this period of history (Brown 2001, 21, 29). Brown notes that moralism's "tiresome tonality and uninspiring spirit" is characteristic of the discourse of the right, center, and left, but her main concern is moralism among leftists (with liberals thrown in) insofar as righteous moralism has become "particularly intense in left activist and academic life" in contemporary North America (21–22). She contends that moralism is "a *symptom* of a certain kind of loss," specifically, that entailed by shattered aspirations for a more humane and egalitarian world in the face of the collapse of alternatives to capitalism and liberalism and the ubiquity of capitalist and liberal institutions not only in the present but in the future as well (18–21; her emphasis). Leftists, she argues, remain attached to "total critique and total transformation" of liberal capitalist society, even though "the historical ground and political and philosophical foundations of that critique and that project have been compromised beyond recognition" (18, 21). Similarly, liberals remain attached to Enlightenment notions of universalism and progress even in the face of theoretical and political challenges that have called both into question (20–21).

---

35. Three important differences exist between the shaming that ACT UP engaged in as a movement and the shaming that occurred inside ACT UP during its conflicts: one is that externally directed shaming, even when against an individual, usually was a critique of the institution that person represented, while internal shaming was almost always intensely personal, directed at specific individuals and others in the same identity category. Second, shaming of institutions had an object—a change in policy—whereas internal shaming had no such clear objective. Third, the internal shaming brought rancor and animosity into a context that once had experienced a high degree of camaraderie, a sentiment that was nonexistent in ACT UP's relations with those it targeted as enemies in the fight against AIDS.

"The consequence of living these attachments as ungrievable losses—
ungrievable because they are not fully avowed as attachments and hence
are unable to be claimed as losses—is theoretical as well as political im-
potence and rage, which is often expressed as a reproachful political
moralism" (21).

I find Brown's account too dismissive of the left, and I also think she
fails to consider affective states other than melancholia that can give rise
to moralism on the left,[36] but two aspects of her argument seem particularly relevant for thinking about why moralism arose in ACT UP. One is
her Nietzschean point about the association between the experience of
impotent rage and the adoption of a moralizing rhetorical register. The
feelings of despair and desperation coursing through ACT UP in this period were a version of impotent rage, and they did lead to moralism. The
second is Brown's contention that moralism has become the "dominant
political sensibility" (29) in this historical period. Moralism has become
a readily available rhetorical register that one might adopt regardless of
one's own relationship to the ungrievable losses at the heart of Brown's
argument.[37]

36. Sociologist Rebecca Klatch (2004) suggests that judgementalism and guilt-
tripping—forms of moralism—had a devastating impact on Students for a Democratic Society in the 1960s, long before the fall of the Berlin Wall and the crisis facing the left in the
1990s.

37. Even as I find Brown's essay enormously useful, I have two additional disagreements. First, at points Brown seems to see reason and feeling as antithetical and to want to
evacuate some feelings from activism, particularly impassioned feelings regarding social,
political, and economic subordination. For example, she contrasts "the compulsive quality of moralism"—in its addiction to moralizing—with a notion of activism that she seems
to favor: "measured, difficult, and deliberate action that implicates rather than simply enacts the self" (2001, 23). From Brown's perspective, a turn toward moralism can never be
measured or spurred through deliberation, and activism should entail such qualities of
reasoning and not, implicitly, be influenced by heightened passions that Brown suggests
interfere with reason. I disagree that moralism is so unthinking, that passion necessarily
interferes with reason, or that impassioned feelings can or should be evacuated from activism. Second, Brown participates in a widespread disparagement of leftist activists when
she caricatures them as "naive" and "confused" (36) about how the state and mainstream
institutions operate. She argues, for example, that activists who condemned the NIH for
not treating the lives of gay men, prostitutes, and drug users with HIV as a political priority failed to understand that the state has specific political and economic investments and
that it is the codification of various dominant social powers. In deriding activists here—and
specifically ACT UP, which she does not name—Brown misconstrues their strategic thinking and glosses over their successes. Could it be that activists know perfectly well how
power works but moralize against the state's failures to live up to its rhetorics of citizenship
and inclusion as a strategic means of forcing its hand? And, why does Brown fail to mention ACT UP's tremendous successes at the NIH, which, by allowing activists and people

We can also understand some ACT UP members' moralism in terms of the general political climate in the United States in the early 1990s, which was dominated by the "culture wars" and the right's attacks against multiculturalism and "political correctness." This phase of the longer-term reaction against the social movements of the 1960s and early 1970s was characterized by immense resentment among some white men, often those in economically precarious situations, toward people of color and women for the "special rights" they allegedly were receiving in response to discrimination. As part of their anti-PC campaign, the right attacked affirmative action as "reverse discrimination." They depicted university and college campuses as overrun by "tenured radicals" and liberal "thought police" who were politicizing the classroom. People questioning ongoing inequalities in society were accused of being divisive and anti-American and were written off as extremists. The very label "PC" became a way to trivialize concerns about ongoing racism and sexism in society and to disregard those raising such concerns. Those attacking "PC" never substantiated their claims, but their allegations circulated widely. In the face of a hostile context where concrete gains from the 1960s and 1970s were being rolled back, and in the face of that sort of nonrecognition—being told that neither you nor your concerns matter—feminists and antiracists fought back. But there was an increasing sense of being under siege and of powerlessness; in that context, some turned to moralism. Moralism, of course, was only one register in which feminist and antiracist politics were taken up in this period, but it became more common, as Brown argues, especially in leftist academic circles.

More specific to ACT UP's context, the "PC Wars" occurred in lesbian and gay communities as well, launched by a few white, gay, male journalists and other writers (Edwards 2000b, 502–3). These writers created a perception that "political correctness" had taken over the lesbian and gay movement, and ACT UP as well. In articles with a distinctly antifeminist bent, lesbians were accused of putting concerns about racism and sexism before concerns specific to the lesbian and gay commu-

---

with AIDS to help set research priorities and design clinical drug trials, undoubtedly have prolonged millions of people's lives and helped to, in Steve Epstein's words (1991, 1996), "democratize" the workings of science? With such dramatic and life-saving successes in mind, one has to wonder how Brown can substantiate her claim that activism targeting the NIH was merely "gestural" and even "regressive" (36). As Lisa Duggan has written, Brown adopts a "pedagogical mode laced with a tone of admonishment, and even sometimes contempt" in addressing leftist activists (Duggan 2003, 79–80).

nity.[38] In that charged context, when lesbians in ACT UP raised issues about the role of racism and sexism in the AIDS crisis, their comments were easily, if erroneously, read as suggesting disdain for the concerns of white gay men with AIDS. (Although gay men sometimes raised similar issues, their commitment to gay men usually was not questioned, suggesting the important role that ideas about identities and identifications were playing in the conflicts during this period.) This context created fertile terrain for moralizing on both sides.

The mutual recriminations in ACT UP substantiate a point that Eve Sedgwick has made about the importance of understanding the dynamics of shame, which she sees as deriving from the experience of nonrecognition, for making sense of things like "trashing" in political organizations: "Can anyone suppose that we'll ever figure out what happened around political correctness if we don't see it as, among other things, a highly politicized chain reaction of shame dynamics?" (Sedgwick 2003, 64). Both sides in ACT UP's conflicts, each feeling unrecognized by the other, turned to moralism—with accusations of impurity, violation of ACT UP's sacred principles, and other forms of being "incorrect"—as a way to deal with those feelings.

Finally, of immense importance in this context was the growing despair in ACT UP. Many of us really had thought that we were going to be able to stop AIDS, and to save the lives of people with AIDS, but the ever-increasing number of deaths, especially within the movement, pointed to our inability to stop the dying. Moralizing may find particularly fertile ground in a moment of impasse, when activists are politically depressed and grasping for explanations about why their efforts seem futile. Blaming can easily morph into shaming.

Conflicts and Desperation

The relationship between the growing despair and desperation and ACT UP's conflicts was complex. Despair fueled the conflicts: with people continuing to die all around us, and at an increasing rate, many in ACT UP felt that we were not doing enough, and some looked at the movement itself to try to figure out what obstacles were standing in our way.

38. See, for example, Wockner 1990c, 1991a, 1992a, and especially 1992c. See also Shilts 1991.

The obstacles were not primarily in the room, but in desperation we looked there anyway and blamed one another for our inability to stop the dying. People in the movement recognized this connection between despair and the conflicts. ACT UP/NY member Andrew Velez, for example, wrote an open letter to ACT UP, explaining why he opposed the moratorium proposal, but in it he tried to reconcile the two sides by pointing toward despair and desperation as the culprits:

> This is a difficult time for us in the fight against AIDS. So many of our friends have died in just the past few weeks, and so many others are struggling to stay alive. The news about drugs, treatments and funding is very discouraging. The government, and our society in general remain essentially ignorant and indifferent to what is going on. We cannot permit that to cause us in our despair to turn on and decimate one another. (Velez 1991)

The conflicts were also a defense against despair. Not only might anger toward others in the movement be easier to feel than despair, it also might allow one to fend off despair. Rather than falling into hopelessness, one could hold on to the possibility that there really might be something ACT UP could do that would save lives, *if only* one's comrades would get in line, *if only* HIV-negatives would "get out of the way." That "if only," then, was not simply an angry accusation, it was also a form of conditional thinking that warded off despair.

The context of despair made the internal conflicts simply unendurable for many in the movement. ACT UP/NY member Risa Denenberg sees ACT UP's decline as in part attributable to their conjunction: "The conflict that came up in ACT UP is part of the reason that ACT UP is not a viable organization right now. Just in the experience of so many people dying, so much loss, and all of our collective bereavement, the conflict just was unbearable" (Denenberg 1993).

Reflecting on ACT UP/Chicago's conflicts, Ferd Eggan noted the despair of people with AIDS in particular, and the inability of all of us to address their despair and accompanying rage. He wished he had been able to recognize "the rage that comes from having to pre-mourn your own death" and speak it aloud, by saying to Danny Sotomayor, for example, "Look, your problem isn't that . . . the demonstration isn't going the way you want, or this that or the other. The problem is you have AIDS, you're gonna die, and you're unhappy. And there's nothing we can do about that. You know, we can't demonstrate you out of dying; we can't do anything about it, because it's just what's happening." In retrospect, Eggan said, "I know I wish that I had known and understood and been able to confront that" (Eggan 1999).

Exhausted, frustrated, desperate, overwhelmed—of course we were unable to address the emotional undercurrents that were shaping the substance, velocity, and intensity of ACT UP's conflicts. The historian in me, however, wants to emphasize that the fracturing of solidarity in ACT UP was never inevitable. It may be that *assuming* solidarity in the early years—an assumption that derived in part from our shared anger— prevented us from doing more trust-building work in those years. ACT UP's emotional habitus provided us with a pedagogy for some feelings, especially emotions oriented toward taking action such as anger. But it did not provide much instruction—beyond anger—for dealing with feelings of betrayal and nonrecognition by one's comrades, or for the feelings of rage that Eggan describes above. Anger was one of our primary idioms, and we turned it against ourselves in a manner that made it difficult to work with one another. Largely unacknowledged, feelings of rage, fear, betrayal, nonrecognition, mistrust, and anger went unaddressed and took an enormous toll on individuals and on the movement. This is not about blaming the movement culture we built—a culture that served ACT UP well for many years—but to remind us that the unfolding of the conflicts was contingent. That is true of conflicts in all movements. Detailing the dynamics of ACT UP's internal conflicts can provide knowledge and insights that might allow current activists to address bad feelings that sometimes arise amid the action.

Despairing

Despair and Movement

D espair destroyed ACT UP. Other phenomena helped, as the previous two chapters indicate, but the despair generated by accumulating deaths in the early 1990s was immense, and its effects on the national direct-action AIDS movement cannot be overstated. There is no great surprise in pointing toward despair to explain ACT UP's decline. Scholars and activists alike tend to put movement and hope in one basket and demobilization and despair in another. And in the moment of ACT UP's decline, there was certainly reason to despair. Even amid striking victories, more and more ACT UP members were dying. The death toll was staggering. ACT UP/NY's meeting minutes from November 12, 1990, announce the deaths of three members during the previous week: Ray Navarro, Vito Russo, and Kevin Smith. Minutes from the meeting the following week announce the death of another member, Oliver Johnston. Minutes from a meeting the following month announce the death of Ortez Alderson, a member of both ACT UP/NY and ACT UP/ Chicago. Deaths in 1991 piled onto the deaths from 1990, and on and on it went. The deaths of our own were simply unrelenting in 1990, 1991, 1992, 1993, . . . even as our activism achieved enormous victories. There were times during the early 1990s when memorial services for ACT UP members were more frequent than ACT UP actions.

It is easy to presume that despair and its companion affective states (e.g., desperation, despondency, depression) hold no political potential, that they necessarily destroy movements, but that is not always the case.[1] Despair sometimes flattens political possibilities, exacerbating a sense of political inefficacy and hopelessness and generating apathy and withdrawal, but it also sometimes works to open new political horizons, alternative visions of what is to be done and how to do it.[2] The period when the direct-action AIDS movement emerged illustrates the latter; the period of its decline illustrates how despair and its companions sometimes do paralyze and demobilize. We need to explore why and under what conditions despair and its companions have the one effect rather than the other. Those engaged in fighting for a more just, equitable, and joyous world have an urgent need to reckon with the pervasiveness of feelings of powerlessness, political inefficacy, apathy, and despair, and to explore how such sentiments influence struggles for social change.

This chapter continues the discussion of activists' emotion work. All of the emotion work that AIDS activists engaged in—including harnessing grief to anger, elevating pride about being queer and in the streets, rerouting gay shame—was crucial for ACT UP's emergence and growth, but the emotional habitus that we generated and that shaped our activism did not provide us with ways to deal with the despair that eventually took hold within the movement. Indeed, ACT UP's emotional habitus prohibited despair, and that made it difficult to deal with that bad feeling. That is not the only reason why despair took a toll. Given the course of the AIDS epidemic in the early 1990s and how overwhelming the despair was in that context, I am not sure whether efforts to deal with it would have lessened its destructive impact on the movement. But I explore the movement's ethos about and approach to despair in some detail because it allows us to see that the effects of despair are contingent, and not necessarily depoliticizing or demobilizing. In this case, in the years of ACT UP's decline, despair *was* depoliticizing and demobilizing. Whereas anger had been collectivizing, despair individualized. And it challenged and worked to unravel ACT UP's emotional habitus. The discussion, then, explores the role of despair in ACT UP's undoing and also allows us to consider alternative routes for despair.

1. For analyses that explore the generative and creative political potential of loss (of bodies, ideals, places), see *Loss,* edited by David Eng and David Kazanjian 2003. See also the work of Feel Tank Chicago: www.feeltankchicago.net.

2. Solnit 2004 makes a similar point.

I begin with a timeline of hope and despair in lesbian and gay communities with regard to AIDS, from the point when direct-action AIDS activism emerged until its decline. Most of the chapter analyzes how despair functioned within ACT UP, exploring its sources, its scope, its effects on individuals, and how and why it became a factor in the unraveling of the direct-action AIDS movement. At the end, I consider whether movements can respond to such bad feelings in ways other than by denying them or defending against them.

From Despair to Activism

Reconfiguring Desperation and Despair

The story begins in despair, in the second half of 1986, when the number of recorded AIDS cases was approximately 25,000 and the total number of known deaths from AIDS-related conditions was more than 15,000.[3] In 1981, the year marking the official start of the epidemic, about 250 people died from AIDS-related complications. By the time of the Supreme Court's *Bowers v. Hardwick* ruling in June 1986 and the emergence of direct-action AIDS groups in the weeks following, the number of deaths per year had surpassed 7,000, a 2,700 percent increase over the first year.[4] By January 1987, half a year later and just months before the founding of ACT UP/NY, the number of deaths per year was closer to 12,000.[5] When ACT UP/NY held its first meeting on March 12, 1987, the numbers of diagnoses and deaths per year were rising exponentially, and there were no FDA-approved drugs to treat AIDS.[6] The period prior to the emergence of direct-action AIDS activism, then, was a period of

3. Centers for Disease Control and Prevention (1986, 5). Because the number of cases and deaths in any given moment is not known precisely, the numbers in these reports are always estimates, and subsequent reports often show revised figures for earlier years. For example, in December 1986, the CDC had recorded about 15,000 deaths from January 1981 through June 1986; by December 1987, the number of deaths recorded for the same period was now almost 20,000 deaths (Centers for Disease Control and Prevention 1987, 5). In thinking about the effect on lesbian and gay communities of sheer numbers of deaths, both the 15,000 and the 20,000 figures are important, the former because it is the perceived number of deaths by June 1986 and the latter because it is closer to the actual number of deaths.

4. Centers for Disease Control and Prevention 1987, 5.

5. Centers for Disease Control and Prevention 1989, 17.

6. One week later, on March 19, 1987, the FDA announced that it had licensed the pharmaceutical company Burroughs Wellcome to produce AZT, the first antiviral (and

horror and growing despair, not only because of the deaths, but also because "legitimate" forms of activism like lobbying and holding candlelight vigils were not moving the government and scientific-medical establishment to an effective and compassionate response, yet anything more confrontational was beyond the political horizon for most AIDS and lesbian and gay activists. Lesbians' and gay men's powerlessness vis-à-vis all levels of government—and the dire consequences of that powerlessness—were clear. As thousands of gay and bisexual men died while the government aggressively ignored the epidemic, people became pessimistic about saving the lives of people with AIDS. A palpable desperation and despair took hold in lesbian and gay communities.

How did those feelings influence lesbian and gay political responses to AIDS? When we think about action born of despair or desperation, we tend to conjure up a negative image of people taking irrational risks and doing crazy and destructive, even self-destructive, things. But the ideological work performed by the negative connotations of the terms should not obscure the creativity that such feelings can induce. Desperate circumstances can inspire risk-taking, an abandonment of the tried and true (but evidently ineffective) path in order to strike out in new, untested directions. In this case, feelings of hopelessness and desperation, rather than foreclosing political activism, spurred lesbian and gay support for confrontational tactics that had long been abandoned by the mainstream, establishment-oriented gay movement. As Epstein contends, "One response to these difficult times was a rebirth of activism, epitomized by the actions of groups like ACT UP" (1996, 117). People's despair helped to wrench open the existing political horizon. Under the very specific conditions of the post-*Hardwick* moment, activists successfully reframed the political context, in effect tapping into, but then unraveling, sentiments of despondency and desperation about the AIDS crisis by offering street AIDS activism—oppositional, self-consciously confrontational, uncompromising, indecorous—as a legitimate and necessary route to save lives. Activists altered the affective experience of despair by coding it as "having nothing left to lose"; rather than paralyzing, despair became freeing. That activist work collectivized and politicized despair and directed it toward street-based AIDS activism. The desperation, despondency, and despair of this period helped to launch the movement.

highly toxic) AIDS therapy. Burroughs Wellcome set the price at $10,000 annually, making AZT the most expensive drug in history. See Crimp and Rolston (1990, 27–29).

With our retrospective knowledge of ACT UP's emergence, and
given a widespread view that hope is necessary to activism,[7] we might be
tempted to say that despair could not have been prevalent in lesbian and
gay communities in this period. Despair connotes utter hopelessness, a
sense that nothing can be done to change oppressive circumstances, and
thus cannot have been present in a moment of movement emergence; despairing people do not act up. I want to challenge this form of reasoning
not only because it is tautological but also because it fails to understand
the nonstatic, combinatory, and indeterminate nature of feelings and the
political dimensions of those qualities. *Nonstatic:* even feelings of complete hopelessness oscillate and change, sometimes due to a momentous
event, sometimes due to the engagements of everyday life—gathering
with people, having a conversation, viewing a work of art, reading history, listening to music, seeing graffiti on the street. *Combinatory:* feelings come bundled together; despair can coexist not only with grief and
sadness, as it did in ACT UP's later years, but also with anger, as it did
in the 1986–87 period. How it combines with other feeling states affects
its political potential. *Indeterminate:* feelings do not produce fixed effects; despair *can* demobilize, but it need not. The empirical record supports these claims: the evidence cited in chapters 1 and 2 indicates despair (as well as other feelings) prior to the *Bowers v. Hardwick* decision,
prompted by unending deaths, the lack of AIDS treatments, an indiffer-
ent, and often hostile, state and society. My insistence here is also political: despair is not the end of the story in an activist context: there is no
necessary connection between despair and demobilization; how activists
navigate that negative affective state matters. This example of the mobilizing potential of despair and the subsequent discussion of the role of
despair in ACT UP's demise can help us to think about the varied routes
that despair may take.

ACT UP's Antidote to Despair

From its start, ACT UP's activism—both because of its origins in despair
and its stunning effectiveness—provided an enormous sense of empowerment and political efficacy for participants; it brought some tremen-

---

7. Although Doug McAdam's notion of "cognitive liberation" is more oriented toward
thought and belief than feelings, the notion that in order to act people need to believe that
something is "both unjust and *subject to change*" (1999, 34; emphasis his) suggests that
hope or optimism is necessary to action. See also Aminzade and McAdam 2001, 31–32.

dous victories for people living with HIV/AIDS and people perceived to be at risk.

ACT UP/NY held its first action two weeks after it formed, on March 24, 1987.[8] Shutting down Wall Street, ACT UP targeted the FDA's slow drug-approval process as well as the profiteering of the drug company Burroughs Wellcome. Activists snarled traffic for several hours; they hung FDA Commissioner Frank Young in effigy. Seventeen people were arrested, and the demonstration made national news. Several weeks later, Commissioner Young announced that the FDA was going to speed up its drug-approval process. CBS News anchor Dan Rather attributed the change in FDA policy to ACT UP's demonstration (Crimp and Rolston 1990, 29). Members of ACT UP experienced this as an enormous victory that had the potential to get experimental, possibly life-prolonging, drug treatments to people with AIDS much more quickly. Corroborating that sense of victory, in December 1987, Burroughs Wellcome dropped the price of AZT by 20 percent.

The movement's actions were not always immediately successful, but even then, they fostered a sense of power and hope. For example, in January 1988, protesters with the AIDS Action Pledge (precursor to ACT UP/San Francisco) marched fifteen miles from San Francisco to Burroughs Wellcome's regional offices in Burlingame to demand a further reduction in the price of AZT. AIDS Action Pledge members scaled the building and hung two banners that read "End AIDS Profiteering" and "Burroughs Un-Wellcome." Nineteen activists were arrested. Although Burroughs Wellcome did not meet activist demands immediately, two people who had participated in the action wrote a letter to the *San Francisco Sentinel* claiming that "the hundreds of people who took part in some aspect of the protest came away feeling a sense of empowerment" (Sutton and Griffith 1988, 8).

News reporting of a C-FAR action at the headquarters of the pharmaceutical company Lyphomed in May 1988 suggests a similar effect. Demanding that Lyphomed reduce the price of its drug pentamidine, used to combat *Pneumocystis carinii* pneumonia (PCP), an opportunistic infection that was a leading killer of people infected with HIV, protesters used their bodies to create a cemetery on the corporation's front lawn. Ten were arrested. An article in the *Windy City Times* a few weeks

8. My account of this action is from ACT UP/NY n.d. a, 1; and Crimp and Rolston 1990, 27–29.

later quoted C-FAR members talking about their civil disobedience. Their action was not immediately successful, but everyone quoted indicated how empowered and effectual they felt as a result of participating in the action. One PWA stated,

> The demonstration brought out a strength in me I didn't know I had. An urge to fight back and make a difference. . . . A sense of love and support grew as we marched. We approached the Lyphomed plant, and the first thing I noticed was the line of riot police. I'd never experienced them before, and I proceeded with urgency in my heart and uncertainty about what would happen. But how powerful I am when I'm motivated from my beliefs and the rights of the gay and lesbian community! . . . And if asked if I would do it again, I'd say my feet are two steps in front of me. (Members of C-FAR 1988, 10)

Direct-action AIDS activism instilled in participants a sense of power and hope.

One of the most significant and successful actions held by the direct-action AIDS movement in its first years was on October 11, 1988, when one thousand AIDS activists from across the country shut down the FDA. The day of actions was sponsored by ACT NOW and organized by ACT NOW and ACT UP/NY. Demanding that the FDA expedite its drug-approval process, allow expanded access to drugs that had been deemed safe but were still undergoing trials for effectiveness, use markers other than placebos to test drug safety and efficacy, enroll people from all affected populations in drug trials, and include people with HIV/AIDS in the trial-review process, affinity groups staged actions throughout the nine-hour demonstration, literally closing down the building and stopping "business as usual" at the government agency. Throughout the day, groups of protesters blocked entrances (fig. 25), held die-ins, snuck into the building, hung President Reagan in effigy, stickered the building and hung banners from it, used street theater to dramatize the failures of the FDA and the Reagan administration, and blocked buses that were taking those arrested to jail.

The demonstration received massive media coverage and brought tremendous victories for people with AIDS and for the AIDS movement. Just one week after ACT NOW's shut-down, the FDA announced plans to speed the approval of drugs for the treatment of AIDS and other life-threatening diseases, cutting the testing time by as much as 50 percent ("Faster" 1988). Within the year, Dr. Anthony Fauci, director of NIAID,

FIGURE 25. A PISD affinity group action at the FDA demonstration, Rockville, MD, October 11, 1988. Photo by Rex Wockner.

announced his support for ACT UP's parallel-track idea, according to which patients unable or unwilling to enroll in an official clinical trial for a drug would still be able to receive the drug (Kolata 1989). The FDA had halved the time it took to approve most new drugs, and it began to make experimental drugs for life-threatening illnesses available before their effectiveness was established. The *Washington Post* declared that AIDS activists had "demanded a revolution" and won, successfully forcing a transformation in the way experimental drugs were being tested in the United States (Specter 1989, A1). Fauci said that a great deal of AIDS activists' criticism of AIDS drug trials "was absolutely valid" (A1). Suggesting just how great ACT UP's inroads into the scientific-medical establishment were, the *Post* reporter claimed that Fauci and FDA officials had begun to sound like "shadow spokesmen for groups like ACT UP" (A14). Fauci also threw his weight behind community-based drug trials as a way to speed up the research process and align it more explicitly with patient needs. The *Wall Street Journal* quoted a scientist who credited ACT UP with the changes in drug research and testing: "If people weren't sitting in at FDA, and chaining themselves to the wall of Burroughs Wellcome Co., none of this would be happening" (Chase 1989b, A12). Moreover, within a year of the ACT NOW shut-down of the FDA, researchers had "all but abandoned the use of

DESPAIRING 403

placebos . . . in drug trials," instead comparing new drugs against AZT (Garrison 1989, A8). By the summer of 1989, AIDS activists were regularly being invited to meetings at the FDA (A8).

Within a year, then, the scientific-medical establishment was addressing almost all of the demands that the national direct-action AIDS movement had issued at its FDA action. At the start of 1990, the *New York Times* quoted New York City Health Commissioner Dr. Stephen Joseph, who said that "there's no doubt that [ACT UP has] had an enormous effect. We've basically changed the way we make drugs available in the last year" (DeParle 1990, B1). It also quoted Fauci praising ACT UP for its parallel-track idea (B4).

In its first three years, the direct-action AIDS movement engaged in dozens of actions, many of which were similarly successful and empowering. During an NIH hearing in February, 1989, for example, ACT UP/NY protested the FDA's denial of access to an experimental drug— DHPG (ganciclovir)—for the treatment of an AIDS-related opportunistic infection, cytomegalovirus (CMV). As a result of the protest, the FDA made DHPG available under its "compassionate use" guidelines, and approved the drug for wider distribution three months later.[9] Another example was ACT UP's continuing campaign against Burroughs Wellcome. It already had succeeded in forcing Burroughs Wellcome to reduce the price of AZT by 20 percent. In April 1989, four ACT UP/NY members barricaded themselves inside a Burroughs Wellcome office in North Carolina, demanding another cut in the price of AZT. Five months later, seven ACT UP/NY members infiltrated the New York Stock Exchange, chained themselves to a balcony, drowned out the opening bell with foghorns, and unfurled a banner reading "SELL WELLCOME." ACT UP/NY held a simultaneous demonstration outside the exchange, and on the same day ACT UP/San Francisco and ACT UP/London protested Burroughs Wellcome as well (Erni 1994, 19). Four days later, responding to the pressure, Burroughs Wellcome reduced the price of AZT by an additional 20 percent.[10]

In June 1989, AIDS activists from across the United States and from Canada took over the stage at the opening ceremonies of the Fifth International Conference on AIDS in Montreal, and, according to the *Wall Street Journal,* "stole the show" (Chase 1989a, A1). They demanded a

9. ACT UP/NY, n.d. a, 2.
10. Ibid., 2–3.

greater role for people with AIDS in the conduct of AIDS research, accelerated testing of promising AIDS drugs, and the implementation of their parallel-track drug-testing plan to make experimental drugs available to people not able to enroll in clinical trials. In the week following the Fifth International, ACT UP members were invited to discuss the latter idea with Anthony Fauci, and days later Fauci announced that the FDA would soon implement it.[11]

Not only were AIDS activists' demands being met, there also was relatively good news on the AIDS drug-treatment front. According to Epstein, the conventional wisdom that emerged at the Montreal conference was that "HIV infection might soon become a chronic manageable illness" (1996, 237). Activists shared scientists' optimism. A *Wall Street Journal* article written just after the conference quoted Larry Kramer as saying, "I'm excited. Between [drugs like] ddI . . . compound Q and the polymerase inhibitor, we seem to be on our way. We have the scientific tools, the only thing in our way is bureaucratic red tape" (Chase 1989a). In August, the new conventional wisdom out of Montreal "received a sharp boost . . . with the release of the latest news about AZT" (Epstein 1996, 237). Two clinical drug trials, ACTG 019 and ACTG 016, found that AZT delayed the onset of AIDS in people infected with the virus but with no symptoms (237). These studies generated enormous optimism.

These are only a few examples, but they indicate that the period from 1987 through 1989 was filled with important activist victories and promising information about AIDS drugs. With collective direct action unquestionably working, activists were feeling their political efficacy. The actions themselves also ushered in a new constellation of feelings. Activists' enactments of anger and hope in the streets helped to produce those very sentiments, warding off or repressing the gloom that had preceded ACT UP and that threatened to return in the face of continuing deaths. Looking back on that period, ACT UP/NY's Theo Smart connected ACT UP's many accomplishments to activists' optimism, writing, "We believed that we could indeed win the battle against AIDS" (Smart 1992, 43). Our victories corroborated and bolstered a newly emergent optimism that we could force the powers-that-be to listen to and respond to us, that we could force change, that we could, and would, save lives. Additionally, the direct-action AIDS movement was receiving a lot of press, both mainstream and in lesbian and gay communities across the

11. Ibid., 2.

country, and was growing rapidly in response. Most likely as a result of their effectiveness, direct-action AIDS organizations garnered support from more mainstream lesbian and gay organizations, leaders, and individuals, as noted in chapter 5. Although some criticized the movement's militancy, a pervasive sentiment during this period was hope-filled optimism that street activism would change the course of the AIDS epidemic, prolonging and potentially saving the lives of countless gay and bisexual men.

From Activism to Despair

That optimism began to fade in ACT UP's later years. The persistence of the AIDS crisis itself generated new feeling states that posed enormous challenges to ACT UP's emotional habitus—to the obligatory anger, to the faith that our direct action would save lives, and especially to the prohibition against despair. Despondency about the accumulating deaths and pessimism about the movement's ability to save lives began to circulate and proved difficult to navigate. Activists continued to express, enact, and evoke anger, and to do the other emotion work that earlier had generated and regenerated the movement's emotional habitus. But our efforts stopped working as effectively, due, I would argue, to the changed context: street activism had been tried and had worked up to a point, and yet the epidemic was continuing, unabated.

The Instability of Hope

The year 1990 marks a pivot point of sorts, when good news and hope mixed with growing anxiety about the prospects for an adequate political and medical response to the crisis. Throughout the year, activists' sentiments oscillated between optimism and pessimism. A high point for many of us in Chicago occurred in April on the heels of a national action for universal health care sponsored by ACT NOW and organized by ACT UP/Chicago. Hundreds of AIDS activists from across the country converged on Chicago to highlight the relationship between the AIDS crisis and the inadequacies and inequities in the delivery of health care in the United States. The overarching demand was for national health insurance, viewed by many in the movement as necessary for the fight against AIDS. A weekend of activities, including a conference focusing

2off

FIGURE 26. ACT UP/Chicago members take over Cook County Building balcony during national ACT UP demonstration, downtown Chicago, April 23, 1990. Photo by Rex Wockner.

on AIDS in communities of color and a twenty-four-hour encampment in front of the severely underfunded and understaffed Cook County Hospital, laid out ACT UP's critique of both the private insurance industry as well as the faltering public health system.[12] The weekend of activities culminated in a raucous Monday morning march through downtown Chicago. Staging actions at the offices of various insurance companies, affinity groups from Los Angeles and New York targeted the high price of private insurance and the discriminatory red-lining practices of the industry. Another New York affinity group held a die-in at the national headquarters of the American Medical Association, targeting it for its opposition to national health insurance. An ACT UP/ Chicago affinity group took over a balcony of the Cook County Building and hung a banner demanding equal health care (fig. 26). Women from around the country put a dozen mattresses in a busy intersection to create an AIDS ward for women, drawing attention not only to the exclusion of HIV-positive women from the AIDS ward at Cook County Hos-

12. Cook County Hospital is Chicago's public hospital; it is governed and funded by the Cook County Board.

pital but also to the broader concerns of women with HIV/AIDS (figs. 27 and 28). More than 130 activists were arrested over the course of the five-hour demonstration.

In a moment all-too-rare in activism, we could declare victory immediately following the protest: after months of inaction, Cook County Hospital opened its AIDS ward to women one day after the demonstration.[13] To be sure, our demand for national health insurance went unmet, and remains so today. But we felt euphoric, not only because we had successfully dramatized the inequities of the current health care system and not only because poor women with AIDS would now receive coordinated and compassionate medical care in Cook County Hospital,[14] but also because we were able to experience, to viscerally feel, our collective power to make change. I remember marveling at the instant effectiveness of our activism, feeling like we really might be able to save lives. I was hooked on direct action. Sentiments of elation and a heady sense of our own potency took hold in ACT UP/Chicago, at least for a while.

AIDS activists from around the country demonstrated against the NIH in May 1990, when AZT was still the only available AIDS drug, and that demonstration too generated exhilaration and a sense of political agency and efficacy among participants. Government studies of experimental AIDS drugs, conducted under the auspices of NIAID's ACTG, were focusing mostly on studies of the already approved AZT, neglecting other antivirals as well as drugs that might treat the opportunistic infections killing people with AIDS. Storming the NIH campus and the nearby office of the director of the AIDS division at NIAID, activists demanded that the NIH study antiviral drugs that worked differently than AZT, put more emphasis on testing drugs designed to fight opportunistic infections, admit people from all affected populations into the clinical drug trials (including women, people of color, injection-drug users, and children), and consult with people with AIDS and their advocates when designing clinical trials. It was another spectacular demonstration. Over the course of the day, activists scaled a building, took

13. Mount (1990, sec. 2, 7). As often happens, even when the efficacy of direct action is so brilliantly demonstrated, the director of AIDS services at Cook County Hospital denied that women were admitted to the AIDS ward because of the ACT UP demonstration (Olson 1990b, 1).

14. The victory was tremendous for women with HIV/AIDS. In the words of ACT UP/Chicago member Saundra Johnson, HIV-positive women now would "have a coordinated schedule of care, . . . food delivered by people without gloves on their hands, and . . . [care] by people who are not afraid of touching them" (Olson 1990b, 1).

FIGURES 27 (*top*) AND 28 (*bottom*). Women's Caucus action at national ACT UP demonstration, downtown Chicago, April 23, 1990. Photos by Genyphyr Novak (fig. 27) and Linda Miller (fig. 28).

over an office, dramatized the exclusion of women from ACTG trials, staged die-ins, set off smoke bombs, and entangled themselves in red tape to dramatize the bureaucratic barriers slowing down the research process. Activists won many of their demands: the ACTG system was soon opened to activists, for example, and more changes were forthcoming. ACT UP chapters across the country and the movement as a whole were having similar successes.[15] These victories helped to prolong people's lives and gave us a strong sense of the importance and value of our work.

At the same time, however, there was little hope in the realm of actual drug treatments. There are indications that some were starting to feel demoralized about the prospects for getting effective AIDS drugs anytime soon. In an article about the NIH demonstration, the *Washington Post* quoted ACT UP/NY member Mark Harrington: "There's a lot of pessimism in the AIDS community right now because there is no new drug on the horizon that gives people hope" (Cimons 1990, A16). Even the victories following the NIH demonstration could not counter the growing sense that a cure for AIDS would not be found in the lifetime of people currently infected with HIV. Activists knew that the backlog in the ACTG drug-testing system meant that new, potentially promising treatments would not be available for years—years that many HIV-positive people simply did not have.[16]

Of course, people find hope at different tempos and for different reasons. The preliminary findings of a small study on the combined use of AZT and another antiviral, ddC, presented in June 1990 at the Sixth International Conference on AIDS in San Francisco generated a great deal of interest because the study found that the combined regimen increased patients' T-cell counts, indicating that it was boosting their immune systems.[17] Epstein writes that "belief in the efficacy of the ddC/AZT combination regimen swept through the AIDS movement with the force of a juggernaut" (1996, 267).[18] But Epstein also notes that well before the FDA's approval of ddC in June 1992, "the hopes of researchers, doctors, and activists had moved well beyond the infertile terrain of the nucleoside analogues," that is, beyond drugs like ddC (280–81). As early as

15. See, for example, ACT UP/NY, n.d. a, 2–3; ACT NOW, 1990, 3.
16. See Epstein 1996, 281.
17. Ibid., 266.
18. By "AIDS movement," Epstein is not referring to ACT UP specifically, but to the broader AIDS community, including doctors, PWAs, and drug-buyers clubs.

June 1990, ACT UP/NY questioned the optimism about ddC and combination therapy and claimed that there was a growing pessimism in AIDS communities about drug treatments. Its "AIDS Treatment Research Agenda," distributed at the Sixth International Conference on AIDS, asserted, "This year, the hopes of many in the AIDS communities have reached a low ebb. It is clear to all that anti-HIV agents such as AZT, ddC, and ddI will not, in any conceivable combination, stop the progression of HIV infection—at most, for those who are lucky, they will significantly slow it" (quoted in Epstein 1996, 281).

Epstein also writes that within a year of the announcement in Montreal that AIDS was becoming a "chronic manageable illness," it became increasingly apparent that that declaration had been "more than a little premature" (Epstein 1996, 281). Writing in *OutWeek* in October 1990, Larry Kramer noted as much: "AIDS is not a manageable disease, and there is nothing at present that makes me think that it is going to be a manageable disease in my lifetime or the lifetime of the other 20 million HIV infected. ANYONE WHO TELLS YOU OTHERWISE IS A LIAR" (quoted in Epstein 1996, 281; emphasis in original).

As I said earlier, activists were oscillating between optimism and pessimism. In comparison to his statement in May 1990 that there was immense pessimism in the AIDS community because of the lack of promising AIDS treatments, Mark Harrington sounded a more optimistic note in an August 1990 *OutWeek* column in which he touted the impending changes in the ACTG system as a result of ACT UP's pressure, particularly its demonstration at the NIH (Harrington 1990).[19] But again, those changes, while crucial in terms of gaining activist input into the drug-trial process, were not expected to generate promising AIDS drugs in the near future.

The headline of an October 1990 article in the *Dallas Morning News* indicates the instability of hope in this moment—"'90s AIDS Outlook Grim, Experts Say; But Medical Advances Deemed Likely." The reporter asked, "What lies ahead for AIDS in its second decade?" and answered, "Small rays of hope on a horizon of despair" (Camia 1990, 1A). The article quoted AIDS researchers predicting a vaccine by the mid-1990s, but in the realm of treatment, the reporter noted, "AZT remains the only federally approved AIDS drug" (7A). A growing despair among

19. This is the column that provoked the contention within the AIDS movement discussed in the previous chapter.

activists was apparent in a comment from ACT UP/NY member Robin Haueter: "The feeling we have is that for all we've done, we haven't done enough. People are still dying" (7A). People *were* still dying, in ever-growing numbers, and no promising drugs were on the way.

Desperation and Violence

An eruption of talk about turning to violent tactics revealed a growing desperation in lesbian and gay communities.[20] In October 1990, the cover of *OutWeek* had a picture of a pistol, pointing toward the reader, with the headline "Taking Aim at Bashers." The cover also announced an essay inside, "Should Queers Shoot Back?"[21] The cover story, with photographs of (ostensibly queer) people aiming guns on five of its six pages, reported on discussions then occurring in New York's lesbian and gay community about queers arming themselves in self-defense against queer bashers (Reyes 1990b). These discussions were primarily in response to a documented increase in queer bashing in New York City and around the country in the summer and fall of 1990 (Solomon 1990), but feelings of hopelessness and pessimism regarding the AIDS epidemic played a role as well. The discussion about taking up guns frequently gestured toward the horrors of the AIDS epidemic to explain the call for gays to bash back, and even to justify it. In their manifesto, "Should Queers Shoot Back?" which laid out in dire terms the effects of antiqueer violence on queer lives, the authors—"Three Anonymous Queers"—used tropes of death, extinction, and genocide that were already widely circulating in queer discourses about the AIDS epidemic. Blurring any distinctions between deaths from AIDS, deaths from queer bashings, and the sapping of the queer soul from living in a homophobic society, they wrote "Life under genocide demands extreme measures" (Three Anonymous Queers 1990). An article in the *Village Voice* by Alisa Solomon also connected the AIDS epidemic and the emerging calls for queers to "bash back." Noting that many of those calling for gays to carry guns were white, middle-class, gay men, she claimed that "10 years of official negligence in the face of a virulent epidemic has made the gay bourgeoisie confront its status as an endangered species" (Solomon 1990).

20. I would not generalize this statement. In other contexts, discussion of political violence, or even the embrace of it, might or might not indicate desperation.
21. *OutWeek,* 17 October 1990.

Meanwhile, a somewhat parallel discussion was occurring within ACT
UP as some members began to voice frustration with what they saw as
the growing ineffectiveness of the AIDS movement's nonviolent tactics.
In the spring of 1990, Larry Kramer, in despair over the state of AIDS
drug-treatment research, had called for activists to escalate their tactics
by rioting at the Sixth International Conference on AIDS that June.[22]
Others in ACT UP dismissed Kramer's calls for riots, but some indicated that they, too, were deeply frustrated and could understand how a
sense of desperation might prompt someone to turn toward violence.

I recall a discussion around this time among some people with AIDS
in ACT UP about launching suicide missions to assassinate public officials who were seen as hindering the fight against AIDS. In an interview,
an ACT UP member corroborated my recollection, telling me a story
that I had until then heard only via the AIDS activist gossip network. He
represented a local ACT UP chapter at the national level and in that capacity attended an ACT UP/Network meeting in Dallas.[23]

> I remember sitting around the pool talking with these guys who were all from
> the PISD caucus from different parts of the country. There were guys there
> from St. Louis, from New York, from San Francisco, L.A., Texas, Ohio, Phil-
> adelphia, and we were talking about what would be our next strategy, and
> someone brought up the idea about how we, as people with AIDS, owed it to
> the rest of the community to make change happen faster. And this is really
> true, this really did happen, people actually talked about assassination. . . . I
> did not bring up the idea, but there was someone there, I don't even remem-
> ber who it was, but they said, you know, what we should start thinking about
> doing is, maybe a PWA who's really on their last leg who knows they don't
> have much time left, maybe they should go up to Jesse Helms with a bomb
> strapped to them and blow themselves up for the movement and assassinate
> him. . . . People were so desperate. (Anonymous 2000)

They were desperate about the government's callous indifference to the
deaths of tens of thousands of queers, about the unavailability and inadequacy of AIDS drugs, about the never-ending deaths. I do not want

---

22. For discussion of Kramer's call to riot, see Clark 1990; Cowley 1990; Gross 1990; Israels 1990; and Kirp 1990.
23. ACT UP/Network was the movement's national umbrella organization.

to romanticize these considerations of political violence, but I want to suggest that this desperation was not desperation in the sense of being driven to what some might cast as senseless rage, destruction, and self-destruction. Rather, it was desperation in the sense of being driven to consider unexplored paths, new modes of political activism, different tactics for confronting power, alternative ways of putting one's body on the line.

With that understanding of desperation in mind, we might understand these discussions about turning toward violent means, occurring both within and outside ACT UP, as indicating some lesbians' and gay men's immense frustration with the extant repertoire of activist tactics; the devastation AIDS was wreaking in lesbian and gay communities helped to shape both that frustration and an openness to other activist means.[24]

Deepening Despair

During the early 1990s, there were sometimes brief moments when hopes rose because a drug seemed to be promising in the early stages of a research study, but more often than not the news was bad, and getting worse. Writing in late 1992 about the increasingly pervasive despair among treatment activists, ACT UP/NY member Theo Smart describes T&D meetings in mid-1991 in which the core members would feverishly discuss and debate treatment issues, while twenty or thirty people would sit in the back of the room, "waiting for a revelation" (Smart 1992, 43). He continues, "The revelation, when it came, wasn't uplifting" (43). By mid-1991 it was apparent that the nucleoside analogue anti-HIV drugs being tested (such as AZT, ddI, and ddC) "were not the magic bullets for which activists and PWAs alike had been hoping" (43). In fact, "there didn't seem to be a difference in survival rates between those who took AZT and those who didn't" (43). Intensifying the despondency, the next generation of anti-HIV drugs was taking an excruciatingly long time to be tested in trials. "The news [in the fall of 1991] that this second generation of drugs had failed was nothing short of shattering. So many hopes had been pinned to their effectiveness" (44).

---

24. Neither the turn toward guns to address gay bashing nor suicide missions carried out by people with AIDS ever materialized.

Epstein corroborates Smart's account, writing that "the ever fragile optimism of treatment activists strained to the breaking point in late
1991" (1996, 295). Despondency set in when the second generation of antiviral AIDS drugs—"the non-nucleoside reverse-transcriptase inhibitors that had been engineered specifically to fight HIV and that had
looked so promising in vitro" (295)—seemed to fail in clinical trials. The
prospect of saving lives faded further. As Epstein notes, "The avowed
goal had been to use the little-loved nucleoside analogues, AZT, ddC,
and ddI, to keep people alive just long enough to get better drugs into
circulation. Now people would have to depend on the first-generation
drugs for much longer—while those who ceased benefiting from them
would have no obvious therapeutic recourse standing between them
and complete immune collapse" (295). Theo Smart suggests that among
some treatment activists in late 1991, "the conviction that a cure would
not be found in their lifetime began to take root" (1992, 44). Meanwhile,
the deaths were relentless. ACT UP/Los Angeles member Mark Kosto-
poulos acknowledged his frustration: "We've worked for three years to
help change the way AIDS is thought about, but all our successes haven't
changed the fact that people continue to die" (Barker 1991).

An article in the *San Francisco Examiner* in February 1992 highlighted activists' despondency, noting that "slow progress in AIDS drug
research has cast a pall over the once burgeoning AIDS activist movement" (Garrison 1992, A10). It quoted Peter Staley (who had just left
ACT UP/NY to form the new, invitation-only TAG) saying, "It's hard to
have hope, to have much fight left, especially as an activist who unfortunately knows too much. As far as I'm concerned I'm going to die, Magic
Johnson is going to die, and the million Americans who are presently infected will die. Maybe something will come along that will save millions
worldwide who become infected in the future. But it won't save us today" (A10).

Larry Kramer sounded a similar note, indicating a shift in the emotional climate of ACT UP, with despair overtaking anger and hope:
"The morale in the activist community is as low as it could be. The anger's been replaced by despondency. Every drug in the pipeline is turning out to be a dud. And none of us knows what to do" (A10).

British gay/AIDS activist and writer Simon Watney described the affective landscape similarly, writing that the gay world was "a community
approaching despair" (Watney 1992b, 18). In a list that explained why

people were feeling despair and cited evidence supporting the contention itself, Watney wrote, "Ninety-seven thousand gay men . . . have already died in the U.S. At least 50 per cent of gay men in New York are
thought to be HIV-positive. Many of the original core of ACT UP/NY
are now dead, or seriously ill. The suicide rate amongst HIV-*negative*
gay men is alarmingly high" (18; emphasis in original).

   Despair and desperation inspired a new tactic, political funerals, that
I discussed in chapter 4. Describing the "Ashes Action" that ACT UP/
NY held in Washington, D.C., in October 1992, Watney wrote, "That
it should come to this—the spectacle of human remains on the White
House lawns—is enough to suggest something of how desperate the situation has . . . become" (Watney 1992b; see also Harrington 2002b). With
its political funerals, ACT UP was continuing the work of harnessing
grief to anger, but despair was creeping in.

The Short-Lived Hope of Clinton's Election,
and ACT UP's Further Decline

The growing despair in the direct-action AIDS movement took an interesting turn in November 1992 when Bill Clinton won the presidential
election. During the campaign, Clinton promised a dramatic increase in
AIDS funding, implementation of the recommendations of the National
Commission on AIDS (including controversial proposals in favor of explicit safe-sex education and needle-exchange programs), further expe-
dition of the FDA's drug-approval process, expansion of clinical drug
trials for promising treatments, and admission into the United States
for HIV-positive Haitians being held without medical care in camps at
Guantánamo Bay Naval Base. Many people with AIDS and others in
the AIDS movement felt a sense of urgency about the election. As HIV-
positive New York City councilman Tom Duane put it, "I'm personally
desperate to get Bill Clinton elected. I don't think I have a chance to live
if he doesn't get elected" ("Angry" 1992). Upon Clinton's election, optimism swept through the AIDS movement that, unlike the Reagan/Bush
administrations, this new administration "would offer a sustained and
comprehensive federal effort to address AIDS" (Rimmerman 2002, 90).

   How did that resurgence of hope about the AIDS epidemic affect
ACT UP? While scholars have noted that hope seems necessary to social movement mobilization (Aminzade and McAdam 2001, 31–32), the

revival of hope following Clinton's election seems to have contributed to ACT UP's decline.[25] In a sense, that little twist in the narrative actually is not all that odd. Clinton had promised to implement many of the demands that AIDS activists themselves were making, so why wouldn't his victory generate hope as well as an exodus from the direct-action AIDS movement, which apparently would have a friend in the White House and thus no longer be quite so necessary? We miss an important part of the story, however, if we focus only on this resurgence of hope. To better understand how Clinton's election affected ACT UP, we need to explore why a number of street AIDS activists had faith in this newly elected President. ACT UP was a politically savvy organization, and many members were deeply cynical about elected officials; we had heard tantalizing promises before, and we knew that politicians almost never fulfilled them. Why would we now believe a politician, even one whose rhetoric was in some ways coincident with our own? As well, the despair in the movement was by then enormous and growing. Why would the promises of a newly elected but still untested president be able to convert that despair into hope?

Indeed, this hope regarding Clinton is best understood through the lens of despair. By the time of his election, direct-action AIDS activists were exhausted and many were in despair, creating a desire to relinquish responsibility and hand it over to the newly elected president who had promised to implement many of the demands of AIDS activists. We were ripe for hearing that someone else would fight the battle, and that is essentially what Clinton offered. That is part of what despair *does;* it crushes an individual's belief or faith in her own agency, in her own ability to effect change. ACT UP/Chicago member Tim Miller suggested that ACT UP members wanted to trust in Clinton, indeed, given our exhaustion and despondency, *needed* to see him as a savior who would take over for us and finally solve the crisis. As he puts it, "Everybody just breathed a sigh of relief [when Clinton won]." He continued in a mock-

---

25. As I argue below, this finding is unsurprising, but it nevertheless is instructive about the need for close study of the relationship between a given feeling or set of feelings and a specific movement process. Generalizations about such relationships (e.g., hope is necessary for movements, despair is depoliticizing, anger leads people to the streets) may be useful in providing direction to our inquiries, but the particulars of each situation often require pushing up against such generalizations in order to see how a relationship is working in practice.

ing and self-mocking tone, and then offered an incisive analysis about the forceful desire to cede our agency to the government:

> "Oh, our savior is here. We're done with the Reagan/Bush folks. Now we've got this liberal youngster in the White House who's gonna give us everything that we could ever ask for." . . . I think people were exhausted and were happy to pass on the torch to the White House. And hopefully they were gonna take care of everything. Make everything beautiful again. And even when that didn't occur, I didn't see the anger resurge. Why that is? I don't know. People were probably still too tired or something. It was like, let's not awake that beast. . . . So yeah, I mean, [Clinton's] a smart guy. And we bought it. I bought it, and I think a lot of people bought it. We wanted to buy it. And yeah, we should've returned it. (Miller 1999)

We should have "returned it" because not only did Clinton fail to implement his AIDS-related campaign promises, but transferring any remaining hopes we might have had from ourselves and our own activism to Clinton, and thereby surrendering our power to him, contributed to the demise of the direct-action AIDS movement. In Miller's view, Clinton's election and the hopeful belief among many ACT UP members that Clinton would be "our savior" was "the worst thing to ever happen to the [AIDS] activist movement. Although, I mean, I voted for him. I was so happy that Bush was not in office. But I think it was the worst thing that ever happened to the activism. It just fell apart. That was a major part of it. That was the final straw" (Miller 1999).

ACT UP/Chicago member Darrell Gordon similarly links the decline of ACT UP to the hope that Clinton, as our protector, would allow us to retreat from the political realm. "There was this hope that Clinton . . . was going to save us. I think it had a great effect [on ACT UP]. I think that people thought that, again, Clinton was going to take care of us, take care of the people in the queer community" (Gordon 2000). Karin Timour from ACT UP/NY suggests that the election of Clinton, along with ACT UP's victories, lessened our sense that nobody was listening to us and that if we didn't do it, nobody would. In that context, "more and more people started to believe that the world is a good place and a safe place, and you don't need to really be watching what elected officials are doing. . . . They'll do the right thing" (Timour 2003, 58). We experienced Clinton's election as offering relief from tending to this crisis largely on our own, with almost no government assistance and, indeed, in the face of unrelenting government hostility. After twelve years of murderous inaction and punitive policymaking from the government, of escalating deaths, of caretaking and taking to the streets, of unceasing vigilance in fighting the crisis, all of that amid growing exhaustion and despair, we needed and wanted a break from activism.

There is, of course, no necessary connection between intense activism and activist depletion and exhaustion; indeed, engagement in activism is often rejuvenating. What the demobilizing hope in Clinton reveals is a combination of exhaustion and burn-out with a forceful despair. The prospect of someone else taking up our battle, the President no less, was absolutely alluring. The contrast between what Clinton seemed to stand for and what had occurred during the Reagan/Bush years—the criminal negligence, the punitive legislation, the foot-dragging, the active ignorance, the intense homophobia that rendered acceptable the deaths of tens of thousands of gay and bisexual men—was dramatic. How could we *not* feel some hope? Many ACT UP members, of course, were cynical about Clinton; indeed, ACT UP handed out fliers during a demonstration at the 1992 Democratic National Convention that criticized Clinton's "meager state funding" for AIDS programs while governor of Arkansas ("Angry" 1992). Nevertheless, the contrast between the Reagan/Bush years and the possibility of better leadership on AIDS from the top was so clear that the skepticism and criticism were initially rather muted. Only in retrospect did many decide that the hope had been misplaced. Billy McMillan from ACT UP/Chicago recalled being thrilled when Clinton won, and moved to tears.

> I remember thinking, "He's got to be better than what we've had for twelve years." I was watching his inauguration at home alone. Maya Angelou was reading her poem, and I was just bawling my eyes out. I was very moved, in part because I survived the Reagan-Bush Era and many of my friends didn't. And I really had hope that maybe we were going to be moving into a new era, that maybe something positive would happen. The Democrats were back in the White House, and I really believed that Clinton was somehow going to help improve things. I was very naive. (McMillan 2000)

I asked if there was a sense among ACT UP members that there was no longer a need to be in the streets. McMillan replied, "Yes. I think there was a sense of that among a lot of people. Because Clinton talked the talk. He had a lot of charisma. He actively engaged in dialogue with gay people, and many of us felt a sense of inclusion for the first time" (2000). Like Tim Miller and Darrell Gordon, McMillan thought that the hope placed in Clinton contributed to ACT UP's demise: "I think what happened after Clinton's election was that a lot of people felt that things were going to be different and better. Many of us let our guard down and placed hope and trust in him. Other stuff contributed, but I think that was probably the final nail in the coffin of a lot of ACT UPs" (2000).

Rather than bolstering the movement, this resurgence of hope prompted more ACT UP members to exit the movement, exhaustedly optimistic that the U.S. government would now do its job without activist pressure. The hope did not last long: Clinton hardly mentioned AIDS in his first six months in office, during which time close to twenty thousand people in the United States died of AIDS-related complications. Even worse, he did not act on many of his AIDS-related campaign promises. Meanwhile, the news on the drug treatment front was looking worse and worse.

The Despair of Concorde and Berlin

Pessimism and despair about AIDS treatments intensified in April 1993 when European AIDS researchers released their Concorde study. In the words of Mark Harrington, "The results were grim" (Harrington 2002a). The Concorde study found that early intervention with AZT neither prolonged patients' lives nor kept them free from opportunistic infections longer.[26] The study also found that "the benefits of early AZT were so transient as to be eliminated after three years of therapy" (2002a). The Concorde trial was the longest study of AZT conducted thus far; its finding that AZT seemed to provide no benefit was devastating.

The news out of the Ninth International Conference on AIDS, held in June 1993 in Berlin, was even worse. The *Advocate*'s coverage of the conference was headlined, "No News Is Bad News" and subtitled, "Silver Linings Are Few and Far Between at this Year's International AIDS Conference" (Bull 1993). The reporter began by citing new medical evidence indicating that HIV's attack on the immune system was so complex that any hope that AIDS would soon be treated with a single "magic bullet" drug was wholly smashed (24). In no sense was AIDS a "chronic, manageable illness," as some had predicted at the Montreal

26. See Epstein 1996, 300–305.

conference in 1989. To the contrary, the conference confirmed that, in the words of Executive Director of NGLTF, Torie Osborn, "AIDS is part of the landscape and will be for a very long time." Osborn continued, "There is no good news on the AIDS front, and it's profoundly depressing" (Biddle 1993). The *Advocate* quoted Fauci at the Berlin conference, who sounded increasingly pessimistic about available antiviral drugs: "Even with clinical benefits of AZT, the benefits of antivirals are limited at best" (Bull 1993, 25). Also quoted in the *Advocate,* Mark Harrington said, "It's pretty depressing. Drugs are crashing right and left. It seems that the more we know, the less secure we become about where to go with research and how to treat this disease" (24). Ferd Eggan recalled the Berlin conference as "the downest time . . . the worst."

> Essentially, the reports were that there was nothing that was working and that there was no hope to be had whatsoever. And everybody *was* dying. I mean, all the people who had gone on AZT and had been healthy for a while all started dying. And so I think there was a feeling of futility, a feeling that we had done a lot, and maybe stretched it as far as we could, you know, the Ryan White Care Act was paying for care for people, the government had finally begun to respond, but at the same time, there was no cure; there was no treatment; there was no nothing. (Eggan 1999)

ACT UP/NY and TAG member David Barr also pointed to 1993 as "the low point," the moment when activists' treatment strategy "just collapsed" (Barr 2002). In response, according to Barr, a lot of people left activism, which was appearing increasingly ineffective in keeping people alive, and "turned to service provision, [thinking] 'We're in this for the long haul. I've got to find a way of doing something that feels grounded'" (2002). The situation was equally bleak through 1994 and 1995.

The decisive shift away from despair occurred in late 1995 and early 1996 when clinical trials of a new class of anti-HIV drugs, protease inhibitors, found that the drugs seemed to reduce the amount of HIV in people's bodies and cut the death rate in half (Epstein 1996, 323–24). The direct-action AIDS movement had declined by that point, prior to this new, and longer-lasting, surge in optimism. A few ACT UP chapters remain active and continue doing important activism, even into the twenty-first century, but by 1995 ACT UP was unquestionably a reduced and less effective presence than it had been in the late 1980s and early 1990s.

Why Despair?

What happens to a movement when deaths of its members and of people in the surrounding community accumulate, one after another, in an endless amassing of dead bodies? Accumulating AIDS deaths generated despair in ACT UP in two interrelated ways. First, the endless stream of illnesses and deaths, and the sense that the deaths would not cease or even slow down anytime soon, generated a physical and emotional exhaustion among many members of ACT UP that was fertile ground for despair. Second, the accumulating deaths, with no end in sight, shattered ACT UP's hopeful vision that its street activism would save lives.

Daily Life in the AIDS Movement

The vast majority of people dying from AIDS-related complications in the first decade and a half of the epidemic in the United States were people in their twenties, thirties, and forties, mostly gay and bisexual men. In an advanced, industrialized country like the United States, young people are not supposed to die. Neither are they supposed to witness the deaths of their peers, and certainly not of their full social circle, to say nothing of losing close to their entire generation. Of course, recent periods of gun violence—by police, by gangs—have threatened young people, particularly in poor black communities. Those deaths also unsettle us at least in part because they veer from the expected trajectory of living and dying. Parents are not supposed to bury their children. ACT UP/NY member Candido Negron noted how AIDS reversed the positions of younger and older generations. Twenty-seven years old, he commented, "I've lost more friends than my parents—and they're twice my age" (Jennings and Gladwell 1990, B7).[27]

In their daily lives during the early 1990s, along with planning and executing numerous demonstrations, ACT UP members visited friends and fellow activists in the hospital; changed diapers and cleaned bed sores; drove friends to doctor appointments; watched lovers be reduced to needing help to eat and go to the bathroom; feared seroconverting and getting sick; felt guilty about being unable to stand the thought of

27. For a moving discussion of how AIDS and other illnesses challenge the "normal" generational narrative, see Sedgwick 2003, 148–49.

visiting yet another friend in the hospital; learned how to hook up a cath-
eter; helped friends move into hospice; learned about more friends testing HIV-positive; listened as loved ones said they had decided to stop
taking their meds; went to memorial service after memorial service;
stopped knowing what to say or how to help; helped lovers and friends
kill themselves.[28]

The narrator in Rebecca Brown's book *Gifts of the Body* (1994), a
home-care worker who assists people with AIDS, poignantly speaks
to the emotional roller coaster, the swings from pessimism to hope and
back again, that characterized this period for so many queer folks.[29] Referring to the condition of many of the people she was assisting and her
own emotional responses, she writes,

> Usually they'd be sick but maintaining. Then they'd get a bout of something
> worse and be hospitalized and you'd think they were going to die but they'd
> pull through. Then they'd get another bout and you'd think they were really
> going to die but they didn't again, so then you got to thinking that they would
> keep pulling through until there was a cure. You'd start thinking they weren't
> going to die. (101)

Brown captures the way that hope tantalizes; surely *someone* will get
better, will beat this horror, surely *someone* will survive. But they all
eventually died, and the hope that your client, friend, lover, or comrade
might be able to hang on for a little longer, until the next medical "mir-
acle" was available, became more difficult to hold onto. We became increasingly tired of false hopes, indeed, exhausted by them. Any hopes
we might have had were demolished.

28. While writing this chapter, I reread Douglas Crimp's important essay from 1989
about AIDS activists' difficulties in mourning the deaths and devastation wrought by
AIDS in queer communities—"Mourning and Militancy." Crimp also created a list of
daily activities, a list "of the problems we face," as a way to convey the psychic enormity of
what gay men were facing (1989, 15–16). The coincidence made me consider why one might
turn to the genre of the list to convey what daily life amid the epidemic was like. A list
seems particularly apt for conveying the sheer immensity and horror of a crisis like AIDS:
it can indicate the scale and scope of a crisis, as well as the complex relationships of differently positioned people to it. A list can also suggest its own incompleteness and thus create
a sense of enormity and vastness.

29. Mary Patten reminded me about this wonderful book. See also Cvetkovich (2003a,
222–26).

The emotional roller coaster wore us out. In describing why she eventually left ACT UP/NY, Jean Carlomusto acknowledged the role played by the never-ending deaths and her consequent exhaustion: "I just got really burnt out and sort of withdrew from life in general for a period of time. A lot of that was about the cumulative amounts of deaths that happened. I just got really introspective" (Carlomusto 2002, 42). ACT UP was quick-paced and all-consuming; caretaking, which many of us were involved in to one degree or another, was similarly absorbing. The pace allowed little time to pause and almost no space for an interior life.

If you were HIV-positive or had AIDS, daily life also entailed gagging on pills that eventually were revealed to be ineffective; fearing every flu and cold; incessant nausea; loss of appetite and weight; constant fatigue; witnessing your body become unrecognizable to you; consoling (or not) friends who were freaking out about your visible deterioration, angry at you for succumbing, unable to face your approaching death, who no longer could stand to be near you; denying/acknowledging your impending death; losing your independence; considering whether to enter hospice; planning your memorial service; watching your body fail the latest pill regimen; experiencing excruciating pain; deciding whether to hold onto life until the bitter end or to kill yourself, and, if the latter, how to do so. I'll always remember getting a phone call at the bookstore where I worked from a very ill friend who asked me to bring him a copy of Derek Humphry's *Final Exit,* a how-to book for killing oneself in the face of a terminal illness.

For everyone living so close to AIDS, daily life was physically and emotionally draining. Marion Banzhaf points to the amassing of deaths as being particularly traumatic: "It got to be too much. You can't sustain that level of loss without becoming traumatized by it" (2002). Jeanne Kracher had a similar analysis about the toll that the accumulating deaths was taking on people in ACT UP. "I think people were exhausted. When you asked before about how did we manage all the grief, how can you manage that? I mean, how does anybody manage? I think it'd be interesting to look at these societies that have been at war for ten, fifteen years. And how do they manage that? How do people come out of that sane?" (Kracher 2000). Others have also made the analogy to war, where the attacks are relentless, and bodies just keep adding up all around you. Emily Nahmanson points to the way that the accumulating deaths changed the feel of ACT UP/NY. "I left ACT UP when I moved out of New York, in 1992. The passion was gone, a lot of the people were gone. . . . A lot of people were dead. I mean, people were just dying and dying and dying" (Nahmanson 2003, 30). In this climate of utter exhaustion, surrounded by unrelenting death and illness, with no end in sight and no good prospects on the treatment front, despair easily edged out hope.

As if that wasn't enough, daily life for many AIDS activists during the early 1990s also included political despair, intimately connected to the unending illnesses and deaths. No matter what we did, no matter our astonishing victories, people continued to die. They started to live longer, but then they died anyway. Dudley Saunders recalls, "ACT UP had all these incredible successes so quickly. New York still has the best insurance laws in America. It's incredible, the things we got done. We'd won all these battles, but the war—we were all still dying. There really was no hope. It was horrible" (Saunders 2003). Tim Miller from ACT UP/Chicago also juxtaposes the victories and the deaths. "Even if we had a success every day it might not have been enough success. Because people were still getting sick. And in Chicago, I think people were relatively healthy for a great period of time. And then all of a sudden, a lot of people started getting ill. A lot of people started dying. And that's demoralizing" (Miller 1999).

Social movements offer a vision of a different future and a way to get there. As I argued in part 2, they are efforts at world-making. As ACT UP's hopeful vision of activism leading to a cure faltered, a vision of unremitting illness and suffering, of early deaths of lovers, friends, and fellow activists, of decimated queer communities, of continuing societal neglect and attacks from the right, and of an ever-exploding crisis took over. We had no other vision to offer; every imaginable future seemed bleak. Despair, then, arrived on the heels of ACT UP's hopeful but receding vision, and as despair took hold, it depleted many ACT UP members' activist energy, replacing their rousing desire and forward momentum, sometimes even their anger, with frustration, exhaustion, and immobility.

Rebecca Brown's narrator describes the emptiness that remains after someone dies: "There was always a hole when someone died. It was always in the middle of people" (1994, 157). During the early 1990s, the hole in ACT UP grew immense. Unconsciously, we tried to fill it with demonstrations and fact sheets; with pithy and poignant agit-prop, angry chants, and campy humor; with flirtation, sex, and another angry action.[30] Still, no matter how much we all tried, the hole became more gaping, more devastating. The growing despair became harder to cover over. A sense of political efficacy and optimism initially helped us to navigate the daily toll of the AIDS epidemic. But as the deaths continued unabated, many people's faith in activism began to falter. It became harder to believe our own hopeful rhetoric that action equaled life, as one ACT UP catchphrase put it.

George Eliot wrote that "there is no despair so absolute as that which comes with the first moments of our first great sorrow, when we have not yet known what it is to have suffered and be healed, to have despaired and to have recovered hope."[31] But consider the possibility of even greater despair, one that emerges after having despaired but then recovered hope, only to have such hope repeatedly smashed until you feel utter despair, having reached the limits of hopefulness, sensing that every shred of hope is false and that holding to it will only exacerbate your sense of helplessness, of futility. The saying "Don't get your hopes up" suggests a belief that hopes dashed might be worse than no hope at all, that it might be better to give up on hope and get off the emotional roller coaster altogether. In any event, it is hard to hold onto the hope that through your action you will be able to save lives when all your actions, even those that are unqualified successes, feel entirely inadequate to the task. As Jeff Edwards has noted, after years of "intensive, all-consuming political involvement in which ACT UP had exploited every tactic short of violence, people were still dying, with no end in sight; maybe, some were coming to think, political action was fruitless" (2000b, 493). Sensing that they were up against the absolutely intractable, many ACT UP activists felt that they had reached the limits of activism, which sapped their hope and generated an even more absolute despair.

The Crush of Great Expectations Betrayed

The force of political despair and its effects on activism vary depending on the context in which the despair arises. In a situation where hopes are

30. What I am saying here should not be read as suggesting that ACT UP's street activism is reducible to the fulfillment of psychic needs. My argument throughout the book belies any such interpretation, but I do want to argue, as I also have done throughout this book, for the important role that unconscious and nonconscious processes play in activism.

31. *Adam Bede,* chap. 31.

not especially high to begin with, despair might be fairly unexceptional, less a confounding element than a long-standing part of the texture of daily life, ordinary and ubiquitous even while devastating. The power of the political despair that overtook ACT UP derived in part from its extraordinariness. As discussed in chapter 2, many in the movement had high expectations about their ability to push the system to respond to their demands. Not only were many ACT UP members, by virtue of their race, class, or gender privilege, able to tap into their own sense of entitlement, but many were raised to believe that the government is, if not compassionate, at least responsive to its citizenry; that hard work is rewarded. Again, this sense of entitlement was not unproblematic; many people's anxiety about sexual difference blocked feelings of entitlement. But in the changed context after the *Hardwick* ruling, such sentiments became easier to ignite and mobilize. David Barr acknowledged the high expectations of some in ACT UP: "I think we lived within this myth that through our anger and our hard work we could end the AIDS crisis" (Barr 2002; see also Miller 1999).

For many, high expectations coincided with a faith in science. Mark Harrington recalls his own optimistic expectations: "I certainly didn't think I was going to be involved for several years or have a career out of AIDS work. I thought that we were going to do a push for a few months or a year or two maybe max, and then . . . we'd have mobilized the resources, and science would sort of find a cure or something. I think that was the fantasy" (Harrington 2002b). The fantasy held for a period of time, in part because ACT UP's early, dramatic successes made it seem true; the illusion was created that we would succeed in getting what was needed, that we could push government bureaucrats and scientists to do the right thing, that we had some control over this crisis. David Barr indicates how devastating it was when he realized that ACT UP's hard work, would, in fact, *not* be enough, particularly in light of the limits of science. "We could get the government to respond, we could get the industry to respond, but you couldn't change the virus. . . . It's a disease, and the crisis, we could handle the crisis, I could respond to the crisis. I could . . . respond to this political crisis, but the disease, the virus is just chaos, it's just horror, and so I can't, there's nothing I can do about it" (Barr 2002).

Their hopes and expectations crumbling, people increasingly felt powerless in the face of the virus. From their perspective, the virus was simply outwitting science, and there was nothing that ACT UP could do about that. The force of the despair was all the stronger because of the long distance traveled from the earlier high hopes and expectations.

Despair's Temporalities

Despair has different tempos for different individuals, and although despair was prevalent in the early 1990s, not all of us consciously felt it. I remember feeling anger, only anger. Grief and despair about the deaths and about our seeming political inefficacy emerged for me only during ACT UP/Chicago's last year or two, and it only intensified once the group disbanded. Soon after, especially as I began my research for this project, I was flooded with those feelings, a deluge that suggested to me the extent of my previous denial, a psychic process that I return to below. Prior to that point, I was mainly aware of my anger: about the AIDS crisis, about government negligence, about the right wing's use of AIDS to advance its homophobic agenda, about the illnesses and deaths of friends and comrades, about the disappearance of a vital world.

The reasons why some of us did not feel intense despair are varied. Crimp (2002) argues that many in the movement wished to defend against the pain of despair and repressed that constellation of feelings. I explore Crimp's argument in greater detail below. Another reason is that the emotional habitus within ACT UP disallowed affects and feelings of despair, countering such discouraging sentiments with anger and hopeful optimism about the efficacy of direct-action activism; I also explore these dynamics in greater detail below. As well, we all occupied different positions in the epidemic: some members were HIV-positive, others were not sure of their HIV status, while others knew they were negative; some members had lost numerous lovers and friends, while others had been largely spared at that point. There was much to despair about, but our different experiences of the epidemic generated different tempos of despair and different ways of dealing with it.

Another part of the explanation, particularly with regard to political despair, is that some ACT UP members simply never had held particularly high expectations, perhaps because of their own experiences with the intransigence of the system, perhaps because of their previous activist endeavors, which usually brought incremental change at best and rarely translated into dramatic victories. Those who had previous experience with the scientific-medical establishment, women in particular, had less faith in science than others who imagined science would discover a "silver bullet" cure. Although they were distressed by the pessimistic news on the treatment front, they did not lose faith in activism altogether. They did not agree that the problems regarding AIDS drug treatments lay at the limits of science and outside the realm of politics, and, in any event, they argued that there were still many treatment issues that required activist pressure (e.g., drug prices and availability, opening clinical trials to all affected populations, getting more drugs into the pipeline, etc.). They also pointed to the many other arenas in the AIDS fight where street activism was necessary and could potentially prolong lives.

Still, during the years of ACT UP's decline, there was a great deal of despair in the direct-action AIDS movement. But in other political contexts we see ongoing activism alongside despair, so if, as I suggested earlier, despair does not necessarily lead to demobilization, what was it about *this* despair that contributed to ACT UP's decline?

What Despair Does

Two factors help to explain why and how despair did its destructive work. First, the unconscious processes that it set in motion had extraordinary force and were difficult for individuals and for the movement to navigate. Second, ACT UP's emotional habitus not only provided no means for activists to address the growing despair except through denial, but itself began to unravel in the face of that despair.

Despair and Unconscious Processes

In a 1993 speech Douglas Crimp posed the question "Why do we despair" and offered the following answer: "Surely because we seem no closer now than we did when ACT UP was formed in 1987 to being able to save our lives. And unlike that moment, when the very fact of our growing activism afforded the hope that we could save ourselves, very few of us still truly believe that the lives of those now infected can be saved by what we do" (2002, 227–28). Our street activism was exhausted, no longer offering hope. Crimp continued, "Without hope for ourselves and our friends many of us now turn away from these battles" (227–28). Despair about AIDS activism and its prospects might have led some to a conscious, even rational, decision to leave the movement; it seemed to be no longer working, so why continue with it? But, more powerfully, despair set unconscious forces to work as well. The pain of despair, the devastating sensations that the AIDS crisis would not end soon, that AIDS deaths would continue no matter what activists did are feelings that AIDS activists might want to deny. In Crimp's words, "It should come as little surprise to us that we might now find AIDS an idea that has become unbearable and against which we might wish to defend" (227) and that we might also require "a psychic defense against our despair about AIDS" (228). That is, AIDS activists might want to defend against the pain of grief and of despair; against the shame and guilt about feeling that in despairing you were somehow giving ground to and, even worse, becoming complicit with those who wanted to see gay men dead, that you were deserting your own people and thus in some sense abandoning your gay and perhaps HIV-positive self as well.

Given that constellation of painful feelings associated with the growing despair, AIDS activists might turn away from AIDS and AIDS activism, perhaps feeling exhausted and numb but not necessarily even aware of their own despair. They might turn toward, as Crimp notes, activism that was emphasizing healthy gay bodies rather than dying ones, fighting to lift the ban on gays in the military, for example (2002, 228). Alternatively, they might turn away from activism altogether, overwhelmed by the deaths and consequent grief, demoralized by a sense of political inefficacy, wracked by guilt both about surviving and about giving up, and simply unable to feel activist rage any longer.

Or, in a contrary way, and I am again drawing from Crimp here, the pain of despair, the shame at feeling yourself giving up, might have encouraged some to disavow those sentiments via a moralistic deploring of *other* activists who were ostensibly "abandoning" the fight. Reacting to a shift in focus in lesbian and gay politics away from AIDS and toward issues like the ban against gays in the military, some AIDS activists demanded of former comrades and of others in the lesbian and gay community, "Where's your anger?!" alongside exhortations to "feel your anger" and "remember AIDS." For Crimp, this moralistic "hectoring" by some remaining AIDS activists indicated the direct-action AIDS movement's disavowal of despair and our collective failure "to assess the depths of our despair" (2002, 222, 227, 244). Projecting despair onto others in some sense warded off the pain associated with one's own despair, but at the cost of alienating others, including potential participants.

Feelings of betrayal are an important part of the story as well. Crimp's emphasis here is on the relationship between despair and moralizing, and although he does not discuss betrayal, I think that is in part what he is getting at. Activists who experienced their own creeping despair as in some sense a betrayal of people with AIDS might, overcome by shame, project the act of betrayal onto others. To understand some activists' sense of being betrayed by their comrades, we also need to remember that, throughout the course of the AIDS epidemic, lesbian and gay individuals and communities *have* been betrayed, by state and society, by families and friends. Indeed, feelings of betrayal have shaped lesbians' and gay men's experiences of the epidemic from its start. The early 1990s was a time of heightened desperation as AIDS activists witnessed both the explosion of the epidemic and attendant deaths, and the decline of the movement needed to fight the crisis, so it is not surprising that activists remaining in ACT UP would feel betrayed by those who were leaving. Some activists' self-righteous (and surely ineffective) attempts to mobilize people into the movement, then, might have been a response to feeling betrayed. Their hectoring might have been a defense against the pain of such feeling states, a way to establish their own righteousness and simultaneously to defend against the pain of others' "betrayal" by casting those who had left or who had never joined the movement as morally suspect.

People felt extraordinarily guilty about leaving the movement, whatever their reasons for doing so. ACT UP members' self-understanding helps to explain why: we saw ourselves as committed to ending the AIDS crisis and in solidarity with people with AIDS; thus, leaving the movement was easily experienced not only as abandoning the fight, but also as betraying people with AIDS. One might feel guilty even if one was HIV-positive, as the following quotation from Gregg Bordowitz indicates.

> You didn't leave ACT UP. It was like a relationship. You left ACT UP in the dishonest way you left a relationship you didn't want to actually acknowledge was breaking up. You just stopped showing up. Or you showed up occasionally. And you would make excuses to your friends, like, "Oh, I had something to do. I couldn't be at the meeting." "I haven't seen you around in a while, what's going on?" "Oh, nothing. Everything's fine. I've just been really busy." So, you'd skip a meeting, and then you'd skip another couple meetings. Then maybe a month would go by and you would check in. You would show up, but you would stay in the back. Finally, at some point I stopped going. . . .

Other people were leaving too. That crowd of people who I was involved with were also playing their little game of showing up, not showing up. (Bordowitz 2002b, 64–65)

The difficulty, Bordowitz suggests, did not simply derive from the pain of endings. The really hard thing was to acknowledge to his fellow activists and to himself that he was leaving, that he was in some sense giving up on ACT UP and the potential it once had signaled. Bordowitz's avoidance strategies, and other people's as well, warded off the pain of facing one's own despair as well as the pain of seeing oneself as betraying one's comrades.[32]

Despair affected different ACT UP members differently: some left the movement when despair and its companion sentiments overwhelmed their anger and hope; some felt despair but disavowed it, and some of those turned their attention toward more hopeful and less devastating activist endeavors like gays in the military, while others remained in ACT UP. Some of those who remained denied their own despair by moralistically deploring others' supposed "abandonment" of the struggle. Some were slower to despair; some felt less despair because they were more suspicious of science, had never had particularly high hopes regarding the powers-that-be, and thus had different expectations about what their activism could accomplish. The different tempos of despair notwithstanding, once the feeling developed among a number of members of ACT UP, it affected the organization as a whole, draining many people's energies and effectively (and affectively) depleting the ranks.

The unconscious processes that despair set in motion occurred in part because ACT UP's emotional habitus disallowed despair. Indeed, the emergence of despair and various activist responses to it indicate both the limits of and an unraveling of the movement's emotional habitus.

Forbidding Despair

Despair was verboten in ACT UP, the constitutive outside of the movement's emotional habitus. Anger and rage were the valid and expected

32. The discussion here provides additional insight into the psychic force of the accusations of betrayal that occurred amid ACT UP's internal conflicts (chapter 6). In a context of growing despair, where some people already were consciously or unconsciously anxious about having "given up" on people with AIDS, accusations of betrayal might be uncomfortably, even guiltily, resonant and thus especially incendiary.

emotions, as were optimism about a better future and faith in direct action as the way to get there. AIDS activism entailed an assertion of heroic agency: never mind the enormous barriers standing in our way, we *would* save our lives and the lives of our lovers, friends, and fellow activists. Given the alternative, we needed to see ourselves this way. In this context, there was no space for despair, which, following Jaggar (1989), might best be described as an "outlaw emotion."

In offering street activism as a response to despondency about the horrors of the AIDS crisis and to the sense of political impotency that was widespread in the mid-1980s, ACT UP fashioned itself as an antidote to despair, a place to "turn your grief into anger." Our practices were oriented toward doing just that. In the early 1990s, ACT UP/ Chicago rejected one member's proposal that ACT UP start its meetings with a moment of silence to commemorate our dead, voting instead to begin meetings with a "moment of rage" in the form of a loud chant. Jeff Edwards noted that anger stifled any grief that might have been expressed at ACT UP/Chicago's meetings: "There [was] just such a demand to take action, to not waste time. The meetings [were] about getting angry and taking action. And grieving just [did not] fit in there" (Edwards 2000a; see also Span 1989, D4). We viewed grief and despair as individualizing and depoliticizing, in contrast to anger, which we believed to be a main impetus for taking to the streets.

But as David Barr pointed out, although ACT UP "didn't have a discourse about emotions other than anger . . . they were all there"— there, but unacknowledged. Barr's sense was that the emotional habitus of ACT UP required feelings like grief and despair to be submerged for fear that permitting their expression somehow would destroy the organization; the ethos was as follows: "We just better not stop being angry, because that will open up all this other stuff and then we're really in trouble" (Barr 2002). So, while despair and its companions were banned, anger was required, as was the optimistic belief that ACT UP's collective action would save lives, especially the lives of people with AIDS *in the room*. The movement held out a hopeful vision—codified in the ACT UP maxim ACTION = LIFE—that in a sense disavowed death. You were not supposed to dwell on death at all, except as a spur to greater anger and intensified activism in honor of the deceased, so that their deaths would not be in vain. Instrumentalizing death for strategic purposes was allowed as well, in order to accuse the government and other institutions of genocide, of murdering our comrades and thousands of other people with AIDS. Doing so not only provided an effective framing of the crisis, it also defended us against the feelings of grief and loss that the accumulating deaths stirred up. It was a way of not giving in to grief and despair.

What lay behind the proscription against despair in some ways differed for HIV-negative and HIV-positive members. HIV-negatives demonstrated solidarity with HIV-positives by expressing anger about the crisis, by indicating their faith in and commitment to activism, by putting their bodies on the line, by holding onto hope for a cure or at least better drug treatments. Therefore, despairing of the crisis ever ending, of being able to save the lives of those now infected, might flood one with shame about failing to be a properly hopeful AIDS activist as well as guilt about giving up on the struggle and thereby in some sense abandoning people with AIDS. It was thus difficult to admit, even to yourself, that you were despairing of an end to the crisis, that you were feeling both helpless and hopeless.

In the following quotation, Rebecca Brown's narrator is referring to quitting her home health aid job, but her acknowledgment of how difficult it was to admit to herself that she was in the process of quitting is instructive about the psychic difficulties faced by HIV-negative ACT UP members when encountering their own feelings of despair and a desire to leave the movement: "I wasn't consciously thinking about quitting, but I was acting like it. But I would have felt bad to quit because it would be, for me, like giving up. Although in some ways I think I already had" (1994, 132). To despair of an end to the crisis, to despair of ACT UP's capacity to save lives, was to give up on HIV-positive people. For an AIDS activist, that was close to abomination.

You really could not succumb to despair, therefore, and if you began to feel it, you certainly could not reveal it to anyone else. Feeling such sentiments, how, for example, would you face people with AIDS? How could you let on that you were losing hope? Anxiety about betraying people with AIDS might propel you to disavow your despair and fight all the harder. And, indeed, many of us were so steeped in ACT UP's emotional habitus that all we felt was anger and conviction that our activism would succeed; it was hard to acknowledge or even to recognize any sentiments of hopelessness, helplessness, despair. But if you were unable to deny your despair, you might quietly leave the movement so as to avoid being in the room with desperate people with AIDS who needed your help and were holding onto hope when you were no longer able to.

You might slink away so as to avoid facing other HIV-negative people who somehow still were hopeful and committed, so as to avoid having to see yourself as someone who was betraying people with AIDS as well as abandoning the movement when it most needed more troops.

While people with HIV/AIDS within the movement, particularly those who were relatively healthy, had to navigate some of those issues as well, they also had to shoulder a different burden. They had to assume the role of the hopeful and persevering person with AIDS, heroically determined to fight the virus and survive the crisis. They had to embody the "empowered PWA" who was living with AIDS, not dying from it, and thereby substantiate ACT UP's assertion that AIDS was not a death sentence.[33] To preserve the vision that ACT UP's activism was saving lives, to inspire the uninfected to keep fighting on their behalf, they had to cloak their own dying. They were supposed to protect the healthy from the knowledge that, despite ACT UP's victories, AIDS was continuing to devastate and decimate and kill, even among ACT UP's own. HIV-positives certainly were not allowed to fall into despair, or, if they did succumb, to reveal to others their feelings of hopelessness and despondency. For both HIV-negatives and HIV-positives, then, to despair was to breach one's proper role as an AIDS activist and thereby *affectively* ditch the movement and (other) people with HIV/AIDS.

That was the ethos against despair, but in the early 1990s, many in the movement, both HIV-negative and HIV-positive, *did* start to feel despair and even to articulate it. The unrelenting deaths anesthetized many members' feelings of anger and overwhelmed their hope that activism would be able to slow or even stop the dying. Crimp observes that rather than attend to this growing despair, ACT UP members were more likely to ignore its depths, disavow its prevalence, and badger people because they were "succumbing" to it, none of which helped people overcome despair (Crimp 2002, 227). ACT UP's emotional habitus, born in a moment of despair and consequently oriented toward dealing with despair through overcoming it, offered no other solutions; under the pressure of growing despair, it began to unravel. Activists continued to elevate and authorize anger, but the force of the despair began

---

33. As problematic as they were, these representational demands need to be understood within a context of dominant society's negative portrayals of people with AIDS. As Bordowitz notes, these were "legitimate responses to the overwhelmingly prejudicial representations of PWAs generated by the commercial media in the early days of the epidemic" (2004, 249).

to numb people to anger, lessening the effectiveness of activists' emotion work.

Ferd Eggan recalled the shift in his own feeling states. While in C-FAR and ACT UP/Chicago, "the anger about people dying sustained [him]." But by the summer of 1990, when he moved to Los Angeles and began working in an ASO, everything "had become too complex and too human to just be angry." He recalls, "It was easier when the government wasn't doing anything. Then the government was doing something, but the something was inadequate. Then ultimately it wasn't just the question of whether it was *quantitatively* inadequate; it was *qualitatively* inadequate. 'Cause there was no resolution to the crisis, because there was no medication, there was no treatment, there was no cure" (Eggan 1999; emphases his). The complexity of AIDS, the unending deaths, and the lack of positive prospects on the treatment front overtook Eggan's anger. He continued, "Kevin Farrell [from ACT UP/L.A.] and I and a couple other people just said, 'Well, you know, mainly we just feel *bad*. We don't feel fiery demandful for something, because there isn't any *something*'" (Eggan 1999; emphases his). For Eggan, the death in 1992 of a close friend in ACT UP/L.A., Mark Kostopolous, marked the moment when ACT UP's emotional habitus seemed exhausted.

> All of these ACT UP veterans got together, [Mark's] friends, people who had been in ACT UP for years, and we wanted to have a political funeral down the street. But at the same time, there was also a lot of discussion at that meeting. . . . A lot of us just wanted to feel sad. We didn't particularly want to have a political funeral. We just wanted to feel sad, to mourn. I mean, we had just sort of reached the end of righteous indignation. (1999)

Eggan notes that "others were still very much full of anger" (1999), but sadness, grief, despair were overwhelming anger for some.

Gregg Bordowitz's 1993 video *Fast Trip, Long Drop,* illustrates this affective shift toward despair and proposes that AIDS activists reflect on how death and despair, and the movement's failures to grapple with both, were affecting their activism. Having made the video in "a period of hopelessness" directly following the 1993 Berlin Conference, at which doctors "announced to the world that no cure was on the horizon," Bordowitz writes that he "needed to openly confront the burn-out and despair that many activists felt" (Bordowitz 2004, 249). Where Bordowitz's earlier projects had adopted an "almost mandatory hopefulness" regarding the lives of PWAs, *Fast Trip, Long Drop* showed Bordowitz and other PWAs looking at their own deaths head on. Bordowitz writes, "When I made *FTLD* I was tired of pretending for the sake of others that I would survive. I became preoccupied with the burdens that sick people bear on behalf of those around them who are well" (249–50). For Bordowitz, the role of the heroic and hopeful person with AIDS, one that he and others in ACT UP had helped to propel, was wearing thin, unable to address the growing despair among HIV-positives and among AIDS activists more broadly. Bordowitz writes that he made the video "to get a handle on despair and put it out there as a political problem to be recognized and discussed," indicating that in his view the AIDS movement had not come to terms with death and despair, even as late as 1993 when (in part as a result of those sentiments and the inability to navigate them) the movement was already in the throes of decline (249–50).

Along with unconscious processes, then, the movement's ethos against despair contributed to its inability to attend to it when it did emerge. What is notable here is both the power of ACT UP's emotional habitus to structure its members' affects and emotional expressions—effectively suppressing and repressing despair—as well as the limits of that power insofar as that emotional habitus did not rid people of the negative affect itself. Because it forbade despair, the emotional habitus could not provide helpful tools for navigating that affective state when it arose despite efforts to exile it. It was a shameful secret not to be divulged to anyone. In that context, despair emerged in a way that individualized and depoliticized the feeling.

Anger, in contrast, had united us. In fact, ACT UP chapters across the country opened their weekly meetings by saying, "ACT UP is a diverse, nonpartisan group of individuals *united in anger* and committed to direct-action to end the AIDS crisis" (www.actupny.org; emphasis mine). Our anger was an important part of our collective self-definition. Even if our anger often had different sources and targets, there was a sharedness about the feeling, and it seemed like we all could relate to one another through our collective anger about the AIDS crisis. Whereas anger had been collectivizing, despair was individuating, particularly insofar as it violated ACT UP's emotion norms and, in part as a result, went largely unacknowledged. With no collective space carved out for its expression within ACT UP, members who were starting to feel despair had no way of interjecting it into their activist lives. As Crimp argues, ACT UP as an organization disavowed despair. As a result, it remained illegible to the room at large, an unacknowledged presence, but one that was nevertheless *felt* by many. But to *feel* it placed one outside of ACT UP's culture, outside of the collective space. It created a feeling chasm that seemed impossible to bridge: How does despair legibly speak to anger? How does anger speak to despair, except by asking "Where's your anger?" As the movement declined, that question was asked over and over during ACT UP meetings, "as if checking other people for I.D.," in the words of ACT UP/NY member John Weir. Where "rage bestow[ed] authenticity" (Weir 1995, 11), despair only created alienation from fellow activists and from ACT UP itself. Where anger had made participants feel like they were part of something vibrant and larger than themselves, despair made people feel alone and guilt-ridden and sad and bad, and thus less inclined to stay in the movement.

The Indeterminacy of Despair

My contention that despair helped to destroy ACT UP is itself depressing, tempting me to find some grain of hope on which to conclude. But to do so risks glossing over the hard feelings that sometimes accompany activism, and given their occasional prevalence in the contemporary political landscape, it seems important to acknowledge negative political feelings like despair in order to consider their sources and consequences. We need to think of ways to work *with* despair other than through denial and conversion into the (ostensibly) requisite hope.

By way of conclusion, then, I want to return to a point I made at the outset about the indeterminacy of despair. In this specific historical case, despair helped to destroy the movement, but that outcome was never inevitable. We need to return to ACT UP's emotional habitus and to the emotion work that generated it in order to understand why despair contributed to ACT UP's undoing. ACT UP's emotion work responded to the emotional habitus and political horizon that prevailed in the early 1980s. AIDS activists understandably focused their efforts on channeling grief into direct action, authorizing anger, burying the despair that characterized the period just prior to the emergence of the direct-action AIDS movement. Despair is not necessarily depoliticizing, but it seemed to be in the earlier period, and it also was painful to feel. AIDS activists therefore wanted to suppress it, in themselves and in others, and their emotion work succeeded for a long period. But the accumulating deaths and a growing sense of our inability to save lives altered the terrain in a manner that lessened the effectiveness of that emotion work.

I'm not sure we could have addressed the growing despair. The work of activism makes it difficult to deal with despair, as Crimp notes. And we have few models for dealing with bad feelings like despair that are not individualizing and depoliticizing. But it is something to consider. Just as ACT UP collectivized anger—as the women's liberation and other movements had done before it—so it might have addressed the despair, somehow, some way. Indeed, that is precisely what queer folks did in the 1986–87 period when the direct-action AIDS movement was born. They collectivized desperation and despair, conjoined those bad feelings with anger, and by doing so helped to launch the direct-action AIDS activist movement. With standard ways of thinking and acting coming up empty, despair acted as a goad to consider different forms of activism. And with ACT UP's many early victories and its elevation of anger the despair faded. When despair reemerged—this time in an especially deflating way because there was no ready activist solution as there had been in 1986–87—anger could no longer do the work it once had. We had no other route for dealing with despair.

Parts of the political left more generally prohibit despair, and my sense is that doing so impedes leftist activism.[34] Why go to a meeting or action only to be made to feel bad that you feel bad? Rather than requiring outrage and optimism, perhaps we should recognize that people feel all kinds of feelings regarding the state of the world, and acknowledging those feelings rather than denying them or requiring their conversion is a first step toward seeing their political potential. To be sure, when in the depths of despair, it can be hard to open toward fresh political possibilities, but that perhaps is some of the most important work of an activist, and of a movement. Bad as it feels, despair can be the provocation to "take the next forward step as activists" (Crimp 2002, 248). The route for despair is not fixed, and while some circumstances, like those facing direct-action AIDS activists in the early 1990s, make despair extremely difficult to address, how we do address it shapes the effects it will have.

34. Solnit argues precisely the opposite, that audible elements of the left only focus on the "bad news" of the world, thus bolstering an identity that is "masculine, stern, disillusioned, tough enough to face facts" (2004, 15–16). I agree that the left tends toward apocalyptic narratives about the world, but I also think that the emotional demand of those narratives is to be outraged and to not give in to despair.

CONCLUSION

Moving Politics

The title of this book, *Moving Politics,* contains two related claims, and I have structured this conclusion around them: first, emotion is fundamental to political life and always a factor in the realm of activism, something that stirs, inhibits, intensifies, modulates, impedes, incites; second, there is nothing fixed or stationary about political activism—its tactics, character, aspirations, are variable, changeable, movable.

Bringing Emotion Back In:
General Concepts and Lines of Inquiry

[A key argument of *Moving Politics* is that to understand the sources and character of political action requires tangling with emotion.] My narrative analysis of the emergence, development, and decline of the direct-action AIDS movement provides a general conceptual apparatus for doing so. I discuss here the concepts and lines of inquiry that have organized my account and that I believe can advance important analytical work in all studies of contentious politics.

I began my investigation with questions regarding political horizons, a line of inquiry that should be useful whatever one's empirical case in that a sense of political possibilities or impossibilities is a crucial factor that spurs and shapes political action or blocks it altogether. A community with grievances might encounter encouraging conditions for contentious activism—a supportive local politician and an influx of resources, for example—but if there is little sense among community members that change is possible or that any political action aside from voting is acceptable, it is unlikely that those conditions will lead to activism. Even when it is not the decisive factor, a political horizon influences whether and how people turn to collective action. And the very concept requires consideration of emotion because a *sense* of political (im)possibilities is itself an emotional state.

The concept of a political horizon opens fruitful avenues for research. To illuminate an instance of political action or inaction, we would want to know the contours and direction of a specific political horizon as well as the factors that generated it and, if change is evident, what expanded or contracted that sense of political possibility. This line of inquiry appropriately links feelings to their contexts and to history. Many factors, at various levels of analysis, might generate, reproduce, or transform a sense of possibility: in addition to some of those discussed in the book—an event like the *Bowers v. Hardwick* decision, closing or opening political opportunities, sentiments of exhilaration or desperation—we can imagine many other important phenomena, such as large-scale economic shifts, altered everyday routines, a change in resources, or spillover from other movements' successes or defeats. What makes any such factor matter with regard to senses of political possibility are the affective charges that attach to it and the way people interpret and respond to it.

That leads me to practice and to the concepts of emotional habitus and emotion work. As much as external factors play a significant role in shaping a sense of political possibility, those desiring social change must generate and regenerate that sense, intentionally or not, and they do so in conditions not of their own choosing. In the U.S. context, multiple barriers stand in the way. Most generally, activists confront prevailing emotional and political norms that tend to militate against contentious activism. There is widespread pessimism and cynicism about the possibilities of significant social change and a strong bias against angry, direct-action politics. Activists therefore need to engage in emotion and other interpretive work that helps to authorize and, even better, make axiomatic the challenges their efforts necessarily pose to the prevailing emotional habitus and its attendant political horizon.

Along with this generally inhospitable environment, activists face the

[handwritten marginal note: what did AIDS crisis do for Bowers?]

specifics of their context, which also shape the sorts of emotion and interpretive work that might be necessary. Early AIDS activists, for example, had to contend with gay shame, fear of social rejection, and consequent distancing from AIDS by many in lesbian and gay communities. They did so in part through emotion work that elevated pride in caretaking. Their efforts—conscious and not—primarily bolstered but also mildly challenged aspects of the existing emotional habitus in lesbian and gay communities and helped both to establish and circumscribe a specific political horizon in those communities. Later AIDS activists transformed the object of gay pride, harnessing it to radicalism, to furious and queer direct-action politics. That and other emotion work helped to generate and reinforce a counterhegemonic emotional habitus that expanded the sense of political possibilities by authorizing—even obliging—anger and tethering it to confrontational activism. A movement's emotional habitus and the emotion work it makes probable can sometimes hamper the movement's efforts, as occurred later in ACT UP's life when the disposition toward anger made it difficult to address some members' despair. This reminds us that emotion work does not always work, and the force of feelings, their bodily, visceral components—their affective dimension—helps to explain why.

Like the other concepts, affect illuminates processes and dynamics important to movement emergence, development, and decline. The nonconscious, noncognitive, nonlinguistic components of our feelings affect our sense of political possibilities and in other ways both incite and hinder political action. A focus on affect reminds us to take the visceral and bodily components of politics seriously, preserving for the concept of "experience" some of its felt quality, some of the sense of being moved by the world around us.

My case pointed me toward the important role of lesbian and gay ambivalence in political responses to the AIDS crisis. The shape and political contours of that constellation of contradictory feelings are specific to lesbian/gay/queer communities, but other marginalized groups who face other forms of oppression likely experience widespread ambivalence about self and society as well. More generally, bringing a concept of ambivalence into studies of contentious politics reminds us of the conflictual feelings, the contradictory pushes and pulls, that shape political behavior.

In my view, the best way to excavate the relation between emotion and politics is with a social, cultural, and historical approach that allows inquiry into the conditions of possibility for any given feeling. This allows us to move across various levels of analysis as necessary and to see both the swirl of feelings at any one juncture as well as the fluidity of emotional dynamics and change over time. It also ensures that we do not isolate feelings from other important factors or naturalize them and their effects. Feelings arise and play out in contexts, and although a given occurrence might tend to produce a specific set of feelings, which in turn might lead to specific sorts of political action, any such unfolding is always contingent, influenced by numerous contextual factors. As Barbalet notes, emotion does not compel behavior but inclines one to act in a particular way, shaping rather than determining one's actions (1998, 27). [The task, then, is to explore why and how given political feelings arise and shape the course of political action.]The general concepts I have offered here came out of my research, but they suggest lines of inquiry useful for doing precisely that.

Affecting Political Imaginaries

Two experiences with some of my students reveal some of what has been at stake for me in writing this book. The first happened in a seminar I was teaching on the social and political aspects of AIDS. We were well into the semester, and most students by then were participating in class discussions. I began a session on AIDS activism by asking if anyone in the class had ever participated in a social movement or protest action. No one answered; a few students looked down, seemingly embarrassed by the topic. Not quite able to interpret the pregnant silence, I tabled the question, and we turned to the assigned texts. At the end of the class, I raised the issue again and wondered aloud about why they had met my question with silence. One student explained her discomfort. She had participated in a walk-out from her high school in 1991 to protest the U.S. bombing of Iraq. When she returned to school the next day, she was met with a barrage of critical questions from other students about why she had walked out. They had accused her of being uninformed, unpatriotic, and radical. She still felt embarrassed, even ashamed, about the incident.

[A few years later, I went to an anti-sweatshop rally at the University of Chicago.]Student organizers were asking the university to join a consortium that monitors transnational corporations to ensure that their products are not being produced in sweatshop conditions. After a few speeches at the flagpole, the students who had organized the action decided to march into the administration building to deliver a petition with that demand. Fifty protesters marched into the building, asked to see the dean, and presented him with the petition. The dean accepted it and then stated that the university would not join the consortium, but he would nonetheless look over the petition. The students thanked him and began to file out of his office. The polite demeanor of the organizers shifted only after another participant in the action suggested that they were letting the dean off the hook and that we all might want to use this opportunity to ask some questions and press the demands. A few students then began to question the dean more vociferously, and some in the crowd loudly and angrily challenged his evasive answers. Just as things started heating up, the leaders ended the protest, again thanking the dean and quickly exiting the office.

Activism is intense, by which I mean it is charged with affect. It can be exhilarating, fun, scary, anxiety-producing. The preceding stories indicate in particular the embarrassment of doing political activism, of acting on your desire to live in a different world and of transgressing borders of decorum in order to do so. Hegemonic discourses in U.S. society tend to circumscribe the political and pronounce what is appropriate to that domain in a manner that ratifies the existing social order and impedes political activism oriented toward social transformation. To engage in activism that envisions alternative ways of organizing society and alternative ways of being is to risk membership in society, a sense of belonging, however partial it may be. Activism can make us vulnerable because it is so obviously about wanting something beyond what *is,* and to have a political desire often is construed as wanting too much. Beyond the specifics of the preceding stories, my general point is that *emotion,* in the word's fullest sense—sensations, feelings, passions, whether conscious or not—conditions the possibilities for oppositional activism. It does so by facilitating, and blocking, our political imaginations, our political horizons, our ideas about the politically (im)possible, (un)desirable, (un)necessary in a given moment. Our affective states can constrict our political imaginaries—as I think occurred with the students in the above stories—as well as extend them in new, unexpected directions.

Through protests and other activist manifestations, social movements unravel commonsense knowledges, counter the subtle and not-so-subtle power relations that pervade our lives, and assert that the way things are is not necessarily natural or the way they must or should be. They reveal sizable cracks in people's apparent complacency and indicate a conviction among participants that social arrangements are neither inevitable nor immutable. Activist interventions not only puncture the taken-for-granted, they also offer alternative ways of understanding and being in the world. They are a testament to the ever-present possibility of change.

   My agenda in this book is to encourage people to think about our individual and collective political horizons and to consider what forecloses and what enlarges our imaginings of what is to be done to bring desired worlds into being. The story of the AIDS movement is a story of political possibilities, of what can happen when people collectivize their efforts to address their grievances and enact their desires. The additional story here, the story of the direct-action AIDS movement specifically, is one of political horizons being blown open, of an embrace of unorthodox tactics in the face of intransigence by state and society. It is a story of political defiance and opposition that helped to change the course of the AIDS epidemic and thus the course of history. Studying this history and especially attending to its affective dimensions will, I hope, help pry open alternative, more expansive political imaginings for the contemporary moment.

Lesbian and Gay Newspapers

This appendix provides information about the lesbian and gay newspapers that I researched for this project. By 1985, lesbian and gay newspapers in the United States had a total circulation of eight hundred thousand; by 1990, that number had risen to one million (Streitmatter 1995).

Advocate

Published in Los Angeles, with national circulation, this was the most widely read gay newspaper when AIDS hit (Clendinen and Nagourney 2001, 466). It had a circulation of eighty thousand in 1984 (Streitmatter 1995).

I looked at every issue from June 1981 through June 1982, selected issues in 1983, every issue from 1984 through 1987, selected issues from 1988 through 1989, and every issue from 1990 through 1993.

Bay Area Reporter

Published in San Francisco, largest gay paper in San Francisco. Circulation was twenty-five thousand in 1983 (Streitmatter 1995), and more than thirty thousand in 1986 (*B.A.R.* editorial, 26 June, 1986).

I looked at every issue from 1983 through 1987, and selected articles from other years that I found in the ACT UP files at the Gay, Lesbian, Bisexual, Transgender Historical Society.

Gay Community News

Published in Boston by a leftist collective, with national circulation of sixty thousand by 1990 (Streitmatter 1995).

I looked at every issue from July 1981 through April 1983 and selected articles from 1983–1995 that were in my personal ACT UP archive and in Lou Snider's ACT UP archive.

Gay Life

Published in Chicago, with local circulation (circulation figures unknown).

I looked at every issue from June 1981 to January 1986, when the paper ceased publishing.

New York Native

Published in New York, with national circulation during the first years of the AIDS crisis. Circulation was twenty thousand in 1981 when the epidemic began, and the gay grapevine spread it far beyond that number; its circulation increased to twenty-five thousand between 1985 and 1989 (Streitmatter 1995).

I looked at every issue from June 1981 through 1987. I also looked at articles from other years from my personal archive, from Lou Snider's archive, from ACT UP collections at the New York Public Library (Manuscripts, Archives, and Rare Books Division) and at the Gay, Lesbian, Bisexual, Transgender Historical Society.

The *New York Native* was the only lesbian and gay paper in New York City during the early years of AIDS. As a source, it presents some problems. It is useful for exploring early lesbian and gay understandings of the epidemic because, unlike any other lesbian/gay paper, it provided consistent coverage from the very first reports. Because of its persistent coverage, and in light of "mainstream media silence," the *Native* became the newspaper where lesbians and gay men around the country got most of their information about AIDS in the earliest years (McGarry and Wasserman 1998, 223); it is also one of the important places where lesbians and gay men in New York and elsewhere discussed central issues about AIDS.

By 1985, however, the *Native*'s credibility had fallen significantly. Much of the reporting reads like a polemic designed to advance specific theories of the causation of AIDS while demoting others. James Kinsella writes that publisher and editor Charles Ortleb "grew frantic" as the deaths among his friends mounted. "His 'tips' moved from the provocative to the preposterous" (Kinsella 1989, 25). The cover of the August 24, 1987, issue prompted a complete loss of credibility: showing a picture of a jumping dolphin, the headline connected mysterious deaths of dolphins to AIDS and warned people to stay out of the ocean. Two gay men who were living in New York at the time have independently told me that that issue put the nail in the *Native*'s coffin for most gay men. In 1987 AIDS activist and cultural critic Douglas Crimp criticized the *Native*, writing, "Rather than performing a political analysis of the ideology of science, Ortleb merely touts the crackpot theory of the week, championing whoever is the latest outcast from the world of academic and government research" (1987c, 238). As sociologist Steven Epstein writes, the *Native*'s "fascination for unorthodox and speculative theories had left it with tarnished credibility even among its intended readership of gay men" (1996, 111; see also Altman 1994, 21; Gross 2001, 103; Streitmatter 1995, 289–91; McGarry and Wasserman 1998, 267). For these reasons, I have avoided using the *Native*'s sensationalized stories and editorials as data except when a part that is relevant to me is unaffected by that polemicism.

Nightlines
Published in Chicago, with local circulation (circulation figures unknown).
I read articles from my archive and from Lou Snider's archive, covering 1988 through 1995.

NYQ
Published in New York, with national circulation (circulation figures unknown).
NYQ published a number of issues in 1991 and 1992 before becoming *QW;* I looked at every issue.

Outlines
Published in Chicago, with local circulation (circulation figures unknown).
I read articles from my archive and from Lou Snider's archive, covering 1988 through 1995.

OUT/LOOK
Published in San Francisco, with national circulation (circulation figures unknown).
I looked at selected, relevant articles that were in my personal archive and in Lou Snider's archive.

OutWeek
Published in New York, with national circulation. Circulation was about twenty thousand according to Features Editor Michelangelo Signorile (2003), and perhaps as high as thirty thousand according to Streitmatter (1995).
I looked at every issue that was published, from June 1989 until July 1991.

QW
Published in New York, with national circulation (circulation figures unknown).
I looked at every published issue (May through November 1992).

Sentinel/Sentinel USA/San Francisco Sentinel
Published in San Francisco, with local circulation. Circulation was eighteen thousand in 1984 (editorial in *Sentinel,* 26 April 1984, 5).

I looked at every issue from 1983 through 1987 and selected articles from other years that were in the ACT UP collection at the Gay, Lesbian, Bisexual, Transgender Historical Society.

TITA (Tell It To ACT UP)

Published weekly by ACT UP/NY member Bill Dobbs as ACT UP/NY's internal complaint and suggestion broadsheet.

I looked at every published issue (February 1990 through June 1, 1992).

Washington Blade

Published in Washington, D.C., with national circulation (circulation figures unknown).

I looked at issues surrounding important events in my narrative: January through June 1983; June through December 1985, July through August 1986. I also looked at articles from other years from my personal archive, from Lou Snider's archive, and from ACT UP collections at the New York Public Library and at the Gay, Lesbian, Bisexual, Transgender Historical Society.

Windy City Times

Published in Chicago, with local circulation (circulation figures unknown).

I read every issue from its first issue in September 1985 through 1988. I also read articles from my own personal archive and from Lou Snider's archive that covered ACT UP through January 1995.

Glossary with Notes on Terms

ACTG. AIDS Clinical Trials Group, a government-sponsored group that conducts most AIDS drug research.

ACT NOW. AIDS Coalition to Network, Organize, and Win; the umbrella organization of direct-action AIDS groups across the country (it later changed its name to ACT UP/Network).

ACT UP. AIDS Coalition to Unleash Power. I use the name ACT UP when referring to the national direct-action AIDS movement, even though ACT UP was neither the first nor the only direct-action AIDS group. Earlier AIDS activist organizations such as Citizens for Medical Justice in San Francisco and DAGMAR in Chicago eventually became ACT UP chapters. Some direct-action AIDS groups, such as the Washington, D.C., group OUT (Oppression Under Target), affiliated with ACT UP on a national level but never adopted the name.

AIDS. Acquired immune deficiency syndrome.

ASO. AIDS service organization.

B.A.R. *Bay Area Reporter,* one of San Francisco's gay newspapers in this period.

CDC. Centers for Disease Control and Prevention.

C-FAR. Chicago for AIDS Rights.

CLGR. Coalition for Lesbian and Gay Rights.

CMJ. Citizens for Medical Justice.

DAGMAR. Dykes and Gay Men against Repression/Racism/Reagan/the Right Wing.

Direct-action AIDS activism; direct-action AIDS movement. I use these phrases to describe ACT UP's style of activism, which tended to be oppositional and often entailed civil disobedience and similar tactics, and to contrast ACT UP with other forms of AIDS activism that emphasized service provision and advocacy. The term *direct action* is multivalent; I use it to refer to activism that seeks social change and is self-consciously involved in a struggle for power in any arena. Along with strikes, sit-ins, die-ins, disruptions, and street demonstrations, direct-action activism often entails the production of knowledge and interventions in the cultural realm. It also sometimes involves creating alternative, self-organized services to meet needs unmet by the state and other major institutions.

FDA. Food and Drug Administration.

GLAAD. Gay and Lesbian Alliance against Defamation.

GLADL. Gay and Lesbian Anti-Defamation League (GLAAD's initial name).

GMHC. Gay Men's Health Crisis.

HIV. Human immunodeficiency virus, the virus thought by most scientists to cause AIDS.

HRCF. Human Rights Campaign Fund.

Lesbian and gay. Naming the members of a social group is always an exclusionary process. The phrase *lesbian and gay* was commonly used during part of the historical moment under study (the 1980s), but it obscured the roles of bisexuals, transgendered people, and other sexual and gender minorities in the events in question. Alternatives such as *queer* and *LGBT* (lesbian/gay/bisexual/transgender), however, are anachronistic; *queer*, which some had used in earlier decades, did not become a widespread self-descriptor until about 1990, a shift that I discuss in chapter 4. While many actors in my narrative likely engaged in sexual and gender practices that today might furnish one with a transgender or bisexual identity, those categories were infrequently invoked during the early years of the period under study. I thus ambivalently use the phrase *lesbian and gay,* sometimes qualifying it to acknowledge that people who identified differently were also actors in this history. (I occasionally use the phrase "queer folks" for brevity.)

Lesbian and gay communities. I use the phrase *lesbian and gay communities* to refer to the groupings of individuals and institutions from which the grassroots response to AIDS emerged. Invocations of the term *community* often obscure the historical contingency of any given community as well as struggles over who is inside and who is outside. I understand the term as a fiction that is always in process, a *becoming* rather than a *being,* and one that is always contested, though it may resonate strongly for many.

MAA. Mobilization against AIDS.

MAC. Majority Action Committee, ACT UP/NY's first caucus for people of color.

NGLTF. National Gay and Lesbian Task Force.

NGTF. National Gay Task Force (NGLTF's name before it included lesbians in its title).

NIAID. National Institute of Allergy and Infectious Diseases, the body that oversees the government's AIDS research effort.

NIH. National Institutes of Health, which oversees NIAID.

PCP. *Pneumocystis carinii* pneumonia.

PISD. People with Immune System Disorders caucus.

PWA. Person with AIDS.

T&D. ACT UP/NY's Treatment and Data Committee.

TAG. Treatment Action Group.

References

"$10 Million Cutback Sought in AIDS Funding." 1985. *Gay Life*, 21 February, 5.

"1985." 1985. Editorial. *Windy City Times*, 26 December, 11.

"ACTG 076 Is Bad Science and Is Unethical." 1991. Fact Sheet. 10 March. Primary Source Microfilm, Gay Rights Movement—Series 3: *ACT UP: The AIDS Coalition to Unleash Power*, reel 46, box 63, folder 4. Produced by Gale CENGAGE Learning; see their Web site at http://www.gale.cengage.com/servlet/BrowseSeriesServlet?region=9&imprint=745&titleCode=PSM5&edition=.

"Acting Up Wins Results—and Enemies." 1990. Editorial. *Economist*, 23 June, 23.

ACT NOW. 1990 [ca. June]. "A Capsule History of ACT UP/San Francisco." Document available in the "ACT UP" file at the GLBT Historical Society (San Francisco).

"ACT UP, AIDS and the Persian Gulf." 1991. Editorial. *Windy City Times*, 31 January, 11.

ACT UP/Chicago. 1990. *Get It: Newsletter of ACT UP/Chicago*. July–August. Document housed in my personal ACT UP archive.

ACT UP/Chicago. 1991a. "ACT UP Lists Broad Agenda." Letter to the editor. *Windy City Times*, 14 February, 10.

———. 1991b. "The AIDS Epidemic, Eleven Years Later. This War's Not Over." Leaflet. 30 June. Document housed in my personal ACT UP archive.

———. 1992. Pride speech. June. Document housed in my personal ACT UP archive.

ACT UP/Chicago PWA Caucus. 1990. Letter to the editor. *Windy City Times*, 30 August, 11.

ACT UP/Chicago Women's Caucus. 1989. "The Women's Caucus of ACT UP Is Acting Up Against Sexism." 3 October. Document housed in my personal ACT UP archive.

"ACT UP Disrupts Yale Speech by Federal Health Secretary." 1990. *New York Times*, 29 November, B12.

ACT UP/Los Angeles. n.d. [ca. January 1988]. "The FDA and the Methodology of Death." Document housed in my personal ACT UP archive.

ACT UP/New York. n.d. a. "ACT UP/NY Capsule History." Primary Source Microfilm, Gay Rights Movement—Series 3: *ACT UP: The AIDS Coalition to Unleash Power,* reel 1, box 1, folder 8. Produced by Gale CENGAGE Learning; see their Web site at http://www.gale.cengage.com/servlet/BrowseSeries Servlet?region=9&imprint=745&titleCode=PSM5&edition=.

——. n.d. b. "ACT UP Chapters outside the United States." Document housed at New York Public Library, Manuscripts and Archives Section, ACT UP/ New York Records, box T-38.

——. 1987a. "Meeting Minutes, March 12, 1987." (Written by Bradley Ball.) Document housed in the New York Public Library, Manuscripts and Archives Section, ACT UP/New York Records, box T-14.

——. 1987b. "ACT UP/NY Meeting Minutes, April 20, 1987." Document housed in my personal ACT UP archive.

——. 1987c. "ACT UP/NY Meeting Minutes, May 18, 1987." Document housed in my personal ACT UP archive.

——. 1988a. "Meeting Minutes, May 30, 1988." Document housed in the New York Public Library, Manuscripts and Archives Section, ACT UP/New York Records, box T-14.

——. 1988b. "Show Your Anger to the People Who Helped Make the Quilt Possible: Our Government." Leaflet. October. Document housed in my personal ACT UP archive.

——. 1990. *A Critique of the AIDS Clinical Trials Group.* (Written by Mark Harrington.) May. Document housed in my personal ACT UP archive.

——. 1991. "Meeting Minutes, March 18, 1991." Primary Source Microfilm, Gay Rights Movement—Series 3: *ACT UP: The AIDS Coalition to Unleash Power,* reel 3, box 5, folder 6. Produced by Gale CENGAGE Learning; see their Web site at http://www.gale.cengage.com/servlet/BrowseSeriesServlet? region=9&imprint=745&titleCode=PSM5&edition=.

——. 1992. "Bring Your Grief and Rage about AIDS to a Political Funeral." Leaflet. Document housed in my personal ACT UP archive.

ACT UP/NY Majority Actions Committee. 1990 (ca. January–March). "Memo to ACT UP; Issue: Cultural Sensitivity and Communication." Primary Source Microfilm, Gay Rights Movement—Series 3: *ACT UP: The AIDS Coalition to Unleash Power,* reel 6, box 8, folder 5. Produced by Gale CENGAGE Learning; see their Web site at http://www.gale.cengage.com/servlet/BrowseSeriesS ervlet?region=9&imprint=745&titleCode=PSM5&edition=.

ACT UP/NY T&D Committee. 1991. "The Treatment and Data Digest." 18 March, 1–8. Document housed in my personal ACT UP archive.

ACT UP/NY Women and AIDS Book Group. 1990. *Women, AIDS, and Activism.* Boston, MA: South End Press.

Adam, Barry. 1995. *The Rise of a Gay and Lesbian Movement*. Rev. ed. New York: Twayne.

Adkins, Barry. 1985. "Gay Anti-Defamation League Announces Town Meeting." *New York Native*, 18–24 November, 10.

Agosto, Moisés. 2002. Interview conducted by ACT UP Oral History Project. Available at www.actuporalhistory.org.

Ahmed, Sara. 2004. *The Cultural Politics of Emotion*. New York: Routledge.

AIDS Action Pledge. n.d. (ca. 1987). "AIDS Action Pledge of Protest and Support, for Love and for Life." Document housed in my personal ACT UP archive.

"AIDS Activists Arrested." 1990. *U.S.A. Today*, 22 May.

"AIDS and Misdirected Rage." 1990. Editorial. *New York Times*, 26 June, A22.

"AIDS: Now a Respectable Disease." 1985. Editorial. *Gay Life*, 27 June, 11.

Alexander, David. 1989. "Time to Grow Up." Letter to the editor. *Bay Area Reporter*, 21 September.

Alexander, Keith. 1991. "AIDS Protester Freed on Bond of $25,000." *Chicago Tribune*, 26 June.

Altman, Dennis. 1987. *AIDS in the Mind of America*. New York: Anchor Books.

———. 1994. *Power and Community: Organizational and Cultural Responses to AIDS*. London: Taylor and Francis.

"Alzheimer's Morass" 1991. Editorial. *Wall Street Journal*, 26 March, A2.

Aminzade, Ron, and Doug McAdam. 2001. "Emotions and Contentious Politics." In *Silence and Voice in the Study of Contentious Politics*, ed. Ron Aminzade, Jack A. Goldstone, Doug McAdam, Elizabeth J. Perry, William H. Sewell, Jr., Sidney Tarrow, and Charles Tilly, 14–50. Cambridge: Cambridge University Press.

Anderson, Benedict. 1983. *Imagined Communities: Reflections on the Origin and Spread of Nationalism*. London: Verso.

Andriote, John-Manuel. 1999. *Victory Deferred: How AIDS Changed Gay Life in America*. Chicago: University of Chicago Press.

Anger, David. 1988. "On ACT UP." *ARTPAPER*. October, 10. Document housed in the New York Public Library, Manuscripts and Archives Section, ACT UP/New York Records, and in my personal ACT UP archive.

"Angry AIDS Activists Rally Near Convention." 1992. *Christian Science Monitor*, 16 July.

Anonymous. 1986. Letter to the editor. *Washington Blade*, 11 July, 21.

———. [Mark Fisher]. 1992. "Bury Me Furiously." *QW*, 25 October, 48.

———. 2000. Interview conducted by Deborah Gould. Interview housed in my personal ACT UP archive.

———. 2002. Interview conducted by Deborah Gould. Interview housed in my personal ACT UP archive.

Appadurai, Arjun. 1990. "Topographies of the Self: Praise and Emotion in

Hindu India." In *Language and the Politics of Emotion,* ed. Catherine Lutz and Lila Abu-Lughod, 92–112. Cambridge and New York: Cambridge University Press.

"Apuzzo, Enlow Testify for AIDS Research." 1983. *Gay Life,* 19 May, 3.

"Apuzzo Testifies for AIDS in Congress; Requests $100 Million for Research." 1983. *Bay Area Reporter,* 19 May, 4.

Apuzzo, Virginia. 1986. "Stonewalling." *New York Native,* 28 July, 11.

ARC & AIDS Vigil. n.d. [ca. February 1986]. "Background on the ARC & AIDS Vigil." Document housed at GLBT Historical Society (San Francisco), ARC/AIDS Vigil Records, 1985–1990.

Armstrong, Elizabeth A. 2002. *Forging Gay Identities: Organizing Sexuality in San Francisco, 1950–1994.* Chicago: University of Chicago Press.

Arno, Peter S., and Karyn L. Feiden. 1993. *Against the Odds: The Story of AIDS Drug Development, Politics, and Profits.* New York: HarperPerennial.

Arvanette, Steven C. 1983. "Thousands in Vigil Demand Millions for AIDS." *New York Native,* 23 May–5 June, 9–10.

"As AIDS Treatment Activists." 1991 (10 March). Primary Source Microfilm, Gay Rights Movement—Series 3: *ACT UP: The AIDS Coalition to Unleash Power,* reel 46, box 63, folder 4. Produced by Gale CENGAGE Learning; see their Web site at http://www.gale.cengage.com/servlet/BrowseSeriesServlet?region=9&imprint=745&titleCode=PSM5&edition=.

Auerbach, Jane. 1991 (12 March). Letter from Life Force (signed by Auerbach). Primary Source Microfilm, Gay Rights Movement—Series 3: *ACT UP: The AIDS Coalition to Unleash Power,* reel 46, box 63, folder 4. Produced by Gale CENGAGE Learning; see their Web site at http://www.gale.cengage.com/servlet/BrowseSeriesServlet?region=9&imprint=745&titleCode=PSM5&edition=.

Baim, Tracy. 1985. "House Hearing on AIDS Held in Frisco." *Gay Life,* 11 July, 4.

———. 1988. Editorial. "This Generation's Holocaust." *Outlines,* July, 4.

———. 1993. "Off the Cuffs." *Nightlines,* 21 July, 8.

———. 2001. Interview conducted by Deborah Gould, July 21, Chicago. Interview housed in my personal ACT UP archive.

Ball, Bradley. 1987. "Letter of May 25, 1987." In Goldberg 1997.

Banzhaf, Marion. 2000. Interview conducted by Ann Cvetkovich, March, New York. Interview housed in my personal ACT UP archive.

———. 2002. Interview conducted by Deborah Gould, September 12, New York. Interview housed in my personal ACT UP archive.

Barbalet, Jack M. 1998. *Emotion, Social Theory, and Social Structure: A Macrosociological Approach.* Cambridge: Cambridge University Press.

Barker, Karlyn. 1991. "Taking AIDS Battle to Capitol Hill." *Washington Post,* 29 September, B4.

Barr, David. 2002. Interview conducted by Deborah Gould, September 11, New York. Interview housed in my personal ACT UP archive.

Barron, James. 1991. "Judge Denounces 'Lawless' Beating by Police at Rally." *New York Times,* 1 October.

Beardemphl, W. E. 1983. "Destroying the Myth of AIDS." Editorial. *Sentinel,* 9 June, 5.

Beck, Joan. 1990. "Protests Threaten to Drown Science at AIDS Conference." *Chicago Tribune,* 14 May.

Beegan, Daniel. 1985. "Studds Says Reagan Has Shown Little Concern over AIDS." Associated Press, 19 September.

Beldekas, John. 1985. "Int'l Conference on AIDS Attended by 2,300 Scientists and Health Care Workers." *New York Native,* 6–19 May, 10–11.

Benford, Robert D. 1993. " 'You Could Be the Hundredth Monkey': Collective Action Frames and Vocabularies of Motive within the Nuclear Disarmament Movement." *Sociological Quarterly* 34, no. 2:195–216.

———. 1997. "An Insider's Critique of the Social Movement Framing Perspective." *Sociological Inquiry* 67, no. 4:409–30.

Bengston, Don. 1984. "Piggy Classified Make Bad PR." Letter to the editor. *New York Native,* 2–15 January, 6.

Berezin, Mabel. 2001. "Emotions and Political Identity: Mobilizing Affection for the Polity." In Goodwin, Jasper, and Polletta, 2001a, 83–98.

Bergman, David. 1991. *Gaiety Transfigured: Gay Self-Representation in American Literature.* Madison: University of Wisconsin Press.

Berkowitz, Richard, Michael Callen, and Richard Dworkin. 1983. *How to Have Sex in an Epidemic.* New York: News from the Front Publications. Reprinted in Blasius and Phelan 1997, 571–74.

Berlandt, Konstantin. 1983. "New York Marches and Rallies for AIDS." *Bay Area Reporter,* 12 May, 4.

Berlant, Lauren. 2007. "Nearly Utopian, Nearly Normal: Post-Fordist Affect in *La Promesse* and *Rosetta.*" *Public Culture* 19, no. 2:273–301.

Berlant, Lauren, and Elizabeth Freeman. 1993. "Queer Nationality." In *Fear of a Queer Planet: Queer Politics and Social Theory,* ed. Michael Warner, 193–229. Minneapolis: University of Minnesota Press.

Bersani, Leo. 1995. *Homos.* Cambridge, MA: Harvard University Press.

Bérubé, Allan. 1984. "Resorts for Sex Perverts." Reprinted as "Prophesy, 1984" in *Harvard Gay and Lesbian Review* (Spring 1998): 10.

———. 1988. "Caught in the Storm: AIDS and the Meaning of Natural Disaster." *Out/Look* (Fall): 8–19.

Berzon, Betty. 1994. "Acting Up." In Thompson 1994, 307–8.

Biddle, Frederic M. 1993. "ACT UP's Last Act?" *Boston Globe Magazine,* 5 September.

Black, Kate. 1996. *Fighting for Life: Lesbians in ACT UP.* MA thesis. Department of Sociology, University of Kentucky.

Blasius, Mark, and Shane Phelan. 1997. *We Are Everywhere: A Historical Sourcebook of Gay and Lesbian Politics.* New York: Routledge.

Bockman, Philip. 1986. "A Fine Day." *New York Native,* 25 August, 12–13.

Boffey, Philip. 1985. "Reagan Defends Financing for AIDS." *New York Times,* 18 September, B7.

Bommer, Lawrence. 1988. "Naming Our Dead: Our Evergreen Memorial Day." *Windy City Times,* 16 June, 10.

Bommer, Lawrence, and Albert Williams. 1984. "AIDS Claims Two Well-Known Chicago Gay Men." *Gay Life,* 11 October, 1.

Bordowitz, Gregg. 1987. "Picture a Coalition." *October* 43 (Winter): 182–96.

———. 1993. "The AIDS Crisis Is Ridiculous." In *Queer Looks: Perspectives on Lesbian and Gay Film and Video,* ed. Martha Gever, John Greyson, and Pratibha Parmar, 209–24. New York: Routledge.

———. 2002a. Interview conducted by Deborah Gould, September 3, Chicago. Interview housed in my personal ACT UP archive.

———. 2002b. Interview conducted by ACT UP Oral History Project. Available at www.actuporalhistory.org.

———. 2004. *The AIDS Crisis Is Ridiculous and Other Writings: 1986–2003.* Cambridge, MA: MIT Press.

Bordowitz, Gregg, and David Deitcher. 1998. "Art, Activism, and Everyday Life." *Documents* 11 (Winter): 30–37.

Bourdieu, Pierre. 1977. *Outline of a Theory of Practice.* Cambridge: Cambridge University Press. (Orig. pub. in French, 1972.)

———. 1990. *The Logic of Practice.* Stanford, CA: Stanford University Press. (Orig. pub. in French, 1980.)

———. 2001. *Masculine Domination.* Stanford, CA: Stanford University Press. (Orig. pub. in French, 1998.)

Bourdieu, Pierre, and Loïc J. D. Wacquant. 1992. *An Invitation to Reflexive Sociology.* Chicago: University of Chicago Press.

Bowden, Mark. 1992. "Rude Awakenings." *Philadelphia Inquirer Magazine,* 14 June, 18–23.

Brady, Judith, ed. 1991. *1 in 3: Women with Cancer Confront an Epidemic.* Pittsburgh: Cleis Press.

Braverman, Gedalia. 2003. Interview conducted by ACT UP Oral History Project. Available at www.actuporalhistory.org.

Braverman, Phil. 1990. Letter to the editor. *Wall Street Journal,* 15 January.

Brennan, Teresa. 2004. *The Transmission of Affect.* Ithaca, NY: Cornell University Press.

Brier, Jennifer. 2007. "Locating Lesbian and Feminist Responses to AIDS, 1982–1984." *Women's Studies Quarterly* 35, nos. 1–2:234–48.

Bronski, Michael. 1982. "AIDing Our Guilt and Fear." *Gay Community News,* 9 October, 8–10.

———. 1986. "The Effect of Death-Fear on the Decadence of the 1970s." *Advocate,* 7 January, 8–9.

———. 1994. "1984: Culture Clash." In Thompson 1994, 259–60.

———. 1998. *The Pleasure Principle: Sex, Backlash, and the Struggle for Gay Freedom.* New York: St. Martin's Press.

Brown, David E. 1985. "Striking Back." *New York Native,* 2–8 December, 23.

Brown, Rebecca. 1994. *Gifts of the Body.* New York: HarperCollins.

Brown, Wendy. 2001. *Politics Out of History.* Princeton, NJ: Princeton University Press.

Brysk, Alison. 1995. "'Hearts and Minds': Bringing Symbolic Politics Back In." *Polity* 27, no. 4:559–85.

Buckley, William F., Jr., 1986. "Identify All the Carriers." *New York Times,* 16 March.

Bull, Chris. 1991. "Spy Allegations Pit Pennsylvania Police Against Activists." *Advocate,* 26 February.

———. 1993. "No News Is Bad News; Silver Linings Are Few and Far between at This Year's International AIDS Conference." *Advocate,* 13 July.

Burkes, William. 1986. "Sodomy: The Effect of '*Bowers v. Hardwick.*'" *Windy City Times,* 10 July, 1–2.

———. 1988. "Chicago Activists: Life after the Supreme Court CD." *Outlines,* February.

Burkett, Elinor. 1995. *The Gravest Show on Earth: America in the Age of AIDS.* New York: Houghton Mifflin.

Bush, Larry. 1983a. "Action and Reaction: Coping with a Crisis: The Community Responds to a Serious Health Problem." *Advocate,* 17 February, 19–21.

———. 1983b. "Reagan Response Blasted in AIDS Hearings." *New York Native,* 15–28 August, 14–15.

"Bush Should Have Come: President Missed a Chance to Show That His Heart Is in the Battle against AIDS." 1990. Editorial. *San Francisco Examiner,* 26 June, 14.

Butler, Judith. 1993. "Critically Queer." *GLQ* 1, no. 1:17–32.

———. 1997. *Excitable Speech: A Politics of the Performative.* New York: Routledge.

———. 1999. *Gender Trouble: Feminism and the Subversion of Identity.* 10th anniversary ed. New York: Routledge. (Orig. pub. 1990.)

Byron, Peggy. 1983. "AIDS and the Gay Men's Health Crisis of New York." *Gay Community News,* 6 August.

———. 1986. "Georgia Decision Ignites Demonstrations Nationwide." *Washington Blade,* 11 July, 1.

Calhoun, Craig. 2001. "Putting Emotions in Their Place." In Goodwin, Jasper, and Polletta 2001a, 45–57.

Califia, Pat. 1994. "1985: Turning Point." In Thompson 1994, 275–76.

"Call 1-(202) 456–7639." 1983. Editorial. *Gay Life*, 28 April, 4.

Callen, Michael, and Richard Berkowitz, with Richard Dworkin. 1982. "We Know Who We Are: Two Gay Men Declare War on Promiscuity." *New York Native*, 8–21 November, 23.

Camia, Catalina. 1990. "'90s AIDS Outlook Grim, Experts Say, but Medical Advances Deemed Likely." *Dallas Morning News*, 29 October.

Carlomusto, Jean. 2002. Interview conducted by ACT UP Oral History Project. Available at www.actuporalhistory.org.

Cecchi, Robert L. 1983. "Dear Mr. President." *New York Native*, 23 May–5 June, 10.

"Celebrating Liberty: For Straights Only." 1986. Editorial. *Windy City Times*, 3 July, 9.

Centers for Disease Control and Prevention. 1986 (29 December). *AIDS Weekly Surveillance Report*, 1–5.

———. 1987 (28 December). *AIDS Weekly Surveillance*, 1–5.

———. 1989 (January 1990). *HIV/AIDS Surveillance, Year End Edition*, 1–22.

———. 1997. *HIV/AIDS Surveillance Report*, vol. 9, no. 1:1–37.

"Central Park Memorial." 1983. *Advocate*, 21 July, 11.

C-FAR. n.d. "Fight Back, Fight AIDS!" Document housed in my personal ACT UP archive.

———. n.d. (ca. April 1988). "Over 30,000 Have Died." Leaflet. Document housed in my personal ACT UP archive.

———. 1988a (7 April). "Dear Friend of C-FAR." Document housed in my personal archive.

———. 1988b. Agenda for October 25, 1988 meeting. Document housed in my personal ACT UP archive.

Chambré, Susan M. 2006. *Fighting for Our Lives: New York's AIDS Community and the Politics of Disease*. New Brunswick, NJ: Rutgers University Press.

Chase, Marilyn. 1989a. "Activists Steal Show at AIDS Conference." *Wall Street Journal*, 12 June, A1.

———. 1989b. "Shock Troops: Activist Risk-Takers May Gain Legitimacy in the War on AIDS; FDA and Researchers Hope 'Community' Drug Trials Will Produce Good Data; Euphoria over Compound Q." *Wall Street Journal*, 28 July, A1.

Chauncey, George. 1995. *Gay New York: Gender, Urban Culture, and the Making of the Gay Male World, 1890–1940*. New York: Basic Books.

Chesley, Robert. 1981. "Letters." Letter to the editor. *New York Native*, 7–21 October.

Chibbaro, Lou, Jr. 1990. "1,000 Demonstrators Storm the NIH." *Washington Blade*, 25 May.

Chibbaro, Lou, Jr., and Steve Martz. 1983. "Pressure for More Federal AIDS Dollars Is Increasing." *Washington Blade*, 6 May, 1.

Chou, Lei. 2003. Interview conducted by ACT UP Oral History Project. Available at www.actuporalhistory.org.

Church, Bart. 1983. Letter to the editor. "Required Reading." *New York Native,* 11–24 April, 5–6.

Cimons, Marlene. 1990. "Demonstrators Demand More AIDS Research." *Los Angeles Times,* 22 May.

City of Chicago Department of Health. 1991. "AIDS Chicago: AIDS Surveillance Report, 1981–1991."

"City, State Should Press for AIDS Funding." 1983. Editorial. *Gay Life,* 21 July, 4.

"Civil Disobedience vs. Uncivilized Behavior." 1989. Editorial. *New York Daily News,* 12 December.

Clark, Keith. 1990. "Will There Be Violence at AIDS Conference?" *Windy City Times,* 7 June.

Clendinen, Dudley, and Adam Nagourney. 2001. *Out for Good: The Struggle to Build a Gay Rights Movement in America.* New York: Touchstone.

Cohen, Cathy J. 1993. *Power, Resistance and the Construction of Crisis: Marginalized Communities Respond to AIDS.* PhD diss. Department of Political Science, University of Michigan.

———. 1996. "Contested Membership: Black Gay Identities and the Politics of AIDS." In *Queer Theory/Sociology,* ed. Steven Seidman, 362–94. Cambridge, MA: Blackwell.

———. 1999. *The Boundaries of Blackness: AIDS and the Breakdown of Black Politics.* Chicago: University of Chicago Press.

Cohen, Jon. 1991. "ACTing StUPid Over AIDS: Activists Hurt Themselves by Disrupting the Florence Conference." *Washington Post,* 30 June, C4.

Cohen, Peter Franzblau. 1998. *Love and Anger: Essays on AIDS, Activism, and Politics.* New York: Harrington Park Press.

Collins, Randall. 1990. "Stratification, Emotional Energy, and the Transient Emotions." In Kemper 1990, 27–57.

———. 1993. "Emotional Energy as the Common Denominator of Rational Choice." *Rationality and Society* 5, no. 2:203–30.

———. 2001. "Social Movements and the Focus of Emotional Attention." In Goodwin, Jasper, and Polletta 2001a, 27–44.

———. 2004. *Interaction Ritual Chains.* Princeton, NJ: Princeton University Press.

"A Condom Too Far." 1990. *Economist,* 15 December, 27.

"Congratulations—And Let's Pitch In!" 1983. Editorial. *Gay Life,* 6 October, 4.

Conkey, Kathleen, Gregory Kolovakas, Rosemary Kuropat, and Darrell Yates-Rist. 1988. "Zapping the Mayor or Zapping Gays?" Letter to the editor. *New York Native,* 4 July, 6.

Conkin, Dennis. 1989. "Bridge Blockade Angers Commuters, Attracts Media." *San Francisco Sentinel,* 2 February.

Cook, Timothy E., and David C. Colby. 1992. "The Mass-Mediated Epidemic: The Politics of AIDS on the Nightly Network News." In *AIDS: The Making of a Chronic Disease*, ed. Elizabeth Fee and Daniel M. Fox, 84–122. Berkeley and Los Angeles: University of California Press.

Corea, Gena. 1993. *The Invisible Epidemic: The Story of Women and AIDS*. New York: HarperPerennial.

Cotton, Paul. 1985a. "Marchers Remember Losses to AIDS." *Gay Life*, 30 May, 1.

———. 1985b. "AIDS: A 1985 Perspective." *Windy City Times*, 26 December, 7.

Cowley, Geoffrey, with Mary Hager and Nadine Joseph. 1990. "Taking Up Arms Against AIDS: Scientists and Activists Discover Common Ground." *Newsweek*, 2 July, 44.

Craig, Sarah. 1989. "Demonstrators Bring Demands Downtown." *Windy City Times*, 30 November, 1.

Crane, Rick. 1983. "AIDS Awareness Week." *San Francisco Sentinel*, 28 April, 4.

Crimp, Douglas, ed. 1987a. "AIDS: Cultural Analysis/Cultural Activism." Special issue. *October* 43 (Winter).

Crimp, Douglas. 1987b. "AIDS: Cultural Analysis/Cultural Activism." *October* 43 (Winter): 3–16.

———. 1987c. "How to Have Promiscuity in an Epidemic." *October* 43 (Winter): 237–71.

———. 1989. "Mourning and Militancy." *October* 51 (Winter): 3–18.

———. 1992. "Right On, Girlfriend!" *Social Text* 33:2–18.

———. 2002. *Melancholia and Moralism: Essays on AIDS and Queer Politics*. Cambridge, MA: MIT Press.

Crimp, Douglas, and Adam Rolston. 1990. *AIDS Demo Graphics*. Seattle, WA: Bay Press.

Crossley, Nick. 2002. *Making Sense of Social Movements*. Buckingham, UK: Open University Press.

———. 2003. "From Reproduction to Transformation: Social Movement Fields and the Radical Habitus." *Theory, Culture and Society* 20, no. 6:43–68.

Crump, Joseph. 1990. "The Angriest Queer." *Chicago Reader*, 17 August, 1.

Cvetkovich, Ann. 2003a. *An Archive of Feelings: Trauma, Sexuality, and Lesbian Public Cultures*. Durham, NC: Duke University Press.

———. 2003b. "Legacies of Trauma, Legacies of Activism: ACT UP's Lesbians." In Eng and Kazanjian 2003, 427–57.

d'Adesky, Anne-Christine. 1986a. "Glaad Tidings." *New York Native*, 30 June, 32–33.

———. 1986b. "Gays on Two Coasts Protest Supreme Court Sodomy Ruling." *New York Native*, 14 July, 8–9.

———. 1987. "Civil Disobedience and the Wedding: 840 Arrested at Supreme Court Action; 2,000 Gay Couples Get Hitched." *New York Native*, 26 October, 9.

d'Adesky, Anne-Christine, and Phil Zwickler. 1987. "The Names Project: The Quilt That Woke Up America; 1,920 Panels Memorialize PWAs." *New York Native*, 26 October, 6.

DAGMAR. 1994. "The Real History behind ACT UP/Chicago." *Windy City Times*, 8 December.

DAGMARR (Dykes and Gay Men against Racism and the Right Wing). 1986. Letter to the editor. "Gays Urged to Be Educated about KKK and Nazis." *Windy City Times*, 11 September, 10.

"Daley Was Right to March Against Violence." 1992. Editorial. *Windy City Times*, 16 April.

Damasio, Antonio R. 1994. *Descartes' Error: Emotion, Reason, and the Human Brain*. New York: Avon Books.

———. 1999. *The Feeling of What Happens: Body and Emotion in the Making of Consciousness*. New York: Harcourt.

Damski, Jon-Henri. 1989. "Two, Five, and Eleven." *Windy City Times*, 14 December.

———. 1992a. "PISD." *Windy City Times*, 9 April.

———. 1992b. "Mad Gaiety and the Political Carnival." *Windy City Times*, 23 April, 15.

Davidson, Craig. 1988. Letter to the editor. *New York Native*, 4 July, 9–10.

Dawsey, Darrell. 1989. "80 Arrested as AIDS Protest Is Broken Up." *Los Angeles Times*, 7 October, sec. 2.

de Beauvoir, Simone. 1989. *The Second Sex*. New York: Vintage Books. (Orig. pub. 1952.)

Deitcher, David. 1995. "Law and Desire." In *The Question of Equality: Lesbian and Gay Politics in America Since Stonewall*, ed. David Deitcher, 136–81. New York: Simon & Schuster.

De La Roche, Michel. 1989. Letter to the editor. *Bay Area Reporter*, 9 February.

De la Vega, Ernesto. 1986. "A Solitary Vigil for Human Rights." *New York Native*, 7 April, 17.

D'Emilio, John. 1992. *Making Trouble: Essays on Gay History, Politics, and the University*. New York: Routledge, Chapman, and Hall.

———. 1997. "A Meaning for All Those Words: Sex, Politics, History and Larry Kramer." In *We Must Love One Another or Die: The Life and Legacies of Larry Kramer*, ed. Lawrence D. Mass, 73–85. New York: St. Martin's Press.

———. 1998. *Sexual Politics, Sexual Communities: The Making of a Homosexual Minority in the United States, 1940–1970*. 2nd ed. Chicago: University of Chicago Press.

D'Eramo, James. 1983. "Not a Bureaucrat." *New York Native*, 9–22 May, 13.

Denenberg, Risa. 1993. Interview conducted by Kate Black, September 25. Interview housed at the Lesbian Herstory Archives, Brooklyn, New York.

DeParle, Jason. 1990. "Rude, Rash, Effective, ACT UP Shifts AIDS Policy." *New York Times*, 3 January, B1.

Dessau, Alfred. 1990. Letter to the editor. *Wall Street Journal,* 15 January.

Diani, Mario. 1996. "Linking Mobilization Frames and Political Opportunities: Insights from Regional Populism in Italy." *American Sociological Review* 61, no. 6:1053–69.

DiPhillips, Raymond, M.D. 1981. "Fatal Infections and Cancer in Gay Men." *Chicago Gay Life,* 18 December, 1.

Dobson, Jesse. 1990. "Why ACT UP Split in Two." *San Francisco Sentinel,* 20 September, 4.

Dorow, Heidi. 1990. Letter to the editor. *OutWeek,* 22 August, 5–6.

Douthwaite, Gregory, and Karen M. Everett. 1989. "A Fight at the Opera: SANE Activists Clash with Socialites During Opening Night AIDS Protest." *Bay Area Reporter,* 14 September.

Dowd, Maureen. 1991. "Bush Chides Protesters on 'Excesses.'" *New York Times,* 17 August.

Dowie, Mark. 1998. "What's Wrong with the *New York Times*'s Science Reporting?" *Nation,* 6 July, 13–14.

Du Bois, W. E. B. 1989. *The Souls of Black Folk.* New York: Bantam, Doubleday, Dell. (Orig. pub. 1903.)

Duggan, Lisa. 2003. *The Twilight of Equality? Neoliberalism, Cultural Politics, and the Attack on Democracy.* Boston, MA: Beacon Press.

Duggan, Lisa, and Nan D. Hunter. 1995. *Sex Wars: Sexual Dissent and Political Culture.* New York: Routledge.

Dunne, Michael. 1989. "The Here and Now." Letter to the editor. *Bay Area Reporter,* 5 October.

Dunne, Richard D. 1987. "Vetoing Vito." Letter to the editor. *New York Native,* 1 June, 6.

Durkheim, Emile. 1995. *The Elementary Forms of Religious Life.* Trans. Karen E. Fields. New York: Free Press. (Orig. pub. 1912.)

"Editorial." 1983. *New York Native,* 25 April–8 May, 3.

Edwards, Jeff. 2000a. Interview conducted by Deborah Gould, April 21, Chicago. Interview housed in my personal ACT UP archive.

———. 2000b. "AIDS, Race, and the Rise and Decline of a Militant Oppositional Lesbian and Gay Politics in the U.S." *New Political Science* 22, no. 4: 485–506.

Eggan, Ferd. 1988. "PISD Off and Fighting Back." Keynote speech from ACT NOW AIDS Teach-in in Washington, 8 October. Document housed in my personal ACT UP archive.

———. 1999. Interview conducted by Deborah Gould, October 30, Chicago. Interview housed in my personal ACT UP archive.

Eigo, Jim. 2002. "The City as Body Politic/The Body as City Unto Itself." In Shepard and Hayduk 2002, 178–195.

———. 2004. Interview conducted by ACT UP Oral History Project. Available at www.actuporalhistory.org.

Elbaz, Gilbert. 1992. *The Sociology of AIDS Activism: The Case of ACT UP/ New York, 1987–1992.* PhD diss. Department of Sociology, City University of New York.

———. 1995. "Beyond Anger: The Activist Construction of the AIDS Crisis." *Social Justice: A Journal of Crime, Conflict, and World Order* 22, no. 4:43–76.

Emirbayer, Mustafa, and Chad Goldberg. 2005. "Pragmatism, Bourdieu, and Collective Emotions in Contentious Politics." *Theory and Society,* 34 (December): 469–518.

Eng, David L., and David Kazanjian. 2003. *Loss: The Politics of Mourning.* Berkeley and Los Angeles: University of California Press.

Epstein, Eric. 1990. "An Open Letter to Larry Kramer." April 23. Primary Source Microfilm, Gay Rights Movement—Series 3: *ACT UP: The AIDS Coalition to Unleash Power,* reel 6, box 8, folder 6. Produced by Gale CENGAGE Learning; see their Web site at http://www.gale.cengage.com/ servlet/BrowseSeriesServlet?region=9&imprint=745&titleCode=PSM5& edition=.

Epstein, Steven. 1991. "Democratic Science? AIDS Activism and the Contested Construction of Knowledge." *Socialist Review* 21, no. 2:35–64.

———. 1996. *Impure Science: AIDS, Activism, and the Politics of Knowledge.* Berkeley and Los Angeles: University of California Press.

———. 1997. "AIDS Activism and the Retreat from the 'Genocide' Frame." *Social Identities* 3, no. 3:415–38.

———. 1999. "Gay and Lesbian Movements in the United States: Dilemmas of Identity, Diversity, and Political Strategy." In *The Global Emergence of Gay and Lesbian Politics: National Imprints of a Worldwide Movement,* ed. Barry D. Adam, Jan Willem Duyvendak, and Andre Krouwel, 30–90. Philadelphia, PA: Temple University Press.

Erni, John Nguyet. 1994. *Unstable Frontiers: Technomedicine and the Cultural Politics of "Curing" AIDS.* Minneapolis: University of Minnesota Press.

Fain, Nathan. 1982. "Is Our 'Lifestyle' Hazardous to Our Health? Part 2." *Advocate,* 1 April, 17–21.

Fall, John A. 1985a. "The New Stonewall?" *New York Native,* 25 November– 1 December, 11.

———. 1985b. "Anti-Defamation League Zaps *New York Post:* 800 Protesters Express Rage in Peaceful Demonstration." *New York Native,* 16–22 December, 10–11.

———. 1986. "LaRouche Group Seeks AIDS Quarantine Referendum; Gay and Lesbian Community Forms Coalition to Defeat Measure." *New York Native,* 16 June, 9–10.

Fanon, Frantz. 1967. *Black Skin, White Masks.* New York: Grove Press. (Orig. pub. 1952.)

"Faster Drug OK Vowed; FDA to Speed AIDS, Cancer Treatments." 1988. *Chicago Sun-Times,* 20 October, 3.

"FBI Reportedly Spied on AIDS Activists: Agency Feared Protesters Would Throw Tainted Blood." 1995. *San Francisco Examiner,* 15 May, A6.

Ferree, Myra Marx. 1992. "The Political Context of Rationality: Rational Choice Theory and Resource Mobilization." In *Frontiers in Social Movement Theory,* ed. Aldon D. Morris and Carol McClurg Mueller, 29–52. New Haven, CT: Yale University Press.

Finder, Alan. 1986. "Police Halt Rights Marchers at Wall St." *New York Times,* 5 July, 32.

Finkelstein, Avram. 1992a. "Activism in Wonderland." *QW,* 2 August, 48.

———. 1992b. "The Other Quilt." *QW,* 25 October, 10.

———. 1992c. "Furious Burial: The First Political Funeral for an AIDS Activist." *QW,* 15 November, 10.

Flam, Helena. 1990. "Emotional 'Man': 1. The Emotional 'Man' and the Problem of Collective Action." *International Sociology* 5, no. 1:39–56.

———. 2005. "Emotions' Map: A Research Agenda." In Flam and King 2005, 19–40.

Flam, Helena, and Debra King, eds. 2005. *Emotions and Social Movements.* Abingdon, UK: Routledge.

"Forced AIDS Tests. Then What?" 1987. Editorial. *New York Times,* 7 June.

Ford, Dave. 1986. "Vigil Ups Ante." *Sentinel USA,* 6 June, 1.

———. 1989. "AIDS: Words from the Front." *Spin Magazine,* January, 60–62.

France, David. 1988. "ACT UP Fires Up." *Village Voice,* 3 May, 36.

Franetic, Dennis. 1987. "Hearing the Call." Letter to the editor. *New York Native,* 27 July, 6.

"Frank Criticism of Civil Disobedience." 1988. *Windy City Times,* 14 April, 4.

Freeman, William. 1983. Letter to the editor. *Bay Area Reporter,* 1 December, 8.

Freiberg, Peter. 1985a. "Apuzzo Blasts New York City on Lack of Money for AIDS Services." *Advocate,* 5 February, 9.

———. 1985b. "Gay Anti-Defamation League Forms in New York: Activists Outraged by Cuomo's Policies, Media Sensationalism." *Advocate,* 24 December, 14–15.

———. 1986a. "Gays Protest *NY Post* Homophobia." *Advocate,* 7 January, 16–17.

———. 1986b. "Supreme Court Decision Sparks Protests; 'New Militancy' Seen in Angry Demonstrations." *Advocate,* 5 August, 12–13.

———. 1986c. "LaRouche AIDS Initiative." *Advocate,* 19 August, 10–11.

Freiberg, Peter, Rick Harding, and Mark Vandervelden. 1988. "The New Gay Activism: Adding Bite to the Movement." *Advocate,* 7 June, 10–11.

Freiberg, Peter, Stephen Kulicke, and Dave Walter. 1985. "Future Think: Forecasting 1985." *Advocate,* 8 January, 16–19.

Freud, Sigmund. 1953. "The Interpretation of Dreams." In *The Standard Edition of the Complete Psychological Works of Sigmund Freud*, vols. 4 and 5, ed. James Strachey, 1–625. London: Hogarth Press. (Orig. pub. 1900.)

———. 1955. "A Phobia in a Five-Year-Old Boy." In *The Standard Edition of the Complete Psychological Works of Sigmund Freud*, vol. 10, ed. James Strachey, 3–149. London: Hogarth Press. (Orig. pub. 1909.)

———. 1958. "Recommendations to Physicians Practicing Psycho-Analysis." In *The Standard Edition of the Complete Psychological Works of Sigmund Freud*, vol. 12, ed. James Strachey, 91–96. London: Hogarth Press. (Orig. pub. 1912.)

———. 1959. *Group Psychology and the Analysis of the Ego.* New York: W. W. Norton. (Orig. pub. 1921.)

———. 1963. "Introductory Lectures on Psycho-Analysis, Part 3: General Theory of the Neuroses." In *The Standard Edition of the Complete Psychological Works of Sigmund Freud*, vol. 16, ed. James Strachey, 243–463. London: Hogarth Press. (Orig. pub. 1916–17.)

Friday, Wayne. 1983. "Politics and People: AIDS and the Congressional Aide." *Bay Area Reporter*, 24 March, 17.

Friedlander, Julia, Ron Vachon, Barbara Stanley, Lori Watts, William H. Bellotti, Ron Hellman, Thomas W. Baker, Michael Pantaleo, Victoria Soliwoda, David M. Wertheimer, Paula Ettelbrick, Angie Rosga, Azadeh Khalili, and Ron Divito. 1988. "An Open Letter to the Members of ACT UP." *New York Native*, 4 July, 8–9.

"From the Desk." 1989. Editorial. *San Francisco Sentinel*, 2 February.

Gallagher, Donna. 1992. "Why Doesn't ACT UP Begin to Act Its Age?" *Philadelphia Inquirer*, 28 October, A13.

Gamson, Josh. 1989. "Silence, Death, and the Invisible Enemy: AIDS Activism and Social Movement 'Newness.'" *Social Problems* 36, no. 4:351–67.

Gamson, William. 1992. *Talking Politics.* New York: Cambridge University Press.

Gans, Ronald. 1986a. "The New Dred Scott." *New York Native*, 28 July, 14.

———. 1986b. "Putting Out the Fire This Time." *New York Native*, 4 August, 12.

———. 1986c. "Quid Erat Demonstration." *New York Native*, 25 August, 14.

———. 1986d. "Whither the Gay Movement." *New York Native*, 1 September, 14.

Garcia, Rick. 1992. "Support for Activists." Letter to the editor. *Outlines*, April.

Garrison, Jayne. 1989. "AIDS Activists Being Heard; Researchers Willing to Move Procedures on Testing, Therapy." *San Francisco Examiner*, 5 September, A1.

———. 1992. "Activists Despondent and the Movement Is Splintering." *San Francisco Examiner*, 2 February, A10.

Gay Men's Health Crisis. 1983. Public Service Announcement. "Together This Is What We're Doing." *New York Native*, 7–20 November, 22.

———. 1991. 1990–1991 Annual Report. "The First Ten Years."

Geertz, Clifford. 1973. *The Interpretation of Cultures*. New York: Basic Books.

Gerber, Judy. 1990. "Southern Discomfort: ACT UP/Atlanta Hosts Two Days of Protests against Sodomy Laws and the CDC." *Gay Community News*, 14–20 January, 1.

"Getting Drugs to the Dying Faster." 1990. Editorial. *Chicago Tribune*, 18 November.

Giteck, Lenny. 1986. "Is This Any Way to Run a Movement? Six National Gay Leaders Respond." *Advocate*, 10 June, 42–49.

Glenn, John K., III. 1999. "Competing Challengers and Contested Outcomes to State Breakdown: The Velvet Revolution in Czechoslovakia." *Social Forces* 78, no. 1:1–25.

Goffman, Erving. 1959. *The Presentation of Self in Everyday Life*. New York: Anchor.

———. 1963. *Stigma: Notes on the Management of Spoiled Identity*. New York: Simon & Schuster.

Goldberg, Ron. 1997. "ACT UP's First Days; The Direct-Action Group That Revolutionized Patient Advocacy Began with Strong Convictions—Of Both the Political and Police Variety." *POZ*, March, 62–65.

Gomez, Jewelle. 1995. "Out of the Past." In *The Question of Equality: Lesbian and Gay Politics in America Since Stonewall*, ed. David Deitcher, 17–65. New York: Simon & Schuster.

Gonsalves, Gregg. 2004. Interview conducted by ACT UP Oral History Project. Available at www.actuporalhistory.org.

Goodstein, David B. 1982. "Opening Space." Editorial. *Advocate*, 18 March.

Goodwin, Jeff. 1997. "The Libidinal Constitution of a High-Risk Social Movement: Affectual Ties and Solidarity in the Huk Rebellion." *American Sociological Review* 62, no. 1:53–69.

Goodwin, Jeff, and James Jasper, eds. 2004. *Rethinking Social Movements: Structure, Meaning, and Emotion*. Lanham, MD: Rowman & Littlefield.

———. 2006. "Emotions and Social Movements." In *Handbook of the Sociology of Emotions*, ed. Jan E. Stets and Jonathan H. Turner, 611–35. New York: Springer.

Goodwin, Jeff, and Steven Pfaff. 2001. "Emotion Work in High-Risk Social Movements: Managing Fear in the U.S. and East German Civil Rights Movements." In Goodwin, Jasper, and Polletta 2001a, 282–302.

Goodwin, Jeff, James Jasper, and Francesca Polletta. 2000. "Return of the Repressed: The Fall and Rise of Emotions in Social Movement Theory." *Mobilization* 5, no. 1:65–84.

———, eds. 2001a. *Passionate Politics: Emotions and Social Movements*. Chicago: University of Chicago Press.

———. 2001b. "Introduction: Why Emotions Matter." In Goodwin, Jasper, and Polletta 2001a, 1–24.

———. 2004. "Emotional Dimensions of Social Movements." In *The Blackwell*

Companion to Social Movements, ed. David A. Snow, Sarah A. Soule, and Hanspeter Kriesi, 413–32. Malden, MA: Blackwell.

Gordon, Darrell. 2000. Interview conducted by Deborah Gould, March 22, Chicago. Interview housed in my personal ACT UP archive.

Gordon, S. L. 1989. "Institutional and Impulsive Orientations in Selectively Appropriating Emotions to Self." In *The Sociology of Emotions: Original Essays and Research Papers,* ed. David D. Franks and E. Doyle McCarthy, 115–36. Greenwich, CT: JAI Press.

Gottlieb, M. S., R. Schroff, H. M. Schanker, J. D. Weisman, P. T. Fan, R. A. Wolf, and A. Saxon. 1981. "*Pneumocystis Carinii* Pneumonia and Mucosal Candidiasis Found in Previously Healthy Homosexual Men." *New England Journal of Medicine* 305 (December): 1425–31.

Gould, Deborah. 2000. *Sex, Death, and the Politics of Anger: Emotions and Reason in ACT UP's Fight Against AIDS.* PhD diss. Department of Political Science, University of Chicago.

———. 2001. "Rock the Boat, Don't Rock the Boat, Baby: Ambivalence and the Emergence of Militant AIDS Activism." In Goodwin, Jasper, and Polletta 2001a, 135–57.

———. 2002. "Life During Wartime: Emotions and the Development of ACT UP." *Mobilization* 7, no. 2:177–200.

———. 2004. "Passionate Political Processes: Bringing Emotions Back into the Study of Social Movements." In Goodwin and Jasper 2004, 155–75.

———. 2006. "Solidarity and Its Fracturing in ACT UP." *AREA Chicago: Arts, Research, Education, Activism* 3 (Summer–Fall): 10–13.

———. 2009. "The Shame of Gay Pride in Early AIDS Activism." In *Gay Shame,* ed. David Halperin and Valerie Traub, 221–55. Chicago: University of Chicago Press.

Green, Jesse. 1989. "Shticks and Stones." *7 Days,* 8 February, 21–26.

Greenberg, Jon. 1992. "Speech for Mark Lowe Fisher's Funeral." Given on November 3, 1992. Document available at DIVA TV's Web site: http://www.actupny.org/diva/synGreenberg.html.

Griffith, Keith. 1986. Letter to the editor. *Sentinel,* 18 July, 2.

Gross, Ken. 1990. "Larry Kramer." *People Weekly,* 9 July.

Gross, Larry. 2001. *Up from Invisibility: Lesbians, Gay Men, and the Media in America.* New York: Columbia University Press.

Grossberg, Lawrence. 1992. *We Gotta Get Out of This Place: Popular Conservatism and Postmodern Culture.* New York: Routledge.

Grover, Jan Zita. 1987. "AIDS: Keywords." *October* 43 (Winter): 17–30.

Groves, Julian McAllister. 1995. "Learning to Feel: The Neglected Sociology of Social Movements." *Sociological Review* 43, no. 3:435–61.

Halberstadt, Mitchell. 1986. "Gay Leaders Call for National March." *New York Native,* 4 August, 6–7.

Halberstam, Judith. 2005. "Shame and White Gay Masculinity." *Social Text 84/85* vol. 23, nos. 3–4:219–33.

Halcli, Abigail. 1999. "AIDS, Anger, and Activism: ACT UP as a Social Movement Organization." In *Waves of Protest: Social Movements Since the Sixties,* ed. Jo Freeman and Victoria Johnson, 135–50. Lanham, MD: Rowman & Littlefield.

Hall, Stuart. 1973a. "A World at One with Itself." In *The Manufacture of News: Social Problems, Deviance and the Mass Media,* ed. Stanley Cohen and Jock Young, 85–94. Beverley Hills, CA: Sage.

———. 1973b. "The Determinations of News Photographs." In *The Manufacture of News: Social Problems, Deviance and the Mass Media,* ed. Stanley Cohen and Jock Young, 176–90. Beverley Hills, CA: Sage.

———. 1974. "Deviance, Politics, and the Media." In *Deviance and Social Control,* ed. Paul Rock and Mary McIntosh, 261–305. London: Tavistock.

———. 1986. "On Postmodernism and Articulation: An Interview with Stuart Hall (edited by Lawrence Grossberg)." *Journal of Communication Inquiry* 10, no. 2:45–60.

Halley, Janet E. 1993. "The Construction of Heterosexuality." In *Fear of a Queer Planet: Queer Politics and Social Theory,* ed. Michael Warner, 82–102. Minneapolis: University of Minnesota Press.

Halley, Jon. 1991. "Police Clash with ACT UP: An impromptu 300-person-strong demonstration in front of a police station turns into a melee as club-wielding cops storm the crowd." *Gay Community News,* 24 February, 1.

Hamilton, Andrea. 1995. "Gay Groups Are Spied Upon, FBI Data Show." *Boston Globe,* 16 May, 3.

Hanania, Ray. 1989. "15 Arrested in Gay Protest." *Chicago Sun-Times,* 22 November, 3.

Handelman, David. 1990. "ACT UP in Anger." *Rolling Stone,* 8 March, 80.

Hansen, Eileen. 1987. "Pledge for Our Lives." *AIDS Action Call: The Newsletter of the AIDS Action Pledge* (Autumn–Winter): 1–2. Document housed in my personal ACT UP archive.

"Harassing NIH." 1990. Editorial. *Washington Post,* 22 May.

Harding, Rick. 1987. "Civil Disobedience at Supreme Court: Demonstration of Gay Outrage Results in Mass Arrests." *Advocate,* 10 November, 26–27.

———. 1991. "Activist Women Debate Tactics at AIDS Meeting." *Advocate,* 15 January, 21.

Hardy, Robin. 1991. "Die Harder: AIDS Activism Is Abandoning Gay Men." *Village Voice,* 36, no. 27:33–34.

Harrington, Mark. 1990. "Let My People In: The Results of Direct Action Have Been Fruitful, Further Validating the Activist Approach to Medical Bureaucracy." *OutWeek,* 8 August, 34–35.

———. 1991. "ACTG Protocol 076: Summary Problems, Alternatives, and Recommended Changes: A Report to the CCG 076 Working Group." Primary Source Microfilm, Gay Rights Movement—Series 3: *ACT UP: The AIDS Coalition to Unleash Power,* reel 46, box 63, folder 4. Produced by Gale CENGAGE Learning; see their Web site at http://www.gale.cengage.com/servlet/BrowseSeriesServlet?region=9&imprint=745&titleCode=PSM5&edition=.

——. 1996. "Deconstructing the Drama: Former ACT UP/NY Scientific Wunderkind Denounces Movement as 'Messianic Utopianism'; AIDS Activism as Religious Cult." *TAGline* 3, no. 5. Available at http://www.thebody.com/TAG/may96c/html (accessed 15 October 2004).

——. 1997. "Some Transitions in the History of AIDS Treatment Activism: From Therapeutic Utopianism to Pragmatic Praxis." In *Acting on AIDS: Sex, Drugs, and Politics,* ed. Joshua Oppenheimer and Helena Reckitt, 273–86. London: Serpent's Tail.

——. 1998. "From Acting Up to Acts of Congress, AIDS Activist Reviews and Critiques a Decade of Social Change." *TAGline* (December). Available at http://www.nmac.org/NewsLetters/TAG/yr98/tg9812.htm (accessed 2 July 2001).

——. 2002a. "Once We Were Warriors: Activist Corpses Borne in Protest, Furtive Legislative Coups, and the Devastation That Was Berlin." *TAGline,* March. Available at http://www.thebody.com/content/art1601.html (accessed 25 December 2008).

——. 2002b. Interview conducted by Deborah Gould, September 10, New York. Interview housed in my personal ACT UP archive.

——. 2003. Interview conducted by ACT UP Oral History Project. Available at www.actuporalhistory.org.

Hartley, John. 1982. *Understanding News.* London: Routledge.

Hass, Robert. 1985. "Becoming an AIDS Volunteer." *Sentinel USA,* 20 June, 6.

Hayse, Carol. 2000. Interview conducted by Deborah Gould, April 2, Chicago. Interview housed in my personal ACT UP archive.

"Health Dept. Timing Is Off Again." 1985. Editorial. *Gay Life,* 11 April, 4.

"Health Secretary Cuts Ties with Activist AIDS Group." 1990. *Chicago Tribune,* 4 July.

"Heckler Stirs Clinton Anger: Excerpts from the Exchange." 1992. *New York Times,* 28 March, 9.

Heim, Chris. 1982a. "'Gay Deficiency' Diseases Examined." *Gay Life,* 6 August, 5.

——. 1982b. "AIDS: What's Being Done?" *Gay Life,* 20 August, 5.

Helquist, Michael. 1986. "Emotional S.F. Protest Greets O'Connor." *Washington Blade,* 25 July, 1.

Higginbotham, Evelyn Brooks. 1993. *Righteous Discontent: The Women's Movement in the Black Baptist Church, 1880–1920.* Cambridge, MA: Harvard University Press.

Highleyman, Liz. 2002. "Radical Queers or Queer Radicals? Queer Activism and the Global Justice Movement." In Shepard and Hayduk 2002, 106–20.

Hilts, Philip J. 1990. "82 Held in Protest on Pace of AIDS Research." *New York Times,* 22 May.

Hippler, Mike. 1985. "A Year to Celebrate: Coming Up with New Strategies for Surviving in the Age of AIDS." *New York Native,* 18–24 November, 30–31.

———. 1986. "The Vigil: A Profile in Gay Courage." *Advocate,* 15 April, 42–47.

Hiraga, Martin. 1988. "Finding Solidarity." *Gay Community News,* 16–22 October, 8.

Hochschild, Arlie Russell. 1979. "Emotion Work, Feeling Rules, and Social Structure." *American Journal of Sociology* 85, no. 3:551–75.

———. 1983. *The Managed Heart.* Berkeley and Los Angeles: University of California Press.

Hodge, G. Derrick. 2000. "Retrenchment from a Queer Ideal: Class Privilege and the Failure of Identity Politics in AIDS Activism." *Environment and Planning D: Society and Space* 18, no. 3:355–76.

Hoffer, Eric. 1951. *The True Believer.* New York: Harper & Row.

Hollibaugh, Amber. 1993. "We *Can* Get There from Here." *Nation,* 5 July, 27–28.

———. 1995. "Lesbian Denial and Lesbian Leadership in the AIDS Epidemic: Bravery and Fear in the Construction of a Lesbian Geography of Risk." In *Women Resisting AIDS: Feminist Strategies of Empowerment,* ed. Beth Schneider, 219–30. Philadelphia, PA: Temple University Press.

Hopkins, Drew, and Phil Zwickler. 1988. "Acting Up or Acting Out? Looking Back on ACT UP's First Year." *New York Native,* 27 June, 33–38.

Hunter, B. Michael, ed. 1993. "Allan Robinson, AIDS Activist." In *Sojourner: Black Gay Voices in the Age of AIDS,* ed. Michael B. Hunter, 54–61. New York: Other Countries Press.

"IGLTF Delivers 2' × 26' letter to Gov. Thompson." 1987. *Outlines,* 13 August, 9.

Ison, John. 1990. "Los Angeles's John Fall: Spurred to Action by a Death in the Family." *Advocate,* 13 February, 36.

Israels, David. 1990. "Larry Kramer: The Angriest AIDS Activist." *San Francisco Bay Guardian,* 13 June.

Jackson, Liddell. 2002. "Jacks of Color: An Oral History (Benjamin Shepard interviews Liddell Jackson)." In Shepard and Hayduk 2002, 172–77.

Jaggar, Alison M. 1989. "Love and Knowledge: Emotion in Feminist Epistemology." In *Gender/Body/Knowledge,* ed. Alison M. Jaggar and Susan R. Bordo, 145–71. New Brunswick, NJ: Rutgers University Press.

James, William. 1890. *The Principles of Psychology.* New York: Henry Holt.

Jasper, James M. 1997. *The Art of Moral Protest: Culture, Biography, and Creativity in Social Movements.* Chicago: University of Chicago Press.

——. 1998. "The Emotions of Protest: Affective and Reactive Emotions in and around Social Movements." *Sociological Forum* 13, no. 3:397–424.

Jefferson, Scott. 1985a. "When a Kiss Is *Not* Just a Kiss." *New York Native*, 2–8 December, 24–25.

——. 1985b. "Just the Facts, Ma'am." *New York Native*, 23–29 December, 26–27.

Jennings, Veronica T., and Malcolm Gladwell. 1990. "1,000 Rally for more Vigorous AIDS Effort: 82 Arrested at NIH in Demonstration to Support Additional Research, Expanded Testing." *Washington Post*, 22 May.

Johnson, J. H. 1986a. "Outspeak: John Lorenzini." *Windy City Times*, 4 September, 8.

——. 1986b. "Outspeak: Darrell Yates Rist." *Windy City Times*, 23 October, 6.

——. 1987. "'Equal Justice!' Demand Protesters at Supreme Court." *Windy City Times*, 22 October, 1.

Johnston, Hank, and John A. Noakes. 2005. "Frames of Protest: A Road Map to a Perspective." In *Frames of Protest: Social Movements and the Framing Perspective*, ed. Hank Johnston and John A. Noakes, 1–29. Lanham, MD: Rowman & Littlefield.

Jones, Brian. 1987. "7 Days in June: Anger Dominates Parade Week; Victory in November." *Bay Area Reporter*, 1 January, 1.

Jones, Cleve. 1985. "Text of Speech, City Hall Steps, November 27, 1985." Reprinted in *Sentinel USA*, 5 December, 10.

——. 2000. *Stitching a Revolution: The Making of an Activist*. New York: HarperCollins.

Jurrist, Charles. 1982. "In Defense of Promiscuity: Hard Questions about Real Life." *New York Native*, 6–19 December, 27.

Kane, Anne. 2001. "Finding Emotion in Social Movement Processes: Irish Land Movement Metaphors and Narratives." In Goodwin, Jasper, and Polletta 2001a, 251–66.

Kantrowitz, Arnie. 1986. "Friends: Gone with the Wind." *Advocate*, 2 September, 42–47.

Kaplan, Esther. 1991. "ACT UP under Siege: Phone Harassment, Death Threats, Police Violence: Is the Government Out to Destroy This Group?" *Village Voice*, 16 July, 35–36.

Karlin, Rick. 1990. "E.T.C." *Gay Chicago Magazine*, 1–11 February, 46.

Kastor, Elizabeth. 1993. "The Gay Moment: Today Just Didn't Happen; It Took a Lot of Yesterdays." *Washington Post*, 25 April, F1.

Kauffman, L. A. 2002. "A Short History of Radical Renewal." In Shepard and Hayduk 2002, 35–40.

Keen, Lisa M. 1986a. "High Court Upholds Sodomy Law." *Washington Blade*, 4 July, 1.

————. 1986b. "'Devastating' Opinion Could Reap Some Benefits, Changes." *Washington Blade*, 4 July, 7.

Kelley, William B. 1981. "New Findings on Fatal Illness Told." *Chicago Gay Life*, 18 December, 1.

Kemper, Theodore D., ed. 1990. *Research Agendas in the Sociology of Emotions*. Albany: State University of New York Press.

Kilpatrick, James. 1991. "AIDS Activists Hurt Their Own Cause." *Chicago Sun-Times*, 26 July, 29.

King, Charles. 2007. "The Many Faces of AIDS: A Message to My Brothers and Sisters in the Gay Community." Speech given in San Francisco, December 1, 2007. Available at http://www.hwupdate.org/update/2007/12/the_many_faces_of_aids_a_messa.html (accessed 22 September 2008).

Kinsella, James. 1989. *Covering the Plague: AIDS and the American Media*. New Brunswick, NJ: Rutgers University Press.

Kinsman, Gary. 1996. "'Responsibility' as a Strategy of Governance: Regulating People Living with AIDS and Lesbians and Gay Men in Ontario." *Economy and Society* 25, no. 3:393–409.

Kirp, David. 1990. "The Scientists from ACT UP." *San Francisco Examiner*, 27 June.

Kirschenbaum, David E. 1988. "Why ACT UP Zapped Koch." Letter to the editor. *New York Native*, 4 July, 6.

————. 1990. "Further Dilemmas with ACTG 076." 26 December. Primary Source Microfilm, *ACT UP: The AIDS Coalition to Unleash Power*, reel 46, box 63, folder 4. Produced by Gale CENGAGE Learning; see their Web site at http://www.gale.cengage.com/servlet/BrowseSeriesServlet?region=9&imprint=745&titleCode=PSM5&edition=.

Klatch, Rebecca. 2004. "The Underside of Social Movements: The Effects of Destructive Affective Ties." *Qualitative Sociology* 27, no. 4: 487–509.

Kolata, Gina. 1989. "AIDS Researcher Seeks Wide Access to Drugs in Tests." *New York Times*, 26 June, A1.

————. 1990. "Advocates' Tactics on AIDS Issues Provoking Warnings of a Backlash." *New York Times*, 11 March.

Koopmans, Ruud, and Jan Willem Duyvendak. 1995. "The Political Construction of the Nuclear Energy Issue and Its Impact on the Mobilization of Anti-Nuclear Movements in Western Europe." *Social Problems* 42, no. 2:235–51.

Koziak, Barbara. 1999. "Homeric *Thumos:* The Early History of Gender, Emotion, and Politics." *Journal of Politics* 61, no. 4:1068–91.

Kracher, Jeanne. 1993. Interview conducted by Kate Black, July 5 and November 6, Chicago. Interview housed at the Lesbian Herstory Archives, Brooklyn, New York.

————. 2000. Interview conducted by Deborah Gould, February 15, Chicago. Interview housed in my personal ACT UP archive.

"Kramer and Russo vs. GMHC." 1987. Letters to the editor. *New York Native,* 16 February, 6–9.

Kramer, Larry. 1981. "A Personal Appeal." *New York Native,* 24 August–6 September. Reprinted in Kramer 1990a, 8–9.

———. 1983a. "1,112 and Counting." *New York Native,* 14–27 March, 1. Reprinted, with commentary, in Kramer 1990a, 33–51.

———. 1983b. "1,112 and Counting." *Bay Area Reporter,* 17 March, 1.

———. 1983c. "AIDS Crisis: Your Life Is on the Line" *Gay Life,* 28 April, 1.

———. 1985. *The Normal Heart.* New York: Plume.

———. 1987a. "An Open Letter to Richard Dunne and Gay Men's Health Crisis, Inc." *New York Native,* 26 January, 1.

———. 1987b. "Our Voice Is Our Power—Only If We Use It." *Windy City Times,* 25 June, 22.

———. 1987c. "Taking Responsibility for Our Lives." *New York Native.* 29 June, 37–40.

———. 1987d. "Oh, My People . . . " *New York Native,* 7 December, 15–16.

———. 1990a. *Reports from the Holocaust: The Making of an AIDS Activist.* New York: Penguin Books.

———. 1990b. "From Larry Kramer." Letter, April 16. Primary Source Microfilm, *ACT UP: The AIDS Coalition to Unleash Power,* reel 6, box 8, folder 6. Produced by Gale CENGAGE Learning; see their Web site at http://www.gale .cengage.com/servlet/BrowseSeriesServlet?region=9&imprint=745&title Code=PSM5&edition=.

Kulp, Denise. 1988. "On Working with My Brothers: Why a Lesbian Does AIDS Work." *Off Our Backs,* August–September, 22.

Laplanche, Jean, and J.-B. Pontalis. 1973. *The Language of Psycho-Analysis.* Tr. Donald Nicholson-Smith. New York: W. W. Norton. (Orig. pub. 1967 by Presses Universitaires de France.)

Lasswell, Harold D. 1986. *Psychopathology and Politics.* Midway reprint. Chicago: University of Chicago Press. (Orig. pub. 1930.)

Lavender Hill Mob. n.d. "The Rise of Militant AIDS Activism." Document housed in my personal ACT UP archive.

———. 1987. "Gay Pride Issue." *Lavender Hill News.* June. Document housed in my personal ACT UP archive.

Layman, Dan. 1987. "On Epidemics, Contras, and Strange Bedfellows." *Windy City Times,* 11 June, 7.

Leavitt, David. 1989. "The Way I Live Now." *New York Times Magazine,* 9 July, 28–32.

Leo, John. 1989. "Today's Uncivil Disobedience." *U.S. News & World Report,* 17 April, 64.

———. 1990a. "When Activism Becomes Gangsterism." *U.S. News & World Report,* 5 February, 18.

———. 1990b. "The AIDS Activist with Blurry Vision." *U.S. News & World Report,* 9 July, 16.

Leonard, Arthur S. 1986. "Letting the Cops Back into Michael Hardwick's Bedroom." *New York Native,* 14 July, 11.

"Letters." 1983. Letters to the editor. *New York Native,* 28 March–10 April, 4–7.

Lewis, Bill. 1982. "The Real Gay Epidemic: Panic and Paranoia." *Body Politic,* November, 38–40.

Lewis, Helen B. 1971. *Shame and Guilt in Neurosis.* New York: International Universities Press.

Linebarger, Charles. 1985a. "The Spark Lives at Memorial Vigil." *Bay Area Reporter,* 30 May, 3–4.

———. 1985b. "Budget Cuts Protested; AIDS Funds Demanded." *Bay Area Reporter,* 11 July, 2.

———. 1985c. "People with AIDS Lead Protest in San Francisco." *Advocate,* 24 December, 21–22.

———. 1986. "Court Protest Takes Anger to the Streets." *Bay Area Reporter,* 24 July, 1.

———. 1987a. "New AIDS/ARC Vigil Begun: Activists Chain Themselves to County Building to Protest Delay in Funding." *New York Native,* 12 January, 6–7.

———. 1987b. "Lots of Red Tape but No Arrests in S.F. Sit-In." *Bay Area Reporter,* 4 June, 13.

———. 1987c. "64 Arrested in White House Sit-In." *Windy City Times,* 11 June, 1.

Link, Derek. 1991a (ca. March/April). "On Meetings and Moratoria III." Letter. New York Public Library, Manuscripts and Archives Section, ACT UP/New York Records, box 8, folder 10.

———. 1991b (ca. March/April). "HIV Negatives: Get Out of Our Way." Primary Source Microfilm, Gay Rights Movement—Series 3: *ACT UP: The AIDS Coalition to Unleash Power,* reel 3, box 5, folder 7. Produced by Gale CENGAGE Learning; see their Web site at http://www.gale.cengage.com/servlet/BrowseSeriesServlet?region=9&imprint=745&titleCode=PSM5&edition=.

Lorch, Paul. 1983. "The Price of Bad News." Editorial. *Bay Area Reporter,* 7 July, 6.

Lorenzini, John. 1987. "AIDS and Civil Disobedience." In *Out & Outraged, For Love, Life & Liberation: Non-Violent Civil Disobedience at the U.S. Supreme Court,* ed. National March on Washington for Lesbian and Gay Rights, 23–24. Document housed in my personal ACT UP archive.

Loughery, John. 1999. *The Other Side of Silence. Men's Lives and Gay Identities: A Twentieth-Century History.* New York: Henry Holt.

Lowe, David M. 1986a. "Where Do We Go from Here?" *Sentinel USA,* 1 August, 5.

———. 1986b. "Activists Stage State Sit-In: AIDS at Duke's Door." *San Francisco Sentinel,* 26 September, 1.

———. 1987. "Scratch N Sniff." *San Francisco Sentinel,* 29 May, 7.

Lutz, Catherine. 1986. "Emotion, Thought, and Estrangement: Emotion as a Cultural Category." *Cultural Anthropology* 1, no. 4:287–309.

———. 1988. *Unnatural Emotions: Everyday Sentiments on a Micronesian Atoll and Their Challenge to Western Theory.* Chicago: University of Chicago Press.

Lutz, Catherine, and Lila Abu-Lughod. 1990. *Language and the Politics of Emotion.* Cambridge: Cambridge University Press.

Lyman, Peter. 1981. "The Politics of Anger: On Silence, Ressentiment, and Political Speech." *Socialist Review* 11, no. 3:55–74.

Lynch, Michael. 1982. "Living with Kaposi's Sarcoma and AIDS." *Body Politic,* November, 31–37.

Ma, Ming Yuen S. 2003. Interview conducted by ACT UP Oral History Project. Available at www.actuporalhistory.org.

Maggenti, Maria. 2003. Interview conducted by ACT UP Oral History Project. Available at www.actuporalhistory.org.

Malliaris, Tony. 1991. "ACT UP/New York Operational Proposal–Draft." November. Primary Source Microfilm, Gay Rights Movement—Series 3: *ACT UP: The AIDS Coalition to Unleash Power,* reel 3, box 5, folder 7. Produced by Gale CENGAGE Learning; see their Web site at http://www.gale.cengage.com/servlet/BrowseSeriesServlet?region=9&imprint=745&titleCode=PSM5&edition=.

"Man and Woman of the Year '86." 1986. *San Francisco Sentinel,* 26 December, 1.

Mansbridge, Jane. 1983. *Beyond Adversary Democracy.* Chicago: University of Chicago Press.

Markson, R. J. 1987. "This Parade Should Pass By." *New York Native,* 15 June, 19.

Marquardt, Joan. 1989. "Terry Sutton, AIDS Activist 1955–1989." *Workers World,* 11 May.

Martz, Steve. 1983a. "Gay Groups Vote to Create New National Lobby." *Washington Blade,* 17 June, 1.

———. 1983b. "Government's Effort to Fight AIDS Slammed as 'Too Little, Too Late.'" *Sentinel,* 4 August, 1–2.

Mason, Kiki. 1988. "FDA: The Demo of the Year; with the Troops in Washington." *New York Native,* 24 October, 13–16.

Mass, Lawrence. 1982. "Congress Looks at the Epidemic." *New York Native,* 10–23 May, 16–17.

———. 1983. "The Case against Medical Panic." *New York Native,* 17–30 January, 23–25.

Massumi, Brian. 1987. "Notes on the Translation and Acknowledgments." In *A*

Thousand Plateaus: Capitalism and Schizophrenia, by Gilles Deleuze and Félix Guattari, xvi–xix. Tr. B. Massumi. Minneapolis: University of Minnesota Press.

———. 2002. *Parables for the Virtual: Movement, Affect, Sensation.* Durham, NC: Duke University Press.

———. 2003. "Navigating Movements: An Interview with Brian Massumi." In *Hope: New Philosophies for Change,* ed. Mary Zournazi, 210–42. New York: Routledge.

McAdam, Doug. 1999. *Political Process and the Development of Black Insurgency, 1930–1970.* 2nd ed. Chicago: University of Chicago Press.

McAdam, Doug, John D. McCarthy, and Mayer N. Zald, eds. 1996a. *Comparative Perspectives on Social Movements: Political Opportunities, Mobilizing Structures, and Cultural Framings.* Cambridge: Cambridge University Press.

———. 1996b. "Introduction: Opportunities, Mobilizing Structures, and Framing Processes." In McAdam, McCarthy, and Zald 1996a, 1–20.

McAdam, Doug, Sidney Tarrow, and Charles Tilly. 2001. *Dynamics of Contention.* New York: Cambridge University Press.

McCarthy, John D., and Mayer N. Zald. 1973. *The Trend of Social Movements in America: Professionalization and Resource Mobilization.* Morristown, NJ: General Learning Press.

———. 1977. "Resource Mobilization and Social Movements: A Partial Theory." *American Journal of Sociology* 82, no. 6:1212–41.

McConnell, Vicki. 1992. "Changing Channels: This Season, TV Viewers Tuned in More Gay Themes and Characters Than Ever Before." *Advocate,* 14 January.

McGarry, Molly, and Fred Wasserman. 1998. *Becoming Visible: An Illustrated History of Lesbian and Gay Life in Twentieth-Century America.* New York: Penguin Books.

McMillan, Bill. 2000. Interview conducted by Deborah Gould, August 23, Chicago. Interview housed in my personal ACT UP archive.

"MECLA 10th Annual Awards Dinner." 1987. *San Francisco Sentinel,* 1 May, 13.

Members of C-FAR. 1988. "Experiencing Civil Disobedience." *Windy City Times,* 26 May, 10.

"Memorials across America." 1986. Editorial. *Windy City Times,* 22 May, 9.

Mendenhall, George. 1984. "300 at Rally to Decry Baths Closure." *Bay Area Reporter,* 1 November, 3–4.

———. 1986. "Fight LaRouche with Gay Anger, Says Britt." *Bay Area Reporter,* 19 June, 3.

Meredith, Linda. 1990. Letter to the editor. *OutWeek,* 22 August, 5.

Merla, Patrick. 1985. "Love and Death at the Public Theater: Larry Kramer Talks about *The Normal Heart.*" *New York Native,* 8–21 April, 37–38.

Merton, Robert K., and Elinor Barber. 1963. "Sociological Ambivalence." In *Sociological Theory, Values, and Sociocultural Change: Essays in Honor of Pitirim A. Sorokin*, ed. Edward A. Tiryakian, 91–120. London: Free Press of Glencoe.

Michael, Miles. 1986. "In Fascist America." *New York Native*, 29 September, 18–19.

Michaud, Chris. 1990. "Other Voices, Separate Views from ACT UP/NY." *Advocate*, 28 August, 50.

Millenson, Michael L., and Keith L. Alexander. 1991. "AIDS Group in a Clash with Police." *Chicago Tribune*, 25 June.

Miller, Tim. 1999. Interview conducted by Deborah Gould, July 13, San Francisco. Interview housed in my personal ACT UP archive.

Minkowitz, Donna. 1990. "ACT UP at a Crossroads." *Village Voice*, 5 June, 19–22.

——. 1992. "The Democrats' Queer Quotient." *Advocate*, 25 August, 15.

Moore, Patrick. 2003. Interview conducted by ACT UP Oral History Project. Available at www.actuporalhistory.org.

"More Than 1,000 Attend Gay Health Conference." 1987. *Windy City Times*, 16 April, 5.

Morgan, Tracy. 1990. Letter to the editor. *OutWeek*, 22 August, 6.

Morgen, Sandra. 1983. "The Politics of 'Feeling': Beyond the Dialectic of Thought and Action." *Women's Studies* 10, no. 2:203–23.

——. 1995. "'It Was the Best of Times, It Was the Worst of Times': Emotional Discourse in the Work Cultures of Feminist Health Clinics." In *Feminist Organizations: Harvest of the New Women's Movement*, ed. Myra Marx Ferree and Patricia Yancey Martin, 234–47. Philadelphia, PA: Temple University Press.

Morris, Sidney. 1985. "Beloved Friend." *New York Native*, 4–10 November, 23.

——. 1986. "Gay Vanishing Act." *New York Native*, 18 August, 15.

Mount, Charles. 1990. "AIDS Ward Is Opened to Women." *Chicago Tribune*, 27 April.

Murray, Tom. 1984. "The Real Revolution." *Sentinel USA*, 30 August, 10.

——. 1986. "Deflated Justice." *Sentinel*, 1 August, 2.

Nahmanson, Emily. 2003. Interview conducted by ACT UP Oral History Project. Available at www.actuporalhistory.org.

National Gay Task Force. 1983. Press Release. "Apuzzo Testifies at House Appropriations Subcommittee on AIDS Funding." 12 May, 1–3. Document housed in my personal ACT UP archive.

National March on Washington for Lesbian and Gay Rights, ed. 1987. *National March on Washington for Lesbian and Gay Rights*. [Official Handbook for 1987 March on Washington]. Document housed in my personal ACT UP archive.

Nesline, Michael. 2003. Interview conducted by ACT UP Oral History Project. Available at www.actuporalhistory.org.

Obejas, Achy. 1987. "Our Anger Should Not Be 'Gentle.'" *Windy City Times*, 8 October, 12.

———. 1991. "Why Is Daley So Afraid of Daniel?" *Windy City Times*, 22 August.

O'Connors, P., and Donald Johnson. 1987. Letter to the editor. "Please, Mr. President." *Windy City Times*, 23 July, 11–12.

Odets, Walt. 1995. *In the Shadow of the Epidemic: Being HIV-Negative in the Age of AIDS*. Durham, NC: Duke University Press.

———. 1996. "Why We Stopped Doing Primary Prevention for Gay Men in 1985." In *Policing Public Sex*, ed. Dangerous Bedfellows, 115–40. Boston, MA: South End Press.

"Offensive Display at AIDS Meeting." 1990. Editorial. *San Francisco Chronicle*, 26 June, A18.

"Off to a Good Start." 1985. Editorial. *Gay Life*, 6 June, 9.

O'Loughlin, Ray. 1986a. "Gays Not Protected by Constitution, Says High Court." *Bay Area Reporter*, 3 July, 1.

———. 1986b. "Ruling Called 'Judicial Bashing.'" *Bay Area Reporter*, 3 July, 2.

Olson, Dave. 1988. "ACT NOW Groups Mull Future Protest Plans." *Windy City Times*, 20 October, 6.

———. 1990a. "Injured Protesters Claim Police Used Excessive Force." *Windy City Times*, 26 April.

———. 1990b. "First Woman Admitted to County AIDS Ward; Access to Facilities Limited by Lack of Participating Staff." *Windy City Times*, 3 May.

———. 1991a. "Police, Protesters Clash in AMA Demonstration." *Windy City Times*, 27 June.

———. 1991b. "Chicago Rock Bottom in AIDS Spending; Daley Administration Blamed for 'Appalling' Figures." *Windy City Times*, 26 December.

———. 1992. "Demonstrators Assail Bush on Gay, AIDS Issues." *Windy City Times*, 27 August.

O'Neill, Cliff. 1990a. "Activists Lay Siege to National Institutes of Health; 82 Arrested in Demands for New Treatments, Broader Access to Trials." *Windy City Times*, 7 June, 8.

———. 1990b "Health Secretary Louis Sullivan Criticizes ACT UP; Other Organizations Defend Street Activist 'Fringe Group.'" *Windy City Times*, 9 August.

"Opera Protest." 1989. *San Francisco Chronicle*, 12 September.

Ortleb, Charles L. 1982. Editorial. *New York Native*, 16–29 August, 3.

———. 1985. Editorial. "AIDSGATE." *New York Native*, 3–16 June, 4.

———. 1987. Editorial. "Thank You, Lavender Hill Mob." *New York Native*, 9 March, 5.

Osborne, Duncan. 1993. "ACT UP and the FBI." *Advocate,* 29 June, 60–61.

O'Sullivan, Sue, and Pratibha Parmar. 1992. *Lesbians Talk (Safer) Sex.* London: Scarlet Press.

"Our Heritage Compels Us to Take Another Step." 1988. Editorial. *Windy City Times,* 23 June, 11.

Padgug, Robert A., and Gerald M. Oppenheimer. 1992. "Riding the Tiger: AIDS and the Gay Community." In *AIDS: The Making of a Chronic Disease,* ed. Elizabeth Fee and Daniel M. Fox, 245–78. Berkeley and Los Angeles: University of California Press.

Patten, Mary. 1993. Interview conducted by Kate Black, July 5, Chicago. Interview housed at the Lesbian Herstory Archives, Brooklyn, New York.

———. 1998. "The Thrill Is Gone: An ACT UP Post-Mortem (Confessions of a Former AIDS Activist)." In *The Passionate Camera,* ed. Deborah Bright, 385–406. New York: Routledge.

Patton, Cindy. 1985. *Sex and Germs: The Politics of AIDS.* Boston, MA: South End Press.

———. 1987. "Resistance and the Erotic: Reclaiming History, Setting Strategy as We Face AIDS." *Radical America* 20, no. 6:68–78.

———. 1989. "The AIDS Industry: Construction of 'Victims,' 'Volunteers' and 'Experts.'" In *Taking Liberties: AIDS and Cultural Politics,* ed. Erica Carter and Simon Watney, 113–25. London: Serpent's Tail.

———. 1990. *Inventing AIDS.* New York: Routledge.

———. 1996. *Fatal Advice: How Safe-Sex Education Went Wrong.* Durham, NC: Duke University Press.

Payne, Ralph. 1987. "Thoughts from Cell Block 'B.'" *San Francisco Sentinel,* 12 June, 8.

Pepper, Rachel. 1990. "Schism Slices ACT UP in Two: San Francisco Chapter Splits in Debate over Focus." *OutWeek,* 10 October.

Perry, David. 1992. "State of the Arts: It's Been a Banner Year for Up-Front Queer Culture in the Mainstream." *Advocate,* 14 January, 68–69.

Petrelis, Michael. 2003. Interview conducted by ACT UP Oral History Project. Available at www.actuporalhistory.org.

Pick, Grant. 1993. "Outward Mobility: Chicago's Gays and Lesbians Are Gaining Acceptance—and Power." *Chicago Tribune Magazine,* 7 February, 12–16.

Pierson, Ransdell. 1983. "The Federal Government's Cold Shoulder." *New York Native,* 25 April–8 May, 15–16.

Piven, Frances Fox, and Richard A. Cloward. 1992. "Normalizing Collective Protest." In *Frontiers in Social Movement Theory,* ed. Aldon D. Morris and Carol McClurg Mueller, 301–25. New Haven, CT: Yale University Press.

"Police Committee Has Work Ahead." 1991. Editorial. *Windy City Times,* 4 July.

Polletta, Francesca. 2002. "Plotting Protest: Mobilizing Stories in the 1960 Student Sit-Ins." In *Stories of Change: Narrative and Social Movements*, ed. Joseph E. Davis, 31–52. Albany: State University of New York Press.

Popham, Paul. 1982. "We've Got Heart." *New York Native*, 26 April–9 May, 13.

Power, Ed. 1983. "Time for Action Not Panic." *San Francisco Sentinel*, 31 March, 4.

———. 1984. "AIDS War Enters Third Year." *S.F. Sentinel*. 5 January, 5.

POZ: The ACT UP Issue. 1997 (March).

Price, Deb. 1990. "Soldiers of Misfortune; Grieving and Angry, AIDS Activists Turn Their Rage on Those Who Turn Their Backs." *Detroit News*, 19 November.

"The Pros and Cons of AIDS Funding Bill." 1983. Editorial. *Gay Life*, 22 September, 4.

"Protest the N.Y. Post." 1985. Advertisement for GLADL demonstration. *New York Native*, 2–8 December, 14.

Purnell, John. 1992. "Power, People, Parties, Platforms: Lesbians and Gays Flex Their Muscles at This Year's Democratic Convention." *Advocate*, 14 July, 42–43.

PWA Coalition. 1987. "PWA Coalition Portfolio." In *October* 43 (Winter): 147–68.

Quinby, Brian Eric. 1985. "A Call for More Activism." *Windy City Times*, 14 November, 10.

"Quotelines." 1991a. *Outlines*, August.

"Quotelines." 1991b. *Outlines*, September.

Rafsky, Robert. 1992. "I'm Not Dying Anymore." *QW*, 12 July, 51.

Rand, Erica. 2005. *The Ellis Island Snow Globe.* Durham, NC: Duke University Press.

Rayside, David. 1998. *On the Fringe: Gays and Lesbians in Politics.* Ithaca, NY: Cornell University Press.

"Reagan Calls for 20% Cut in AIDS Funding." 1986. *Windy City Times*, 27 February, 3.

Reddy, William M. 1997. "Against Constructionism: The Historical Ethnography of Emotions." *Current Anthropology* 38, no. 3:327–51.

———. 1999. "Emotional Liberty: Politics and History in the Anthropology of Emotions." *Cultural Anthropology* 14, no. 2:256–88.

———. 2000. "Sentimentalism and Its Erasure: The Role of Emotions in the Era of the French Revolution." *Journal of Modern History* 72, no. 1:109–52.

———. 2001. *The Navigation of Feeling.* Cambridge: Cambridge University Press.

Reed, Jean-Pierre. 2004. "Emotions in Context: Revolutionary Accelerators, Hope, Moral Outrage, and other Emotions in the Making of Nicaragua's Revolution." *Theory and Society* 33, no. 6:653–703.

Reed, T. V. 2005. *The Art of Protest: Culture and Activism from the Civil Rights*

Movement to the Streets of Seattle. Minneapolis: University of Minnesota Press.

Reger, Jo. 2004. "Organizational 'Emotion Work' through Consciousness-Raising: An Analysis of a Feminist Organization." *Qualitative Sociology* 27, no. 2:205–22.

Regnier, Derek. 1985. "Statewide AIDS Advisory Council Set." *Gay Life,* 28 November, 1.

"Reporting on Opera Protest Is Corrected." 1989. *San Francisco Chronicle,* 13 September.

Reyes, Nina. 1990a. "Queerly Speaking: The Three-Word Title of an Essay Has Hurled the Lesbian and Gay Community into Yet Another Raging Controversy. Why Has 'I Hate Straights' Ignited Such a Furor?" *OutWeek,* 15 August, 40–42.

———. 1990b. "Reign of Terror." *OutWeek,* 17 October.

Richter, Frank. 1987. "AIDS Protest Week Planned." *AIDS Action Call: The Newsletter of the AIDS Action Pledge,* Autumn–Winter, 3.

Rieder, Ines, and Patricia Ruppelt. 1988. *AIDS: The Women.* San Francisco: Cleis Press.

Rimmerman, Craig. 2002. *From Identity to Politics: The Lesbian and Gay Movements in the United States.* Philadelphia, PA: Temple University Press.

Rist, Darrell Yates. 1985a. "Going to Paris to Live: The Hope of HPA-23." *New York Native,* 1–14 July, 26–33.

———. 1985b. "No More Lies!" *New York Native,* 9–15 December, 20–21.

———. 1986. "Sexual Slander: Why Gays Should Stop Taking the Blame for AIDS and Start Fighting Back." *Advocate,* 13 May, 42–47.

———. 1987. "The Top Gay Stories of 1986." *New York Native,* 5 January, 11–16.

Roberts, Stan. 1989. "The Opera Isn't the Enemy." Letter to the editor. *Bay Area Reporter,* 14 September.

Robinson, David. 1990. "Letter to ACT UP/NY from David Robinson." 2 July. New York Public Library, Manuscripts and Archives Section, ACT UP/New York Records, T-5.

Robles, Jennifer Juarez. 1988. "Eight Years into Epidemic, City AIDS Office Only Now Gets Underway." *Chicago Reporter,* 17, no. 3:1.

Roeder, Pam. 1992. "Damaging Protest." Letter to the editor. *Chicago Tribune,* 16 December.

Rofes, Eric. 1986. "A Call to Resist: Gays Must Return to Activism." *Advocate,* 27 May, 9.

———. 1990. "Gay Lib vs. AIDS: Averting Civil War in the 1990s." *Out/Look* (Spring): 8–17.

———. 1996. *Reviving the Tribe: Regenerating Gay Men's Sexuality and Culture in the Ongoing Epidemic.* New York: Haworth Press.

Rogers, Buck, and Alan Selby. 1984. Letter to the editor. *Bay Area Reporter*, 26 July, 7.

Román, David. 1998. *Acts of Intervention: Performance, Gay Culture, and AIDS*. Bloomington: Indiana University Press.

Rosaldo, Michelle Z. 1984. "Toward an Anthropology of Self and Feeling." In *Culture Theory: Essays on Mind, Self, and Emotion*, ed. Richard A. Shweder and Robert A. Levine, 137–57. Cambridge: Cambridge University Press.

Rosco, Jerry. 1986. "Letter from New York: Supreme Court Ruling Sparks New Militancy in the Big Apple." *Bay Area Reporter*, 17 July, 11.

Rose, Jacqueline. 1987. *Sexuality in the Field of Vision*. London: Verso.

Rosett, Jane. 1997a. "The Buddy Line: A Love Song for a Fallen Fighter." *POZ*, March, 40.

———. 1997b. "Dressed for Arrest." *POZ*, May. Available at http://www.poz .com/articles/240_12313.shtml (accessed 15 December 2005).

Ross, Bob. 1986. "Forward Together." Editorial. *Bay Area Reporter*, 26 June, 8.

Ross, Judith Wilson. 1988. "An Ethics of Compassion, a Language of Division: Working Out the AIDS Metaphors." In *AIDS: Principles, Practices, and Politics*, ed. Inge Corless and Mary Pittman-Lindeman, 81–95. New York: Harper & Row.

Roth, Benita. 1998. "Feminist Boundaries in the Feminist-Friendly Organization: The Women's Caucus of ACT UP/LA." *Gender & Society* 12, no. 2:129–45.

Rubin, Gayle S. 1991. "The Catacombs: A Temple of the Butthole." In *Leatherfolk: Radical Sex, People, Politics, and Practice*, ed. Mark Thompson, 119–41. Boston, MA: Alyson Publications.

———. 1997. "Elegy for the Valley of Kings: AIDS and the Leather Community in San Francisco, 1981–1996." In *In Changing Times: Gay Men and Lesbians Encounter HIV/AIDS*, ed. Martin P. Levine, Peter M. Nardi, and John H. Gagnon, 101–44. Chicago: University of Chicago Press.

Rupp, Leila J., and Verta Taylor. 1987. *Survival in the Doldrums: The American Woman's Rights Movement, 1945 to the 1960s*. New York: Oxford University Press.

Ruschmeyer, Henry C. 1986. "Scapegoats of the Majority." *New York Native*, 21 July, 18.

Russo, Vito. 1988a. "Zapping the Mayor or Zapping Gays?" Letter to the editor. *New York Native*, 4 July, 6.

———. 1988b. "Viewpoints: It Isn't Happening to Them." *Windy City Times*, 28 July, 10–11.

Saalfield, Catherine, and Ray Navarro. 1991. "Shocking Pink Praxis: Race and Gender on the ACT UP Frontlines." In *Inside/Out: Lesbian Theories, Gay Theories*, ed. Diana Fuss, 341–69. New York: Routledge.

Sack, Kevin. 1990. "Cuomo Defuses Protest and Still Makes a Point." *New York Times,* 4 January, B5.

Salholz, Eloise, Tony Clifton, Nadine Joseph, Lucille Beachy, Patrick Rogers, Larry Wilson, Daniel Glick, and Patricia King. 1990. "The Future of Gay America: The '90s Reflect a New Spirit of Anger, Activism and Political Clout. But How Far Will the Limits of Tolerance Extend?" *Newsweek,* 12 March, 20–25.

Salinas, Mike. 1987a. "Kramer, Mob, Others Call for Traffic Blockade." *New York Native,* 30 March, 6.

———. 1987b. "ACT UP Goes to Washington; Peaceful Demonstration, Despite Arrests." *New York Native,* 15 June, 13–15.

San Francisco AIDS/KS Foundation. 1983. "A Report to the Community from the San Francisco AIDS/KS Foundation." December. Document housed in my personal ACT UP archive.

Saunders, Dudley. 2003. Interview conducted by ACT UP Oral History Project. Available at www.actuporalhistory.org.

Savage, Dan. 1997. "Death Takes a Holiday: Welcome to the End of the AIDS Crisis. No One Said It Was Going to Be Pretty." *Chicago Reader,* 14 February, 1.

Scannell, Teresa. 1983. "AIDS: A Lesbian Perspective." *Bay Area Reporter,* 13 October, 15.

Scheff, Thomas J. 1988. "Shame and Conformity: The Deference-Emotion System." *American Sociological Review* 53, no. 3:395–406.

———. 1990a. *Microsociology: Discourse, Emotion, and Social Structure.* Chicago: University of Chicago Press.

———. 1990b. "Socialization of Emotion: Pride and Shame as Causal Agents." In Kemper 1990, 281–304.

———. 1992. "Rationality and Emotion: Homage to Norbert Elias." In *Rational Choice Theory: Advocacy and Critique,* ed. James S. Coleman and Thomas J. Fararo, 101–19. Newbury Park, CA: Sage.

Scheman, Naomi. 1993. *Engenderings: Constructions of Knowledge, Authority and Privilege.* New York: Routledge.

Scherer, Klaus. 1984. "On the Nature and Function of Emotion: A Component Process Approach." In *Approaches to Emotion,* ed. Klaus Scherer and Paul Ekman, 293–317. Hillsdale, NJ: Lawrence Erlbaum Associates.

Schmalz, Jeffrey. 1992. "Gay Politics Goes Mainstream." *New York Times Magazine,* 11 October, 18.

Schmitz, Dawn. 1991. "PWAs Abused in Wisconsin: Inmates and Activists Stage Concurrent Demonstrations Protesting Prison Abuses of People with HIV Disease." *Gay Community News,* 21 September, 3.

Schoofs, Mark. 1988. "ACT UP Proliferates Nationwide." *Windy City Times,* 22 December, 16–17.

———. 1997. "The AIDS Shock Troopers Who Changed the World." *Village Voice*, 25 March, 42.

Schulman, Sarah. 1985a. "Committee Resolves to Close Baths; Councilmember Maloney Joins Anti-Gay Sellout; Gay Activist Arrested." *New York Native*, 2–8 December, 11–13.

———. 1985b. "'Becoming an Angry Mob—In the Best Sense': Lesbians Respond to AIDS Hysteria." *New York Native*, 2–8 December, 27–28.

Schweikhart, Gary. 1983. "The Real AIDS Victims." Editorial. *Sentinel*, 21 July, 5.

Scondras, David. 1985. "With a Carrot *and* a Stick." *New York Native*, 28 October–3 November, 15.

Seabaugh, Cathy. 1993. "President Clinton Hosts Historic Meeting with Gays and Lesbians." *Outlines*, May, 13.

Sedgwick, Eve Kosofsky. 2003. *Touching Feeling: Affect, Pedagogy, Performativity*. Durham, NC: Duke University Press.

Sedgwick, Eve Kosofsky, and Adam Frank, eds. 1995. *Shame and Its Sisters: A Silvan Tomkins Reader*. Durham, NC: Duke University Press.

Seidman, Steven. 1988. "Transfiguring Sexual Identity: AIDS and the Contemporary Construction of Homosexuality." *Social Text* 19, no. 20:187–205.

"Sense of Hope, Sense of Urgency in AIDS Drug Battle: Waging War in the Fog." 1989. Editorial. *San Francisco Sentinel*, 9 February.

Sewell, William H., Jr. 1996. "Historical Events as Transformations of Structures: Inventing Revolution at the Bastille." *Theory and Society* 25, no. 6: 841–81.

Shepard, Benjamin Heim. 1997. *White Nights and Ascending Shadows: An Oral History of the San Francisco AIDS Epidemic*. London: Cassell.

———. 2002. "Introductory Notes on the Trail from ACT UP to the WTO." In Shepard and Hayduk 2002, 11–16.

Shepard, Benjamin Heim, and Ronald Hayduk, eds. 2002. *From ACT UP to the WTO: Urban Protest and Community Building in the Era of Globalization*. New York: Verso.

Shilts, Randy. 1983. "When the Diagnosis Is AIDS." *San Francisco Chronicle*, 8 August.

———. 1985. "Horror Stories and Excuses: How New York City Is Dealing with AIDS." *New York Native*, 25 March–7 April, 21–23.

———. 1987. *And the Band Played On: Politics, People and the AIDS Epidemic*. New York: St. Martin's Press.

———. 1989. "Politics Confused with Therapy." *San Francisco Chronicle*, 26 June, A4.

———. 1991. "The Queering of America: Looking Back at 1990 and the Resurrection of the Gay Movement." *Advocate*, 1 January, 32–38.

Shouse, Eric. 2005. "Feeling, Emotion, Affect." *M/C Journal* 8, no. 6 (December). Available at http://journal.media-culture.org.au/0512/03-shouse.php (accessed 24 February 2007).

Sieple, Frank. 1999. Interview conducted by Deborah Gould, July 8, San Francisco. Interview housed in my personal ACT UP archive.

Signorile, Michelangelo. 1992. "Out at the *New York Times*." *Advocate*, 5 May, 34–42.

———. 1993. *Queer in America: Sex, the Media, and the Closets of Power*. New York: Random House.

———. 2003. Interview conducted by ACT UP Oral History Project. Available at www.actuporalhistory.org.

Smart, Theo. 1992. "This Side of Despair." *QW*, 13 September, 43–44.

Smelser, Neil J. 1998. "The Rational and the Ambivalent in the Social Sciences: 1997 Presidential Address." *American Sociological Review* 63, no. 1:1–16.

Smith, Barbara. 1993. "Queer Politics: Where's the Revolution?" *Nation*, 5 July, 12–15.

Smith, James Monroe. 1992. "Praise for ACT UP." Letter to the editor. *Windy City Times*, 26 March, 13.

Snitow, Ann, Christine Stansell, and Sharon Thompson, eds. 1983. *Powers of Desire: The Politics of Sexuality*. New York: Monthly Review Press.

Snow, Bill. 2003. Interview conducted by ACT UP Oral History Project. Available at www.actuporalhistory.org.

Snyder, Will. 1985. "AIDS Activist Chains Himself to Fed Building: John Lorenzini Protests Budget Cuts, Neglect." *Bay Area Reporter*, 27 June, 17.

Soehnlein, Karl. 2003. Interview conducted by ACT UP Oral History Project. Available at www.actuporalhistory.org.

Solnit, Rebecca. 2004. *Hope in the Dark: Untold Histories, Wild Possibilities*. New York: Nation Books.

Solomon, Alisa. 1989. "AIDS Crusaders ACT UP a Storm." *American Theatre* October, 39–40.

———. 1990. "Fired Up: Should Gays Carry Guns?" *Village Voice*, 27 November, 43–44.

Sonnabend, J. A. 1982. "Promiscuity Is Bad for Your Health: AIDS and the Question of an Infectious Agent." *New York Native*, 13–26 September, 21.

Span, Paula. 1989. "Getting Militant About AIDS: ACT-UP's Mission and the Escalating Protest." *Washington Post*, 28 March, D1.

Sparta, Christine. 2002. "Emergence from the Closet." *U.S.A. Today*, 11 March.

Specter, Michael. 1989. "Pressure from AIDS Activists Has Transformed Drug Testing." *Washington Post*, 2 July, A1.

———. 1990a. "Letter from the AIDS Conference: Painting the Picture with Street Surrealism." *Washington Post*, 23 June, A8.

———. 1990b. "More Theatrics Than Science: Many Question Need for International Meeting." *Washington Post*, 26 June.

Spiers, Herb. 1988. "Fighting the AIDS Beast: Strategies and Consequences." *Windy City Times,* 23 June, 36.

Sprecher, Mark. 1990. "CSW March, June 24." *ACT UP/LA Newsletter* 3, no. 3:16.

Staley, Peter. 1991. "Has the Direct-Action Group ACT UP Gone Astray?" *Advocate,* 30 July, 98.

———. 2002. Interview conducted by Deborah Gould, September 13, New York. Interview housed in my personal ACT UP archive.

"Stay Vigilant Against AIDS Panic." 1983. Editorial. *Gay Life,* 23 June, 4.

Stearns, Carol Zisowitz, and Peter N. Stearns. 1986. *Anger: The Struggle for Emotional Control in America's History.* Chicago: University of Chicago Press.

Stearns, Peter N., and Jan Lewis, eds. 1998. *An Emotional History of the United States.* New York: New York University Press.

Stein, Arlene. 1998. "Whose Memories? Whose Victimhood? Contests for the Holocaust Frame in Recent Social Movement Discourse." *Sociological Perspectives* 41, no. 3:519–40.

Steinberg, Marc W. 1999a. *Fighting Words: Working-Class Formation, Collective Action and Discourse in Early Nineteenth-Century England.* Ithaca, NY: Cornell University Press.

———. 1999b. "The Talk and Back Talk of Collective Action: A Dialogic Analysis of Repertoires of Discourse among Nineteenth-Century English Cotton Spinners." *American Journal of Sociology* 105, no. 3:736–80.

Stockdill, Brett C. 2003. *Activism against AIDS: At the Intersections of Sexuality, Race, Gender, and Class.* Boulder, CO: Lynne Rienner.

Stoller, Nancy E. 1997. "From Feminism to Polymorphous Activism: Lesbians in AIDS Organizations." In *In Changing Times: Gay Men and Lesbians Encounter HIV/AIDS,* ed. Martin P. Levine, Peter M. Nardi, and John H. Gagnon, 171–89. Chicago: University of Chicago Press.

———. 1998. *Lessons from the Damned: Queers, Whores, and Junkies Respond to AIDS.* New York: Routledge.

"The Storming of St. Pat's." 1989. Editorial. *New York Times,* 12 December.

Streips, Karlis. 1983a. "NGTF's Apuzzo Blasts U.S. Government on Response." *Gay Life,* 18 August, 1.

———. 1983b. "$2.97 Million Federal Grant Awarded to Chicago Clinic for AIDS Research." *Gay Life,* 6 October, 1.

Streitmatter, Rodger. 1995. *Unspeakable: The Rise of the Gay and Lesbian Press in America.* Boston, MA: Faber and Faber.

Sturken, Marita. 1997. *Tangled Memories: The Vietnam War, the AIDS Epidemic, and the Politics of Remembering.* Berkeley and Los Angeles: University of California Press.

Sullivan, Andrew. 1993. "The Politics of Homosexuality." *New Republic,* 10 May, 24–26.

———. 1996. "When AIDS Ends." *New York Times Magazine,* 10 November, 52–62.

"Sullivan Will Curtail ACT UP Role." 1990. *Washington Post,* 4 July, A6.

"Support AIDS Research Benefits." 1982. Editorial. *Gay Life,* 24 September, 4.

"Supreme Court Comes to Town." 1986. Advertisement for CLGR demonstration. *New York Native,* 11 August, 28.

"The Supreme Court Opinion." 1986. *New York Native,* 14 July, 12–18.

Sutherland, John. 1991. "ACT UP Would Be Wise to Shut Up." *Philadelphia Inquirer,* 28 October, A11.

Sutton, Terry, and Keith Griffith. 1988. "New Levels." Letter to the editor. *San Francisco Sentinel,* 26 February, 8.

Tarrow, Sidney. 1994. *Power in Movement: Social Movements, Collective Action and Politics.* Cambridge: Cambridge University Press.

———. 1998. *Power in Movement: Social Movements and Contentious Politics,* 2nd ed. New York: Cambridge University Press.

Taylor, Paul. 1990. "AIDS Guerrillas: ACT UP's Tactics Can Be Outrageous, but They Seem to Be Working." *New York Magazine,* 12 November, 65–73.

Taylor, Verta. 1989. "Social Movement Continuity: The Women's Movement in Abeyance." *American Sociological Review* 54:761–75.

———. 1995. "Watching for Vibes: Bringing Emotions into the Study of Feminist Organizations." In *Feminist Organizations: Harvest of the New Women's Movement,* ed. Myra Marx Ferree and Patricia Yancey Martin, 223–33. Philadelphia, PA: Temple University Press.

———. 1996. *Rock-a-by Baby: Feminism, Self-Help, and Postpartum Depression.* New York: Routledge.

Taylor, Verta, and Nancy E. Whittier. 1992. "Collective Identity in Social Movement Communities: Lesbian Feminist Mobilization." In *Frontiers in Social Movement Theory,* ed. Aldon D. Morris and Carol McClurg Mueller, 104–29. New Haven, CT: Yale University Press.

———. 1995. "Analytical Approaches to Social Movement Culture: The Culture of the Women's Movement." In *Social Movements and Culture,* ed. Hank Johnston and Bert Klandermans, 163–87. Minneapolis: University of Minnesota Press.

Tell It To ACT UP (TITA). Internal ACT UP/NY broadsheet, published almost every week from February 1990 through June 1, 1992. Documents housed in my personal ACT UP archive.

Tester, Griff. 2004. "Resources, Identity, and the Role of Threat: The Case of AIDS Mobilization, 1981–1986." *Research in Political Sociology* 13:47–75.

Thistlethwaite, Polly. 1993. Interview conducted by Kate Black, September 26. Interview housed at the Lesbian Herstory Archives, Brooklyn, New York.

Thoits, Peggy A. 1990. "Emotional Deviance: Research Agendas." In Kemper 1990, 180–203.

Thomas, Kendall. 2002. Interview conducted by Deborah Gould, September 11, New York. Interview housed in my personal ACT UP archive.

Thompson, Mark, ed. 1994. *Long Road to Freedom: The Advocate History of the Gay and Lesbian Movement.* New York: St. Martin's Press.

Thompson, Michael. 2000. Interview conducted by Deborah Gould, March 19, Chicago. Interview housed in my personal ACT UP archive.

Three Anonymous Queers. 1990. "Should Queers Shoot Back?" *OutWeek,* 17 October, 38.

Tilly, Charles. 1978. *From Mobilization to Revolution.* New York: McGraw Hill.

"The Time for Gay Rage Is Now!" 1986. Editorial. *Advocate,* 5 August, 18.

Timour, Karin. 2003. Interview conducted by ACT UP Oral History Project. Available at www.actuporalhistory.org.

Treichler, Paula A. 1987. "AIDS, Homophobia, and Biomedical Discourse: An Epidemic of Signification." *October* 43 (Winter): 31–70.

Tuller, David. 1988. "AIDS Protesters Showing Signs of Movement's New Militancy." *San Francisco Chronicle,* 27 October, A4.

Turner, Jonathan H. 2007. *Human Emotions.* New York: Routledge.

Turner, Jonathan H., and Jan E. Stets. 2006. "Sociological Theories of Human Emotions." *Annual Review of Sociology* 32 (August): 25–52.

Turner, Ralph H., and Lewis M. Killian. 1957. *Collective Behavior.* Englewood Cliffs, NJ: Prentice-Hall.

"Turning Up the Lights." 1990. Editorial. *Windy City Times,* 10 May, 11.

Vaid, Urvashi. 1995. *Virtual Equality: The Mainstreaming of Gay and Lesbian Liberation.* New York: Anchor Books.

Vance, Carole S., ed. 1989. *Pleasure and Danger: Exploring Female Sexuality.* London: Pandora Press.

Vandervelden, Mark. 1987a. "Gay Health Conference: Comegys Calls for Nationwide Civil Disobedience." *Advocate,* 28 April, 12.

———. 1987b. "Civil Disobedience: Are We Entering a New Militant Stage in the Struggle for Gay Rights?" *Advocate,* 29 September, 45–48.

Varnell, Paul. 1987. "We're Making Progress." *Windy City Times,* 25 June, 22.

Vazquez-Pacheco, Robert. 2002. Interview conducted by ACT UP Oral History Project. Available at www.actuporalhistory.org.

Velez, Andrew. 1991. "An Open Letter to ACT UP." 1 April. Primary Source Microfilm, *ACT UP: The AIDS Coalition to Unleash Power,* reel 6, box 8, folder 10. Produced by Gale CENGAGE Learning; see their Web site at http://www.gale.cengage.com/servlet/BrowseSeriesServlet?region=9&imprint=745&titleCode=PSM5&edition=.

Walsh, Edward J. 1981. "Resource Mobilization and Citizen Protest in Communities around Three Mile Island." *Social Problems* 29, no. 1:1–21.

Walter, Dave. 1983. "AIDS Vigil Brings High Emotion, but Low Turnout." *Washington Blade,* 14 October, 1.

———. 1985. "Openly Gay Elected and Appointed Officials Hold 'Historic' Meeting." *Advocate,* 24 December, 10–13.

———. 1986. "High Court Upholds Sodomy Law." *Advocate,* 5 August, 10–11.

———. 1987a. "CDC AIDS Conference." *Advocate,* 31 March, 10–11.

———. 1987b. "D.C. AIDS Protests: Activists Blast Reagan." *Advocate,* 7 July, 10–11.

Walters, Suzanna. 2001. *All The Rage.* Chicago: University of Chicago Press.

Warner, Michael. 1999. *The Trouble with Normal: Sex, Politics, and the Ethics of Queer Life.* New York: Free Press.

Warner, W. L. 1989. "Reflections on Activism." *Bay Area Reporter,* 12 October.

"Washington—By Way of Stonewall." 1993. Editorial. *New York Times,* 27 April.

Watney, Simon. 1989. *Policing Desire: Pornography, AIDS, and the Media.* 2nd ed. Minneapolis: University of Minnesota Press.

———. 1992a. "The Possibilities of Permutation: Pleasure, Proliferation, and the Politics of Gay Identity in the Age of AIDS." In *Fluid Exchanges: Artists and Critics in the AIDS Crisis,* ed. James Miller, 329–67. Toronto: University of Toronto Press.

———. 1992b. "Political Funeral." *Village Voice,* 20 October, 18.

———. 1994. *Practices of Freedom: Selected Writings on HIV/AIDS.* Durham, NC: Duke University Press.

———. 1995. "AIDS and the Politics of Queer Diaspora." In *Negotiating Lesbian and Gay Subjects,* ed. Monica Dorenkamp and Richard Henke, 53–70. New York: Routledge.

Webb, Steven. 1987. "Where Were You?" Letter to the editor. *New York Native,* 27 July, 6.

Weir, John. 1995. "Rage, Rage." *New Republic,* 13 February, 11–12.

Weisberg, Louis. 1997. "A Decade of Rage: ACT UP Commemorates Ten Years of Street Activism." *Windy City Times,* 3 April, 1.

Wentzy, James. 1995. *Political Funerals.* Video. AIDS Community Television.

Wetzl, John. 1985. "Feds Book Civil Protester." *Sentinel USA,* 4 July, 1.

———. 1986. "Top Court's Decision Bashes Gays." *Sentinel.* 4 July, 1, 2, 4.

———. 1987. "ARC/AIDS Vigil Vows Fight: Ordered to Move Tuesday." *San Francisco Sentinel,* 13 February, 1.

"We've Got to Help Ourselves." 1985. Editorial. *Gay Life,* 11 April, 4.

Whiting, Sam. 1990. "AIDS Groups That Vow to Act Up: They Seek to Influence as Well as Inconvenience." *San Francisco Chronicle,* 31 January, B3.

Whittier, Nancy. 1995. *Feminist Generations: The Persistence of the Radical Women's Movement.* Philadelphia, PA: Temple University Press.

William, Dan. 1982. "If AIDS Is an Infectious Disease . . . A Sexual Syllogism." *New York Native,* 16–29 August, 33.

Williams, Albert. 1987. "AIDS, Politics, and 'The Normal Heart': An Interview with Playwright Larry Kramer." *Windy City Times,* 19 February, 23–24.

Williams, Raymond. 1977. *Marxism and Literature*. Oxford: Oxford University Press.

Winnow, Jackie. 1992. "Lesbians Evolving Health Care: Cancer and AIDS." *Feminist Review* 41 (Summer): 68–76.

Wockner, Rex. 1988. "Gay Pride and Backpack Flirtations." *Outlines*, July, 29.

———. 1989a. "ACT UP Havoc Oct. 6." *Outlines*, October, 21.

———. 1989b. "ACT UP/Chicago Ideology Clash." *Outlines*, November.

———. 1989c. "Mayor Daley Storms Out of Gay Meeting: Community 'Cut Off' from Administration; Activists Arrested in City Hall." *Outlines*, December, 26–27.

———. 1989d. "Activists: City AIDS Campaign 'Useless.'" *Outlines*, December, 25.

———. 1990a. "Chicago's Frank Sieple: No Time for Closets." *Advocate*, 13 February, 35.

———. 1990b. "Chicago Rejects Miller Boycott, but Marlboro Blacklisted." *Nightlines*, 15 August, 10.

———. 1990c. "Cartoonist Sotomayor Quits ACT UP/Chicago." *Bay Area Reporter*, 23 August.

———. 1990d. "Helms Files Complaint Against Activists Over Miller/Marlboro; Activists Set Up 800 Number; Chicago Rejects Miller Call." *Outlines*, September, 19.

———. 1991a. "ACT UP/Portland Explodes." *Outlines*, March.

———. 1991b. "President Bush Blasts ACT UP." *Outlines*, June.

———. 1991c. "25 Arrests, Brutality at ACT UP AMA Demo." *Nightlines*, 3 July, 26–28.

———. 1991d. "President Bush Worried about ACT UP Labor Day Invasion." *Outlines*, September, 13.

———. 1991e. "1,500 March on Kennebunkport; Bush Calls for 'Behavioral Change' to Curb AIDS." *Outlines*, October.

———. 1992a. "The AIDS Activist the Mayor Feared." *Nightlines*, 12 February, 28–29.

———. 1992b. "Inside the Mind of Richard M. Daley; ACT UP, Mayor Argue at CPNA Dinner; CPNA Ejects ACT UP, then Grills Mayor on Issues." *Outlines*, March, 25.

———. 1992c. "Boys Town." *Nightlines*, 28 October.

Wofford, Carrie. 1991. "Sitting at the Table." *OutWeek*, 3 April, 22–23.

Wojnarowicz, David. 1992. Reading at the Drawing Center, New York City. Available at http://www.actupny.org/reports/CBwoj.html (accessed 17 April 2007).

Wolfe, Maxine. 1990a. "AIDS and Politics: Transformation of Our Movement." In *Women, AIDS, and Activism*, ed. ACT UP/NY Women and AIDS Book Group, 233–37. Boston, MA: South End Press.

———. 1990b. "Would You Trust These Men with Your Life?" *ACT UP Reports* (Fall–Winter): 2–3.

———. 1991 (ca. March). "Of Meetings and Moratoria: Reality vs. Rumor: An Open Letter to NY ACT UP." New York Public Library, Manuscripts and Archives Section, ACT UP/New York Records.

———. 1992. "To: ACT UP Members, From: Maxine Wolfe." Letter. 21 April. New York Public Library, Manuscripts and Archives Section, ACT UP/New York Records.

———. 1993. Interview conducted by Kate Black, September 21. Interview housed at the Lesbian Herstory Archives, Brooklyn, New York.

———. 1994. "The AIDS Coalition to Unleash Power (ACT UP): A Direct Model of Community Research for AIDS Prevention." In *AIDS Prevention and Services: Community Based Research*, ed. Johannes P. Van Vugt, 217–47. Westport, CT: Bergin and Garvey.

———. 1997. "This Is about People Dying: The Tactics of Early ACT UP and Lesbian Avengers in New York City; an Interview with Maxine Wolfe by Laraine Sommella." In *Queers in Space: Communities, Public Places, Sites of Resistance*, ed. Gordon Brent Ingram, Anne-Marie Bouthillette and Yolanda Retter, 407–37. Seattle, WA: Bay Press.

———. 2004. Interview conducted by ACT UP Oral History Project. Available at www.actuporalhistory.org.

Yang, Guobin. 2000. "Achieving Emotions in Collective Action: Emotional Processes and Movement Mobilization in the 1989 Chinese Student Movement." *Sociological Quarterly* 41, no. 4:593–614.

Yang, Jacob Smith. 1991. "AIDS Activists Brutalized in Chicago; Dozens of Protesters Are Arrested at the American Medical Association's Annual Conference; Many Level Charges of Police Brutality." *Gay Community News*, 13 July, 1.

"The Yin and Yang of Activism." 1991. Editorial. *Windy City Times*, 24 October.

Yingling, Thomas. 1991. "AIDS in America: Postmodern Governance, Identity, and Experience." In *Inside/Out: Lesbian Theories, Gay Theories*, ed. Diana Fuss, 291–310. New York: Routledge.

Youngblood, Tom. 1989. "Ashamed." Letter to the editor. *San Francisco Sentinel*, 21 September.

Zonana, Victor F. 1990. "Did AIDS Protest Go Too Far? Conference: ACT UP Draws Fire and Praise after Activists Shouted Down a Cabinet Official in San Francisco." *Los Angeles Times*, 2 July, A3.

———. 1992. "Kramer vs. the World." *Advocate*, 1 December.

Zwickler, Phil. 1987. "AIDS Activists Convene; Conference Calls for Week of Protests in 1988." *New York Native*, 26 October, 11.

Index

Daley, Richard, 7, 43, 249n20, 251, 254,
    280–81, 303–4, 314, 321
Damasio, Antonio, 16–17n20, 17, 19–20n23
Damski, Jon-Henri, 7, 251
Dannemeyer, William, 161
death: ACTION = LIFE maxim, 425, 432;
    AIDS deaths as murder, 2, 93, 110–11,
    165–66, 169–70, 171, 226, 239–41, 254,
    284, 432–33; antiqueer violence and,
    411; despair/desperation and, 395–438;
    direct-action AIDS activism and, 229–
    33, 238–41; disavowal of, 432–33; emo-
    tion work and, 229–33, 238–41; fear
    of, 82, 84, 104, 375–76, 385; gay sexual
    practices and, 61, 71–72, 73–74, 75, 76,
    78–79, 82, 86–87, 91, 170, 257, 261, 262,
    264; genocide frame and, 165–72, 174,
    230–32, 239, 432–33; instrumentaliz-
    ing of, 229–33, 238–41, 432–33; politi-
    cal funerals, 8, 229–33, 229n11, 415,
    435; premourning one's own, 393–94;
    queer sensibilities and, 257, 261, 262;
    SILENCE = DEATH and, 171; despite
    victories, 414, 424–25
decline of direct-action AIDS activism,
    267–438; affect and, 269–70, 338–41,
    436; anger and, 270, 364, 386, 393, 394;
    betrayal and, 320–23, 330, 341, 348–
    49, 354, 364–65, 368, 369, 375–76, 394,
    430; Clinton-era optimism and, 415–19;
    criticism and, 273–74, 303–5, 305, 311–
    15, 318–20, 325, 326; cultural openings
    and, 307–8, 308–11; "drugs into bodies"
    debate and, 337, 339–40, 339n6, 349–
    55, 363, 364, 370, 372, 376n30, 380–81;
    emotional habitus and, 340–41, 394,
    396, 405, 427, 428, 431, 431–37, 437–38,
    441; exhaustion and, 312, 394, 416–19,
    421–25, 428, 429, 435; gays in the mili-
    tary campaign and, 323–24, 429, 431;
    hope and, 303, 415–19; increasing gay
    visibility and, 307–11, 311n30; isolation
    and, 320–23; overwhelmedness and,
    338–39, 374–75, 376, 394, 396, 429, 431,
    435; police brutality and, 269, 269n3;
    political openings and, 305–7, 308–11,
    311–15, 320, 323–25; politics of exper-
    tise and, 330; scarcity mentality and,
    338–39, 348–49, 350, 353–54, 375, 381;
    shifting affective landscape within

ACT UP and, 338–41; social accep-
    tance and, 311–15, 315–20, 323–26; Vaid
    on, 280; victories and, 269, 270. *See
    also* conflicts; despair/desperation; me-
    dia, lesbian/gay; moralism/moralizing
    rhetoric; solidarity
Deitcher, David, 122–23, 139
De la Vega, Ernesto, 108n67
D'Emilio, John, 65, 94–95, 98n57, 132n14,
    299–300
democracy ideology: *Bowers v. Hardwick*
    decision and, 134, 135; vs. confronta-
    tional activism, 46, 99, 214, 253, 273–74,
    288, 318–19; delegitimization of protest
    and, 253; disillusionment and, 134, 174
Denenberg, Risa, 393
Denver Principles, 68
despair/desperation, 395–438; ACT UP as
    antidote to, 335, 399–405, 405–9, 432;
    anger and, 393, 394, 399, 405, 414, 424,
    429, 431–37, 438, 441; betrayal and,
    338–39, 341, 349, 369, 374–75, 375–76,
    377, 430–31, 431n32, 433; Clinton-era
    optimism and, 415–19; Concorde trial,
    419; conflicts and, 338, 349, 390, 392–
    94; Crimp on, 323–24, 338, 427, 428–30,
    434, 436–37, 438; daily life of activists
    and, 421–25; death and, 395–438; dis-
    avowal of, 429, 431, 433, 434, 436–37;
    emotional habitus and, 394, 396, 405,
    427, 428, 431–38, 441; exhaustion and,
    394, 416–19, 421–25, 429, 435; expecta-
    tions and, 425–27, 427–28, 431; as for-
    bidden, 431–37, 438, 438n34; as genera-
    tive, 396, 396n1, 398–99; guilt and, 429,
    430–31, 431n32, 433, 437; HIV-positive/
    HIV-negative people and, 433–34, 435–
    36; hope as, 415–19; indeterminacy of,
    399, 437–38; as individualizing, 396,
    432, 436–37, 438; moralism and, 390,
    392, 392–94, 429–30; as nonstatic,
    399; political despair, 338–39, 349, 354,
    396, 424–25, 425–27, 427–28, 428–29,
    430–31, 433–34, 438; political funerals
    and, 415, 435; political horizons and,
    396, 398–99, 437–38; political ineffi-
    cacy and, 338–39, 349, 354, 396, 424–25,
    425–27, 427–28, 428–29, 430–31, 433–
    34, 438; political violence and, 411–13;
    recovered hope and, 425; scarcity men-

tality and, 338–39, 348–49, 350, 353–
54, 375, 381; scientific-medical research
and, 407, 409–11, 413–14, 419–20, 426–
27; shame and, 429–30, 433, 436; solidarity and, 392–94, 430–31, 433; suicide missions, 289n16, 412–13, 413n24;
temporalities of, 427–28, 431; treatment
activists and, 413–15; unconscious processes of, 424–25, 425n30, 428–31
Deukmejian, George, 109, 114–15, 128, 150
Dinkins, David, 286
direct-action AIDS activism: as antidote to
despair, 335, 399–405, 405–9, 432; buyers' clubs as, 68, 68n25; emergence of,
49–53, 121–22, 127–32, 133–43, 163–
64, 165–72, 172–75; emotional habitus
of, 8–10, 164–65, 214–15, 237, 249, 255,
341, 394, 405, 431–37, 438, 441; impact
of *Hardwick* decision on, 121–22, 128–
32, 133–34, 141–42, 142–43, 155–57,
157–63, 163–64, 172–75; lesbian/gay critiques of, 152–53, 157–63, 280–84, 289–
91, 291n19, 300, 301–2, 303, 305, 311–
15, 315–20, 320–23, 323–26; lesbian/
gay support for, 150–55, 155–57, 219–
21, 299–302, 303–5, 315; mainstream
critiques of, 249n20, 275–80, 284–89;
mainstream support for, 187–88, 292–
99; political horizons and, 5, 127–32,
133–34, 137, 139–43, 146–50, 150–55,
155–57, 157–63, 163–64, 170, 173–75,
211–12, 216–21, 265, 398, 441, 444; rationality of, 50, 171, 226, 253–55, 263;
use of term, 449–50. *See also* ACT UP;
AIDS/ARC Vigil; C-FAR; confrontational activism; decline of direct-action
AIDS activism; Lavender Hill Mob;
SANOE
Dittman, Laurie, 304
Dobbs, Bill, 348n15, 448
Dobson, Jesse, 347
Dornan, Robert, 276
Dorow, Heidi, 357–59, 361, 362, 363, 365
"drugs into bodies" debate, 337, 339–
40, 339n6, 349–55, 363, 364, 370, 372,
376n30, 380–81. *See also* Treatment &
Data committee (ACT UP/NY)
Duggan, Lisa, 390–91n37
Dunne, Richard, 147, 152–53
Durkheim, Emile, 207, 207n11, 210, 241, 244

Dyke March (1993), 342n10
Dykes and Gay Men Against Repression/
Reagan/the Right Wing (DAGMAR).
See DAGMAR (Dykes and Gay Men
Against Repression/Reagan/the Right
Wing)

early AIDS activism (1981–1986), 55–120;
ACT UP as overshadowing, 55–56;
AIDS/ARC Vigil, 115–16, 115n75, 119,
149; ambivalence and, 52–53, 63–65,
69–71, 77–79, 84, 85–88, 91–104, 104–
14; anger and, 91–100, 104–11, 108n67,
111–14, 114–19, 125 154, 157; anxiety
and, 73–77, 78n36, 85–90, 87n42, 91–92,
95, 107–9, 111, 113–14; ASOs and, 56–
57, 65–66, 65n17, 67, 67n23, 68, 69n26,
85–90; buyers' clubs, 68, 68n25; candlelight vigils, 24, 51, 68, 90, 92–93, 98,
100, 107–8, 108–9, 125, 133, 154, 223–
24, 398; caretaking, 45, 51, 55–57, 63–
64, 65, 68–71, 85–90, 94, 104, 116–17,
133, 441; as community self–determi-
nation, 65, 65n17, 66, 70; vs. confrontational activism, 91–100, 100–103,
105–11, 111–14, 114–19, 157; "Denver
Principles" (1983), 68; distancing from
AIDS, 82–85; electoral strategies, 24,
45, 50, 51, 55, 57, 64, 68–69, 71, 90, 93,
94, 96, 98, 99–100, 104, 106, 107, 109–
10, 111, 113–14, 118; emotional habitus
during period of, 58, 62–65, 81–82, 85,
89–90, 91–92, 97–98, 100–104, 106–7,
111–14, 114–19, 157; emotion work during period of, 63–64, 67–71, 82, 85–90,
92–94, 95–99, 100–103, 104, 105–11,
111–14, 116–19, 440–41; government ac-
countability and, 57, 69, 91–100, 100–
101, 105, 108, 110–11, 112, 113, 115–16,
118, 145, 165–66; government inaction
and, 57, 61, 65, 67n23, 68, 91–100, 105,
106, 112, 113, 115–16; grassroots nature
of, 65; heroic narrative of, 56–57, 57–58,
65, 70–71, 78n36, 82, 83, 85; historical
erasure of, 44–45; lesbians and, 66–67;
lobbying and, 24, 45, 50, 51, 55, 57, 64,
68–69, 71, 93, 94, 96, 98, 99–100, 104,
106, 107, 109n68, 113–14, 118, 173, 174–
75; Mobilization against AIDS (MAA),
109, 109n68, 114–15, 115n75; mobili-

412–13, 433–34; discrimination against, 49, 128, 138, 146–47, 353, 406; early AIDS activism and, 56–57, 68; the "empowered" PWA, 434, 434n33; HIV-negatives' identification with, 333, 344, 344n12, 349, 356, 357, 367n26, 381–82; HIV-status differences in ACT UP, 333–34, 336, 346, 347–48, 366–67, 367n26, 369–74, 374–78, 380–81, 393; inclusion in research decision-making, 4–5, 294–95, 355–56, 403–4, 407–9; as leaders of movement, 346–47, 370, 381–82; March on Washington (1987) and, 131; negative portrayals of, 434n33; People with Immune-System Disorders (PISD) Caucus, 190, 191, 206, 381, 402, 412; quarantine of, 11, 50, 61, 76, 109, 118, 119, 128–29, 133, 138, 141, 162, 166, 167, 168, 168n36, 169–70, 203, 236, 388n34; self-determination of, 346–47, 370, 381–82; self-empowerment movement, 68; solidarity and, 187, 203, 205–6, 207, 333–34, 335–36, 346–48, 348–49, 358–61, 362–63, 366–68, 369–78, 381–82, 385, 430–31, 433–34; suicide mission discussions, 412–13, 413n24; tattooing of, 50, 118, 168–69, 168n36; women with HIV/AIDS, 5, 67, 206, 337, 342, 343, 344, 344n12, 350–51, 350n16, 352, 353, 355–63, 365–67, 365–66n24, 366n25, 368, 372, 374–75, 406–7, 407nn13–14

People with Immune-System Disorders (PISD) Caucus, 190, 191, 206, 381, 402, 412

Perry, Troy, 142–43, 143n19

Petrelis, Michael, 152

Phil Donahue Show (1990), 289

PISD Caucus (People with Immune-System Disorders Caucus), 190, 191, 206, 381, 402, 412

Piven, France Fox and Richard Cloward, 253

police presence at protests, 125, 159, 189–90, 197, 199, 206, 207n12, 269, 269n3, 276–77, 401

political action/inaction: affect and, 3, 16, 18–19, 22–29, 32, 41, 58, 64, 64n16, 90, 102–3, 119–20, 134, 163–64, 172–73, 439–42, 442–44; ambivalence and, 24, 24n30, 63–64, 102–3, 441–42; black po-

litical action, 133, 167n35; emotion and, 3, 16, 18–19, 22–29, 32, 41, 58, 64, 64n16, 68–70, 90, 102–3, 119–20, 134, 163–64, 172–73, 439–42, 442–44; emotional habitus and, 32, 41–42, 46–47, 53, 55, 58, 63–65, 85, 90, 98, 101–3, 111–13, 119, 134, 157, 163–64, 170–72, 173, 174–75, 214–15, 216, 233–35, 235–38, 255, 256, 265, 439–42; emotion work and, 213, 214–15, 219–21, 223, 226, 238, 241, 265, 440–41; feeling/feelings and, 3, 16, 18–19, 22–29, 32, 41, 58, 64, 64n16, 68–70, 90, 102–3, 119–20, 134, 163–64, 172–73, 439–42, 442–44; moral shock and, 137, 139, 140–42; nonrecognition/recognition and, 57–58; political opportunities and, 133, 167n35; pride and, 57, 58, 63–64, 68–71, 85–90, 105–6, 111–13, 116–17, 118–19, 119–20, 157, 245–49, 255, 265, 441; respectability and, 90; shame and, 58, 63–64, 70–71, 85–90, 98, 101, 119–20, 249–52; social movement theories, 51, 51n2. See also political horizons

political correctness, 283, 345, 362, 369, 377, 383, 384–85, 391–92

political despair, 338–39, 349, 354, 396, 424–25, 425–27, 427–28, 428–29, 430–31, 433–34, 438

political funerals, 8, 229–33, 229n11, 231, 239, 415, 435

political horizons: affect and, 3, 24, 32, 46–47, 55, 119–20, 139, 163–64, 396, 440, 441–42, 443; ambivalence and, 24, 24n30, 63–64, 102–3, 113–14, 441–42; anger and, 91–111, 111–14, 114–19, 122–32, 134, 142–43, 146–49, 149–50, 150–51, 153–57, 163–64, 173–75, 219, 223–33, 238–41, 241–45, 255, 265; caretaking and, 63–64, 90, 98, 104, 105–6, 108, 111–13, 116–17, 118–19; confrontational activism as beyond the political horizon, 24, 63–64, 90, 98, 104, 105–6, 108–11, 111–14, 118–19; despair and, 396, 398–99, 437–38; direct-action activism and, 5, 127–32, 133–34, 137, 139–43, 146–50, 150–55, 155–57, 157–63, 163–64, 170, 173–75, 211–12, 216–21, 265, 398, 441, 444; early AIDS activism and, 5, 24, 56, 58, 62–64, 85, 90, 91–100, 100–103,